"A volume which merits a place on even the smallest bookshelf."

—New York Herald Tribune

In the golden days of Greek civilization, four hundred years before the birth of Christ, the philosopher Plato wrote the DIALOGUES *which, to this day, comprise the most influential body of philosophy of the Western world. Written in the form of debates, the* DIALOGUES *are filled with philosophy's continual search for truth and the moving drama of intellectual conflict.*

The Republic, a brilliant discussion of the ideal state, presents Plato's basic concepts of education, justice and the philosopher-king, the wise and just prototype of a ruler who could cure the world's ills. In the dialogues, *Apology, Crito,* and *Phaedo,* the imposing figure of Socrates, Plato's beloved mentor, emerges as Socrates discusses respect for law and authority, human virtue, and the immortality of the soul. The additional dialogues contain the great philosopher's thinking on subjects of such universal and ageless interest as art, virtue and the nature of love and beauty.

Now rendered into fresh, exact and lucid English, this comprehensive paperbound edition of Plato's *Dialogues* provides hours of enlightening reading.

"In Rouse's pages Socrates' strength of mind, his dedication to philosophical truth, are borne in on the modern reader with something of the power that impressed and disturbed the ancient Greeks."—*Time* Magazine

W. H. D. Rouse, one of the world's greatest classical scholars, made the world-famous translations of Homer's *The Odyssey* and *The Iliad,* volumes which have sold about a million copies. Dr. Rouse was educated at Cambridge University, where he became an Honorary Fellow of Christ's College.

Other MENTOR Books of Special Interest

THE GREEK PHILOSOPHERS *edited by Rex Warner*
Basic writings of philosophers from Thales to Plotinus, revealing the roots of Western philosophy in ancient Greece. (#MP442—60¢)

THE ORIGINS OF SCIENTIFIC THOUGHT
edited by Giorgio de Santillana
This collection of the basic writings of the ancient philosophers of science from Anaximander to Proclus (600 B.C. to 500 A.D.), with commentaries by the editor, is the first book in the new series, *The Mentor History of Scientific Thought*. (#MQ336—95¢)

THE GREEK WAY TO WESTERN CIVILIZATION
by Edith Hamilton
A noted scholar reveals the glorious achievements of ancient Greece in literature, art, science, democracy. (#MD32—50¢)

GREEK CIVILIZATION AND CHARACTER
edited by Arnold J. Toynbee
Brilliant translations of Hellenic experience and life that shed light on contemporary problems.
(#MP501—60¢)

GREAT DIALOGUES
OF *Plato*

Translated by W.H.D. Rouse

EDITED BY ERIC H. WARMINGTON
AND PHILIP G. ROUSE

A MENTOR BOOK
Published by THE NEW AMERICAN LIBRARY

© 1956 BY JOHN CLIVE GRAVES ROUSE

All rights reserved

FIRST PRINTING, MARCH, 1956
NINTH PRINTING, APRIL, 1963

Library of Congress Catalog Card No. 56-7927

MENTOR TRADEMARK REG. U.S. PAT. OFF. AND FOREIGN COUNTRIES
REGISTERED TRADEMARK—MARCA REGISTRADA
HECHO EN CHICAGO, U.S.A.

MENTOR BOOKS are published *in the United States* by
The New American Library of World Literature, Inc.,
501 Madison Avenue, New York 22, New York,
in Canada by The New American Library of Canada Limited,
156 Front Street West, Toronto 1, Ontario,
in the United Kingdom by The New English Library Limited,
Barnard's Inn, Holborn, London, E.C. 1, England

PRINTED IN THE UNITED STATES OF AMERICA

Editors' Note

This translation was one of Dr. Rouse's many labours, and he was unfortunately prevented, by the volume of other work which he undertook, from giving it a final revision in detail before his death in February 1950.

In carrying out this revision, the Editors have tried to clear up the few inaccuracies and obscurities they found, and at the same time to interrupt as little as possible the distinctive character of Dr. Rouse's translation.

By far the greater part of his work remains unaltered, but in fairness to him it should be stated that the Divided Line diagram, the Banquet and Cave diagrams, and some of the footnotes have been subsequently added, so any faults in these should be imputed not to Dr. Rouse but to the Editors. The Summary of the *Republic*, which is also an addition, was written by J. C. G. Rouse, who also assisted in the work of editing.

Except for one or two well-known names (such as Plato) Dr. Rouse retained consistently the ancient Greek spelling of names; e.g. Phaidon, instead of Phaedo, the familiar Anglicised form; but for readers' convenience it has been decided to adopt the more generally accepted form for the titles of the dialogues.

The numbers and letters in parentheses at the top of each right-hand page of the translation refer to the pages of the standard Greek text.

ERIC H. WARMINGTON
PHILIP G. ROUSE

Preface

Socrates (469-399 B.C.) lived in the great age of Greece, after the two Persian invasions had been defeated (Darius, 490, Xerxes, 480-479 B.C.) and the Carthaginians overcome (Sicily, 480)—the great barbarian pincer-movements—after big political changes, and through the marvellous growth of drama, history, architecture and sculpture in Athens.

Athens in the days of Socrates was a small country town (by our measurements) where everybody knew everybody else, but they had no printed books, no newspapers, no broadcasting to satisfy an insatiable curiosity; when they wanted news they walked about and gossipped, and the central fount of gossip was the market place. There in halls or under the colonnades or in the open air parliament met (every grown man was a member) and lawsuits were tried (any man might be called to the jury or the bench—for the cases were put to the vote, a ballot vote), there public ministers or military commanders were elected by lot, and there the Athenian Tribes presided in regular order.[1] Groups of friends could gather and talk of all that attracted their minds, and if the subjects were interesting they discussed them in a friendly house or the gymnasium or any hall that might be available, or on the racecourse. The streets were narrow, the suburban roads were wide, and the scenes may be imagined.

Dion Chrysostom[2] sketches the spectacle which might be seen in any great city "of Greece or Italy" in his day, about the year 70 A.D., and things were much the same four hundred years earlier on a smaller scale:

> One may see in all the crowd and cram and crush everyone calmly doing his own business; the piper piping and teaching to pipe often in the street with his pupils, while the crowd passes by and does not interfere with him; the trainer producing his dancers for a stage play without noticing a few fights going on, and buying and selling and so forth, harping and painting pictures; most remarkable of all, schoolmasters sit in the streets with their boys, teaching or learning for all that multitudinous mob. Once, out for a walk across the racecourse, I myself saw people doing all sorts of things there, piping, dancing, one giving a show, one reciting a poem, one singing, one reading a story or fable, and not one of them preventing anyone else from his own particular business.

[1] See *Defence*, p. 438, n. 1.
[2] Dion Chrysostom, Speech 20, §9, edition by H. von Arnim.

But the whole Hellenic[1] race, in cities of the Aegean world from Asia Minor to South Italy and Sicily, was most interested in the sciences of matter and mind, what was the origin of things, what were sun, moon and stars, what was man and whence came he, and whither was he bound; and a great many philosophers propounded their theories, and all the world discussed them. In time a number of men appeared, called generally "Sophists" (students of philosophy) who travelled from city to city professing to teach their chosen doctrines, including conduct in private and public life and the right use of words, rhetoric and the art of persuasion, like travelling university professors, and asking for fees. None of the famous ones came from Athens, but they all tended to come to Athens, and several appear in Plato's dialogues. These are all represented as making speeches, and discussion is mentioned only of one. But Socrates was a born critic, and by his questions he created general definition and logical method, induction (from details to generals) and deduction (from generals to details).

Socrates, a small man of great courage,[2] was a stonemason and carver, and very poor; his wife was always reproaching him for neglect of his family. But he believed that he had a divine mission to test all statements, and that a "voice"[3] guided him in all his acts by warning him not to do things if they would be wrong. And so we see him questioning public and private men, and proving them wrong if their statements were untrue, which naturally amused the young men, who all thronged about him.

> When you agree to listen to the talk of Socrates, it might seem at first to be nothing but absurdity; such words and phrases are wrapped round it, like the hide of a boisterous satyr. Pack-asses and smiths and shoemakers and tanners are what he talks about, and he seems to be always saying the same things in the same words, so that any ignorant and foolish man would laugh at them. But when they are opened out, and you get inside them, you will find his words, first, full of sense, as no others are; next, most divine and containing the finest images of virtue, and reaching farthest, in fact reaching to everything which it profits a man to study who is to become noble and good.[4]

Socrates wrote nothing himself; but, after his death, his favourite and most brilliant pupil, Plato, (427–347 B.C.), set up a school of philosophy in 386 B.C. in a place called

[1] Greek. See p. 28, n. 3.
[2] See *Banquet*, p. 114 for his behaviour as a soldier in war.
[3] See *Defence*, p. 437.
[4] Extract from the speech of Alcibiades in praise of Socrates; see *Banquet*, p. 115 (inserted in this Preface by P. G. Rouse).

Academy[1] in an olive grove on the outskirts of Athens, and wrote his memories of what he had heard, and made this into a more or less complete system, adding much of his own, no doubt, but grouping all under the name of his beloved teacher. Plato did write his own work, and kept his records under constant revision, discussing them with his pupils.

The dialogues as recorded are some didactic—that is, they recommend or explain something, as the *Republic* or the *Laws* (Plato's latest work)—some negative, that is they expose or disprove a mistake; but many of them state or show a difficulty without giving a solution. Socrates himself described his object as that of a midwife, to bring other men's thoughts to birth, to stimulate them to think and to criticise themselves, not to instruct them. Thus the reader may be disappointed in finding no solution at the end, but he is encouraged to go on searching for himself.

Another of the pupils of Socrates was Xenophon, a matter-of-fact man of the world, and the hero of the grand book of adventures[2] which describes the advance and retreat of the Ten Thousand, whom he led home from Mesopotamia over the wild Armenian mountains. Xenophon has left a book of *Memorabilia*, reminiscences of Socrates and his conversations, sometimes describing scenes which Plato has described, but looking on all in a blunt man's way.

Love is the underlying subject of the *Banquet*, and a word is necessary about the vice of boy-loving, which disfigured much of ancient Greece. In some states, notably in military Sparta, it was accepted even in law; but not so in Athens, where law discouraged it. There it was only one of the extravagances of young men, in a society where the wife was not the centre of the home but only a manager of the household. Socrates turns even this to noble effect, when he draws men's thoughts from vulgarity to the noble aspect of love in seeking for ideal beauty of mind and spirit.

W. H. D. ROUSE

Histon Manor,
Cambridge.

---

[1] See there the olive grove of Academe,
  Plato's retirement, where the Attic bird (*the nightingale*)
  Trills her thick-warbled notes the summer long;
  Milton, *Paradise Regained*, iv. 244 ff.

[2] Xenophon, *Anabasis (The March Up Country)*.

Contents

ION	13
MENO (Menon)	28
SYMPOSIUM (The Banquet)	69
THE REPUBLIC	
Summary	118
Book I	125
Book II	155
Book III	182
Book IV	217
Book V	246
Book VI	281
Book VII	312
Book VIII	341
Book IX	369
Book X	393
THE APOLOGY (The Defence of Socrates)	423
CRITO (Criton)	447
PHAEDO (Phaidon)	460
The Greek Alphabet	522
Pronouncing Index	523

ION

Socrates, Ion

Introductory Note

This is a dialogue between Socrates and the "rhapsode" or reciter, Ion of Ephesus, who declares himself unequalled as a reciter and exponent of Homer. The rhapsodes ("song-stitchers") were men who made a living by giving public recitations from the great epic poets, chiefly Homer. The most successful held large audiences spellbound and moved them to amazement, laughter or tears. They also lectured or taught.

Socrates suggests to Ion that his skill as a reciter and his hold on his audiences are due to divine inspiration passed down to him through the poet, and shows up as absurd the claims of the reciters to teach practical rules of conduct from Homer.

The dialogue foreshadows the views on art as a whole which are explained in the Republic *(see pp. 406-407).*

SOCRATES: Good morning, Ion. Where have you now come from in your travels? From home, from Ephesus?

ION: Oh no, Socrates, from Epidauros; I have been at the feast of Asclepios.

SOCRATES: Do the Epidaurians hold a contest of reciters[1] of poetry in honour of the god?

ION: Yes, of course, and in other fine arts also.

SOCRATES: Well! and did you compete, please? And how did your contest go?

ION: First prize is what I won, Socrates.

SOCRATES: Well done! Now then, we must win the Panathenaia[2] too!

ION: So we will, please God.

[1] See Introductory Note.
[2] A great festival at Athens.

SOCRATES: I have often envied you reciters that art of yours, Ion. You have to dress in all sorts of finery, and make yourselves as grand as you can, to live up to your art! And you are, at the same time, bound to spend your time on no end of good poets, especially Homer, the best and most divine of all poets; you have to learn his meaning thoroughly, not only his verses, another enviable thing. For no one could be a good reciter unless he understood what the poet says. Yes, the reciter must be the interpreter of the poet's mind to the audience; and to do this, if he does not understand what the poet says, is impossible. So all that very properly makes one envy.

ION: Very true, Socrates. At least I found this myself the most troublesome part of the art; and I believe I can speak on Homer better than any other man alive. Not Metrodoros of Lampsacos, not Stesimbrotos the Thasian, not Glaucon, nor anyone else who ever was born could utter so many fine thoughts on Homer as I can.

SOCRATES: I'm glad to hear it, Ion, for it is clear you won't mind giving me a show.

ION: I will most certainly. You'll find it a treat to hear, Socrates, how finely I have decked out Homer! I believe I've earned a golden crown from the Homer Association.[1]

SOCRATES: Many thanks. I'll make leisure to hear it some time, but just answer me one question now: Are you as good at Hesiod and Archilochos, or only Homer?

ION: Only Homer, no one else; I think Homer's quite enough.

SOCRATES: But is there anything which both Homer and Hesiod speak about, and say the same?

ION: Yes, I think so, a good many things.

SOCRATES: Well then, in such matters could you explain what Homer says better than what Hesiod says?

ION: Oh, just the same, Socrates, when they say the same.

SOCRATES: What about when they don't say the same? For example, they both say something about divination?

ION: Yes, certainly.

SOCRATES: Well then, could a good diviner explain better what these two poets say about divination, both when they say the same and when they don't, or could you?

[1] There was a group in Chios called the Homeridai, "the clan or family of Homer," who claimed descent from him; but there is no evidence that they had anything to do with the reciters.

ION: A diviner could.

SOCRATES: But if you were a diviner, and if you were able to explain what was said the same, you would know how to explain what was said otherwise?

ION: That's obvious.

SOCRATES: Then how comes it that you are good at Homer but not at Hesiod and the other poets? Does not Homer speak about those very things which all other poets speak of? War, now—has not he said nearly everything about war, and the intercourse of men together, good men and bad men, craftsmen and laymen, about the gods' dealings with men and with each other, how they do it, about what happens in heaven and in the house of Hades, and the origins of gods and heroes? Are not these the things about which Homer made his poetry?

ION: That is quite true, Socrates.

SOCRATES: And the other poets, did not they speak of these same things?

ION: Yes, they did, Socrates, but not as Homer did.

SOCRATES: What then—worse than Homer?

ION: Much worse.

SOCRATES: And Homer did it better?

ION: Better indeed, I should think so, by Zeus!

SOCRATES: Now listen, dear heart alive! Suppose there are several people talking about number, and one speaks much better than the rest; I suppose somebody will be able to pick out the good speaker?

ION: I should say so.

SOCRATES: Will it be the same person who can also pick out the bad speakers, or somebody else?

ION: The same, I suppose.

SOCRATES: Well, this will be the person who has arithmetic, the art of numbers?

ION: Yes.

SOCRATES: Very well. Suppose a number of people discussing which foods are healthy, and one speaking much the best; will the same person recognise that the best speaker speaks best and the worse worse, or will one person recognise the best and another the worse?

ION: The same, that's clear, I suppose.

socrates: Who is he? What's his name?

ion: Doctor.

socrates: So we should say that in general the same person will always know who speaks well and who speaks badly, when a number of people are speaking about the same things; or else, if he does not know the bad speaker, it is clear he will not know the good speaker either about one and the same thing.

ion: Just so.

socrates: Then the same person is good at both?

ion: Yes.

socrates: Very well. You say, then, that both Homer and the other poets, two of them being Hesiod and Archilochos, speak about the same things, but not in the same way: that Homer speaks well, and the others not so well?

ion: Yes, I do say so, and it is true.

socrates: Then if you recognise the one who speaks well, you would recognise the ones who speak worse, and know that they do speak worse?

ion: Yes, so it seems.

socrates: Then, my dear fellow, if we say Ion is good at Homer and good at the other poets alike, we shan't be wrong, since you admit yourself that the same person is a sufficient judge of all that speak about the same things, and the poets pretty well all poetise the same things.

ion: Very well, Socrates, kindly explain the reason for something I am about to tell you. When someone speaks about any other poet, I can't attend. I can't put in one single remark to the point, I'm just in a doze—but only mention Homer and I'm wide awake in a jiffy, and I attend, and I have plenty to say!

socrates: Oh, that's not hard to guess, old fellow. Anyone can see that not by art and science are you able to speak about Homer; for if art made you able, you would be able to speak about all the other poets too; for there is, I suppose, an art of poetry as a whole; isn't there?

ion: Yes.

socrates: Well now, if one gets a grasp of any other art whatever, the whole of it, the same way of looking at your problem holds good for all the arts, doesn't it? Would you like me to say what I mean, my dear Ion?

ION: I should indeed, my dear Socrates; I love to listen to a clever man like you.

SOCRATES: I only wish that were true, my dear Ion. But clever! *You* are the clever ones, you reciters and actors, and the poets whose verses you chant;[1] all I can do is to tell the truth, as any plain man can do. Just look at my question; how plain and simple it is; Everyone recognises, as I said, that if one takes any art as a whole, it is the same problem for all arts. Suppose for our discussion we take, say, painting; there is a general art of painting, isn't there?

ION: Yes.

SOCRATES: And there have been also many painters, good and bad?

ION: Certainly.

SOCRATES: Well, have you ever seen anyone who was good at Polygnotos, son of Aglaophon, and could show which of his paintings are good and which are not, but with the other painters was incapable? When someone shows him works of other painters, does he just doze, and has nothing to say, and can't put in a remark: but when he has to give an opinion about Polygnotos, or any other one painter that you may choose, does he wake up and take notice, and does he find plenty to say?

ION: Oh dear me, no, not at all.

SOCRATES: Well then, take sculpture: Did you ever see anyone who was good at Daidalos, Metion's son, or Epeios, Panopeus' son, or Theodoros the Samian, or any other one sculptor, and could explain all his good work, but before the work of the other sculptors is dumbfounded, starts dozing, and has nothing to say?

ION: Oh dear me, no, I have not seen him either.

SOCRATES: Go on, then, to piping and harping and singing to the harp and reciting poetry; you saw never a man, as I think, who was good at discoursing on Olympos or Thamyras or Orpheus, or Phemios[2], the Ithacan reciter, but is struck dumb before Ion the Ephesian, and has no remark to make when he recites well or ill!

[1] Cf. *Republic*, p. 196, n. 2.
[2] Olympos was one of the mythical discoverers of music; Thamyras and Orpheus were, in tradition, bards of Thrace; Phemios was forced to sing to Penelope's suitors in the *Odyssey*.

ION: I can't contradict you there, Socrates. But one thing I do know about myself: I speak about Homer better than any other man alive, I have plenty to say and all declare that I speak well; but yet about the others, no. Do just see what that means.

SOCRATES: I do see, my dear Ion, and I'm going to show you what I think that means. Really, as I said just now, this is no art in you to speak well about Homer; no, some divine power is moving you, such as there is in that stone which Euripides called the Magnesian, but most people call it the Heracleian stone[1]. This magnet attracts iron rings, and not only that, but puts the same power into the iron rings, so that they can do the same as the stone does; they attract other rings, so that sometimes there is a whole long string of these rings hanging together, and all depend for their power on that one stone. So the Muse not only inspires people herself, but through these inspired ones others are inspired and dangle in a string. In fact, all the good poets who make epic poems use no art at all, but they are inspired and possessed when they utter all these beautiful poems, and so are the good lyric poets; these are not in their right mind when they make their beautiful songs, but they are like Corybants out of their wits dancing about. As soon as they mount on their harmony and rhythm, they become frantic and possessed; just as the Bacchant women, possessed and out of their senses, draw milk and honey out of the rivers, so the soul of these honey-singers does just the same, as they say themselves. The poets, as you know, tell us that they get their honey-songs from honey-founts of the Muses, and pluck from what they call Muses' gardens, and Muses' dells, and bring them to us, like honeybees[2], on the wing themselves like the bees; and what they say is true. For the poet is an airy thing, a winged and a holy thing; and he cannot make poetry until he becomes inspired and goes out of his senses and no mind is left in him; so long as he keeps possession of this, no man is able to make poetry and chant oracles. Not by art, then, they make their poetry with all those fine things about all sorts of matters—like your speeches about Homer—not by art, but by divine dispensation; therefore, the only poetry that each one can make is what the Muse has pushed him to make, one ecstatic odes, one hymns of praise, one songs for dance or pantomime, one epic, one satiric iambic; in every other

[1] Magnesia was a city in Caria in Asia Minor, where also were several called Heraclea.
[2] He plays on the words for song, *melos*, and honey, *meli*, and bee, *melitta*.

ION (533C–535C)

kind each one of them is a failure. For not by art do they speak these things, but by divine power, since if an art taught them how to speak well in one kind, they could do it also in all the other kinds. Therefore God takes the mind out of the poets, and uses them as his servants, and so also those who chant oracles, and divine seers; because he wishes us to know that not those we hear, who have no mind in them, are those who say such precious things, but God himself is the speaker, and through them he shows his meaning to us. A very strong piece of evidence for the argument is Tynnichos of Chalcis, who never made one poem which a man would think worth mentioning except only the hymn of praise which all the world sings,[1] well-nigh most beautiful of all lyrics, really and truly "a godsend from the Muses" as he calls it himself. Here most of all I think God has shown us, beyond all dispute, that these beautiful poems are not human, not made by man, but divine and made by God; and the poets are nothing but the gods' interpreters, possessed each by whatever god it may be. Just to prove this, God purposely sang the most beautiful of songs through the meanest of poets. Don't you think I speak the truth, my dear Ion?

ION: Upon my word I do! You touch my soul in some way by your words, my dear Socrates! I feel sure that a divine dispensation from heaven for us makes good poets the interpreters in these things.

SOCRATES: And don't you reciters interpret the poet's works?

ION: That is quite true also.

SOCRATES: So you are interpreters of interpreters?

ION: We are indeed.

SOCRATES: Then go on and tell me something more, my dear Ion; don't hide it, just answer my question. When you speak your verses well, and astound the audience most—you know, when you sing how Odysseus leaps onto the threshold, and reveals himself to the wooers, and spreads out the arrows before his feet,[2] or how Achilles rushes on Hector,[3] or one of those touching scenes about Andromache[4] or Hecuba or Priam[5] —are you in your right mind then, or do you get beside yourself, does your soul feel itself inspired and present in the action which you describe, somewhere in Ithaca or at Troy or wherever the epic scene is?

[1] Like the poet of "The Burial of Sir John Moore at Corunna," Charles Wolfe.
[2] Homer, *Odyssey*, xxii. 2 ff.
[3] Homer, *Iliad*, xxii, 312 ff.
[4] *Iliad*, vi. 370-502; xxii. 437 ff.
[5] *Iliad*, xxii. 430-436; xxiv. 747-759; xxii. 408-428, xxiv. 144 ff.

ION: Clear as daylight I see your proof, my dear Socrates! I will not hide it, I will tell you frankly. Why, whenever I speak of sad and touching scenes, my eyes are full of tears; when it is something terrible or awful, my hair stands up straight with fear and my heart leaps!

SOCRATES: Well then, my dear Ion, could we say such a man is for the time being in his right senses who, decked out in gorgeous raiment and golden crown, bursts out crying at a sacrifice or a festival, when he has lost none of these fine things? Or who is terrified, with more than twenty thousand friendly faces about him, when no one robs him or wrongs him?

ION: No, upon my word, not at all, my dear Socrates, to tell the honest truth.

SOCRATES: And do you know that you reciters make most of the audience do the very same?

ION: Oh yes, indeed I do! I always look down from my platform, and there they are crying and glaring and amazed, according to what I say. Indeed, I'm bound to pay careful attention to them. If I leave them crying in their seats, I shall laugh at my pockets full of money; if I leave them laughing, I myself shall cry over the money lost.

SOCRATES: Then do you know that the member of the audience is the last of those rings which I described as getting power from each other through the magnet? You the reciter and the actor, are the middle ring, and the first is the poet himself; but God through all these draws the soul of men whithersoever he will, by running the power through them one after another. It's just like that magnet! And there is a great string of choristers and producers and under-producers all stuck to the sides of these hanging rings of the Muse. And one poet hangs from one Muse and another from another—we call it "possessed," and it is very like that, for he is held fast; and from these first rings, the poets, different people again, hang on each to his own poet, some to Orpheus, and some to Musaios, but most hang on to Homer, and they are possessed and held fast through the poet. And you are one of them, Ion; you are possessed through Homer; and whenever someone recites who belongs to another poet, you go to sleep and have nothing to say, but whenever someone chants a melody of this poet, you are awake in a jiffy and your soul dances and you have plenty to say; for it is not by any art or science of Homer that you say what you say, but by divine dispensation and possession. Just so with the wild Corybants; the only melody which they quickly perceive is that which belongs to the god of whom they are possessed, whoever he is, and for that melody they have plenty of dances and songs, but they care nothing about the rest. The same with you, my dear Ion. Let anyone mention Homer, you are ready; for anyone else you are dumb. And this is the reason why, this answers your question why you have plenty to say about Homer and nothing about the others; because no art, but divine dispensation, makes you Homer's great encomiast.

ION: That is excellently said, Socrates. But I should be surprised if you could be eloquent enough to persuade me that I am always possessed and mad when I praise Homer. If you heard me speaking about Homer, I believe you would not think so yourself.

SOCRATES: Well, that's just what I want to hear—but not until you answer one more question: What in Homer do you speak well about? Not everything, I suppose.

ION: Every mortal thing, my dear Socrates, I assure you.

SOCRATES: Surely not when he speaks about something which *you* do not know?

ION: And what is there that Homer speaks about which I don't know?

SOCRATES: Why, does not Homer speak often enough about arts and crafts? For example, driving a chariot—if I can remember the verses, I will repeat them.

ION: Oh, I'll say them, I remember.

SOCRATES: Then tell me what Nestor says to his son Antilochos, in the horse race at the funeral of Patroclos, when he advises him to be careful in turning the post.[1]

ION: This is what he says:

> Lean yourself over in your polished car
> A little to the left of both your steeds;
> Call to the right-hand horse and goad him on,
> And slacken with your hand his reins. Then let
> The left horse swerve close round the turning post,
> So that the nave of well-made wheel may seem
> To reach the stone's edge: but avoid to graze it!

[1] *Iliad*, xxiii, 335 ff.

SOCRATES: That will do. Now then, Ion, which would know better whether that is good or bad advice, a doctor or a charioteer?

ION: A charioteer, I suppose.

SOCRATES: Because that's his own art, or why?

ION: Because it is his art.

SOCRATES: Well, has God granted to each of the arts to be able to know some particular work? For example, what we know by the art of the pilot we shall not know by the art of physic.

ION: Of course not.

SOCRATES: And what we know by the art of physic, we shall not know by the art of carpentry.

ION: Of course not.

SOCRATES: And is that true of all arts—what we know by one we shall not know by another? But before that, answer me this: Do you agree that there are different arts?

ION: Yes.

SOCRATES: Do you distinguish as I do—would you call them different arts when they are the knowledge of different things?

ION: Yes.

SOCRATES: For I suppose that if one were only a knowledge of the same things as another, there would be no reason to call the arts different, when you would know the same things from both. For example, I know that here are five fingers, and you know the same about them as I do; then if I asked you if we both knew it by the same art, arithmetic, or a different one, you would say, "by the same," I suppose?

ION: Yes.

SOCRATES: Very well, now tell me what I was going to ask you just now, is this what you think about all arts in general: by the same art we must know the same things, but by another art not the same things—if it is another art, we must know different things by that?

ION: Yes, that is what I think, Socrates.

SOCRATES: Then if anyone has not a certain art, he will not be able to know what is said or done well in that art?

ION: Quite true.

SOCRATES: Then take those verses which you repeated: Will you or a charioteer know better whether Homer speaks well or ill?

ION: A charioteer.

SOCRATES: Because you are a reciter, not a charioteer.

ION: Yes.

SOCRATES: And the reciter's art is different from the charioteer's art?

ION: Yes.

SOCRATES: If it is different, then, it is also a knowledge of different things?

ION: Yes.

SOCRATES: Well then, when Homer says how Nestor's woman Hecamede gives wounded Machaon a posset to drink, it goes something like this—[1]

> With Pramnian wine, and over it she grates
> With a bronze grater goat's-milk cheese, and adds
> An onion as a relish for the drink.

Whether this is good or bad in Homer, what will decide properly, the art of physic or the art of reciting?

ION: Physic.

SOCRATES: Again when Homer says—[2]

> Into the deep she plunged, like a lead weight
> Set in an ox horn, which goes hurtling down
> With death for greedy fishes.

Do we say this is rather for the fisherman's art to judge than the reciter's, whether it is good or bad?

ION: The fisherman's art, Socrates, that is clear.

SOCRATES: Look here then. If you were asking the questions, and if you should say, "Ah well, Socrates, so much for these arts; you find the places in Homer where each of these ought to decide, but kindly find something about a seer and his divination, which are the bits which he ought to be able to decide and say whether they are done well or badly." If you were to say that, see how easily and truly I shall answer. He speaks of these in many passages in the *Odyssey*,

[1] *Iliad*, xi. 639.
[2] *Iliad*, xxiv. 80.

for example what that seer of Melampus' family says[1] to the wooers, Theoclymenos, I mean—

> Poor souls, what mischief's on you? Night is wrapt
> About your heads and faces, down to your feet—
> There is a blaze of wailing, cheeks bedabbled—
> The porch is full, the hall is full of spectres,
> Hurrying to hell and darkness; and the sun
> Put out in heaven, a foul mist covers all.

There are many places in the *Iliad*, too, as in the battle at the wall, where he says—[2]

> A bird came over as they tried to cross,
> An eagle flying high, skirting their left,
> With a great serpent bleeding in his talons,
> Alive and struggling still, not yet forgetful
> Of battle's joy. Bent back it struck the bird
> That held it on the breast, hard by the neck.
> The eagle hurled it from him to the ground
> In agony, and down among the crowd
> It fell; he shrieked, and flew on puffs of wind.

These and other such things I should say it is proper for the seer to examine and to decide.

ION: Yes, you are right in what you say, Socrates.

SOCRATES: So are *you*, Ion. Well now, come, I have picked out from both *Odyssey* and *Iliad* pieces which belong to the seer, and to the doctor, and to the fisherman; will you kindly pick out for me, since you are better up in Homer than I am, pieces which belong to the reciter, my dear Ion, and the reciter's art, which are proper for the reciter to examine and judge beyond the rest of mankind.

ION: My reply, my dear Socrates, is all Homer.

SOCRATES: Oh dear me, Ion, surely not all? Have you such a bad memory? Surely a reciter ought not to have a bad memory.

ION: Why, what have I forgotten?

SOCRATES: Don't you remember that you said the reciter's art was different from the charioteer's?

ION: Yes, I remember.

SOCRATES: Did you not agree that, being different, it would know different things?

[1] *Odyssey*, xx. 351.
[2] *Iliad* xii. 200.

ION: Yes.

SOCRATES: Then the reciter and his art will not know all Homer, according to your argument.

ION: All except, perhaps, a few things like that.

SOCRATES: By things like that, you mean all the business of the other arts, pretty well. But what will he know then, since he will not know everything?

ION: What is proper for a man to say—so at least *I* take it, or what for a woman, what for a slave or what for a free man, what for a subject or what for a ruler.

SOCRATES: Do you mean, what is proper to say for the ruler of a ship in a storm at sea? Will the reciter know that better than the pilot?

ION: Oh no, the pilot will know that better.

SOCRATES: And what the ruler of a sick man ought to say: Will the reciter know that better than the doctor?

ION: No, he won't know that either.

SOCRATES: But you say he knows what a slave ought to say?

ION: Yes.

SOCRATES: If, for example, the slave is an oxherd, and his cattle are wild and he wants to calm them, you say the reciter will know what he ought to say, and not the oxherd?

ION: Oh dear, no.

SOCRATES: Then, what a woman ought to say about working wool, a woman whose business is to spin?

ION: No.

SOCRATES: Then he will know what a man ought to say if he is a general encouraging his troops?

ION: Yes, that is the sort of thing a reciter will know.

SOCRATES: Oh, the reciter's art is the general's art?

ION: I should know, at any rate, what the general ought to say.

SOCRATES: Perhaps you are something of a general, Ion. In fact, if you were something of a horseman as well as a harpist, you might know when horses were well or badly managed; but then I might ask you, "Which of the two arts, Ion, makes you know the well-managed horses? The art by which you are a horseman, or the art by which you are a harpist?" What would you answer me then?

ION: That which makes me a horseman.

SOCRATES: Well, if you could distinguish good performances on the harp, would you agree that you did it as being a harpist and not as a horseman?

ION: Yes.

SOCRATES: Well, since you understand military matters, do you do so as being a bit of a general, or as being a good reciter?

ION: I think there's no difference.

SOCRATES: How's that—no difference? Do you say that reciting and generalship are one art, or two?

ION: One, I think.

SOCRATES: Then whoever is a good reciter is also really a good general?

ION: Certainly, my dear Socrates.

SOCRATES: Then whoever is really a good general is also a good reciter?

ION: No, I don't think that.

SOCRATES: But you do think that whoever is a good reciter is also a good general?

ION: By all means.

SOCRATES: Well, you are the best reciter in Hellas?

ION: Much the best, my dear Socrates.

SOCRATES: Then are you also the best general in Hellas?

ION: Yes, I assure you, Socrates; and I learnt it all from Homer.

SOCRATES: Good heavens, my dear Ion! You are the best man of the nation, both reciter and general! Then why do you career all round Hellas reciting, and don't general at all? Do you think there is a great need for a reciter in our nation, with a golden crown on his head, and no need at all for a general?

ION: The reason is, my dear Socrates, that my own city of Ephesus is under your state's rule and generalship, and needs no general of its own; and your state and Lacedaimon[1] would

[1] Sparta.

not choose me as general, for you think you are enough by yourselves.

SOCRATES: Dear old fellow, don't you know Apollodoros of Cyzicos?

ION: Who is he?

SOCRATES: One whom the Athenians have often chosen as general over themselves, although he is a foreigner. And Phanosthenes of Andros, and Heracleides of Clazomenai, they are both foreigners, but they proved themselves men of merit, and so this our city invites them in for generalships and other high offices. But not Ion of Ephesus, it seems! Will she not choose him as general, and honour him, if he is considered a man of merit? Why, aren't you Ephesians really Athenians in origin, and is not Ephesus no mean city?

But really, my dear Ion, if you are telling the truth when you say that by art and knowledge you are able to praise Homer, you are cheating me. You declared to me that you know any number of fine things about Homer, and you promised to make an exhibition; but you only deceive me, and there is no exhibition—far from it! You will not even tell me what these things are in which you are so clever, although I have been imploring you all this time. You are really nothing but a new Proteus, changing into all sorts of shapes, and twisting up and down, and at last you escaped me and turned into a general, all to avoid showing me how clever you are in the lore of Homer. Well, if you are an artist, and if you just promised to exhibit your art, and then deceived me, as I said just now, you are cheating; if you are not an artist, but are possessed by divine dispensation through Homer, and say all those fine things about the poet without knowing anything, as I described you, then you are not cheating. Choose, then, which you prefer us to believe you, a cheat or one divine.

ION: A great difference there, Socrates! It is much finer to be considered divine!

SOCRATES: Then that finer thing is yours, Ion, in our belief; you are divine, and not an artist, when you eulogize Homer.

MENO (Menon)

Menon, Socrates, A slave of Menon, Anytos

Introductory Note

This dialogue is a discussion of the nature of virtue and particularly the question whether virtue can be taught.

Menon was a wealthy young Thessalian nobleman. He took part, probably not long afterwards, as a Thessalian general in the famous expedition of the Ten Thousand under Cyrus in 401 B.C. against the King of Persia; he was captured, and was put to death by the King. Xenophon considered him a treacherous, self-seeking character (The March Up Country, ii. 5.28, translated by W. H. D. Rouse).

Anytos appears later as one of the three accusers at Socrates' trial.

MENON: Can you tell me, Socrates—can virtue be taught? Or if not, does it come by practice? Or does it come neither by practice nor by teaching, but do people get it by nature, or in some other way?

SOCRATES: My dear Menon, the Thessalians have always had a good name in our nation—they were always admired as good horsemen and men with full purses. Now, it seems to me, we must add brains to the list. Your friend Aristippos is a very good example, and his townsmen from Larissa. Gorgias[1] is the man who set it all going. As soon as he got there, all the Aleuadai[2] were at his feet—your own bosom friend Aristippos was one—not to mention the rest of Thessaly. Here's a custom he taught you, at least—to answer generously and without fear if anyone asked you a question; quite natural, of course, when one knows the answer. Just what he did himself; he was a willing victim of the civilised world of Hellas[3]—any Hellene might ask him anything he liked, and every mortal soul got his answer!

But here, my dear Menon, it is just the opposite. There is a regular famine of brains here, and your part of the world

---

[1] A celebrated Sophist from Leontini in Sicily; he taught rhetoric based upon impressive language. He visited Athens in 427 B. C., and travelled about Greece, lecturing. See also *Banquet*, p. 93, n. 5.
[2] As it were, the leaders of society in Thessaly.
[3] Greece. The ancient Greeks called themselves Hellenes, and their country Hellas; it was later called Graecia by the Romans.

seems to hold a monopoly in that article. At least, if you do ask anyone here a question like that, all you will get is a laugh and—"My good man, you must think I am inspired! Virtue? Can it be taught? Or how does it come? Do I know that? So far from knowing whether it can be taught or can't be taught, I don't know even the least little thing about virtue, I don't even know what virtue is!"

I'm in the same fix myself, Menon. I am as poor of the article as the rest of us, and I have to blame myself that I don't know the least little thing about virtue, and when I don't know what a thing is, how can I know its quality? Take Menon, for example: If someone doesn't know in the least who Menon is, how can he know whether Menon is handsome or rich or even a gentleman, or perhaps just the opposite? Do you think he can?

MENON: Not I. But look here, Socrates, don't *you* really know what virtue is? Are we to give that report of you in Larissa?

SOCRATES: Just so, my friend, and more—I never met anyone who did, so far as I know.

MENON: What! Did not you meet Gorgias when he was here?

SOCRATES: Oh, yes.

MENON: Didn't you think *he* knew?

SOCRATES: I have rather a poor memory, Menon, so I can't say at the moment whether I did think so. But perhaps he did know, or perhaps you know what he said; kindly remind me, then, what he did say. You say it yourself, if you like; for I suppose you think as he thought.

MENON: Oh, yes.

SOCRATES: Then let us leave him out of it, since he is not here; tell me yourself, in heaven's name, Menon, what do you say virtue is? Tell me, and don't grudge it; it will be the luckiest lie I ever told if it turns out that you know and Gorgias knew, and I went and said I never met anyone who did know.

MENON: That is nothing difficult, my dear Socrates. First, if you like, a man's virtue, that is easy; this is a man's virtue: to be able to manage public business, and in doing it to help friends and hurt enemies, and to take care to keep clear of such mischief himself. Or, if you like, a woman's virtue, there's no difficulty there: she must manage the house well, and keep the stores all safe, and obey her husband. And a child's virtue is different for boy and girl, and an older man's, a freeman's, if you like, or a slave's, if you like. There are a very large number of other virtues, so there is no difficulty in saying what virtue is; for according to each of our activities and ages each of us has his virtue for doing each sort of work, and in the same way, Socrates, I think, his vice.

SOCRATES: I seem to have been lucky indeed, my dear Menon, if I have been looking for one virtue and found a whole swarm of virtues in your store. However, let us take up this image, Menon, the swarm. If I asked you what a bee really is, and you answered that there are many different kinds of bees, what would you answer me if I asked you then: "Do you say there are many different kinds of bees, differing from each other in being bees more or less? Or do they differ in some other respect, for example in size, or beauty, and so forth?" Tell me, how would you answer that question?

MENON: I should say that they are not different at all one from another in beehood.

SOCRATES: Suppose I went on to ask: "Tell me this, then—what do you say exactly is that in which they all are the same, and not different?" Could you answer anything to that?

MENON: Oh, yes.

SOCRATES: Very well, now then for virtues. Even if there are many different kinds of them, they all have one something, the same in all, which makes them virtues. So if one is asked, "What is virtue?" one must have this clear in his view before he can answer the question. Do you understand what I mean?

MENON: I think I understand; but I do not yet grasp your question as I could wish.

SOCRATES: Do you think that virtue alone is like that, Menon—I mean one thing in a man and another in a woman, and so forth, or do you also say the same of health and size and strength? Do you think health is one thing in a man, and another in a woman? Or is the essence the same everywhere if it be health, whether it be in a man or in anything else whatever?

MENON: I think health is the same thing in both man and woman.

MENO (71E–73C)

SOCRATES: And what of size and strength? If a woman is strong, is it the same essence and the same strength which will make her strong? By the same strength I mean this: the strength is not different in itself whether it be in a man or a woman. Do you think there is any difference?

MENON: Why, no.

SOCRATES: Yet virtue will differ in itself in a boy and in an old man, in a woman and in a man?

MENON: I can't help thinking, Socrates, that this is not quite like those other things.

SOCRATES: Very well: Did you not say that man's virtue is to manage public affairs well, and woman's to manage a home?

MENON: Yes, I did.

SOCRATES: Then is it possible to manage a state or a house or anything well, without managing temperately[1] and justly?

MENON: Certainly not.

SOCRATES: If, then, they manage temperately and justly, they will manage with temperance and justice?

MENON: Necessarily.

SOCRATES: Then both need the same things, if they are to be good, both woman and man—justice and temperance.

MENON: So it seems.

SOCRATES: What of the boy and the old man? If they are reckless and unjust, could they ever be good?

MENON: Certainly not.

SOCRATES: But they must be temperate and just?

MENON: Yes.

SOCRATES: Then all men are good in the same way? For when they have the same things, they are good.

MENON: So it seems.

SOCRATES: Then I suppose if they had not the same virtue, they would not be good in the same way.

MENON: Certainly not.

---
[1] The Greek word translated "temperately" means rather "with soundness of mind."

SOCRATES: Since therefore the same virtue is in all, try to tell me, and try to remember, what Gorgias says it is, and what you say too.

MENON: What can it be but to be able to rule men? If you want something which is the same in all.

SOCRATES: That is just what I do want. But is it the same virtue in a boy, Menon, and a slave, for each of them to be able to rule his master? And do you think he that ruled would still be a slave?

MENON: No, Socrates, I certainly don't think that.

SOCRATES: For it isn't reasonable, my good fellow. But here is another thing to consider. You say, "able to rule": shall we not add to it justly, not unjustly?

MENON: I think so, yes; for justice is virtue, Socrates.

SOCRATES: Virtue, Menon, or *a* virtue?

MENON: What do you mean by that?

SOCRATES: The same as in anything else. For example, if you please, take roundness: this I would say is *a* figure, not simply thus—figure. I would say so because there are other figures.

MENON: What you said was quite right, since I agree that there are other virtues besides justice.

SOCRATES: What are they, tell me, just as I would tell you other figures if you ask; then you tell me some other virtues.

MENON: Very well. Courage, I think, is a virtue and temperance and wisdom and high-mindedness and plenty more.

SOCRATES: Here we are again, Menon: We looked for one virtue and found many, although that was in another way; but the one that is in all these things we cannot find!

MENON: I can't see my way yet, Socrates, to find the one virtue you seek in them all, as we did with the other things.

SOCRATES: That is quite likely; but I will do my best to bring us a step forward, if I can. You understand, no doubt, that it is the same with everything: if someone should ask you what I mentioned just now: "What is figure, Menon?" and you said to him: "Roundness"; and if he asked you, as I would: "Is roundness figure or a figure?" I suppose you would say: "A figure."

MENON: Yes, to be sure.

MENO (73C–75B)

SOCRATES: Because there are other figures, isn't that the reason?

MENON: Yes.

SOCRATES: And if he asked further: "What other figures?", you would tell him?

MENON: So I would.

SOCRATES: And again, if he asked you in the same way what colour is, and you said, "White," the man would ask next, "Is white colour, or a colour?" And you would say, "A colour," because there are others.

MENON: I should.

SOCRATES: And if he requested you to tell him other colours, you would tell him others that are no less colours than white?

MENON: Yes.

SOCRATES: If then he followed up the argument, like me, and said, "We always arrive at a multitude. I don't want that; but since you call these many by one name, and say they are all figures without exception, and that too even if they are opposite to each other, what is this which contains the round no less than the straight? You name it indeed figure, and say the round is no less figure than the straight." Is not that what you say?

MENON: It is.

SOCRATES: Well, when you say that, do you then mean that the round is no more round than the straight, or the straight no straighter than the round?

MENON: Not at all, Socrates.

SOCRATES: Yet you do say that the round is no more figure than the straight, or the straight than the round.

MENON: Quite true.

SOCRATES: Then what is this name, figure? Try to tell me. If someone asked you like that about colour or figure, and you said, "My good man, I don't understand what you want, and I don't know what you mean," perhaps he would have been surprised, and would have said, "Don't you understand that I am looking for the common element in these?" Or would you have nothing to say, if someone should ask, "What is there in the round and straight and so forth, all that you call figures, the same in all?" Try to say, that you may have a little practice for your reply about virtue.

MENON: No, no, Socrates, *you* say.

SOCRATES: Shall I grant you that favour?

MENON: Please do!

SOCRATES: And then will *you* do me the favour of telling me about virtue?

MENON: Yes, yes.

SOCRATES: Then I must do my best; it is worth while.

MENON: That it is.

SOCRATES: Come along, then, let me try to tell you what figure is. Just think a moment: Will you accept this for it— let us suppose that figure is the only thing in the world which is always found along with colour. Good enough, eh? Or do you want something else? If you give me an answer like that about virtue, I shall be quite content, I assure you.

MENON: But that's silly, my dear Socrates.

SOCRATES: How do you mean?

MENON: That figure, according to your statement, is what always goes with colour. Very well; but if someone said he didn't know what colour is, and if he were in the same difficulty as about figure, what do you think you should have answered them?

SOCRATES: Only the truth! And if my questioner were one of these clever fellows, who just chop logic and argue to win, I should answer him, "I have said my say; if I am wrong, it is your business to take up the argument and to refute it." But if we were friends, like you and me now, who wished to have a talk together, you see I must answer more gently and more like friends talking together; and perhaps it is more like friends talking together, not only to answer with truth, but to use only what the one who is questioned admits that he knows.

Then that is how I will try to talk with you. Tell me, if you please: Do you speak of an end of anything? I mean something like this, a boundary or a verge—these are all the same thing. Perhaps Prodicos[1] might not agree with us, but you at any rate say that a thing is bounded and ended; that's the sort of thing I mean, nothing elaborate.

MENON: Oh yes, I use those words, and I think I understand you.

[1] A noted Sophist of Ceos; see p. 49, n. 1.

MENO (75B–76D)

SOCRATES: Very well; you speak of a surface, or a solid as it may be, like those things in geometry.

MENON: Yes, I use those words.

SOCRATES: There's enough then already for me to explain what I call figure. With every figure, I say that to which the solid extends is the figure; to put it shortly, I would say that figure is the boundary of a solid.

MENON: And what is colour, Socrates?

SOCRATES: You're a bully, Menon; you worry an old man to answer questions, and you won't trouble to remember what Gorgias says virtue is.

MENON: Oh, I'll tell you that as soon as you tell me this, my dear Socrates!

SOCRATES: Anyone could tell you're a handsome man and have lovers, by only hearing you talk, even if he were blindfolded!

MENON: Why, pray?

SOCRATES: Because in your talk you do nothing but lay commands on people, like young society beauties who are regular tyrants as long as they are young and good-looking. And perhaps you have found me out already; I can't resist the handsome! So I will do you the favour of answering.

MENON: Yes, do me that favour.

SOCRATES: Then do you wish me to answer in the style of Gorgias, so that you could most easily follow?

MENON: Of course I do.

SOCRATES (*imitating Gorgias*): Well, you people say that emanations, *or films,* are given off from things—that is the science of Empedocles.

MENON: Certainly.

SOCRATES: And there are pores, *or passages,* and the emanations go *pouring* into them and through them?

MENON: Quite so.

SOCRATES: And some of the films fit some of the *pores,* but some are too small or too large?

MENON: That is true.

SOCRATES: You speak of sight also?

MENON: Yes.

SOCRATES: Then from these things "Comprehend what I tell thee," as Pindar said: Colour is an emanation from figures, and is symmetrical with sight and perceptible by sense.

MENON (*laughing*): That is an excellent answer of yours, my dear Socrates.

SOCRATES: Perhaps because you are used to the way it is put. And at the same time, I think, you notice that you could define in this way what sound is, and smell, and many other such things?

MENON: Certainly, yes.

SOCRATES: Because the answer is in high poetic style, so you like it better than the one about figure.

MENON: I do, certainly.

SOCRATES: But it is not so good, my dear son of Alexidemos; I am convinced the other is better. And I think you would agree with me, if you were not obliged to go off before the Mysteries, as you said yesterday; you have only to stay and be initiated.

MENON: Oh, I would stay, my dear Socrates, if you would only go on talking like this!

SOCRATES: Indeed, my will shall not be wanting; I would go on talking like this for both our sakes, but I fear I shall not be able to go on talking like this for long. But now please try yourself to keep your promise to give me a general description of virtue—what it is; no more turning the singular into the plural, as witty people say whenever you smash something; just leave virtue sound and whole, and tell me what it is—I have shown you how to do it by my examples.

MENON: Then, my dear Socrates, virtue seems to me to be, as the poet says, "to rejoice in what is handsome and to be able"; I agree with the poet, and I say virtue is to desire handsome things and to be able to provide them.

SOCRATES: Do you say that the man who desires handsome things is desirous of good things?

MENON: By all means.

SOCRATES: Do you imply that there are some that desire bad things, and others good? Don't you think, my dear fellow, that all desire good things?

MENON: No, I don't.

SOCRATES: But some desire bad things?

MENON: Yes.

SOCRATES: Thinking the bad things to be good, you mean, or even recognising that they are bad, still they desire them?

MENON: Both, I think.

SOCRATES: Do you really think, my dear Menon, that anyone, knowing the bad things to be bad, still desires them?

MENON: Certainly.

SOCRATES: What does he desire, do you say—to have them?

MENON: To have them; what else?

SOCRATES: Thinking that the bad things benefit him that has them, or knowing that they injure whoever gets them?

MENON: Some thinking that the bad things benefit, some also knowing that they injure.

SOCRATES: Do those who think that the bad things benefit know that the bad things are bad?

MENON: I don't think that at all.

SOCRATES: Then it is plain that those who desire bad things are those who don't know what they are, but they desire what they thought were good whereas they really are bad; so those who do not know what they are, but think they are good, clearly desire the good. Is not that so?

MENON: It really seems like it.

SOCRATES: Very well. Those who desire the bad things, as you say, but yet think that bad things injure whoever gets them, know, I suppose, that they themselves will be injured by them?

MENON: They must.

SOCRATES: But do not these believe that those who are injured are miserable in so far as they are injured?

MENON: They must believe that too.

SOCRATES: Miserable means wretched?

MENON: So I think.

SOCRATES: Well, is there anyone who wishes to be miserable and wretched?

MENON: I think not, Socrates.

SOCRATES: Then nobody desires bad things, my dear Menon, nobody, unless he wishes to be like that. For what is the depth of misery other than to desire bad things and to get them?

MENON: It really seems that is the truth, Socrates, and no one desires what is bad.

SOCRATES: You said just now, didn't you, that virtue is to desire good things and to be able to provide them.

MENON: Yes, I did.

SOCRATES: Well, one part of what you said, the desiring, is in all, and in this respect one man is no better than another.

MENON: It seems so.

SOCRATES: It is clear, then that if one is better than another, he must be better in the ability.

MENON: Certainly.

SOCRATES: Then according to your argument virtue is the power to get good things.

MENON: My dear Socrates, the whole thing, I must admit, seems to be exactly as you take it.

SOCRATES: Now let us see whether your last is true—perhaps you might be right. You say virtue is to be able to provide the good?

MENON: Quite so.

SOCRATES: Don't you call good such things as health and wealth?

MENON: Yes, and to possess gold and silver and public honour and appointments.

SOCRATES: Don't you say some other things are good besides these?

MENON: No, at least, I mean all such things as those.

SOCRATES: Very well; to provide gold and silver is virtue, according to Menon, the family friend of the Great King.[1] Do you add to your providing, my dear Menon, the qualification "fairly and justly"? Or does that make no difference to you, and if a man provides them unjustly, you call it virtue all the same?

[1] The King of Persia, the owner of fabulous riches.

MENO (78B–79C)

MENON: Oh dear me no, Socrates.

SOCRATES: It is vice then.

MENON: Dear me, yes, of course.

SOCRATES: It is necessary then, as it seems, to add to this getting, justice or temperance or piety or some other bit of virtue; or else it will not be virtue, although it provides good things.

MENON: Why, how could it be virtue without these?

SOCRATES: And not to get gold and silver when that is not just, neither for yourself nor anyone, is not this not-getting also virtue?

MENON: It looks like it.

SOCRATES: Then the getting of such good things would not be virtue any more than the not-getting; but as it seems, getting with justice would be virtue, and getting without such qualifications, vice.

MENON: I think it must be as you put it.

SOCRATES: Now we said a little while ago that each of them is a bit of virtue, justice and temperance and all things like that.

MENON: Yes.

SOCRATES: Then are you making fun of me, Menon?

MENON: How so, Socrates?

SOCRATES: Because I begged you just now not to break virtue into bits, or give me virtue as a handful of small change, and I gave you specimens to show how you ought to answer; and you simply paid no attention—now you tell me virtue is to be able to get good things with justice, and justice, you say, is a bit of virtue!

MENON: Yes, that is what I say.

SOCRATES: It follows, then, from what you agree, that to do whatever we do along with a bit of virtue is virtue; for you say justice is a bit of virtue, and so with each of those bits. Well, why do I say this? Because when I begged you to tell me what whole virtue is, instead of telling me that (far from it!) you say that every action is virtue if it be done with a bit of virtue, just as if you had explained what virtue is as a whole and I should know it at once even if you chopped your coin up into farthings. Then I must put the very same question from the beginning, as it seems: My dear friend Menon, what is virtue, if a little bit of virtue would make any action virtue? For that is as much as saying, whenever anyone says it, that all action with justice is virtue. Don't you think yourself that I must put the same question again, or do you believe that we can know what a bit of virtue is, when we do not know virtue itself?

MENON: I don't believe that.

SOCRATES: Perhaps you remember that when I answered you about figure a while ago, we excluded such an answer as might try to explain things by using what was not yet agreed between us but what we were seeking still.

MENON: We did right to exclude that.

SOCRATES: Then don't *you* do it now, my dear fellow! We are still trying to find out what virtue is as a whole, and pray do not believe you will make that clear to anyone by using bits of virtue in your answer. You will never explain anything to anyone by this same manner of speaking, but you will again come up against the same question, what this virtue is which you bring into your explanation. Do you think there's something in what I say?

MENON: I think you are quite right.

SOCRATES: Then begin again and answer: What is virtue, according to you and your friend?

MENON: Well now, my dear Socrates, you are just like what I always heard before I met you: always puzzled yourself and puzzling everybody else. And now you seem to me to be a regular wizard, you dose me with drugs and bewitch me with charms and spells, and drown me in puzzledom. I'll tell you just what you are like, if you will forgive a little jest: your looks and the rest of you are exactly like a flatfish and you sting like this stingray—only go near and touch one of those fish and you go numb, and that is the sort of thing you seem to have done to me. Really and truly, my soul is numb and my mouth is numb, and what to answer you I do not know. Yet I have a thousand times made long speeches about virtue, before many a large audience, and good speeches, too, as I was convinced; but now I have not a word to say at all as to what it is. I must say you are wise not to sail away or travel abroad; for if you did this as a foreigner in a foreign city, you would probably be run in for a wizard.

SOCRATES: You are a young rogue, Menon, and you almost took me in.

MENO (79C–81A)

MENON: How, Socrates?

SOCRATES: I know why you made that comparison of me.

MENON: Why, do you think?

SOCRATES: That I might make another of *you*.[1] I know this—that all the famous beauties love being put into comparisons; it pays them, you see, for comparisons of the beautiful are beautiful, I think; but I will not do it with you in return. Well, if this stingray is numb itself as well as making others numb, I am like it; if not, I am not. For I am not clear-headed myself when I make others puzzled, but I am as puzzled as puzzled can be, and thus I make others puzzled too. So now, what virtue is I do not know; but you knew, perhaps, before you touched me, although now you resemble one who does not know. All the same, I wish to investigate, with your help, that we may both try to find out what it is.

MENON: And how will you try to find out something, Socrates, when you have no notion at all what it is? Will you lay out before us a thing you don't know, and then try to find it? Or, if at best you meet it by chance, how will you know this is that which you did not know?

SOCRATES: I understand what you wish to say, Menon. You look on this as a piece of chop-logic, don't you see, as if a man cannot try to find either what he knows or what he does not know. Of course he would never try to find what he knows, because he knows it, and in that case he needs no trying to find; or what he does not know, because he does not know what he will try to find.

MENON: Then you don't think that is a good argument, Socrates?

SOCRATES: Not I.

MENON: Can you tell me why?

SOCRATES: Oh yes. I have heard wise men and women on the subject of things divine—

MENON: And what did they say?

SOCRATES: True things and fine things, to my thinking.

MENON: What things, and who were the speakers?

SOCRATES: The speakers were some priests and priestesses who have paid careful attention to the things of their ministry, so as to be able to give a reasoned explanation of them; also

[1] A favourite game in society.

inspired poets have something to say, Pindar and many others. What they say I will tell you; pray consider, if they seem to you to be speaking truth. They say that the soul of man is immortal, and sometimes it comes to an end—which they call death—and sometimes it is born again, but it is never destroyed; therefore we must live our lives as much as we can in holiness: for from whomsoever

> Persephone shall accept payment for ancient wrong,
> She gives up again their souls to the upper sun in the ninth year;
> From these grow lordly kings, and men of power and might,
> And those who are chief in wisdom; these for time to come
> Are known among men for holy heroes.[1]

Then, since the soul is immortal and often born, having seen what is on earth and what is in the house of Hades, and everything, there is nothing it has not learnt; so there is no wonder it can remember about virtue and other things, because it knew about these before. For since all nature is akin, and the soul has learnt everything, there is nothing to hinder a man, remembering one thing only—which men call learning[2]—from himself finding out all else, if he is brave and does not weary in seeking; for seeking and learning is all remembrance. Then we must not be guided by this chop-logic argument; for this would make us idle, and it is pleasant for soft people to hear, but our way makes them active and enquiring. I have faith that this is true, and I wish with your help to try to find out what virtue is.

MENON: Yes, Socrates. But what do you mean by saying that we do not learn, but what we call learning is remembering? Can you teach me how this is?

SOCRATES: You are a young rogue, as I said a moment ago, Menon, and now you ask me if I can teach you, when I tell you there is no such thing as teaching, only remembering. I see you want to show me up at once as contradicting myself.

MENON: I swear that isn't true, my dear Socrates; I never thought of that, it was just habit. But if you know any way to show me how this can be as you say, show away!

SOCRATES: That is not easy, but still I want to do my best for your sake. Here, just call up one of your own men from all this crowd of servants, any one you like, and I'll prove my case in him.

MENON: All right. *(To a boy)* Come here.

[1] From Pindar. Persephone was Pluto's consort in Hades.
[2] I.e., the one thing needed to remember is how to learn; also remembering is learning. Both statements are covered here.

SOCRATES: Is he Greek, can he speak our language?

MENON: Rather! Born in my house.

SOCRATES: Now, kindly attend and see whether he seems to be learning from me, or remembering.

MENON: All right, I will attend.

SOCRATES: Now my boy, tell me: Do you know that a four-cornered space is like this? [*Diagram 1*][1]

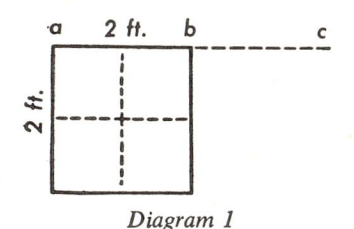

Diagram 1

BOY: I do.

SOCRATES: Is this a four-cornered space having all these lines[2] equal, all four?

BOY: Surely.

SOCRATES: And these across the middle, are they not equal too?

BOY: Yes.

SOCRATES: Such a space might be larger or smaller?

BOY: Oh yes.

SOCRATES: Then if this side is two feet long and this two, how many feet would the whole be? Or look at it this way: if it were two feet this way, and only one the other, would not the space[3] be once two feet?

BOY: Yes.

SOCRATES: But as it is two feet this way also, isn't it twice two feet?

BOY: Yes, so it is.

---
[1] There are no diagrams in the Greek text; they and the lettering have been added to assist the reader.
[2] I.e., sides.
[3] I.e., area.

SOCRATES: So the space is twice two feet?

BOY: Yes.

SOCRATES: Then how many are twice two feet? Count and tell me.

BOY: Four, Socrates.

SOCRATES: Well, could there be another such space, twice as big, but of the same shape, with all the lines equal like this one?

BOY: Yes.

SOCRATES: How many feet will there be in that, then?

BOY: Eight.

SOCRATES: Very well, now try to tell me how long will be each line of that one. The line of this one is two feet; how long would the line of the double one be?

BOY: The line would be double, Socrates, that is clear.

SOCRATES: *(aside to MENON)*: You see, Menon, that I am not teaching this boy anything: I ask him everything; and now he thinks he knows what the line is from which the eight-[square] foot space is to be made. Don't you agree?

MENON: Yes, I agree.

SOCRATES: Does he know then?

MENON: Not at all.

SOCRATES: He *thinks* he knows, from the double size which is wanted?

MENON: Yes.

SOCRATES: Well, observe him while he remembers bit by bit, as he ought to remember.

Now, boy, answer me. You say the double space is made from the double line. You know what I mean; not long this way and short this way, it must be equal every way like this, but double this—eight [square] feet. Just look and see if you think it will be made from the double line.

BOY: Yes, I do.

SOCRATES: Then this line [ac][1] is double this [ab], if we add as much [bc] to it on this side.

[1] In Diagram 1.

BOY: Of course!

SOCRATES: Then if we put four like this [ac], you say we shall get the eight-foot space.

BOY: Yes.

SOCRATES: Then let us draw these four equal lines [ac, cd, de, ea].[1] Is that the space which you say will be eight feet?

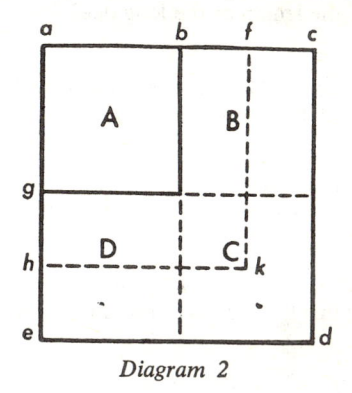

Diagram 2

BOY: Of course.

SOCRATES: Can't you see in it these four spaces here [A, B, C, D] each of them equal to the one we began with, the four-foot space?

BOY: Yes.

SOCRATES: Well, how big is the new one? Is it not four times the old one?

BOY: Surely it is!

SOCRATES: Is four times the old one, double?

BOY: Why no, upon my word!

SOCRATES: How big, then?

BOY: Four times as big!

SOCRATES: Then, my boy, from a double line we get a space four times as big, not double.

BOY: That's true.

[1] In Diagram 2.

SOCRATES: Four times four is sixteen, isn't it?

BOY: Yes.

SOCRATES: But what line will make an eight-foot space? This line makes one four times as big, sixteen, doesn't it?

BOY: That's what I say.

SOCRATES: And this four-foot space [*A*] comes from this line [*ab*], half the length of the long one?

BOY: Yes.

SOCRATES: Good. The eight-foot space will be double this [*double A*] and half this [*half A, B, C, D*].

BOY: Yes.

SOCRATES: Then its line must be longer than this [*ab*], and shorter than this [*ac*]. What do you think?

BOY: That's what I think.

SOCRATES: That's right, just answer what you think. Tell me also: Was not this line [*ab*] two feet, and this [*ac*] four?

BOY: Yes.

SOCRATES: Then the line of the eight-foot space must be longer than this line of two feet, and shorter than the line of four feet.

BOY: Yes, it must.

SOCRATES: Try to tell me, then, how long you say it must be.

BOY: Three feet.

SOCRATES: Three feet, very well: If we take half this bit [*half of bc*] and add it on, that makes three feet [*af*], doesn't it? For here we have two [*ab*], and here one [*bf*], the added bit; and, on the other side, in the same way, here are two [*ag*], here one [*gh*]; and that makes the space you say [*afkh*].

BOY: Yes.

SOCRATES: Then if the space is three feet this way and three feet that way, the whole space will be three times three feet?

BOY: It looks like it.

SOCRATES: How much is three times three feet?

BOY: Nine.

SOCRATES: How many feet was the double to be?

MENO (83C–84C)

BOY: Eight.

SOCRATES: So we have not got the eight-foot space from the three-feet line after all.

BOY: No, we haven't.

SOCRATES: Then how long ought the line to be? Try to tell us exactly, or if you don't want to give it in numbers, show it if you can.

BOY: Indeed, Socrates, on my word I don't know.

SOCRATES: Now, Menon, do you notice how this boy is getting on in his remembering? At first he did not know what line made the eight-foot space, and he does not know yet; but he thought he knew then, and boldly answered as if he did know, and did not think there was any doubt; now he thinks there is a doubt, and as he does not know, so he does not think he does know.

MENON: Quite true.

SOCRATES: Then he is better off as regards the matter he did not know?

MENON: Yes, I think so too.

SOCRATES: So now we have put him into a difficulty, and like the stingray we have made him numb, have we done him any harm?

MENON: I don't think so.

SOCRATES: At least we have brought him a step onwards, as it seems, to find out how he stands. For now he would go on contentedly seeking, since he does not know; but then he could easily have thought he would be talking well about the double space, even before any number of people again and again, saying how it must have a line of double length.

MENON: It seems so.

SOCRATES: Then do you think he would have tried to find out or to learn what he thought he knew, not knowing, until he tumbled into a difficulty by thinking he did not know, and longed to know?

MENON: I do not think he would, Socrates.

SOCRATES: So he gained by being numbed?

MENON: I think so.

48   *GREAT DIALOGUES OF PLATO*

SOCRATES: Just notice now that after this difficulty he will find out by seeking along with me, while I do nothing but ask questions and give no instruction. Look out if you find me teaching and explaining to him, instead of asking for his opinions.

Now, boy, answer me. Is not this our four-foot space [A]?[1] Do you understand?

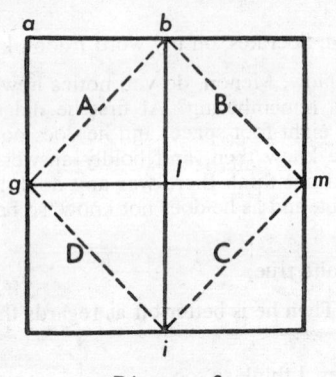

Diagram 3

BOY: I do.

SOCRATES: Shall we add another equal to it, thus [B]?

BOY: Yes.

SOCRATES: And a third equal to either of them, thus [C]?

BOY: Yes.

SOCRATES: Now shall we not also fill in this space in the corner [D]?

BOY: Certainly.

SOCRATES: Won't these be four equal spaces?

BOY: Yes.

SOCRATES: Very well. How many times the small one is this whole space?

BOY: Four times.

SOCRATES: But we wanted a double space; don't you remember?

[1] In Diagram 3.

BOY: Oh yes, I remember.

SOCRATES: Then here is a line running from corner to corner, cutting each of these spaces in two parts [*draws lines bm, mi, ig, gb*].

BOY: Yes.

SOCRATES: Are not these four lines equal, and don't they contain this space within them [*bmig*]?

BOY: Yes, that is right.

SOCRATES: Just consider: How big is the space?

BOY: I don't understand.

SOCRATES: Does not each of these lines cut each of the spaces, four spaces, in half? Is that right?

BOY: Yes.

SOCRATES: How many spaces as big as that [*blg*] are in this middle space?

BOY: Four.

SOCRATES: How many in this one [*A*]?

BOY: Two.

SOCRATES: How many times two is four?

BOY: Twice.

SOCRATES: Then how many [square] feet big is this middle space?

BOY: Eight [square] feet.

SOCRATES: Made from what line?

BOY: This one [*gb*].

SOCRATES: From the line drawn from corner to corner of the four-foot space?

BOY: Yes.

SOCRATES: The professors[1] call this a diameter [diagonal]: so if this is a diagonal, the double space would be made from the diagonal, as you say, Menon's boy!

BOY: Certainly, Socrates.

SOCRATES: Now then, Menon, what do you think? Was there one single opinion which the boy did not give as his own?

MENON: No, they were all his own opinions.

[1] Sophists, experts in some subject who gave lessons for a fee.

SOCRATES: Yet he did not know, as we agreed shortly before.

MENON: Quite true, indeed.

SOCRATES: Were these opinions in him, or not?

MENON: They were.

SOCRATES: Then in one who does not know, about things he does not know, there are true opinions about the things which he does not know?

MENON: So it appears.

SOCRATES: And now these opinions have been stirred up in him as in a dream; and if someone will keep asking him these same questions often and in various forms, you can be sure that in the end he will know about them as accurately as anybody.

MENON: It seems so.

SOCRATES: And no one having taught him, only asked questions, yet he will know, having got the knowledge out of himself?

MENON: Yes.

SOCRATES: But to get knowledge out of yourself is to remember, isn't it?

MENON: Certainly it is.

SOCRATES: Well then: This knowledge which he now has—he either got it sometime, or he had it always?

MENON: Yes.

SOCRATES: Then if he had it always, he was also always one who knew; but if he got it sometime, he could not have got it in this present life. Or has someone taught him geometry? For he will do just these same things in all matters of geometry, and so with all other sciences. Then is there anyone who has taught him everything? You are sure to know that, I suppose, especially since he was born and brought up in your house.

MENON: Well, I indeed know that no one has ever taught him.

SOCRATES: Has he all these opinions, or not?

MENON: He has, Socrates, it must be so.

SOCRATES: Then if he did not get them in this life, is it not clear now that he had them and had learnt at some other time?

MENON: So it seems.

SOCRATES: Is not that the time when he was not a man?

MENON: Yes.

SOCRATES: Then if both in the time when he is a man and when he isn't there are to be true opinions in him, which are awakened by questioning and become knowledge, will not his soul have understood them for all time? For it is clear that through all time he either is or is not a man.

MENON: That's clear.

SOCRATES: Then if the truth of things is always in our soul, the soul must be immortal; so that what you do not know now by any chance—that is, what you do not remember—you must boldly try and find out and remember?

MENON: You seem to me to argue well, Socrates. I don't know how you do it.

SOCRATES: Yes, I think that I argue well, Menon. I would not be confident in everything I say about the argument; but one thing I would fight for to the end, both in word and deed if I were able—that if we believed that we must try to find out what is not known, we should be better and braver and less idle than if we believed that what we do not know it is impossible to find out and that we need not even try.

MENON: I think you argue well there too, Socrates.

SOCRATES: Very well. Since we agree that we must try to find out about what we do not know, shall we do our best to find out together what is virtue?

MENON: By all means. However, my dear friend, I should very much like to consider and to hear what I began by asking, whether we ought to tackle what virtue is as being something which can be taught, or as if men get it by nature or in some other way.

SOCRATES: But if I were your master, Menon, as well as master of myself, we should not consider beforehand whether virtue can be taught or not until we had tried to find out first what virtue really is. But since you make no attempt to master yourself—I suppose you want to be a free man—but you do attempt to master me, and you do master me! I will give way to you—for what else am I to do?—and it seems we must consider what qualities a thing has when we don't know yet what it is. Please relax at least one little tittle of your mastery, and give way so far that we may use a hypothesis to work from, in considering whether it can come by teaching or in some other way. I mean by hypothesis what the geometricians often envisage, a standing ground to start from; when they are asked, for instance, about a space, "Is it possible to inscribe this triangular space in this circle?" They will say, "I don't know yet whether it can be done, but I think I have, one may say, a useful hypothesis to start from, such as this: If the space is such that when you apply it to the given line[1] of the circle, it is deficient by a space of the same size as that which has been applied, one thing appears to follow, and if this be impossible, another.[2] I wish, then, to make a hypothesis before telling you what will happen about the inscribing of it in the circle, whether that be possible or not."

There now, let us take virtue in that way. Since we don't know what it is or what it is like, let us make our hypothesis or ground to stand on, and then consider whether it can be taught or not. We proceed as follows: If virtue is a quality among the things which are about the soul, would virtue be teachable, or not? First, if it is like or unlike knowledge, can it be taught or not, or as we said just now, can it be remembered —we need not worry which name we use—but can it be taught? Or is it plain to everyone that only one thing is taught to men, and that is knowledge?

MENON: So it seems to me at least.

SOCRATES: Then if virtue is a knowledge, it is plain that it could be taught.

MENON: Of course.

SOCRATES: We have soon done with that—if it is such, it can be taught, if not such, not.

MENON: Certainly.

SOCRATES: Now we have to consider, as it seems, whether virtue is a knowledge or something distinct from knowledge.

MENON: Agreed, that must be considered next.

SOCRATES: Very well. Don't we say that virtue is a good thing? This hypothesis holds for us, that it is good?

MENON: We do say so.

SOCRATES: Then if there is something good, and yet separate from knowledge, possibly virtue would not be a knowledge, but if there is no good which knowledge does not contain, it would be a right notion to suspect that it is a knowledge.

[1] Diameter.
[2] Mr. Ivor Thomas is thanked for help here. The matter is explained by him in his *Greek Mathematical Works*, vol. 1, p. 395 ff. (Loeb Classical Library).

MENO (87A–88C)

MENON: That is true.

SOCRATES: Further, by virtue we are good?

MENON: Yes.

SOCRATES: And if good, helpful; for all good things are helpful. Are they not?

MENON: Yes.

SOCRATES: And virtue, therefore, is helpful?

MENON: That must follow from what we have agreed.

SOCRATES: Let us consider then, taking up one by one, what sorts of things are helpful to us. Health, we say, and strength, and good looks, and wealth, of course; these and things like these we say are helpful, eh?

MENON: Yes.

SOCRATES: And these same things we say do harm sometimes also; do you agree with that?

MENON: I do.

SOCRATES: Consider then what leads each of these when it is helpful to us, and what leads each when it does harm. Are they not helpful when led by right use, and harmful when they are not?

MENON: Certainly.

SOCRATES: Let us pass on then, and consider the things that concern the soul. You speak of temperance and justice and courage and cleverness at learning and memory and highmindedness, and all such things?

MENON: Yes.

SOCRATES: Look now; such of these as seem to you to be not knowledge but different from knowledge, are they not sometimes harmful and sometimes helpful? For example courage, if courage is not intelligence but something like boldness; is it not true that when a man is bold without sense, he is harmed, but when with sense, he is helped?

MENON: Yes.

SOCRATES: Is it not the same with temperance and cleverness at learning? When things learnt are accompanied by sense and are fitted in their proper places they are helpful; without sense, harmful?

MENON: Very much so.

SOCRATES: Then, in short, all the stirrings and endurings of the soul, when wisdom leads, come to happiness in the end, but when senselessness leads, to the opposite?

MENON: So it seems.

SOCRATES: Then if virtue is one of the things in the soul, and if it must necessarily be helpful, it must be wisdom: since quite by themselves all the things about the soul are neither helpful nor harmful, but they become helpful or harmful by the addition of wisdom or senselessness.

According to this argument, virtue, since it is helpful, must be some kind of wisdom.

MENON: I think so.

SOCRATES: Very well then, come now to the other things we mentioned a while since, wealth and so forth, and said they were sometimes good and sometimes harmful. When wisdom led any soul it made the things of the soul helpful, didn't it, and senselessness made them harmful: so also with these, the soul makes them helpful when it uses them rightly and leads them rightly, but harmful when not rightly?

MENON: Certainly.

SOCRATES: The sensible soul leads them rightly, the senseless wrongly?

MENON: That is true.

SOCRATES: Then cannot we say this as a general rule: In man everything else depends on the soul; but the things of the soul itself depend on wisdom, if it is to be good; and so by this argument the helpful would be wisdom—and we say virtue is helpful.

MENON: We do.

SOCRATES: Then we say virtue is wisdom, either in whole or in part?

MENON: I think what we say is well said, Socrates.

SOCRATES: Then if this is right, nature would not make men good.

MENON: I think not.

SOCRATES: Here is another thing, surely: If good men were good by nature, we should have persons who could distinguish those young ones who were good in their nature, and we might take them over as they were indicated and keep them safe in the acropolis, and hallmark them more care-

MENO (88C–90A)

fully than fine gold, that no one might corrupt them, but that when they grew up they should be useful to their cities.

MENON: Quite likely that, Socrates.

SOCRATES: Then since the good are not good by nature, is it by learning?

MENON: I really think that must be so; and it is plain, my dear Socrates, according to the hypothesis, that if virtue is knowledge, it can be taught.

SOCRATES: Yes, by Zeus, perhaps, but what if we were wrong in admitting that?

MENON: Well, it did seem just then to be a right conclusion.

SOCRATES: But what if we ought not to have agreed that is was right enough for then only, but for now also and all future time, if it is to be sound?

MENON: Why, what now? What makes you dissatisfied and distrustful? Do you think virtue is not knowledge?

SOCRATES: I will tell you Menon. It can be taught if it is knowledge; I do not wish to dispute the truth of that statement. But I have my doubts whether it is knowledge; pray consider if there is any reason in that. Just look here: If a thing can be taught—anything, not virtue only—must there not be both teachers and learners of it?

MENON: Yes, I think so.

SOCRATES: On the contrary, again, if there are neither teachers nor learners, we might fairly assume the thing cannot be taught?

MENON: That is true; but don't you think there are teachers of virtue?

SOCRATES: I have in truth often tried to find if there were teachers of it, but, do what I will, I can find none. Yet there are many on the same search, and especially those whom I believe to be best skilled in the matter. (*Enter* ANYTOS) Why look here, my dear Menon, in the nick of time here is Anytos, he has taken a seat beside us. Let us ask him to share in our search; it would be reasonable to give him a share. For in the first place, Anytos has a wealthy father, the wise Anthemion, who became rich not by a stroke of luck or by a gift, like Ismenias the Theban who got "the fortune of a

Polycrates" the other day,[1] but he got his by his own wisdom and care. In the next place, his father has a good name generally in the city; he is by no means overbearing and pompous and disagreeable, but a decent and mannerly man; and then he brought up our Anytos well, and educated him well, as the public opinion is—at least, they choose him for the highest offices. It is right to ask the help of such men when we are looking for teachers of virtue, if there are any or not, and who they are. Now then, Anytos, please help us, help me and your family friend Menon here, to find out who should be teachers of this subject. Consider it thus: If we wished Menon here to be a good physician, to whom should we send him to be his teachers? To the physicians, I suppose?

ANYTOS: Certainly.

SOCRATES: And what if we wanted him to be a good shoemaker, we should send him to the shoemakers?

ANYTOS: Yes.

SOCRATES: And so with everything else?

ANYTOS: Certainly.

SOCRATES: Something else, again, I ask you to tell me about these same things. We should be right in sending him to the physicians, we say, if we wanted him to be a physician. When we say this, do we mean that we should be sensible, if we sent him to those who profess the art, rather than to those who do not, and who also exact a fee for this very thing and declare themselves teachers, for anyone who wants to come and learn? If we looked to such things and sent him accordingly, should we not be doing right?

ANYTOS: Yes.

SOCRATES: Then the same about pipe-playing[2] and the rest. If we want to make anyone a piper, it is great folly to be unwilling to send him to men who undertake to teach the art, and exact a fee for it; and instead to make trouble for others by letting him seek to learn from people who neither pretend to be teachers nor have a single pupil in the art which we want the person we send to learn from them. Don't you think that is plain unreason?

ANYTOS: Yes, by Zeus. I do, even stupidity.

[1] A proverb from the life of Polycrates, tyrant of Samos. This Theban had helped Anytos and the other banished Athenians the year before the supposed date of this dialogue.

[2] The pipe was a wind instrument, blown at the end like an oboe; see also *Republic*, p. 198, n. 2, 3.

MENO (90A–92A)

SOCRATES: You are right. Now you can join me in consulting together about our friend Menon here. The fact is, Anytos, he has been telling me this long time that he desires the wisdom and virtue by which men manage houses and cities well and honour their parents, and know how to entertain fellow-citizens and strangers and to speed them on their way, as a good man ought to do. Then consider whom we should properly send him to for this virtue. Is it not clear from what has just been said that we should send him to those who profess to be teachers of virtue, and declare themselves to be public teachers for any of the Hellenes who wish to learn, with a proper fee fixed to be paid for this?

ANYTOS: And who are these, my dear Socrates?

SOCRATES: *You* too know, I suppose, that these are the men who are called Sophists.

ANYTOS: O Heracles! Hush, my dear Socrates! May none of my relations or friends, here or abroad, fall into such madness as to go to these persons and be tainted! These men are the manifest canker and destruction of those they have to do with.

SOCRATES: What's that, Anytos? These are the only men professing to know how to do us good, yet they differ so much from the rest that they not only do not help us as the others do, when one puts oneself into their hands, but on the contrary corrupt us? And for this they actually ask pay, and make no secret of it? I, for one, cannot believe you. For I know one man, Protagoras, who has earned more money from this wisdom than Pheidias did for all those magnificent works of his, or any ten other statue-makers. This is a miracle! Those who cobble old shoes or patch up old clothes could not hide it for thirty days if they gave back shoes and clothes worse than they got them, for if they did that they would soon starve to death: but Protagoras, it seems, hid it from all Hellas, and corrupted those who had to do with him, and sent them away worse than he got them, for more than forty years!—for I think he was nearly seventy when he died, after forty years in his art—and in all that time to this day his great name has lasted! And not only Protagoras, but very many others, some born before his time and others living still. Are we to suppose, according to what you say, that they knew they were deceiving and tainting the young, or did they deceive themselves? And shall we claim that these were madmen, when some call them wisest of all mankind?

ANYTOS: Anything but madmen, Socrates; the young men are much madder who pay them money; and madder still those, their relations, who entrust young people to them; maddest of all, the cities which allow them to come in and do not kick them out—whether he is a foreigner or native who attempts to do such a thing.

SOCRATES: Why, Anytos, have you ever been wronged at all by Sophists? What makes you so hard on them?

ANYTOS: Good God, I have never had anything to do with one, and I would never allow anyone else of my family to have to do with them.

SOCRATES: Then you are quite without experience of these men?

ANYTOS: And I hope I may remain so.

SOCRATES: Astonishing! Then how could you know anything about this matter, whether there is anything good or bad in it, if you are quite without experience of it?

ANYTOS: Easily. At least I know who these are; whether I have experience of them or not.

SOCRATES: Perhaps you are a prophet, Anytos; since how indeed otherwise you could know about them, from what you say yourself, I should wonder. But we were not trying to find out who those are that Menon might go to and become a scoundrel—let them be Sophists if you like—but those others, please tell us and do good to this, your family friend, by showing him some to whom he should go in all this great city, who could make him of some account in that virtue which I described just now.

ANYTOS: Why didn't *you* show him?

SOCRATES: Well, I did say whom I thought to be teachers of these things, but it turns out I made a mess of it, so you say; and perhaps there is something in what you maintain. Now pray take your turn, and tell him which of the Athenians he should try. Tell us a name, of anyone you like.

ANYTOS: Why ask for[1] the name of one man? Any wellbred gentleman[2] of Athens he might meet will make him better than Sophists can, every single one of them, if he will do as he is told.

[1] Literally, "Why must you hear."
[2] Literally, Any of "the beautiful and good"; a usual term for "gentleman."

MENO (92B–93E)

SOCRATES: Did these well-bred gentlemen become like that by luck? Did they learn from no one, and can they nevertheless teach other people what they themselves never learnt?

ANYTOS: I suppose they learnt from their fathers, who were also gentlemen before them; or do not you think there have been plenty of fine men in our city?

SOCRATES: I think, Anytos, that there are plenty of men here good at politics, and that there have been plenty before no less than now; but have they been also good teachers of their virtue? For this is what our discussion is really about—not if there are or have been good men here, but if virtue can be taught—that is what we have been considering for so long. And the point we are considering is just this: whether the good men of these times and of former times knew how to hand on to another that virtue in which they were good, or whether it cannot be handed on from one man to another, or received by one man from another—that is what we have been all this while trying to find out, I and Menon. Well then, consider it thus, in your own way of discussing: Would you not say Themistocles[1] was a good man?

ANYTOS: Indeed I should, none better.

SOCRATES: And also a good teacher of his own virtue, if ever anyone was?

ANYTOS: That is what I think, of course if he wished.

SOCRATES: But don't you think he would have wished others to be fine gentlemen, especially, I take it, his own son? Or do you think he grudged it to him, and on purpose did not pass on the virtue in which he was good? I suppose you have heard that Themistocles had his son Cleophantos taught to be a good horseman. At least, he could remain standing upright on horseback, and cast a javelin upright on horseback, and do many other wonderful feats which the great man had him taught, and he made him clever in all that could be got from good teachers. Haven't you heard this from older men?

ANYTOS: Oh yes, I have heard that.

SOCRATES: Then no one could have blamed his son for lack of good natural gifts.

ANYTOS: Perhaps not.

SOCRATES: What do you say to this, then: that Cleophantos became a good and wise man in the same things as

[1] Who during the wars with Persia laid the foundations of the navy—and of the greatness—of Athens.

his father Themistocles, did you ever hear that from young or old?

ANYTOS: No, indeed.

SOCRATES: Are we to believe, then, that he wished to educate his son in these things, but not to make the boy better than his neighbours in that wisdom in which he was himself wise—are we to believe this, if virtue can really be taught?

ANYTOS: Well, upon my word, perhaps not.

SOCRATES: There you have a grand teacher of virtue, whom you admit yourself to be one of the best men of the past! Let us consider another, Aristeides,[1] Lysimachos' son. Do not you admit that he was a good man?

ANYTOS: I do, most assuredly.

SOCRATES: Then this one educated his own son Lysimachos, as far as teachers went, in the best that the Athenians could provide; but did he make him better than anyone else—what do you think? I take it you have met him yourself and you see what he is. Or Pericles[2], if you like, a man magnificently wise— you know he brought up two sons, Paralos and Xanthippos?

ANYTOS: Oh yes.

SOCRATES: Well, he taught them (you know that, as I do) to be horsemen as good as any in Athens; he educated them in the fine arts and gymnastics and all the rest, to be as good as any as far as education goes; yet he did not wish to make them good men? Oh yes, he wished, as I think, but I take it the thing can't be taught. You must not suppose only a few of our people, or the meanest of them, could not do it: remember Thucydides[3] again—he brought up two sons, Melesias and Stephanos, and gave them a proper education; in particular they were the best wrestlers in Athens—Xanthias was trainer for one, Eudoros for the other—and these had the name of being the best wrestlers. Don't you remember?

ANYTOS: Oh yes, I have heard of them.

SOCRATES: Is it not clear then, that, if virtuous things could be taught, this father would never have had his own children taught these other things, for which fees had to be paid for teaching, and moreover he would never have failed to teach them these virtuous things, by which he could make them

[1] Another Athenian statesman, renowned for nobility of character; a contemporary of Themistocles.
[2] Famous leader of Athens and her empire for thirty years.
[3] Not the famous historian, but an honourable opponent of Pericles in imperial policy.

good men, without needing to spend anything? But perhaps Thucydides was a mean creature, perhaps he had not crowds of friends in Athens and among our allies![1] And he came of a great house, he had great power in the city and all through the nation of Hellenes: so if this could be taught, he would have found the man who could make his sons good, some foreigner or native, in case he himself had no leisure because of his care of the state. The truth is, my dear friend Anytos, I fear virtue cannot be taught.

ANYTOS: My dear Socrates, you seem to speak ill of men easily. I would advise you to be careful, if you will listen to me. Perhaps it is easier to do people harm than good in other cities, but it is very easy in this. I think you yourself knew that perfectly well. (*Exit* ANYTOS.)

SOCRATES: Menon, I am afraid Anytos is angry, and I don't wonder, for he thinks firstly that I am defaming these men, and secondly he believes he is one of them, himself. But if he ever learns what it is to speak ill, he will no longer be angry; he does not know now. Answer me, please, are there not well-bred, fine gentlemen in your part of the country also?

MENON: Certainly.

SOCRATES: Well then, are they ready to offer themselves to young men as teachers? Do they agree that they are teachers themselves and virtue can be taught?

MENON: No, upon my word, Socrates! but sometimes you might hear them say that it can be taught, sometimes that it cannot.

SOCRATES: Are we to say, then, that they are teachers of virtue, when not even this point is agreed on by them?

MENON: I don't think so, Socrates.

SOCRATES: What next, then: these Sophists of yours who alone make the claim—do you think they are teachers of virtue?

MENON: Gorgias in particular always makes me surprised, Socrates, because you will never hear such a promise from him; indeed he laughs at the others when he hears them promising; making men clever at speaking is what he thinks their job is.

---

[1] Thucydides protested against Pericles' use of tribute, paid by Athens' subject allies, towards paying the cost of public buildings in Athens.

SOCRATES: Then do you not think the Sophists are such teachers either?

MENON: I really can't say, Socrates. I have felt about it much the same as most people; sometimes I think they are, sometimes I don't.

SOCRATES: Well, do you know this: You are not alone, nor are the others who are public men, in thinking sometimes that it can be taught, sometimes not? Theognis the poet says the same, do you know that?

MENON: In what passage?

SOCRATES: In the elegiacs, where he says,

> Eat and drink with those that have great power,
> Sit with those, give them a pleasant hour.
> You'll learn good from the good; those who are not,
> If you mix with them, spoil the sense you've got.

Do you know that he speaks there as if virtue can be taught?

MENON: It looks like it.

SOCRATES: Elsewhere he says, changing a little,

> Could sense be made and put into a man,

then he goes on something like this,

> Many a handsome fee would people earn.

—those who could do it, he means: and again,

> A good man's son, obeying wisdom's words,
> You'd scarcely find grown bad. But yet you would
> Never by *teaching* make the bad man good.

You see he contradicts himself about the same things!

MENON: It looks like it.

SOCRATES: Then can you tell me of any other subject whatever where those who profess to be teachers are, like these, not accepted as teachers of others, and not only that, but they are believed not to understand it themselves but to be rotten in the very subject which they profess to teach! And, moreover, where those who are accepted for well-bred, fine gentlemen say sometimes it can be taught and sometimes it cannot! When people are so confused about anything, could you properly call them teachers of that thing?

MENON: No indeed, by God.

SOCRATES: Then if neither the Sophists, nor those who are themselves well-bred, fine gentlemen, are teachers of the subject, it is clear that there are no others?

MENON: Quite clear, I think.

SOCRATES: And if there are no teachers, there are no learners?

MENON: I think so too.

SOCRATES: But we have agreed that if there are neither teachers nor learners of any given thing, this cannot be taught.

MENON: We have.

SOCRATES: No teachers of virtue appear, then?

MENON: No.

SOCRATES: And if no teachers, no learners?

MENON: So it seems.

SOCRATES: Then virtue could not be taught?

MENON: It looks like it, if our enquiry has been right. So I am wondering now, Socrates, whether there are no good men at all, or what could be the way in which the good men who exist come into being.

SOCRATES: We are really a paltry pair, you and I, Menon; Gorgias has not educated you enough, nor Prodicos me. Then the best thing is to turn our minds on ourselves, and try to find out someone to make us better by hook or by crook. In saying this I have my eye on our recent enquiry, where we were fools enough to miss something; it is not only when knowledge guides mankind that things are done rightly and well; and perhaps that is why we failed to understand in what way the good men come into being.

MENON: What do you mean by that, Socrates?

SOCRATES: This: That the good men must be useful; we admitted, and rightly, that this could not be otherwise.

MENON: Yes.

SOCRATES: Yes, and that they will be useful if they guide our business rightly, we admitted also: was that correct?

MENON: Yes.

SOCRATES: But that it is not possible to guide rightly unless one knows, to have admitted that looks like a blunder.

MENON: What do you mean?

SOCRATES: I will tell you. If someone knows the way to Larissa, or where you will, and goes there and guides others, will he not guide rightly and well?

MENON: Certainly.

SOCRATES: Well, what of one who has never been there, and does not know the way; but if he has a right opinion as to the way, won't he also guide rightly?

MENON: Certainly.

SOCRATES: And so long as he has a right opinion about that of which the other has knowledge, he will be quite as good a guide as the one who knows, although he does not know, but only thinks, what is true.

MENON: Quite as good.

SOCRATES: Then true opinion is no worse guide than wisdom, for rightness of action; and this is what we failed to see just now while we were enquiring what sort of a thing virtue is. We said then that wisdom alone guides to right action; but, really, true opinion does the same.

MENON: So it seems.

SOCRATES: Then right opinion is no less useful than knowledge.

MENON: Yes, it is less useful; for he who has knowledge would always be right, he who has right opinion, only sometimes.

SOCRATES: What! Would not he that has right opinion always be right so long as he had right opinion?

MENON: Oh yes, necessarily, I think. This being so, I am surprised, Socrates, why knowledge is ever more valued than right opinion, and why they are two different things.

SOCRATES: Do you know why you wonder, or shall I tell you?

MENON: Oh, tell me, please.

SOCRATES: Because you have not observed the statues of Daidalos.[1] But perhaps you have none in your part of the world.

MENON: What are you driving at?

[1] Daidalos (*Daedalus*), the mythical sculptor and craftsman; the ancient Greeks attributed to him the masterpieces whose origins they did not know.

MENO (97A–98D)

SOCRATES: They must be fastened up, if you want to keep them; or else they are off and away.[1]

MENON: What of that?

SOCRATES: If left loose there is not much value in owning one of his works—like a runaway slave; it doesn't stay; but chained up it is worth a great deal; for they are fine works of art. What am I driving at? Why, at the true opinions. For the true opinions, as long as they stay, are splendid and do all the good in the world; but they will not stay long—off and away they run out of the soul of mankind, so they are not worth much until you fasten them up with the reasoning of cause and effect. But this, my dear Menon, is remembering, as we agreed before. When they are fastened up, first they become knowledge, secondly they remain; and that is why knowledge is valued more than right opinion, and differs from right opinion by this bond.[2]

MENON: I do declare, Socrates, you have a good comparison there.

SOCRATES: Well, I speak by conjecture, not as one who knows; but to say that right opinion is different from knowledge, that, I believe, is no conjecture in me at all. That I would say I know; there are few things I would say that of, but this I would certainly put down as one of those I know.

MENON: You are quite right in saying this, Socrates.

SOCRATES: Now then, is this not right: True opinion guiding achieves the work of each action no less than knowledge?

MENON: Yes, I think that also is true.

SOCRATES: Then right opinion is nothing inferior to knowledge, and will be no less useful for actions; and the man who has right opinion is not inferior to the man who has knowledge.

MENON: Yes.

SOCRATES: Again, the good man we have agreed to be useful.

MENON: Yes.

SOCRATES: Since, then, not only by knowledge would men be good and useful to their cities (if they were so) but also by right opinion, and since neither knowledge nor true opinion comes to mankind by nature, being acquired[3]—or do you think that either of them does come by nature, perhaps?

[1] A common saying.
[2] "Opinion in good men is knowledge in the making."—Milton, *Areopagitica*.
[3] The text of Plato is uncertain here.

MENON: No, not I.

SOCRATES: Therefore they come not by nature, neither could the good be so by nature.

MENON: Not at all.

SOCRATES: Since not by nature, we enquired next whether it could be taught.

MENON: Yes.

SOCRATES: Well, it seemed that it could be taught if virtue was wisdom.

MENON: Yes.

SOCRATES: And if it could be taught, it would be wisdom.

MENON: Certainly.

SOCRATES: And if there were teachers, it could be taught, if no teachers, it could not?

MENON: Just so.

SOCRATES: Further, we agreed that there were no teachers of it?

MENON: That is true.

SOCRATES: We agreed, then, that it could not be taught, and that it was not wisdom?

MENON: Certainly.

SOCRATES: But, however, we agree that it is good?

MENON: Yes.

SOCRATES: And that which guides rightly is useful and good?

MENON: Certainly.

SOCRATES: Again, only these two things guide rightly, right opinion and knowledge; and if a man has these, he guides rightly—for things which happen rightly from some chance do not come about by human guidance: but in all things in which a man is a guide towards what is right, these two do it, true opinion and knowledge.

MENON: I think so.

SOCRATES: Well, since it cannot be taught, no longer is virtue knowledge.

MENON: It seems not.

SOCRATES: Then of two good and useful things one has been thrown away, and knowledge would not be guide in political action.

MENON: I think not.

SOCRATES: Then it was not by wisdom, or because they are wise, that such men guided the cities, men such as Themistocles and those whom Anytos told us of; for which reason, you see, they could not make others like themselves, because not knowledge made them what they were.

MENON: It seems likely to be as you say, Socrates.

SOCRATES: Then if it were not knowledge, right opinion is left, you see. This is what politicians use when they keep a state upright; they have no more to do with understanding than oracle-chanters and diviners, for these in ecstasy tell the truth often enough, but they know nothing of what they say.

MENON: That is how things really are.

SOCRATES: Then it is fair, Menon, to call those men divine, who are often right in what they say and do, even in grand matters, but have no sense while they do it.

MENON: Certainly.

SOCRATES: Then we should be right in calling these we just mentioned divine, oracle-chanters and prophets and the poets or creative artists, all of them; most of all, the politicians, we should say they are divine and ecstatic, being inspired and possessed by the god when they are often right while they say grand things although they know nothing of what they say.

MENON: Certainly.

SOCRATES: And the women, too, Menon, call good men divine; and the Laconians[1] when they praise a good man say, "A divine man that!"

MENON: Yes, and they appear to be quite right, my dear Socrates, although our friend Anytos may perhaps be angry with you for saying it.

SOCRATES: I don't care. We will have a talk with him[2] by and by, Menon. But if we have ordered all our enquiry well and argued well, virtue is seen as coming neither by nature nor by teaching; but by divine allotment incomprehensibly[3]

[1] The Spartans.
[2] Anytos was one of the accusers in his trial for life. See the *Defence of Socrates*.
[3] Literally, "without mind."

to those to whom it comes—unless there were some politician so outstanding as to be able to make another man a politician. And if there were one, he might almost be said to be among the living such as Homer says of Teiresias among the dead, for Homer says of him that he alone of those in Hades has his mind, the others are flittering shades.[1] In the same way also here on earth such a man would be, in respect of virtue, as something real amongst shadows.

MENON: Excellently said, I think, Socrates.

SOCRATES: Then from this our reasoning, Menon, virtue is shown as coming to us, whenever it comes, by divine dispensation; but we shall only know the truth about this clearly when, before enquiring in what way virtue comes to mankind, we first try to search out what virtue is in itself.

But now it is time for me to go; and your part is to persuade your friend Anytos to believe just what you believe about it, that he may be more gentle; for if you can persuade him, you will do a service to the people of Athens also.

[1] *Odyssey*, x. 494.

SYMPOSIUM (The Banquet)

Apollodoros and Friend
Aristodemos, Socrates, Agathon, Pausanias, Aristophanes,
Eryximachos, Phaidros, Alcibiades

Introductory Note

The banquet took place in Agathon's house in 416 B.C.; a few days previously Agathon, the handsome young tragic poet then aged about thirty-one, had won the prize, his first "victory," when one of his tragedies was first performed at a dramatic festival in the Theatre of Dionysos, the theatre at the foot of the Acropolis at Athens, which accommodated about 30,000 spectators; on page 89 Socrates refers to Agathon's courage in facing such a huge audience. Agathon appears to have been the first to insert into his tragedies choral odes unconnected with the plot of the drama. He gave this banquet to his friends on the next evening after he and his chorus had offered their sacrifice of thanksgiving for his victory.

Of his guests:

SOCRATES *was then aged fifty-three.*

PHAIDROS *(Phaedrus), who was invited to preside, was a friend of Plato. The famous dialogue* The Phaedrus, *not included in this volume, on the subject of love, was named after him.*

PAUSANIAS *was a disciple of Prodicos, the Sophist, of Ceos.*

ARISTOPHANES, *the famous comic poet, was then about thirty-two. In his comedy* The Clouds, *first performed five years previously, he had made fun of Socrates.*

ALCIBIADES, *the eminent statesman then about thirty-five, a man of remarkable beauty and talent, but unscrupulous and dissolute, was a great admirer of Socrates, as his speech at the banquet shows. Socrates saved his life in battle when Alcibiades was about twenty.*

The story of the banquet, as told by Aristodemos, who attended it with Socrates, is here retold by Apollodoros to a friend while they were out walking together about fifteen years after. Apollodoros is described in the dialogue Phaidon (Phaedo) *as being present weeping at Socrates' death about a year later.*

APOLLODOROS: I think I am pretty well word-perfect in what you are inquiring about. It so happened a day or two ago that I was coming up to town from Phaleron, when someone I knew caught sight of me and called out from behind, some distance away, in a bantering tone—"Hullo, you Phalerian there!" he shouted. "Apollodoros! Halt!" I halted and stood still.

Then he said, "Well, Apollodoros, I was just looking for you. I wanted to know about Agathon's party, Socrates and Alcibiades and the others who were at the dinner then, and the speeches they made about love. Somebody else told me the story; he heard it from Phoinix, Philip's son, and he said you knew too. But he had nothing very clear to say, so you must tell it to me; you are the best man to report your friend's speeches. But tell me first of all," he went on, "were you at the party yourself, or not?"

Then I said, "It is obvious that the story he told was not clear, if you think this party you ask about was held lately, so that I might have been there myself."

"That *is* what I thought," he said.

"How could you think that, my dear Glaucon?" I said. "Don't you know that Agathon has been abroad for many years, and it's only in the last three years I have been spending my time with Socrates, and taking care every day to know whatever he says or does? Before that I used to run all over the place, anywhere, and I thought myself a grand fellow, but I was more miserable than anyone—just as *you* are now, when you think you would do anything rather than be a philosopher."

"Oh, don't jeer," said he, "just tell me when that party was."

I said, "It was when we were boys, and Agathon won the prize with his first tragedy—on the next day after he and his chorus offered the sacrifice of thanksgiving."

"Then that is a long time ago," he said, "as it seems. But who told you the story—was it Socrates?"

"Oh dear me, no," I said, "the same man who told Phoinix; he was a Cydathenaian, Aristodemos, a little man who never wore shoes. He was at the party, a lover of Socrates as much as anyone else in those days, I think. I did ask Socrates himself about some things too, which I heard from this man, and he agreed with all the other had told me."

"Well, I think you might tell me now," he said, "certainly

SYMPOSIUM (172A–174B)

the road to town will do well enough for us to talk and listen as we go."

So as we went along we talked about all this; and hence, as I told you to begin with, I am pretty well word-perfect. Well, if I must tell you people the story too, then I must. The truth is that whenever I speak about philosophy myself or hear others doing so, I am highly delighted, besides believing that it does me good. But when I hear other kinds of talk, especially among you rich men and moneymakers, it annoys me, and I pity you, my friends, because you are doing nothing while you think you are doing something. Well, perhaps again you believe I am a poor devil, and I think you think right; but I don't *think* you are, I *know* it well.

FRIEND: Always the same, Apollodoros! Always abusing yourself and everybody else. You really seem to think everyone wretched except Socrates, beginning with yourself! Where you got that nickname of madman, I don't know exactly, but in what you say you are always mad enough—you rave against yourself and everybody except Socrates!

APOLLODOROS: O my dear man, surely it is plain that I am mad and crazy, if I have such a notion about myself and you all!

FRIEND: It is not worth while quarrelling about this now, Apollodoros; but please do what I begged you—don't say no, but tell me what the speeches were.

APOLLODOROS: Well, they were something like this—but I will try to tell you the story from the beginning as Aristodemos[1] told it.

Aristodemos said that he met Socrates coming from the bath, with evening shoes on,[2] which he did not often wear; and he asked him where he was going so smart; he said, to dinner at Agathon's; yesterday he had refused him at the victory feast, to avoid the crowd; but he accepted for today. "That's why I made myself pretty," he said, "to go pretty to a pretty man! But look here," he continued, "how about you yourself feeling willing to go to dinner uninvited?"

And I replied (said Aristodemos), "As you like."

"Come with me, then," said Socrates, "and we will pervert the proverb a bit, and say, 'When gents give dinners, gents may just walk in.'[3] For Homer has really perverted this proverb, and made it vulgar too. He draws Agamemnon as a very perfect

---

[1] The reader must be careful to remember that Plato represents the banquet and the speakers as described by Aristodemos, one of the guests.
[2] Socrates usually went unshod, so he was evidently going somewhere in dress.
[3] The Greek text is uncertain, but the proverb seems to have been something like "When snobs give dinners, gents may just walk in." Socrates makes a perfect pun on Agathon's name, which means "the gentleman." Homer's passage is in *Iliad*, xvii. 588-90.

gentle knight, and Menelaos as a 'weak warrior': and when Agamemnon gave a feast and a sacrifice, he brings in Menelaos to the feast uninvited, although he is a low man and the other high."

Hearing this, my friend said, "Well, perhaps I'll risk it too, not as you suggest, Socrates, but, as in Homer, I, a poor creature, will go uninvited to a wise man's feast. Then just think what you will say about it, for I certainly will not admit that I came uninvited, I'll tell him that you invited me."

He said, "'Two heads are better than one';[1] we will plan what we shall say. Well, let us go."

So after some such talk, they started off. On the way, Socrates fell behind, absorbed in his own thoughts; and when my friend was waiting, Socrates told him to go on ahead. When he came to Agathon's house, he found the door open, and there (he said) something rather ridiculous happened; for a servant from inside met him at once, and led him where the others were on their couches, and he came upon them as they were about to begin dinner. But as soon as Agathon saw him, he said, "My dear Aristodemos, you are just in time to join us at dinner; if you have come for something else, put it off to another time; yesterday I looked for you to invite you, but I could not see you anywhere. But why have you not brought us Socrates?" I turned round (continued Aristodemos) but I could not see Socrates following; so I said I had come with Socrates and he had invited me there to dinner. "Very nice of you to come," he said, "but where is the man?"

"He was coming in behind me just now; I wonder myself where he could be."

"You there, you boy," said Agathon, "look about and bring in Socrates. And you take your place here, Aristodemos, beside Eryximachos."

Then the boy washed his feet, that he might take his place; and another boy came, and reported, "Socrates went into the porch next door and there he is standing, but though I call him he won't come in."

"That's odd," said he, "just ask him again and don't let him go."

But my friend said, "Don't do that, leave him alone. That is only his way; he often goes off and stands anywhere. He will come soon, I think. Don't interfere with him, let him alone."

Agathon said, "Very well, if you think so, we must do so. Serve the feast for the rest of us, you boys, and put before us just what you choose, whenever no one directs you (I never

[1] *Iliad* x. 224. Literally, "When two go together, one thinks things out before the other," (ἐνόησεν is understood from *Iliad*.)

SYMPOSIUM (174B–175D) 73

tried this before!).[1] Now then, imagine that I also as well as the others here have been invited by you to dinner, and serve us so as to earn our compliments."

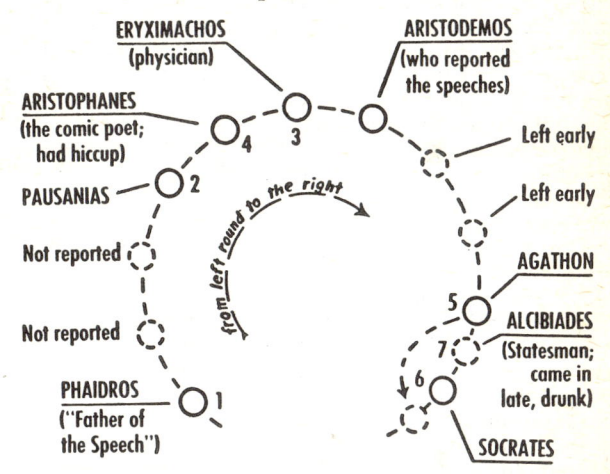

ERYXIMACHOS (physician)
ARISTODEMOS (who reported the speeches)
ARISTOPHANES (the comic poet; had hiccup)
PAUSANIAS
Not reported
Not reported
PHAIDROS ("Father of the Speech")
Left early
Left early
AGATHON
ALCIBIADES (Statesman; came in late, drunk)
SOCRATES

from left round to the right

THE BANQUET AT AGATHON'S HOUSE (416 B.C.)
Diagram showing order of reported speeches

NOTE: The diagram is drawn circular for convenience; it is not known how the couches were arranged. The couches usually accommodated two persons each, but some were made longer. From representations on ancient vases it seems that each diner reclined towards his left, supported under his left arm by a large cushion and with his right hand free to help himself from a low stool or table in front of the couch. They had no knives or forks. The wine was usually drunk mixed with water, about three parts of water to two of wine. See *A Dictionary of Greek and Roman Antiquities*, by W. Smith, W. Wayte, and G. E. Marindin, 3rd edition (1891), p. 393 on "Cena" and p. 741 on "Symposium."

After this, he said, they fell to, but no Socrates appeared. Agathon kept on giving orders to send for him, but my friend would not let him. However he did come, after not so long delay as usual, and found them about the middle of dinner. Then Agathon, who was reclining on the lowest seat[2] alone, on the right, said, "This way, Socrates, come by me, I want to get hold of you, to enjoy that wise thought which came to you in the porch. For it is clear you found it and have it still, or you would never have come away."

[1] An "aside" to his guests.
[2] Lowest in dignity, at the end on the right. It was taken in politeness by the host. They reclined in twos.

Socrates sat down, and said, "What a blessing it would be, Agathon, if wisdom could run from the fuller amongst us to the emptier, while we touch one another, as when two cups are placed side by side a bit of wool conveys water from the fuller to the emptier! If wisdom is like that, I think it precious to be beside you, for I think I shall be filled up with fine wisdom. Mine would be poor stuff and questionable, like a dream, but yours brilliant and fast growing; see how it has blazed out of you while you are still young, and showed itself to us the other day before over thirty thousand of our nation!"

"You are a scoffer, Socrates!" said Agathon. "Well, we will come into court before long about this, you and I, on our claim for wisdom, and the judge shall be Dionysos:[1] now first turn to dinner."

After this (Aristodemos said), Socrates reclined, and he and they all had their dinner; they poured the drops of grace, and sang a chant to the god, and did the usual things, and settled down to drinking. Then (he continued) Pausanias began the talk like this: "Look here, gentlemen," he said, "how shall we manage our drinking most conveniently? I tell you I am really not up to the mark myself after yesterday's bout and I want some rest, and so do most of you, I think—for you were present yesterday; just consider then how we could manage our drinking most conveniently."

Then Aristophanes said, "Now that is good advice, Pausanias, to make the drinking as comfortable as we can; I am one of those myself who had a good soaking yesterday."

So Eryximachos, Acumenos' son, when he heard them, said, "Quite right, you two. And one thing more I want to know, how Agathon feels about being fit to drink."

"No," said Agathon, "I don't feel very fit myself either."

The other said, "It seems it would be a bit of luck for us, me and Aristodemos and Phaidros and our friends here, if you with the strongest heads for drinking have thrown up the sponge; for we are always the weaklings. I do not count Socrates; he can do both ways, and it will content him whichever we choose. Then since it seems no one present votes for a hearty bout of deep wine-drinking, perhaps I should not give offence if I tell you the truth about the effect of getting drunk. I think I have seen quite clearly as a physician that drunkenness is a dangerous thing for mankind; and I am not willing to go far in drinking myself, nor would I advise another to do it, especially if he still has a headache from yesterday."

Phaidros the Myrrhinusian responded, "Well, I always take your advice, especially on matters of physic and health; and

[1] Dionysos or Bacchus, god of wine, who loosens care and inspires to music and poetry.

SYMPOSIUM (175D–177E)

the rest of us will be wise to do the same now." So all agree after hearing this not to drink too much during the present party, but everyone should drink just to please himself.

"Very well," said Eryximachos, "since the motion is passed that each one may drink as much as he likes, but no one *must* drink, my next motion is, that the piping-girl who has just come in may go out again, and play to herself, or if she pleases to the women inside, and that today we entertain each other with talk; and with your leave, I will propose what kind of talk." They all agreed, and gave leave, and told him to propose away.

"I will begin," said Eryximachos, "by quoting from the *Melanippe* of Euripides:[1] 'the story is not mine' which I am going to tell, it belongs to Phaidros. For Phaidros is always complaining to me, 'It's a shame, Eryximachos, that many other gods have hymns and paeans made for them by the poets, but Love, that ancient mighty god, has not a single one; of all the thousands of poets who have lived, not one has ever made even an ode to praise him! Or look at the worthy professors,[2] if you please; they compose praises of men like Heracles in prose, as the excellent Prodicos did,[3] perhaps that is not so surprising, but lately I came across a book by some wise man where salt was lauded to the skies for its usefulness, and you could find many other such things praised up. Just think—to make such a fuss about things like salt, when no human being has ever dared to this day to hymn Love worthily! What neglect for so great a god!' I think Phaidros is quite right there. So I wish to make my small contribution, and to offer it to him; and at the same time it seems to me proper on this occasion for us now present to glorify the god. If you vote with me, we should find plenty to amuse us in the speeches; for my proposal is that we should deliver a full-dress oration in praise of Love, each one from left to right, and Phaidros must begin first, since he is in the first place[4] and he is also father of the speech."

Then Socrates said, "No one will vote against you, Eryximachos. I could not refuse myself, I suppose, when love is the only thing I profess to know about; nor will Agathon, I suppose, and Pausanias, nor indeed Aristophanes, who devotes all his time to Dionysos[5] and Aphrodite, nor any other of those I see here. However, it is not quite fair on us who are last.[6] But if those before us give us some really good speeches, that will do for us. Then let Phaidros be the first, and speak in

---

[1] Euripides, *Fragment* 488.
[2] "Sophists," see *Meno*, p. 49, n. 1.
[3] In his famous *Choice of Heracles* (Hercules), Xenophon, *Memorabilia* ii. 1.21.
[4] He sat furthest on the left, in the place of honour.
[5] As the patron of comedy.
[6] Socrates and Agathon on the lowest couch on the right.

and good luck to him." All the others agreed, to do as Socrates suggested. However, what each all said, Aristodemos could not remember, nor ber all he told me. But what I do remember, and ght most worth remembering, I will tell you of each of the speeches.

Well, as I say, Phaidros, according to Aristodemos, was the first, and he began hereabouts; that Love was a great god and wonderful on earth and in heaven, especially in his birth. "The god is honourable as being among the most ancient of all," he said; "and a proof is, that parents Love has none, nor are they mentioned by anyone, poet or not, although Hesiod does say that Chaos came first,[1]

> And then
> Broad-breasted Earth, the everlasting seat
> Of all, and Love.

Acusileōs also agreed with Hesiod; he says that after Chaos were produced these two, Earth and Love. But Parmenides says of Birth, that she

> Contrivèd Love the first of all the gods.

Thus many agree that Love is most ancient among them. And being most ancient, he is cause of the greatest good for us. For I cannot say what is a greater good for a man in his youth than a lover, and for a lover than a beloved. For that which ought to guide mankind through all his life, if it is to be a good life, noble blood cannot implant in him so well, nor office, nor wealth, nor anything but Love. And what do I mean by that? I mean shame at ugly things, and ambition in beautiful things; for without these neither city nor man can accomplish great and beautiful works. I say then of a man who loves, that if he should be detected in doing something ugly, or allowing himself to be treated in ugly fashion because through cowardice he did not defend himself, he would suffer less pain to be seen by father or friends or anyone else than by his beloved. In the same way we see that the beloved is particularly ashamed before the lover, when seen in any ugly situation. Then if any device could be found how a state or an army could be made up only of lovers and beloved, they could not possibly find a better way of living, since they would abstain from all ugly things and be ambitious in beautiful things towards each other; and in battle side by side, such troops although few would conquer pretty well all the world. For the lover would be less willing to be seen by his beloved than by all the rest of the

[1] Hesiod, *Theogonia*, 116.

world, leaving the ranks or throwing away his arms, and he would choose to die many times rather than that; yes, and as to deserting the beloved, or not helping in danger, no one is so base that Love himself would not inspire him to valour, and make him equal to the born hero. And just as Homer says that the god 'breathes fury'[1] into some of the heroes, so does Love really give to lovers a power coming from himself.

"And to die for another—this only lovers are willing to do, not only men, but women. Alcestis, Pelias' daughter,[2] gives sufficient evidence of this to prove it to our nation; she alone was willing to die for her husband, although he had a father and a mother; these the wife so much surpassed in love because of her affection for her husband that she showed they were aliens to their own son and were relatives only in name. Having done this, she was thought, not only by men, but by gods also, to have done so nobly that they sent up her soul from the dead in admiration for her deed, although of all the many who have done noble deeds one might easily count those to whom the gods gave the privilege of having their souls sent up again from Hades. Thus the gods also honour especially earnestness and valour in love. But Orpheus, Oiagros' son, they sent back unsuccessful from Hades, showing him a phantom of his wife for whom he came, but not giving her real self because they thought him soft, being a zither-player, and they thought he did not dare to die for his love like Alcestis, but managed to get into Hades alive. For this reason, therefore, they punished him, and made his death come about by women, unlike Achilles, the son of Thetis; but they honoured Achilles and sent him to the Islands of the Blest,[3] because when his mother told him that if he killed Hector he would die, but if he did not kill him he would return home and live to be an old man, he dared to choose, by helping his lover Patroclos and avenging him, not only to die for him, but in his end to perish over his body: hence therefore the gods, admiring him above measure, honoured him particularly, because he set so high the value of his lover. (But Aeschylus is absurd[4] when he says Achilles was the lover and Patroclos the beloved, when he was more beautiful not only than Patroclos but than all the heroes, and was yet beardless, and again much younger, as Homer says.[5]) But in fact the gods do most greatly honour this valour for love's sake; yet they still more respect and admire and reward when the beloved feels affection for the lover, than when the lover does for his beloved. For a lover is more divine than the be-

---

[1] *Iliad* x. 482 and elsewhere.
[2] See Euripides' famous play *Alcestis*, produced in 438 B.C.
[3] Pindar, *Olympian* ii. 78.
[4] In a lost play called *The Myrmidons*.
[5] *Iliad* xi. 786.

loved, since he is inspired. Therefore they honoured Achilles more than Alcestis, and sent him to the Islands of the Blest.

"Thus then I say, that of the gods Love is at once oldest, and most precious, and has most power to provide virtue and happiness for mankind, both living and dead."

Such or something like it was the speech of Phaidros, as related to me by Aristodemos; and after Phaidros there were some others which he did not remember well; so he passed them by, and reported the speech of Pausanias, who said, "I do not think, Phaidros, that the rules were properly laid down, I mean that we should just simply belaud Love. For if Love were one, that would do, but really he is not one; and since he is not one, it is more proper to say first which we are to praise. Then I will try to set this right, and say first which Love we ought to praise, and then praise that god worthily. For we all know that Aphrodite[1] is never without a Love: if she were one, Love would be one; but since there are really two, there must be two Loves. Of course there are two goddesses. One I take it is older, and motherless, daughter of Heaven, whom we call Heavenly Aphrodite, the other younger, a daughter of Zeus and Dione, whom we call, as you know, Common. It must be then, you see, that Love too, the one who works with this Aphrodite, should be called Common Love, and the other Heavenly Love. It is true we must praise all gods, but I must try to say what is the province of each of these two. For the performance of every action is, in itself, neither beautiful nor ugly. So what we are doing now, whether drinking or singing or speaking, is not itself beautiful, but according as it is done, so it comes out in the doing: when it is done well and rightly, it is beautiful, but when not rightly done, it is ugly. Just so with being in love, and with Love himself; he is not all beautiful and worthy to be praised, but only so far as he leads to right loving.

"The Love, then, which belongs to Common Aphrodite is really and truly common and works at random; and this is the love which inferior men feel. Such persons love firstly women as well as boys; next, when they love, they love bodies rather than souls; and next, they choose the most foolish persons they can, for they look only to getting something done, and care nothing whether well or not. So what happens to them is that they act at random, whether they do good or whether they do its opposite; for this Love springs from the goddess which is much younger than the other, and in her birth had a share of both female and male.

[1] Goddess of love.

But the other Love springs from the Heavenly goddess, who firstly has had no share of the female, but only of the male; next, she is the elder, and has no violence in her: consequently those inspired by this love turn to the male, because they feel affection rather for what is stronger and has more mind. One could recognise even in boy-love those who are driven by this Love pure and simple; for they do not fall in love with those who are little boys, but with those who begin to have mind, and that is nearly when they show the down on their chins. For those who begin to love them from this age, I think, are ready to be with them always for all their lives, and to live with them together; they do not wish to get a boy in the foolishness of youth, and then deceive him and laugh at him and go off running to another. There ought to have been a law against loving little boys, that a great deal of earnestness might not have been spent on what is uncertain; for it is uncertain how little boys will turn out, as regards vice and virtue, both of body and soul. Now those who are good place this law before themselves unbidden; but it ought to be made compulsory for those common lovers, just as we make it compulsory as far as we can that they shall not make love to freeborn women. For these are they who bring reproach on the whole thing, so that some dare to say that it is ugly to gratify lovers; they say this with their eye on those common ones, when they see their tactlessness and injustice; since I suppose nothing done decently and lawfully could fairly bring discredit.

"Again, here and in Lacedaimon the law about love is confusing, but that in other states is easy to understand. In Elis and Boeotia, and where people are not clever speakers, it is simply laid down that it is right to gratify lovers, and no one young or old would call it ugly; as I think, they wish not to have the trouble of convincing the young, because they cannot argue; but in many other parts of Ionia it is considered ugly, where they are under barbarians. For the barbarians because of the rule of despots call this ugly, as well as philosophy and sports; I suppose it is profitable to their rulers that the subjects should not be great in spirit or make strong friendships and unions, which things love is wont to implant more than anything else. In fact, our own despots[1] here found that out by experience; for the love of Aristogeiton, and the friendship of Harmodios, grown strong, brought their rule to an end. So where it has been laid down as ugly to gratify lovers, that was from the evil condition of

[1] Hippias and his brother Hipparchos, joint tyrants of Athens, 514 B.C.

those that made the laws, the grasping habits of the rulers and the cowardice of the ruled; and where it was thought simply good, that was from laziness of soul in those who made the laws. But in these parts, much of the law and custom is better, and as I said, it is not easy to understand.

"For consider that it is called better to love openly than secretly, and especially to love the highest and noblest born, even if they are uglier than others; and consider how wonderfully all encourage the lover—not as if he were doing something ugly, which if he wins is thought beautiful, and if he does not win, ugly; and how the law has allowed the lover, in trying to win, to be praised for doing extraordinary things, which if a man should dare to do in pursuit of anything else except this, or should even wish to accomplish, he would reap the greatest disgrace. For if, wishing to get money from someone, or to win public office, or to get any other power, a man should behave as lovers do towards their beloved, begging and beseeching them in their petitions, and swearing solemn oaths, and sleeping at their doors, and being willing to do slavish services such as no slave would do, he would be hindered both by friends and by enemies from doing his business thus: the friends would be ashamed of such things and warn him, the enemies would upbraid him for flattery and bad manners. But the lover has a grace when he does all this, and the law allows him to do it without discredit, as a thing wholly beautiful; and strangest of all, he alone, as the people say, is pardoned by the gods for breaking the oath he has sworn—for it is said an oath of love simply has no force. Thus both gods and men have given full licence to the lover, as the law here says; so far, then, one might think it was considered wholly beautiful in this city both to love and to feel affection for a lover. But on the other hand when fathers place tutors over the loved ones and forbid them to converse with their lovers, and the tutor is ordered to see to it; when age-mates and companions reproach them if they see anything like this going on; and lastly when the older men do not stop these from reproaching them, nor scold them for talking nonsense—if one looked at this, one would think such a thing was considered very ugly here. The fact is, I think, the case is not simple: as I said at the beginning, it is neither beautiful nor ugly by itself, but beautifully done it is beautiful, and uglily done it is ugly—uglily, is to gratify a base man and basely; beautifully, is to gratify a good man and beautifully. A base man is that common lover who loves the body rather than the soul; for he is not lasting since he loves a thing not lasting. For as soon as the flower of the body fades, which is what he loved, 'He takes to the wing and away he flies,'[1] and violates any number of vows and promises; but the lover of a good character remains faithful throughout life, since he has been fused with a lasting thing. These, then, our law wishes to test well and thoroughly; for these reasons, then, it enjoins to pursue the one and eschew the other, setting them tasks and testing them to see which class the lover belongs to, and which class the beloved. Thus you see it is on these grounds that, first of all, to be won quickly is considered ugly—for time should come in, which seems to test everything well; next, to be won by money and political power is ugly, whether it means shrinking from suffering and lack of endurance, or failure to despise the benefits flowing from money or political achievements; for none of these things appears to be firm and lasting, not to mention that genuine affection is never bred from them. Then only one road is left for our law, if the beloved is to gratify the lover beautifully. For our law is, that as it was not counted flattery or disgrace for lovers to be willing slaves in any slavery to the beloved, so for the beloved, there is only one willing slavery which is no disgrace—and that is in pursuit of virtue.

"For we have a custom that if one wishes to serve another, because he thinks that the man can make him better either in wisdom or any other part of virtue, this willing slavery is not ugly and it is no flattery. Then let us compare these two customs, that which concerns boy-lovers and that which concerns philosophy and virtue in general, if we are to infer that when the beloved gratifies the lover it is beautiful. For when lover and beloved come together each with his law—the one, that when he serves the consenting beloved in anything whatever the service is right, the other, that by doing any service whatever to one who makes him wise and good he does right service, the one able to contribute something for wisdom and virtue in general, the other desiring to get this for education and wisdom in general—then, you see, these laws meet together, and then only it follows that for beloved to gratify lover is beautiful, but never otherwise. In this case, even to be deceived is not ugly; in all others both to be deceived and not to be deceived is ugly. For if one in pursuit of riches gratifies a lover supposed to be rich, and is deceived and gets no money because the lover turns out to be poor, it is no less ugly; for such a one is thought to show, as far as in him lay, that for money he would do anyone and everyone any and every service, and that is not beautiful.

[1] Agamemnon thus speaks about a dream. *Iliad* ii. 71.

By the same argument observe that even if one gratifies another as being good, expecting to be better himself because of his affection for the lover, but since the other turns out to be bad and not possessed of virtue, he is deceived, nevertheless the deceit is beautiful; for he again is thought to have shown, as far as in him lay, that for virtue and to become better he was ready with everything for everyone. And this again is the most beautiful thing of all; so in every case it is beautiful to gratify for the sake of virtue.

"This is the love of the heavenly goddess, love both heavenly and precious to city and men; for it compels both lover and beloved to take all possible care for virtue. But all other loves belong to the other goddess, the common one. Here, my dear Phaidros, you have my humble contribution on Love, as well as I could make it at the moment."

Pausanias paused upon this clause—that's how the stylists teach me to jingle!—and Aristodemos said that Aristophanes ought to have spoken next, but he had a hiccup from surfeit or something, and couldn't speak. However, he managed to say to Doctor Eryximachos, who was reclining in the place just below him, "My dear Eryximachos, it's your job either to stop my hiccup, or to speak instead until I stop myself."

And Eryximachos answered, "Well, I will do both; I will speak in your turn, and when you stop the hiccup you shall speak in mine. And while I am speaking, hold your breath a long time and see if the hiccup will stop; if it won't, gargle water. But if it still goes strong, pick up something to tickle your nose with, and sneeze; do this once or twice, and stop it will, even if it is very strong."

"Look sharp," says Aristophanes, "speak away, and I'll do all that."

Then (continued Aristodemos) Eryximachos said, "Pausanias began well, but ended feebly, so I think I must try to put a good end to his oration. He said Love was double, and I think he was right in dividing him. But I think I have seen from our art of medicine how great and wonderful the god is, and how he extends over everything human and divine; he is not only in the souls of mankind and directed towards beautiful people, but he is in all the rest, and directed towards many other things; he is in the bodies of all living creatures, and in what grows in the earth, and, one may say, in everything there is. I will begin my speech with medicine, that we may do special honour to my art. The natural body has this double Love; for bodily health and disease are by common consent different things and unlike, and what is unlike desires and loves things unlike. Then there is one love in the healthy, and another in the diseased. So you see just as, according to what Pausanias said just now, it is beautiful to gratify good men, and ugly to gratify the intemperate, so in the bodies themselves, to gratify the good things in each body and the healthy things is beautiful and must be done, and this gratification is what is called the healing art, but to gratify what is bad and diseased is ugly and must not be done, if one is to practise that art. For the healing art, to put it shortly, is knowledge of the body's loves for filling and emptying, and one who distinguishes the beautiful and the ugly love in these things is the most complete physician; and one who makes them change, so that they get one love instead of the other, and, where there is no love when there ought to be, one who knows how to put it in, and to take out love that is in, he would be a good practitioner. You see one must be able to make loving friends of the greatest enemies in the body. Now the greatest enemies are the most opposite, hot and cold, bitter and sweet, dry and wet, and so forth; our ancestor Asclepios,[1] as our poets[2] here say and I believe, composed our art because he knew how to implant love and concord in these. Then the healing art, as I say, is all guided by this god, and so is gymnastic and agriculture; music too is clearly in the same case with this, as it is plain to anyone who thinks for a moment; and perhaps that is what Heracleitos means, since his words are not very clear. He says, 'The One at variance with itself is brought together again, like a harmony of bow and lyre.'[3] It is quite illogical to say that a *harmony* is *at variance* with itself or is made up of notes still *at variance*. But perhaps he meant to say that it was made from the high and low notes—first at variance, then afterwards reconciled together by the art of music. For I suppose there could not be harmony from high and low notes still at variance, for harmony is symphony and symphony is a kind of agreement; but agreement there cannot be of things at variance so long as they are at variance. But what is at variance, and yet is not unable to be brought into agreement, it is possible to harmonize. Just so rhythm is made from quick and slow, first differing, then brought into agreement. But

[1] Father of medicine.
[2] Agathon and Aristophanes.
[3] The reader may find Eryximachos' explanation which follows easier to understand if he thinks of "at variance" as meaning "out of tune," and "reconciling" as tuning the strings, and of a bow as giving out a deep faint musical note when the arrow leaves it. "Harmony" and "symphony" had not to the Greeks all the meaning they have to us as musical terms. Harmony was rather the relation between single notes which sounded well in sequence, and symphony the sound of those notes played together. (Unison was one form of harmony, and sounds in unison one form of symphony; steady motion, a compromise of quick and slow, is one form of rhythm). See also *Republic*, p. 196, n. 3.

music places agreement here in all these, just as there the art of healing does, by implanting concord and love for each other; and music again is the knowledge of love affairs concerning harmony and rhythm. And in the very composition of harmony and rhythm it is not difficult to distinguish the love affairs, although the double love is not there yet; but whenever one must use rhythm and harmony for men, either composing (which they call melody-making), or rightly using the melodies and verses made (which is called education), that is the time when there are difficulties, and a good craftsman is wanted. Then the same old argument comes round again, that decent men must be gratified, and also those not yet quite decent that they may become so, and their Love must be protected; and this is the beautiful Love, the Heavenly Love, the Love belonging to the 'Heavenly' Muse Urania; but that of 'Manyhymn' Polymnia is the common one, who must be offered to people with great care whenever he is offered, to let them reap the pleasure from him, but not to implant any intemperance: just so in our art, it is a great business to use well the desires concerned with the art of cookery, so that people may reap the pleasures without disease. So you see, both in music and in physic and in everything else earthly and heavenly, we must watch and protect both Loves as far as we can, for both are there.

"See how the composition of the seasons of the year is full of these two: and so, whenever the things I mentioned just now, hot and cold and dry and wet, have the decent Love towards each other, and get a harmony and a temperate mixture, they come bringing a good season, with health for mankind and the other animals and vegetables and plants, and then they do no harm; but when the violent Love has more power on the seasons of the year, he does harm, and destroys much. For pestilences often come as a result, and many other discordant diseases in wild beasts and growing things: hoarfrosts and hails and blights come from the grasping habits and indecency of such love affairs, knowledge of which as regards the courses of the stars and the seasons of the year is called astronomy. Moreover, all sacrifice and the domain of divination (this is the communion of gods and men together), all this is concerned solely with the protection and healing of Love. For all impiety is wont to occur, as concerns parents both living and dead, and gods, if one does not gratify the decent Love and honour him and put him first in every work, but honours the other. So you see this is what divination is ordered to do, to supervise these Loves and to treat them as a physician; and divination is again the craftsman of friendship between men and gods, by its knowledge of the love affairs of mankind which tend towards good law and piety.

"So Love as a whole has great and mighty power, or rather in a word, omnipotence; but the one concerned with good things, being accomplished with temperance and justice, both here and in heaven, has the greatest power, and provides all happiness for us, and makes us able to have society together, and to be friends with the gods also, who are higher than we are. Perhaps indeed I also omit much in praising Love; but I can't help it. If I have omitted something, it is your part, Aristophanes, to fill up the gap; or if you intend to praise the god in some other way, go on and do so, since your hiccup is gone."

So Aristophanes (said Aristodemos) took his turn next, and said, "Oh yes, it has quite gone, but not until sneezing was applied to it; which makes me wonder if the decency of the body desires noises and ticklings like a sneeze; for it stopped at once when I applied the sneeze to it."

Then Eryximachos said, "My good man, look what you're doing! You are playing the fool when you are about to make a speech! You compel me to keep a watch on your speech and look out for something laughable, when you might speak in peace!"

And Aristophanes answered, with a laugh, "Quite right, Eryximachos, I take back what I said. But don't watch me, for as to what I am going to say, I am not at all afraid I may say something laughable, for that would be clear gain and natural to our Muse—but lest the things I say may be just ridiculous!"

"So you think you are going to hurl your shaft, Aristophanes," he said, "and get off scot free? Take care, take care, and be sure you will have to account for yourself. But perhaps I will let you off, if I am so disposed."

"Well, Eryximachos," said Aristophanes. "I intend to speak in a different way from you and Pausanias. For it seems to me that mankind have wholly failed to perceive the power of Love; if they had, they would have built to him their greatest sanctuaries and altars, and they would have made their greatest sacrifice to him; but now nothing of the sort is done, although it most assuredly ought to be done. For he is the most man-loving of gods, being the helper of man, and the healer of those whose healing would be the greatest happiness to the human race. Therefore I will try to introduce you to his power, and you shall teach the others.

"First you must learn about the nature of man and the

history of it. Formerly the natural state of man was not what it is now, but quite different. For at first there were three sexes, not two as at present, male and female, but also a third having both together; the name remains with us, but the thing is gone. There was then a male-female sex and a name to match, sharing both male and female, but now nothing is left but the title used in reproach.[1] Next, the shape of man was quite round, back and ribs passing about it in a circle; and he had four arms and an equal number of legs, and two faces on a round neck, exactly alike; there was one head with these two opposite faces, and four ears, and two privy members, and the rest as you might imagine from this. They walked upright as now, in whichever direction they liked; and when they wanted to run fast, they rolled over and over on the ends of the eight limbs they had in those days, as our tumblers tumble now with their legs straight out. And why there were three sexes, and shaped like this, was because the male was at first born of the sun, and the female of the earth, and the common sex had something of the moon, which combines both male and female; their shape was round and their going was round because they were like their parents. They had terrible strength and force, and great were their ambitions; they attacked the gods, and what Homer said of Otos and Ephialtes is said of them, that they tried to climb into heaven intending to make war upon the gods.[2]

"So Zeus and the other gods held council what they should do, and they were perplexed; for they really could not kill the tribe with thunderbolts and make them vanish like the giants —since then their honours and the sacrifices of mankind would vanish too—nor could they allow them to go on in this wild way. After a deal of worry Zeus had a happy thought. 'Look here,' he said, 'I think I have found a scheme; we can let men still exist but we can stop them from their violence by making them weaker. I will tell you what I'll do now,' says he, 'I will slice each of them down through the middle! Two improvements at once! They will be weaker, and they will be more useful to us because there will be more of them. They shall walk upright on two legs. And if they choose to go on with their wild doings, and will not keep quiet, I'll do it again!' says he, 'I'll slice 'em again through the middle! And they shall hop about on one leg! Like those boys that hop on the greasy wineskins at the fair!'[3] says he; and then he sliced men through the middle, as you slice your serviceberries through the middle

[1] Hermaphrodite.
[2] *Odyssey* xi. 305 ff. Otos and Ephialtes were the giants, who, to climb into heaven, piled Mt. Pelion on Mt. Ossa.
[3] This was done at the country feast of Dionysos.

for pickle, or as you slice hard-boiled eggs with a hair. While he sliced each, he told Apollo to turn the face and half the neck towards the cut, to make the man see his own cut and be more orderly, and then he told him to heal the rest up. So Apollo turned the face, and gathered up the skin over what is now called the belly, like purses which you pull shut with a string; he made one little mouth, and fastened it at the middle of the belly, what they call the navel. Most of the wrinkles he smoothed out, and shaped the breasts, using a tool like the shoemaker's when he smooths wrinkles out of his leather on the last; but he left a few, those about the navel and the belly, to remind them of what happened. So when the original body was cut through, each half wanted the other, and hugged it; they threw their arms round each other desiring to grow together in the embrace, and died of starvation and general idleness because they would not do anything apart from each other. When one of the halves died and the other was left, the half which was left hunted for another and embraced it, whether he found the half of a whole woman (which we call woman now), or half of a whole man; and so they perished. But Zeus pitied them and found another scheme; he moved their privy parts in front, for these also were outside before, and they had begotten and brought forth not with each other but with the ground, like the cicadas. So he moved these parts also in front and made the generation come between them, by the male in the female; that in this embrace, if a man met a woman, they might beget and the race might continue, and if a man met a man, they might be satisfied by their union and rest, and might turn to work and care about the general business of life. So you see how ancient is the mutual love implanted in mankind, bringing together the parts of the original body, and trying to make one out of two, and to heal the natural structure of man.

"Then each of us is the tally[1] of a man; he is sliced like a flatfish, and two made of one. So each one seeks his other tally. Then all men who are a cutting of the old common sex which was called manwoman are fond of women, and adulterers generally come of that sex, and all women who are mad for men, and adulteresses. The women who are a cutting of the ancient women do not care much about men, but are more attracted to women, and strumpetesses also come from this sex. But those which are a cutting of the male pursue the male, and while they are boys, being slices of the male, they are fond

[1] Tallies, like half of a broken coin or bone kept by friends or parties to an agreement, or the split laths of the old English exchequer, or the cut parchments of an indenture.

of men, and enjoy lying with men and embracing them, and these are the best of boys and lads because they are naturally bravest. Some call them shameless, but that is false; no shamelessness makes them do this, but boldness and courage and a manly force, which welcome what is like them. Here is a great proof: when they grow up, such as these alone are men in public affairs. And when they become men, they fancy boys, and naturally do not trouble about marriage and getting a family, but that law and custom compels them; they find it enough themselves to live unmarried together. Such a person is always inclined to be a boy-lover or a beloved, as he always welcomes what is akin. So when one of these meets his own proper half, whether boy-lover or anyone else, then they are wonderfully overwhelmed by affection and intimacy and love, and one may say never wish to be apart for a moment. These are the ones who remain together all their lives, although they could not say what they expect to get from each other; for no one could suppose that this is sensual union, as if this could make anyone delight in another's company so seriously as all that. Plainly the soul of each wants something else—what, it cannot say, but it divines and riddles what it wants. And as they lie together suppose Hephaistos[1] were to stand beside them with his tools, and ask, 'What do you want from each other, men?' And if they were at a loss, suppose he should ask again, 'Is it only that you desire to be together as close as possible, and not to be apart from each other night or day? For if that is what you desire, I am ready to melt you and weld you together, so that you two may be made one, and as one you may live together as long as you live, and when you die you may die still one instead of two, and be yonder in the house of Hades together. Think if this is your passion, and if it will satisfy you to get this.' If that were offered, we know that not a single one would object, or be found to wish anything else; he would simply believe he had heard that which he had so long desired, to be united and melted together with his beloved, and to become one from two. For the reason is that this was our ancient natural shape, when we were one whole; and so the desire for the whole and the pursuit of it is named Love.

"Formerly, as I say, we were one, but now because of doing wrong we have been dispersed by the god, as the Arcadians were dispersed by the Lacedaimonians. There is fear then, if we are not decent towards the gods, that we may be sliced in half again, and we may go about like so many relief carvings of persons shown in half-view on tombstones, sawn right

[1] The god of fire.

through the nose, like tally-dice cut in half. For these reasons we must exhort all men in everything to be god-fearing men, that we may escape this fate and attain our desire, since Love is our leader and captain. But let no man oppose Love—and whoever is the gods' enemy does oppose him. For when we are friends with this god and reconciled to him, we shall find and enjoy our very own beloved, which now few are able to do. And don't let Eryximachos chip in and make fun of my speech, and say that I mean Pausanias and Agathon; I should not be surprised if they are really of this class, and both males by nature, but indeed I speak in general of all men and women, that the way to make our race happy is to make love perfect, and each to get his very own beloved and go back to our original nature. If this is the best thing possible, the best thing to our hand must of course be to come as near it as possible, and that is to get a beloved who suits our mind. Then if we would praise the god who is the cause of this, we should rightly praise Love, who in the present gives us our chief blessing by bringing us home to our own, and for the future offers the greatest hopes; that if we duly worship the god, he will restore us to our ancient nature and heal us and make us blessed and happy.

"There is my speech about Love, Eryximachos, very different from yours. Then, as I begged you, do not make fun of it, but let us hear what each of the others will say, or rather, each of the two others; for only Agathon and Socrates are left."

"I will do as you ask," said Eryximachos, "for I did very much enjoy hearing that speech. And if I did not know that both Socrates and Agathon were experts in love matters, I should be afraid they might be puzzled what to say when such a world of things has been said already. But as it is, I don't fear at all."

Then Socrates said, "You played your part well yourself, Eryximachos; but if you were where I am now, or rather perhaps where I shall be, when Agathon has made his speech, you would be very much afraid, and like me now, you wouldn't know where you were."

"You want to put a spell on me, Socrates," said Agathon, "and make me shy through thinking that the audience has great expectations of a fine speech from me!"

Socrates answered, "I should have a very bad memory, Agathon, if I thought you would be shy now before a few people like us, since I saw your courage and spirit when you mounted the platform along with the actors, and faced all that huge audience, ready to display your compositions without the smallest sign of confusion."

"What!" said Agathon, "my dear Socrates, you don't really think I am so full of the theatre that I don't know a few men with minds are more formidable to a man of sense than many without minds!"

"I should make a mistake, my dear Agathon," Socrates said, "if I imagined anything vulgar about you; I am quite sure that if you were in company with any you thought intelligent, you would rate them above the many. However, perhaps we are not intelligent—for we were there too, and we were among the many—but if you should meet with others who are, you would be ashamed of doing before them anything which you might think ugly. What do you say to that?"

"Quite true," said he.

"And before the many, would you not be ashamed if you thought you were doing something ugly?"

Then Phaidros put in a word, and said, "My dear friend Agathon, if you answer Socrates, he will not care what becomes of our business here! He won't care anything about anything, so long as he can have someone to converse with, especially someone beautiful. For myself, I like hearing Socrates arguing, but it is my duty to care about the praise of Love, and to exact from each one of you his speech. So just pay up to the god, both of you, and then you may argue."

"Quite right, Phaidros," said Agathon, "I am ready to speak; Socrates will be there another time, and often, to talk to.

"First, then, I wish to describe how I ought to speak; then to speak. It seems to me that all who have spoken so far have not praised the god, but have congratulated mankind on the good things which the god has caused for them: what that god was himself who gave these gifts, no one has described. But the one right way for any laudation of anyone is to describe what he is, and then what he causes, whoever may be our subject. Thus, you see, with Love: we also should first praise him for what he is, and then praise his gifts.

"I say then that all gods are happy, but if it is lawful to say this without offence, I say that Love is happiest of them all, being most beautiful and best. And how he is most beautiful, I am about to describe. First of all, Phaidros, he is youngest of the gods. He himself supplies one great proof of what I say, for he flies in full flight away from Old Age, who is a quick one clearly, since he comes too soon to us all. Love hates him naturally and will not come anywhere near him. But he is always associated with the young, and with them he consorts, for the old saying is right, 'Like ever comes to like.' I am ready to admit many other things to Phaidros, but one I do not admit, that Love is older than Cronos and Iapetos;[1] no, I say he is youngest of the gods, and ever young; but that old business of the gods, which Hesiod and Parmenides tell about, was done through Necessity and not through Love, if they told the truth; for if Love had been in them, there would have been no gelding or enchaining of each other and all those violent things, but friendship and peace, as there is now, and has been ever since Love has reigned over the gods. So then, he is young, and besides being young he is tender; but we need a poet like Homer to show the god's tenderness. For Homer says of Ate[2] that she was a god and tender—at least her feet were tender—when he says that

> Tender are her feet; she comes not near
> The ground, but walks upon the heads of men.

I think he gives good proof of her tenderness, that she walks not on the hard but on the soft. Then let us use the same proof for Love, that he is tender. For he walks not on the earth nor on top of heads, which are not so very soft, but both walks and abides in the softest things there are; for his abode is settled in the tempers and souls of gods and men, and again, not in all souls without exception; no, whenever he meets a soul with a hard temper, he departs, but where it is soft, he abides. So since he always touches with feet and all else the softest of the soft, he must needs be tender. You see, then, he is youngest and tenderest, but besides this his figure is supple, for if he were stiff, he could not fold himself in everywhere, or throughout every soul, and come in and go out unnoticed from the first. A great proof of his good proportion and supple shape is his gracefulness, which, as we all know, Love has in high degree; for there is always war between gracelessness and Love. Colours and beauty are testified by the god's nestling in flowers; for where there is no flower, or flower is past, in body and soul and everything else, Love sits not, but where the place is flowery and fragrant there he both sits and stays.

"Of the god's beauty much more might be said, but this is enough; the virtue of Love comes next. Chief is that Love wrongs not and is not wronged, wrongs no god and is wronged by none, wrongs no man and is wronged by none. Nothing that happens to him comes by violence, for violence touches not Love; nothing he does is violent, for everyone willingly serves Love in everything, and what a willing person grants to a

[1] In Greek mythology these were two of the Titans who were children of Ouranos (Heaven) and Gaia (Earth). They existed even before Zeus.
[2] Atē, presumptuous Madness, something like Sin. *Iliad* xix. 92.

willing, is just— so say 'the city's king, the laws,'[1] And besides justice, he is full of temperance. It is agreed that temperance is the mastery and control of pleasures and desires, and that no pleasure is stronger than Love. But if they are weaker, then Love would master and control them; and being master of pleasure and desires, Love would be especially temperate. Furthermore, in courage 'not even Ares[2] stands up against Love,' for it is not Ares that holds Love, but Love Ares— love of Aphrodite, as they say; stronger is he that holds than he that is held, and the master of the bravest of all would be himself bravest. Now the justice and temperance and courage of the god have been spoken of, and wisdom is left; so one must try to do the best one is able to do. And first, that I may honour our art as Eryximachos honoured his, Love is so wise a poet that he can make another the same; at least, everyone becomes a poet whom Love touches, even one who before that, had 'no music in his soul'.[3] This we may fittingly use as a proof that Love is a good poet[4] or active maker in practically all the creations of the fine arts; for what one has not or knows not, one can neither give to another nor teach another. Now take the making of all living things; who will dispute that they are the clever work of Love, by which all living things are made and begotten? And craftsmanship in the arts; don't we know that where this god is teacher, art turns out notable and illustrious, but where there is no touch of Love, it is all in the dark? Archery, again, and medicine and divination were invented by Apollo, led by desire and love, so that even he would be a pupil of Love; so also the Muses in music and Hephaistos in smithcraft and Athena in weaving and Zeus in 'pilotage of gods and men.' Hence you see also, all that business of the gods was arranged when Love came among them—love of beauty, that is plain, for there is no Love in ugliness. Before that, as I said at the beginning, many terrible things happened to the gods because of the reign of Necessity—so the story goes; but when this god Love was born, all became good both for gods and men from loving beautiful things.

"Thus it seems to me, Phaidros, that Love comes first, himself most beautiful and best, and thereafter he is cause of other such things in others. And I am moved to speak something of him in verse myself, that it is he who makes

---

[1] Quoted from Alcidamas, a stylist.
[2] Ares, god of war. The quotation is from Sophocles' lost play *Thyestes*, fragment 235 N.
[3] Euripides, *Stheneboea*, fragment 663 N.
[4] The Greek word ποιητής, poet, means a maker, and he uses this here to indicate creative arts and crafts and even the "creation" of living things.

SYMPOSIUM (196C–198C)

Peace among men, calm weather on the deep,
Respite from winds, in trouble rest and sleep.[1]

He empties us of estrangement, and fills us with friendliness, ordaining all such meetings as this one, of people one with another, in feasts, in dances, in sacrifices becoming men's guide; he provides gentleness and banishes savagery; he loves to give good will, hates to give ill will; gracious, mild; illustrious to the wise, admirable to the gods; enviable to those who have none of him, treasured by those who have some of him; father of luxury, daintiness, delicacy, grace, longing, desire; careful of good things, careless of bad things; in hardship, in fear, in drinking,[2] in talk a pilot, a comrade, a stand-by[3] and the best of saviours; of all gods and men an ornament, a guide most beautiful and best, whom every man must follow, hymning him well, sharing in the song he sings as he charms the mind of gods and men.

"This, Phaidros, is my speech," he said; "may the god accept my dedication, partly play, partly modest seriousness, and the best that I am able to do."

When Agathon had spoken (Aristodemos told me), all applauded; the young man was thought to have spoken becomingly for himself and for the god. Then Socrates looked at Eryximachos, and said, "Now then, son of Acumenos, do you think there was no reason to fear in the fears I feared?[4] Was I not a prophet when I said, as I did just now, that Agathon would make a wonderful speech, and leave me with nothing to say?"

"Yes, to the first," said Eryximachos, "you were a prophet there, certainly, about the wonderful speech; but nothing to say? I don't think so!"

"Bless you," said Socrates, "and how have I anything to say, I or anyone else, when I have to speak after that beautiful speech, with everything in it? The first part was wonderful enough, but the end! The beauty of those words and phrases! It was quite overwhelming for any listener. The fact is, when I considered that I shall not be able to get anywhere near it, and I have nothing fine to say at all—I was so ashamed that I all but took to my heels and ran, but I had nowhere to go. The speech reminded me of Gorgias,[5] and I really felt quite

---
[1] Compare *Odyssey* v. 391.
[2] This word "drinking" is doubtful in the Greek text.
[3] The three words used by Plato mean a ship's pilot, a fighter (not the driver) in a chariot or a marine on a ship, and a man who stands by another in battle.
[4] He puts in his own little drop of parody.
[5] Gorgias, the celebrated Sophist, adopted an artificial, affected style. See *Meno* p. 28, n. 1.

as in Homer's story;[1] I was afraid that Agathon at the end of his speech might be going to produce the Gorgon's head of Gorgias—the terror in speech-making—directed against *my* speech, and turn me into stone with dumbness. And I understood then that I was a fool when I told you I would take my turn in singing the honours of Love, and admitted I was terribly clever in love affairs, whereas it seems I really had no idea how a eulogy ought to be made. For I was stupid enough to think that we ought to speak the truth about each person eulogised, and to make this the foundation, and from these truths to choose the most beautiful things and arrange them in the most elegant way; and I was quite proud to think how well I should speak, because I believed that I knew the truth. However, apparently this was not the right way to praise anything, but we should dedicate all that is greatest and most beautiful to the work, whether things are so or not; if they were false it did not matter. For it seems the task laid down was not for each of us to praise Love, but to seem to praise him. For this reason then, I think, you rake up every story, and dedicate it to Love, and say he is so-and-so and the cause of such-and-such, that he may seem to be most beautiful and best, of course to those who don't know—not to those who do, I suppose—and the laudation is excellent and imposing. But indeed I did not know how an encomium was made, and it was without this knowledge that I agreed to take my part in praising. Therefore the tongue promised, but not the mind,[2] so good-bye to that. For I take it back now; I make no eulogy in this fashion: I could not do it. However, the truth, if you like: I have no objection to telling the truth, in my own fashion, not in rivalry with your speeches, or I should deserve to be laughed at. Then see whether you want a speech of that sort, Phaidros. Will you listen to the truth being told about Love, in any words and arrangement of phrases such as we may hit on as we go?"

Phaidros and the others (continued Aristodemos) told him to go on just as he thought best. "Then, Phaidros," he said, "let me ask Agathon a few little things, that I may get his agreement before I speak."

"Oh, I don't mind," said Phaidros, "ask away." After that Socrates began something like this:

"Indeed, my dear Agathon, I thought you were quite right in the beginning of your speech, when you said that you must first show what Love was like, and afterwards come to his

[1] *Odyssey* xi, 634. Odysseus, at the end of his visit to the Kingdom of the Dead, grew pale with fear that Persephone might out of Hades send upon him a Gorgon-head, and turn him to stone.
[2] A modification of Euripides' *Hippolytos* 612.

works. That beginning I admire very much. Now then, about Love: you described what he is magnificently well, and so on; but tell me this too—is Love such as to be a love of something, or of nothing? I don't mean to ask if he is a love of mother or father; for that would be a ridiculous question, whether Love is love for mother or father; I mean it in the sense that one might apply to 'father' for instance; is the father a father of something or not? You would say, I suppose, if you wanted to answer right, that the father is father of son or daughter. Is that correct?"

"Certainly," said Agathon.

"And the same with the mother?"

This was agreed.

"Another, please," said Socrates, "answer me one or two more, that you may better understand what I want. What if I were to ask: 'A brother now, in himself, is he brother of something?' "

He said yes.

"Of a brother or sister?"

He agreed.

"Then tell me," he said, "about Love. Is Love love of nothing or of something?"

"Certainly he is love of something."

"Now then," said Socrates, "keep this in your memory, what the object of Love is;[1] and say whether Love desires the object of his love?"

"Certainly," said Agathon.

"Is it when he *has* what he desires and loves that he desires and loves it, or when he has not?"

"Most likely, when he has not," said he.

"Just consider," said Socrates, "put 'necessary' for 'likely'; isn't it necessary that the desiring desires what it lacks, or else does not desire if it does not lack? I think positively myself, Agathon, that it is absolutely necessary; what do you think?"

"I think the same," said he.

"Good. Then would one being big want to be big, or being strong want to be strong?"

"Impossible, according to what we have agreed."

"For I suppose he would not be lacking in whichever of these he is?"

"True."

"For if being strong he wanted to be strong," said Socrates, "and being swift he wanted to be swift, and being healthy he wanted to be healthy—you might go on forever like this, and you might think that those who were so-and-so and had such-

[1] Agathon had just said it was beauty.

and-such did also desire what they had; but to avoid our being deceived I say this—if you understand me, Agathon, it is obvious that these *must* have at this present time all they have, whether they wish to or not—and can anyone desire that? And when one says, 'I am healthy and want to be healthy,' 'I am rich and want to be rich,' 'I desire what I have,' we should answer, 'You, my good man, being possessed of riches and health and strength, wish to go on being possessed of them in the future, since at present you have them whether you want it or not; and when you say, "I desire what I have," consider—you mean only that you want to have in the future what you have now.' Wouldn't he agree?"

Agathon said yes.

Then Socrates went on, "Therefore this love for these blessings to be preserved for him into the future and to be always present for him—this is really loving that which is not yet available for him or possessed by him?"

"Certainly," he said.

"Then he, and every other who desires, desires what is not in his possession and not there, what he has not, and what he is not himself and what he lacks? Those are the sorts of things of which there is desire and love?"

"Certainly," he said.

"Come now," said Socrates, "let us run over again what has been agreed. Love is, first of all, of something; next, of those things which one lacks?"

"Yes," he said.

"This being granted, then, remember what things you said in your speech were the objects of Love. I will remind you, if you wish. I think you said something like this; the gods arranged their business through love of beautiful things, for there could not be a love for ugly things. Didn't you say something like that?"

"Yes, I did," said Agathon.

"And quite reasonably too, my friend," said Socrates; "and if this is so, would not Love be love of beauty, not of ugliness?"

He agreed.

"Well now, it has been agreed that he loves what he lacks and has not?"

"Yes," he said.

"Then Love lacks and has not beauty."

"That must be," said he.

"Very well: do you say that what lacks beauty and in no wise has beauty is beautiful?"

"Certainly not."

"Then if that is so, do you still agree that Love is beautiful?"

Agathon answered, "I fear, Socrates, I knew nothing of what I said!"

"Oh no," said he, "it was a fine speech, Agathon! But one little thing more: don't you think good things are also beautiful?"

"I do."

"Then if Love lacks beautiful things, and good things are beautiful, he should lack the good things too."

"Socrates," he said, "I really could not contradict you; let it be as you say."

"Contradict the truth, you should say, beloved Agathon," he replied; "you can't do that, but to contradict Socrates is easy enough.

"And now you shall have peace from me; but there is a speech about Love which I heard once from Diotima of Mantineia,[1] who was wise in this matter and in many others; by making the Athenians perform sacrifices before the plague she even managed to put off the disease for ten years. And she it was who taught me about love affairs. This speech, then, which she made I will try to narrate to you now, beginning with what is agreed between me and Agathon; I will tell it by myself, as well as I can. You will see that I must describe first, as you did, Agathon, who Love is and what like, and then his works. I think it easiest to do it as the lady did in examining me. I said to her very much what Agathon just now did to me, that Love was a great god, and was a love of beautiful things; and she convinced me by saying the same as I did to Agathon, that he is neither beautiful, according to my argument, nor good. Then I said, 'What do you mean, Diotima? Is Love then ugly and bad?' And she said, 'Hush, for shame! Do you think that what is not beautiful must necessarily be ugly?' 'Yes, I do.' 'And what is not wise, ignorant? Do you not perceive that there is something between wisdom and ignorance?' 'What is that?' 'To have right opinion without being able to give a reason,' she said, 'is neither to understand (for how could an unreasoned thing be understanding?) nor is it ignorance (for how can ignorance hit the truth?). Right opinion is no doubt something between knowledge and ignorance.' 'Quite true,' I said. 'Then do not try to compel what is not beautiful to be ugly, or what is not good to be bad. So also with Love. He is not good and not beautiful, as you admit yourself, but do not imagine for that reason any the more that he must be ugly and bad, but something between these two,' said she. 'Well, anyway,' I said,

[1] A well-known Greek city in the Peloponnesus. The names perhaps suggest "the prophetess Fearthelord of Prophetville."

'he is admitted by all to be a great god.' 'All who don't know,' she said, 'or all who know too?' 'All without exception.' At this she said, with a laugh, 'And how could he be admitted to be a great god, Socrates, by those who say he is not a god at all?' 'Who are these?' said I. 'You for one,' said she, 'and I for another.' And I asked, 'How can that be?' She said, 'Easily. Tell me, don't you say that all the gods are happy and beautiful? Or would you dare to say that any one of them is not happy and beautiful?' 'Indeed I would not,' said I. 'Then don't you call happy those possessed of good and beautiful things?' 'Certainly.' 'Yet you admitted that Love, because of a lack of good and beautiful things, actually desired those things which he lacked.' 'Yes, I admitted that.' 'Then how could he be a god who has no share in beautiful and good things?' 'He could not be a god, as it seems.' 'Don't you see then,' said she, 'that you yourself deny Love to be a god?'

" 'Then what could Love be?' I asked. 'A mortal?' 'Not at all.' 'What then?' I asked. 'Just as before, between mortal and immortal.' 'What is he then, Diotima?' 'A great spirit, Socrates; for all the spiritual is between divine and mortal.' 'What power has it?' said I. 'To interpret and to ferry across to the gods things given by men, and to men things from the gods, from men petitions and sacrifices, from the gods commands and requitals in return; and being in the middle it completes them and binds all together into a whole. Through this intermediary moves all the art of divination, and the art of priests, and all concerned with sacrifice and mysteries and incantations, and all sorcery and witchcraft. For God mingles not with man, but through this comes all the communion and conversation of gods with men and men with gods, both awake and asleep; and he who is expert in this is a spiritual man, but the expert in something other than this, such as common arts or crafts, is a vulgar man. These spirits are many and of all sorts and kinds, and one of them is Love.'

" 'Who was his father,' said I, 'and who was his mother?' She answered, 'That is rather a long story, but still I will tell you. When Aphrodite was born, the gods held a feast, among them Plenty,[1] the son of Neverataloss. When they had dined, Poverty came in begging, as might be expected with all that good cheer, and hung about the doors. Plenty then got drunk on the nectar—for there was no wine yet—and went into Zeus's park all heavy and fell asleep. So Poverty because of her penury made a plan to have a child from Plenty, and lay by his side and conceived Love. This is why Love has become

[1] So Spenser calls him in the "Hymn to Love"; Lamb has "Resource, the son of Cunning," in his translation in the Loeb Classical Library.

follower and servant of Aphrodite, having been begotten at her birthday party, and at the same time he is by nature a lover busy with beauty because Aphrodite is beautiful. Then since Love is the son of Plenty and Poverty he gets his fortunes from them. First, he is always poor; and far from being tender and beautiful, as most people think, he is hard and rough and unshod and homeless, lying always on the ground without bedding, sleeping by the doors and in the streets in the open air, having his mother's nature, always dwelling with want. But from his father again he has designs upon beautiful and good things, being brave and go-ahead and high-strung, a mighty hunter, always weaving devices, and a successful coveter of wisdom, a philosopher all his days, a great wizard and sorcerer and sophist. He was born neither mortal nor immortal; but on the same day, sometimes he is blooming and alive, when he has plenty, sometimes he is dying; then again he gets new life through his father's nature; but what he procures in plenty always trickles away, so that Love is not in want nor in wealth, and again he is between wisdom and ignorance. The truth is this: no god seeks after wisdom or desires to become wise—for wise he is already; nor does anyone else seek after wisdom, if he is wise already. And again, the ignorant do not seek after wisdom nor desire to become wise; for this is the worst of ignorance, that one who is neither beautiful and good[1] nor intelligent should think himself good enough, so he does not desire it, because he does not think he is lacking in what he does not think he needs.'

"'Then who are the philosophers, Diotima,' said I, 'if those who seek after wisdom are neither the wise nor the ignorant?' 'That's clear enough even to a child,' she answered; 'they are those between these two, as Love is. You see, wisdom is one of the most beautiful things, and Love is a love for the beautiful, so Love must necessarily be a philosopher, and, being a philosopher, he must be between wise and ignorant. His birth is the cause of this, for he comes of a wise and resourceful father, but of a mother resourceless and not wise. Well then, dear Socrates, this is the nature of the spirit; but it was no wonder you thought Love what you did think. You thought, if I may infer it from what you say, that Love was the beloved, not the lover. That was why, I think, Love seemed to you wholly beautiful; for the thing loved is in fact beautiful and dainty and perfect and blessed, but the loving thing has a different shape, such as I have described.'

"Then I said, 'Very well, madam, what you say is right; but

[1] The Greeks meant by this what we might call a cultured gentleman.

Love being such as you describe, of what use is he to mankind?' 'I will try to teach you that next, Socrates,' she said. 'Love then is like that, and born like that, and he is love of beautiful things, as you said he is. But suppose someone should ask us: "Socrates and Diotima, what is meant by love of beautiful things?"—I will put it more clearly: "He that loves beautiful things loves what?"' Then I answered, 'To get them.' 'Still,' she said, 'that answer needs another question, like this: "What will he get who gets the beautiful things?"' I said I could not manage at all to answer that question offhand. 'Well,' said she, 'suppose one should change "beautiful" to "good" and ask that? See here, Socrates, I will say: "What does he love who loves good things?"' 'To get them,' said I. 'And what will he get who gets the good things?' 'That's easier,' said I; 'I can answer that he will be happy.' 'Then,' said she, 'by getting good things the happy are happy, and there is no need to ask further, why he who wishes to be happy does wish that, but the answer seems to be finished.' 'Quite true,' said I. 'But do you think this wish and this love is common to all mankind,' Diotima said, 'and do you think that all men always wish to have the good things, or what do you say?' 'That's it,' said I, 'it's common to all.' 'Why then, Socrates,' said she, 'do we not say that all men are lovers, if they do in fact all love the same things and always, instead of saying that some are lovers and some are not?' 'That surprises me too,' I said. 'Don't let it surprise you,' she said. 'For we have taken one kind of love, and given it the name of the whole, love; and there are other cases in which we misapply other names.' 'For example?' said I. 'Here is one,' she said. 'You know that poetry is many kinds of making;[1] for when anything passes from not-being to being, the cause is always making, or poetry, so that in all the arts the process is making, and all the craftsmen in these are makers, or poets.' 'Quite true,' I said. 'But yet,' said she, 'they are not all called poets; they have other names, and one bit of this making has been taken, that concerning music and verse, and this is called by the name of the whole. For this only is called poetry, and those who have this bit of making are called poets.' 'That is true,' I said. 'So with love, then; in its general sense it is all the desire for good things and for happiness—Love most mighty and all-ensnaring; but those who turn to him by any other road, whether by way of moneymaking, or of a taste for sports or philosophy, are not said to be in love and are not called lovers, but only those who go after one kind and are earnest about that have the name of the whole, love, and are said to love and to be lovers.' 'I think you are right there,'

[1] See p. 92, n. 4.

said I. 'And there is a story,' said she, 'that people in love are those who are seeking for their other half,[1] but my story tells that love is not for a half, nor indeed the whole, unless that happens to be something good, my friend; since men are willing to cut off their own hands and feet, if their own seem to them to be nasty. For really, I think, no one is pleased with his own thing, except one who calls the good thing his own and his property, and the bad thing another's; since there is nothing else men love but the good. Don't you think so?' 'Yes,' I said. 'Then,' said she, 'we may say simply that men love the good?' 'Yes,' I said. 'Shall we add,' she asked, 'that they love to have the good?' 'Yes, add that,' I said. 'Not only to have it, but always to have it?' 'Add that too.' 'Then to sum up,' she said, 'it is the love of having the good for oneself always.' 'Most true, indeed,' I said.

"She went on, 'Now if love is the love of having this always, what is the way men pursue it, and in what actions would their intense earnestness be expressed so as to be called love? What is this process? Can you tell me?' 'No,' said I, 'or else, Diotima, why should I, in admiration of your wisdom, have come to you as your pupil to find out these very matters?' 'Well then, I will tell you,' she said. 'It is a breeding in the beautiful, both of body and soul.' 'It needs divination,' I said, 'to tell what on earth you mean, and I don't understand.' 'Well,' she said, 'I will tell you clearer. All men are pregnant, Socrates, both in body and in soul; and when they are of the right age, our nature desires to beget. But it cannot beget in an ugly thing, only in a beautiful thing. And this business is divine, and this is something immortal in a mortal creature, breeding and birth. These cannot be in what is discordant. But the ugly is discordant with everything divine, and the beautiful is concordant. Beauty therefore is Portioner and Lady of Labour at birth. Therefore when the pregnant comes near to a beautiful thing it becomes gracious, and being delighted it is poured out and begets and procreates; when it comes near to an ugly thing, it becomes gloomy and grieved and rolls itself up and is repelled and shrinks back and does not procreate, but holds back the conception and is in a bad way. Hence in the pregnant thing swelling full already, there is great agitation about the beautiful thing because he that has it gains relief from great agony. Finally, Socrates, love is not for the beautiful, as you think.' 'Why not?' 'It is for begetting and birth in the beautiful.' 'Oh, indeed?' said I. 'Yes indeed,' said she. 'Then why for begetting?' 'Because begetting is, for the mortal, something everlasting and immortal. But one must desire immortality along with the

[1] See Aristophanes' story, p. 87.

good, according to what has been agreed, if love is love of having the good for oneself always. It is necessary then from this argument that love is for immortality also.'

"All this she taught me at different times whenever she came to speak about love affairs; and once she asked, 'What do you think, Socrates, to be the cause of this love and desire? You perceive that all animals get into a dreadful state when they desire to procreate, indeed birds and beasts alike; all are sick and in a condition of love, about mating first, and then how to find food for their young, and they are ready to fight hard for them, the weakest against the strongest, and to die for them, and to suffer the agonies of starvation themselves in order to feed them, ready to do anything. One might perhaps think that man,' she said, 'would do all this from reasoning; but what about beasts? What is the cause of their enamoured state? Can you tell me?' And I said again that I did not know; and she said, 'Then how do you ever expect to become expert in love affairs, if you do not understand that?' 'Why, Diotima, this is just why I have come to you, as I said; I knew I needed a teacher. Pray tell me the cause of this, and all the other love lore.'

"'Well then,' she said, 'if you believe love is by nature love of that which we often agreed on, don't be surprised. For on the same principle as before, here mortal nature seeks always as far as it can be to be immortal; and this is the only way it can, by birth, because it leaves something young in place of the old. Consider that for a while each single living creature is said to live and to be the same; for example, a man is said to be the same from boyhood to old age; he has, however, by no means the same things in himself, yet he is called the same: he continually becomes new, though he loses parts of himself, hair and flesh and bones and blood and all the body. Indeed, not only body, even in soul, manners, opinions, desires, pleasures, pains, fears, none of these remains the same, but some perish and others are born. And far stranger still, this happens to knowledge too; not only do some kinds of knowledge perish in us, not only are other kinds born, and not even in our knowledge are we ever the same, but the same happens even in each single kind of knowledge. For what is called study and practice means that knowledge is passing out; forgetting is knowledge leaving us, and study puts in new knowledge instead of that which is passing away, and preserves our knowledge so that it seems to be the same. In this way all the mortal is preserved, not by being wholly the same always, like the divine, but because what grows old and goes leaves behind something new like its past self. By this device, Socrates,' said she, 'mortality partakes of immortality, both in body and in all other respects; but it cannot otherwise. Then do not be surprised that everything naturally honours its own offspring; immortality is what all this earnestness and love pursues.'

"I heard this with admiration; and I said, 'Really, Diotima most wise! Is that really and truly so?' She answered as the complete Sophists do,[1] and said, 'You may be sure of that, Socrates. Just think, if you please, of men's ambition. You would be surprised at its unreasonableness if you didn't bear in mind what I have told you; observe what a terrible state they are in with love of becoming renowned, "and to lay up their fame for evermore"[2] and for this how ready they are to run all risks even more than for their children, and to spend money and endure hardship to any extent, and to die for it. Do you think Alcestis would have died for Admetos, or Achilles would have died over Patroclos, or your Codros[3] would have died for the royalty of his sons, if they had not thought that "immortal memory of Virtue" would be theirs, which we still keep! Far from it,' she said; 'for eternal virtue and glorious fame like that all men do everything, I think, and the better they are, the more they do so; for the immortal is what they love. So those who are pregnant in body,' she said, 'turn rather to women and are enamoured in this way, and thus, by begetting children, secure for themselves, so they think, immortality and memory and happiness, "Providing all things for the time to come;"[4] but those who are pregnant in soul—for there are some,' she said, 'who conceive in soul still more than in body, what is proper for the soul to conceive and bear; and what is proper? wisdom and virtue in general—to this class belong all creative poets, and those artists and craftsmen who are said to be inventive. But much the greatest wisdom,' she said, 'and the most beautiful, is that which is concerned with the ordering of cities and homes, which we call temperance and justice. So again a man with divinity in him, whose soul from his youth is pregnant with these things, desires when he grows up to beget and procreate; and thereupon, I think, he seeks and goes about to find the beautiful thing in which he can beget; for in the ugly he never will. Being pregnant, then, he welcomes bodies which are beautiful rather than ugly, and if he finds a soul beautiful and generous and well-bred, he gladly welcomes the two body and soul together, and for a human being like that he has plenty of talks about virtue, and

[1] That is, she made a speech rather than answered questions.
[2] A line of poetry.
[3] A legendary King of Athens, who gave his life for this in the Dorian invasion.
[4] A line of poetry.

what the good man ought to be and to practise, and he tries to educate him. For by attaching himself to a person of beauty, I think, and keeping company with him, he begets and procreates what he has long been pregnant with; present and absent he remembers him, and with him fosters what is begotten, so that as a result these people maintain a much closer communion together and a firmer friendship than parents of children, because they have shared between them children more beautiful and more immortal. And everyone would be content to have such children born to him rather than human children; he would look to Homer and Hesiod and the other good poets, and wish to rival them, who leave such offspring behind them, which give their parents the same immortal fame and memory as they have themselves; or if you like,' she said, 'think what children Lycurgos[1] left in Lacedaimon, the saviours of Lacedaimon and, one may say, of all Hellas. Honour came to Solon also, in your country, by the begetting of his laws; and to many others in many countries and times, both Hellenes and barbarians, who performed many beautiful works and begat all kinds of virtue; in their names many sanctuaries have been made because they had such children, but never a one has been so honoured because of human children.

" 'These are some of the mysteries of Love, Socrates, in which perhaps even you may become an initiate; but as for the higher revelations, which initiation leads to if one approaches in the right way, I do not know if you could ever become an adept. At least I will instruct you,' she said, 'and no pains will be lacking; you try to follow if you can. It is necessary,' she said, 'that one who approaches in the right way should begin this business young, and approach beautiful bodies. First, if his leader leads aright, he should love one body and there beget beautiful speech; then he should take notice that the beauty in one body is akin to the beauty in another body, and if we must pursue beauty in essence, it is great folly not to believe that the beauty in all such bodies is one and the same. When he has learnt this, he must become the lover of all beautiful bodies, and relax the intense passion for one, thinking lightly of it and believing it to be a small thing. Next he must believe beauty in souls to be more precious than beauty in the body; so that if anyone is decent in soul, even if it has little bloom, it should be enough for him to love and care for, and to beget and seek such talks as will make young people better; that he may moreover be compelled to

[1] The Spartan lawgiver.

contemplate the beauty in our pursuits and customs, and to see that all beauty is of one and the same kin, and that so he may believe that bodily beauty is a small thing. Next, he must be led from practice to knowledge, that he may see again the beauty in different kinds of knowledge, and, directing his gaze from now on towards beauty as a whole, he may no longer dwell upon one, like a servant, content with the beauty of one boy or one human being or one pursuit, and so be slavish and petty; but he should turn to the great ocean of beauty, and in contemplation of it give birth to many beautiful and magnificent speeches and thoughts in the abundance of philosophy, until being strengthened and grown therein he may catch sight of some one knowledge, the one science of this beauty now to be described. Try to attend,' she said, 'as carefully as you can.

" 'Whoever shall be guided so far towards the mysteries of love, by contemplating beautiful things rightly in due order, is approaching the last grade. Suddenly he will behold a beauty marvellous in its nature, that very Beauty, Socrates, for the sake of which all the earlier hardships had been borne: in the first place, everlasting, and never being born nor perishing, neither increasing nor diminishing; secondly, not beautiful here and ugly there, not beautiful now and ugly then, not beautiful in one direction and ugly in another direction, not beautiful in one place and ugly in another place. Again, this beauty will not show itself to him like a face or hands or any bodily thing at all, nor as a discourse or a science, nor indeed as residing in anything, as in a living creature or in earth or heaven or anything else, but being by itself with itself always in simplicity; while all the beautiful things elsewhere partake of this beauty in such manner, that when *they* are born and perish *it* becomes neither less nor more and nothing at all happens to it; so that when anyone by right boy-loving goes up from these beautiful things to that beauty, and begins to catch sight of it, he would almost touch the perfect secret. For let me tell you, the right way to approach the things of love, or to be led there by another, is this: beginning from these beautiful things, to mount for that beauty's sake ever upwards, as by a flight of steps, from one to two, and from two to all beautiful bodies, and from beautiful bodies to beautiful pursuits and practices, and from practices to beautiful learnings, so that from learnings he may come at last to that perfect learning which is the learning solely of that beauty itself, and may know at last that which is the perfection of beauty. There in life and there alone, my dear Socrates,' said the inspired woman,[1] 'is life worth living for man, while he contemplates Beauty itself. If ever you see this, it will seem to you to be far above gold and raiment and beautiful boys and men, whose beauty you are now entranced to see and you and many others are ready, so long as they see their darlings and remain ever with them, if it could be possible, not to eat nor drink but only to gaze at them and to be with them. What indeed,' she said, 'should we think, if it were given to one of us to see beauty undefiled, pure, unmixed, not adulterated with human flesh and colours and much other mortal rubbish, and if he could behold beauty in perfect simplicity? Do you think it a mean life for a man,' she said, 'to be looking thither and contemplating that and abiding with it? Do you not reflect,' said she, 'that there only it will be possible for him, when he sees the beautiful with the mind, which alone can see it, to give birth not to likenesses of virtue, since he touches no likeness, but to realities, since he touches reality; and when he has given birth to real virtue and brought it up, will it not be granted him to be the friend of God, and immortal if any man ever is?'

"This then, Phaidros and gentlemen, is what Diotima said, and I am quite convinced, and, being convinced, I try to persuade other people also to believe that to attain this possession one could not easily find a better helper for human nature than Love. And so I say that every man ought to honour Love, and I honour love matters myself, and I practise them particularly and encourage others; and now and always I sing the praises of Love's power and courage, as much as I am able. Then let this be my speech of eulogy to Love, if you please, Phaidros, or call it anything else you like."

When Socrates had done speaking, there was applause from the rest, and Aristophanes started to say something about Socrates' allusion to his own speech, when suddenly there came a knocking on the courtyard door and a great din as of some party of revellers, and they heard a girl-piper's notes. Then Agathon said to the staff, "Boys, go and see about that. If it is one of our friends, ask him in; if not, say we are not drinking now, we are just going to bed." In a few minutes they heard the voice of Alcibiades in the yard, very drunk and shouting loud, asking where Agathon was, and take him to Agathon. So he was brought in to them by the piping-girl, who with some others of his company supported him; he came

[1] The Greek word is Μαντινική —see p. 97, n.

to a stand at the door crowned with a thick wreath of ivy and violets and wearing a great lot of ribands on his head, and said, "Good evening, you fellows, will you have a very drunken man to drink with you, or shall we only put a garland on Agathon, which we came for, and then go? For I tell you this," he said, "I could not get at him yesterday, but here I come with the ribands on my head, that I may take them off my head and just twine them about the head of the cleverest and most beautiful of men, if I may say so. Will you laugh at me because I'm drunk? I tell you, even if you laugh, that this is true and I know it. Look here, tell me straight, do I come in on those terms or not? Will you drink with me or not?"

Then they all cheered and told him to come in and take his place, and Agathon gave him a formal invitation. So he came in leaning on those people, pulling off the ribands at the same time to put them on Agathon, and as he held them in front of his eyes, he did not see Socrates, but sat down beside Agathon, between Socrates and him, for Socrates made room for him. He sat down and embraced Agathon and crowned him. Then Agathon said, "Take off Alcibiades' shoes, you boys, and let him make a third on our couch."

"All right," said Alcibiades, "but who is fellow-drinker number three here?" At the same time he turned round and saw Socrates; when he saw him, he jumped up and cried, "What the deuce is this? Socrates here? You lay there again in wait for me, as you are always turning up all of a sudden where I never thought to see you! And now what have you come for? And again, why did you lie there, not by Aristophanes or some other funny man or would-be funny man, but you managed to get beside the handsomest of the company!"

Then Socrates said, "Agathon, won't you defend me? I find that this person's love has become quite a serious thing. From the time when I fell in love with him, I am no longer allowed to look at or talk with a handsome person, not even one, or this jealous and envious creature treats me outrageously, and abuses me, and hardly keeps his hands off me. Then don't let him try it on now, but do reconcile us, or if he uses force, defend me, for I'm fairly terrified at his madness and passion."

"No," said Alcibiades, "there's no reconciliation between you and me! My word, I'll punish you for this by and by; but now, Agathon," he said, "give me some of the ribands, and let me wreath this fellow's wonderful head—there!—so he can't quarrel with me and say I wreathed you and didn't wreath the man who beats all the world at talking, not only the other day like you, but always!" While he spoke he took some of the ribands and wreathed Socrates, and then reclined himself.

When he was settled, he said, "I say, men, I think you are sober. That won't do, you must drink! We agreed on that. Then I choose as prince of the pots, to see that you drink enough, myself. Let 'em bring it in, Agathon, the biggest goblet you have! No, better than that! You, boy there; bring that cooler," said he, for he saw it would hold more than half a gallon; first he filled that and drank it off himself, then told the boy to fill for Socrates, saying, "For Socrates, men, my trick is nothing; he drinks as much as anyone tells him, and never gets drunk one bit the more."

So the boy filled for Socrates, and he drank; then Eryximachos said, "Well, Alcibiades, what do we do? Are we just to say nothing over the cup, and to sing nothing, but only to drink like thirsty men?"

Alcibiades answered, "Good evening to you, Eryximachos, best son of a best father you, and he was very sober too!"[1]

"Same to you," said Eryximachos, "but what are we to do?"

"Whatever you say," he replied, "for we have to obey you. 'One medicine man is worth a host of laymen.'[2] Command what you will."

"Then listen," said Eryximachos. "Before you came in, we decided that each one in turn from left to right[3] should recite the most excellent speech he could as a eulogy in honour of Love. All the rest of us, then, have made their speeches; but since you have made none, and since you have drunk your bumper, you are the proper one to speak; and when you have spoken, lay your commands on Socrates, what you like, and let him do the same with the next man to the right[4] and so with the rest."

"Good," said Alcibiades, "but look here, Eryximachos, I don't think it's fair to tell a drunken man to risk a speech before sober men! And at the same time, bless you my dear! do you really believe anything of what Socrates has just said? Don't you know that the truth is exactly the opposite of what he stated? For if *I* praise anybody in his presence, god or man other than himself, this man will not keep his two hands off *me*."

[1] Alcibiades' Greek becomes poetic!
[2] *Iliad* xi. 514.
[3] and [4] From the left of the company clockwise, round to the right; see diagram, p. 73.

SYMPOSIUM (213E–215D)

"Won't you shut up?" said Socrates.

"On my honour, you need not make any objection," said Alcibiades. "I would not praise a single other person in your presence!"

"Very well, do this if you like," said Eryximachos; "praise Socrates."

"What's that?" said Alcibiades. "Must I, Eryximachos? Am I to have at the man and punish him before your faces?"

"Hullo," said Socrates, "what's your notion? To praise me and raise a laugh, or what will you do?"

"I'll tell the truth! Will you let me?"

"Oh yes, let you tell the truth, I even command you to do that."

"Then I'll do it at once!" said Alcibiades. "Look here, this is what I want you to do. If I say anything that is not true, stop me in the middle, and say that I am lying; for I won't tell any lies if I can help it. But if I speak higgledy-piggledy trying to remember, don't be surprised, for it is not easy to set out all your absurdities nicely in order, for one in my state.

"I am to speak in praise of Socrates, gentlemen, and I will just try to do it by means of similes.[1] Oh yes, he will think perhaps it is only for a bit of fun, but my simile will be for truth, not for fun. I say then, that he is exactly like a Silenos, the little figures which you see sitting in the statuaries' shops; as the craftsmen make them, they hold Panspipes or pipes, and they can be opened down the middle and folded back, and then they show inside them images of the gods. And I say further, he is like Marsyas[2] the Satyr. Well anyway, Socrates, your face is like them, I don't suppose you will deny that yourself! In everything else, too, you are like them, listen what comes next. You are a bully! Aren't you? If you don't admit that I will find witnesses. Well, aren't you a piper? Yes, a more wonderful performer than that Marsyas! For he used to bewitch men through instruments by the power of his mouth, and so also now does anyone who pipes his tunes; for those Olympos[3] piped, I say were from Marsyas who taught him; then it is his tunes, whether a good artist plays them or a common piping-girl, which alone enravish us and make plain those who feel the need of the gods and their mysteries, because the tunes are divine. The only difference between you is, that *you* do the very same without instruments by bare words! We, at least, when we hear someone else making other

[1] A favourite game in society. Socrates obviously plays up, and makes signs or grimaces as Alcibiades goes on, and the other turns to him and to the company in turn.
[2] In Greek mythology a celebrated player on the pipe. See also *Republic*, p. 198.
[3] A Phrygian musician.

speeches, even quite a good orator, nobody cares a jot, I might say; but when one hears you, or your words recited by another, even a very poor speaker, let a woman hear, or a man hear, or a boy hear, we are overwhelmed and enravished. I, indeed, my friends, if you would not have thought me completely drunk, would have taken a solemn oath before you, and described to you how this man's words have made me feel and still make me feel now. When I hear them my heart goes leaping worse than frantic revellers', and tears run from my eyes at the words of this man, and I see crowds of others in the same state. When I heard Pericles, and other good orators, I thought them fine speakers, but I felt nothing like that, and no confusion in my soul or regret for my slavish condition; but this Marsyas here has brought me very often into such a condition that I thought the life I lead was not worth living. And that, Socrates, you will not say is untrue! And even now at this moment, I know in my conscience that if I would open my ears I could never hold out, but I should be in the same state. For he compels me to admit that I am very remiss, in going on neglecting my own self but attending to Athenian public business. So I force myself, and stop my ears, and off I go running as from the Sirens, or else I should sit down on the spot beside him till I become an old man. I feel towards this one man something which no one would ever think could be in me—to be ashamed before anybody; but I *am* ashamed before him and before no one else. For I know in my conscience that I cannot contradict him and say it is not my duty to do what he tells me, yet when I leave him, public applause is too much for me. So I show my heels and run from him, and, whenever I see him, I am ashamed of what I confessed to him. Often enough I should be glad to see him no longer among mankind; but if that should happen, I am sure I should be sorrier still, so I don't know what to do with the fellow.

"The pipings of this satyr have put many others into the same state as me; but let me tell you something else to show how like he is to my simile, and how wonderful his power is. I assure you that not one of you knows this man; but I will show you, since I have begun. You see, of course, that Socrates has a loving eye for beauty, he's always interested in such people and quite smitten with them, and again he is ignorant of everything and knows nothing; that is his pose. Isn't that Silenosity? Very much so! He wraps that round him like a cloak, like the outside of the carved Silenos figure; but inside, when he is opened—what do you think he is full of, gentlemen pot-fellows? Temperance! Let me say that he cares not a straw if one is a beauty, he despises that as no one would ever believe; and the same if one is rich, or has one of those mob distinctions which people think so grand. He thinks all those possessions are worthless and we are nothing, yes, I tell you! Pretending ignorance and making fun of his fellows all his life—that's how he goes on. But when he's in earnest, and opened out—I don't know if anyone has seen the images inside; but I saw them once, and I thought them divine and golden and all-beautiful and wonderful, so that one must in short do whatever Socrates commands. I thought he was in earnest over my youthful bloom, I thought I had found a godsend and a wonderful piece of luck, in that by gratifying Socrates I had the chance to hear all he knew; I thought a lot of my blooming beauty, you know, an awful lot. With this notion—you see, before that, I never used to visit him alone without an attendant—but after that I sent my attendant away and always went in alone; for I must tell you all the truth; now Socrates, attend and refute me if I tell a lie. Well, I paid him visits, gentlemen, I alone and he alone, and I thought he would talk to me as a lover would talk to his darling in solitude, and I was happy. Nothing came of it, nothing, he just talked as usual, and when we had had a nice day together, he always went off. Next I challenged him to gymnastics with me, and I went through it hoping for something then; well, he exercised with me, and we wrestled together often, with nobody there. What's the good of talking? I got nothing by it. Since I was none the better for all that, I resolved to try stronger measures with the man, and not to give in after I had undertaken something, but to find out what was behind the business. So I invited him to dinner with me, exactly like a lover with designs on his beloved. For a long time he would not even consent to come, but at last I persuaded him. The first time he came he wanted to go after dinner. That time I was ashamed, and let him go; but I made my plot again, and after we had dined, I went on talking till late at night, and when he wanted to go, I forced him to stay by pretending it was late. So he rested on the couch next to mine, where he had dined, and no one else was sleeping in the room, only we two. So far I could tell my story to anyone; but what follows you would never have heard me tell, only first, wine is true, as they say —whether children are there or not[1]—secondly, to hide a superimperious deed of Socrates is unfair, I think, for one who has come to sing his praises. Moreover, I too have

[1] The proverb was: "Wine and children are true."

'felt the viper's bite,' as the saying goes. You know they say that one who felt it would not tell what it was like except to other people who had been bitten, since they alone would know it and would not be hard on him for what he allowed himself to do and say in his agony. Well, I have been bitten by a more painful viper, and in the most painful spot where one could be bitten—the heart, or soul, or whatever it should be called—stung and bitten by his discourses in philosophy, which hang on more cruelly than a viper when they seize on a soul young and not ungenerous, and make it do and say anything—and when I see men like Phaidros, Agathon, Eryximachos, Pausanias, Aristodemos, too, and Aristophanes— Socrates himself I need not mention—and how many more! For you have all shared in the philosopher's madness and passion! Then you shall all hear; for you will not be hard on what was done then and what is being said now; but you servants, and anyone else who is common and boorish, clap strong doors on your ears!

"Well then, gentlemen, when the lamp was out and the servants outside, I thought it necessary not to mince matters but to say freely what I felt; so I stirred him up, and said, 'Asleep, Socrates?' 'Not at all,' said he. 'Do you know what is in my mind?' 'What is it?' he asked. 'I think,' said I, 'that you are the only lover I have ever had worthy of me, and now you won't speak a word to me. I'll tell you how I feel: I consider it simply silly not to gratify you in this, and anything else you want of my property or from my friends. For myself, I think nothing more precious than to attain the height of excellence, and to help me in this there is no one more competent than you. Then I should be much more ashamed before the wise if I did not gratify such a man than I should be ashamed before the multitude of fools if I did.' He answered, playing the innocent as usual, quite like himself, 'My dearest Alcibiades, you are really and truly no bad hand at a bargain, if what you say is really true about me, and if there is in me some power which can make you better; you must see some inconceivable beauty in me immensely greater than your own loveliness. If then you spy it there, and if you are trying to do a deal and exchange beauty for beauty, you want to get very much the better of me, you want to get real beauties for sham, and indeed to exchange "golden for bronze."[1] Bless you, my dear, spy better, and you'll see I am nothing. The sight of the mind begins to see sharp when the sight of the eyes is losing its keenness, and you are far from

[1] An allusion to Homer, where Diomedes exchanges his bronze armour for Glaucos' golden; *Iliad* vi. 236.

that still.' I heard him, and said, 'That is what I have to tell you, and I have said exactly what I mean; consider yourself, then, what you believe best for you and me.' 'That's well said,' he answered, 'another time we will consider, and do whatever seems best for us both in this and other matters.'

"When I heard this and said this, and as it were shot my shafts, I thought he was wounded; so I got up, and without letting this man[1] say another word, I threw my own mantle over the man and crept in under this man's threadbare cloak —for it was winter—and threw my arms round this man, this really astonishing and wonderful man, and there I lay the whole night! You will not say that is a lie, either, Socrates! Though I had done all this, yet this man was so much above me and so despised me and laughed at my bloom, and insulted me in the point where I did think I was something, gentlemen of the jury—for jury you are, to give a verdict on the super-imperiosity of Socrates—that I swear by the gods, I swear by the goddesses, when I got up I had no more slept with Socrates than if I had been with a father or elder brother.

"How do you think I felt after that! I thought I had been disgraced, and yet I admired the way this man was made, and his temperance and courage; and I had met such a human being for wisdom and endurance as I never expected to find in the world, so that I could not bring myself to quarrel and lose his company, nor could I think of any way to attract him. For I knew quite well that to money he was much less vulnerable than Aias to steel, and in what I thought would alone win him, he had escaped me. So I was at a loss, and I walked about, a slave to the creature as no one ever was to anyone. Well, all this happened before our expedition went to Poteidaia;[2] we were both in it, and we were messmates there. And first of all, in bearing hardships he not only beat me but everyone else; when we were cut off somewhere, and had to go without food, as happens on campaign, the others were nothing for endurance. Yet when there was plenty of good cheer, he was the only one who could really enjoy it; particularly, although he did not care for drinking, when he was compelled to drink he beat them all, and what is most wonderful of all, no one in the world has ever seen Socrates drunk. That we shall be able to test presently, as I think. That was not all; in his endurance of the cold winter— the winters were dreadful there—he did wonders, and here is a specimen. Once there was a most dreadful frost, and no one would go out of doors, or if he did he put on an awful

[1] With each phrase he points at Socrates.
[2] 432 B.C., when Socrates was about thirty-seven and Alcibiades about nineteen.

lot of things, and swathed his legs, and wrapped up his feet in felt and sheepskin, but this man went out in that weather wearing only such a cloak as he used to wear before, and unshod he marched over the ice more easily than others did with boots on. The soldiers looked black at him thinking he despised them.

"So much for that;
But here's a doughty deed the strong man did,[1]

once on that expedition, and it is worth hearing. He got some notion into his head, and there he stood on one spot from dawn, thinking, and when it did not come out, he would not give in but still stood pondering. It was already midday, and people noticed it, and wondered, and said to one another that Socrates had been standing thinking about something ever since dawn. At last when evening came, some of the Ionians after dinner—it was summertime then—brought out their pallets and slept near in the cool, and watched him from time to time to see if he would stand all night. He did stand until it was dawn, and the sun rose; then he offered a prayer to the sun and walked away.

"Now with your leave we will take the battles; for it is fair to pay him his due. When there was that battle[2] after which the generals actually gave me the prize of valour, this man, when not a single other person came to my rescue, saved my life. I was wounded, but he would not leave me, and saved my weapons and me too. Then I begged the generals myself, Socrates, to give you the prize for valour, and here you will not find fault with me or say I am lying; but the fact is, when the generals looked at my rank and wanted to give me the prize, you were more eager than the generals that I should get it and not yourself. Again, gentlemen, it was worth while to see Socrates when the army was routed and retreating from Delion.[3] I happened to be there on horseback, and he on foot. This man and Laches were retreating together in the rout; I met them, and told them to cheer up, and said I would not desert them. There indeed I had an even better view of Socrates than at Poteidaia, for I had less to fear, being on horseback. First I saw how he kept his head much better than Laches; next I really thought, Aristophanes, to quote your words,[4] that he marched exactly as he does here, 'with swaggering gait and rolling eye,' quietly looking round at friends and enemies, and

[1] *Odyssey* iv. 242.
[2] During the activities at Poteidaia, 432-429 B.C.
[3] Delium, 424 B.C.
[4] Aristophanes, *Clouds*, 362.

making it quite clear to everyone even a long way off that if anyone laid a finger on this man, he would defend himself stoutly. And therefore he came off safe, both this man and his companion; for in war where men are like that, people usually don't touch them with a finger, but pursue those who are running headlong.

"One could quote many other things in praise of Socrates, wonderful things: of his other habits one might perhaps say much the same about another man, and yet it is his not being like any other man in the world, ancient or modern, that is worthy of all wonder. Men like Achilles might be found, one might take, for example, Brasidas and others; and again men like Pericles[1], such as Nestor and Antenor, and there are more besides; and so we might go on with our comparisons. But as for this man, so odd, both the man and his talk, none could ever be found to come near him, neither modern nor ancient, unless he is to be compared to no man at all, but to the Silenoses and satyrs to which I have compared him—him and his talk.

"For indeed there is something which I left out when I began, that even his talk is very like the opening Silenoses. When you agree to listen to the talk of Socrates, it might seem at first to be nothing but absurdity; such words and phrases are wrapped outside it, like the hide of a boisterous satyr. Pack-asses and smiths and shoemakers and tanners are what he talks about, and he seems to be always saying the same things in the same words, so that any ignorant and foolish man would laugh at them. But when they are opened out, and you get inside them, you will find his words first full of sense, as no others are; next, most divine and containing the finest images of virtue, and reaching farthest, in fact reaching to everything which it profits a man to study who is to become noble and good.

"This, gentlemen, is my laudation of Socrates; and I have mixed in as well some blame, by telling you of the way he insulted me. I am not the only one he has treated so; he has done the same to Charmides, Glaucon's son, and Euthydemos, Diocles' son, and very many others, whom he has tricked as a lover and made them treat him as beloved instead. That is a warning to you, Agathon, not to be deceived by this man; try to learn from our experience, and take care not to be the fool in the proverb, who could only learn by his own."[2]

When Alcibiades had ended his speech, there was much

[1] Pericles was the great leader of the Athenians from 460 to 429 B.C.; Brasidas was a fine Spartan officer who served his city well against the Athenians from 431 to 422 B.C.
[2] *Iliad* xvii. 33.

laughter at his frankness, because he seemed to be still in love with Socrates. But Socrates said, "You're sober, I think, Alcibiades, or you would never have wrapped all that smart mantle round you in trying to hide why you have said all this, and put your point in a postscript at the end; for your real aim in all you said was to make me and Agathon quarrel: you think I ought to be your lover and love no one else, and Agathon should be your beloved and loved by no one else. But I see through you; your satyric and silenic drama has been shown up. Now, my dearest Agathon, don't let him gain anything by it; only take care that no one shall make you and me quarrel."

Then Agathon said, "Upon my word, Socrates, that's the truth, I am sure. I notice how he reclined between me and you in order to keep us apart. Then he shall gain nothing by it, and I will come past you and recline there."

"Yes do," said Socrates, "recline here below me."

"Oh Zeus!" cried Alcibiades, "how the creature treats me! He thinks he must have the best of me everywhere! Well, if nothing else, you plague, let Agathon recline between us."

"Impossible!" said Socrates. "For you have sung my praises, and it is my duty to praise the next man to the right.[1] Then if Agathon reclines below you—I don't suppose he is going to praise me again, before I have praised him as I should? Then let him alone, you rascal, and don't grudge my praise to the lad; for I want very much to sing his glory."

"Hooray, hooray!" cried Agathon, "I can't stay here, Alcibiades. I must and will change my place, and then Socrates will praise me!"

"Here we are again," said Alcibiades, "the usual thing; where Socrates is, there is no one else can get a share of the beauties! And now how easily he has invented a plausible reason why this one should be beside him!"

Then Agathon got up to go and lie down beside Socrates, but suddenly a great crowd of revellers came to the doors; seeing them open as someone was going out, they marched straight in and found places among the diners, and the whole place was in an uproar. No order was kept any longer and they were forced to drink a great deal of wine. Eryximachos and Phaidros and some others went out and departed (so Aristodemos told me), and he fell asleep himself, and slept soundly for a long time, as the nights were long then, and he woke up towards day when the cocks were already crowing. When he awoke he saw the others were either asleep or had gone, but Agathon and Aristophanes and Socrates were the

[1] I.e., the next man beyond or "below" Socrates; see diagram, p. 73.

only ones still awake, and they were drinking out of a large bowl from left to right. Socrates was arguing with them; Aristodemos told me he could not remember much of what was said, for he was not listening from the beginning and he was rather drowsy, but he told me the upshot of it was that Socrates was compelling them to admit that the same man ought to understand how to compose both comedy and tragedy, and that he who has skill as a tragic poet has skill for a comic poet. While they were being forced to this, and not following very well, they began to nod, and first Aristophanes fell asleep, and while day was dawning, Agathon too. Socrates made them comfortable, then got up and went away, and Aristodemos himself followed as usual. Socrates went to the Lyceum and had a wash, and spent the day as he generally did, and after spending the day so, in the evening went home to bed.

THE REPUBLIC

ocrates, Glaucon, Polemarchos, Thrasymachos,

Adeimantos, Cephalos

Summary

Book I. Polemarchos invites Socrates and Glaucon to visit his father Cephalos' house. Various other friends are there as well. Cephalos talks about old age: eventually the conversation turns to the subject of justice. How do you define justice? asks Socrates. Polemarchos puts forward Simonides' definition—to render what is due—but this on examination proves unsatisfactory. Here Thrasymachos breaks in, maintaining that the whole conversation so far has consisted of nothing but pious platitudes. Justice, he says, is whatever suits the strongest best. Might is right. A ruler is always just. Socrates suggests that even a ruler sometimes makes a mistake, and orders his subjects to do something which is really not to his advantage at all. Is he just when he does this? Thrasymachos answers that in so far as he is mistaken he is not a true ruler. Socrates then argues that a doctor is primarily concerned to heal the sick, and only incidentally to make money: similarly, medicine seeks not its own advantage but the advantage of the human body. By analogy a ruler seeks the advantage of his subjects, not of himself.

Thrasymachos then rushes off on a new tack. Injustice, he says, is virtuous, and justice is vicious. Justice is everywhere at the mercy of injustice, which is reviled not because men fear to do it but because they fear to suffer it. Socrates sets out to disprove this view, and establishes that justice is apparently wise and virtuous, and at the same time more profitable than injustice. But, he says, he is still without a definition of justice.

Book II. Glaucon and Adeimantos then develop further objections to Socrates' conclusions. Is justice, says Glaucon, any more than society's refuge from the consequences of the doctrine that true success depends on being as unjust as possible? Has it really a value for its own sake? Whereupon his brother Adeimantos adds that everybody is in fact as unjust as he can be without being found out; is there any value in justice itself, he asks, as distinct from a reputation for justice?

At this stage Socrates suggests that the nature of justice is more easily to be discovered in the macrocosm, the state, than in the microcosm, the individual. This is agreed and the discussion shifts to the origins and composition of a city-state. People associate for mutual support, because different men have different abilities. Society flourishes because it is efficient: it enables each person to devote himself to the task he is best fitted for, and saves him from dispersing his energies in other tasks he is not fitted for at all, and which he will therefore perform indifferently.

Socrates then describes the various classes of persons in a city, ending with the highest class, the rulers or guardians, who require the highest qualities. They must be both courageous and philosophical, both brave and wise. How are these qualities to be developed?

This leads to the subject of education, which, Socrates says, seems to consist of gymnastic for the body and music (in the broad sense of the arts) for the soul. He takes literature, a part of music, first of all, because education begins, he says, in the nursery, with fables and fairy stories. These must be very carefully censored to ensure a suitable moral tone; and in particular the gods must always appear in a virtuous light. God must be portrayed as the author of good only, not of evil, and as incapable of falsehood.

Book III. Literature, Socrates continues, must deal only with suitable subjects, and only in a suitable manner. He prescribes in some detail as to both subject and form: in effect, the poet may tell only plain stories of virtuous people. The same considerations apply to music, as we mean the word: none but the Dorian and Phrygian, the manly and sober modes, are to be allowed, and those rhythms expressive of an orderly and brave life. The practice in the other arts is to be similarly regulated; and in the result a noble art, purified of unwholesomeness and extravagance, will develop in the young the characteristics of nobility. By learning to appreciate the good and the beautiful in art, they will learn to love them in life.

In gymnastic, as in music, a wholesome simplicity is prescribed. There will be in the city little disease and few lawsuits. But care must be taken to hold the balance between music and gymnastic: excess in the former leads to effeminacy, and excess in the latter to harshness. It is a mistake to suppose that music trains the soul while gymnastic trains the body: gymnastic is as much a part of the soul's education as music is, and the noblest natures, at once brave and wise, require a harmonious blend of the two.

From the noblest natures, Socrates goes on, the rulers of the city will be chosen—the best of the older men, selected for their devotion to the state by various tests and carefully groomed for office. They will be assisted by the lower class of guardians, the auxiliaries or soldiers. Their rule over the city will be supported by the mystical sanction of the myth of the three metals, gold, silver and iron. And they will not live the life of princes, but the simple life of soldiers, free from the distractions of wealth and luxury.

Book IV. Adeimantos remarks that the arrangements for the guardians do not sound very inviting. Socrates replies that this is not the point, even if it is a true criticism, which he doubts; he is concerned not with the happiness of parts but with one harmonious whole, the happy city. The unity of this city, he says, depends mainly on three principles—equal shares for all, so that there are no rich and no poor; a physical limit of size; and the recognition of merit regardless of birth. These precepts are to be safeguarded by the educational system previously laid down, and all else will then follow—a perfectly arranged city which will endure as long as the purity of the system itself is maintained.

If this is the perfect city it must contain justice, and besides, wisdom, courage and temperance. Wisdom, says Socrates, is to be found in the thinking element, the guardians, and it is the knowledge in the light of which they lead the city. Courage or spirit, the quality of the soldiers, is the preserver of the constitution from the twin dangers of war and sedition. Temperance is common to all three classes, and is the harmonious and beneficial relationship between them. Now for justice—which is the virtue that enables all the others to flourish, and is none other than the old principle put forward in Book II, by which each class does the work for which it is fitted without presuming upon the preserves of the others.

So much for the city. Applying this argument to the individual, Socrates finds that the three classes in the state are reflected in three elements in the soul, the reasoning, the spirited, and the desiring, corresponding to the counsellors, the assistants or soldiers, and the producers. Justice is therefore the due arrangement of these three elements in their proper stations in the soul, namely that the reasoning part rules, with its auxiliary the spirited part, over the desiring part.

Socrates then begins to discuss the nature of injustice, and the five types of political structure. One type, the only good one, has been dealt with; the other four are all more or less bad.

Book V. Socrates is here interrupted by Polemarchos, who asks him to fill in the outline of the perfect city in more detail, before going on to the degenerate ones. This leads to a long digression, the main theme being picked up again at the start of Book VIII.

After a little preliminary skirmishing Socrates deals with the position of women in the perfect city. Woman, he says, is the weaker sex; but there are no occupations for which a woman is unfitted merely because she is a woman. He then describes a society in which all institutions and relationships are ruthlessly subordinated to the preservation of the unity of the state, and private life as well as private property are rejected. The city-state thus becomes the smallest as well as the largest—in fact the only—unit of social life. Socrates is just starting to investigate the nature of wars, and the difference between civil war and foreign war, when Glaucon asks the fundamental question whether the perfect city, desirable as it may be, can ever possibly be achieved in fact. No, replies Socrates, unless there comes about a union of wisdom and power in the person of the philosopher-king.

In the rest of Book V Socrates defines what he means by philosopher, a *lover of wisdom*. True knowledge is concerned not with the physical world of the senses but with the qualities, the realities, that are inherent in the everyday world—with Beauty, not with beautiful sounds and colours. The changing world of the senses is the object of opinion, but the unchanging world of realities is the object of true knowledge or wisdom, and it is this wisdom that true philosophers love.

Book VI. The guardians of the city, then, are to be true philosophers in this strict sense. Socrates is describing their other good qualities when Adeimantos objects that in fact philosophers have a very different reputation—of being knaves or fools or both. Socrates explains the reasons for this. A philosopher will never be a popular hero, because he has no time to waste on mere party politics, and it is success in this lower sphere alone which earns the plaudits of the crowd. But he admits that a large number of professed philosophers are rascals. Once corruption sets in, the very excellence of the philosophic qualities leads to great temptation and great evildoing. In an unsympathetic, if not actively hostile, world only a few remain faithful to the principles of true philosophy. These few must be helped and encouraged by means of the educational system already described; but philosophy is not a subject which can be acquired at school or in the teens, it is a lifelong study, and extra facilities must be provided accordingly. In sum, says Socrates, his proposals are desirable if they can be realised, and their realisation is difficult but not impossible.

Socrates then reverts to his definition of justice in Book IV. This, he says, was a superficial treatment of the subject. Now he speaks of the highest truth of all, which underlies justice and all the other virtues. This, the Idea of the Good, the guiding star of the soul, is the end of the philosopher's study. As the sun is to the world of sight, the Idea of the Good is to the world of mind. He goes on to the four divisions of the Divided Line, a refinement of the distinction between these two worlds, as already sketched in Book V. The physical world of the sun, the domain of opinion, contains in its lower class images, such as shadows and reflections, and in its higher class physical objects, such as animals and trees. The corresponding division in the world of mind, the domain of knowledge, is between, on the one hand, concepts of a mathematical type, which depend on given postulates, and, on the other hand, the eternal verities, the Ideas or Ideals, comprehended by dialectic in the light of the Idea of the Good. The four categories are the subjects of conjecture, belief, understanding, and the exercise of reason respectively, and partake in ascending order of clearness and truth.

Book VII. Socrates goes on to the story of the cave, which illustrates the escape of the philosopher from the fetters and darkness of the physical world of the senses to the freedom and dazzling radiance of the world of mind. But, he says, the philosopher must afterwards return to the cave to enlighten and set at liberty those still imprisoned there.

How is this escape made possible? By the study of a class of subjects which deal in abstractions: these are arithmetic, the study of numbers, and, of less importance, plane and solid geometry, astronomy so far as it concerns the principles of movement of solids, and harmonics, the study of sound. All these have a practical application, but their real value lies in their power to lead the soul out of the darkness of the changing world of the senses towards the light of the unchanging world of mind. Fortified by these exercises in abstract thought, the soul at last learns, through the study of dialectic, to comprehend the Idea of the Good.

In the last part of Book VII Socrates describes in more detail the practical application of his curriculum. After the standard education in music and gymnastic the selected student passes on to the abstract subjects and thence to dialectic, with frequent tests on the way. The few who reach the summit, at about the age of fifty—and Socrates reminds his hearers that they may be men or women—divide the rest of their lives between philosophy and the affairs of state.

Finally, Socrates repeats that his proposals will only be realised by a philosopher-king, an unlikely combination perhaps, but not an impossible one.

Book VIII. The perfect city and the kingly or aristocratic character having now been fully described, Socrates reverts to the point reached at the end of Book IV, and proceeds to deal with the four degenerate forms of constitution and the four corresponding types of individual.

The aristocratic constitution degenerates into the timocratic (or honour-loving) when the warrior class prevails over the wisdom-loving class, and imposes a militant policy dictated by ambition and the love of glory. Similarly, in the soul of the timocratic man the spirited part gains precedence over the reasoning part, and the result is a valiant but contentious and ambitious nature.

The timocratic constitution degenerates into oligarchy (the rule of the few) when honour-loving turns to money-grubbing. The city is divided into rich rulers and poor subjects. In the soul of the oligarchic man, pleasure-loving but ungenerous, the desiring part prevails over the reasoning and spirited parts.

The oligarchic constitution degenerates into democracy (the rule of the people) when the poor in the oligarchic state revolt. All are then set free to do as they wish—and, says Socrates in effect, to go to the devil in their own way. Where the oligarchic man, thrifty at heart, gave way only to the moneymaking (or *necessary*) desires, the democratic man, casting off even this restraint, gives free rein to the spendthrift (or *unnecessary*) desires, and liberty is thus complete.

The democratic constitution degenerates into tyranny when men tire at last of the lawlessness of a liberty which has become licence. They appoint a strong man to restore order; he raises a bodyguard or private army to suppress the irresponsible elements in society; and, unperceived, tyranny is established in the city.

Book IX. The tyrannic man, continues Socrates, is ruled by the worst class of the unnecessary desires. To the lawlessness of the democratic man he adds the frenzy of lust; utterly without scruple, he is driven to boundless excess by passions he can never sate. The tyrannic man, like the tyrannic state, is slave to fear, want, every sort of misery and every sort of wickedness: he is last in happiness, below the kingly man, the oligarchic man and the democratic man in descending order.

This is Socrates' first answer to Thrasymachos' argument in Book I, that injustice is more profitable than justice. He continues with another. The three elements in the soul distinguished in Book IV lead the three classes of men in which they respectively rule in pursuit of wisdom, honour and pleasure. Each class will maintain its own aim to be the highest, but clearly the best opinion will be that of the wisdom-loving or philosophical man, because he will be the most experienced and the best equipped to judge. We must agree with him that wisdom-loving is superior to honour-loving and honour-loving to pleasure-loving.

Yet a third argument follows. Socrates analyses the kinds of pleasure enjoyed by the three classes: the philosopher's pleasure in wisdom is best because it partakes most of the unchanging world of truth and real being; the pleasures of victory and honour come next; and last of all is the pleasure of gratified desire, which is no more than a fleeting shadow of true pleasure.

Finally Socrates deals with the question raised by Glaucon and Adeimantos in Book II, whether justice is valuable for its own sake. The three elements in the soul are likened to a man, a lion and a monster: in the soul of the just the man rules, in the soul of the unjust the monster rules. Clearly the first condition is intrinsically of more value than the second, and a spurious appearance of justice cannot make injustice any more praiseworthy.

Socrates ends Book IX by saying that whether or not the perfect city exists on earth, it is laid up in heaven as a pattern for mankind.

Book X. Socrates now returns to his criticism of the artist. He distinguishes three levels of reality, instancing the ideal bed, the bed you sleep on, and the image of a bed in a picture. The artist functions at the lowest level; he only portrays the actual, not the ideal bed: art is mere imitation of an appearance of reality. Now, imitation is essentially an activity inferior to doing or making; and moreover the artist will never even be able to imitate particularly well, because his knowledge of his subject is bound in every case to be inferior to a practical knowledge of it. However diverting, art cannot be a serious occupation.

Nevertheless, art does appeal to some element in the soul —not, says Socrates, the rational element, but the irrational. In literature, for example, the poet will not imitate the reasonable man but the foolish and unstable man, because the latter will, he thinks, give more scope for effect, and will also be a more congenial subject for the foolish and unstable part of the soul. The tendency of art to corrupt even the best of natures, by thus encouraging the lower element at the expense of the higher, is all the more dangerous because of art's undoubted fascination; and the soul in pursuit of virtue must be ceaselessly on guard against it.

The last section of Book X follows the fortunes of the just and the unjust to the after life. Everything, says Socrates, has its own evil, tending to corrupt and destroy, and its own good, tending to preserve. The soul is corrupted by its evil, vice, but is not destroyed by vice; it is hardly likely, therefore, to be destroyed by the evil of the body, disease. In fact disease and death do not affect the soul at all—obviously they do not make it more unjust. The soul, therefore, does not perish with the body; in the after life, as on earth, it fares according to its deserts, the just soul being eternally rewarded and the unjust soul eternally punished. With the fable of Er, in which these conclusions of the argument are given mystical form, the *Republic* ends.

BOOK I

I went down to the Peiraeus yesterday with Glaucon, Ariston's son, to pay my devoirs to the goddess,[1] and at the same time I wanted to see how they would manage the festival, as this was the first time they held it. A fine procession I thought it which our people made, but the Thracians' seemed to be quite as good. We made our prayers then, and saw the show, and set off for the city.

Someone caught sight of us from a distance just as we had started for home, Polemarchos, Cephalos' son, and he sent his boy after us to tell us to wait for him. The boy caught me from behind by the cloak, and said, "Polemarchos wants you to wait for him."

I turned round and asked where the master was. "There he is," he said, "coming behind; do wait!"

"Oh, we'll wait," said Glaucon.

In a little while Polemarchos came up, and Glaucon's brother, Adeimantos, and Niceratos, Nicias' son, and a few others, from the show it seemed. Polemarchos said, "My dear Socrates, you seem to have just set out towards the city and to be going to leave us."

"Not a bad guess," I said.

[1] Bendis, whose festival had been introduced into Athens from Thrace.

"Well," said he, "do you see how many we are?"

"Oh yes!"

"Very well, then," he said, "either stay here, or fight for it."

"Surely there's a third choice," I said, "if we can persuade you that you ought to let us go?"

"If you can!" said he. "Could you persuade us if we refused to listen?"

"Of course not," said Glaucon.

"Then make up your minds that we shan't be listening!"

And Adeimantos said, "Don't you really know there's to be torch on horseback this evening, for the goddess?"

"Horseback?" said I, "that's something new! What do you mean? A relay race on horseback, handing the torches on?"

"That's it," said Polemarchos, "and they are going to have a night festival—worth seeing! We shall rise directly after dinner, and see this night show, and meet a lot of young fellows there, and have a good talk. Do stay, don't say no!"

Glaucon said, "It seems we must stay."

"Well, if you say so," said I, "we must do so."

Accordingly we went home with Polemarchos, and there we found Lysias and Euthydemos, his brothers, and, besides, Thrasymachos from Chalcedon, and Charmantides of the Paianian parish, and Cleitophon, Aristonymos' son; Cephalos, the father of Polemarchos, was at home too. A very old man he seemed to be; it was long since I had seen him. He sat on a chair with a cushion; he had a garland on, for he had just sacrificed in the courtyard.

So we seated ourselves beside him, for there were chairs ready in a circle. As soon as he saw me, Cephalos greeted me, and said, "My dear Socrates, you don't often come to see us in the Peiraeus; you really should! You know there would be no need for you to come here, if only I were strong enough to walk up to the city easily; I should go to see you. But now you really must come here oftener. My other pleasures are withering away now, my bodily pleasures, but just as fast grows my pleasure in talking, and my desire for that. So I do beg you to visit us regularly, and make yourself at home here as among friends, and be a companion to these young men."

"Indeed, Cephalos," I said, "what I enjoy most is talking with men who are really old. It seems right to enquire of them, as if they had traversed a long journey which we perhaps will have to traverse, to ask what the journey is like, rough and difficult, or easygoing and smooth. And so I would gladly enquire of you what you think about it, since you are now at that time of life which the poets call the threshold of old age. Is it a difficult time of life, or what do you say of it?"

"Well, my dear Socrates," he said, "I will tell you how I feel. We often meet, a few of much the same age, like to like as the old proverb says. Most of us when we meet are full of lamentations; we miss the pleasures of youth, we talk of our old love affairs, and drinking and feasting, and other such things; and we regret them as if we had been robbed of great things, as if that were real life, and we were hardly alive now. Some even complain of mud-spatterings of old age by their nearest and dearest, and so they chant forever what evils old age has brought on them. But I think the blame does not lie there, Socrates; for if that were the reason, I too should have suffered the same for my old age, as the others who have come to my time of life. But in fact I have met others who don't feel like that about it, Sophocles the poet, for instance. I was with him once, when somebody asked him, 'What about love now, Sophocles? Are you still able to serve a woman?' 'Hush, man,' he said, 'I've escaped from all that, thank goodness. I feel as if I had escaped from a mad, cruel slave driver.' I thought it was a good answer, and I think so still. Indeed, there is great and perfect peace from such things in old age. When desires go slack and no longer tighten the strings, it is exactly what Sophocles said; perfect riddance of frantic slave drivers, a whole horde of them. No, Socrates, both here and in family life there is only one reason for what happens; not old age, but the man's character. For if they are decent, even-tempered people, old age is only moderately troublesome; if not, then youth is no less difficult than age is for such people."

I thought this admirable, and wanted to hear some more; so I stirred him on by saying, "My dear Cephalos, I don't think most people would agree with you there. You bear old age easily, they think, not because of character, but because you have a large fortune; rich people have many consolations, they say."

"Quite true," said he, "they don't believe it. Indeed there is something in what they say, though not so much as they think. No, Themistocles was right when that Seriphian told him off and said his fame came from Athens and not from himself; he answered, you know, 'I should never have been famous if I were a Seriphian, nor would you if you were an Athenian.' You could say the same of those who are not rich and bear old age badly. Even a reasonable man would not bear old age quite easily in poverty, but the unreasonable man, if he were rich, would not be at peace with himself."

"What you have, Cephalos," I asked then, "did you inherit most of it, or did you get it yourself?"

"What, get it?" he said. "I am somewhere between father and grandfather as a moneymaker. My grandfather, whose name was the same as mine, inherited about as much property as I now have, and made it many times as great; but my father Lysanias made it even less than it is now. I am content if I leave it to these lads not less than I inherited, but a trifle more."

"What made me ask," said I, "was that you seemed to me not to care much for money. Those who don't are generally those who have not earned it; those who have welcome money twice as much as the others. They care for it as poets do for their poetry, and fathers for their children; in the same way, I suppose, those who have earned money take it seriously as their own work, not only for its use as the rest do. So they are difficult people to deal with, because they will praise nothing but money."

"True," he said.

"Yes indeed," said I. "But one more question, please. What do you think the greatest good you have gained from getting great wealth?"

"Something," he said, "which I could perhaps not make most people believe. Know well, Socrates," said he, "that when a man faces the thought that he must die, he feels fear and anxiety about what did not trouble him before. Think of the tales they tell of the next world, how one that has done wrong here must have justice done him there—you may have laughed at them before, but then they begin to rack your soul. What if they are true! And the man himself, whether from the weakness of old age, or because he is nearer, has a better sight of them. Suspicion and fear fill him then, and he runs up his account, and looks to see whether he has wronged anyone. If he finds many wrongs in his life, he often starts up out of his sleep like a child, in terror, and lives with evil expectations; but one who has no wrong on his conscience has always Hope beside him, lovely and good, the old man's nurse, as Pindar puts it. That is a charming bit of his—you know it, Socrates—where he says that when one has lived justly and piously,[1]

> A lovely companion by his side cheers his heart,
> The old man's nurse, Hope, who chiefly guides
> The wayward mind of mortals.

A noble saying that, very much so indeed. In this respect then, I put down possession of wealth as worth a great deal, not to every man, but to the decent man. Never to deceive anyone even unconsciously, never to be dishonest, nor to be debtor

[1] Pindar, *Fragment* 214 in the Loeb edition.

to any god for sacrifices or any man for money, and so go to that world in fear—to possess money contributes a great share in avoiding all this. It has other uses, many indeed; but setting one thing against another, I would put this as the chief thing for which wealth is most useful to a sensible man."

"Excellently said, Cephalos," I replied. "But this very thing justice—are we to say that it is just simply to pay back what one has received from anyone? Or is it true that this may be sometimes just and sometimes unjust? For example: Suppose you have received weapons from a friend when in his right mind, everyone would say that you should not give such things back if he were mad when he asked for them. Then it would not be right and just to give them back, or always to tell him the whole truth in such a condition."

"You are right," he said.

"Then this is not the definition of justice, to speak the truth, and to give back whatever one has received."

"But indeed it is," Polemarchos put in, "at least if we must believe Simonides."

"Oh well," said Cephalos, "I hand over the word to you people; it is high time now for me to see after the sacred rites."

"Then," said Polemarchos, "I, Polemarchos, am son and heir to what is yours?"

"Quite correct," said Cephalos with a laugh, and at once went off to the sacrifice.

"Come along then," I said, "Mr. Heir to the conversation, what's that Simonides said about justice, and correctly, according to you?"

"He said," was the reply, "that to give back what is owed to each is just; in saying that I think he was right."

"Well in any case," I said, "Simonides is not to be easily disbelieved. A wise man, a man inspired by God. But what does this mean? Perhaps you know, Polemarchos, but I don't. For he certainly does not mean what we were speaking of just now, to give anything and everything back on demand when the depositor is not in his right mind; yet the deposit is a debt owed, isn't it?"

"Yes."

"But one must by no means give back on demand when the depositor is not in his right mind?"

"True," said he.

"Then it seems Simonides means something else, something different from that, when he said it is just to give back what is owed."

"No doubt of it," said he, "for he believes that friends owe friends something good, not to do them harm."

"I understand," said I; "whoever gives back a sum of gold to the depositor does not give back what is owed, if the giving back and the taking do harm, and if the giver and the taker are friends. Is not that what Simonides means, according to you?"

"Exactly."

"Oh, and it should be given back to enemies, whatever the thing owing may be?"

"Certainly," he said, "what is owing to them. And from enemy to enemy, that debt is surely something evil, as is right and proper."

"It was a riddle, then, it seems," I said, "when Simonides told us what justice was. He intended to say, as it appears, that justice is to give back what is proper to each, and this is what he called the thing owed."

"Well, what do you think?" he asked.

"Oh, good heavens," I said, "look here. Suppose the question were put to Simonides, 'What does the art called medicine give as owing and proper to what?' Say what you think he would answer."

"Clearly," he said, "it gives drugs and food and drinks to bodies."

"And what does the art called cookery give to what, as owing and proper?"

"Flavourings to vittles."

"Then what art, giving back what to what, should be called justice?"

"If we must follow these models, Socrates, the art which gives back benefits to friends and hurts to enemies."

"Then to do well to friends and to do ill to enemies he calls justice?"

"I think so."

"But who is best able to do well to sick friends and ill to sick enemies as regards disease and health?"

"The physician."

"And who, when they are on board ship, as regards the dangers of the sea?"

"The pilot."

"Now then, the just man; in what action and for what work is he best able to benefit friends and hurt enemies?"

"In war and alliance, I think."

"Very good. If men are not sick, however, the physician is useless."

"True."

"And if not at sea, so is the pilot."

"Yes."
"Then is the just man useless if they are not at war?"
"Not at all, I don't think that."
"So justice is useful even in peace?"
"Yes, it is."
"So is agriculture, isn't it?"
"Yes."
"For getting crops."
"Yes."
"And shoemaking too?"
"Yes."
"Yes, for getting shoes, I think you would say."
"Certainly."
"Well, then, justice; for what use or getting would you say it is useful?"
"For contracts, Socrates."
"By contracts you mean partnerships, or what?"
"Partnerships, of course."
"In a game of checkers,[1] is the just man a good and useful partner, or the good checkers player?"
"The checkers player."
"For laying bricks and stones, is the just man a better and more useful partner than the builder?"
"Not at all."
"What partnership is the just man a better partner for than the builder or the harp-player, as the harp-player is better than the just man for playing music?"
"Money partnerships."
"Except in using money, perhaps, Polemarchos, when, for instance, the partners must buy or sell a horse for money; then the man who knows about horses is better, eh?"
"So it appears."
"Yes, and with a boat, the boatbuilder or the pilot."
"It seems so."
"Very well, when is the just man more useful than the others? To do what with gold or silver together?"
"In making a deposit, Socrates, and keeping it safe."
"You mean when it is not to be used at all, but to be hoarded?"
"Exactly."
"So when the money is useless, justice is useful about it?"
"It looks like that."
"And when you want to take care of a pruning-knife, justice is useful both in partnership and in private; when you want to use it, you want the vine-dresser's art?"

[1] Usually called "draughts" in England.

"So it seems."

"And you will say that when you want to take care of a shield and a harp and not to use them, justice will be useful, but when you want to use them, the art of arms or music?"

"Necessarily."

"So then in general, in the use of each justice is useless, but in their uselessness useful?"

"It looks like that."

"Well then, my friend, justice is nothing very serious, if it really is useful only for useless things. Let us look at this in another way. Is not the best at attack in battle or boxing or anything else, also the best at defence?"

"Certainly."

"Then in disease: he who is good at keeping it away, the same man is best at putting it in[1] without being found out?"

"It seems so to me."

"And on a campaign: a good guardian is the one who can best steal the enemy's plans for his various doings."

"Certainly."

"Then if a man is a good guardian of anything, he is also a good thief of the same thing?"

"It looks like it."

"Then if the just man is good at guarding money, he is good at stealing it?"

"At least that is what the argument indicates!"

"So the just man has been shown to be a thief, as it seems! You must have learnt that from Homer. For Homer loves Autolycos, the grandfather of Odysseus on his mother's side, and says he was 'first of all the world in thievery and swearing his oath.' So it seems, according to you, and according to Homer, and according to Simonides, that justice is a kind of thievery, for the benefit of friends, however, and the hurt of enemies. Didn't you say that?"

"Upon my word and honour, I don't know any longer what I did say! However, I still think justice is to help your friends and hurt your enemies."

"Which do you call friends—those whom anyone thinks to be good, honest men, or those who really are, even if he thinks they are not, and the same with enemies?"

"It is natural to love those you think to be good, honest men, and to hate those you think bad."

"Don't people make mistakes about this? Don't they think many to be honest men when they are not, and the opposite?"

"They do."

---

[1] E.g., poison.

"Then to these are good men enemies, and the bad men friends?"

"Yes, indeed."

"But nevertheless it is just, then, for these to help the bad ones and to hurt the good?"

"It seems so."

"Yet the good are just and not such as do wrong."

"True."

"Then by your reasoning it is just to do ill to those who are doing no injustice!"

"No, no, not that, Socrates; the reasoning seems to be bad."

"Then," said I, "it is just to harm the unjust, and to benefit the just."

"That seems a better way of putting it."

"Then see what will often happen, Polemarchos: when people have made mistakes in their men, it will be just both to hurt their friends—for they have bad ones, and also to benefit their enemies—for they have good ones. So we shall go clean contrary to what we said Simonides meant."

"Well, really," he said, "that is the result. But let us change a bit, for it looks as if we put the friend and enemy wrong."

"How, Polemarchos?"

"That the one thought good and honest was the friend."

"How should we change it now?" said I.

"The one," said he, "who is both thought good and is good is the friend; but the one who is not good, but thought good, only seems a friend and is not; so also with the enemy."

"Very well, as it seems by this reasoning, the good one will be a friend, and the bad one an enemy."

"Yes."

"We said first it was just to do well to the friend and to do ill to the enemy: now we must add something to this 'just,' and say it is just to do well to the friend if he is good, and to injure the enemy if he is bad?"

"Certainly," he said. "That seems right to me now."

"And yet," said I, "is it right for the just man to injure any man at all?"

"Of course it is," he said, "to injure bad men and enemies."

"Take horses: When injured do they become better or worse?"

"Worse."

"Worse in the virtue of a dog, or in the virtue of a horse?"

"Worse in the virtue of a horse."

"And dogs being injured become worse in the virtue of a dog, not of a horse?"

"That is necessary."

"And what about men, my friend? Are we not to say that they become worse in human virtue when they are injured?"

"Certainly."

"Is not justice a human virtue?"

"That is necessary too."

"Then, my friend, if men are injured, they must necessarily become more unjust."

"So it seems."

"Take music, now: Is it possible for the musical to make men unmusical by means of music?"

"No."

"Or horsemen bad horsemen by horsemanship?"

"Impossible."

"But can the just make men unjust by justice? Or in general, can the good make men bad by means of virtue—is that possible?"

"No, impossible."

"For it is not the work of heat to make cold, but the opposite?"

"Yes."

"And it is not the work of what is dry to make things wet, but the opposite?"

"Certainly."

"Nor is it the work of the good to injure, but the opposite?"

"So it seems."

"And the just man is good?"

"Certainly."

"Then it is not the work of the just man to injure, Polemarchos, whether to injure a friend or anyone else,[1] anyone —but that is the work of the unjust man."

"I think you are absolutely right, Socrates."

"Then if one says it is right to give back what is owing to each, and means by this that injury is owing to his enemies from the just man and benefit to his friends, the one who said it was no wise man; for he did not speak the truth, since it has been shown that to injure anyone is never just anywhere."

"I grant it," said he.

"Then shall we fight him," said I. "Shall we be partners, you and I, if anyone says that this has been laid down by Simonides, or Bias, or Pittacos,[2] or any other of the wise and blessed men?"

"I'm ready, at least," he said, "to be your partner in the battle."

"But do you know," said I, "whose doctrine I think this

[1] Plato is the first person known to have said this.
[2] Some of the Seven Wise Men.

THE REPUBLIC Book I (335C–337A)

to be, that it is just to benefit your friends and to injure your enemies?"

"Who said it?" he asked.

"I believe Periandros, or Perdiccas, or Xerxes,[1] or Ismenias the Theban, or someone else who thought no end of his power, some rich man."

"Very true indeed," he said.

"Very well, then," said I, "since it has been shown that justice is no more this than what we thought at first, what else could we affirm it to be?"

While we were talking, Thrasymachos had often tried to break in and take a hand in the argument and he was prevented by the other sitters who wished to hear the talk. But when we paused after my last words, he kept quiet no longer; he gathered himself up, and leapt on us like a wild beast to tear us to pieces. Polemarchos and I were frightened out of our wits, as he roared out to the company, "What's all this stuff and rubbish, Socrates! There are you two, bowing and scraping to each other all this time like a pair of simpletons! But if you really want to know what justice is, don't go on like that, merely asking questions and trying to trip him up whatever he answers, which you think is a grand thing! You know quite well it's easier to ask than to answer. Now answer yourself, and tell me what you think justice to be. Don't say it is what is due, or useful, or profitable, or what pays and what benefits, tell me simply and clearly what you mean. I won't accept it if you give me nonsense like that."

I was confounded on hearing this, and frightened to look at him, and I really think I should have been struck dumb if I had not seen him before he saw me.[2] But when he began to go mad at our talk, I fixed my eyes on him first so that I was able to answer, and I said, trembling a little, "My dear Thrasymachos, don't be cross with us. If we two have made mistakes in our discussion, we could not help it, I assure you. If we were prospecting for gold, we should not go bowing and scraping to each other in the search if we could help it; we should only lose our chance of finding it. We were prospecting for justice, a thing worth more than much gold—should we be such fools as to truckle to each other and not do our best to find it? Think so if you like, my friend; but I believe that find it we cannot. Pity is more natural for us to expect than anger from clever men like you."

He gave a great guffaw, and, laughing bitterly, he said, "By Heracles, here's the famous irony of Socrates! I knew

[1] Despots.
[2] According to the proverb, "If a wolf sees you first you go dumb." Theocritus, xiv. 22.

it, and I told these gentlemen all along—you will never answer, only play simplicity and do anything rather than answer, if someone asks a question!"

"That's because you are a wise man, Thrasymachos," I said. "Suppose you asked someone, 'How many are twelve?'—and suppose you said to him beforehand, 'Don't say twice six, man, or three times four, or six times two, or four times three; I won't accept it if you give me nonsense like that.' It's plain, I think, that no one would answer such a question, and you know that quite well. But suppose he said to you, 'What do you mean, Thrasymachos? I must not give any of those answers which you forbade? You surprise me! Not even if one of them is right? Must I answer something which is not true, or what do you mean?' What would you say to that!"

"Pooh!" he said. "Much alike, aren't they, this case and that!"

"There's nothing to hinder their being so," said I, "but even if they are not alike and if the man thinks they are, do you believe he will any the less answer what appears to him, whether we forbid him or not?"

"Is that what you are going to do, then?" he said. "Will you give one of the answers I barred?"

"I shouldn't be surprised if I did," was my reply, "if I thought so after consideration."

"All right," he said, "what if I show you another answer about justice, different from all those, and better? What punishment do you think you deserve?"

"Nothing," said I, "except the proper punishment for one who does not know. I suppose that is to learn from one who does; and that is the punishment I think I deserve."

"I like that!" he said. "But besides the learning, you must pay a fine."

"When I've got it to pay," I answered.

"Oh, the money's here!" said Glaucon. "The money's all right, Thrasymachos, you go on; we will all make a collection for Socrates."

"Oh yes, of course," he said, "so that Socrates may be up to his usual games, I suppose, answer nothing himself and only pick holes in what other people say."

"My dear old fellow," said I, "how could anyone answer if he doesn't know in the first place, and doesn't profess to know, and in the second place, if he is forbidden to give any notions he may have, and that by a man of reputation? But surely you ought to speak, that's more reasonable; for you do profess to know, and to be able to tell us. Don't refuse. Please answer, and I shall be grateful myself; and don't grudge a lesson to Glaucon and the rest."

When I said this, Glaucon and the others begged him to be kind. Thrasymachos plainly was eager to speak, because he thought he had a splendid answer, and expected to get glory by it; but he pretended to insist that I should be the answerer. At last he gave way, and then said, "There you have the wisdom of Socrates! Not to be willing to teach anything himself, but to go about learning from others and not even saying thank you!"

"I do learn from others," I said, "that's true, Thrasymachos; but when you say that I pay no thanks, that is false. I do pay, all I can; but I can only pay praises, for money I have none. How gladly I do that, if I think anyone speaks well, you shall see directly as soon as ever you answer, for I think you will speak well."

"Then listen," said he. "I declare justice is nothing but the advantage of the stronger. Why don't you applaud that? Because you won't!"

"If I may learn first what you mean," I said, "for I don't know yet. The advantage of the stronger you say is just. And what do you really mean by that, Thrasymachos? It cannot be anything like this: If Pulydamas, the all-around athlete, is stronger than we are, and if a diet of beef is an advantage to his body, then this diet is an advantage, and just, for us the weaker."

"Damn you, Socrates!" he said. "You take me just in the way to spoil the whole thing!"

"Not at all, my good sir," I said, "only tell me more clearly what you mean."

"Don't you know then," said he, "that some states are under despots, and some are governed by a democracy, and some by an aristocracy?"

"Of course."

"Is not the strong power in each the ruling power? And each power lays down the laws so as to suit itself, a democracy democratic laws, and a despotism despotic laws, and so with the rest; and in laying them down, they make it clear that this is a just thing for their subjects, I mean their own advantage; one who transgresses these they chastise as a breaker of laws and a doer of injustice. Then this is what I mean, my good friend: that the same thing is just in all states, the advantage of the established government. This I suppose has the power, so if you reason correctly, it follows that everywhere the same thing is just, the advantage of the stronger."

"Now I understand what you mean," said I. "Whether it is

true or not, I will try to find out. You have answered as we did, that justice is advantage, yet you forbade me to say that. It is true you have added something to it, 'of the stronger.' "

"Only a small addition, perhaps," he said.

"It is not clear yet whether it is small or great; but we must consider whether what you say is true, that's clear. For I myself admit that justice is some advantage, and you add a bit, and say it is the advantage of the stronger. I don't know, and so we must consider."

"Consider away," said he.

"So I will," said I. "You say also, don't you, that to obey rulers is just?"

"I do."

"Are the rulers in each state infallible, or can they make a mistake?"

"Oh, they can certainly make mistakes," he said.

"Then when they undertake to lay down laws, do they sometimes do the job well and sometimes not well?"

"I believe so."

"To do it well is to lay down what has advantage for themselves, and not well, what is not to their advantage? What do you say about it?"

"I agree."

"Whatever they lay down, their subjects must do, and this is justice?"

"Of course."

"Then by your reasoning, it is not only just to do what is an advantage to the stronger, but also the opposite, what is not."

"What's that you are saying?" he replied.

"Only what *you* say, I think; but let us consider and put it better. Was it not agreed that the rulers, in telling their subjects what to do, sometimes make a mistake, and miss their own advantage, but whatever the rulers enjoin upon them it is just for their subjects to do? Was not this agreed?"

"I believe so," he said.

"Then," said I, "you will have to believe it is just to do what is not an advantage to the rulers, that is, the stronger, by your own admission, whenever the rulers unintentionally command things evil for themselves, and it is just, as you say, for the subjects to do what the rulers have commanded. Must it not then follow of necessity, most wise and sapient Thrasymachos, that in this case it is just to do exactly the opposite of what you say? For surely the weaker are commanded to do what is not to the advantage of the stronger."

"Yes, upon my word, Socrates," said Polemarchos, "that's as plain as can be."

"Yes, if you are the witness,"[1] Cleitophon said, breaking in.

"And where's the need of a witness?" he asked. "Thrasymachos himself admits that sometimes the rulers command things evil for themselves, and it is just for the subjects to do them."

"To be obedient to their rulers' commands, Polemarchos, was what Thrasymachos affirmed to be just."

"Yes, Cleitophon, but he also affirmed that the advantage of the stronger was just. And after affirming both these things, he admitted that sometimes the stronger commanded the weaker, their subjects, what was not to the stronger's advantage. From these admissions, advantage of the stronger would be no more just than their disadvantage."

"But," said Cleitophon, "the advantage of the stronger he said was what the stronger believed to be his advantage; that was what the weaker had to do, and that he affirmed to be justice."

"Well, he didn't say so," said Polemarchos.

"That doesn't matter, Polemarchos," I said, "but if Thrasymachos now says that, let us take it from him so.

"Tell me now, Thrasymachos. Was that what you wished to say justice was, that which the stronger thought to be his advantage, whether it is or not? Are we to say you meant that?"

"Not at all," he said. "Why, do you believe that I call one who makes mistakes the stronger at the time when he is mistaken?"

"I did believe you meant that," said I, "when you admitted that the rulers are not infallible but could make mistakes."

"You are a quibbler, Socrates! Just take a doctor, for example. Would you call one who made mistakes about his patients a doctor in the very mistakes he makes? Or an arithmetician, when he makes mistakes in a sum, at the time when he makes his mistake and in the mistake he makes? I suppose we do say loosely that the doctor has made a mistake, or the arithmetician, or the scholar; but the truth is, that each of these as far as he is what he is called, never makes a mistake; so to speak exactly in your own exact style, no artist or craftsman ever makes a mistake. Knowledge fails, and the man makes a mistake, in so far as he is no craftsman; thus no craftsman, no wise man, no ruler, ever makes a mistake so long as he is a ruler, although everyone would say the doctor was wrong,

[1] The only witness allowed, in the method of Socrates, was the opponent.

or the ruler was wrong. That's how you must take me to answer now; but the extreme exactitude is really that the ruler, as far as he is a ruler, makes no mistakes, and, making no mistakes, he lays down what is best for himself, and this the subject must do. So as I said from the first, I say now it is just to do what is the advantage of the stronger."

"Oh, my dear Thrasymachos!" I said, "do you think I am quibbling?"

"Indeed I do," he said.

"Then you think I did it on purpose to discredit you when I asked those questions?"

"I'm sure of it," said he, "and you shall gain nothing by it, for you could not hide your wrecking scheme, and if you can't hide it you could never force me by your talk."

"But bless you," I said, "I should never even try! However, I don't want anything else of that sort to come between us; so please define your ruler and your stronger, as to whether you mean the so-called or the exactly so, to use your own phrase, whose advantage, as being stronger, it will be just for the weaker to provide."

"I mean the ruler in the most exact sense of the word. Now wreck and quibble, if you can, I ask no mercy. But you will never be able to do it!"

"Do you believe I would be so mad," I said, "as to try to beard a lion, or to quibble with Thrasymachos?"

"You at least did try just now," he said, "feeble though you were at it!"

"Enough of these compliments!" I said. "Please tell me; what about the doctor in the most exact sense of the word, to use your phrase; is he a moneymaker or one who serves the sick? I mean the real healer."

He replied, "One who serves the sick."

"And the pilot—is the true pilot a sailor, or a ruler of sailors?"

"A ruler of sailors."

"We need not take into account, I think, that he sails in a ship, nor must we call him a sailor; for he is named pilot not because he sails in a ship, but from his art and his rule over sailors."

"True," he said.

"Well, each of these persons has an advantage of his own?"

"Certainly."

"Again, this art," said I, "is to seek and provide the advantage for each, and that is why it exists."

"That is why," he said.

"Then has each of the arts any other advantage for itself

than to be as perfect as possible?"

"What do you mean by that?"

"To take an example," said I; "if you should ask me if it is enough for a body to be a body, or if it is in want of something more, I should say certainly, it does want more. That is why this art has now been invented, the healing art, because body is ill and it is not enough for it simply to be body; and so this art has been made to provide what is for its advantage. Do you think I am right in putting it so?"

"Quite right," he said.

"Very well. Is this healing art itself ill? Or is there any other art which is in want of some virtue (as eyes want sight, and ears hearing, so that there is need for an art over these senses, to enquire and provide what is advantageous for them)? Is there some illness in art itself, and do we need for each art another art to enquire what it wants, and for the enquiring art another such, and so *ad infinitum?* Or shall the art enquire for itself as to the advantage it wants? Or on the contrary, does it need neither itself, nor any other art for any illness of its own, to enquire for its advantage, and is there no illness and no fault at all in any art at all; and is it improper for an art to seek advantage for anything except that of which it is the art, the art in itself being faultless and untainted and right so long as each art is what it is, exact and whole? Consider the matter in your exact way of speaking: Is it so, or not?"

"Apparently it is so," said he.

"Then," I said, "the art of healing seeks no advantage for the art of healing, but for a body."

"Yes," he said.

"Nor horsemanship for horsemanship, but for horses; and no other art for itself, since it needs nothing, but for that of which it is the art."

"So it appears," he said.

"Furthermore, Thrasymachos, the arts rule and have power over that of which they are arts." He agreed to this, but very reluctantly. "Then no science seeks or commands the advantage of the stronger, but the advantage of the weaker, that which is subject to it." He agreed to this also at last, but he tried to fight it; and when he agreed, I said, "Then is it not true that no doctor, so far as he is a doctor, seeks or commands the advantage of the doctor, but only the advantage of the patient? For we have agreed, haven't we, that a doctor in the exact sense is a ruler and not a moneymaker." He said yes. "And that a pilot in the exact sense is a ruler of sailors, and not a sailor?"

"Yes."

"Then such a pilot and ruler will enquire and command not what is the advantage of the pilot, but the advantage of the sailor, his subject." He agreed, reluctantly. "Then, Thrasymachos," said I, "no one else in any place of rule at all, in so far as he is a ruler, enquires or commands what is his own advantage, but the advantage of his subjects and that of which he is craftsman; that only he keeps in view, and what is its advantage, and what is proper for that, while he says what he says and does what he does, always."

When we had come so far in the discussion, and it was quite clear to all that the definition of justice had been turned upside down, Thrasymachos made no reply; but he asked instead, "Have you a nurse at home, Socrates? Tell me that."

"Hullo," said I, "ought not you to answer, instead of putting questions like that?"

"If you want to know," he said, "I ask because she takes no notice when you are snuffling[1] and doesn't wipe your nose though you ask for it, and she can't get you to know the difference between shepherd and sheep."

"What makes you say that?" I asked.

"Because you think shepherds and oxherds look for the good of their sheep and cattle. Why do they fatten them and take care of them? Only because they look out for their own good and their masters'! Just so the rulers in states, those who really rule, are to their subjects what people are to sheep! Can you conceive of anything else? What do you think they look for night and day but how to get benefit for themselves! You are a long way out about justice and the just, injustice and the unjust, when you don't know that justice and the just are really another man's good, the advantage of the stronger, the ruler, but the private damage of the subject, the servant. Injustice is the opposite, and rules those who are really simple creatures and just ones; but the subjects do what is the advantage of the other who is stronger, and they make him happy by serving him, but themselves not at all. You must consider, my most simple Socrates, that a just man comes off worse than an unjust man everywhere. First of all in contracts with one another, wherever two such are in partnership, and the partnership is dissolved, you would never find the just man getting the better of the unjust, but he always gets the worst of it. Secondly, in public affairs, when there are taxes and contributions, the just man pays more and the unjust less from an equal estate; when there are distributions the one gains nothing and the other much. Again, when these

[1] With another sense of "drivelling."

two hold public office, the just man gets his private affairs, by neglecting them, into a bad state, if he has no other loss, and he has no profit from the treasury because he is just; besides, he is unpopular with friends and acquaintances if he will not serve them contrary to justice; but it is quite the opposite with the unjust man. I mean the man that I spoke of before, the one who can gain great profits. Consider him then, if you wish to decide how much greater advantage he finds it personally to be unjust rather than just. You will understand it most easily, if you come to the most perfect injustice, which makes the unjust man most happy, and makes those who are wronged and will not be unjust most miserable. That is a despotism, which takes away others' property, not in little bits secretly and by force, but all in a lump, things sacred and things profane, things private and things public. In small parts of these, if a man is caught doing wrong, he is punished and has the greatest disgrace: in sacrilege and kidnapping and housebreaking, swindling and thievery, the piecemeal criminals have names from their crimes; but whenever someone not only takes people's money but kidnaps and enslaves all the citizens of a city, instead of these ugly names he is called happy and blessed, both by the citizens themselves and by all who hear of the man who has committed the whole and perfect injustice. For those who call injustice a shame do so because they fear suffering the injustice, not doing it. So, my dear Socrates, injustice when it is grand enough is more mighty than justice, more generous, more masterly; and as I began by saying, the just really is the advantage of the stronger; but the unjust is to his own profit and advantage."

When Thrasymachos had finished, he had it in mind to go away, after he had poured this flood of oratory over our ears like a bathman. But the company would not let him go; they forced him to stay and give an account of what he had said. I begged him urgently myself, and said, "What a speech to throw among us, my dear man! And now you want to go off without sufficient proof or disproof whether it is so or not! Do you believe this is a small thing you try to define? Is it not rather the whole conduct of living, how each one of us may live the most profitable life?"

"Well, could I possibly think otherwise?" said Thrasymachos.

"You appear to," I said, "or else you have no thought for us, and don't care a bit whether we shall live better or worse in our ignorance of what you say you know. Now be kind, there's a good fellow, and prove it to us. If you do a good turn to all this company you will not find it a bad investment. I tell you for my own part at once; I am not convinced and I don't believe that injustice is more profitable than justice, not even if you leave it free and let it do what it likes. Well then, my good friend, let there be an unjust man, and let him be able to do wrong either by keeping it unobserved or by forcing it through; all the same, he does not convince me that it is more profitable than justice. Perhaps I am not alone, but some other among us feels the same. Convince us then, be so kind, convince us that we are not right in valuing justice more highly than injustice."

"And how can I convince you?" said he. "For if you are not convinced by what I have said, what more can I do? Am I to serve up my argument and feed it to your soul like tidbits?"

"Oh, please don't," I said. "But first of all, either stand by what you say, or if you vary it, vary openly and do not cheat us. Now you see, Thrasymachos—let us look at the earlier part again—see how you define the true man of healing; but afterwards you do not think it necessary to be so exactly careful with the shepherd—you think that he fattens the sheep, in so far as he is a shepherd, not with a view to what is best for the sheep, but with his eye on good fare, like some diner going to have a feast, or with a view to selling, like a moneymaker and no shepherd. But the art of shepherding, I take it, cares simply and solely for what it is set over, how to provide the best for that; since for itself all has been sufficiently provided, that it shall be at its best so long as it does not fall short of being the shepherd's art. In the same way, I thought it now necessary for us to admit that every kind of rule, both public and private, so long as it is really rule, enquires only what is best for the ruled, that which is in its care. Do you believe that the rulers in cities, those who are truly rulers, rule willingly?"

"I don't believe that," said he. "I know it."

"Why, Thrasymachos," said I, "what of the other kinds of rule? Don't you observe that no one chooses willingly to rule, but they all demand pay, thinking there will be no benefit for themselves from ruling, but only for the subjects? Look here, tell me this: When we speak of a number of different arts, is not the difference that each has a different power? Pray don't answer contrary to your opinion, my dear fellow, or we shall never get on."

"Yes," he said, "that is the difference."

"And each offers us its own benefit, not all the same; thus the medical art gives health, the pilot's art a safe voyage, and so forth?"

"Certainly."

THE REPUBLIC Book I (345A–347A) 145

"Then the wage-earning art gives a wage?—for this is its power. Unless you call medicine and piloting the same art! Suppose a pilot finds sailing on the sea to be an advantage, and becomes healthy in consequence, you would not call his art medical any more for that reason, if you wish to define exactly, as you proposed to do."

"Certainly not," he said.

"Nor, I suppose, would you call the wage-earning art medical, if someone becomes healthy by earning a wage."

"Certainly not."

"Well, would you call the healing art moneymaking, if one makes money by healing?" He said no. "Well, we agreed that the benefit from each art is peculiar to itself?"

"So be it," he said.

"Any benefit then, which all craftsmen gain in common, they gain from something else which they all use in common besides their art."

"It seems so," he said.

"Very well; we say that the benefit craftsmen receive by earning a wage comes to them from their using the wage-earning art in addition to their own." He agreed, reluctantly.

"Then this benefit, the receipt of the wage, does not come to each from his own art; but to put it exactly, the medical art makes health and the wage-earning art makes the wage; the builder's art makes a house, and the wage-earning art, going with it, makes the wage; and so with all the others, each works out its own work, and benefits that which is in its care. But if a wage is not added, does the craftsman get any benefit from his art?"

"It seems not," said he.

"But does he confer no benefit, then, supposing he works for nothing?"

"I think he does, indeed!"

"Surely then, Thrasymachos, it is clear by this time that no art or rule provides what is a benefit to itself, but as we have said all along, it both provides and commands the benefit of the subject, and looks for the advantage of that, being weaker, and not the advantage of the stronger. This is the reason, my dear friend Thrasymachos, why I have said all along that no one chooses to rule, and take other people's troubles in hand to set them right, willingly, but he asks a wage; because one who means to practise his art properly never does what is best for himself, nor commands it when he commands according to his art, but what is best for the subject; and therefore pay must be found for those who shall be willing to rule, either money, or honour, or a penalty if he will not rule."

Glaucon now asked, "What do you mean by that, Socrates? The two wages I understand; but the penalty which you call a kind of wage, I do not understand."

"Then you don't understand the wage of the best men, for which the most distinguished rule, when they are willing to rule. Don't you know that place-hunting and greed are reputed to be a disgrace, and are a disgrace?"

"Yes," he said.

"For this reason, then," I said, "good men are not willing to rule either for money or for honour. They do not wish to exact pay openly for their rule, and to be called hirelings, and they do not wish to take it themselves from their rule secretly, and be called thieves; nor again for honour, for they are not place-hunters. Therefore constraint must be put upon them, and a penalty if they are to become willing to rule,[1] and that is really why it has come to be thought an ugly thing to present yourself willingly for office and not to wait for constraint. But the greatest penalty is to be ruled by a worse man, if one is not oneself willing to rule. This I think distinguished men fear when they do accept office; and then they enter upon their office, not as coming into something good, or expecting to enjoy it, but as a grim necessity, being unable to entrust it to men better than themselves, or as good. For in fact if a city of good men could be, they would fight to avoid ruling, just as they fight now to rule; and then it would become quite manifest that indeed a true ruler's nature is to look for the subject's advantage, not his own. So every man who knows what is what would choose rather to have benefit from another than to benefit another and have no end of trouble. This therefore I in no way concede to Thrasymachos, that justice is the advantage of the stronger. But we will leave that question for another time; what he says now seems to me something bigger, when he declares the life of the unjust man is better than the life of the just man. Then which way do you choose, Glaucon? Which seems to you more true?"

"I choose," he said, "that the just man's life is more profitable."

"You heard," I said, "all the good things which Thrasymachos just now described and gave to the unjust man?"

"I heard," said he, "but I do not believe."

[1] Plato means that the threat of a penalty must be used to change their unwillingness to willingness.

THE REPUBLIC Book I (347A–348E)

"Shall we try to persuade him then, if we can find any way, that he does not speak the truth?"

"That's what I wish, of course," said he.

"If, then, we give him speech for speech," said I, "and recount all the good things which the just man has, and let him make another speech, and then make another speech ourselves, we shall have to count the good things, and measure them, in each of the speeches, and then we shall need judges to decide; but if as before we come to some agreement between ourselves, we shall be ourselves both pleaders and judges."

"By all means," he said.

"It shall be as you please," I said.

"That pleases me," said he.

"Very well," said I. "Now, Thrasymachos, begin once again, and answer us. Do you say that perfect injustice is more profitable than perfect justice?"

"Assuredly I do," said Thrasymachos, "and I have told you why."

"Very well, here is something general to consider; tell us what you say. I suppose you call one of these things virtue, and the other vice?"

"I don't see why not."

"Justice virtue, and injustice, vice?"

"What delightful innocence! That's likely, isn't it, when I say injustice is profitable, and justice unprofitable!"

"Well, what then?"

"The opposite," said he.

"Do you mean that justice is vice?"

"No, but a generous simplicity."

"Then you call injustice a bad disposition?"

"No, good prudence."

"Sensible and good, then, Thrasymachos, is what you think the unjust are."

"Yes, those capable of doing injustice to perfection, able to put cities and nations of men under their power. But you perhaps think I mean a lot of cutpurses; there is profit even in that sort of thing," he said, "I grant it, if they are not caught; but such things are not worth mentioning, only what I was speaking of just now."

"I understand quite well," said I, "what you mean; but I was surprised if you placed injustice in the class of virtue and wisdom, and justice in the opposite class."

"That is certainly what I do."

"That's firmer footing for you, my friend," I said, "and it is not easy now to find what to say. If you had affirmed that injustice was profitable, but admitted that it was vice or something ugly, like other people, we should have something to say on accepted principles; but as it is you clearly mean to say it is beautiful, and strong, and you will add to it all the other descriptions which we used to give to the just, since you have been so bold as to class it with virtue and wisdom."

"You are among the truest prophets!" he said.

"Now, I take it," said I, "you are giving your real opinion, and so long as that is so, I must not shrink from following up your lead. For I believe you are really not jesting now, Thrasymachos, but saying what you really think."

"What's the difference to you," he said, "whether I think so or not? Why don't you tackle me?"

"Oh, it's all the same," said I. "Please try to answer one more question: Do you think the just man would wish to get the better of the just?"

"Not a bit," he said, "or he would not be the nice, simple creature he is."

"Or of the just action?"

"Nor of the just action," said he.

"But get the better of the unjust man—would he claim to do that, and think that just, or would he not think it just?"

"Think so, and claim it, yes," he said, "but he couldn't do it."

"But that is not what I ask," said I; "is this what you say—the just man does not claim or wish to get the better of the just, but he does of the unjust?"

"That's how it is," he said.

"Well, what of the unjust? Does he claim to get the better of the just man and the just action?"

"Of course, since he claims to get the better of all."

"Then the unjust man will get the better of the unjust man and action also, and he will strive to get most of all?"

"That is correct."

"Well," I said, "let us put it in this way: The just man does not get the better of his like, but his unlike, and the unjust man of both."

"Excellent," he said.

"And further," I said, "the unjust is sensible and good, the just neither."

"That's good, too," said he.

"Then," said I, "the unjust is like the prudent and good, but the just is not?"

"Well, if he is so-and-so," he said, "of course he will be like so-and-so, and the other unlike."

"Good. Then each of them is such as he is like."

"What else do you expect?" he said.

"Very well, Thrasymachos. Again: You say one man is musical, and another unmusical?"

"Yes."

"Which is sensible and which insensible?"

"The musical I take to be sensible, and the unmusical insensible."

"Then he is good where he is sensible, and bad where he is insensible?"

"Yes."

"The same with the medical?"

"The same."

"Suppose that a musical man, my good friend, is tuning a harp, does he wish to get the better of another musical man in tightening and loosening the strings, and want to overreach him?"

"I don't think so."

"But he does wish to get the better of an unmusical man?"

"Necessarily."

"And the medical man; in diet or drink would he wish to get the better of another medical man or action?"

"Surely not."

"But of one not medical?"

"Yes."

"In every form of knowledge and ignorance, do you think anyone who knows would want to choose to do or say more than another who knows would do or say, and not the very same as his like would do in the same action?"

"Well," said he, "perhaps it is necessary that he would do the same in such cases."

"And what of one who does not know? Would he not try to get the better both of his like and his unlike?"

"Perhaps."

"But the one who knows is wise?"

"I say so."

"And the wise, good?"

"I say so."

"Then the good and wise will not wish to get the better of his like, but of his unlike and opposite?"

"So it seems," he said.

"But the bad and ignorant, both of like and unlike?"

"It appears so."

"Then, Thrasymachos," I said, "our unjust man gets the better of both unlike and like—you said that, didn't you?"

"I did," he said.

"But the just man will not get the better of his like, but only of his unlike?"

"Yes."

"Then," said I, "the just man is like the wise and good, the unjust like the ignorant and bad."

"That seems to follow."

"But, further, we agreed that each is such as he is like."

"We did indeed."

"Then our just man has been shown to be good and wise, and the unjust ignorant and bad."

Thrasymachos made all these admissions not easily, as I now record them, but dragged with difficulty, and with any amount of sweat, it being high summer. And then I saw something which I never saw before, Thrasymachos blushing. At last, after we had agreed that justice was virtue and wisdom, and injustice vice and ignorance, I went on.

"Very well, we have settled that. But I think we said injustice was also strong; don't you remember, Thrasymachos?"

"I remember," said he, "but I don't approve of what you say now, either, and I have something to say about it. But if I should make a speech, I am sure you would call it mob oratory. Then either let me say all that I wish, or ask away if you wish me to answer questions, and I will merely say, 'Just so!' and nod my head or shake my head, as we do to old wives when they tell a story."

"Please don't," I said, "if it is not your opinion."

"Just to please you," he said, "since you won't let me make a speech. Why, what else do you want?"

"Nothing else, I declare," said I, "but since you are ready to do this, do it, and I'll ask my questions."

"Ask away," said he.

"Then I ask you," said I, "the same as before, that we may examine the reasoning step by step, and find out what justice is as compared with injustice. I think it was said that injustice was both stronger and more powerful than justice; but now," I said, "since justice is a kind of wisdom and virtue, it will easily be shown, I believe, that it is stronger than injustice, since injustice is ignorance. No one could fail to see that any longer. But I do not wish simply to put it so, Thrasymachos; let us try another way. You would say that it is unjust for a city to try to enslave other cities unjustly, or to have done it already, and to keep many enslaved under itself?"

"Of course," he said, "and this the best city will do most, the city most perfectly unjust."

"I understand," said I, "that that is what you affirmed, but there is something else I am asking about it, whether the city becoming stronger than another city will have this power without justice, or must it necessarily be combined with justice?"

"If it is true," he said, "as *you* said just now, that justice is wisdom, it must be combined with justice; but if true as *I* said, with injustice."

"I admire you, Thrasymachos," said I, "you don't only nod your head and shake your head, but you answer very nicely."

"To please you," he said.

"I'm much obliged," said I, "but do please me once more, and tell me: Do you think a city, or an army, or a gang of robbers or thieves, or any other body of men that set out for some unjust purpose in common would be able to achieve their object if they dealt unjustly with each other?"

"Not at all," he said.

"They would do it better if they were not unjust?"

"Certainly."

"For factions and hates and battles among themselves are what injustice gives them, I suppose, Thrasymachos, but justice gives friendship and a single mind; doesn't it?"

"Let it be so," he said, "I don't want to quarrel with you."

"Many thanks, my good friend. Tell me this again: If the work of injustice is to implant hatred wherever it is, then where it is found, whether among slaves or free men, it will make them hate one another, and form factions, and they will be unable to act together in common?"

"Certainly."

"Well, if it is found in two, won't they quarrel and be enemies both to each other and to the just?"

"They will," he said.

"Well then, suppose injustice be in one, my clever friend, surely it will not lose its special power; will it not keep it just the same?"

"Granted, it certainly keeps it," he said.

"Then this seems to be the kind of power it has: Wherever it is, city or nation or army or anything else, first it makes it unable to act with itself because of factions and quarrels, next it is an enemy both to itself and to every adversary and to the just. Is that correct?"

"Quite."

"Then in one person, I think, it will work all which its nature is to do; first it will make him unable to act, because he is in rebellion within and not of one mind with himself; next, it will make him an enemy both to himself and to the just, isn't that so?"

"Yes."

"And the gods also are just, my friend?"

"If you like."

"Then the unjust man is an enemy of the gods also, Thrasymachos, and the just man a friend."

"Enjoy your feast of reason," he said; "don't be afraid, I am not going to oppose you, or I shall annoy these people."

"Then please serve me up in full the rest of the feast, and go on answering as you are doing. Now when we say that the just are shown to be wiser and better and more able to act effectively, and the unjust to be incapable of accomplishing anything together, and when on the other hand we add that in fact those who do accomplish something with strong united action are yet sometimes unjust people—then we are not saying what is wholly true; for they could not have kept their hands off each other if they were absolutely unjust; it is clear that some justice was in them, which kept them from wronging each other as well as those they attacked, and by this justice they accomplished as much as they did. They set out on their unjust way only demidevils in wickedness, since whole villains, and men perfectly unjust, are perfectly unable to act effectively. That I understand to be the truth of the matter, not what you supposed at first.

"We now come to the second question which we proposed. Have the just a better life of it than the unjust? Are they happier? Indeed they appear to be so already, as I think, from what we have said, but let us examine still more carefully. The matter is no chance trifle, but how we ought to live."

"Examine away," said he.

"Here goes then," said I. "Kindly tell me—do you think a horse has his work?"

"I do."

"Then would you put down as the work of a horse, or anything else, that which you could do only with the thing, or best with it?"

"I don't understand," he said.

"Look here, now: Could you see with anything but eyes?"

"No."

"Well, could you hear with anything but ears?"

"No."

"Then we say rightly that sight and hearing are the works of eyes and ears."

"Certainly."

"Again: You could cut a vine twig with a sheath-knife, or chisel, or many other things?"

"Of course."

"But with nothing so well, I think, as a pruning-knife, which is made for the purpose."

"True."

"Then shall we not put this down as the pruning-knife's work?"

"We will, by all means."

"Now then, I think, you could understand better what I meant by asking if the work of each thing is what the thing alone could do, or better than anything else could."

"Oh," he said, "I understand now, and I agree that this is the work of each thing."

"Very good," said I. "Do you think there is a virtue in each thing which has a work appointed for it? Let us run over the same things. Eyes, we say, have a work?"

"They have."

"Then have eyes a virtue too?"

"They have a virtue too."

"Well, the ears had a work?"

"Yes."

"And a virtue too?"

"True."

"But what about all the other things? Does not the same hold good?"

"It does."

"One moment, now. Could the eyes do their work well if they had not their own proper virtue, but instead of the virtue a vice?"

"How could they?" he said—"I suppose you mean blindness instead of sight."

"Which is their virtue," I said, "but I do not ask that yet; I ask if their proper virtue makes them do well the work which they do, and vice makes them do it badly?"

"That is true so far," he said.

"Then ears also, deprived of their own virtue, will do their work badly."

"Certainly."

"Do we say the same of all the other things?"

"I think so."

"Consider the next point, then. Soul has a work, which you could not do with anything else? Something of this sort; to care, to rule, to plan, and all things like that. Is there anything but soul to which we could rightly entrust them and say they are its own?"

"Nothing else."

"What, again, of life? Shall we say it is a work of soul?"

"Most certainly," said he.

"And do we not say that soul has a virtue also?"
"Yes."
"Then will soul ever do its work well, Thrasymachos, deprived of its proper virtue? Is that not impossible?"
"Impossible."
"A bad soul then must needs rule and care badly, but a good soul must needs do all these things well."
"It must needs be so."
"Now did we not agree that soul's virtue was justice, and soul's vice injustice?"
"We did."
"Then the just soul and the just man will live well, and the unjust man badly."
"So it appears by your reasoning."
"But, further, he who lives well is blessed and happy,[1] he that does not is the opposite."
"Of course."
"The just man then is happy,[2] and the unjust miserable."
"Let it be so," he said.
"But to be miserable is not profitable, to be happy, is."
"Of course."
"Then, O Thrasymachos, blessed among men! injustice is never more profitable than justice!"

"Here endeth your banquet, Socrates, at the Feast[3] of Bendis!"

"I have to thank you for the banquet, Thrasymachos," I said, "because you have become gracious to me and you are angry no longer. But I have not had a good dinner—my own fault, not yours. Greedy people—how they grab at every dish that is brought in, and take a taste, before they have decently enjoyed the one before! I think I am like that. Before we had found what we first looked for, what justice is, I let that go and dashed at questions about it—whether it is vice and ignorance, or wisdom and virtue; then comes another story tumbling on the top of us, that injustice is more profitable than justice, and I left the first and hunted this—I simply couldn't help it. So the upshot of our talk is now that I know nothing at all! When I don't even know what justice is, I shall hardly know whether it is really a virtue or not, and whether one who has it is happy or not happy."

[1] The natural phrase in Greek for enjoying life.
[2] εὐδαίμων, happy and fortunate.
[3] See note on p. 125.

BOOK II

When I said this, I thought I had done with talk, but after all, this was only the prelude. For Glaucon is always the bravest of the brave, and he showed it then. He would not accept Thrasymachos' great renunciation, but said, "Socrates, do you want really and truly to persuade us that in every way it is better to be just than unjust, or only to seem to have persuaded us?"

"Really and truly," I said, "is what I would choose, if the choice were with me."

"Then," he said, "you are not doing what you wish. For tell me—do you think that there is a kind of good which we should be glad to have for its own sake alone, not because we desire what comes from it? Like joy, and those pleasures which are harmless, and afterwards nothing happens because of them except that you keep on being happy."

"Yes," I said, "I think there is something like that."

"And again one kind that we love both for its own sake and for what comes from it? For example, to have good sense, and to see, and to be healthy; such things I suppose we welcome for both reasons."

"Yes," I said.

"And do you see a third kind of good which athletic sports belong to, and to be cured by treatment when sick, and the art of healing, and the other ways of making money? These are laborious, you might say, but they give us benefit; we should not care to have them alone for their own sakes, but for the sake of the wages and the other things which come from them."

"Yes, true," I said, "there is also this third kind. But what then?"

"Where do you put justice?" he said. "In which class?"

"My own opinion is," I said, "that it belongs to the noblest class, which is to be loved both for its own sake, and for what comes from it, if you mean to be perfectly happy."

"Well," said he, "that's not what the many think. They put it in the laborious class, which has to be practised both for its wages and the praises of public opinion, but for its own sake is to be avoided as hard."

"I know," said I, "that they think so, and I know that is just why Thrasymachos has been finding fault with it all this while, and praising injustice. But I am a bad pupil, I fear."

"Do let me speak too," he said, "and see if you agree with

me. I think Thrasymachos has let himself be charmed by you like a charmed snake sooner than he ought; but I am not yet satisfied with the proof offered about justice or injustice. For I desire to hear both what each is, and what power each has in itself, when it is in the soul, and to leave aside the wages and what comes from each. That's what I will do, then, if you please. I will run over Thrasymachos' account once more; first I will say what most people think justice is and whence it comes; secondly, that all who practise it practise unwillingly, as a necessary thing but not as a good; thirdly, that they have some reason in that; for to hear them talk it does seem that the life of the unjust is much better than the life of the just. I don't think so myself, Socrates, please understand me, but I am puzzled when this is dinned into my ears; this is what I hear from Thrasymachos and countless others, but I have never heard any account of justice such as I want, to show it is better than injustice, and I want to hear it commended for its own sake. And I think I am most likely to hear that from you. Therefore I will strain every nerve to praise the unjust life, and in speaking I will show how I wish to hear you speak, when you dispraise injustice and praise justice. Does that meet your wishes?"

"Most assuredly," said I, "what else could please me so much to speak and hear about often?"

"Quite right," said he, "and first hear what I have to say, as I promised, on what justice is, and whence it comes.

"They say, then, that to be unjust is good, and to suffer injustice is bad, and the excess of evil in suffering injustice is greater than the excess of good in being unjust; so that when people do and suffer injustice in dealing with one another, and taste both, those who cannot both escape the one and take the other think it profitable to make an agreement neither to do nor to suffer injustice; from this they begin to make laws and compacts among themselves, and they name the injunction of the law lawful and just. This, they say, is the origin and nature of justice, which is something between the best, namely to do wrong and not to pay for it, and the worst, to suffer wrong and not to be able to get vengeance. Justice, they say, is between these two, and they are content with it not as a good, but as honoured in the weakness of injustice; since one who was able to do injustice, if he were truly a man, would never make an agreement with anyone neither to wrong nor to be wronged—he would be mad to do so. Then this and such is the nature of justice, Socrates, and such is its origin, as they say.

"But we could perceive most clearly that those who practise

justice do so unwillingly and because they cannot do injustice, if we should put a case in imagination; let us grant licence to each, both just and unjust, to do whatever he wishes, and let us follow this up by seeing where his desire will lead each. Then we should catch the just man in the act; he would go the same way as the unjust through self-seeking, the way which every creature naturally follows as a good, only the law leads him forcibly astray to honour fair dealing. This licence I speak of would be very much the same as the power which Gyges had, the ancestor of Gyges the Lydian. They say he was a shepherd serving the then ruler of Lydia. A great storm came and an earthquake; and there was a split in the earth, and a chasm opened in the place where he kept his flocks; he saw it, and wondered, and went down. There he saw many wonderful things which the story tells, and in particular a brazen horse, hollow, with windows in the side; he peeped in and saw a dead body, as it appeared, larger than human, with nothing on but a golden ring on the hand, which he took off and came out again. It was the custom among the shepherds to hold a monthly meeting, and then report to the king all about the flocks; this meeting he attended wearing the ring. As he sat with the others, he happened to turn the collet of the ring round towards himself to the inside of his hand. As soon as this was done he became invisible to the company, and they spoke of him as if he had left the place. He was surprised, and fingered the ring again, turning the collet outwards, and when he turned it he became visible. Noticing that, he made trial of the ring, to see if it had that power; and he found that whenever he turned the collet inside, he was invisible, when he turned it outside, visible. After he found this out he managed to be appointed one of the messengers to the king; when he got there, he seduced the king's wife, and with her set upon the king, and killed him, and seized the empire. Then if there could be two such rings, and if the just man put on one and the unjust the other, no one, as it would be thought, would be so adamantine as to abide in the practise of justice, no one could endure to hold back from another's goods and not to touch, when it was in his power to take what he would even out of the market without fear, and to go into any house and lie with anyone he wished, and to kill or set free from prison those he might wish, and to do anything else in the world like a very god. And in doing so he would do just the same as the other; both would go the same way. Surely one would call this a strong proof that no one is just willingly but only under compulsion, believing that it is not a good to him personally; since wherever each thinks he will be able to do injustice, he does injustice. There is more personal profit, as everyone clearly believes, from injustice than from justice, and he is right in his belief, as those will say who give this account of the matter; since if anyone had this licence and yet would do no injustice or touch other men's property, he would be thought a miserable fool by any who perceived it. But they would praise him to each other, deceiving each other for fear of suffering injustice themselves. So much then for that.

"We shall be able to judge rightly between those two lives only if we confront the superlatively just and the superlatively unjust, and not otherwise. How do we set them out clearly against each other? Thus: Let us take nothing of injustice from the unjust, and nothing of justice from the just, but suppose each of them perfect in his own practice.

"First of all, then, the unjust man: Let him act as expert craftsmen do. The tiptop pilot, for example, or physician, distinguishes what is possible and what is impossible in his art. He undertakes the one and not the other; besides, if he happens to make any slip, he is able to recover. Just so the unjust man will undertake his injustices in the right way, and then he must not be found out if he is to be great in wrongdoing; one who is caught must be considered a bad workman, for the extreme injustice is to be thought just when one is not. So we must grant to the perfectly unjust perfect injustice and take nothing away; but we must allow the one who does the greatest wrongs to get the greatest fame for justice, and to recover if he does make a slip. He must be able to persuade if he is denounced for his wrongdoings; and to compel whenever force is needed, because of his courage and strength and because of his store of wealth and friends.

"Having set up this unjust man as having these qualities, let us in our theory set against him the just; a man simple and generous, one who wishes not to seem good, but to be good, as Aeschylus says. So we must take away the seeming. For if he is to be thought just, honour and gifts will be his because he is thought just, and then it would not be clear whether he were such because of his justice or because of the gifts and honours. He must be stripped naked of all but justice, and made the opposite of the former; doing no wrong, let him have the greatest possible repute of injustice, that he may be tested for justice through not being softened by infamy and all that comes of it. So let him go on his way unchanging until death, believed to be unjust all through life while he is just; that both may go to the extreme, one of justice and one of injustice, and it may be judged which of them is happier and more fortunate."

"Lord bless us, my dear Glaucon!" I said. "How forcibly

THE REPUBLIC Book II *(360D–362E)* 159

you do carve them out and polish them up, like a pair of statues for a competition!"

"I do my best," he said. "There they both are; and, as I think, it is no longer difficult to discuss what kind of life awaits each. So now I must go on; and if my words are rather rough, don't suppose me to be speaking, Socrates, but those who praise injustice above justice. This is what they will say: The just man in those circumstances will be scourged, racked, chained, have his eyes burnt out; at last, after every kind of misery, he will be set up on a pole;[1] and he will know that one ought to wish not to be just, but to seem just. And the words of Aeschylus[2] were, then, much more rightly applicable to the unjust. For they will say that really the unjust man practises a thing which clings close to truth, and he does not live for opinion—he wishes not to seem but to be unjust,

> Reaping, from furrow deep, within his mind,
> Whence careful counsels grow.

First he will hold public office because he is thought to be just; then he will marry into any family he chooses, and give his children to marry anyone he chooses, and make partnerships and contracts with any he likes, and besides all this he will benefit by gaining profit because he does not mind being unjust. In legal actions public or private, he will overcome and get the better of his enemies; and by this he will grow rich and able to benefit a friend and hurt an enemy, and to sacrifice and dedicate offerings to the gods properly and magnificently, and to serve gods and men, if he will, much better than the just, so that he may reasonably expect that the gods will care for him more than for the just man. So they say, Socrates, that both gods and men have provided life better for him than for the just."

When Glaucon finished, I had in mind to say something to this, but his brother Adeimantos interrupted.

"Surely you don't think, Socrates," he said, "that the case has been stated completely enough?"

"What else is there?" I asked.

"The very thing," said he, "which ought most to be said, has not been said!"

"I see," said I, "it's the old saying, 'A brother to a man's help'! So back him up and help him, if he leaves anything out; though even what he has been saying already is enough to lay me flat, helpless to render aid to justice."

He answered, "Nonsense! But listen to something more. We ought to run over also the arguments which are the opposite

[1] Crucified. Cf. Luke xxiii: 33, 47.
[2] Aeschylus, *Seven Against Thebes*, 592-3.

of the ones put forward by our friend—arguments which praise justice and dispraise injustice, to make clearer what I think Glaucon means. Fathers, of course, admonish their sons, and so do all those who have the care of others, and tell them one must be just; but they do not commend justice itself, only the good reputation which comes from it, that one who is thought to be just may get from this opinion offices and marriages and the other things which Glaucon mentioned just now, which come to the just man from his good reputation. But the people I am talking of speak still more about reputations. They throw in men's good reputations among the gods, and they can mention a heap of good things for the pious which they say the gods give. Take the noble poets Hesiod and Homer, for example. Hesiod says the gods make oak trees provide for the just:

Acorns upon the top, bees in the middle,
And the fleecy sheep (says he) are heavy with their wool[1]

and many other good things akin to these. The other says very much the same:

> For a good, upright king who fears the gods
> And upholds justice, the black earth brings forth
> Barley and wheat, the trees are heavy with fruit,
> The sheep have many lambs, the sea gives fish.[2]

Musaios and his son have still gayer gifts for the just from the gods; for they take them to Hades in their story and recline them at table, and provide a banquet of the saints, where with garlands on their heads they spend all their time in carousing. Thus they consider the finest wages of virtue to be eternal intoxication. Others make the heavenly wages last for generations to come; the pious man, they say, who keeps his oath, leaves children's children to follow and his race remains. For such things then, and others too, they commend justice; but the impious and unjust they bury deep down in the mud in the next world, and compel them to fetch water in a sieve. While they still live they bring them into evil repute; and all the punishments which Glaucon recounted about the just considered to be unjust, these the poets tell of the unjust, but they have nothing else. So much for the praise and dispraise of the two.

"Besides this, Socrates, consider another kind of speaking about justice and injustice, as told by poets and other men too. All sing with one mouth how beautiful is temperance[3] and

[1] Hesiod, *Works and Days*, 232.
[2] *Odyssey* xix. 109.
[3] σωφροσύνη is the word here used; it is usually translated "temperance" or "self-control." A closer rendering would be "sound-mindedness"; the word always implies both feeling and intellect.

justice. But it is a hard thing and laborious; licentiousness[1] and injustice are pleasant and easy to get and ugly only in opinion and custom. Unjust things are more profitable than just for the most part, they say; bad men rich and holding other powers they call happy, and they are ready to honour them willingly in public and in private, and to dishonour and despise any who are at all weak and poor, although they admit they are better than the others. But in all these things the most surprising is what they say of the gods and virtue; that the gods apparently have allotted to many good men misfortunes and an evil life, but to the opposite an opposite portion. Begging priests and seers are at the doors of the rich, persuading them that they themselves have power, granted them from the gods by sacrifices and incantations, if any wrong has been done by the man himself or his forefathers, to heal it with pleasures and feasts; and if he wishes to wound an enemy, at small expense they will damage just and unjust alike by certain charms and spells, because thus they persuade the gods to be their own servants. And they call in poets to witness all these tales. Some sing about the plentiful ease of vice—

> Vice can be found in plenty and with ease;
> She lives hard by, and smooth is the road to Vice:
> But sweat the gods have placed in front of Virtue,[2]

and a road long and uphill. Others will bring Homer to witness the seduction of gods by mankind, when he said,

> Prayer can persuade the gods themselves; at times
> With sacrifice and gentle supplication,
> Drink offering, fragrant smoke, mankind may turn
> The gods by praying, should one transgress and sin.[3]

They bring in a whole crowd of books by Mousaios and Orpheus. These, they say, were descendants of Moon and the Muses, in whose names they do their rites; and they persuade cities as well as private men that there are ransoms and purifications for sin by means of sacrifices and pleasurable sport while men yet live, and others for the dead, which they call mystic rites, which absolve us from evil in the next world, whereas without sacrifice terrible things await people.

"All these things, Socrates my dear friend, so many and so great, which they say about virtue and vice, and how both gods and men respect them—how do we think they will work on the souls of young people when they hear them—at least those who are clever, and able to flit from one thing to another, and to gather from all they hear what one ought to be, and

---

[1] Literally, "unchasteness," unchastity in all passions and conduct, licentiousness.
[2] Hesiod, *Works and Days*, 287-9.
[3] *Iliad* ix. 497-501, slightly changed.

what way to go, in order to make the best of life? Most likely a young man would ask himself Pindar's question:

> By justice, or by crooked craft—
> A loftier tower[1]

shall I climb, and live out my life with that rampart around me? What they say is, that to be just, unless I am believed to be just, is no profit to me, but plain loss, toil and trouble; but if I manage to get the name of being just when I am not, a heavenly life is what they say! Then since 'the seeming,' as wise men tell me, 'overpowers even the truth,' since this is lord of happiness, to this I must turn my whole heart! Porches and pretences I must build around me, and paint an impressionist scene of virtue about me, and drag behind me the fox of most wise Archilochos, greedy and crafty. But, someone says, it is not easy to be wicked and not to be found out. Ah, but nothing is easy, we will say, none of the great things. However, if we are to be happy, this is the way to go, where the trail of our stories leads. To keep all secret, we will make clubs and conspiracies; there are professors of persuasion who teach the art of speaking to assemblies and courts; and thus we will now persuade, and now compel, so that we may gain the advantage and not be punished. 'Yes, but the gods cannot be deceived or compelled!' Why, if there are none, or if they care nothing for mankind, we need care nothing in case they find out; if there are gods, and if they do care, we know of them and hear of them only from the tales and genealogies of poets; and these very same do say that sacrifices and gentle prayers and votive offerings can persuade them and seduce them. We must believe the poets in both, or in neither; if we have to obey, after all, let us do wrong and sacrifice from our ill-gotten gains. If we are just, we shall certainly be unpunished by the gods, but we shall refuse the gains of injustice; unjust, we shall have the gains, and then if we transgress and sin, we will pray and beseech them and come off unpunished after all. 'Yes, but in the next world we shall have justice done upon us for our injustice here, either ourselves or our children or children's children!' 'Ah, my friend,' the calculating man will say, 'the mystic rites, again, have great power, and the absolving gods; so the greatest cities declare, and those sons of the gods, who have become poets and interpreters of the gods, the ones who give all this information.'

"Then what reasoning would lead us to choose justice rather than the supreme injustice? If we take that along with a false outward show of propriety, we shall fare well before gods and men both living and after death, as the words of the multi-

[1] *Fragment* 213 in the Loeb Pindar.

tude and of the best authorities declare. To judge from all that has been said, Socrates, what could possibly induce a man to choose to have any value for justice, if he has power of soul or wealth or body or family? He would just laugh at anyone praising justice! Well then, see, if anyone can show what we have said to be false, if anyone is sufficiently convinced that justice is best, he can find many excuses for the unjust; he is not angry with them, but he knows that of all men no one ever is willingly just except one who is born with a divine hatred of injustice or one who has learnt reasons why he should eschew it; otherwise cowardice or old age or some other weakness makes him dispraise injustice because he is unable to do it. That is true, clearly; for the first of such men who gets the power is the first to be unjust as far as he is able. And the only cause of all this is that from which we started, my friend and I, when we said to you, Socrates, 'Here is a surprising thing! All you who profess to commend justice, beginning with the primeval heroes, all those whose words remain, down to the present generation of men—not one of you has ever praised justice or dispraised injustice except in terms of the reputations and honours and gifts which come from them. What each of them is, by its own power, in the soul of him that has it, hidden from gods and men, no one has ever described properly either in poetry or in private talk; no one has shown that injustice is the worst evil that the soul has in itself, and justice the greatest good. If you had all said this from the beginning, and if you had proved it to us in our youth, we should not be guarding against injustice from each other, but each one would be his own best guard, for fear of doing wrong and being housemate to the worst of evils.'

"Thrasymachos and others would no doubt say this and even more, Socrates, about justice and injustice. They would interchange their powers, like common men, as I think; but I have tried my best to speak as strongly as I can, because I longed to hear you say the opposite; for I don't want to hide anything from you. So I beg you not simply to show in argument that justice is stronger than injustice; we want to know what each of them does, by its own nature, to its possessor, which makes the one a good thing, the other bad. Leave out the reputations, as Glaucon asked you; for if you do not take away the true ones on each side and add the false ones, we shall say you are praising not justice but the seeming, and dispraising not injustice but the seeming, that you are only exhorting the unjust not to be found out; we shall think you agree with Thrasymachos that justice is another's good and the advantage of the stronger, and that injustice is profit and advantage to oneself but against the advantage of the weaker. You have agreed that justice is one of the greatest goods, those which are worth getting for what comes from them but much more for their own sakes, such as sight, hearing, sense, health and all the other goods which are creative by their own nature and not by opinion; then show that justice has exactly this in it—that it blesses the possessor in itself, and that injustice damages him. Leave wages and opinions for others to praise. I might accept such praises from others, if they praised justice and dispraised injustice for such reasons, if they lauded or laughed at their reputations and wages, but not from you, unless you told me to do it, because all your life you have been investigating this matter and nothing else. Then pray don't prove to us only that justice is stronger than injustice, but show what it is that each of them does by its own pervasive[1] action to its possessor, whether gods and men notice it or not, which makes the one a good thing, the other bad."

I had always admired the character of Glaucon and Adeimantos, but I never had been so pleased as I was when I heard them now. I said, "You are true sons of your honoured father, and Glaucon's admirer began his elegies with a line that fits you not badly, when he sang the praises of your distinguished services at the battle of Megara

> O sons of Ariston[2] the Excellent, offspring divine
> Of an illustrious father!

That seems to me, my friends, to be very apt; for you have a really divine inspiration[3] if you refuse to be convinced that injustice be better than justice, when you can put the case for it so ably. And I think you truly are not convinced. I judge that from your general characters, since from your arguments alone I should disbelieve you; but the more I believe you, the less I know what to do about it. I don't see how to help you, and indeed I think I have not the power myself; my evidence for this is that I did think that what I said to Thrasymachos proved that justice was better than injustice; you would not accept that. But then I don't see how I can refuse to help. I fear it would be a real sin and shame to stand by and hear justice being slandered, and to shirk it and refuse to help while there is breath in my body and I can utter a word. The best thing is then to do what I can to defend her."

Then Glaucon and the rest begged me by all means to help and not to drop the matter; they begged me to search out

[1] Literally, "itself through itself."
[2] The father's name, Ariston, meant "Excellent" or "Best," and it is an indirect compliment here. The two young men were Plato's brothers. It was a great family.
[3] They spoke as the mouthpiece of God without regard to logic or eloquence or anything else, like poets. See the dialogue *Ion*.

thoroughly what each is, and which way the truth lies about the benefit of each. I said then what I thought: "The search we undertake is no small matter, but one that needs a sharp eye, as it seems to me. Well then, since we are not clever, I think," said I, "that we should make the following kind of search for our object. Suppose we had been told by someone to read an inscription in small letters a good way off, and we had not very sharp sight; and then someone noticed the same inscription somewhere else, in larger letters on a larger tablet, that would be a great piece of luck, I think. We could read the large ones first, and then examine the smaller, to see if they were the same."

"That's true enough," said Adeimantos, "but what do you see like it in the search about justice?"

"I'll tell you," said I. "There is justice of one man, we say, and justice of a whole city, I suppose?"

"Certainly."

"Well, a city is larger than one man?"

"Of course it is," he said.

"Then perhaps there would be a larger justice in the city and easier to understand. If you like, then, let us enquire first what it is in the cities; then we will examine it in the single man, looking for the likeness of the larger in the shape of the smaller."

"That is a good proposal," said he.

"Then," said I, "suppose we should imagine we see a city in the making, we might see its justice, too, in the making, and the injustice?"

"Possibly," he said.

"So when it is made, there is hope to see what we seek more easily?"

"Yes, a good hope."

"Then ought we to try to do this task? I think it will be no small labour; so pray consider."

"We have considered," said Adeimantos. "Please do so."

"Very well then," said I. "A city, I take it, comes into being because each of us is not self-sufficient but needs many things. Can you think any other beginning could found a city?"

"No," said he.

"So we each take in different persons for different needs, and needing many things we gather many persons into one dwelling place as partners and helpers, and to this common settlement we give the name of city. Is that correct?"

"Certainly."

"Then one man gives a share of something to another or

takes a share, if he gives or takes, because he thinks he will be the better for it?"

"Yes."

"Now then," said I, "let us imagine that we make our city from the beginning. Our need will make it, as it seems."

"Of course."

"Well, first indeed and greatest of our needs is the provision of food that we may live and be."

"Assuredly."

"Second, the need of housing, third of clothes and so forth."

"That is true."

"The next thing to ask is," said I, "how the city shall suffice for all this provision. Will not one be a farmer, one a builder, one a weaver? Shall we add a shoemaker to the list and someone else to look after the body's needs?"

"Certainly."

"Then the smallest possible city will consist of four or five men?"

"So it seems."

"Very good. Must each of these contribute his work to all in common—I mean must the farmer, who is only one, provide food for four and spend four times as much time and trouble in providing food, and share it with the others; or shall he neglect them, and provide only food for himself, the fourth part of the food, in a fourth part of the time, and spend the other three parts of the time one on the house, one on the clothes, one on the shoes? Is he to avoid the bother of sharing, and only to look after himself and his own affairs?"

Adeimantos said, "Perhaps the first way is easier, Socrates."

"That is quite likely, by heaven," said I, "for it comes into my mind when you say it, that we are not born all exactly alike but different in nature, for all sorts of different jobs, don't you think so?"

"Yes, I do."

"Then would one man do his work better working at many crafts, or one man at one craft?"

"One man at one craft."

"And again, I think, it is clear that a man just wastes his labour if he misses the time when it is wanted."

"Yes, that is clear."

"For I don't imagine the work will await the workman's leisure; the workman must follow his work and not just take it by the way."

"He must, indeed!"

"Consequently, more things of each kind are produced, and better, and easier, when one man works at one thing, which suits his nature, and at the proper time, and leaves the others alone."

"Most certainly."

"Then we need more citizens, Adeimantos, more than four to provide all we said. For the farmer, as it seems, will not make his own plow, if it is to be a good plow, nor his mattock, nor the other tools for working the land. Nor will the builder, and he, too, wants many others. So also the weaver and the shoemaker."

"True."

"Carpenters, then, and smiths, and many other such craftsmen, become partners in our little city and make it big."

"Certainly."

"Yet it would still not be so very large, even if we were to add oxherds and shepherds and the other herdsmen, that the farmers might have oxen for the plow, and the builders draught-animals to use along with the farmers for carriage, and that the weavers and shoemakers might have fleeces and skins."

"And not so very small either, if it had all these!"

"Furthermore," I said, "to settle the city in such a place that imports will not be needed is almost impossible."

"Yes, impossible."

"Then it will need others to import what it wants from another city."

"It will."

"But again, if our assistant goes empty, without taking with him any of the things needed by those from whom people get what they need, he will return empty, won't he?"

"I think so."

"Then they must make at home not merely enough for themselves, but enough for those people of whom they have need, and such things as those same people need."

"So they must."

"More farmers, then, and more other craftsmen will be necessary for our city."

"Yes, indeed."

"And more of the other assistants, I suppose, to export and import the various things. These are traders, aren't they?"

"Yes, they are."

"So we shall want traders too."

"Certainly."

"And if the trade goes by sea, many others will be wanted besides who understand commerce overseas."

"Many others, indeed."

"Now, in the city itself, how will they exchange the things

which each class makes? For that is the reason why we founded the city as a partnership."

"By selling and buying," he said, "that is clear, surely."

"We shall have a market, then, as a result of this, and coinage as a token of the exchange."

"By all means."

"Suppose the farmer, then, brings in some of his products to market, or suppose any of the other craftsmen do, and suppose he comes at a time when those who want to exchange his goods for their own are not there, he will sit in the market and waste time from his work?"

"Not at all," said he; "there will be some who, seeing this, appoint themselves for this particular purpose. In cities properly managed these are generally the men weakest in body and useless for other work. They must remain on the spot, about the market, and exchange money for the goods with those who want to sell, or give them goods for money if any people want to buy anything."

"Then," said I, "this need creates a class of shopkeepers in our city. We call them shopkeepers or retail dealers, don't we, when they are settled in the market to serve us in selling and buying, but those who travel from city to city we call traders or merchants?"

"Certainly."

"And there are others, I believe, who serve us, who have strength enough for the labours of bodily work, but nothing particular in their minds which makes them worthy to be partners. These sell the use of their strength for a price which they call wages, and therefore, no doubt, they are called wage-earners; what do you say?"

"I agree."

"Wage-earners also then help to fill up our city."

"Yes."

"Now then, Adeimantos, has our city grown to perfection?"

"Perhaps."

"Then where would justice and injustice be in it? What place has it among those we have described?"

"I do not quite see, Socrates," he said, "unless perhaps in some need which all these actually have in their dealings together."

"Well perhaps you are right," I said, "we must try and see, without shrinking.

"First let us consider how, thus provided, they will spend their lives. Making food and wine and clothes and shoes, I suppose. They must build houses; in summer they will generally work stripped and barefoot, in winter with wraps on and their feet sufficiently protected. To feed them they will make meal from barley and flour from wheat; some they will cook, some they will knead into fine flat-cakes and loaves which they lay on reeds or clean leaves; they will lie on pallets strewn with yew and myrtle, enjoying good cheer with their children, and drinking it down with wine, garlanded and singing hymns to the gods, pleased with each other's company, having no more children than they can afford in their care against poverty or war."

Glaucon now interrupted: "Nothing more, then?" he said. "You seem to give the men no relish at their feast!"

"True," I said, "I forgot that; they will have something more,[1] salt, of course, and olives, and cheese, onions and greens to boil, such as they have in the country. And I suppose we shall give them dessert, figs and chickpeas and beans, and they will toast myrtle berries and acorns[2] before the fire, with a drop to drink, not too much. So they will spend their days in health and peace, living to old age as you might expect and leaving another such life to their children."

He said then, "But if you were founding a city of pigs, Socrates, what other fodder than this would you give them?"

"Why, how ought they to live?" said I.

"In the usual manner," he said. "Let them recline on couches, if they don't want to be uncomfortable, and dine off tables, and have the relishes and dessert which people have now."

"Oh, I understand," said I. "The question before us is not simply how a city comes into being, but a luxurious city. That's not a bad notion, perhaps. A city of that sort might show us possibly how justice and injustice grow up in states. However, the real city seems to me what we have described, a healthy sort; but if you wish us to examine one in a high fever, there is nothing to hinder. Some people will not be satisfied with a life like this, as it seems; they will have their couches and tables and other furniture, they will have fine food, too, and ointments and incense and pretty girls and cakes, all sorts of each! Then what we said at first will no longer be the bare necessaries, I mean houses and clothes and boots; no, we must get painting on the go, and embroidery, we must provide gold and ivory and everything of that sort! Is that so?"

"Yes," he said.

"Then we must make the city larger again," I said, "for that healthy city is not enough now; it must be swollen and filled

---

[1] Glaucon uses a word ὄψον which properly means "relish," usually meat or fish, eaten with bread. Socrates misunderstands him on purpose.

[2] φηγός, edible acorns from a kind of oak, not the Latin *fagus* (beech).

with people and things which are not in cities from necessity—hunters of all sorts, imitative artists, crowds concerned with figures and colours, crowds with music, poets with their attendants—reciters, actors, choric dancers, contractors, makers of all sorts of furniture and fittings, not forgetting those who provide the adornment of women. And besides, we shall want more servants. Don't you think we shall want boys' tutors, wet-nurses and nannies, tirewomen, barbers, cooks and pastrycooks? And besides we shall want swineherds; there were none in our first city, because they were not wanted, but they will be wanted in this one, and lots of all kinds of other pasturing animals will be wanted if anyone is to eat them. That's all true, isn't it?"

"Quite so."

"And shan't we need physicians much more than before in such a manner of life?"

"Yes, indeed, we shall."

"Take the land also; what was enough to feed them then will not be enough now, it will be too small, don't you think so?"

"Yes," he said.

"Then we must take a slice of our neighbours' land, if we are to have enough for grazing and plowing, and they also must take a slice of ours, if they, too, pass the bounds of the necessary, and give themselves to the boundless getting of wealth."

"That must be so, Socrates," he said.

"The next thing is, we shall go to war, Glaucon, or what will happen?"

"That is what will happen," he said.

"Don't let us say yet," said I, "whether war produces either anything bad or anything good, but only that we have discovered the origin of war now, from that whence cities get most of their troubles[1] both for each citizen and for the whole public."

"Certainly."

"Then, my friend," I said, "we want a still larger city; not a little larger, but a whole army larger, that it may go out and fight against all attackers in defence of those we have described and for all we have."

"Why, aren't the people enough?" he said.

"No," said I, "for you and we all made that clear when we were moulding the city. I think we agreed, if you remember, that it was impossible for one man to exercise many arts well."

"Quite true," said he.

[1] From greed, that is; the source of all evil, in Plato's mind.

"Very well, then," said I. "The struggle of war is an art, isn't it?"

"Very much so," said he.

"If so, must we care for the art of shoemaking but not for the art of war?"

"Oh no," said he.

"Well, we forbade the shoemaker to try to be a farmer or weaver or builder; he was to make shoes, that the work of shoemaking might be properly done for us. Just so we sorted out the others, according to their natural gifts; each was to leave other things alone, and to spend his life on this one occupation and to lose no chance of doing his work well; and is it not most important that the business of war shall be well done? Or is that so easy that even a farmer shall be a man of war, and a shoemaker, and anyone else working at any other art? Even a checkers player or a dicer could never be a good one if he treated it as a sideline instead of practising from boyhood. Is it enough to pick up a shield or some other war tool and weapon, and you will be able on that very day to be a competent fighter in the heavy-arm battle or in the other branches of warfare? No other tool will ever make one a craftsman or athlete by just picking it up, and it will be useless for one who has not acquired its science and has not given it enough practice."

"If only that were so," he said, "tools would be precious things!"

"Then," I said, "since the guardian's work is the greatest, it needs more leisure than all the others, and more practice, and further, more skill and care."

"That is my view," he said.

"Does it need also a nature fit for this pursuit?"

"Of course."

"It will be our business then, as it seems, to pick out if we can which persons and which natures are fitted to guard the city."

"So it will."

"I declare," said I, "this is no small task we have taken upon us! But we must not be cowards, as far as our powers allow."

"No, indeed," he said.

"Do you think there is much difference," I said, "between a well-bred dog and a well-bred lad[1] for this guarding?"

"What do you mean, exactly?"

"Each of them must be keen in perception, and light in chasing the instant that he perceives, and strong also if he

[1] He puns on the words *skylax* and *phylax*, a doggie and a bobby (British nickname for a policeman).

catches and has to fight it out."

"Yes," he said, "they want all those things."

"And brave too, if he is to fight well."

"Of course."

"Will anything want to be brave if it is not high-spirited in temper, whether horse or dog or any other animal? Have you not noticed how invincible and irresistible is high temper? With this present, every soul is fearless against all and unconquerable."

"Yes, I have noticed that."

"Then what the guardian must be in body is clear."

"Yes."

"And in soul he must be of spirited temper."

"That also."

"Well," said I, "if such is their nature, how will they avoid being savage to the other citizens and to each other?"

"Not easily, I vow," said he.

"Yet they must be gentle towards their own people, but rough towards their enemies; otherwise they will not wait for others to destroy them, they will do it themselves first."

"True," said he.

"Then what shall we do?" said I. "Where shall we find a nature which is both gentle and full of high temper? For these are opposite things."

"So it appears."

"Yet if either of the two be lacking, a good guardian he will never be; these look like impossibilities, and it follows that a good guardian cannot possibly be."

"It looks like that," he said.

I felt quite at a loss, but as I thought over what went before, I said, "We are naturally at a loss, my friend; for we have forgotten the comparison which we made."

"How so?"

"We did not notice that there are natures such as we thought there were not, which have all these opposite things."

"Why, where?"

"It may be seen in other animals, but specially in the one we compared with the guardian. You know, I suppose, that the character of well-bred dogs is naturally to be as gentle as can be to those they are used to, those they know, but the opposite to strangers."

"Oh yes, I know that."

"Then the thing is possible," I said, "and we don't go against nature in seeking such a guardian."

"It seems not."

"Do you not think, then, that one who is to be guardian-like needs something more besides a spirited temper, and that is to be in his nature a lover of wisdom?"[1]

"How so?" he said. "I don't understand."

"You will see another thing in dogs," I said, "and it is a wonderful thing in the creature."

"What?"

"Whenever he sees a stranger, he is angry, although the man has done him no harm; when he sees anyone he knows, he welcomes him, although the man may have done him no good. Has that never surprised you?"

"No," he said, "I never paid any attention to that before, but he does, it is clear."

"But there is something refined in that feeling in his nature, and it shows a real love of wisdom."

"Why, how?" he asked.

"Because he recognises friendly and hostile looks simply and solely from knowing one and not knowing the other. Then how could he not be a lover of learning if he distinguishes his own and others' by understanding and ignorance?"

"Of course he must be," said he.

"But surely," said I, "love of learning and love of wisdom are the same thing."

"The same," he said.

"Then we can confidently set down the same as true of a man also; if he is to be gentle to his own people, whom he knows, he must be a lover of learning and a true lover of wisdom."

"Let us suppose that," he said.

"A lover of wisdom, then, and high-spirited in temper, and quick and strong, will be the one who is to be a good and true guardian of the city?"

"Most assuredly indeed," he said.

"Then that would be the basis of his character. But how shall our guardians be trained and educated? And if we consider that, will it help us on towards discovering what is the reason for our whole enquiry, how justice and injustice come up in a city? We must not leave the discussion incomplete, but we would not make it tediously long."

And Glaucon's brother said, "Indeed, I expect this enquiry will be of great help for our purpose."

"Then certainly, my dear Adeimantos," I said, "we must not let it go, even if it turns out to be rather long."

"No, indeed."

"Then let us imagine their education, as if we were just

[1] The Greek word is *philosophos*.

telling stories to amuse a long leisure hour."

"That is what we must do."

"Then what is this education? It seems really hard to find one better than our own, which long time has discovered. That is, in short, gymnastic for the body and music[1] for the soul."

"It is."

"Shall we begin our education with music before gymnastic?"

"Very well."

"In music," I said, "you include tales, don't you?"

"Of course."

"There are two kinds of tales, one true and the other false?"

"Yes."

"And we must educate by both, the false ones first?"

"I don't understand what you mean."

"Don't you understand," I said, "that first we tell fables to the children? These are mostly false, but there is some truth in them, and we use fables for the children before athletics."

"That is true."

"That's what I meant by saying that music must be taken up before gymnastic."

"Quite right," he said.

"Now you know the beginning is always the chief thing in every process, especially for whatever is young and tender; for it is then most easily moulded and each takes the shape which you wish to impress upon each."

"Exactly."

"Then shall we just carelessly allow the children to hear any chance fables moulded by chance persons, and to receive in their souls opinions which are generally contrary to those which we believe they ought to have when they grow up?"

"Most certainly not."

"Then first, as it seems, we must set up a censorship over the fable-makers, and approve any good fable they make, and disapprove the bad; those which are approved we will persuade the mothers and nurses to tell the children, and to mould the souls of the children by the fables even more carefully than the bodies by their hands.[2] Most of those they tell now must be thrown away."

[1] "Music" means more in Greek than in English; it includes poetry and letters and things intellectual. The discussion about music for education continues to p. 202, Book III. (It might be mentioned here that the division of the *Republic* into the ten "books" was not made until centuries after Plato wrote it.)
[2] A sort of massage was usual in the nursery.

"What sort do you mean?" he said.

"In the greater fables," I said, "we shall see also the less, for I suppose the same stamp is on great and small, and they have very much the same power in them. Don't you think so?"

"Yes, I do," said he, "but I don't understand which you call the great ones."

"Those which Hesiod and Homer have told us, and the other poets, for these have told us, and still tell us, false fables which they composed."

"Which do you mean," said he, "and what fault do you find in them?"

"One that must be condemned first and most of all, especially if it is an ugly falsehood."

"What is that?"

"When one portrays badly in words what the gods and heroes are, like a painter who paints a portrait not in the least like what he wants to portray."

"Yes, indeed," he said, "it is right to condemn such things. But give some examples."

"First," I said, "the greatest falsehood about the greatest persons was an ugly one, how Uranos did what Hesiod said he did, and how Cronos had his revenge;[1] and what Cronos did, and what his son did to him—even if these things were true, I did not think they ought to be just carelessly told before simple young people; they were best left in silence, but if it were necessary to tell them, as few as possible should hear them as a dead secret, and for that mystery there should be sacrificed, not a pig,[2] but some huge monster, so that the fewest possible in number should ever have heard these tales."

"Oh yes," he said, "those are hard sayings indeed."

"And indeed not to be told at all in our city, Adeimantos," I said; "a young man should not be allowed to hear that he would be doing nothing surprising if he did the worst of wrongs, even if he chastised an erring father in every possible way, but that he would be doing the same as the first and greatest of the gods."

"No, by heaven," he said, "and I don't think myself such things are proper to tell."

"And he must never hear at all that gods war against gods and plot and fight (for that is not true either), if our future guardians of the city are to believe it a very ugly thing to take offence among themselves easily. Far be it from us to

---

[1] The story is summed up by Rose, *Handbook of Greek Mythology*, Methuen, p. 22. An ugly tale of brutality, treachery and mutilation.
[2] Pigs were sacrificed at the mysteries of Eleusis.

fable about wars with the giants, and embroider them on robes, or all those multifarious quarrels of gods and heroes with their friends and kindred. But if we are to persuade them somehow that there has never been any quarrel among any of the citizens, and the thing is simply not done,[1] that rather is the sort of thing to be told by old men and old women to the little children straightaway, and when they grow older, we must compel the poets also to make fables in much the same sense. How Hera was tied up by her son,[2] and how Hephaistos was thrown out of heaven by his father when he wanted to save his mother from a beating, and the battles between gods which Homer describes,[3] we must not admit into our city, whether they are explained as allegory or not. For the young person is not able to judge what is allegory and what is not; but he will keep in his mind indelible and unchangeable whatever opinions he receives at that age. Therefore perhaps we must be specially careful that what they hear first are the noblest things told in the best fables for encouraging virtue."

"Yes," he said, "there is reason in that. But if we were asked what are these things, and which are the fables, what could we say?"

I answered, "My dear Adeimantos, we are not poets just now, you and I, but founders of a city; and founders ought to know the shapes in which the poets ought to make their fables, and if the poets make them different, the founders must not put up with it; but they have not to make fables themselves."

"Quite right," he said, "but this very thing, the shapes of tales of the gods—what would they be?"

"Something like this: The character of the god, that must always be described, no doubt, whether the poetry be epic or lyric or tragic."

"Yes, that is true."

"And is not a god good in reality, and the fable must agree with that?"

"Of course."

"Again, nothing good is harmful, is it?"

"I think not."

"Can what is not harmful do harm?"

"Oh, dear, no!"

"Can what does no harm do evil?"

"Never."

---

[1] The word used means what is lawful by religion and open to anyone to do.
[2] Hephaistos was said to have tied her to her own throne. Another tale told how Zeus threw Hephaistos out of heaven. *Iliad* i. 586 ff.
[3] *Iliad* xx. 1-74; xxi. 385-513.

THE REPUBLIC Book II (378C–380A)

"And what does no evil could not be the cause of anything evil?"

"How could it?"

"Very well; the good is serviceable?"

"Yes."

"The cause of well-being, then?"

"Yes."

"Then the good is cause not of all things, but of those that are well, and no cause of those that are evil."

"By all means," he said.

"It follows then," said I, "that God, since he is good, would not be cause of all things, as most say, but cause of a few things to mankind, and of many no cause; for the goods are much fewer for us than the evils; and of the good things God and no other must be described as the cause, but of the evil things we must look for many different causes, only not God."

"What you say seems to me very true," he said.

"Then," said I, "we must not accept from Homer or any other poet an error like this about the gods, when he foolishly makes the mistake of saying that[1]

> Two jars are standing in the hall of Zeus
> Chock full of fates, one bad fates and one good:
> When Zeus commingles them, and gives them both

to any man,

> He meets with evil now and now with good;

but when he does not, and gives a man one or other sort unmixed,

> Stark hunger drives him round the awesome world;

nor must we accept his statement that Zeus is dispenser to us

> Of things both good and evil.

"And as to the violation of the oaths and the truce violation by Pandaros[2]—if anyone says that this came about through Athena and Zeus we shall not thank him, or if he says the gods' discord and division[3] came about through Themis and Zeus. Nor again must we let the young people

---

[1] *Iliad* xxiv. 527-532, with variations.
[2] *Iliad* iv. 69 ff.
[3] Probably the quarrel over the Apple of Discord, and the judgment of Paris; See *Gods, Heroes and Men of Ancient Greece*, by W. H. D. Rouse, p. 215. But some refer to *Iliad* xx, where Zeus bids Themis summon a general assembly and the gods have battles among themselves.

hear, as Aeschylus says,[1] that

> God plants a fault in mortals
> When he would ruin some house utterly.

But if poets write about the 'Sorrows of Niobe'—in which these iambic lines of Aeschylus occur—or about the tale of the Pelopids, or the Trojan business or anything else of that sort, we must either forbid them to describe these events as the work of God, or else, if they do, they must find out some such explanation as we are looking for now—they must declare that God did a just and good work, and they gained benefit by being chastised. But to describe those who were punished as miserable, and to say that God made them so, is what the poet must not be suffered to do. Yet he may be suffered to say that the evil men were wretched because they needed chastisement, and that God did them good by punishing them. However, to call God a cause of evil to anyone, being good himself, is a falsehood to be fought tooth and nail; no one must allow that to be said in his own city if it is to be well governed, no one must hear it, whether younger or older, no one must fable it whether in verse or in prose; such things if spoken are impious, dangerous for us and discordant in themselves."

"I vote with you for this law," said he. "I am pleased with it."

"Very well," said I, "this would be one of the laws about our gods, one of the shapes within which a speaker must speak and a poet must compose; that God is cause of the good things, not of all things."

"That is quite enough," he said.

"Now then, here is the second. Do you believe God is a wizard? Is he able to show himself on purpose in different forms at different times, sometimes really changing his appearance and passing into many transformations, sometimes deceiving us by making us think we see him so? Or is he really simple and never leaves his own form at all?"

"I can't answer you now offhand," said he.

"Consider then. If something should leave its own form, it is necessary, isn't it, that it either changes itself or is changed by something else?"

"That is necessary."

"Take the second first; things which are in the best condition are least liable to be changed and moved by something else; for instance, a body by food and drink and labour, plants and trees by the sun's heat and wind and such influ-

[1] Aeschylus, *Fragment* 160.

ences; isn't it true that the strongest and healthiest is least altered in this way?"

"Quite true."

"With the soul wouldn't it be the same? The bravest and wisest souls would least be disturbed and altered by any experience from without?"

"Yes."

"The same is true, I suppose, of made-up things, furniture and buildings and dress, those which are well made and in good state are least altered by time or anything else that happens to them."

"Certainly that is true."

"Then everything which is in a good state, either by nature or by art or both, least admits change by something else."

"So it seems."

"But think, God and what is God's is everywhere in a perfect state."

"Of course."

"Then in this respect God would be least likely to take on many transformations."

"Least likely, indeed."

"Now as to himself: Would he change and alter himself?"

"Clearly he would," said he, "if he does alter."

"Does he change himself for the better and more beautiful, or for the worse and more ugly than himself?"

"He must change for the worse," said he, "if he does change, for I suppose we shall not say there is a lack in God of beauty or virtue."

"Quite right," said I; "and if thus perfect, do you think, Adeimantos, that anyone, god or man, would willingly make himself worse than this in any respect?"

"Impossible," said he.

"Then it is impossible," I said, "that God should wish to alter himself. No, as it seems, each of them, being the best and most beautiful possible, abides forever simply in his own form."

"I think that is absolutely necessary," he said.

"Then no poet must tell us, my excellent friend," said I, "that

> Gods like strangers from a foreign land
> Take on all sorts of shapes and visit cities;[1]

and no one shall lie about Proteus[2] and Thetis,[3] and in the

---

[1] *Odyssey* xvii. 485.
[2] He changed into all sorts of shapes to escape capture; *Odyssey* iv. 456.
[3] Thetis did the same because she tried to escape marriage with Peleus; Pindar *Nemean* iv. 62.

tragedies and other poems no one shall bring on Hera[1] disguised as a priestess begging alms

> For the life-giving sons of Inachos,
> The Argive river.

We don't want these and many other such lies. And the mothers, again, shall not be deluded by them and terrify their children by telling nasty fables, how some gods prowl about by night—just imagine it!—in the likeness of a lot of people from the ends of the earth; we won't have them blaspheming the gods and adding to their children's fears at the same time."[2]

"We will not!" said he.

"Well then, next," said I, "the gods themselves cannot change, but do they deceive us and bewitch us and make us think we see them in all these forms?"

"Perhaps," he said.

"What!" said I. "Would a god wish to lie or deceive in word or deed, by putting a pretence before us?"

"I don't know," said he.

"Don't you know," said I, "that what is truly a lie, if that could be said, all gods and men hate?"

"What do you mean?" he asked.

"This," I said; "that to be false in the most vital part of one's being and about the most vital things is what no one willingly chooses, but one fears more than anything to have falsehood there."

"I don't understand even yet," said he.

"Because you think," I replied, "that I am saying something pretentious. I only mean that in the soul, to be false and to be deceived and ignorant about what is real, and to have and keep the falsehood in the soul—no one would ever accept such a thing; all have the greatest hatred for it in such a place."

"Exactly," he said.

"But surely this could most rightly be called the true lie, as I called it just now, this ignorance in the soul, the ignorance of one deceived; since the lie in words is an imitation of the state of the soul, and came later, an image, not the pure lie. Is not that so?"

"Quite so."

"Then the real lie is hated both by gods and by men."

"So I think."

"What then of the lie in words? When is it useful, and

[1] In a lost tragedy by Aeschylus.
[2] He means the well-known bogies, Lamia, Mormo, Empusa, who could take any shapes.

to whom, and so is not hateful? Surely towards enemies? And among those called friends, whenever they try to do something evil, because of madness or some folly; then it becomes a kind of useful preventive medicine to avert this. And in the fables we were speaking of, we make the falsehood as much like the truth as we can, because we do not know what is the truth about ancient things, and so we make it useful."

"Most certainly," he said.

"Then in which of these ways is the falsehood useful to God? Doesn't he know about ancient things, and does he try to make a falsehood as much like them as he can?"

"Oh, that would be absurd," he said.

"There is no lying poet in God then?"

"I think not."

"Would he fear an enemy, and lie?"

"Far from it."

"His friends' madness then, or folly?"

"No indeed," he said, "for no fool or madman is a friend of God."

"Then there is no reason why God should lie."

"None."

"If so, the spiritual and divine is wholly without falsehood."

"It is so beyond a doubt."

"Altogether, then, God is simple and true in word and deed, and neither changes himself nor deceives others, whether by apparitions or by stories or by sending signs in daylight or in dreams."

"That is exactly how it seems to me myself," he replied, "as I hear you say it."

"You agree, then," said I, "that this is the second shape in which to tell stories and make poetry about gods; that they are not wizards who change their forms, and they do not mislead us by falsehood in word or in deed?"

"I agree."

"Then, however much we commend in Homer, here is one thing that we shall not commend, the sending of that dream to Agamemnon by Zeus;[1] nor Aeschylus, when Thetis tells how Apollo singing at her marriage,[2]

> Foreboded her fine progeny
> Long-lasting lives and free from all diseases,
> And after telling all, cried out in triumph
> For my god-friended lot and cheered my heart.
> And I believed the mouth divine of Phoibos

[1] *Iliad* ii. 1-34.
[2] From a lost play.

> Was without falsehood, full of prophecy:
> But he—who sang himself, was there himself
> One of the banquet, said all this himself—
> He is himself the slayer of my child.

When a poet speaks like this of the gods, we shall be angry, and we will refuse him a chorus,[1] we will not allow schoolmasters to use his sayings in educating the young, if our guardians are to be pious and themselves divine as far as human beings can possibly be."

"Most certainly," he said, "I grant you these two shapes, and I would use these as laws."

BOOK III

"As regards the gods, then," said I, "these are the sorts of things, as it seems, which ought and ought not to be heard from childhood, by those who are to honour God and honour their parents, and to hold dear the friendship among themselves."

"And quite right too, as I believe," he said.

"What next, then? If they are to be brave, we must not stop there; we must add such things as will make them never fear death. Do you think anyone will be always brave while he has this fear in him?"

"No, indeed I do not."

"And if he believes in all that about the world of Hades and its terrors, do you think anyone will be fearless, and choose death in his battles rather than defeat and slavery?"

"Not at all."

"Then, as it seems, we must have our censorship about these fables also, to govern those who undertake to tell them; and we must beg them not just simply to decry the other world, but rather to praise it, since what they say now is neither true nor useful for those who are to be warlike."

"We must," he said.

"Let us wipe out, then," I said, "everything of the kind, beginning with this passage from epic poetry—

> I'd rather be a serf or labouring man
> Under some yeoman on a little farm
> Than be king paramount of all the dead,[2]

---

[1] The proper board at Athens heard the plays, and then decided who should have "a chorus," that is a right to exhibit, and to train the actors and chorus of dancers and singers.

[2] Said by Achilles to Odysseus when his ghost was called up from Hades. *Odyssey*, xi. 489.

And this—

> Lest mortals and immortals should set eyes
> Upon these fearsome, danksome dwellings which
> The very gods abhor;[1]

And—

> What! Is there really in the house of Hades
> A soul and phantom, but no sense is left?[2]

And again—

> He only has a mind, but all the rest
> Are flitting shadows;[3]

And—

> The soul flew from his limbs and went to Hades
> Groaning its fate, youth and strength left behind;[4]

And this—

> The soul went down below the earth like smoke,
> Gibbering;[5]

And this—

> Like a string of bats in depths of some vast cave
> Which hang clinging together from the rock;
> If one falls out, they flitter gibbering.
> So the souls gibbered as they marched together.[6]

We will beg Homer and the other poets not to be put out if we strike through such things as these; we do not deny they are good poetry and what most people like to hear, but the more poetical they are, the less we wish our children and men to hear them, those who must be free, and afraid of slavery more than death."

"Most certainly."

"Besides that, we must abolish all those names, those fearful and terrific names, Cocytos, the River of Lamentation, Styx, the River of Hate, the infernals and the corpses dead, and all other names of this type which make those who hear them shiver. Perhaps these may have another use of some kind; but now we are anxious about our guardians; we fear all this shiv-

---

[1] The terrible noise and the quaking of the earth, from the battle raging overhead, made the lord of Hades fear lest the earth above him might be split open and expose Hades to view. *Iliad* xx. 64.
[2] Said by Achilles, when he saw the ghost of Patroclos. *Iliad* xxiii. 103.
[3] Said of Teiresias, *Odyssey* x. 495.
[4] Said of Patroclos, *Iliad* xvi. 856.
[5] *Iliad* xxiii. 100.
[6] *Odyssey* xxiv. 6; the souls of the slain wooers of Penelope.

ering may bring on a hot fit and make them softer than they should be."[1]

"We are right to fear that," he said.

"Then must we abolish these names?"

"Yes."

"But the opposite type we must use in stories and poetry?"

"That is surely clear."

"And the weepings and wailings of famous men?"

"They must go," he said, "if the others do."

"Just consider," I said, "if that will be right or not. We say, I take it, that the good man will not believe death is a terror for his comrade, who also is a good man."

"We do."

"Then he would not lament for him as if he had suffered something terrible."

"He would not."

"Moreover, we say that such a man is most self-sufficient for living well, and least of all needs the help of others."

"True," he said.

"Then it is least terrible for him to lose a son or brother, or wealth or any other such."

"Yes, least of all."

"Then he laments least, and he endures most calmly when any such misfortune befalls him."

"Very true."

"Then we should rightly do away with the dirges of famous men, and leave them for women, not the best women either, and for the mean among men; in order that we may help those whom we talk of bringing up for the guarding of our city to despise doing things like that."

"Quite so," he said.

"Then we will beg Homer again, and the other poets too, not to describe Achilles, the son of a goddess, as

> Lying now on his side, now on his back,
> Now flat upon his face,[2]

and sometimes rising up and 'sailing distracted over the shore of the barren sea,'[3] or 'catching up the sooty dust with both hands, and scattering it over his head,'[4] or weeping and lamenting as long and loud as the poet describes; or Priam again, a near kinsman of gods, as uttering prayers and

---

[1] There seem to be two thoughts here: the cold shiver and feverish heat of disease, and the heating of iron which makes it soft and beatable.
[2] *Iliad* xxiv. 10; Achilles, grieving for his friend Patroclos.
[3] *Iliad* xxiv. 12; Plato substitutes "sailing" for "roaming," perhaps in parody.
[4] *Iliad* xviii. 23.

> rolling on the dungheap,
> And calling loudly on the name of each.[1]

Much more even than these, we shall beg him not to make a god lament and say

> O wretched that I am! O hapless me,
> To bear that noblest son![2]

And if so for *a* god, never to dare to depict the greatest of the gods so ungodlike as to cry

> Good heavens! there's a friend chased round the city—
> I see it with my eyes! my heart laments![3]

and

> Woe's me, that Fate decrees my best beloved
> Sarpedon is to fall before Patroclos,
> Son of Menoitios.[4]

"For, my dear Adeimantos, if our young people should take such things seriously, instead of laughing at them as unworthily said, a mortal man could hardly think them unworthy of himself, or blame himself if it should occur to him to say or do anything of the sort; no, he would not be ashamed and endure his little sufferings, but many a dirge and lament he would sing over them."

"Very true," he said.

"But he must not do it, as our reasoning has shown us; and we must trust our reasoning until someone shall find us a better to convince us."

"He must not, indeed."

"Then again, they must not be too fond of laughter. For usually when one indulges violent laughter, such a thing is apt to bring about in oneself a violent upset of feeling."

"Yes, I think so," he said.

"Then we must not allow it if a poet shows men of mark mastered by laughter, still less gods."

"Far less," he said.

"Then we will not accept this either, from Homer about the gods:

> Inextinguishable laughter rose among the blessed gods,
> When they saw fussy Hephaistos puffing all about the room.[5]

This is not tolerable according to your reasoning."

---

[1] *Iliad* xxii. 414; Priam, on his dead sons.
[2] *Iliad* xviii. 54; Thetis says this of herself.
[3] *Iliad* xxii. 168; Zeus says this when he sees Achilles chasing Hector.
[4] *Iliad* xvi. 433. Zeus speaks.
[5] *Iliad* i. 599.

"If you like to call it mine," he said. "Certainly it is intolerable."

"Truth, however, must be highly valued. For if we were right in saying lately that falsehood is really useless to gods, but to men it is useful as a kind of drug, it is clear that we must allow such a thing to doctors, but laymen must not touch it."

"That is clear," he said.

"Then for the rulers of the city, if for anyone, it is proper to use falsehood, to deal with enemies or indeed with citizens for the benefit of the city; no others must touch anything of the sort, and that a layman should lie to rulers we shall say is the same or a greater offence than that a sick man should lie to a doctor, or a practising pupil should not tell his trainer the truth about the state of his body, or that anyone speaking to a pilot about ships and sailors should not describe exactly how things are being done on board by himself or some other."

"Very true," he said.

"Then if the ruler catches any one of those who are craftsmen telling lies in the city,

Seer, healer of sicknesses, or maker of timbers,[1]

he will chastise him for bringing in a practice as likely to overthrow and destroy the city as it would a ship."

"Yes," he said, " 'if tellings comes to doings.' "

"Again: Will not our young men need temperance?"[2]

"Of course."

"In temperance, the greatest thing for the multitude is to obey the rulers, and for rulers to rule the pleasures of drinking and love making and eating too?"

"I think so."

"Then we shall say that such things as this are good, which Diomedes in Homer says to his friend,

Old chum, sit silent and be ruled by me;[3]

and what comes not long after,

The Achaians marched breathing passion,
In silent fear of their captains,[4]

and all else of the same sort."

"Yes, good."

"Well, what of this,

[1] *Odyssey* xvii. 383.
[2] *Sôphrosýnē*: sound-mindedness. See p. 160, n. 3. This word occurs frequently in the *Republic* and the dialogues, and is translated as "temperance" throughout.
[3] *Iliad* iv. 412.
[4] *Iliad* iv. 431, to which Plato prefixed a phrase from iii. 8; unless he had a different text.

THE REPUBLIC Book III (389B–390E)

> Wine-heavy, with dog's eyes, and heart of deer,[1]

and what follows these words, do you think that good, and all other youthful vulgarities of commoners, which anyone has spoken against rulers in prose or verse?"

"Not good."

"Because, I think, to hear these is not likely to make the young temperate; if it does give them some other pleasure, there is no wonder in that. What do you think about it?"

"I think as you do," he said.

"And then again, to describe the wisest of men as saying that he thinks it the height of bliss when

> Tables are by us full of bread and meat,
> A butler ladling from the mixing bowl
> Wine which he carries round to fill the cups,[2]

—do you think a young man hearing this will find it a help to self-mastery? Or this—

> To starve is the cruellest death a man can die?[3]

Or about Zeus, how, when the other gods, and men, were asleep and he alone was awake, he easily forgot, because of his lustful desire, all those plans which he had been making, and was so overwhelmed by the sight of Hera that he would not go to his bedroom but wanted to lie with her there on the ground; how he said he had never desired her so much, not even when they first visited each other unknown to their dear parents?[4] Or about the enchaining of Ares and Aphrodite by Hephaistos for a similar reason.[5] Will those things be useful for them to hear?"

"Anything but useful, upon my word," said he.

"But deeds of endurance against everything—when such things are spoken or done by famous men, these they ought to see and to hear; for example,

> Striking his breast he thus reproached his heart—
> Endure, my heart! much worse you have endured!"[6]

"Most certainly," he said.

"Furthermore, we must not let them take bribes or be greedy of money."

"We must not."

"Or recite to them

---
[1] *Iliad* i. 225, addressed by Achilles to his king, Agamemnon.
[2] Odysseus says this to his host in the hall of Alcinoös. *Odyssey* ix. 8.
[3] *Odyssey* xii. 342.
[4] *Iliad* xi. 1, xiv. 281.
[5] *Odyssey* viii. 266 ff.
[6] *Odyssey* xx. 17, Odysseus says this to himself.

Gifts persuade gods, gifts persuade reverend kings.[1]
Nor should we praise Phoinix, the guide and instructor of Achilles, as giving decent advice when he told him to accept the Achaians' gifts and defend them, but without gifts not to give up his wrath.[2] Nor shall we think it proper, or believe, that Achilles was so greedy that he accepted gifts from Agamemnon,[3] or took a price for a dead body, and would not release it without."[4]

"No," he said, "it is not right to commend such things."

"I don't like to say," I went on, "for Homer's sake, that it is plain impiety to say such things against Achilles, or to believe them when said; and again how Achilles spoke to Apollo,

Far-shooter, you have failed me now, you worst of all
    the gods;
I'd pay you out, indeed I would, if only I could do it![5]

and how he behaved so disobediently toward the River,[6] who was a god, as to be ready to fight with him; and how he said about his tress of hair, which was consecrated to another river, the Spercheios, that he

Would give Patroclos this hair to take with him,[7]

who was then a dead body, and how he did this; we must not believe these stories. And the dragging of Hector around the barrow of Patroclos, and the slaughtering of the captives over the pyre,[8] all this we shall deny to be true; nor will we allow our young people to believe that Achilles—the son of a goddess and of Peleus, one famous for self-control and the third generation from Zeus[9]—and brought up by Cheiron most wise, was yet so full of confusion that he had within him two opposite diseases, meanness combined with greed, and also overweening contempt for gods and men."

"You are right," he said.

[1] An old saying.
[2] See *Iliad* ix. 515.
[3] *Iliad* xix. 278. But Achilles was not so ungenerous as Plato implies, nor did he say a word about the ransom, he let it pass.
[4] *Iliad* xxiv. 502, and later, as 560.
[5] *Iliad* xxii. 15.
[6] The Scamandros, *Iliad* xxi. 130.
[7] *Iliad* xxiii. 151. Achilles cut off the consecrated tress, and laid it in the dead hand of his friend Patroclos on the funeral pyre.
[8] *Iliad* xxiv. 14; xxiii. 175.
[9] Peleus, king of Phthia, was son of Aiacos, son of Zeus, and in story the most chaste of men: Pindar, *Nemean* iv. 56. Hippolyte, wife of Acastos, fell in love with him; and when he refused the temptress, she accused him to her husband. On a hunting trip Acastos stole the sword of Peleus, and persuaded the centaurs to lie in wait for him, but Cheiron saved him. To reward him for his virtue, the gods gave him Thetis, who gave birth to Achilles.

"Very well," said I, "do not let us believe these things either, or allow anyone to say that Theseus, son of Poseidon, and Peirithoös, son of Zeus, attempted those dreadful rapes,[1] or that any other hero and son of a god would have dared dreadful and irreligious deeds, such as they now falsely allege against them. Let us further compel the poets either to say that these were not their doings, or that they were not sons of gods; both together they shall not say. They must not try to persuade our young people that the gods beget evils, and that heroes are no better than men. For as we have said in our earlier discussion, this is neither pious nor true; for we have shown, I believe, that gods cannot possibly produce evils."

"Of course that is impossible."

"And more, these things damage those who hear. For everyone will find an excuse for himself to be evil, if he believes that such things are done and were done by

> the nearest kin of gods
> Those close to Zeus—their own ancestral altar
> For Zeus stands on mount Ida high in heaven,
> And the gods' blood is not yet dim in them.[2]

For these reasons we must put an end to such fables, or they will breed in the young great readiness for crime."

"Assuredly we must."

"Then what kind of tale is left for us," I said, "now we are defining what should be told and what not? The gods have been properly disposed of, and spirits and heroes and what happens after death."

"Just so."

"So then, what is left would be tales about men?"

"That is clear."

"Well, my friend, it is impossible for us to lay that down at present."[3]

"How so?"

"Because I believe we are about to say that poets and storytellers are wrong about men in the most important matters. They declare that many men are happy though unjust, and wretched although just; that injustice is profitable, if not found out, and justice good for others but plain loss for oneself. Such things we will forbid them to say, and command them to sing and to fable the opposite, don't you agree with me?"

"I'm sure of it," he said.

"Then if you agree that I am right, I will say you have

---

[1] Of Helen, and then of Queen Persephone from the underworld.
[2] From the lost play, *Niobe*, by Aeschylus. Tantalos seems to be meant; Ida was in his land.
[3] It would assume the principles which the *Republic* tries to prove.

admitted the very thing which we have been trying to discover all this while."

"You have taken that point well," he said.

"Then we have to find out first what justice is, and how it is profitable to him that has it, whether he is believed to be just or not; then and not before we will agree that such-and-such tales ought to be told of men."

"Most true," he said.

"So much then, for the matter; and the manner, or style, comes next, as I think; then we shall have examined the whole thing, what is to be said and how."

Here Adeimantos said, "I don't understand what you mean by that."

"Oh, but it is necessary that you should," said I. "Perhaps you will see my meaning more easily this way. Whatever is said by storytellers or poets is really a narrative of what has been, or is, or will be, is that correct?"

"Why, of course," said he.

"And they do this either by simple narrative, or by imitation, or both?"

"This also," he said, "I should like to understand more clearly."

"Oh dear me!" I said; "what a ridiculous, obscure teacher I must be! Then I'll do as people who don't know how to speak; I won't try to show what I mean as a whole, but I will try by taking a bit at a time. Look here; you know the first lines of the *Iliad*, in which the poet says that Chryses besought Agamemnon to release his daughter, and the king was angry; and when Chryses couldn't get her he cursed the Achaians?"

"Yes, I do know."

"You know, then, that as far as the lines

> He prayed the Achaians all,
> But chiefly the two rulers of the people,
> Both sons[1] of Atreus,

the poet himself speaks, he never tries to turn our thoughts from himself or to suggest that anyone else is speaking; but after this he speaks as if he was himself Chryses, and tries his best to make us think that the priest, an old man, is speaking and not Homer. All the narrative about what happened at Troy and in Ithaca and throughout the *Odyssey* is given in much the same way."

"Just so," he said.

"It is narrative, then, both all the speeches which are made and all that comes between the speeches?"

---

[1] *Iliad* i. 15. Agamemnon and Menelaus.

"Certainly."

"And whenever someone makes a speech as if he were someone else, shall we not say that he makes his own manner of speaking as much as he can like the one who he told us beforehand was going to speak?"

"Yes, of course."

"Now to make oneself like another either in voice or in looks is to imitate the person whom one makes oneself like."

"Of course."

"In such a case then, as it seems, he and the other poets make their narrative through imitation."

"Certainly."

"But if the poet should nowhere hide himself, all his poetry and narrative would have been made without imitation. Now please don't say again, 'I don't understand'; I'll tell you how it would be. When Homer had said that Chryses came with the ransom for his daughter, as a suppliant to the Achaians and particularly to the two princes, if the poet had spoken after this, not as if he were Chryses himself but still just as Homer, you know that would have been simple narrative and not imitation. It would have been something like this—I will speak without metre, for I'm nothing of a poet: The priest came and prayed the gods to grant to the Achaians to take Troy and go home in safety, and he besought them to release his daughter to him and accept ransom in reverence for the god. After he had said this, the people all feared God and agreed; but Agamemnon fell into a rage, telling him to go away now and not to come back, or his staff and the wreathings of the god might not help him; before he would give her up, he said she should grow old with him in Argos, told him to be off and not to provoke him, if he wanted to get home safe. When the old man heard this, he was frightened and departed in silence; but after leaving the camp he prayed earnestly to Apollo, calling upon the god by his titles, and reminding him and asking for a return if he had ever offered gifts to his pleasure, in the building of temples or in sacrifices of victims; in return for these things, then, he adjured the god to make the Achaians pay for his tears by his arrows. There, my comrade," said I, "is the plain narrative without imitation."

"I understand that," said he.

"Understand then," said I, "that the opposite of this is when one takes away from the poet all the parts between the speeches, and leaves only the interchange of talk."

"That I understand too," he said. "It is the sort of thing we have in tragedy."

"You take me exactly," said I, "and I think I make clear to you now what I could not before, that poetry and fabling are of two kinds: one wholly through imitation, as you say, tragedy and comedy; the other through the poet's own report of things. You would find this best in the dithyramb.[1] A third kind, using both, is in epic poetry, and in many other places too, if you understand me."

"Oh yes," he said, "I know now what you meant."

"Then just recall what came before that, when we said that we had finished with *what* ought to be told, but next we had to consider, *how*."

"Yes, I remember."

"Well, this then is what I wanted: We must make up our minds whether we will let the poets imitate when they make their narratives, or imitate in parts and narrate in parts, and which parts for each; or whether we will allow no imitation at all."

"O my prophetic soul!" he said. "Your question is, whether we shall admit tragedy and comedy into our city, or not."

"Perhaps," I said, "and perhaps I mean something more than that. For I really don't know myself yet, but wherever the enquiry shall blow us like a breeze, there we must go."

"And quite right too," he said.

"Then keep your eye on this, Adeimantos; should each of our guardians be a bit of a mimic, or not? It follows, doesn't it, from what was said before, that each one could practise one calling well, but not many; if he should try to do this, the jack of many trades would miss competence in all—at least so as to count for anything?"

"That is sure to happen."

"The same surely is true of imitating: one man could not imitate many things well, as he could one thing?"

"He could not."

"Then he will scarcely practise any of the callings worth consideration, and at the same time be a bit of a mimic and imitate many things; since I suppose the same imitators cannot practise well two kinds of imitation at the same time, even those which are thought to be close together, for example, tragedy and comedy. Didn't you call these two 'imitations' just now?"

"I did," he said, "and you say truly that the same men cannot do both."

"Nor can men be both good reciters and good actors."

"True."

"Even the actors in comedy and tragedy are not the same;

[1] A long lyric, a narrative not unlike an ode of Pindar or Bacchylides.

and all these things are imitations, don't you think so?"

"They are."

"And it appears to me, Adeimantos, that human nature has been coined up into small change even smaller than this; so that it is incapable of imitating many things well, or of doing the many things of which these imitations are likenesses?"

"Very true," he said.

"Then if we are to keep the first rule, that our guardians must be released from all other crafts and be master craftsmen of freedom for the city, and practise nothing else that does not lead to this, then they should not do or imitate anything else. If they do imitate, they should imitate from childhood what is proper for their craft—men who are brave and temperate, pious, free and all things of that sort; but things not for the free they should neither do nor be clever at imitating, and nothing else that is ugly, that the imitation may never give them a taste of the real thing. Have you not perceived that imitations settle into habits and become nature if they are continued from early youth, in body and voice and mind?"

"Indeed I have," he said.

"Then any we care for, and think they should become good men, we will not allow to imitate a woman, being men themselves, either a young or older woman, nagging at a husband or quarrelling with gods and boasting, thinking herself happy; or one held in misfortune with mourning and dirge, much less one in sickness or in love or in labour of child."

"Far from it," he said.

"Nor must they imitate slaves whether men or women, doing what slaves do."

"No."

"Nor wicked men, as it seems, cowards, those who do the opposite of what we said just now, scolding, mocking and speaking vilely of each other, whether drunk or sober, and imitating what such men say and do to each other or to themselves with offence. And I think they must not get the habit of making themselves like madmen in word or act. They must know about madmen, of course, and about bad men and women, but they must do nothing of all this nor imitate this."

"Most true," he said.

"And then again," said I, "are they to imitate smiths or other workmen, or rowers of ships-of-war or men in charge of the rowers, or anything else of that kind?"

"How could that be right," he said, "when they will not be allowed to take any notice of such persons at all?"

"Well then—neighing horses and bellowing bulls and roaring rivers and crashing seas, thunders and all such things—

are they to imitate those?"

"No, indeed," he said. "They have been forbidden to be mad or to make themselves like what is mad."

"Then," said I, "if I understand what you mean, there are two kinds of speech and narrative; one which the man really good and noble would use when he had anything to say or narrate, and another different kind which a man of the opposite nature and breeding would keep to in telling his tale."

"What are these, pray?" he asked.

"It seems to me," I said, "that when the decent man in his narrative comes to sayings or doings of a good man, he will wish to report them as though he were himself the man; he will not be ashamed to imitate in that way, especially to imitate the good man acting firmly and sensibly, but less willingly and less often a good man shaken by disease or passions, or again by drunkenness or some other misfortune. But when he comes to one unworthy of himself, he will not wish to make himself really like a worse man, except now and again if the man does something good; he will be ashamed. He is unpractised, you see, in imitating such persons; and at the same time he resents modelling and fitting himself into the shapes of the worse. He disdains it in mind, unless it be just a bit of fun."

"That is likely," he said.[1]

"It follows that he will use a narrative like what we described a while ago in speaking of Homer's epic poetry. His manner of speech will have something of both, imitation and simple narrative, but only a small part of imitation in a long story—or is there nothing in what I say?"

"A great deal," he said: "that must be exactly the model of such a speaker."

"On the other hand," I said, "one of a different sort, the worse he is the readier he will be to imitate everything; he will think nothing unworthy of himself, so he will try to imitate everything in earnest and before a large audience; even what I mentioned just now, claps of thunder and the sounds of winds and hailstorms, of axles and windlasses, the notes of trumpets and pipes and Pan's-pipes and all manner of instruments; he will bark like a dog and bleat like a sheep and twitter like a bird. Will not all the speech of this man be made with the sounds and gestures of imitation, or will there be just a little of narrative in it?"

"That must be so too," said he.

"These are what I spoke of," said I, "the two manners of speech."

[1] In Book X Plato deals with this subject, and he uses "imitation" here to include the sympathy of the spectator.

"So they are," said he.

"Then one manner of the two has few changes and modulations; and if we give the words a suitable scale[1] and rhythm,[2] the correct speaker will in his speaking keep almost in one musical scale, for there are few modulations, and very nearly indeed in the same rhythm likewise."

"Well really," he said, "that is quite true."

"And what of the other manner of speech? Does it not want the opposite: all the scales, all the rhythms, if it also is to fit the words, since it contains modulations in all manner of shapes?"

"That is most certainly true."

"Well, all poets and all who have anything to tell hit on either one or the other kind of style, or else mix the two up together?"

"It must be so," he said.

"Then what shall we do?" said I. "Are we to accept all these into the city, or one of the unmixed styles, or the mixed style?"

"If my vote is to win," he said, "the pure style imitating the good."

"Ah, but my dear Adeimantos, the mixed style is delightful too; and much the most delightful to children and tutors alike is the opposite to the one you choose—the most delightful also to the world at large."

"So it is."

"But perhaps you would say it would not suit our state, because man with us is not twofold or manifold, since each does only one thing."

"No, it does not suit."

"Then this," I said, "is why such a city is the only one where we shall find the shoemaker always a shoemaker and not a pilot in addition to his shoemaking, and the farmer always a farmer and not a judge in addition to his farming, and the soldier always a soldier and not a moneymaker in addition to his soldiering, and so forth?"

"True," he said.

"Suppose then there were a man so clever that he could take all kinds of shapes and imitate anything and everything, and suppose he should come to our city with his poems to give a display, what then? We should prostrate ourselves[3] before him

---

[1] The Greek "harmony," i.e., the tune or scale regulating the musical intervals, differs in meaning from our modern use of the word. See p. 196, n. 3.
[2] The rhythm is the scansion or succession of longs and shorts. See p. 199, n. 1.
[3] The Greek word seems to have meant originally "throw a kiss to," but in Plato's time it meant "prostrate oneself before."

as one sacred and wonderful and delightful, but we should say that we cannot admit such a man into our city; the law forbids, and there is no place for him. We should anoint his head and wreathe about it a chaplet of wool, and let him go in peace to another city; but ourselves we should employ the more austere and less pleasing poet and storyteller, for our benefit. He should imitate for us the speech of the good, and should tell his tales on those patterns for which we made our laws at the beginning, when we were trying to educate the soldiers."

"That is just what we should do," he said, "if we had the power."

"And now, you see," said I, "we have completely finished that part of music[1] which is concerned with stories and fables; and we have decided what is to be said, and how."

"I agree with that," said he.

"There remains after this," I said, "the manner of song and melody."[2]

"Yes, clearly."

"Surely everyone could find out at once in what terms we ought to describe them, if we are to be in tune with what we have said already?"

And Glaucon said, with a laugh, "I am afraid everyone does not include me, Socrates; I can't divine for you well enough at present what sorts of things we ought to say, but I have some suspicion."

"At least you can say well enough," said I, "that lyric poetry is made up of three parts, words and tune[3] and rhythm."

"Oh yes, I see that," he said.

"Then as far as words go, there is no difference, I suppose, between words when sung and words when spoken, but both

---

[1] See p. 174, n. 1.

[2] Greek lyric poetry was always sung to a melody, just as it used to be in England in the days of Queen Elizabeth I.

[3] ἁρμονία. The Greek word "harmony" seems to have had several shades of meaning; see also pp. 231, and 242, n. 1., *Banquet*, p. 83, n. 1 and *Phaedo* p. 490. Here the "harmonies" meant what we might term tunes or scales regulating the musical intervals. Our Western ears have been trained for centuries to music based on tones and semitones (each tone being one-sixth of an octave) and on major and minor scales all using these intervals. Consequently some oriental music based on intervals and scales of different sizes and arrangements from ours may sound almost incomprehensible or barbaric to us. The Greeks, in the composition of their melodies, used scales more varied in their intervals and more numerous than ours; their smallest interval was probably a quarter of and their largest probably twice our tone. Thus they were able, choosing also their "pitch," to suit their melodies to their moods. They gave these scales ("harmonies," as they called them) descriptive names—Dorian, Lydian, Phrygian, etc. The Dorian resulted in melodies of plain, warlike, manly character; those of the Lydian were gentle and relaxing. The lyre, which then had probably seven to ten strings, was probably retuned to whatever "harmony" was being used. The Greeks sang the melodies as solos or in unison, not in harmony as we understand the word.

For further information about Greek music and rhythm, see the article on "Music" in *The Oxford Classical Dictionary*, Clarendon Press, Oxford, England, 1949.

must follow the same shapes we have already described, and the same manner?"

"True," he said.

"And tune and rhythm must follow the words."

"Of course."

"However, we said we did not want dirges and lamentations also among the words."

"No, we did not."

"Then what are the tunes and scales[1] which belong to dirges? Tell me that, for you are a musical man."

"Mixed Lydian," he said, "and high or sharp Lydian, and a few like them."

"Then we must do away with these," I said, "for they are useless even for women if they are to be decent, much more for men."

"Certainly."

"Again, drunkenness is most unbecoming for guardians, and softness and idleness."

"Of course."

"Then what scales are soft and fit for a drinking party?"

"Ionian," said he, "and some of the Lydians are also called relaxing."[2]

"Well then, my friend, could you have any use for these with men of war?"

"None at all," said he, "but that seems to leave for you Dorian and Phrygian."

"I don't know the scales," I said, "but leave the particular scale which could suitably imitate the notes and tones of a brave man in warlike action and in all violent doings, or defending himself against fortune steadily with endurance when he has had bad luck and faces wounds or death or falls into any other trouble. And leave another for the works of peace without violence, when a man acts of his own free will, whether persuading or beseeching someone for something, as praying to a god or instructing or admonishing a man, or on the other hand when he is yielding to another who beseeches or instructs or persuades him; and if he wins his object by these means, he is not overbearing or triumphant, but temperate and moderate in every case and well content with what follows. Leave them these two scales—the violent scale and the free-will scale, such as will imitate best the tones of men unhappy or well off, temperate and brave."

"But," said he, "these which you ask me to leave are just the

---

[1] See page 196, n. 3.
[2] As Milton wrote in "L'Allegro": "Lap me in soft Lydian airs."

ones I mentioned, Dorian and Phrygian."[1]

"Well, then," said I, "we shall not want a host of strings and endless modulations from key to key in our songs and melodies. So we will have no psalteries or gitterns or instruments of many strings and many keys, and the craftsmen of these we will not harbour."

"So it seems."

"Very well, will you receive makers or players of pipes[2] into the city? Or is not this the most many-stringed[3] of instruments itself, and don't the many-key instruments simply imitate the pipe?"

"Yes, clearly," said he.

"You have left, then," said I, "lyre and harp, and they are useful in the city; in the country, again, the herdsmen would have some sort of Panspipes."

"At least that seems to be indicated by what we have been saying."

"Well, my friend," said I, "we are doing nothing new if we judge that Apollo and Apollo's instruments are better than Marsyas'[4] and his instruments."

"I should think not, upon my word!" said he.

"Aye, by the Dog!" I said, "and we never noticed that we were purging the city clean again, which we said just now was luxurious."

"And very wisely, too," said he.

"Come on, then," said I, "let us do the rest of the cleansing. The next thing after the scales is the matter of rhythms; we must not seek for complex rhythms or variety of metrical steps, but consider what are the rhythms of a manly and orderly life; then with this in view we must compel the foot and the melody to follow the words of such a life, not let the words follow the foot and the melody. But what these rhythms would be is your business to indicate, as with the musical scales."

"Well upon my word," he said, "I can't tell. There are three shapes or forms from which the steps are combined, just as there are four from which all the scales are built; I have seen

---

[1] The ancients had different views of the moral influence of the "harmonies" or scales, but, as we see, Plato thought the Dorian manly, and the Phrygian sober. Yet he rejected the pipes, which were generally associated with the Phrygian. He represents Socrates as favouring two particular types of scales, one such as to promote music inspiring courage and sobriety in times of war and trouble, and another—the free-will scale—for music suggestive of men acting on their own free will in works of peace.

[2] The *aulos* (pipe) was not a flute, as often translated. It was blown at the end, like an oboe.

[3] Pipes, of course, were not stringed instruments. But "many-stringed" is what Plato seems to say, unless the word is metaphor and means "having many notes." We have no equivalent names for the Greek instruments, but that does not obscure the argument.

[4] Marsyas the Satyr challenged Apollo to a contest (with pipe against Apollo's lyre). Apollo was adjudged victor by the Muses, and he put Marsyas to death.

THE REPUBLIC Book III *(399C–400D)* 199

that and so I can tell you.[1] But which are the imitations of which life, I cannot tell."

"Oh, well," said I, "we will ask Damon's[2] advice as to which are the proper steps of vulgarity or violence or madness or any other vice, and what rhythms we must leave for their opposites. I seem to remember myself hearing him say something not very clever about an up-in-arms[3] rhythm, a compound rhythm; and a dactyl and a heroic rhythm, arranging them goodness knows how and making up and down equal,[4] topsy turvy, and coming to short and long; yes, and I think he named one iambic and another trochaic, and stuck on longs and shorts to them. And in some of these I think he praised or blamed the time of the foot no less than the rhythms themselves, or a bit of both; I really can't say.[5] But as I said, this may all be referred to Damon, for it is no small business to disentangle it. Don't you think so?"

"Yes, indeed I do!"

"But so much you can disentangle—that the graceful or the graceless goes along with fine rhythm or no rhythm!"

"Of course."

"And further, fine rhythm follows a good style of speech and is like it, and no-rhythm goes with the opposite, and the well-tuned and badly tuned in the same way; since as we said, rhythm and tune follow the word,[6] not word follows these."

"Sure enough," said he, "these must follow the word."

"And what of the manner of speaking," said I, "and the speech itself? Do they not follow the spirit of the soul?"

"Of course."

"And the others follow the speaking?"

"Yes."

---

[1] All the Greek metrical "feet" are derived from steps of the human foot, in march or dance. Glaucon has seen the feet move as the voice sings, and so he knows that. The three were called "the three equal," where the foot is allowed equal time to fall and rise: — —, ♩♩ ; or — ᴗᴗ, ♩ ♫ ; or ᴗᴗ —, ♫ ♩ . The "feet" where the step came down first (as in dactyl — ᴗᴗ, and trochee — ᴗ) were generally thought to be more vigorous than where it came second (as in anapaest ᴗᴗ —, and iambus ᴗ —).
The four tonic elements mentioned are probably the tetrachord, but it is uncertain.
With the Dorian musical scale the rhythm was simple and even, having two figures in various arrangements: (1) one or more dactyls followed by a spondee — —, and (2) the equivalent in time of two spondees. The same rhythm in English would be: "|How can he|find it in|Hyde Park?|Ask a|pleecemanǃ" (policeman) The metrical "feet" are indicated by the vertical divisions. With the Ionian ("the soft scale fit for a drinking party," p. 198), the rhythm was commonly | ♫ ♩♩ | ♫ ♩♩ | etc. or | ♩♩♫ | ♩♩♫ | etc. or the "Anacreontic." | ♫ ♩♩♩♫♩♩.

[2] A musical expert, mentioned again on p. 222.

[3] ἐνόπλιον.

[4] The rise and fall of the foot taking equal time.

[5] The time of — ᴗ — for example, in a series of such figures was ♩ ♪♩, the second long having the time of a dotted note. The speech is comically confused on purpose.

[6] Because each Greek word had one syllable a musical fifth above the normal monotone, and the speech sounded like a musical recitative.

"Good speaking then, and good concord, and good gracefulness and good rhythm, each follows good spirit—not the good nature which we mildly call simplicity when it is really silliness, but the mind really well and truly constructed in its character."

"Exactly so," he said.

"Then must not these be everywhere pursued by the young, if they are to do their part?"

"They must indeed."

"And painting is full of these, and all such arts and crafts, weaving is full of them and embroidery and architecture and moreover all the making of furniture and, besides, the very nature of animal bodies and of plants and trees, for in all these is either gracefulness or ungracefulness. And gracelessness and disproportion and discord are akin to evil speaking and evil spirit, but the opposites are symbols of the opposite, and akin to it—to sound mind and good spirit."

"Entirely true," he said.

"Then are only the poets in question? Must we have supervision over them only, and compel them only, to implant the image of good spirit in their poems or else to make no poems at all amongst us? Must we not have the same supervision over the other craftsmen, and stop their implanting this spirit so evil and dissolute, so ungenerous and unseemly, whether in the likenesses of living things, or in buildings, or in any other thing made by craftsmen?[1] One that cannot obey must not be tolerated as a workman among us, or else our guardians will be fed on images of vice like poisonous weeds, culling and cropping large quantities every day in little bits from all sides until they unconsciously collect one great mass of corruption in their souls. But we must search for those craftsmen who by good natural powers can track out the nature of the beautiful and the graceful, and then our young people, dwelling, as it were, in wholesome country, will take in good from every direction; with works of beauty around them meeting their sight and hearing there will be, as it were, breezes blowing health to them from favourable regions, and, from childhood up, bringing them unconsciously into likeness and love and harmony with the beauty of speech."

"Ah," he replied, "that would be the best of education for them!"

"It follows then, Glaucon," said I, "that education in music and the fine arts is most potent, because by this chiefly rhythm and harmony sink into the inmost part of the soul and fasten

[1] The duty to make all things beautiful for the education of the young is Plato's own precept; and in recent times it was proclaimed by Ruskin and others.

most firmly upon it, bringing gracefulness and making it graceful if one is well trained, but otherwise just the opposite: and again, because if any things are defective or badly made or badly grown, one trained as he should be in that way would perceive it at once and would be pleased or pained with true taste. He would praise the beautiful things, and eagerly receive them into his soul, and feed on them, and become himself beautiful and good; but the ugly things he would blame with true taste, while still too young to have reason by which to understand about them, and when reason came to him he would gladly welcome her as a friend whom he recognised by a sense[1] of affinity. Don't you think so?"

"At least that is my opinion," said he; "such are the reasons why music is the way of their education."

"It's like learning to read," I said. "We were quite satisfied then, if we knew the letters at sight, as they were dancing about, only a few elements in all the words; whether in a small word or a large word we did not disregard them and think them not necessary to notice, but everywhere we took pains to distinguish them, believing that we should never be men of letters until we could."

"True," he said.

"And images of letters—if we should ever see them in water or in a mirror, we shall not know them unless we first know the letters themselves, but knowing the reflections belongs to the same art and practice?"

"Assuredly."

"Then is it not true, in heaven's name, that in the same way we cannot be musical ourselves, nor can those whom we say we have to educate, our guardians, until we can recognise the shapes of self-control and courage and generosity and loftiness, and all things akin to these, and again their opposites, where they are dancing about everywhere, and until we can perceive them in the things in which they are; we must know them and know their images, and never disregard them whether in little or in large, but we must believe that both image and original belong to the same art and practice?"

"Very necessary," he said.

"Then," said I, "when both are there together—beautiful manners in the soul, and in the bodily form what agrees and concords with these and is of the same type, would it not be the most beautiful sight for one who is able to see it?"

"Much the most beautiful."

"And besides, the most beautiful is most lovable."

"Of course."

[1] Resulting from education.

"Then the musical one would fall in love with persons who are most completely of this sort; but he would not love someone in whom there was discord."

"No, not if anything were lacking in the soul," he said, "but some lack in the body he might put up with and love him all the same."

"I understand," said I, "that you have or had a lover of that sort, and I grant it. But tell me this: Is there any communion between temperance and excessive pleasure?"

"How could there be," said he, "when excessive pleasure sends a man out of his mind no less than pain!"

"Or between any other virtue and this?"

"None."

"Well, has excessive pleasure any communion with violence and licence?"

"Most assuredly it has."

"Can you name any pleasure greater and keener than bodily love?"

"No," said he, "and none madder."

"But the right love is to love the orderly and beautiful soberly and in the spirit of music?"

"Indeed it is," he said.

"And nothing mad or akin to licence must be allowed to come near right love?"

"Nothing."

"Then this excessive pleasure must not be allowed to come near, and there must be no communion with it for lover and beloved if they love aright?"

"No indeed, Socrates," he said, "there must be none."

"Very well, for the city which we are founding you will, it seems, lay down the law thus: A lover may kiss his beloved, and be with him and touch him, as his own son, for the grace of the beautiful, and with his consent; in all else, if he cares for anyone, he should be careful to behave in associating with him so that there shall never be a suspicion of anything more intimate than this, or if there is, he will have the blame of bad education and bad taste."

"Just so," he said.

"Now then," said I, "do you think we have here the end of our account of music? At least it has ended where it ought to end; for I take it music ought to end in the love of the beautiful."[1]

"I agree," he said.

"After music comes gymnastic in the education of the young men."

---

[1] This discussion about "music" for education began on p. 174.

"Naturally."

"Of course in this also they must be properly trained from childhood and all through life. I believe this is how the matter stands. Please consider it yourself. I don't think a sound body makes a soul good by its own virtue; on the contrary, I think a good soul by its own virtue provides a body in the best possible condition. What do you think?"

"I think just as you do," he said.

"Should we not be right then," I said, "if we should attend sufficiently to the mind, and pass on to it the care of details about the body, after giving only the general outlines briefly as a guide?"

"Quite right," he said.

"Well, drunkenness we said they must eschew. Surely the guardian is the last man in the world who should be allowed to get drunk and not to know where on earth he is!"

"That would be ridiculous," he said, "a guardian to want a guardian himself!"

"What about food, then? Our guardians are champions in the greatest of contests; or is that not so?"

"Yes, they are."

"Then would the condition of the athletes we see here be suitable for them?"

"Perhaps."

"But that is a sleepy condition and shaky as regards health. Don't you see how they sleep away their lives, and if they depart even a little from their appointed diet and routine, these athletes fall into great and dangerous diseases?"

"I do."

"But the warlike athletes need some more varied training," said I, "since it is necessary for them to be like unsleeping dogs, to see and hear most keenly; they have many changes to endure in their campaigns, changes of drinking water and food, sun's heat and cold weather, and they must never be unsteady in health."

"So it seems to me."

"Then would not the best gymnastic be a sister of the music which we have recently been describing?"

"How do you mean?"

"A simple, reasonable gymnastic, I should think, and particularly that which is concerned with war."

"How, if you please?"

"One could learn this sort of thing from Homer," I said. "You know that on campaign, in the feasts of the heroes, he never gives them fish to eat, although they are on the Hellespont close to the sea; and never boiled meat, only roast, which would be most easy for soldiers to get, of course, for to use fire alone is easier, one might say, everywhere, without carrying pots and pans about with them."

"Exactly."

"And sauces and sweets I believe Homer never mentions. Is not this indeed what every athlete also knows—to have a good habit of body we must eschew all such things."

"They are quite right," he said, "they know it and they do it."

"Then if you think that is right, my friend, I think you do not praise a Syracusan table and a Sicilian variety of relishes."

"Not I."

"So you would not allow a man to have a Corinthian girl as his little dear, if he is to keep fit in body?"

"Certainly not."

"Or the famous[1] luxuries of Attic pastry?"

"Of course not."

"For all this sort of feeding and diet and routine we could rightly liken to the melody making and songs composed in a gallimaufry of all scales and rhythms."

"Of course."

"There the variety engendered licence, here disease; but simplicity in music produces sound soberness in the soul, in gymnastic health in the body?"

"Most true," he said.

"But when licence and diseases multiply in a city, numerous law courts and dispensaries are opened, and the arts of law and medicine hold their heads high when even freeborn men take a serious interest in them."

"That is sure to happen."

"And what greater proof will you find of bad and ugly education in a city when tiptop doctors and juries are wanted not only for common people and artisans, but for those who claim to have been brought up in a liberal style? Don't you think it an ugly thing and a great proof of bad education to have to make use of justice imported from foreigners and let them be your masters and judges, for lack of the homegrown product?"

"The ugliest thing in the world," he said.

"Ah, but don't you think there is an uglier thing," I said; "when a man wastes the greater part of his life in law courts, prosecuting and prosecuted; and not only that, but through lack of taste he is induced to pride himself even on this—being a terrible fellow at wrongdoing, ready to wriggle and

[1] Or "seeming," "imaginary."

twist every way and to get out of any hold by every possible outlet, as slippery as a withy, to avoid paying penalty—and all that for trifles and nothings! He can't see how much more beautiful and better it is to make a life for himself which needs no dozing juryman."

"Indeed," he said, "such behaviour is even uglier than the other."

"And to need doctoring," I said, "isn't that ugly—except for wounds, or the attacks of some seasonal illnesses? But to need it because of sloth or the manner of life we have described, when men fill themselves with floods and winds like so many marshes!—compelling the smart sons of Asclepios[1] to invent names to suit the diseases, and call them flatulences and fluxes!"[2]

"Yes, indeed," he said, "they are truly strange novelties as names for diseases."

"There was nothing like that, I think," said I, "in the days of Asclepios himself. At least I infer it, because before Troy that woman gave wounded Eurypylos handfuls of barley meal sprinkled over Pramnian wine, and cheese grated on, surely an inflammatory mess, and then the sons of Asclepios found no fault, nor did they blame Patroclos, who was attending the man."[3]

"Yes, really," said he, "it was a strange drink for one in such a state."

"Not at all," I said, "if you remember that the Asclepiads did not formerly use the present medicine, which dances attendance on diseases—not before Herodicos was born, as they say. Herodicos was a trainer, and becoming sickly he mingled gymnastic with physic and wore out himself first and worst, and afterwards many another."

"How so?" said he.

"By making his death so long," I said. "He had a mortal disease, and attended it closely; he could not cure himself, I suppose, so he did nothing all his life long but doctor himself, until he wore himself out with worrying if he omitted any of his usual habits, and he lasted to old age, a regular die-hard by means of his science."

"A fine old[4] prize he got for his skill!" said he.

"As might be expected," I said, "when he did not know why Asclepios did not reveal this kind of medicine to his descendants. It was not ignorance or inexperience of it at all;

---

[1] Father of medicine.
[2] Literally "windblasts" and "downflows."
[3] Plato had a different text, or else he confuses two scenes. In *Iliad* xi. 624, Hecamēdē gave the potion to Nestor and Machaon, Asclepios' son. In *Iliad* xi. 844, Patroclos cut out an arrow from Eurypylos' leg and put on a poultice.
[4] Plato puns on *gēras*, old age, and *gĕras*, reward or privilege.

but Asclepios knew that amongst all well-ordered peoples each man in a city has a work laid upon him which he is obliged to do, and no one has leisure to be ill and doctor himself all his life. Absurdly enough we notice this in the craftsmen, but don't notice it in the rich and those who are thought fortunate."

"How?" he asked.

"A carpenter," said I, "when he is ill expects the doctor to give him a drug to drink and so to vomit out his disease, or he expects to get rid of it by downward purging or burning or cutting. But if a doctor orders a long treatment for him with bandages round his head and all that sort of thing, he says at once he has no time to be ill, and life like that is not worth having, if he is always thinking of disease and neglecting the work which lies before him. Then he says goodbye to that kind of doctor, and goes on with his usual life; he gets well doing his business and lives, or if his body is not strong enough to hold out, he dies and gets rid of his troubles."

"For such a man," he said, "that seems the proper way to use the art of medicine."

"Is the reason," I said, "because he had a work to do, and if he did not do it, life was not worth living?"

"That is clear," he said.

"But we don't say that the rich man has any such work laid out before him, from which if he is forced to abstain, life is not worth living?"

"Not so far as I know."

"Why!" said I, "do you never hear the saying of Phocylides 'As soon as a man has got enough to live on, he should then practise virtue'?"

"I think he might do it before too," he said.

"Oh well, don't let us quarrel with him about that," I said, "but let us inform ourselves about this—must the rich man practise this, and is life not worth living if he does not; or is nursing disease no hindrance to him in following the advice of Phocylides, although it is a hindrance to close attention in carpentry and the other crafts?"

"Oh, indeed it is," he said, "almost more than anything else, this excessive care for the body which goes beyond gymnastic. It is troublesome, you know, for household management, and for military service, and for sedentary office in the city. Worst of all, it is difficult with any kind of learning and thinking and self-discipline; it is forever suspecting the headaches or dizziness of a high-strung nature, and throwing the blame on philosophy as the cause of their existence. The result is, that wherever virtue is practised in this manner and tested, it is in every way a hindrance; it always makes one imagine some illness and never to cease agonizing about the body."

"Just what might be expected," I said. "Then we must believe that Asclepios knew all this. So he provided for men, healthy in body by nature and habits, who had some local disease inside themselves; for these and for this condition he revealed the art of healing, thus expelling the disease from them by drugs or cuttings, and told them to go on living as usual that he might not hinder their duties in the city. But bodies which were diseased inwardly all through he did not try to cure by diet and by draining out and pouring in gradually. That only implants other diseases which naturally come from this treatment, so as to make life long and miserable for a man; one who could not live in the established round he thought it not his duty to treat, because he was of no use to himself or the city."

"Asclepios was a statesman then," he said, "as you describe him."

"It is clear that he was," said I, "and his sons—he was such a man—don't you see they showed themselves good men in the war before Troy, besides practising the art of healing as I describe it? Don't you remember how Menelaos was wounded by a shot from Pandaros, and

They sucked the blood, and sprinkled soothing simples.[1]

But what he must eat and drink afterwards they did not tell him, any more than they told Eurypylos. They thought the simples were enough to heal men who were healthy before the wounds, and temperate in their way of living, even if they happened to drink a posset on the spot. But one who was naturally diseased and intemperate they thought was of no use alive to himself or anyone else; their art was not for such men, and they should not try to cure them even if they were richer than Midas."

"Smart lads," he said, "the sons of Asclepios, by your account."

"So they should be," said I. "However, the tragedians and Pindar[2] will not have it our way. They say that Asclepios was a son of Apollo, and he was bribed with gold to cure a rich man then in the throes of death, for which he was struck by lightning. After what has been said before we cannot believe both their tales; if he was the son of a god, we shall

[1] *Iliad* iv. 218.
[2] Pindar, *Pythian* iii. 55, gives the story which follows. He says the man was dead.

maintain that he was not covetous; if he was covetous, he was no son of a god."

"That is right, so far," he said. "But what do you say to this question, Socrates—must we not have good doctors in the city? And would not those be likely to be best who have treated the largest numbers of men both healthy and diseased? So also the best jurymen would be those who have had to do with all sorts of natures."

"Oh yes," I said. "I agree we must have good ones. But do you know which I think good?"

"Not unless you tell me," he said.

"Well, I will try," said I. "But in one question you put two things together which are not alike."

"How?" he asked.

"Doctors," I said, "would become most clever if beginning from childhood, besides learning their art, they should have to do with the largest possible number of the most diseased bodies, and if they had been sick of every disease and were not very healthy in themselves. For they do not cure body by body, I take it; if so, we should not allow their bodies to be or to have been in an evil state. But they cure body by soul, which cannot cure well if it has been an evil soul or is evil."

"You are right," he said.

"But a juryman, my friend, rules soul with soul; and a soul cannot be allowed to be brought up from youth among bad souls and have to do with them, and itself to have run through all sorts of wrongdoing and committed all, in order to infer quickly from itself the wrongs done by others, as with diseases of the body. No. The soul must have been, when young, pure and uncontaminated from evil natures, if it is to be good and true in deciding justice wholesomely. Therefore decent people appear to be simple-minded in youth, and they are easily deceived by the unjust, since they have no models within themselves of like feeling with the bad."

"Yes, indeed," he said, "that is just what happens to them."

"So then," said I, "the good judge or juryman must be old, not young; he must have learned late what injustice is, and not have perceived it as something of his own within his soul, but he must have had long practice in discerning what evil really is, as an alien thing in alien souls, by knowledge, not by experience of his own."

"A real genuine judge, at least," said he, "such a one would be."

"And a good one," said I, "which was your question. For he that has a good soul is good; not that clever one, ever suspicious of evil, who has done much wrong himself and is thought a knowing rogue. When he has to do with his likes he appears to be clever and cautious, with an eye upon the models within himself; but as soon as he comes across good men, and older men, he appears to be only stupid, distrustful at the wrong time and not knowing a wholesome nature when he sees it, because he has no model of such a thing. But because he meets bad men more often than good, he seems to himself and to others to be rather wise than foolish."

"Quite true," said he, "beyond a doubt."

"Then," I said, "the good and wise judge is not such as that, but we must seek the first kind. For wickedness could never know either virtue or itself; but virtue schooled by nature will gain knowledge in time both of itself and of wickedness. Then this one is wise, I think, not the evil one."

"And I agree with you," said he.

"Then the healing art such as we described it, coupled with the art of dispensing justice in this fashion, you will ordain by law in the city; these will care for those of the people who are naturally good in body and soul, but if any are not, those who are not so in body they will leave to die, and those who are naturally bad in soul and incurable they will certainly themselves put to death?"

"The best thing that could happen to them," he said, "and the best thing for the city, as we have seen."

"And the young people," I said, "by using that simple music[1] which as we said engenders temperance and soberness, will clearly be careful not to fall in need of the courtroom art."

"Surely," said he.

"And will not the musician, following these very same tracks in pursuit of gymnastic, manage, if he wishes, to need nothing of medicine unless it is absolutely necessary?"

"I think so."

"Again, he will labour at the exercises themselves and their hard work with an eye to the high-spirited part of his nature, to awaken that, rather than towards mere strength; he will not be like other athletes who go in for diet and hard work only to make themselves strong."

"You are certainly right," he said.

"Very well, then, Glaucon," said I, "those who established our education in music and gymnastic had not the purpose which some believe they had, to care for the soul by one and the body by the other?"

"What, then?" he asked.

[1] I.e., education, "culture."

"Really," said I, "they meant to establish both chiefly for the soul."

"How so?"

"Haven't you noticed," I said, "what is the real state of mind of those who spend their whole lives in association with gymnastic, and do not touch music? and the state of mind of those who have the opposite dispositions?"

"What have you in mind?" he asked.

"Their savagery and hardness," I said, "and the softness and gentleness of the others."

"Oh yes," he said, "I have noticed that those who use undiluted gymnastic turn out more savage than they should, and the others became softer by music than is good for them."

"And yet," said I, "the high-spirited part of our nature would produce the savagery, and if rightly trained it would become courage; but being strained more than is proper it would naturally become hard and disagreeable."

"So I think," he said.

"Well," I said, "gentleness would be in the philosophic nature; and if it were slackened too much it would become too soft, but if it were well trained it would be both gentle and moderate."

"That is true."

"But there ought to be both these two natures in the guardians, we say."

"There ought."

"Then these natures ought to be fitted in concord together?"

"Of course."

"And when there is concord in a man, his soul is both temperate and brave?"

"Certainly."

"But when there is discord, cowardly and boorish?"

"Very much so."

"Now suppose a man allows music to play him lullaby, and pour over his soul through the ears like a funnel a flood of those sweet and soft and melancholy strains which we were talking of just now, and suppose he goes on warbling all his life enraptured with song, what happens? If he had any high spirit he softens it at first like iron, and makes useful the useless and hard; but if he does not slacken in his devotion, and fascinates the spirit, next it begins at once to melt and run, until he has melted all the spirit away, and cut the sinews out of the soul, and made a 'feeble spearman.'"[1]

[1] *Iliad* xvii. 588, which is used here as a proverb.

"Very true," he said.

"And if to begin with," I said, "he receives a spiritless nature, he does all this very soon; but if a high-spirited one, he makes the spirit weak and unstable, one soon flaring up and soon put out by trifles. Then they become sudden and quick to quarrel and full of ill temper instead of high-spirited."

"Exactly so."

"Again, if he works hard at gymnastic, if he is a good trencherman and never touches music and philosophy, at first while his body is in high condition he is full of pride and spirit and at his very bravest?"

"Yes, indeed."

"But then as he does nothing else and has no communion with the Muse at all, what becomes of any love of knowledge which may have been in his soul? With never a taste of any learning, or of research, not a bit of reasoning or anything else musical, it becomes weak and deaf and blind, because it is never awakened or fed, and its senses are never purified."

"Just so," he said.

"Then such a one becomes a hater of reason and culture; he no longer uses reasonable persuasion but does everything by violence and savagery as a wild beast confronting a wild beast—a life of ignorance and ineptitude full of discord and gracelessness."

"That is perfectly true," said he.

"Then to help these two natures, as it seems, I would say some god has given two arts to mankind, music and gymnastic, for the philosophic and the high-spirited parts; not for soul or body particularly, except by the way, but for both together, in order that they may be fitted together in concord, by being strained and slackened to the proper point."

"So it seems," he said.

"Then the one who best mingles music and gymnastic, and most proportionably applies them to the soul, would most rightly be called the perfect musician and master of melody, much rather than the one who tunes together the strings of harps; and that is what we say."

"And with good reason, Socrates."

"Then, my dear Glaucon, shall we need some such person to be always in charge in our city, if the constitution is to be preserved?"

"We shall, most certainly."

"Then these would be the outlines or shapes of their education and breeding. For what would be the use of making a long list of their dancings and huntings and houndings, their gymnastic contests and horse races? It must surely be clear that they will follow the same lines, and there should be no further difficulty in finding them out."

"Probably no difficulty."

"Very well then," I said, "what would be the next thing for us to decide? Must it not be which among these are to rule, and which to be ruled?"

"What else could it be?"

"The older men must be the rulers, and the younger be the ruled, so much is clear."

"Yes, that is clear."

"And the best of them must be the rulers?"

"That is clear too."

"Among farmers, are not the best those who are most perfectly farmers?"

"Yes."

"Then those who most perfectly guard the city must be the rulers, since they are the best of the guardians?"

"Yes."

"So they must be men intelligent in this their business, and capable, and besides, careful for their city?"

"That is true."

"And one would be most careful for what he really loves most?"

"Necessarily."

"And further, he would love most what he believes to have the same interests as himself, when he thinks all is well with him if all is well with that, otherwise the opposite?"

"Exactly so," said he.

"Then we must choose out of the guardians men such as those whom we observe to be most careful for us all their lives long; who do with all their hearts whatever they think will be for the advantage of the city, and would in no way ever wish to do what is not."

"They would be most suitable," he said.

"Then I think we should watch them at every time of life, and see if they are careful guardians of this resolve, and if neither sorcery nor force can move them and make them cast out unconsciously the opinion that they must do what is best for the city."

"What do you mean," he said, "by this casting out?"

"I will tell you," said I. "It appears to me that an opinion leaves the mind either by intention or without intention: by intention, the false opinion of one who learns better; without intention, every true opinion."

"I understand the intentional one," said he, "but I want to hear more about the unintentional."

"Oh, very well," said I. "Don't you believe yourself that men do not intend to lose their good things, but they get rid of the evil things intentionally? And is not to be defrauded of the truth evil, and to possess the truth good? And do you not think that to hold true opinions is to possess the truth?"

"Yes, I think you are right," said he, "and they are unwilling to be deprived of true opinion."

"So when that happens, they have been robbed or bewitched or compelled?"

"Even now I don't understand," he said.

"I must be speaking like a man in a tragedy!"[1] said I. "By 'robbed' I mean they are argued down, or forget; because in the one case argument, in the other, time robs them of their opinions without their knowing it. You understand now, I suppose?"

"Yes."

"By 'compelled,' I mean when some pain or suffering makes them change their opinion."

"I understand that now," he said, "and I think you are right."

"But when I say 'bewitched,' I believe you would agree that the word describes those who change their opinion either charmed by pleasure or terrified by fear of something."

"I agree," said he "that all which deceives, bewitches."

"To return to our task, now, we must examine who are the best guardians of their resolution that they must do whatever they think from time to time to be best for the city. They must be watched from childhood up; we must set them tests in which a man would be most likely to forget such a resolution or to be deceived, and we must choose the one who remembers well and is not easily deceived, and reject the rest. Do you agree?"

"Yes."

"Hard labour again, and suffering, and contests—in all these we must watch them in the same way."

"Quite right," he said.

"Now take the third kind of competitive test, bewitchment —here too we must try them and see what happens. You know how they bring colts among noises and tumults and see if they are timid; in the same way while the men are young we must bring them into situations of terror, and again change the scene to pleasures, and test them even more than gold in the fire. Then see if one proves hard to bewitch, and keeps his graces

[1] In high-flown metaphor.

in all, if he is a good guardian of himself and the music which he has learnt, if he shows himself well in rhythm and concord through all this, and such as would be most useful to the city and to himself. Then whoever is thus tested among boys, youths and men,[1] and comes out immaculate, he must be established as ruler and guardian of the city; honours must be given him while he lives, and at death public interment and other magnificent memorials. Those who fail are to be rejected. Some such method as this, Glaucon, I think there should be in our selection, and so we should appoint our rulers and guardians; but this is only a sketch, not something to be followed in every detail."

"I agree," he said, "it should be done in some such way as that."

"Then really and truly we may call these our perfect and complete guardians? They shall keep watch on enemies without and friends within; they shall see to it that the friends will not wish to injure, and the enemies shall not be able; and they will have the young men whom we called guardians just now as helpers and assistants for the decrees of the rulers."

"I agree with that," he said.

"You remember a while since," I said, "we spoke of necessary lies. Is there any device by which we might tell one genuine lie worthy of the name, and persuade the rulers themselves that it is true, or at least persuade the rest of the city?"

"What may that be?"

"We don't want a novelty," I said; "it is only a sort of Phoenician thing,[2] which has happened already in many places, as the poets tell us, and they were believed; but it never happened in our time and I don't know that it could, and to make it believed needs a good deal of faith."

"You don't seem very willing to speak out," said he.

"You will think I have good reason for that," I said, "when I have spoken."

"Speak out," he said, "and don't be afraid."

"Here goes, then, although I don't know how I shall dare, or what words to use. Well, I will try first to convince the rulers themselves and the soldiers, then the rest of the city; and this is the story. The training and education we were giving them was all a dream, and they only imagined all this was happening to them and around them; but in truth they were being mould-

---

[1] The three regular grades in the public games were Boys, Youths and Men.
[2] He hints at the legends about Cadmos, and perhaps in particular about the crop of men sprung from the dragon's teeth which Cadmos sowed at Thebes. These again are associated with the Doric culture, especially in Sparta, which was one model that Plato had in mind. The Athenians believed themselves to be indigenous, or sprung from the earth where they lived. Plato hints also at the current legend of the Four Ages, Gold, Silver, Brass and Iron.

ed and trained down inside the earth, where they and their arms and all their trappings were being fashioned. When they were completely made, the earth their mother delivered them from her womb; and now they must take thought for the land in which they live, as for their mother and nurse, must plan for her and protect her, if anyone attacks her, and they must think of the other citizens as brothers also born from the earth."

"I am not surprised," he said, "that you were shy of telling that lie!"

"There was good reason for it," I said, "but never mind, listen to the rest of the fable. 'So you are all brothers in the city,' we shall tell them in our fable, 'but while God moulded you, he mingled gold in the generation of some, and those are the ones fit to rule, who are therefore the most precious; he mingled silver in the assistants;[1] and iron and brass in farmers and the other craftsmen. Then because of being all akin you would beget your likes for the most part, but sometimes a silver child may be born from a golden or a golden from a silvern, and so with all the rest breeding amongst each other. The rulers are commanded by God first and foremost that they be good guardians of no person so much as of their own children, and to watch nothing else so carefully as which of these things is mingled in their souls. If any child of theirs has a touch of brass or iron, they will not be merciful to him on any account, but they will give him the value proper to his nature, and push him away among the craftsmen or the farmers; if again one of them has the gold or silver in his nature, they will honour him and lift him among the guardians or the assistants, since there is an oracle that the city will be destroyed when the brass or the iron shall guard it.' Now have you any device to make them believe this fable?"

"No, these people themselves will never believe it; but I see a way to make their sons believe it, and those who come after them, and the rest of mankind."

"I think I understand pretty well what you mean," said I, "but even that would be good for the men themselves; they would be more inclined to care for the city and each other. This will, I suppose, allow some chance for tradition to give a lead in the matter.[2]

"Now let us arm these sons of earth, and lead them forward with their rulers guiding. Let them go and see the best place in the city for a camp. They want a place from which they can best keep in hand those within, if they will not obey the laws;

---

[1] That is, the guardian soldiers, the second class of guardians.
[2] The first would accept it as a useful notion, and their children would learn it as a truth.

and repel those without, if some enemy should come like a wolf on the fold. There let them sacrifice to the proper gods, and there make their beds. What do you say?"

"I agree," said he.

"So arranged as to have shelter in winter and to be all right in summer?"

"Of course," he said, "you mean places to live in, I think."

"Yes," I said, "soldiers' quarters, not places of business."

"What do you mean by this difference?" he asked.

"I will try to tell you," said I. "The most dangerous and the ugliest thing possible for shepherds is to breed such dogs for attendance upon the flocks, and to keep them in such a manner, that licence or hunger or any other evil passion may lead the dogs themselves to set upon and damage the flocks, and to be more like wolves than dogs."

"Dangerous, of course," he said.

"Then we must guard in every way that our assistants may not do anything of the sort to the citizens because they are stronger, and be more like savage masters than friendly allies."

"We must indeed," said he.

"And they would be provided already with the greatest of safeguards if they have been really well educated?"

"Well, so they have been," said he.

And I said, "We have no right to affirm that yet, my dear Glaucon; but we may affirm what we were just saying, that they must receive the right education, whatever it is, if they are to have what will most chiefly make them gentle both to themselves and to those who are guarded by them."

"That is quite right," said he.

"Then besides this education any sensible man would say that we must provide their lodgings and their other property such as will not prevent them from being themselves as good guardians as they can be, and such as will not excite them to do mischief among the other citizens."

"That will be quite true," said he.

"Look here, then," said I; "do you think some such manner of life and lodging as this will do, if they are to be as we describe? First of all, no one must have any private property whatsoever, except what is absolutely necessary. Secondly, no one must have any lodging or storehouse at all which is not open to all comers. Then their provisions must be so much as is needed by athletes of war, temperate and brave men, and there must be fixed allowances for them to be supplied by the other citizens as wages for their guardianship, so much that there shall be plenty for the year but nothing over at the end. They must live in common, attending in messes as if they were in the field. As to gold and silver, we must tell them that they have these from the gods as a divine gift in their souls, and they want in addition no human silver or gold; they must not pollute this treasure by mixing it with a treasure of mortal gold, because many wicked things have been done about the common coinage, but theirs is undefiled. They alone of all in the city dare not have any dealings with gold and silver, or even touch them, or come under the same roof with them, or hang them upon their limbs, or drink from silver or gold. In this way they would be saved themselves and save the city; but whenever they get land of their own and houses and money, they will be householders and farmers instead of guardians, masters and enemies of the rest of the citizens instead of allies; so hating and hated, plotting and plotted against, they will spend all their lives fearing enemies within much more than without, running a course very near to destruction, they and the city together. For all these reasons," I said, "let us agree on this manner of providing our guardians with lodging and all the rest, and let us lay it down by law. What do you say?"

"I agree wholly with you," said Glaucon.

BOOK IV

Adeimantos broke in here, and said, "Defend yourself in this if you can, Socrates. Suppose someone says you are not making these men very happy, and they have themselves to thank for it. The city is theirs in truth, but they get no such joy of it, as others who have gotten lands and builded houses beautiful and large, collecting furniture to suit the houses and making sacrifices of their own to the gods, and entertaining guests; yes, indeed, and possessing what you have just mentioned, gold and silver, and all that is expected for those who are to live in bliss! But these, he would say, appear like hired mercenaries in the city, sitting still and guarding and nothing more!"

"Yes," I said, "and all serving for board and lodging and not even getting pay with their board like the others. They can't even go abroad on a trip if they wish, can't make a present to a pretty girl if they wish, can't spend a penny on anything else, like those who are thought to be having a good time! All this and more like it—what a lot of things you leave out of your list of complaints!"

"All right," said he, "put those in too."

"What defence shall we make, you ask?"

"Yes."

"Let's walk along on the same old path," I said, "and we

shall find what to say. This is what we will say. We should not be surprised if these also would be most happy in this way; yet what we had in mind when we founded the city was not how to make one class happy above the rest, but how to make the city as a whole as happy as it could be. For we believed that in such a city we were most likely to find justice, and injustice again in the worst managed city; then we might examine them and decide the matter which we have been searching all this time. Well then, now, as we believe, we are moulding the happy city; we are not separating a few in it and putting them down as happy, but we take it as a whole. By and by we will examine the opposite kind. Suppose we were putting colour on a statue, and someone came up and found fault because we did not put the finest colours on the finest parts of the figure, for the eyes, a most beautiful part, have, he says, been tinted dark, not crimson. We should think it a reasonable answer to give him if we said, 'Don't be silly! Do you think we ought to paint such a beautiful pair of eyes that they don't look like eyes at all? So also the other parts? But look and see if, by giving all the parts their proper treatment, we are making the whole beautiful!' Just so now, don't force us to tack on such happiness to the guardians as will make them anything but guardians. We could indeed just as well order the farmers to dress in purple and fine linen, and hang gold chains about them, and till the land for their pleasure; we might make the potters put their wheels away, and recline on couches and feast, and have drinking matches at the fire, and send the cup round to the right,[1] and make their pots when they felt so disposed; and we might make all the others live in bliss in that sort of way, and then expect the whole city to be happy! Don't preach to us like that; for if we obey you, farmer will not be farmer, and potter will not be potter, and no other class of those which make a city will have its proper form. The others are really no great matter; cobblers who are bogglers may work badly and pretend to be what they are not, and may go to ruin with no danger to the city; but if guardians of city and laws are not what they are thought to be, you see they destroy the city utterly, and they alone have the opportunity to make it well managed and happy. Then if we are making real and true guardians of the city, not marauders, and if our critic talks of farmers of some kind having a jolly time at a fair or a feast, not in a city at all, he must be talking of something else, not a city. Consider then, with this in our mind, whether we shall arrange that our guardians may have the greatest possible

---

[1] Clockwise, by way of the left, round to the right, as the wine goes now; "through the buttonhole," as Mr. Jingle puts it (Charles Dickens, *Pickwick Papers*, Chapter 2).

happiness, or if we shall keep in view the city as a whole and see how that shall be happy. Then we must compel and persuade these assistants, and all the guardians, to do as I have said, in order that they may be the best possible craftsmen in their own work; we must do the same with all the other craftsmen, and the whole city will increase and be managed well, and we must leave each class to have the share of happiness which their nature gives to each."

"Indeed," he said, "I think you are right."

"Very well," said I, "there is something else akin to this, and I wonder if you will think it reasonable too."

"What is it, exactly?"

"Consider whether it will ruin the other craftsmen also, and make them bad."

"Well, what is it?"

"Wealth and poverty," I said.

"In what way?"

"In this way. Let a potter grow wealthy—do you think he will care about his craft?"

"Oh dear no," said he.

"Then he will become idle and careless, more than before?"

"Much more."

"He becomes a worse potter, then?"

"Yes indeed," he said, "much worse."

"Yet again, if he is too poor to provide himself with tools or anything else needed for his trade, his goods will be worse, and he will not be able to teach his sons or apprentices so well, and they will be worse craftsmen?"

"Of course."

"Then both poverty and wealth make the craftsmen worse and the things they make as well?"

"So it seems."

"Then we have found other things which the guardians must guard against, and must prevent by all means from creeping unnoticed into the city."

"What are these?"

"Wealth," said I, "and poverty too; because wealth creates luxury and idleness and faction, and poverty adds meanness and bad work to the faction."

"Certainly," he said. "But consider, Socrates, how our city will be able to make war without having wealth, especially if it be forced to fight against a great city which has wealth."

"It is rather difficult," I said, "to fight against one, but against two such it is clearly easier."

"How can that be?" he asked.

"First of all," I said, "if there must be a fight, I suppose our men will be athletes of war matched against men of wealth."

"Yes to that," said he.

"Very well, Adeimantos," I said. "One boxer as well trained as he can be, against two non-boxers wealthy and fat—don't you think he would have an easy battle?"

"Perhaps not," he said, "if they came on both at once!"

"Not even if he could retreat and wait for the first man up, and then turn back and strike him, and did it again and again in the stifling heat of the sun? Could not such a boxer beat a lot of men like that?"

"I should say so," he answered. "That would hardly surprise me."

"But don't you think that rich men have more knowledge and experience of boxing than they have of the art of war?"

"I do," he said.

"Then it will be easy for our athletes, in all likelihood, to fight twice or three times their own number."

"I will grant you that," he said, "for I think you are right."

"Then again, suppose they send an embassy to one of the two cities, and tell them the truth; saying 'We use neither gold nor silver, and that is forbidden for us, but not for you; then join us in this war and get what the others have.'[1] Do you think anyone hearing this would choose to fight against a pack of hard, lean dogs, and not to join the dogs and tackle fat, tender sheep?"

"No, I do not! But if the wealth of the others be collected into one city," said he, "does not that bring danger to the one which is not wealthy?"

"Oh blissful ignorance!" I said. "Do you think any so-called city is worthy of the name except the one which we were constructing?"

"Why not?" said he.

"You must have a bigger appellation for the others," I said; "for each one of these greater cities is, as they say in the game,[2] 'Cities, cities everywhere, but city none for me!' Each is at least two cities, one of the poor and one of the rich, enemies to each other; and in each of these two there are very many smaller. If you treat with them as one, you will lose everything; if you treat with them as many, and offer to give the wealth and powers, even also the people themselves, of one or more

[1] Spartan brevity! Sparta also had no gold or silver.
[2] A board, it seems, was marked off into squares, and a game called "City" was played on it with counters. The board was called "city," and probably each square was a city too, which would explain the boy's cry when his own squares were empty, mentioned by Plato here; literally, "There are a great many cities, but not a city." The counters were called "dogs," and two dogs of one colour could take one dog of the other colour by getting one on each side. Plato has been hinting at this game already.

groups of men to other groups, you will always have many allies and few enemies. And so long as your city is managed with soberness as was laid down just now, it will be very great —I do not mean in fame, but in real truth very great, even if it has no more than a thousand men to fight for it. For a great city, one in this sense, you will not easily find either among the Hellenes or among the barbarians, but many you will find which are thought to be as great and many times greater than this is. Don't you agree?"

"Yes, I do," said he.

"Then here we might find the best limit for our rulers," I went on, "to decide how large the city should be, and how much land they ought to enclose for a city of that size, letting the rest go."

"What limit?" he said.

"This, I think," said I; "as long as the growing city is willing to remain a unity,[1] so big let it grow but no farther."

"Excellent," said he.

"Then here is another injunction we must lay upon the guardians—to guard in every way that the city be neither small nor seeming to be large, but be just great enough, and a unity."

"Quite a trifling injunction for them, I should think," he said.

"And another thing," I said, "is more trifling still, I suppose, which we mentioned before, when we said that if a trifling kind of son should be born among the guardians he was to be sent off to the others, and if one showing excellence were born among the others, he should be sent to the guardians. This was meant as a rule for the other citizens also, one man, one work; they were to bring each man to the work which was naturally his, so that each might practise his own work and be one man, not many men, and thus the whole city might grow into one city, not many cities."

"Yes," said he, "this is a smaller injunction than the other."

"Really, my dear Adeimantos," I said, "these are not a host of great injunctions laid on them, as one might think, but all trifles, if only they guard the proverbial one great thing needful, or rather not great but sufficient."

"What is that?" he asked.

"Education," I said, "and training. For if they are well educated and become orderly men, they will easily see the way through all these things, and others, too, that we have not mentioned yet, the possession of wives and marriage and begetting children; they will understand that all these goods, as the proverb goes, must be held in common."[2]

"Yes," he said, "that would be quite correct."

[1] So long as it can be governed with consent.
[2] "Friends' goods are common; what is your friend's is yours," is the proverb.

"Indeed," said I, "when a state once has a proper start, it grows as a circle would grow. Training and education being kept good engender good natures; and good natures holding fast to the good education become even better than those before, both in the power of breeding, like the lower animals, and in other ways."

"That is likely," he said.

"Then to put it shortly, this one thing needful—training and education—is what the overseers of the city must cleave to, and they must take care that it is not corrupted insensibly. They must guard it beyond everything, and allow no innovations in gymnastic and music against the established order, but guard it with all possible care; and when someone says of songs,

> What is it people always want to hear?
> The latest tune that's warbled through the air![1]

they would be anxious lest men may think perhaps that the poet does not mean new songs but a new way of singing, and may praise this. So we must not praise such a thing, or take that to be the meaning. For to change to a new kind of music is a thing we must beware of as risking the whole. For the methods of music cannot be stirred up without great upheavals of social custom and law; so says Damon, and I believe it."

"And you may put me down too," said Adeimantos, "as one of the believers."

"Then the fort of safeguard for the guardians," said I, "must be built somewhere hereabouts, it seems: in music."

"Here at least," he said, "lawlessness easily creeps in unseen."

"Yes," I said, "in the form of play, when it seems likely to do no harm."

"And it does no harm," said he, "if it were not that it makes itself at home little by little, and gently overflows upon manners and practice; from these now stronger grown, it passes to men's business agreements; and from business it moves upon laws and constitutions in a wanton flood, Socrates, until at last all public and private life is overwhelmed."

"Really!" said I, "is that the case?"

"It seems so to me," he said.

"Then, as we were saying at the beginning, our children must hold fast to play of a more law-abiding kind from the first, since when play becomes lawless and the children likewise, it is impossible that law-abiding and serious men can grow out of such children."

"Certainly they must," he said.

[1] *Odyssey* i. 352.

"Indeed it seems that when children begin by playing properly, and receive into themselves law and order through the music, just the opposite happens; good order goes with them in all things and makes them grow, and raises up again whatever of the old state was lying in ruins."[1]

"True indeed," he said.

"Then these discover again the customs, even trifles as they were thought, which those before them had wholly destroyed."

"What customs?"

"Such as silence of the younger in the presence of their elders, which is becoming; and giving place to them and rising before them, and honouring their parents; the cut of the hair, the manner of dress and footgear, their whole bearing and deportment, and everything of that sort. Don't you think so?"

"I do!"

"But to legislate about such customs would be silly, I think. For they are not observed, and they would not last if laid down as laws in word and writing."

"How could they?"

"Anyhow, the fact is, Adeimantos," I said, "that whatever way the education starts them, their future ways are of like quality. It's a case of like always calling for like!"

"What else could happen?"

"And in the end then, I think, we should say it will turn out to be something complete and bold, either good or bad."

"Of course," he said.

"My opinion then, let me tell you," I said, "is that for these reasons I would not try to make laws about such things."

"With good reason," he said.

"Ah, but for goodness' sake," I went on, "do say what you think about all this market business, contracts which different classes of people make in the market, and contracts with artisans if you like, and slander and assault, and filing of declarations and finding juries, or there may be dues to exact or to pay which have to be enforced sometimes in markets or harbours—the whole multitude of market rules or police rules or the harbour rules and all other such—shall we allow ourselves to make any laws about these?"

"No, it would not be worth the trouble," he said, "to give orders to cultured gentlemen. They will easily find out for themselves, I suppose, most of the lawmaking needed."

"Yes, my dear friend," I said, "if only God grants them safe maintenance of the laws which we have described already."

"If he does not," said he, "they will spend their whole lives

[1] He is thinking of Athens, which he thought so degenerate in his day.

making such laws and amending them and expecting to find perfection."

"You make them like sick men," I said, "who are too undisciplined to give up their bad manner of life."

"Exactly."

"Ah, what a charming life they have! Always doctoring themselves, with the sole result that they make their diseases worse and more complicated, and if anyone recommends a medicine, always expecting to be cured by it!"

"Yes," he said, "that is just what happens to men who are sick in that way."

"Yes indeed," said I, "and here's another charming thing about them—they hate worst of all the man who tells them the truth, who tells them that nothing in the world will do them any good—not medicines or burnings or cuttings, no, not incantations or amulets, or anything else until they stop drinking and gorging and wenching and idling."

"Not so very charming," he said; "to be angry with one who gives good advice. There's no charm in that."

"You don't seem to approve of such men," said I.

"No, I do not, I do declare."

"Nor will you approve of the city then, to return to what we were saying, if it does things of that sort as a whole. Do not cities appear to you to do just the same as these sick men, when they are badly governed and forewarn their people not to meddle with their city's constitution—on penalty of death to anyone who tries to do this? But whoever serves them most pleasantly, governed as they are, and heaps favours upon them, and cringes and forestalls their wishes, and shows himself clever in fulfilling them—there's their good man and true, there's their fountain of wisdom, there's the man they will honour!"

"They do seem to me to do just the same," said he, "and I do not approve them at all."

"And what of those who are willing and eager to serve such cities—don't you admire them for courage to carry it off so lightly?"

"I do," said he, "except those who are really deluded, and believe themselves to be real born statesmen, because they are praised by the mob."

"What's that you say? Can't you make some allowance for the poor men?" I said. "Suppose a man can't use a footrule, and suppose a crowd of others, who can't use a footrule either, say he is six feet high, won't he be sure to believe it?"

"Oh, that—I'm sure he will!"

"Then don't be angry, for such men are the most charming of the lot! They go on making laws and amending the laws, as we described, and they always believe they are going to make an end of frauds in all those contracts about which I spoke just now, and they can't see they are only cutting off the Hydra's heads!"[1]

"Yes indeed," he said, "that's exactly what they are doing."

"And really," I said, "I should not have thought the true lawgiver ought to have the trouble of working out things of that sort in laws or constitution, either in a badly or in a well-governed city, in the one because they are useless and do no good, in the other because sometimes they follow naturally from former conduct, or if not anyone could find out what to do."

"Then what more could be left for us," said he, "in our legislation?"

And I answered, "For us, nothing, but for Apollo in Delphi the greatest and finest and first of enactments."

"What are those?" he said.

"The founding of temples and sacrifices and worship of gods and spirits and heroes besides; tombs of the departed, again, and whatever service is due to those who are in the next world to keep them gracious. For these are matters we do not know ourselves, and in founding a city we will obey no man, if we have sense, and we will use no interpreter except the god of our fathers.[2] For this god, as I take it, is the ancestral interpreter on such matters for all mankind; and he sits in the middle of the earth upon the navel,[3] and interprets."

"You are right in saying so," he replied, "and so we must do."

"There it is founded, then," said I, "that city of yours, Mr. Ariston's son.[4] The next thing for you to consider is to find for us in the city a light from somewhere, and invite your brother to help you and Polemarchos and all the others, a light clear and sufficient. Let us try to see where justice can be, and where injustice, and what is the difference between them; and which must be the possession of a man who is to be happy, whether all know him to have it, or whether it is hidden from gods and men."

"That is nonsense," said Glaucon, "for you promised to

---

[1] Heracles and the Hydra; when he cut off one head, two new ones grew.

[2] Apollo was the ancestral god of the Ionians; but here he is appealed to as the centre of the Hellenic world, whose oracle was always consulted before founding a colony.

[3] The *Omphalos*, or navel, a conical stone, has been discovered and is at Delphi still. There was a board of three interpreters at Athens.

[4] Mr. Bestmanson, the Greek formal style of address by the father's name, as used still in Russia.

search for it yourself, because you said it was a sin and a shame not to defend justice by every means in your power."

"True," said I, "now you remind me; yes, I must do so, but you must all help me too."

"Oh, we will do that," said he.

"Then I hope," said I, "to find it in this way. I believe our city, if it has been rightly arranged, is perfectly good."

"That must be so," he said.

"Then clearly it is wise and brave and temperate and just."[1]

"Clearly."

"Then if we find any of these in it, the remainder will be what we have not found?"

"How could it be otherwise?"

"Now take any four things: Suppose we were looking for one of the four in anything, if we recognised it first that would be enough for us; and if we recognised the other three first, that would have shown us the one we were looking for, since it is clearly the one left and nothing else."

"You are right," he said.

"Then since these are four, should we not use the same way with these?"

"Yes, clearly."

"Very well: First of all I seem to see wisdom[2] there very clearly; and there appears to be something strange about it."

"What?" he asked.

"Wise the city really is, as we described it, for it is full of good counsel, isn't it?"

"Yes."

"Further, this same good counsel is a kind of science,[3] that is clear; men contrive their counsels by science, not by ignorance, I suppose."

"That is clear."

"And again, there are manifold and various kinds of science in the city."

"Of course."

"Then is it because of carpenters' science that the city is to be entitled wise and full of good counsel?"

"Not at all," he said; "that would give it the title of good carpenter."

"Then a city should not be called wise because of the science of wooden furniture which gives counsel for its best possible production?"

"Certainly not."

---

[1] The four Greek cardinal virtues.
[2] *Sŏphía*, wisdom, in the highest sense of the word. In Plato's political thought wisdom is the "political" art.
[3] *Epistēmē*, knowledge.

"Well, what of the others, the science of smith's work or anything of that sort?"

"Not any one of these, either."

"Nor the science of growing corn out of the earth? That would give it the title of good farmer."

"So I think."

"Very well," said I. "Is there in our lately founded city any science among some of the citizens, which takes counsel not about some particular thing in the city, but about the city as a whole, how it could best behave to itself and towards other cities?"

"There is, surely."

"What is that," I said, "and in whom is it?"

"This science of guardianship, and it is in these rulers whom we lately named the perfect guardians."

"Because of this science then, what title do you give the city?"

"A city of good counsel," he said, "and really wise."

"Tell me then," said I, "do you think smiths or these true guardians are more numerous in our city?"

"Smiths," he said. "Many more."

"And just so with the others," I said, "who are particularly named after any sciences which they have; the guardians would be fewest of them all?"

"Much the fewest."

"So by reason of the smallest class, the city's smallest part of itself, and the science which is in this, that is, the governing and ruling class, the whole city would be wise as a whole when it is established according to nature. And the class whose place it is to partake of the science which alone of all sciences ought to be called wisdom, is by nature the fewest, as it seems."

"Very true," he said.

"So we have found this one of the four somehow or other, both the thing itself, and where it resides in the city."

"I certainly am convinced," said he, "that we have found it."

"Again, courage itself and its place in the city, by reason of which the city may be called by its name, is not very hard to see."

"How so?"

"Why," said I, "who would call a city cowardly or brave, except in regard of that portion of it which makes war and goes to battle for it?"

"No one would," he said, "for anything else."

"For," said I, "the cowardice or bravery of the other people in it would not, I think, decide the question of its being a city of this quality or that."

"No, indeed."

"Then the city is brave also by some part of itself, because it has in that part such a power as will preserve through everything the belief that whatever the lawgiver declared in their education to be dangerous, that and that only was dangerous. Don't you call that courage?"

"I did not quite understand what you said," he answered. "Please say it again."

"I say that courage is a kind of preservative," said I.

"What kind of preservative can that be?"

"That which preserves the belief about dangers, what is dangerous and what is not, which law has engendered through education. And when I said 'through everything,' I meant that it preserves this both in pain and in pleasure, and does not let it go either in desire or in fear. I'll give you what I think is a good comparison, if you like."

"Yes, I should like that."

"Take the case of dyers, then. When they wish to dye wool so as to hold the sea-purple, they begin, you know, by choosing out of all colours one, the natural white wool; then they prepare it first, treating it with no small care so as to take the bright hue thoroughly, and only after this preparation they soak it in the dye. What they dye in this manner holds the colour fast when dyed, and no washing can get the bright hue out either with soap or without. Otherwise you know the results, if they dye this colour or any other without the proper treatment."

"I know!" he said; "the colours get washed out and the effect is ridiculous."

"Understand then," I said, "that we ourselves were trying our best to do something like this, when we chose out the soldiers and educated them by music and gymnastic; believe me, we were only trying to find a contrivance to make them, under our persuasion, receive the laws like a dye, as thoroughly as possible. We wished their faith to be a fast colour about what they thought to be dangerous, and about everything else, because both nature and training were suited to hold it; and we wished their dye not to be washed out by these soaps, pleasure and pain, which are so dangerously effective in cleansing away; pleasure, which is more dangerously effective in doing this than any detergent powder or abstergent soda, pain and fear and desire more so than any soap. Such a power, I say, and preserver, through everything, of right and lawful faith about what is dangerous or not, is courage; and so I do declare, unless you have anything else to say."

"I have nothing to say," said he; "for I think you mean

that even a right opinion about these same things which is engendered without education, such as a wild beast or a slave might have, does not last,[1] and you call it by another name than courage."

"That is exactly the truth," said I.

"Very well, I accept this as courage."

"Do accept it," I said, "as a citizen's courage, and you will be right. Some other time, if you wish, we will go into it better, but this is not really what we have been looking for—that was justice. As far as courage goes, I think we have done enough for our search."

"You are right there," said he.

"Two other things," I said, "still remain to be found in the city; one is temperance, the other is the object of all our enquiry, justice."

"Exactly."

"How then could we find justice, so that we need not trouble further about temperance?"

"I'm sure I don't know," said he, "and I should be sorry to find justice revealed first if it means we should consider no further about temperance. If you would be so kind, do examine temperance before the other."

"Very well, I am willing," said I, "and I ought not to refuse."

"Do examine it, then," said he.

"I must," said I; "and as we see it now, it looks more like a concord and harmony than the first two."

"How?"

"Temperance is a kind of good order, I imagine," said I, "and a mastery of certain pleasures and desires; you hear people saying 'he is stronger than himself',[2] but how that can be I don't know. And other such things are said which seem to put us on its track. Isn't that so?"

"Most certainly it is," he said.

"That 'stronger than himself' is ridiculous, isn't it! For he who is stronger than himself would be also weaker than himself, I suppose, and he who is weaker would be stronger, for it is the same he all through."

"Of course."

"But," said I, "the meaning of this seems to be that there is in the man himself something about the soul which is better, and something which is worse, and when the naturally better masters the worse, they speak of 'stronger than himself.'

---

[1] So Stobaeus' conjecture μόνιμον. The manuscripts give νόμιμον, which makes the sense "is not lawful," "is not regular."
[2] Or "master of himself," and similarly below "subject to" instead of "weaker than."

Certainly it is praise. But when from bad training or some association the better, being the smaller, is mastered by the worse, this being a multitude, they say the man is weaker than himself in that state, and dissolute, words of reproach and disapproval."

"Yes indeed," he said, "it looks like that."

"Turn your eyes now," I said, "upon our new city, and you will find the former of these conditions within it; you will justly give it the title of stronger than itself—if a place where the better part rules the worse is entitled to be called temperate and stronger than itself."

"I turn my eyes there," said he, "and what you say is true."

"And the manifold and multitudinous desires and pleasures and pains would be found mostly in children and women and servants, or, of those said to be free, among the multitude of common people."

"Certainly."

"But the simple and moderate desires, which are guided by reason along with sense and right opinion, you will find in the few, those who were born with the best nature and had the best education."

"True," he said.

"And don't you see these things in your city too? And the desires in the multitude of common people there, mastered by the desires and the intelligence which is in the fewer and better men?"

"Yes I do," he said.

"Then if any city is to be entitled stronger than pleasures and desires, and stronger than its own self, this is such a city."

"Most assuredly," said he.

"And temperate also in all these things, isn't it?"

"Certainly," said he.

"And moreover this city, if any, will have in it one and the same opinion both in the rulers and the ruled, as to who should rule? Don't you think so?"

"I do indeed," he said, "very strongly."

"Then where will you say temperance will be, in the rulers or in the ruled, when the citizens are in this condition?"

"In both, I should suppose," he said.

"You see then," said I, "that we were good prophets just now, when we said that temperance is like a kind of harmony."

"Why so?"

"Because it is not like courage and wisdom. These did

give the titles of brave and wise to the city, but they were each seated in a single portion. Temperance does not act as these do; it is stretched right through the whole city bringing all the strings into concord,[1] and puts all persons in tune, the strongest and the weakest and the middles in everything just the same—in intelligence, if you like, or strength, if you like, or numbers, or wealth, or anything else of that sort. So we should be perfectly right in calling this unanimous mind temperance, a concord of the naturally better and worse as to which ought to rule whether in a city or in any single person."

"I agree with you entirely," said he.

"Very good," said I, "we have spied three of the four forms in our city, to judge from this line of reasoning. What would be the remaining form, which would give the city a share in still another virtue? It is clear that this is justice."

"Quite clear."

"Now then, Glaucon, we must post ourselves like a ring of huntsmen round the covert, and watch carefully that justice may not escape through us and disappear and be seen no more; it is manifestly somewhere here. Look out then and do your best to get a sight of it before me, and give me a view-halloo!"

"I only wish I could," he said, "but if you will give me a lead, you will find me not a bad second in seeing what you point out."

"Come on, then," said I, "and pray for good luck, and we'll do it together."

"That I will," said he. "Only take the lead yourself."

"Ah well," said I, "it seems a bad place to walk in, and covered in shadow. It is dark at least, and hard for the beaters, but we must go on."

"Yes, we must go on," said he.

Then I saw something and cried, "Halloo, halloo Glaucon! I've really got the trail, and I don't think it will escape us!"

"Good news!" he said.

"Oh, we *are* stupid slackers!" I cried.

"How?"

"Bless you, my dear man, evidently it was rolling before our feet all the time, and we never saw it! What ridiculous fools we have been! People often search about for what they hold in their hands, and we've been doing the same—looking

---

[1] The concord "through all strings" διὰ πασῶν (which we have borrowed in the word "diapason") was the octave, the perfect "concord" to the Greek ear. He means only that all the people are in concord in this opinion. It is of no use to try to identify the divisions with musical notes, although "middle" is a technical term.

away into the distance; and that, perhaps, was why it escaped our notice."

"What do you mean?" he said.

"This," I said: "I think we have been speaking of it and hearing of it, and did not understand ourselves! We were speaking of it all the time in a fashion."

"What a long prelude," said he, "for one who longs to hear!"

"Listen, then," I said, "and see if there's any sense in what I say. Justice is that very thing, I think, or some form of it, which we laid down at first when we were founding the city, as necessary conduct in everything from beginning to end. And what we did lay down and often repeated, if you remember, was that each one must practise that one thing, of all in the city, for which his nature was best fitted."

"We did say so."

"Further, that to do one's own business and not to meddle with many businesses is justice; this also we have heard from many others and we have often said ourselves."

"Yes, we have often said it."

"So now, my friend," said I, "it seems that really this in a sense appears to be justice—to do one's own business; and do you know whence I deduce this?"

"No," he said, "but please tell me."

"It seems to me," said I, "that this is the one thing left of those four which we were examining in our city; there were temperance and courage and intelligence, and here is a thing which makes it possible for the other three to be there at all, and it preserves them there as long as it is in them. Now we said that justice would be the one left if we could find the other three."

"That follows necessarily," he said.

"But however," said I, "if we had to judge which of these will do most towards making our city good when it is present within, it would be difficult. Would it be the single mind of the rulers and the ruled; or the preserving in the soldiers of the opinion bred by law as to what are dangers and what are not; or the intelligence and guardian spirit in the rulers; or would it be this last thing which most makes the city good, present in woman and child, in bond and free, in craftsman and ruler and ruled, that each single one did his own business and meddled in no other businesses?"

"Difficult to judge indeed," said he, "of course."

"Then it seems there would be a regular competition in making the city virtuous, between this power of every man in the city doing his own business, and its rivals, the wisdom of the city and its temperance and its courage."

"Exactly," said he.

"And would you not put down justice as that which competes with these for virtue in the city?"

"By all means," he said.

"Now look at it in another way, to see if you agree. Will you appoint the rulers in the city to try lawsuits?"

"Of course."

"Won't their aim in their judgments be nothing more than this—to provide that each class may not lose what belongs to them and may not keep what belongs to others?"

"Yes, chiefly this."

"As being just?"

"Yes."

"Then by this way of looking at it also, the having and the doing of what is one's own would be admitted to be justice."

"That is true."

"Look here then, and see if you agree with me. Suppose a carpenter tries to do the cobbler's work, or a cobbler the carpenter's, exchanging tools and honours with each other, or even one man trying to do both—do you think that all the other things mixed up like this would do great harm to the city?"

"Not very much," he said.

"Ah, but suppose a craftsman or anyone else who is a moneymaker by nature is excited by wealth or following or strength or anything of that sort, and then tries to push himself into the fighting class, or one of the soldiers into the counsellor and guardian class, being unworthy, and then these exchange each other's tools and honours? Or suppose the same man tries to do all these things at once? Then I believe you would agree that this exchange by these persons and meddling in many businesses would be ruin for the city."

"Most assuredly."

"Then the meddling and interchange between the three classes would be the greatest damage to the city, and would rightly be entitled evildoing in chief."

"Exactly so."

"But will you not say that the greatest evildoing towards one's own city is injustice?"

"Of course."

"So this is injustice. On the other hand, let us put it in this way. The opposite of this, own-dealing of each class, moneymakers, assistants and guardians, each one of these doing its own business in the city, would be justice and would make the city just."

"That seems to me," said he, "exactly the way of it."

"Let us not yet say so quite firmly," said I, "but only if this pattern enters into each single one of our people and is there accepted as justice; then we will grant it at once (for what else shall we say?); if not, there will be another enquiry for us. But at present let us finish the examination we made in which we believed it would be easier to see what sort of thing justice is in one man, if we were to try to inspect it in some larger thing, one of those which contain justice, viewing it there first. We have agreed already that this larger thing is the city, and we founded our city so as to be at its very best, as well as we could, since we knew well that in the good city surely justice would be. What we found there, then, let us apply to the single man; and if it be found to agree, well and good; but if something else becomes manifest in the one man, we will come back to the city and test it. So by examining them side by side and rubbing them together like firesticks, we may very likely make justice flash out, and when it shows itself we may confirm it for ourselves."

"Well," said he, "that seems a good method and we ought to try it."

"Now then," said I, "take anything greater or smaller: if we call both by the same name, are they like or unlike in so far as they have that name?"

"Like," said he.

"And a just man then will not differ from a just city, but he will be like it, as far as the actual pattern of justice goes."

"Yes, like," he said.

"Moreover, we thought a city just when three classes of natures in it each did their own business; and again we thought it temperate and brave and wise because of certain other states and conditions of these same three classes."

"True," said he.

"Then, my friend, here is our claim for the single man: If he has these same patterns in his soul, he is entitled to the same names as the city because of the same conditions."

"That is wholly necessary," he said.

"Oh, my good man," said I, "here is another trifling enquiry we have fallen into about the soul, whether it has these three patterns in it or not!"

"Not so very trifling, I think," said he, "for perhaps the saying is true, Socrates. Fine things are hard."

"So it seems," I said. "And be sure, my dear Glaucon, in my opinion we shall never comprehend this exactly by such methods as we are now using in our discussions. Another way, longer and harder, leads to this; however, perhaps we shall manage not unworthily from what has been said in our earlier enquiry."

"Won't that do, then?" said he. "It would be quite enough for me for the present."

"Oh, well," said I, "that will do very well for me too."

"Then pray don't give up," said he, "but go on."

"Then," said I, "we must necessarily admit that the same patterns and qualities are in each one of us which are in the city, mustn't we? Whence do they come there at all if not from that source? It would be ridiculous to believe that the spirited temper was not engendered in the city from the private persons wherever any have a reputation for such, for example the Thracians and the Scythians or the people up country in general; or the temper of intellectual enquiry, which would be said especially to belong to our own part of the world; or the love of moneymaking, which is reported to be the particular mark of Phoenicians and Egyptians."

"Quite so," he said.

"That's true then," said I, "and quite easy to see."

"Quite easy."

"But now we come to a difficulty. Is it by the same faculty we do each of these; or by three faculties, by one faculty—one, and by another—another?[1] Do we learn by one thing within us, do we feel spirited by another, and by a third do we desire the pleasures associated with eating and drinking and the propagation of our kind and so on; or is each separate thing done by the soul as a whole when we have the impulse? There is the difficulty, and it is hard to decide it as our argument deserves."

"I think so too," he said.

"Then let us try to decide whether these are all the same thing or different."

"But how?"

"It is clear that the same thing will never do or undergo opposite things in the same part of it and towards the same thing at the same time; so if we find this happening, we shall know it was not one thing but more than one."

"Very well."

"Then look here a moment."

"Go on," said he.

"Can the same thing both stand still and move in the same part at the same time?"

"Impossible."

"Let us be even more exact or we may have a dispute some-

[1] The unity of the soul is what Plato has in mind here. He has to be very careful with details in the beginnings of logic.

where before we go on. Suppose a man is standing still, but moving hands and head; if someone were to say the same man is standing still and moving at the same time, we should not allow that to be right, but we should say part of him stands still and part moves. Isn't that right?"

"It is."

"The speaker might go further in this and refine upon it with quite a bit of pretty wit. He might say of a spinning top that the whole thing stands still and turns at the same time, when it fixes the peg in one spot and goes round and round upon it, and so also anything else does this that goes round in a circle in the same place, but we should not accept that. We should say that such things are not resting and revolving in the same parts of themselves, but they have a straight part (the axis) and a circling part (the periphery); in the straight part it moves round; and when it leans the perpendicular to right or left or front or back while it revolves, then it does not stand still anywhere."

"Yes," he said, "they are opposites."

"So such a saying will not dismay us, and it will never convince us that the same thing in the same place towards the same thing could sometimes be or do or suffer two opposites."

"Not me, at any rate," said he.

"However," said I, "we do not wish to have to make a long list and run through all such puzzles and assure ourselves they are not true; so let us take it that this is true and go forward, but let us agree to wipe out all that follows from this if we ever see reason to think otherwise."

"Yes, that is what we must do," he said.

"Then what of these pairs," I said—"to nod down for 'yes' and to nod back for 'no',[1] to want to get something and to refuse; to be attracted and to be repelled—should not these be set down as mutual opposites, whether acts or feelings, for it is equally true of both?"

"Yes," he said," they are opposites."

"Very well," said I; "thirst and hunger and desires in general, and again to wish and to be willing—would you not place all these somewhere in the classes mentioned just now? For example, the soul of the desirer always wants that which he desires, or is attracted to that which he wishes to have; or again, inasmuch as it wants something to be provided for him, it nods 'yes' to itself as if someone had asked the question, reaching forward to the production of the thing. Will you not agree?"

---

[1] The gesture for "no" was, and still is, in modern Greece, to nod the head upwards and backwards.

"I agree," he said.

"Very well; to be unwilling and unwishing and not to desire we will place in the class of repelling and driving away from the soul and in the general class of urges opposite to the former."

"Of course."

"Since that is the case, shall we say desires are all in one class; and the most obvious of these are what we call hunger and thirst?"

"We will," said he.

"One is desire of food, one of drink?"

"Yes."

"Then as far as thirst is thirst, could it be a desire in the soul for something more than what we mean here—drink? I mean, is thirst a thirst for hot drink or cold, for much or little, or in a word for drink of any special kind? Perhaps if there be a hotness added to the thirst, that could provide an added desire of cold, or if there be coldness, a desire of heat? If muchness were present, would there be much thirst providing the desire of much, if littleness little thirst providing the desire for little? And in all cases will thirst itself never be a desire of anything but what it naturally desires, just drink, and the same with hunger desiring food?"

"Yes to that," he said. "Every desire in itself is only for that one thing which each naturally wants; this or that kind is simply an addition."

"But," I went on, "don't let us be caught napping; someone may try to confuse us by saying that no one desires only drink, but good drink,[1] or only food, but good food, for all (he will say) desire good things. If then thirst is a desire, it would be for good drink, and the same with the other desires whatever the desire is for."

"There might be something in that man's statement," he said.

"Remember all the same," said I, "whatever things are such as to be related to something, those of them which are in a way qualified are related to some qualified things, as it seems to me; but those which are simply themselves are each related to something which is simply itself."[2]

"I did not understand that," he said.

"Don't you understand that the greater is such that it must be greater than something?"

[1] "All desire the good" was a Socratic commonplace.
[2] The simplicity of the Greek here is justly admired. The sense is, for example, whatever things are related pairs, if one thing is of a special kind, so is the other; but if one is simply itself, so is the other. Or: if one term of a relation is qualified, so must the other be; if one term is unqualified, so also is the other.

"Oh yes."

"That is, than the less?"

"Yes."

"And the much greater than the much less. Isn't that so?"

"Yes."

"And the sometimes greater than the sometimes less, and what will be greater than what will be less?"

"Why, of course," said he.

"And just so the more are related to the fewer, and doubles to halves, and so forth, and again heavier to lighter and quicker to slower, and, besides, hot to cold, and all other things like these. Is not that so?"

"Certainly."

"What about the sciences, isn't it just the same? Science, or knowledge, by itself is knowledge of learning by itself, or whatever is the proper name of its counterpart; but any special knowledge is of some special thing. Take an example: when the knowledge of building a house came up, it differed from other kinds of knowledge and was called housebuilding."

"Just so."

"And was this not because it was of a kind different from any of the others?"

"Yes."

"So it became knowledge of a certain kind itself because it was knowledge of a thing of a certain kind? And the other arts and sciences in the same way?"

"That is true."

"Then if you really do understand now, please suppose that I meant this, when I said that whatever things are such as to be related to something, those of them which are simply themselves are related to things which are simply themselves; but those of a certain kind—to things of a certain kind. I do not mean that they are of the same kind as the things to which they are related, so that the knowledge of health and diseased things must be healthy and diseased, and the knowledge of good and evil things good and evil; what I mean is that since it was not knowledge of the knowable in general[1] but knowledge of a special thing, and this thing was health and disease, consequently it must be of some special kind itself; and this caused it to be no longer called simply knowledge, but the special kind was added and it was called physic."

"I understand," said he, "and I agree with you."

"Very well then, thirst," said I. "Will you not put it in the class of related pairs, and say that it is what it is for something, thirst for something, that is?"

[1] Literally, "of that of which knowledge is."

"Yes," he said, "for drink."

"Then if the drink is of some special kind, so is the thirst for it, but thirst by itself is neither for much nor for little, neither for good nor for bad, nor in a word for any kind, but thirst pure and simple is for drink pure and simple."

"By all means."

"Then the soul of the thirsty in so far as it thirsts wants to drink and nothing else, reaches out for this, and has impulse for this."

"Clearly."

"So if anything pulls back the soul athirst, it would be something in the soul other than the thirst, which is dragging the thirsty man himself to drink like a beast—for as we said, the same thing with the same part of itself would not do two opposite things at the same time about the same thing."

"That would indeed be impossible."

"Just as, I think, it cannot properly be said of an archer that his hands push away the bow and pull it to him at the same time; what is meant is that the pushing hand is one hand, and the pulling hand another."

"Most certainly," he said.

"Can we say, then, that people who are thirsty sometimes don't want to drink?"

"Oh yes," he said, "many a man and many a time!"

"Then what are we to think about these?" I went on. "There is in their soul that which bids them to drink and also that which forbids them to drink, something different which controls that which bids: will that do?"

"I think so," said he.

"Therefore that which forbids such things whenever it is engendered in them is engendered by the reason, but what drives and drags is engendered by certain affections and diseases—something additional?"

"So it seems."

"Then we shall claim not unreasonably that these are two separate things and different from each other, calling the part of the soul with which it reasons the 'reasoning' part, and that by which it loves and hungers and thirsts, and is all aflutter about the other desires, the 'unreasoning' and 'desiring' part, a comrade of repletions and pleasures."

"Quite fairly," said he. "That is what we should suppose."

"Then let us decide these two," said I, "as two patterns which are in the soul. But now what of the temper or high spirit, that by which we are angry or get into a temper: Will that be a third, or, if not, which of these two is it akin to?"

"One of the two, perhaps," he said, "the desiring temper."[1]

"Well," I said, "once I heard something, and I believe it: Leontios, Aglaion's son, so it was said, was going up from the Peiraeus under the north wall outside, and saw dead bodies lying beside the executioner.[2] He desired to see them and felt disgusted at the same time, and turned away. He resisted awhile and covered his face, but the desire was too much for him. He ran up to the bodies, and pulled his eyes open with his fingers, calling out, 'There, confound you! Stare your fill at the beautiful sight!"

"Yes, I have heard that too," said he.

"The story indicates," I said, "that sometimes anger fights against the desires as one thing against a different."

"It does," he said.

"Yes," I said, "and in many other cases, when desires force one contrary to reason, we see the man reproaching himself, and angry with what is forcing him within himself; we see something like two warring factions in such a man, and the temper as an ally to the reason. But the temper making common cause with the desires, when reason decides that they ought not to act against reason—that I believe is something you never perceived happening in yourself, and never, I fancy, in anyone else."

"No indeed," he said.

"Very well," I said, "when a man thinks he is doing wrong, the nobler he is the less angry he can be, when he suffers hunger and cold and any other such things from him whom he thinks to be causing these things justly, which is exactly what I was saying: his temper does not wish to be roused against the man. Isn't that true?"

"Yes," he said.

"Ah, but when anyone believes he is wronged, does not his temper boil and fume then because he suffers hunger and cold and so forth? Doesn't it fight for what it thinks just? Doesn't it hold out until it conquers, and never cease in noble persons before it succeeds, or dies, or before it is called back and quieted by the reason which is at hand in him, as a dog is quieted by a shepherd?"

"That is an excellent comparison to make," he said; "and surely in our city we placed the assistants like dogs to help the rulers like shepherds of the city."

"Good," said I, "you take my meaning rightly. But besides that, do you notice something more?"

---

[1] There is a play in this passage on the word *thymós*, temper or spirit, and *epithymía*, desire, which is derived from it.
[2] He was throwing them into the pit where malefactors were thrown. The north wall was the northern of two making a corridor between Athens and the port. There was a third farther away enclosing Phaleron.

"What?" he asked.

"That this appears to contradict what we said before about the high-spirited part. Then we thought there was something of desire about it, but we say now far from that; much rather it ranges itself in arms beside the reasoning part in the factions of the soul."

"Exactly," he said.

"Then it is different from reason; or itself a kind of reason, so that there are not three patterns in the soul, but only two, the reasoning and the desiring? Or is the soul like the city: just as three classes held it together, the moneymakers, the state-assistants, and the counsellors, so this high-spirited part in the soul is also a third, which naturally assists the reasoning part, if it be not ruined by bad training?"

"A third part," he said; "that is necessary."

"Yes," I said, "if it is shown to be something different from the reasoning, as it was shown to be different from the desiring."

"Well, that's not hard to show," said he; "look at children, and you will see that. As soon as they are born they are full of temper at once, but reason! Some of them never have any at all, in my opinion, and most of them only get it late."

"Excellent, upon my word!" said I. "In animals too we can see that you are right. Besides, remember what we quoted previously somewhere[1] from Homer; that will bear us out—

Striking his breast he thus reproached his heart.

There as you see, Homer makes a difference between the two; he represents the part of him which has considered about better and worse as striking the part of him which was angry unreasonably."

"You are quite right," he said.

"So far then," I said, "after a hard struggle we have swum these waters; and we are pretty well agreed that both city and each soul of man have their classes, the same in each and the same number."

"That is true."

"Another thing must follow of necessity, that as and whereby the city was wise, so and thereby a particular man is wise?"

"How else, indeed!"

"And therefore whereby and as the particular man is brave, thereby and so the city is brave, and as regards the other virtues, both of them are in the same case exactly?"

"That is necessary."

[1] P. 187.

"Then, Glaucon, I think," said I, "we shall say a man is just in the same way as the city was just."

"That also is absolutely necessary."

"But we have by no means forgotten that the city was just by reason that each single man in its three classes did his own business."

"Oh no, we have not forgotten that, I think."

"We must remember then that each one of us will be doing his own business, and will be just, when each part of him will be doing its own business in him."

"Indeed, we must remember that," he said.

"Then it is proper for the reasoning part to rule, because it is wise and has to use forethought for the whole soul; and proper for the high-spirited part to be its ally and subject."

"Certainly."

"Then, as we were saying, a mingling of music and gymnastic will put them in concord, stringing up the reason and feeding it with beautiful words and teachings, but slackening the temper while it soothes it and makes it gentle by tune[1] and rhythm."

"Exactly," said he.

"These two, then, thus trained and educated, will truly learn their own business; then they will preside over the desiring part, which is the largest part of the soul in each man, and by its nature can never have wealth enough. This they will watch lest it be filled full of what are called the bodily pleasures, and so growing great and strong may no longer do its own business but may try to enslave and rule the classes which it properly should not, and so overturn the whole life of all."

"Certainly," he said.

"And the enemies from outside," said I—"would not these two best guard against them for the whole soul and body, one planning and advising, the other fighting for all and following the ruling part, carrying out those plans by its courage?"

"Yes indeed."

"And when we speak of any man as brave, we call him so because of this part, when his high-spirited temper preserves through both pains and pleasures the reason's teaching as to what is really dangerous or not."

"Quite right," he said.

"Yes, and wise by that small part which was ruling in him and gave these instructions, because that again had in itself knowledge, that is, knew what was the advantage both

[1] ἁρμονίᾳ.

of each single one and of their commonwealth of the three classes."

"Certainly."

"Further: when we speak of him as temperate, it is by the friendship and concord of these very three, whenever the ruler and the two ruled are of one mind, and agree that the reasoning part ought to rule, and make no faction against it."

"Temperance, at any rate," said he, "is this and nothing else, whether in city or in citizen."

"Now we come to justice: he will be just as and whereby we have said so often."

"Absolutely necessary."

"Very well," I said. "I wonder if justice seems perhaps blurred in some way? Do we think it to be anything else in him than what it was shown to be in the city?"

"I think not," said he.

"Well," said I, "we should be able to assure ourselves completely, if any further doubt comes up in our minds, by applying tests from common life."

"What, may I ask?"

"For example, compare that city and the man like to it in nature and training, and see if we should agree whether such a one, if entrusted with a deposit of gold or silver, would be likely to withhold it for himself? Who, think you, would believe that he would be more likely to do that than those who were not such as he?"

"No one would believe that," he said.

"Take sacrilege and theft and treachery, either privately towards friends or publicly towards the state—would he be outside all that?"

"Yes," he said.

"And further, he would not be false to his oath in any way, or to his other agreements."

"How could he?"

"Adultery, again, and dishonour to parents and neglect of divine service are proper to anyone rather than him."

"Anyone else," he said.

"What is the cause of this? Surely that each of the parts in him does its own business about ruling and being ruled?"

"That is the cause," he said, "nothing else."

"Then what are you looking for in justice but this power which produces such men and cities?"

"Nothing but that, I declare," said he.

"Then our dream is come perfectly true, and we have made real what we said we surmised, how at the very beginning of our foundation of the city, some good providence has really been bringing us upon a principle and outline of justice."

"Yes, entirely true!"

"Indeed it really was, Glaucon—and that is why it helps us, a kind of image of justice, that the natural cobbler ought properly to cobble and do nothing else, and the carpenter to carpenter, and so on."

"So it seems."

"But in truth, justice, it appears, was something like this; not, however, in a man's outward practice, but inwardly and truly he must do his own business in himself. He must not have allowed any part of himself to do the business of other parts, nor the parts in his soul to meddle in many businesses with each other; but he must have managed his own well, and himself have ruled himself, and set all in order, and become a friend to himself. He must have put all three parts in tune within him, highest and lowest and middle, exactly like the three chief notes of a scale, and any other intervals between that there may be; he must have bound all these together and made himself completely one out of many, temperate and concordant; and then only do whatever he does, getting of wealth, or care of the body, or even matters of state or private contract. In all these he must believe and name as just and beautiful dealing whatever practice preserves this condition and works along with it, and as wisdom he must name the knowledge which presides over this practice; but as unjust dealing he must name whatever dissolves it, and as brute ignorance, again, the opinion which presides over such."

"What you say, Socrates," he said, "is perfectly true."

"Very well," said I, "if we should say we have found the just man now, and the just city, and what justice really is in them, I think it would hardly be thought a lie."

"By heaven, no," said he.

"Then shall we say so?"

"We will," said he.

"So be it, then," said I. "The next thing is to examine injustice. Surely it must be factions among these three, and meddling in many businesses, and meddling in others' business, and revolt of one part of the soul against the whole in order that this part may rule in the soul though it is not proper for it to do so, being a part suitable by nature to be the slave of that which is the ruling principle. Something like that we shall say, I believe; and the confusion of these and their error will be injustice and riot and cowardice and ignorance—complete vice, in a word."

"Just that," he said.

THE REPUBLIC Book IV (443C–445B)

"Then," said I, "to practise injustice and to do wrong, and on the contrary, to do right—all these are clear and manifest already, since justice and injustice are clear?"

"How so?" he said.

"Because," I said, "they are exactly like the healthy things and the diseased things in the body—what these are in the body, those are in the soul."

"How?" he asked.

"Healthy things no doubt implant health, and diseased things disease?"

"Yes."

"Then to do justly implants justice, and to do unjustly injustice?"

"Necessarily."

"And to make health is to settle the parts of the body so as to rule or be ruled together, according to nature; to make disease is to settle that this part rules and that is ruled one by another contrary to nature."

"It is."

"On the other hand," I said, "to implant justice is to settle the parts of the soul so as to rule and be ruled together according to nature; to implant injustice is to settle things so that one part rules and one part is ruled one by another contrary to nature?"

"Exactly so," said he.

"Virtue then, it seems, would be a kind of health and beauty and fine fitness of the soul; vice is disease and ugliness and weakness."

"That is so."

"Is it not true, then, that beautiful pursuits lead to the getting of virtue, ugly pursuits to vice?"

"It must be."

"Then what is left for us now, as it seems, is to enquire if it is profitable to do justly and pursue beautiful things, and to be just, whether known or unknown to be such; or if it is profitable to do wrong and to be unjust if indeed one is not punished and does not become better by being chastised."

"Oh my dear Socrates!" he said. "The enquiry seems to me to become from now absurd! If we think life is not worth living when the bodily nature is ruined, even with all the meats and drinks in the world and all the wealth and all the power there is, how could life be worth living when the very nature of that by which we live is corrupted and destroyed, if a man may do whatever he wishes, one thing excepted—to get rid of vice and injustice, and to get justice and virtue, now that these have been shown to be each as we described them."

"Absurd indeed," I said. "However, since we have come so far as to be able to see quite clearly that these things are true, we must not give up in weariness."

"No, I swear," he said, "we must of all things not give up."

"This way, then," said I. "Look and see how many kinds of vice there are to my thinking—at least I will mention those that are worth looking at."

"I am following," said he. "Go on."

"Well now," said I, "we have climbed up to a kind of gazebo here in our discussion, and I seem to see that there is only one kind of virtue, but infinite kinds of vice, and four among these are worth mentioning."

"What do you mean?" he asked.

"There are as many manners of soul," I said, "as there are manners of political constitutions."

"How many, then?"

"Five of constitutions," I said, "and five of soul."

"Tell me what they are," said he.

"I tell you," said I, "that one would be this manner of constitution which we have described, but it might have one of two names. If there arose one man in it among the rulers distinguished above the rest it would be called a kingdom; if more than one,[1] aristocracy."[2]

"True," said he.

"I call this one form," said I, "because neither one ruler, nor more than one so arising would disturb any of the city's laws worth considering, if he possessed the training and education which we have described."

"No, that is not likely," said he.

BOOK V

"Then good and upright I call such a city and constitution, and such a man; bad and blundering the others, if this one is right, both in the management of cities and their manner of furnishing the soul of individual citizens; they are classable in four conditions of wickedness."

"What are these?" he asked.

I was going on to give a list of them in order, as they appeared to follow one after another, when Polemarchos (who sat a little away from Adeimantos) stretched out a hand and

---

[1] There may be one chief or a few more, but never many.
[2] Government by the best.

caught hold of the upper part of his brother's wrap near the shoulder, pulled him towards himself and, leaning forward, whispered something in his ear. We could not catch what it was, except this: "Shall we let him off, then" (says he), "or what shall we do?"

"Let him off—no!" said Adeimantos, speaking aloud now.

I said, "What exactly won't you two let off?"

"You," said he.

"But why, exactly?" I said.

"You are shirking, we think," said he. "You are cheating us out of a whole chapter of the discussion, and by no means the smallest, because you don't want to discuss it. Do you imagine you will get away with the remarks you dropped in that light way? What was it about women and children—clear to anyone, did you say—that friends will have all in common?"

"Well, wasn't that quite right, Adeimantos?" I asked.

"Yes," he said, "but just that 'quite right' wants explaining, like the rest of it, how they shall be in common; there might be many ways, so don't fail to tell us which way you mean. We have been waiting ever so long hoping to hear what you will have to say about child-getting. How will they get children, how will they train them when they have come? And all this community of wives and children of which you speak—we think it will have a great and capital effect on the state according as it is rightly or wrongly done. You are putting your hand to another constitution before you have properly finished this; and so, as you heard, we are now resolved not to let you go before you discuss all these things like the rest."

"Put me down too," said Glaucon, "as voting likewise for that."

And Thrasymachos said, "Oh yes, we are all decided on this, Socrates, take that for granted."

"Oh dear me," said I, "what a thing you have done in challenging me like this! What a debate you are stirring up! It looks like doing the constitution again from the beginning. I thought I had finished now and glad indeed I was, quite happy if it could just be accepted and left alone as described. And now you demand all this too; you can't imagine what a hornet's nest of words you are waking; but I saw it, and passed it by to prevent trouble."

"My dear man," said Thrasymachos, "that's what these people have come for—they left all to come and hear words! Do you suppose they are looking for a gold mine?"[1]

---

[1] Literally, "smelting gold from ore," a proverb taken from an old story, where the people left their proper duties to hunt for a reputed find of gold.

"Words, yes," I said, "but not words without end. You must draw the line somewhere."

"Draw the line at the end of life, Socrates," said Glaucon, "for men having sense, when words can be heard such as these. But never mind us, just get on and answer our questions; tell the story in your own way, only don't give up. What will be this community of wives and children among our guardians, and the training of them while they are quite young, which comes in the time between birth and education, the most troublesome task of all, as we understand? Try to tell us how this ought to be managed."

"Bless you, that is not easy," said I. "There are many incredibilities in it, even more than in what we discussed before. If we say it can be done, they will say, 'Incredible!' and, if it could be done, that it would be the best thing—again, 'Incredible!' So I shrink a little from touching the matter, for fear that my story may seem just a pious wish, my dear comrade."

"Don't shrink," said he, "for we are not dullards or incredulous or unkind; we will listen."

And I said, "Oh you good, kind man! Do you say that because you want to encourage me?"

"Yes, I do," he said.

"Well then," I said, "you are doing the very opposite. If I knew that my story was true, if I believed it myself, the encouragement would help; to speak before thoughtful hearers and dear friends on supreme matters dear to them, knowing what you say to be true, is a steady and confident march; but being incredulous yourself, to enquire along with them in a discussion is fearful and slippery. This is what I am doing. I do not fear being laughed at, which would be childish; I fear I may slip from the truth, and drag my friends over me in a heap, and lie flat—in matters where a slip is most dangerous. I prostrate[1] myself before Adrasteia, Glaucon, I pray grace of Nemesis for what I am about to say; for I take it indeed that to kill a man unwittingly is a smaller offence than to deceive him about what is beautiful and good and just in laws and customs. That is a risk to run with enemies[2] about you rather than friends, so your encouragement is a grand one, isn't it!"

Glaucon laughed and said, "Well, Socrates, if we come to grief by the discussion, we acquit you of manslaughter and hold you as pure[3] and no deceiver of us. Come, take heart and speak on."

---

[1] For the Greek word used here, see p. 195, n. 3.
[2] If you fail enemies alone will suffer.
[3] A man was impure if he did manslaughter.

"Ah well," said I, "in that case the acquitted man is pure, so saith the law, and that holds here, too, if there."

"Then speak on," he said, "on that basis."

"If I speak," I said, "I must go back again now to what I ought perhaps to have said already, in its proper place. The men have fully played their part on our stage and made their exit; and now perhaps it would be right to call in the women, especially since you invite me to do it.

"For people then, born and educated as we explained, the only right way, in my opinion, for them to get and use children and women is the way we started them to go. You remember we tried in our discourse to establish the men as it were guardians of a herd."

"Yes."

"Then let us follow up by giving the women birth and training like theirs, and see if it is proper for us or not."

"How?" he asked.

"Thus; do we think that the females of the guardian dogs ought to share in the guard which the males keep? Ought they to join in the hunt and whatever else they do? Or should the females keep kennel indoors, as being unable because of the birth and training of pups, and should the males do the hard work and have all the care of the flocks?"

"They ought to do everything together," he said, "except that we treat the males as stronger and the females as weaker."

"But is it possible," I said, "to use animals for the same things, if you do not give them the same training and education?"

"Impossible."

"Then if we are to use the women for the same things as the men, we must teach them the same things."

"Yes."

"Now music and gymnastic were taught to the men."

"Yes."

"So we must teach the women those same two arts, and matters of war too, and use them in the same way."

"That seems fair from what you say," he replied.

"Well then," said I, "perhaps much in our present proposals would appear funny in contrast with usual custom, if they were done in the way we say."

"Likely enough," he said.

"And what will be the biggest joke of all?" I asked. "Surely to see naked women in the wrestling schools exercising with the men—not only the young women, but even the older ones too? Like old men in the gymnasium, all over wrinkles and not pleasant to look at, who still fancy the game!"

"You are right, upon my word!" said he; "it would seem funny as things are now!"

"Very well," said I, "since we have set out to speak, let us not fear the jests of refined people. Let them talk how they like and say what they like of such an upheaval, about gymnastic and music, and not least about wearing armour and riding on horseback."

"Quite right," said he.

"But since we have begun let us march on to the rough part of our law. We will entreat these wits to leave their usual business and be serious for once; we will remind them that it is not so very long since Hellenes thought it ugly and funny, as most barbarians do still, to see men naked; and when the Cretans began naked athletics, and the Lacedaimonians followed, the clever people then were able to make fun of the thing. Don't you agree?"

"Yes, I do."

"But we found by experience that it was better to strip than to hide all such things; and soon the seeming funny to the eyes melted away before that which was revealed in the light of reason to be the best. It showed also that he is a vain fool who thinks anything ridiculous but what is evil; and he is a fool who tries to raise laughter against any sight, as being that of something funny, other than the sight of folly and evil; or in earnest sets up any other mark to aim at than what is honourable and good."

"By all manner of means," he said.

"Then surely we must decide first whether this is possible or not. Next, we must open the debate to all, whether a man chooses to argue in jest or in earnest; and let them discuss whether the female nature in mankind allows women to share the same work with men in everything, or in nothing, or only in some things, and if in some, to which class war belongs. Would not this be the best beginning which would lead most likely to the best end?"

"Much the best," he said.

"Are you willing, then," said I, "that we should defend the others against ourselves, and not take the fort of the counterargument undefended?"

"There's nothing to hinder that," he replied.

"Then let us say on their behalf, 'You need no others to dispute with you, Socrates and Glaucon; you yourselves at the first foundation of your city admitted that each single person must do his own one business according to nature.' 'We admitted it, I think; of course.' 'Is there not all the difference in the world between man and woman according to nature?'

THE REPUBLIC Book V (452B–454B)

'There is a difference, certainly.' 'Then further, is it not proper to appoint work for each according to the nature of each?' 'What then?' 'Then you are mistaken surely, and contradict yourselves, when you say now that men and women must do the same things, although their natures are very different!' Come on now, answer me that and I will thank you!"

"What! all of a sudden!" he said. "That's not altogether easy; but I beg and pray you to interpret our argument for us, whatever that may be."

"That is what I expected, my dear Glaucon," said I, "and there are many other such objections, which I foresaw long ago; that is why I feared and shrank to touch the law about getting and training women and children."

"No, by heaven, it does not look like an easy thing," said he.

"And it is not," said I, "but it's like this: If anyone tumbles into a small swimming pool, or if into the middle of the broad sea, he has to swim all the same."

"Certainly."

"Then we must swim too, and try to save ourselves out of the argument; we may hope for some dolphin to take us on his back, or some other desperate salvation."

"So it seems," he said.

"Come along then," said I, "see if we can find the way out anywhere. We agreed, you know, that a different nature ought to practise a different work, and that man and woman have different natures; now we say that these different natures must do the same work. Is that the accusation against us?"

"Exactly."

"How noble is the power, my dear Glaucon," said I, "of the art of word controversy!"[1]

"How so?" he said.

"Because," I said, "so many seem unable to help falling into it; they think they are arguing, when they are only striving quarrelsomely. The reason is that they don't know how to split up a given utterance into its different divisions, but pursue simply a verbal opposition to what is uttered. They bandy words with each other, instead of using reasoned discussion."

"That certainly does happen," he said, "in many cases; but surely it does not apply to us in this case?"

"It does, by all manner of means," I said; "at any rate we appear to have got into a word controversy without meaning to."

"How?"

---

[1] The Controversialists were almost a sect in Plato's time. They were ready to prove or disprove anything; there are amusing examples in Plato's *Euthydemos*.

"That *different* natures ought not to engage in the *same* practices; we have been chasing the words about with plenty of courage and eristic wrangling, and never thought of enquiring in any way what was the sense of 'different nature' and what was the sense of 'same nature,' and what we were aiming at in our definition when we allotted to a different nature different practices, and to the same nature the same."

"True, we did not," said he.

"It seems we might just as well ask ourselves," I said, "whether the natures of bald men and hairy men are the same or opposite; and in case we agree that they are opposite, we might forbid long-haired men to make shoes if bald men do, and forbid bald men if long-haired men do."

"That would be ridiculous," he said.

"Yes, ridiculous," I said, "but only because we did not then mean the words 'different' and 'same nature' absolutely; we were thinking only of that kind of sameness or difference which had to do with their actual callings. Thus we meant that a man and a woman who have a physician's mind have the same nature, didn't we?"

"Yes."

"But a man physician and a man carpenter different natures?"

"Yes, I suppose so."

"Now," said I, "take the male and the female sex; if either is found to be better as regards any art or other practice, we shall say that this ought to be assigned to it. But if we find that they differ only in one thing, that the male begets and the female bears the child, we shall not take that difference as having proved any more clearly that a woman differs from a man for what we are speaking of; but we shall still believe that our guardians and their wives should practise the same things."

"And rightly so," he said.

"Next, we shall call upon the man who says the opposite, to tell us just this—any art or practise, of those which furnish our city, for which the nature of woman and man is not the same but different."

"That is fair, at least."

"The other man's reply might very likely be what you said a little while ago, that he can't easily answer properly all of a sudden, but give him time to think and it will not be hard."

"Yes, he might say that."

"Then if you please shall we ask our opponent kindly to follow us, and see if we can show him that there is no practice peculiar to woman in the management of a city?"

THE REPUBLIC Book V (454B–456A)

"Certainly."

"We will say to him then, 'Come along, answer. Was it this that you meant by having or not having a natural gift for anything—that one learned easily, the other with difficulty? One after short learning was very inventive in what he learnt, the other after long learning and practice could not even remember what he had learnt? In one the body served the mind properly, in the other it opposed the mind? Was there anything else by which you distinguished good and bad natural gifts for various things?'"

"No one will find anything else," he said.

"Well, do you know anything at all practised among mankind, in which in all these respects the male sex is not far better than the female? Or should we make a long story of it—take weaving, and the careful tending of cakes and boiling pots, in which women think themselves somebody and would be most laughed at if beaten?"

"You are right," he said, "that one sex is much better than the other in almost everything. Many women, it is true, are better than many men in many things, but generally it is as you say."

"Then, my friend, no practice or calling in the life of the city belongs to woman as woman, or to man as man, but the various natures are dispersed among both sexes alike; by nature the woman has a share in all practices, and so has man, but in all, woman is rather weaker than man."

"Certainly."

"Then shall we assign all to man and none to woman?"

"Why, how can we?"

"No, for as I believe, we shall say one woman is musical by nature, one not, one is medical by nature, one not."

"Of course."

"But are we not to add—one woman is athletic or warlike, and another is unwarlike and unathletic?"

"Indeed we are."

"Shall we not say the same of philosophy and misosophy, one loves wisdom and one hates it? One has high spirit, one no spirit?"

"That is so also."

"Then there may be a woman fit to be a guardian, although another is not; for such was the nature we chose for our guardian men also?"

"Yes, it was."

"Then both woman and man may have the same nature fit for guarding the city, only one is weaker and one stronger."

"So it seems."

"Such women, then, must be chosen for such men, to live with them and to guard with them, since they are fit for it and akin to them by nature."

"Certainly."

"Practice and calling must be assigned to both sexes, the same for the same natures?"

"Just the same."

"So we have come round to where we began, and we agree that it is not against nature to assign music and gymnastic to the wives of the guardians."

"By all means."

"Then our law was not impossible, not only like a pious dream; the law we laid down was natural. But rather, it seems, what happens now, the other way of doing things, is unnatural."

"So it seems."

"Our question then was: Is our proposal possible, and is it best?"

"Yes, that was it."

"It is possible, we are both agreed, aren't we?"

"Yes."

"Then the next thing is to agree if it is best."

"Clearly."

"Well, for a woman to become fit to be a guardian, we shall not need one education to make men fit and a different one to make women fit, especially as it will be dealing with the same nature in both?"

"No; the same education."

"Then what is your opinion about the following?"

"What?"

"About the notion in your mind that one man is better, another is worse. Or do you think all men are alike?"

"Not by any means."

"In the city that we were founding, then, which do you think we formed into better men, the guardians educated as we described, or the cobblers educated in cobbling?"

"A ridiculous question," said he.

"I understand," said I, "but tell me—are not the guardians the best of all the citizens?"

"Much the best."

"Very well, will not these women be the best of the women?"

"Again the very best," he said.

"And is there anything better for a city than that both women and men in it should be as good as they can be?"

"There is not."

"But this will be brought about by the aid of music and gymnastic, as we have described?"

"Of course."

"Then the plan we proposed is not only possible, but best for the city?"

"Just so."

"So the women of the guardians must strip, since naked they will be clothed in virtue for gowns; they must share in war and in all the guarding of the city, and that shall be their only work. But in these same things lighter parts will be given to women than men because of the weakness of their sex. And the man who laughs at naked women, exercising for the greatest good, plucks an unripe fruit of wisdom from his laughter;[1] he apparently does not know what he laughs at or what he is doing. For it is and will be the best thing ever said, that the useful is beautiful and the harmful is ugly."

"Assuredly so."

"There goes, let us say, the first wave[2] we have to meet in discussing our women's law—and we are alive! The flood has not quite swallowed us up after ordaining that our guardians and guardianesses must have all their doings in common. The argument makes a humble bow to itself, and admits that what itself says is possible and useful too."

"Yes indeed," he said, "that is no small wave you are surviving."

"No big one, you will say," I answered, "when you see the next."

"Go on, let me see it," he said.

"Another law," said I, "follows this and the others before it, I think."

"What, pray?"

"These women are to be all common to all these men; no one must have a private wife of his own, and the children must be common too, and the parent shall not know the child nor the child its parent."

"A much bigger wave indeed than the other," said he. "It makes one doubt about the possibility and the usefulness of this proposal."

"Oh, about useful," I said, "there would be no doubt there, I think; no one will deny it would be the greatest good to have women in common and children in common. But is it possible? I think there would be the greatest dispute about whether it is possible or not."

"Both would be disputed," he said, "hot and strong."

[1] An allusion to a phrase of Pindar.
[2] The image in his mind is three succeeding waves; the third is proverbial.

"A regular league of logic," said I. "I thought I should escape one of them, if you would agree that it is useful, and that would leave me only possible or not."

"Aha, I spied you trying to slip away," said he; "but you must show reason for both."

"Well, I must pay penalty," said I. "But do me one favour. Let me have a little holiday, and feast my imagination as idle people do walking about alone in a daydream. Such people don't wait to find out how they can get what they want. They do not want to tire themselves out by deliberating about possible and impossible; they let that pass, and suppose that they have what they want; then they arrange all the rest, and describe in high glee the grand things they will do now they have got it, and so they make their idle soul still idler than it was. So I am already going soft myself, and I want to put off the question whether it is possible; we can examine that by and by. Now, assuming that it is among the possibles, with your leave I will examine how the rulers will arrange these things when they have them, and I will try to show that these arrangements would be of the greatest advantage to the city and to the guardians. This first I will consider along with you, and then the other things, by your leave."

"You have my leave," he said, "pray go on."

"I think then," said I, "that the rulers must act up to their name, and their assistants, too, in the same way. Rulers will be willing to give orders, and assistants to do what has been ordered; but the rulers must themselves in some things obey our laws, and in other things exhibit the spirit of those laws in matters which we leave to their discretion."

"Quite reasonable," said he.

"Then suppose you are the lawgiver," I said. "You have picked out the men, and likewise then you will pick out the women of the same nature as far as possible, and give them to the men. These will all have dwellings and messes in common, and no one will have any private property of that kind at all; so they will be together and mingle together in places of exercise and in all their training; then by inborn necessity, I think, they will mingle in union with one another. Don't you think it is a case of necessity?"

"Not the necessity of mathematics," he said, "but the necessity of love, which is really more pressing than the other to persuade and to attract the majority of people."

"Very much so," I said. "But next, Glaucon, to mingle in disorderly fashion with each other, or to do anything else in that fashion, is not to be thought of in a city of happy people; and the rulers will not allow it."

"No," he said, "for that is not just."

"It is plain then, that we shall make marriages as sacred as ever we can; and sacred would mean the most useful."

"By all means."

"Then how will they be most useful? Tell me that, Glaucon. For I see in your house hunting dogs and numbers of pedigree game birds. Pray, have you paid any attention to their matings and breedings?"

"What sort of attention?" he asked.

"First of all, in this admittedly pedigree stock there are some, aren't there, which turn out to be the best?"

"There are."

"Then do you breed from all alike, or do you take the greatest care to choose the best?"

"I choose the best."

"What of their age—do you take the youngest or the oldest, or as far as possible those in their prime?"

"Those in their prime."

"And if the breeding should not be done in this way, you consider the stock will be much worse both in bird and dog?"

"I do," said he.

"What of horses," said I, "and other animals? Is it different in them?"

"That would be odd indeed," he said.

"Bless my soul!" said I. "My friend, what simply tiptop rulers we need to have, if the same is true of mankind!"

"Well, it is," he said, "but why do you say that, pray?"

"Because," said I, "they will have to use all those drugs. We thought even an inferior physician was enough, I take it, for bodies willingly subjected to a proper diet and needing no drugs; but when drugs must be used, we know that the physician must be braver."

"True: but what has that to do with it?"

"This," I said. "Often the rulers will have really to use falsehood and deceit for the benefit of the ruled; and we said all such things were useful as a kind of drugs."

"Yes, and that was right," he said.

"In their weddings and child-gettings, then, it seems this right will be rightest."

"How so?"

"It follows from what we agreed that the best men must mingle most often with the best women, but the opposite, the worst with the worst, least often; and the children of the best must be brought up but not the others, if the flock is to be tiptop. And none must know this to be going on except the rulers alone, if the herd of guardians is also to be as free as possible from quarrels."

"Quite right," he said.

"Then holidays must be provided by law, when we shall bring together the brides and bridegrooms, and there must be festivals, and hymns must be made by our poets suitable to the weddings which come about. But the number of weddings we will leave the rulers to decide, so that they may keep the number of the men as far as possible the same, taking into account war and disease and so forth, in order to keep the city from becoming either too large or too small as far as possible."

"That is right," he said.

"And there must be some clever kind of lots devised, I think, so that your worthless creature will blame his bad luck on any conjunction, not his rulers."

"Just so," he said.

"And I suppose, when young men prove themselves good and true in war or anywhere else, honours must be given them, and prizes, and particularly more generous freedom of intercourse with women; at the same time, this will be a good excuse for letting as many children as possible be begotten of such men."

"That is right."

"Then the officials who are set over these will receive the children as they are born; they may be men or women or both, for offices are common, of course, to both women and men."

"Yes."

"The children of the good, then, they will take, I think, into the fold, and hand them over to certain nurses who will live in some place apart in the city; those of the inferior sort, and any one of the others who may be born defective, they will put away as is proper in some mysterious, unknown place."

"Yes," he said, "if the breed of the guardians is to be pure."

"Those officials, then, will have charge of their nurture; they will bring into the fold the mothers when they are in milk, taking every precaution that no mother shall recognise her own; if these are not able, they shall provide others who have milk. They shall be careful that these mothers do not suckle too long; sleepless nights and other troubles will be left for nurses and nannies."

"What an easy job you make it," he said, "for the guardians' wives to have children!"

"As it should be," I said. "But now let us go on with the

next part of our scheme. We said, you remember, that the offspring ought to be born from parents in their prime."

"True."

"Do you think, as I do, that the prime of life might fairly be counted as lasting twenty years for a woman, and thirty for a man?"

"Which years would you choose?" he asked.

"The woman," I said, "shall bear for the state from the age of twenty to forty; the man shall beget for the state from the time when 'his quickest racing speed is past'[1] to the age of five and fifty."

"At all events," he said, "that is the prime of both in body and mind."

"Then if a man either older or younger than these shall meddle in begetting for the state, we shall say this offence is neither lawful nor right. He has planted a child in the city, which will be born, if the secret is kept, not as one conceived in the grace of sanctity; no holy rite and prayers will be heard over it, such as priestesses and priests will intone for each wedding while the whole city prays that the children born may be better children of good parents, and more useful children of useful parents, from generation to generation; instead it was begotten in darkness with incontinence to the common danger."

"You are right," said he.

"The same law will hold," said I, "if one still within the creative age touch a woman within her age without a ruler's pairing; bastard and unaccredited and unsanctified we shall call that child which he dumps upon the city."

"Quite rightly so," he said.

"But I think, as soon as the women and the men pass the age of begetting, we shall leave the men free to consort with any they will, except with daughter or mother, and daughters' children, and those of an earlier generation than the mother; and the women again free except for son or father or those above and below as before. However, with all this allowance, we must warn them to be as careful as possible not to bring any of such conceptions into the light, not even one; but if a child is born, if one forces its way through, they must dispose of it on the understanding that there is no food or nurture for such a one."

"Yes," he said, "that is quite reasonable too; but how will they recognise each others' fathers and daughters and other relations you spoke of just now?"

"They will not," said I. "But whenever one of them becomes

[1] A poetic quotation, which probably referred to a horse.

a bridegroom, he will call all the male children sons and all the female children daughters, who are born in the tenth month, or indeed the seventh month, counting from the day of his marriage; and they will call him father; and likewise he will call their offspring grandchildren, and they again will call these grandfathers and grandmothers. And those born in that particular time when their mothers and fathers were begetting they will call sisters and brothers. So these will not touch each other in the way we spoke of; but brothers and sisters the law will allow to live together, if the lot falls that way and if the Pythian oracle sanctions."[1]

"Quite right," he said.

"So you see, Glaucon, what is meant by having women and children in common among the city's guardians. Now we must establish by the argument that this fits in with our general constitution and is by far the best. Or what shall we do next?"

"Surely this," he said.

"Surely, then, the beginning of our agreement is to ask ourselves what we can name as the greatest good for furnishing a city which the lawgiver should aim at in laying down the laws; and what is the greatest evil. Then we must enquire whether what we have just described fits the footstep of the good and does not suit that of the bad."

"Most of all," he said.

"Then can we name any greater evil for a city than that which tears it asunder and makes it many instead of one? Or a greater good than what binds it together and makes it one?"

"We cannot."

"Surely community in pleasure and pain binds it together? That is when, as far as possible, all the citizens alike are glad or sorry, on the same occasions of births and successes or deaths and disasters?"

"Certainly," he said.

"But if each has his own feelings apart about such happenings the bonds are cut, if some are very happy and some very much pained while the same things happen to the city and those who are in the city."

"Of course."

"And does not this come because the people do not all utter in unison the words 'mine' and 'not mine,' or likewise the word 'another's'?"

"Exactly so."

[1] The lot will be arranged by the rulers, who know the truth. Something not unlike this confusion of family names exists now among the Lepshas of Sikkim; see G. Gorer, *Himalayan Village*, Michael Joseph, 1938.

"So that city is best managed in which the greatest number say 'mine' and 'not mine' with the same meaning about the same thing?"

"Much the best."

"That is when the city is nearest the single man. For example, what happens when your finger is hurt? The whole community, arranged throughout the body, stretching to the soul as one orderly whole under that which rules in it,[1] feels the pain, and the community has pain all together as a whole when the part is in trouble: so we say the man has pain in the finger, and the same is said of any other of the parts of the man, about pain when a part is in trouble and about pleasure when a part gets better."

"Just the same," he said, "and as you put it, the best governed city comes nearest to such a man."

"Then," I said, "if something either good or bad happens to any one of the citizens, such a city will be most likely to say that the sufferer is part of the city, and it will be happy or unhappy as a whole."

"There is necessity in that," he said, "for the well-managed city."

"Now it is time," I said, "to go back to our city, and see if this has most chiefly the qualities agreed upon in our argument, or if another has them more."

"Yes, that is what we must do," said he.

"Very well then. In other cities, as in this, there are rulers and people?"

"There are."

"All these will call each other citizens?"

"Of course."

"So the people in other cities call their rulers citizens; but what else do they call them?"

"In most cities 'masters,' in democracies by that very name —'rulers.' "[2]

"But what do people in our city call their rulers besides 'citizens'?"

" 'Saviours' and 'helpers,' " he said.

"And what do these call the people?"

" 'Paymasters' and 'maintainers.' "

"What do the rulers in the other cities call their peoples?"

" 'Slaves,' " he said.

"And what do the rulers call each other?"

" 'Fellow-rulers.' "

"And what do our rulers call each other?"

[1] The man, here, not the soul.
[2] That is what the Greek word means; in fact the "rulers" were elected magistrates.

" 'Fellow-guardians.' "

"Can you then say whether any one of the rulers in the other cities would address one of his fellow-rulers as 'one of us,' and another as 'an outsider'?"

"Yes, many."

"Then he considers the one of us as his own, and so speaks of him, but the outsider as not his own?"

"Just so."

"And what of your guardians? Would any one of them be able to consider one of his fellow-guardians an outsider and address him as such?"

"By no means," he said; "for whomever a man meets he will think he is meeting a brother or sister, or a father or mother, or a son or daughter, or their direct descendants or forebears."

"An excellent answer!" said I. "But tell me this, too. Will you ordain these names only as family names for them, or will you make them act up to the names in everything? Will they have to treat the fathers with that honour which the law ordains for a father? Will they have to care for them, and give them a parent's obedience? Will they believe that anything else would be impious and unjust, and that he who did otherwise would find no favour either with gods or men? Will these or different ones be the voices which will from birth sing in the childrens' ears from all the citizens, about those whom anyone points out to them as fathers and about their other kindred?"

"These will be the voices," he said, "for it would be ridiculous for them merely to chant family names on their tongues and do nothing."

"Then in this city most of all they will sing in chorus this word we were speaking of just now—the word 'mine'; if one person is well off or ill off, 'mine' does well, or 'mine' does badly."

"Most true," said he.

"Then with this conviction, and this way of speaking, it comes consequently that pleasures and pains are shared in common; didn't we say so?"

"We did, and rightly."

"So here, most of all, our citizens will have in common that which they will describe as 'mine,' and having this in common they will have completest community in their pleasures and pains?"

"Yes, highly so."

"Then is not the cause of this the community of women

and children among the guardians, besides the general constitution of the city?"

"Most chiefly that," he said.

"But that we agreed, furthermore, was the highest good for the city, and we compared a well-managed city to the body as to how the parts and the whole were connected in pain and pleasure."

"Yes, we were quite right," he said.

"Then the cause of the highest good for the city has been shown to be the community of women and children among the assistants."

"That is true," he said.

"And here we agree with what we said earlier: you remember these assistants were to have no houses of their own, no land or property; they were to be supported by the other citizens, and to spend this wage of their guardianship all in common, if they were to be really guardians."

"We were right," he said.

"Then is it not as I say? Those rules we mentioned, and still more these we speak of now, make them into true guardians, and prevent their tearing the city asunder. They will not use the word 'mine' each of different things, but of the same: one will not drag into his own house whatever goods he can get apart from the rest; another will not drag into his own separate house a separate wife and separate children; they will not bring in private pleasures and pains of their own, but they will have one conviction of what their own means, and they will all pull in the same direction and feel pain and pleasure together as far as possible."

"Exactly so," said he.

"Further, will not lawsuits and accusations against each other vanish almost entirely from among them? For they will have all in common, nothing private except their body; which, you see, makes them free from quarrels and factions, as far as human quarrels come from possessing wealth or children and kindred."

"They will be quite free from that," he said, "beyond all doubt."

"And moreover, lawsuits for violence and assault could never justly be among them. For we shall say, I suppose, that among years-mates self-defence is fair and just, and so we shall compel them to keep their bodies in condition."

"Rightly so," he said.

"And it is equally right that if one should be angry with another by chance, and should work off his temper in such a way, he would be less likely to go on to greater factions."

"Certainly."

"Authority will be given to an elder to command and chastise all younger men."

"That is clear."

"And further, as is to be expected, a younger will not try to compel an older, unless magistrates command it, and particularly will never try to strike him; and I think he will not show him disrespect in any other way, for two guards are sufficient to prevent him, fear and shame. Shame will restrain him from touching one who may be his parent, and his fear will be that others may come to the sufferer's help as sons or brothers or fathers."

"That follows," he said.

"Everywhere the laws will keep them at peace with one another?"

"There will be a great peace!"

"Further, if these do not quarrel amongst themselves there will be no fear that the rest of the city should fall out with them or with each other?"

"None at all."

"Besides, they would be free of those trifling unpleasantnesses which I really don't care to speak of because they are so mean; fawnings on the rich, all want and anxiety such as the poor endure in bringing up children and finding money for the bare necessities of sustenance for their household, now having to borrow, now to repudiate, getting something by any shift and giving it over to wives and servants to manage —all this, my friend, and what they suffer, is plain enough, but it is ignoble and not worth mention."

"Oh, a blind man can see it," said he.

"They will be rid of all these things, then, and they will live a life of bliss, more blest than the life of Olympian victors."

"How so?"

"Those Olympians are congratulated for a small part of the happiness secured for these. The victory of these is more glorious, their public maintenance is more complete; their victory is the salvation of the whole city, they themselves and their children are crowned with free food and free everything else that life needs; alive, they receive honourable prizes from their own city, and in death a worthy burial."

"Fine things indeed," he said.

"You remember," said I, "how awhile since someone or other blamed us for not making the guardians happy; it was in their power to have everything belonging to the citizens, and they had nothing. Our answer was, I believe, that if the matter came up we would consider it by and by, but at present we were making the guardians guardians, and the city as greatly happy as we could make it, and we were not looking at one class in it and trying to make that one happy."

"I remember," he said.

"Very well. If the life of our assistants is really better and more beautiful than that of the conquering heroes of Olympia, can you possibly compare the life of shoemakers with it, or of some of the other craftsmen, or of the farmers?"

"I think not, indeed," said he.

"And indeed I may fairly say again what I said then; if the guardian shall attempt to make himself happy in such a way as to be not a guardian, if a life so reasonable and sure and one that is best, as we say, shall be not enough for him, if a foolish and childish doctrine of happiness falls on him and drives him on to take possession of all in the city just because he can—then he shall learn that Hesiod was really a wise man when he said, 'The half is greater in a way than the whole!'"[1]

"If the man will take my advice," he said, "he will stick to this way of life."

"You grant, then," said I, "that there should be the community of women with men, which we described, in education and in children and in the guardianship of the other citizens; that whether remaining in the city or going to war they must be fellow-guardians, and hunt with them like dogs, and share everything in every way up to their power; and that so doing they will do what is best, and not what is contrary to female nature as compared with male, the natural relation of the two sexes towards each other?"

"I grant it," he said.

"Then," I said, "it remains to decide whether it is really possible for this community to come into being in mankind as in other animals; and if so, in what way."

"You have forestalled me in bringing up the point I was going to raise," said he.

"Well," I said, "take war first; I think it is clear how they will take part in that."

"How?" he asked.

"They will march with the men, and they will also bring along any of the children who are strong enough, that they may watch what they will have to do in their own craft when they grow up, just like the children of the other craftsmen. Besides watching, the children will be servants and ministers in all the business of war, and wait upon their fathers and

[1] The proverb was, "Beginning is half the whole"—well begun is half done; Hesiod, *Works and Days*, 40.

mothers. Have you not noticed in the arts, how potters' children, for example, look on and help for a long time before they touch pot-making?"

"Yes, indeed."

"Then should more care be taken by potters than by the guardians to educate their children by letting them watch and practise their duties?"

"That would be quite ridiculous," he said.

"Then again, every animal will fight harder when its children are present."

"No doubt, but if they are beaten, Socrates, as often happens in war, think of the risk! They may lose their children as well as themselves, and the rest of the city may never recover."

"That's true enough," I said, "but tell me first, do you consider that the chief aim in life is never to run risks?"

"Not at all!"

"Well, if risks must be run, should it not be wherein the victors will be made better?"

"Clearly, of course."

"But do you think it will make only a small difference for them, and be not worth a risk, to see or not to see the business of war as boys, if they are to be men of war?"

"No indeed, for the purpose of which you speak it is a great advantage."

"Then we must begin with this—make the children look on at war, but also provide somehow for their safety, and all will be well. Don't you think so?"

"Yes."

"Of course," said I, "their fathers will not be without human common sense; they will have a bit of knowledge about campaigns, which are risky and which are not."

"Quite likely," he said.

"So they will take them along if they are not risky, and they will be very careful if they are?"

"Rightly so."

"And no doubt," I said, "they will put over them as officers not the poorest specimens but those best fitted to be leaders and guides for children by experience and age."

"Yes, that is proper."

"But we shall remember that many things happen unexpectedly to many people."

"Very much so."

"Well, my friend, we must give the children wings from the first for occasions of that kind, so that if necessary they may escape by flying!"

"What do you mean?" said he.

"Horses!" I said. "Put them on horseback as young as possible; we must teach them to ride and bring them to the spectacle on horses, not high-mettled war horses but the most swift-footed, manageable goers. For in this way they will have the best view of their own business, and if need be, they will most safely preserve their lives by going along with their elderly leaders."

"That seems right and true," he said.

"What, now, of the business of war?" I said. "How are the soldiers to behave towards themselves and the enemy? Am I right in my way of thinking, or not?"

"Tell me what you think," said he.

"First the men themselves; if one of them deserts his post," I said, "or throws aways his arms, or does anything of that sort from cowardice, should he not be degraded to a craftsman or farmer?"

"By all means."

"If one is taken alive by the enemy should we not present him to his captors as a gift, to use their captured game as they like?"

"The very thing!" he said.

"And if one proves a champion and distinguishes himself, in the first place he must be crowned on the field by each lad or boy in the army in turn, don't you think so?"

"Yes, I do."

"And then clasped by the right hand?"

"Yes, that also."

"But you don't agree with my next, I'm afraid. He shall kiss and be kissed by each one."

"But I do," said he, "most certainly! And I add to your law, that so long as they are on that campaign, no one whom he wants to kiss shall be allowed to refuse; with this object, that if anyone is in love with a boy or girl, he may be the more eager to win the prize of valour."

"Good," said I. "We have said already that a brave man shall have more weddings ready for him than the rest, and frequent choice in such matters compared with the others, since we want as many children as possible from such a man."

"Yes, we said so."

"And further, we have it in Homer that it is just to honour in these ways those of the young who are good and true. For Homer describes how after distinguishing himself in the war Aias[1] was honoured at dinner with the long chine,[2] as being

[1] Ajax.
[2] *Iliad* vii. 321.

the proper honour for the brave man in his youthful prime; and from this, besides being honoured, he would increase his strength."

"Quite right," said he.

"Then," said I, "we will obey Homer in this. For we also in our feasts and on all such occasions will honour the good and true, in proportion as they have proved themselves to be so, both with hymns and the privileges we just now described, and besides these with

> High seats, and meats, and bumpers, without end;[1]

since we have in view not honour only, but training, for both good men and good women."

"Excellent," he said.

"Well then; of those who fall on the field—if one dies in glory, shall we not say he is one of the golden stock?"

"Most certainly."

"And shall we believe Hesiod,[2] when he says of his golden people that when they die

> Some dwell upon the earth as holy spirits,
> Good guardians protecting mortal men?"

"Certainly we shall."

"So we will enquire of the god[3] how we ought to inter spiritual and divine men, and what distinction to give them, and we should inter them according as he shall answer."

"So we will indeed."

"And to the end of time we will tend their tombs and worship before them as the sepulchres of spirits; and we will observe these same customs whenever one dies from old age or in any other way, of those who have been judged in life to be pre-eminent."

"At least that is just."

"Next, how shall our soldiers behave towards their enemies?"

"I don't quite understand."

"Take enslavement first: Do you think it just for Hellenes to enslave the people of Hellenic cities, and should they allow another city to do so if they can help it? Should it not be the custom to spare the Hellenic race, foreseeing the danger of racial enslavement under the barbarians?"[4]

"To spare is out and out the best," he said.

---

[1] *Iliad* viii. 162.
[2] *Works and Days*, 121.
[3] Apollo, through his oracle at Delphi.
[4] By "barbarians" the Greeks meant all people who were not Greeks.

"Then they shall not possess a Hellenic slave themselves, nor consent that other Hellenes should possess one."

"Certainly," he said, "and in that way they would be more turned against the barbarians and keep their hands off themselves."

"Well, will they strip the dead," said I, "when they are victors, more than of their arms? Is that good? It may offer an excuse to cowards not to attack the fighting man, as if they were doing part of their duty when poking about the dead man; and many an army has perished because of such robbery."

"Very true."

"Don't you think it mean and greedy to despoil a corpse, and a sign of a petty, womanish mind to think the dead body an enemy, when the foeman has flitted afar, and only what he fought with is left? Do you think there is any difference between those who do this and dogs which worry the stones that strike them and never touch the thrower?"

"Not a bit," said he.

"Then we will have nothing to do with the robbing of corpses and with preventing their being taken up for burial?"

"Nothing, by God!" he said.

"Furthermore, we will not carry the arms to a temple and dedicate them there, least of all the arms of Hellenes, if we care anything for good feeling towards the other Hellenes. Rather than that we shall even fear a pollution in bringing such arms of our own people to a temple, unless the god himself says otherwise."

"Most rightly so," said he.

"And what of ravaging the land of Hellenes and burning their houses? How will your soldiers deal with their enemies in that matter?"

"Tell me your own opinion," said he. "I should be glad to hear."

"Then it seems to me that they should do neither, but only take the year's crops. Shall I tell you why?"

"Pray do."

"My opinion is: Just as there are these two different names, war and faction, so there are two epithets which apply to two kinds of disagreement. The two epithets I mean are, one, domestic and family, the other, alien and outland; faction is the name given to domestic hostility, war to alien."

"That is quite to the point," said he.

"Consider then whether this is equally to the point: I say that the Hellenic race is domestic and family to itself, outland and alien to the barbarian."

"Good," he said.

"Well then—Hellenes fighting against barbarians and barbarians against Hellenes we will say are enemies by nature, and that they are warring against each other, and this hostility should be called 'war'; but Hellenes fighting against Hellenes, whenever they do such a thing, we will say are by nature friends, and that in such a case Hellas is diseased with factions, and a hostility of this sort should be called 'faction.'"

"I fully agree with your way of thinking."

"Consider then this faction," I said, "as it is now understood, whenever something like this happens and a city is divided against itself. If both parties lay waste the farms of each other and burn their houses, the faction is thought abominable and both parties unpatriotic, or else they could never have brought themselves to ravage their mother and nurse; but all think it reasonable for the victors to take the crops of the vanquished—only they must behave as expecting to be friends again someday and not to make war forever."

"Yes," he said, "this is a much more humane feeling than the other."

"Now then," I said, "will not the city which you are founding be Hellenic?"

"It ought to be so," he said.

"Will they not be both good and gentle?"

"Abundantly."

"And will they not love the Hellenic nation? Will they not consider Hellas to be their own, and share in the same temples as the others do?"

"Most assuredly so."

"Then they will consider this quarrel with Hellenes as faction, since it is against their own, and not so much as give it the name of war?"

"Yes, indeed."

"And they will quarrel as expecting one day to be friends again?"

"Certainly."

"Then they will chastise kindly; they will not punish to the extent of slavery or destruction, being chastisers, not enemies."

"Just so," he said.

"Being Hellenes then, they will not ravage Hellas; they will not burn houses; they will not admit all to be their foes in any city, men and women and children, but their foes will always be few—only those who caused the quarrel; and for all these reasons they will never wish to ravage the land, since most of them are their friends, nor to pull down the houses. They will carry on the quarrel only until the guilty ones shall be compelled by the suffering innocents to make amends."

"I, at least, agree," he said; "that is how our citizens ought to behave towards their adversaries, but to barbarians they should do as Hellenes now do to each other."

"Let us lay down this law, then, for our guardians, that they neither lay waste the land nor burn the houses."

"Yes," he said, "and let us agree that these rules are as good as the former ones.

"But if we let you go on like this, my dear Socrates, I think you will never remember the question you thrust aside some time ago before you made all this long talk—is this constitution able to come into being, and if so, how in the world is it possible. If it could ever be, then I agree that all would be fine in the city that had it. I even add something which you omit: against their enemies they would fight at their very best because they would never desert each other, when they knew each other and called one another by these names of 'brother,' 'father,' 'son.' And if women also should be on the campaign, whether in the same rank or posted in the rear, to strike terror into the enemy or in case of some necessity for help at any time, I am sure they would be made quite invincible by that. And they would have many blessings at home which you have not mentioned, I see also. I freely admit that all these good things would be there, and thousands besides, if this constitution could be founded, so you need say no more about it. But the one thing we should try to prove to ourselves is whether it is possible, and if so, how; let us leave the other things to take care of themselves."

"What a sudden assault you have made upon my proposals!" I said. "You have no pity on a poor wretch in a tight corner![1] Perhaps you don't know that this is the third wave; I have only just escaped two, and here you come with the third and largest and most dangerous.[2] As soon as you see it and hear it you will certainly forgive me, and know that I had good reason to shrink and fear before telling such an extraordinary tale and trying to examine it."

"The more you talk in that way," he said, "the less we will let you go; tell us you must how this constitution can come into being. Go on, and don't waste any more time."

"Very well," I said. "First it must be remembered that our quest was for justice, if we could find out what it is, and injustice also; and that has brought us to this stage."

---

[1] The Greek verb used here means "loitering."
[2] See p. 255, n. 2.

"Yes," he said, "but what of that?"

"Oh, nothing; but if we do find what sort of thing justice is, shall we claim that the just man must in no way differ from perfect justice, but must in all respects be such as justice is? Or shall we be content if he gets as near as possible to it and has more justice in him than any other man?"

"Oh, that will content us," he said.

"Very well, then," I said, "what we sought was a model to show us what actual justice is, and the man perfectly just if he could be so, and what he would be if such a man could be; so with injustice again and the utterly unjust man. We kept our eyes on these two, to decide how each would prove to be as regards happiness and unhappiness; so that we might be forced to agree about ourselves also, that each of us would receive a portion most like to theirs according as he was most like to them. We were not trying to show that the thing is possible."

"That is quite true," he said.

"Take a painter now: if he should paint a pattern of the ideally[1] beautiful man, and put into the painting all the details properly, but if he could not prove that such a man is possible, do you think he would be the worse painter for that?"

"Not a bit, I swear," said he.

"Very well," said I, "what we made was a pattern of the good city in words."

"Just that," he said.

"Then if we cannot prove that it is possible to make a real state in the way it was described, do you think our description is any the worse?"

"Not at all," said he.

"Then that is the truth," I said, "and if I must really do my best for you, and show how and in what respect it could most likely be possible, you must make the same concession to me for such a proof."

"What?"

"Is it possible for things to be done exactly as they are said? Or is it natural that doing has less grasp of the truth than saying, even if some do not think so? Come now, do you agree yourself about this or not?"

"I do."

"Then do not force me to prove that what we have discussed in words must be done wholly and exactly in fact. No, if we should be able to find how a city could be managed most nearly as we described it, you must allow that the

[1] Literally, "of what would be the most beautiful man."

thing is possible and your demand has been met. Won't you be satisfied to get that? I should myself."

"So should I," he said.

"Then the next thing is, as it seems, we must try to discover and to show what exactly is now badly conducted in cities, which cause them not to be managed like this one, and what is the smallest change that will bring a city into our kind of constitution: one thing if that is enough, or else two, or as few in number as possible and least farreaching."

"By all means," he said.

"There is one change," said I, "which I think would make the transformation, and I think I can prove it; it is certainly neither small nor easy, but it is possible."

"What is that?" he asked.

"Ah! now," I said. "I am right upon that which we likened to the greatest wave. But I will speak, even if the deluge is going to have the laugh of us and swallow us up utterly in a wave of contempt; do consider what I am going to say."

"Go on," he said.

"The philosophers must become kings in our cities," I said, "or those who are now called kings and potentates must learn to seek wisdom like true and genuine philosophers, and so political power and intellectual wisdom will be joined in one; and the crowds of natures who now pursue one or the other separately must be excluded. Until that happens, my dear Glaucon, there can be no rest from troubles for the cities, and I think for the whole human race. Until then, this constitution which we have now evolved in words will never grow into being, as something possible; it will never see the light of the sun, but it will live only in our description. Now this is what has made me so reluctant so long to speak, because I saw that it would run clean contrary to opinion; for it is not easy to see that no other constitution could give happiness to man or to people."

He answered, "O Socrates! what a speech, what a doctrine, you have thrown at our heads! Say this, and you'll have an army upon you in a jiffy, don't make any mistake, and no contemptible adversaries! They will throw off their coats and come at you stripped, each seizing the first weapon he finds, in a furious rush to wreak signal vengeance. If your logic does not defend you and keep them off, you will pay the penalty and be well and truly jeered at!"

"And it's all your fault," I said.

"And I'm glad of it," said he. "But I won't desert you, I'll help all I can. What I can do is to wish you luck and say,

'Go to it!' Yes, and perhaps I could answer your questions less objectionably than another. Count on my help, then, and try to show unbelievers that what you say is right."

"I must try," said I, "since you provide this mighty alliance. I think it necessary, then, if we are to escape that great army of yours, to define for them clearly whom we mean by the philosophers who ought to rule, as we dare to say. If we can make that clear, a man can make some defence, by showing that it is the proper nature of these to keep hold of true wisdom and to lead in the city, but of the others to leave philosophy alone and follow their leader."

"Yes," he said, "it is high time to define that clearly."

"Come along, then, follow me on my road and see if we can explain it sufficiently somehow."

"Come on!" he said.

"I shall have to remind you, then," said I, "or perhaps you remember, that when we say someone loves a thing he must obviously be fond of it altogether, not loving part of it and lacking love for another part, if we describe him aright."

"I need reminding, as it seems," he said, "for I really don't understand."

"Oh dear," I said, "that remark, Glaucon, would suit someone else better. A lover like you ought not to forget that all youths in their bloom sting and stir somehow or other the lover and courter of boys; they all seem worthy of attention and a kiss. Isn't that how you all feel towards young beauties? You will praise one with a tilted nose and call him Gracie, another's hook, you say, is a royal nose, the one between has the happy mean; swarthy ones are brave to look at, fair are little angels; as for honey-coloured, the very name, you think, must be the invention of a coaxing lover who does not mind a pallid skin one bit if there is bloom behind it. In one word, you make every excuse and blurt out anything and everything so as not to reject any who are in fresh bloom."

"If you wish to infer from me," he said, "that amorous people do so, I grant it, just to help your argument along."

"And then again," I said, "you find those who are fond of wine doing just the same, don't you? They make any and every excuse for welcoming a drink."

"So they do."

"And those who are in love with honour, you find them the same, I think; if they can't become generals they are willing to be captains, and if they can't have honour from great, imposing people they are content to have it from common, little people, but honour of some sort they will have."

"Exactly so."

"Now then, say yes or no to this: When we speak of one who has a desire for something, does he desire the whole thing, whatever it may be, and not only a part?"

"The whole," he said.

"Then we may say the philosopher, the wisdom-lover, desires wisdom so, not merely parts but the whole."

"True."

"So if anyone makes a fuss about his studies, especially one young who does not know what is good or what is not, we shall say he is no lover of learning and no philosopher. He is like a fussy feeder, not really hungry, who has no appetite for his vittles; we don't call him a philosopher of the table, but just a bad trencherman."

"Just the right word, that!"

"But if anyone has a good appetite for study, if he is ready to taste every dish, and tackles learning gladly and never can have enough, we justly call him a philosopher, don't we?"

Glaucon replied, "You will find many of that sort and they are very odd people. Of the same sort, so at least it seems to me, are sight-fanciers always gazing at shows, who delight in learning something; there are lecture-fanciers who love listening, the last persons in the world to be counted philosophers— they will never attend a discussion or any such serious study if they can help it, but their ears are for public hire; they run about to hear all the concerts at festival time,[1] not leaving out one town or one village. So we are to allow all these to be philosophers, all the fanciers of such petty performances?"

"Not at all," said I, "but they are imitation philosophers."

"And which do you call the real ones?" he asked.

"Those who are sight-fanciers of truth," said I.

"Well," he said, "that is right enough, but what do you mean by it?"

"It would not be easy to explain," said I, "to anyone else; but you will agree with me, I think, about this."

"About what?"

"Since the beautiful is opposite to the ugly, these are two."

"Oh, of course."

"Since they are two, each is one."

"Yes, yes."

"The same can be said of other pairs, just and unjust, good and bad, and all such notions: each of these by itself is one, but each appears to be many because each shows itself everywhere in community with the others and with actions and bodies."

---

[1] The country Dionysia, rollicking festivals held about our Christmastime.

"Quite right," he said.

"Then here I draw the line," said I. "On one side are the sight-fanciers and art-fanciers you spoke of, and practical men; on the other side again the subjects of our discussion, those who alone may rightly be named philosophers."

"What do you mean?" he asked.

"The one class, I take it," said I, "sound-fanciers and sight-fanciers, delight in beautiful voices and colours and shapes and all which craftsmen have made from such; but their mind is incapable of seeing and delighting in the beautiful itself."

"That is certainly so," he said.

"But the other class are able to approach the beautiful itself and to see it by itself; and would not these be few?"

"Very few."

"Then if a man believes things to be beautiful, but does not believe in beauty by itself, and cannot follow when he is led towards the knowledge of it, what is his life? Is he awake, or is his life a dream? What do you think? Consider. What is dreaming but this, whether one be asleep or awake: thinking what is like something to be not the likeness but the thing itself?"

"I at least would say," he replied, "that such a one is dreaming."

"Take the opposite case. The man who believes in beauty itself, and can distinguish it from things which partake of it, who does not believe the things with beauty to be beauty, or beauty to be those things: do you think that his life is a dream, or is he awake?"

"He is awake," said he, "no doubt about that."

"Then could we not call this man's state of mind knowledge, as of one who knows, and the other's opinion, as of one who opines?"

"By all means."

"Then suppose the one who opines but does not know, as we say, suppose he is angry with us and challenges us as not speaking the truth; can we console him and peacefully persuade him without telling him plainly that he is not sane?"

"We ought to try," he said.

"Very well, think what we shall say to him. Shall we say that if he knows anything, we won't grudge him that; on the contrary, we shall be delighted to see that he does know something. Then we might add the question, 'Does the knower know something or nothing, please tell us that?' But answer for him yourself."

"I will answer, then," said he, "that he knows something."

"Something which is or which is not?"

THE REPUBLIC Book V (476B–477D)

"Which is—how could he know what is not?"

"Then we are sufficiently convinced that however we may examine it, that which wholly is, is wholly knowable, and that which in no way is, is in every way unknowable?"

"Most sufficiently."

"Good, but if there is anything in such a state as both to be and not to be, that would lie between that which simply is and that which is not at all; is that correct?"

"Yes, between them."

"So since knowledge belongs to what is, and ignorance of necessity to what is not, for this thing between, something must be sought between ignorance and acquired knowledge, if there really is such a thing between?"

"Certainly."

"Do we say there is such a thing as opinion?"

"Of course."

"Is it the same power as knowledge or different?"

"Different."

"Then opinion has been assigned to one thing and knowledge to another, according to the power of each."

"Just so."

"Then knowledge naturally belongs to that which is, to know in what way it is? But stay, here is a distinction I think I must make first."

"How do you mean?"

"We will say that 'powers' are a class of entities—I mean the powers which make us able to do what we are able, and everything else to do what it is able. For example, sight and hearing are powers, if you really understand what sort of things I mean."

"Oh, I understand," said he.

"Then hear what I think about them. In power I see no colour, and no shape, or anything of that kind, such as I see in many other things, which I hold in view when I distinguish objects in my mind, some as being different from others, but in power I look only at one thing, what does it belong to and what does it effect; in this way I always call each of them a power, and if one belongs to the same thing and effects the same thing I call it the same power, but one that belongs to another thing and does another thing I call another power. What about you? What do you do?"

"The same as you," he said.

"Come back again now, my good friend," I went on. "Knowledge—do you say it is a power, or what class do you put it in?"

"This power class," he said, "yes, most mighty of all powers."

"And opinion—shall we put that with power, or with another class?"

"Of course not with another class," he said, "for that with which we are able to opine can be nothing else than opinion."

"But a little while ago you agreed that opinion and knowledge are not the same."

"Yes, no one with common sense would say that the infallible is the same as the fallible."

"Good," said I, "so we are clearly agreed that opinion is different from knowledge."

"Yes, different."

"Then each of them has a different power over a different thing."

"Necessarily."

"Knowledge, I take it, over that which is, to know in what state that is."

"Yes."

"And opinion, we say, has power to opine?"

"Yes."

"To opine the same that knowledge knows? Will the same thing be both knowable and opinable, or is that impossible?"

"Impossible," he said, "from what has been agreed between us; if really different powers belong to different things, and both knowledge and opinion are powers, and they are different, as we say, it follows that knowable and opinable cannot be the same."

"Then if the knowable is that which is, the opinable is different from that which is."

"Yes, different."

"Then does it opine what is not? Or is it impossible to opine what is not? Think a moment: Does not the opiner bring his opinion to something? Or is it possible to opine and yet to opine nothing?"

"Impossible."

"Then the opiner opines some one thing?"

"Yes."

"But that which is not, is not some one thing; it would most properly be named nothing."

"By all means."

"Further, we assigned ignorance to what is not, of necessity, and knowledge to what is?"

"Rightly so," he said.

"Then he does not opine either what is or what is not."

"True."

"Opinion then would be neither ignorance nor knowledge."

"So it seems."

"Then is it outside of both these, surpassing either knowledge in clearness or ignorance in unclearness?"

"Neither."

"So then," I said, "opinion is darker than knowledge and brighter than ignorance? Is that what appears to you?"

"Most certainly," said he.

"And it lies between the two?"

"Yes."

"Between them, that is where opinion lies."

"Exactly so."

"We have already asserted that if anything should be found, as it were, being and not being at the same time, such would lie between what simply is and what wholly is not; and neither knowledge nor ignorance would belong to it but that which was found between knowledge and ignorance."

"You are right."

"And now between these two has been found what we call opinion."

"It has."

"One thing, then, seems to be left for us to find, that which partakes of both being and not-being, which could not be named simply one or the other; so that if it appears, we may justly name it the opinable, assigning thus extremes to extremes and between to between. Don't you think so?"

"I do."

"We have so much then, clear before us. Now let that honest fellow speak out, I will say, now let him answer my question. He does not believe in the beautiful itself, he will have no model of perfect beauty always unchangeable, but he believes in a host of beautiful things; this is that sight-fancier who will not tolerate to be told that the beautiful is one,[1] and the just is one, and so forth. This is my question: 'My good man, of all these beautiful things is there a single one which will not sometimes appear ugly? Of all these just things will one never appear unjust? Of all these pious things, will one never appear impious?'"

"No; it is inevitable," he said, "that they would appear both beautiful in a way and in a way ugly, and so with all you mention in your questions."

"And again, the host of doubles can appear as halves all the same?"

"Every one of them."

"And things great and small, and light and heavy, as we

[1] A separate essence.

call them, cannot they have the opposite names equally well?"

"They can," said he. "Each will have part in both opposites."

"Then is each of these many things really what we call it, or equally is it not what we call it?"

"This is like the double meanings which they play with at table, like the children's riddle about the eunuch, where they riddle how he shot at the bat, what he hit it with and what it sat on.[1] These sayings also have double meanings, and it is impossible to fix any of them firmly in the mind as being or not being, or as both or as neither."[2]

"Then don't you know what to do with them?" said I; "do you know where better to put them than between being and not-being? For they cannot seem brighter than being, so that they should more be, or darker than not-being, so that they should more not-be."

"Very true," he said.

"We have found then, as it seems, that the common beliefs of the multitude about beautiful and so forth are just rolling about between simply and truly being and not being."

"We have."

"But we have agreed already that if any belief of this kind should come to light it ought to be called opinable and not knowable, something astray in the middle and caught by the middle power."

"We have."

"Then if people gaze at many beautiful things, and cannot see the beautiful itself or follow one who leads them to it, and the same with just things and justice itself and so in all cases, we will say they opine all these but know nothing of what they opine?"

"That must be so," he said.

"But what of those who gaze at all these as they are in themselves unchangeable forever? Those do not opine, but know?"

"That also must be so."

"Shall we not say also that those men welcome and love the things to which knowledge belongs, and the others the things of opinion? Do we not remember saying that these love and gaze at beautiful sounds and colours and so on, and will not tolerate the idea of the beautiful itself as something which is?"

---

[1] The riddle was: A man not a man saw and did not see a bird not a bird sitting on a stick not a stick and hit it with a stone not a stone. The answer was: A eunuch caught a glimpse of a bat sitting on a reed and hit it with a piece of pumice.
[2] Phenomena cannot be fixed firmly in the mind because they are always changing.

"We remember."

"Then shall we perhaps give offence by calling them philodoxers rather than philosophers?[1] Will they be very angry with us if we call them that?"

"Not if they take my advice," he said; "for to be angry with the truth is not right."

"And those who welcome that which is, in each case, must be called true philosophers, not philodoxers."

"By all means."

BOOK VI

"So then, Glaucon, they have appeared at last!" I said, "and we know who are the philosophers and who are not, after our argument has travelled a long and difficult road."

"Perhaps," he said, "it would not have been easy by a shorter road."

"So it seems," I said, "though I can't help thinking at least that it might have been better shown if we had only had this to discuss. But there are so many things left to examine for one who means to discover how just life differs from unjust."

"Well, what are we to take next?" he asked.

"Why, the next thing, of course!" I said—"since philosophers alone are able to lay hold of the ever same and unchangeable, and those who cannot do so, but keep wandering amid the changeable and manifold are not philosophers,— which ought to be leaders of a city?"

"I hardly know what to say, without saying too much," he said.

"Whichever of the two," said I, "appear able to guard the laws and habits of cities, set them up as guardians."

"Quite right," he said.

"Here is another question," said I: "Ought a guardian to be blind or sharp-sighted when he watches anything? Is that clear?"

"Of course it is clear," he said.

"Well then, are those any better than blind men who are in truth deprived of knowledge of what truly each thing is? —who have no bright-shining pattern in the soul; who cannot fix their eyes on the truest, like painters, always referring to it and beholding it most exactly, and only thus lay down ordinances here as regards what is beautiful and just and good,

[1] Lovers of opinion rather than lovers of wisdom.

if that is necessary, and preserve and keep safe those already laid down?"

"No indeed," he said, "they are not much better than the blind."

"Then shall we choose to establish these as guardians, or those who do know everything that really is, and in experience are not inferior to the others, and in any portion of virtue, too, are not behind them?"

"Really it would be extraordinary," said he, "to choose others, provided that the philosophers were not otherwise inferior, when they would be superior in this very knowledge—perhaps the greatest of superiorities."

"Then let us say now, in what way the same persons will be able to have both qualifications."

"By all means."

"Then we should first learn their nature, as we said when we began this talk. And I believe that if we can satisfy ourselves as to that, we shall agree both that the same persons are able to have both, and that these and no others ought to be leaders of cities."

"How?"

"One thing in the nature of philosophers let us take as agreed, that they always are in love with learning, that is, whatever makes clear to them anything of that being[1] which is eternal, and does not merely wander about between the limits of birth and death."

"Let that be taken as agreed."

"Further," said I, "they never leave hold of this being, if they can help it, the whole or a part, neither a greater part nor smaller, neither a more honourable part nor less honourable. We have shown that already in discussing lovers of honour and the amorous."

"You are right," he answered.

"Next, consider if there be necessity to have something else, in the nature of those who are to be such as we described."

"What?"

"Truthfulness—never to admit willingly a falsehood, to hate it and to love the truth."

"That is likely," said he.

"Not only likely, my friend," said I; "it is absolute necessity that one who is in love with anything by his nature should be fond of all that is akin to his beloved and at home in his beloved."

[1] "Being," of course, is not a person, but abstract, all that really is, as distinct from what seems to be, or what changes.

"Quite right," said he.

"But could you find anything more at home in wisdom than truth?"

"Of course not," said he.

"Then is it possible for the same nature to love wisdom and to love falsehood?"

"By no means."

"So the real lover of learning must reach after all truth with all his might from youth upwards."

"By all means."

"But further, if the desires in anyone weigh strongly towards some one thing, we know, I suppose, that they are weaker for other things, like a flow of water drawn away to one place by a channel."

"Certainly."

"Well, when the desires in anyone flow towards learning and every such object, their concern would surely be with the pleasure of the soul within itself, and they would leave alone bodily pleasures, if one were a true lover of wisdom, not a sham."

"That is utterly necessary."

"Again, such a one would be temperate, and in no wise a money-lover; for to seek earnestly those things for which wealth with its great expenditure is earnestly sought belongs to anyone but him."

"That is so."

"There is something more which you must ask if you mean to distinguish the philosopher's nature from the sham."

"What is that?"

"Has it a touch of meanness? Don't overlook that; for littleness is the most opposite, I take it, to a soul which is always yearning to reach after what is whole and complete, both human and divine."

"Very true," said he.

"Then if a mind has magnificence, and a view over all time and all being, do you believe such a one thinks human life a great thing?"

"Impossible," said he.

"Then he will consider death to be no terror?"

"Not in the least," said he.

"Then a cowardly and mean nature could have no part in true philosophy, as it seems."

"I think not."

"Very well; one well-ordered and not covetous, not mean

or cowardly, no impostor, could never become a hard bargainer or unjust?"

"It is not possible."

"Here too is something which you must consider in distinguishing the true and sham wisdom-loving soul—whether from childhood the man is just and gentle, or unsocial and savage."

"By all means."

"Another thing you will not omit, I believe."

"What?"

"Is he teachable or unteachable? Do you expect that anyone will ever properly love doing anything when he would only do it painfully and effect little with much work?"

"That could not be."

"Again, what if he could not preserve anything he learnt, being full of forgetfulness? Would not such a one certainly be empty of knowledge?"

"Of course he would."

"So, labouring uselessly, don't you think he will be compelled at last to hate such work and himself too?"

"Of course."

"A forgetful soul, then, we should never include among the souls capable of loving wisdom enough; we must look for one of good memory."

"By all means."

"Again, we should say, bad culture and bad manners in a nature could only draw the man to bad proportion."[1]

"Surely."

"And do you think truth is akin to bad proportion, or to good proportion?"

"Good proportion."

"So, in addition, let us look for a mind also naturally well-proportioned and graceful, which will make the inborn nature easy to lead towards every form of real being."

"Of course."

"Very well. Surely the qualities in our list follow one from another, and they are necessary for a soul which is to apprehend real being sufficiently and perfectly—do you disagree anywhere?"

"No indeed, they are most necessary."

"Then can you find a fault anywhere in such a pursuit, which a man would never be able to practise competently unless he were by nature good at remembering and learning, endowed with magnificence and grace, friendly and akin to truth, justice, courage, temperance?"

---

[1] ἀμετρία, "want of measure."

"Not Fault-finding himself[1] personified," said he, "could find any fault in that."

"Very well," I said, "when such men are perfected by education and ripe age, you would commit the city to them alone, wouldn't you?"

And Adeimantos answered, "What you say, Socrates, no one could contradict. But you should know what happens to those who hear you each time you speak in this way. They feel their own inexperience in question and answer, and they think they are led astray a little in each question, so that at the end of an argument the many littles make a muckle; they stumble badly and find themselves contradicting what they said at first. It is like a game of checkers, when bad players in the end are held in check by the good players and can't make a move: so they also find themselves in check and can't make a speech in this other game with words for counters; and they feel indeed that they have not grasped the truth any better by this game. I speak with an eye to the present case. As things are, one might say that in each question he could not contradict you in argument; but they say what they see in fact is that of those who apply themselves to philosophy and spend a long time in the study, not those who only touch it as a part of education and drop it while still young, most become regular cranks, not to say quite worthless, and those who are considered the finest are made useless to their cities by the very pursuit which you praise."

I listened to this and said, "Then do you think that those who say this are saying untruths?"

"I don't know," said he, "but I would gladly hear your opinion."

"You would hear then," said I, "that they appear to me to be speaking the truth."

"Then how can it be right," said he, "to say that cities will have no end to their miseries until philosophers rule in them, when we admit that philosophers are useless to them?"

"You ask a question," said I, "which must be answered in a parable."[2]

"And you never use parables, of course!" he said.

"Oh, all right!" I said. "You make fun of me after dumping me into an argument so hard to prove! Listen to my parable then, and see more than ever how greedy I am of parables. The fact is, that what happens to the finest philosophers in their relation to cities is hard; there is no single thing in the world like it, but one must compile a parable from all sorts

[1] Momos, the god of blame.
[2] *Eikōn*, a likeness, a comparison.

of things to defend them, like a painter painting a goat-stag[1] and other such mixtures. Imagine a ship or a fleet of ships in the following state. The captain[2] is above all on board in stature and strength, but rather deaf and likewise rather short-sighted, and he knows navigation no better than he sees and hears. The crew are quarrelling about pilotage; everyone thinks he ought to be pilot, although he knows nothing of the art, and cannot tell us who taught him or where he learnt it. Besides, they all declare that it cannot be taught, and they are ready to tear in pieces anyone who says it can; they all keep crowding round the solitary captain, begging and praying and doing anything and everything to get him to hand over the helm to them. Sometimes one party fails but another succeeds better; then one party kills the other, or throws them overboard, and the good, honest captain they bind hand and foot by some opiate[3] or intoxicant or some other means and take command of the ship. They use up all the stores, drinking and feasting, and make such a voyage as you might expect with such men. Besides, they have their votes of thanks: one has a testimonial as Good Navigator, another is a Born Pilot and Master Mariner. These are for any who are good hands at backing them up when they try to persuade or compel the captain to let them rule; for those who will not they have a vote of censure, Good-For-Nothing, and the true pilot is nowhere—they won't listen to him. They fail to understand that he must devote his attention to year and seasons, sky and stars and winds, and all that belongs to his art, if he is really to be anything like a ruler of the ship; but that as for gaining control of the helm, with the approval of some people and the disapproval of others, neither art nor practice of this can be comprehended at the same time as the art of navigation. With such a state of things on board the ships, don't you believe the true-born pilot would be dubbed stargazer, bibble-babbler, good-for-nothing, by those afloat in ships so provided?"

"That he would," said Adeimantos.

"I don't suppose," I said, "you want us to examine the parable bit by bit, and so to see how this is exactly what happens between the true philosopher and the city; I think you understand what I mean."

"Certainly," he said.

"Well, then, if anyone is surprised that philosophers are not honoured in a city, first teach him this parable, and try to

[1] One of the Greek mythical creatures; cf. the centaur, part man and part horse.
[2] The people, in a democracy.
[3] *Mandragoras* (mandrake) in the Greek.

persuade him that it would be much more surprising if they were."

"That I will," said he.

"And tell him he is quite right in saying that the finest philosophers are useless to the multitude; but tell him it is *their* fault for not using them, no fault of these fine men. For it is not natural that a pilot should beg the sailors to be ruled by him; nor that the wise should wait at the rich man's door.[1] No, the author of that neat saying told a lie, but the truth is that the sick man must wait at the doctor's door, whether he is rich or poor; and anyone who needs to be ruled should wait at the door of one who is able to rule him, not that the ruler should petition the subjects to be ruled, if there is truly any help in him. But you will make no mistake in likening the present political rulers to the sailors I described just now, and those whom they call good-for-nothing and stargazing babblers to the true pilots."

"Quite right," said he.

"For these reasons then, and in these conditions, it is not easy for the best of studies to have a good name from those who study the very opposite. But by far the worst and strongest reproach comes upon philosophy because of those who profess to be philosophers; no doubt these were meant by the accuser you mentioned, when he said that most of the students who go to philosophy are worthless, and the best of them are useless, and I agree that you spoke truly. Is not that so?"

"Yes."

"Well, we have discussed why the good ones are useless."

"Certainly."

"Now the worthlessness of the many bad ones: Shall we discuss that next, and try to show, if we can, that this must be so, but that philosophy is not to blame for this any more than the other?"

"By all means."

"Let us listen then, and let us speak; reminding ourselves of the starting point from which we described what must be the inborn nature of one who is to be 'beautiful and good'—a 'gentleman.' The first and leading thing in him, if you remember, was truth, which he was bound to pursue wholly and everywhere, unless he was to be an impostor and never have a part in true philosophy."

"Yes, that was what we said."

[1] Said to be a saying of Simonides.

"Well, is not this one thing clean contrary to the opinion now held of him?"

"It is indeed," he said.

"Then will it not be our reasonable defence that the real lover of knowledge by his nature strives towards real being, and is not content to abide by this multitude of things which exist only in opinion; forwards he always goes, and he is never blunted, and never ceases from that love, until he grasps the nature of what really is in each case, by that part of the soul to which it belongs to grasp such a thing, and that is the part akin to real being; then going in unto this and mingling with the real he would beget mind and truth, he would know, and truly live, and be nourished, and so he would cease from his travail, but never before."

"Most reasonable," he said.

"Well then, will it be in him to be fond of falsehood at all, or will he, on the contrary, hate it?"

"He will hate it."

"Then while truth leads, never, I think we should say, could a train of evils follow her?"

"How could it!" he said.

"But a wholesome and just spirit, accompanied by temperance."

"Quite right," he said.

"So there is no need, I think, to insist on mustering the rest of the train of the philosopher's nature once more from the beginning. You remember, no doubt, that we found belonging to these, courage and magnificence, ready learning and good memory. Then you interposed that all will necessarily agree with what we say, but if they left words alone and fixed their eyes on the persons discussed, they would say that they saw some of them to be useless, and most to be vicious with every vice. And searching for the cause of this prejudice we have now come to ask why most of them are vicious; and that is why we have once more taken up the nature of the true philosopher and defined it, as we were compelled to do."

"That is true," he said.

"Accordingly," I said, "we must survey the corruptions of the true philosopher's nature; it is corrupted in most, but a small portion escapes, those, of course, whom they call not bad but useless. Next again, those who imitate this character and settle down into its pursuits—we must examine what are the natures of their souls, seeing that they enter upon a pursuit which is too good and too great for them, and so give offence in many ways, and everywhere and amongst all men have fastened this repute onto philosophy."

"What are these corruptions?" he said.

"I will try to describe them," I said, "if I can. I suppose at least that such a nature, one that has all we have just mentioned as necessary if he is to be a perfect philosopher, is a rare growth rarely found among men; everyone will agree to that, don't you think so?"

"Very rare indeed."

"Only think how many dangers of destruction, and how great, attend upon these rare few."

"What, pray?"

"One which will be most surprising of all to hear: that each one of the very qualities which we praise in such a nature corrupts the soul which has it, and drags it away from philosophy. I mean courage, temperance and all we described."

"That is amazing," he said.

"Moreover," I said, "besides these, all the reputed good things corrupt and distract, beauty and riches, bodily strength, and powerful kindred in the city, and all that belongs to these. Now you have the sketch of what I mean."

"I have," said he, "and I should be glad to learn more exactly what you mean."

"Grasp it rightly as a whole," said I, "and then it will clearly appear, and what I have just said will not amaze you at all."

"How, exactly?" he asked, "what do you ask me to do?"

"Every seed or growth," I said, "vegetable or animal, the stronger it is the more it falls short of being its proper self, if it lacks the nurture that each ought to have and the proper place and season: for evil is more opposed to the good than to the not-good."

"Of course."

"It is reasonable, then, I think, that the best nature with unsuitable nurture turns out worse than the poor one."

"That is reasonable."

"Then, Adeimantos." I said, "we may likewise say that the souls naturally best become more exceedingly evil if they have evil education. Or perhaps you think that the greatest injustice and unmitigated rottenness come from a poor nature, and not from a vigorous one corrupted by its nurture? Do you think perhaps that a weak nature will ever be the cause of great good or great evil?"

"No," said he, "but I think as you do."

"The philosopher's nature then, as we described it, if it has proper instruction, must, I think, necessarily attain all virtue as it grows; but if it is not sown and grown and nourished in proper surroundings it will grow to everything opposite, unless a god comes to the help. Or perhaps you hold the common opinion; you think it is a case of a few young men corrupted by Sophists, or a few minor Sophists corrupting on their own account, if they are really worth mentioning; you don't see it is the people themselves talking in this way who are the greatest Sophists, and they most perfectly educate everybody to be such as they wish, young and old, men and women."

"When, pray?" he asked.

"When they take their seats in large numbers together," I said, "in parliament, or in the law court, in theatre or in camp, or any other public assembly of a crowd, when they hoot what is said or done with loud roars, or cheer in turn, each extravagantly; they shout and they clap, and besides their own noise the place of meeting and the rocks around re-echo and redouble the din of applause and denunciation. What's the state of the young man's heart, as the saying goes, when that kind of thing happens? What private education will hold out in him? Won't it be deluged by this praising or blaming, and go floating away down the stream wherever that carries him? Won't he say 'yes' to their notions of beautiful and ugly, and follow their practices, and be like them?"

"He can't help it, Socrates," said he.

"Ah," said I, "but we have not yet mentioned the strongest compulsion."

"What is that?" he asked.

"The one these 'educators' and 'Sophists' impose by deed, when they can't convince by word. Don't you know that they chastise the disobedient with disgrace and fines and death?"

"I do indeed," he said.

"What other Sophist then, or what private sermons, do you expect to prevail contending against these?"

"None, I think," said he.

"No," I said, "but even to try is utter madness. For there is not, and never has been, and never will be, a character which has become different from the many as regards virtue, through having been educated towards virtue contrary[1] to the education which the many give—an ordinary human character, I mean, my friend; the divine, however, we must except from the rule, as the proverb says. For you may be quite certain that if anything is saved and becomes such as it ought to be, in the present state of society, it is saved by the

[1] Another possible rendering is "a character which has become different in progress towards virtue, having been educated according to the education which the many give."

providence of God;[1] that you are safe in saying."

"And that is what I think," he said.

"Then kindly think this too," said I.

"What?" said he. "That all these private persons who take pay, whom those politicians call Sophists and think them rivals, teach nothing but these very resolutions[2] which the multitude pass and the opinions which they opine when they gather together; and this they call wisdom. It's like a keeper with a huge, powerful monster in charge. He learns by heart all the beast's whims and wishes, how he must approach, and how touch him, when he is dangerous and when he is tame, and why; learns his language, too—what sounds he usually makes at what, and what sound uttered by another creature quiets him and what infuriates him. The keeper learns these lessons perfectly in the course of time by living with him, and calls it wisdom: then compiles a handbook of veterinary art and sets up as a professor. He knows nothing, in truth, about these resolutions or whims of the multitude, whether any of them is beautiful or ugly, good or evil, just or unjust, but gives a name to each according to the monster's opinions, calling beautiful what pleases the monster and evil what annoys him; he has no other principle whatever in all this, but he calls necessities just and beautiful; and how really different by nature necessity is from good he has never seen himself and he is unable to teach another. Don't you think in heaven's name that such a one would be a strange educator?"

"I do!" said he.

"Isn't he exactly like one who considers it wisdom to have learnt off the temper and pleasures of that vast congregation of incompatibles, in painting or music or, for that matter, in politics? If any expert in poetry or some other art or craft or public service mixes with the multitude and exhibits his work, if he makes the many his masters beyond what he must, then necessity will know no law, as the proverb goes,[3] he will have to do or make whatever they like; but to prove that whatever they like is good and beautiful, did you ever hear anyone offer a reason which was not absolutely ridiculous?"

"I never did," said he, "and I think I never shall."

"Keep this in mind, then, and recall another question. Is it possible that a crowd will ever believe in the beautiful by itself as distinct from the many beautiful things, and each of those other notions by itself in the same way?"

[1] Cf. the words of Christ: "With men it is impossible, but not with God: for with God all things are possible." Mark x:27.
[2] The word used, *dogma*, meaning opinion or doctrine, is also the proper word for a bill or resolution of parliament.
[3] "Diomede's necessity" is the Greek proverb, variously explained, but all meaning that he can't help himself.

"It will not put up with such an idea! Not a bit," said he.

"So then," said I, " a crowd cannot be a lover of wisdom."

"Impossible!" said he.

"And they must necessarily defame all who practise philosophy."

"They must."

"And so must all private persons who company with the crowd and desire to please it."

"That is plain."

"That being so, what safety do you see for one with a philosopher's nature? How can he abide by his practice to the end? Think of it from what we said before. We have agreed, I take it, that ease of learning and memory belong to this nature, and courage and magnificence."

"Yes."

"Then such a one will from boyhood be first among all the boys, especially if his body be naturally well matched with the soul."

"Of course he will," said he.

"So when he grows older, his relatives will, I presume, wish to use him for their own affairs, and so will his fellow-citizens."

"Of course."

"Then they will all be at his feet, supplicating and honouring him, getting hold of his future power in good time, and flattering him in advance?"

"That's what generally happens," he said.

"Then what do you expect such a one will do in such a case," said I, "especially if he belongs to a great city, and if he is rich and highly born in that city, and if, besides, he is handsome and big? Will he not be filled with unlimited hopes? Will he not believe himself to be fit to manage the affairs of both Hellenes and barbarians; and to lift himself high upon this base, infected with 'empty posturing, pretentious pride',[1] without real sense?"

"Very much so," he said.

"Then if someone quietly comes up to him while he is getting into that condition, and tells him the truth, how there is no sense in him and sense is what he needs, but he must work like a slave to win it or he never will—do you suppose he will find it easy to hear through all that evil din?"

"Far from it," he said.

"But supposing there really is one," I said, "who, by good inborn nature and natural affinity for sound advice, understands in some measure and is bent and drawn towards philos-

---

[1] A quotation from some poet.

ophy, what do we think the others will do who believe they are losing his use and fellowship? Will they not leave nothing unsaid and nothing undone to him and his admonisher, that he may never obey and the other may not have the power to warn? What private plots and public prosecutions there will be!"

"No doubt about that," he said.

"Then it is possible that such a one will follow philosophy?"

"Impossible," said he.

"You see then," said I, "that we were not wrong in saying that even the parts of the philosopher's own nature are themselves in a way causes of backsliding from his profession, if they grow up under evil nurture; and so are the reputed advantages, riches and all that sort of equipment."

"Not wrong; we spoke rightly," he said.

"There then," said I, "my excellent fellow, there is the ruin, there is the destruction, how great and how dire! of that noblest nature—rare in any case, as we say—entering the best of all vocations. And from this class, then, come those who work the greatest evil upon cities and upon private men, as well as those who work the greatest good when the flood carries them that way; but a small nature never does anything great either to man or to city."

"Most true," said he.

"And so these, her nearest and dearest, fall away, leaving Philosophy deserted and jilted,[1] and they themselves live a false life, a life not theirs at all. Philosophy is left bereft of kindred, and other persons unworthy of her burst in and insult her and fasten reproaches upon her, such as you say her defamers reproach her with—that some of those who court her are quite worthless and most are worthy of condign punishment."

"Yes," he said, "that, at any rate, is what they say."

"With reason, too," said I. "For others, a lot of manikins, espy this territory empty of men but full of beautiful names and pretences, and, like criminals escaped from prison rushing away into the sanctuaries, are just as glad to jump out of their trades into philosophy, whoever are smartest in their own little trade. For although philosophy is in this plight, nevertheless her dignity remains more magnificent as compared with the other arts; this, of course, is what attracts many whose natures are imperfect—as their bodies are damaged by their arts and crafts, so their souls are doubled up and maimed by their vulgar lives, don't you think that must be so?"

---

[1] This alludes to the law that if property was left to an heiress, the next of kin had to marry her and take both.

"It must be so, certainly," he said.

"To look at them," I said, "don't they remind you of a little bald-headed tinker who has come into money and just been freed from his chains, and has had a wash in the bathing house, with a brand-new robe around him decked out like a bridegroom and going to marry his master's daughter because the poor girl is destitute?"

"There is not any difference," he said.

"Then what will such men probably produce? Mean, bastard offspring, I should expect!"

"They certainly must, indeed!"

"Well, and when men unworthy of culture pay court to philosophy and consort with her above their worth, what sort of thoughts and opinions shall we expect them to beget? Would you not say—things most truly and properly to be called sophisms, nothing genuine, nothing with a touch of true intelligence?"

"Exactly so," he said.

"Very small indeed, Adeimantos," I said, "is this remnant of those who court philosophy as an equal. It may be a character genuine and well bred, overtaken by exile and, in the absence of corruptors, abiding instinctively in philosophy; or it may be a great soul born in some small city, who despises the city's business as dishonourable; or possibly some small number of persons from some craft or other[1] might rightly despise that and come to philosophy by their own fine nature. It may be too that the bridle of our friend Theages[2] is enough sometimes to hold a man back; everything is there ready to make Theages desert philosophy, but bodily ill health holds him back and keeps him out of politics. My own case is not worth mentioning, the spiritual sign,[3] for I believe that such a thing has never or hardly ever happened to anyone before. Those who belong to this little band have tasted how sweet and delectable their treasure is, and they have seen sufficiently the madness of the multitude; they know that in public life hardly a single man does any act that has any health in it, and there is no ally who would stand by anyone going to the help of justice, and would save him from destruction. Such a champion would be like a man fallen among wild beasts; he would never consent to join in wickedness, but one alone he could not fight

---

[1] Another suggested rendering is "or possibly some humble character from some craft or other might . . ."

[2] Theages' bridle (ill health) became a proverb. The point is that ill health, by holding Theages back from politics, keeps him away from political corruptions, thus leaving him one of the remnant fit to be true philosophers.

[3] See Socrates' description in the *Defence*, pp. 437, 444-445, of the spiritual "voice" of which he was frequently conscious warning him to refrain from acts which he contemplated.

all the savages. So he would perish before he could do any good to the city or his friends, useless both to himself and to others. When the philosopher considers all this he keeps quiet and does his own business, like one who runs under a wall for shelter in a storm when dust and sleet is carried before the wind. He sees the others being filled full of lawlessness, and he is content if somehow he can keep himself clean from injustice and impious doings, and so live his life on earth and at the end depart in peace and good will with beautiful hopes."

"But he would have done a great work first," said Adeimantos, "before he departed."

"Yet not the greatest," I said, "if his city had not the constitution that suited him, for in a suitable city he will grow greater himself, and save the common fortunes along with his own.

"I think now I have explained fairly well why that prejudice came upon philosophy, and how unjust it is—unless you have something further to say?"

"No," he answered, "nothing about that; but tell me which of the present constitutions is suitable for it."

"Not a single one," I said, "and that is exactly the fault I find, that no constitution of any existing state is worthy of the philosopher's nature. That is exactly why it is turned and changed. When a foreign seed is sown in another soil it is likely to be overpowered and to fade out into the native culture; just so this philosophic stock no longer holds its own power but degenerates into an alien character; but if it can only get the best constitution, being itself also best, then experience will show that this stock was really divine and the others were merely human both in nature and in practice. Now I am sure you are going to ask, which is this best constitution."

"You are wrong," he said, "I was not going to ask that, but whether it is this which we have described in founding our city, or another."

"Generally speaking, yes," I said, "but don't forget what we also said then: something more there must always be in the city, something which has the same understanding of its constitution as you had when you laid down its laws as lawgiver."

"So we did say," he answered.

"But it was not explained clearly enough," said I, "because I was afraid of those very matters which you seized upon; you have shown that the demonstration was long and difficult, and indeed the part remaining is anything but easy."

"Which is that?"

"How a city shall deal with philosophy so as not to be destroyed itself. For all great things are hazardous, and it is true, as the proverb says, that beautiful things are hard."

"Never mind," he said, "let this be cleared up and let the demonstration be completed."

"There's no want of will," said I, "but want of ability will hinder me, if anything. You shall see my readiness with your own eyes. Just see now how readily and recklessly I shall stand up and say that a city should deal with this way of life not as it does now but just the opposite."

"How so?"

"At present," said I, "those who do take it up are only lads just out of boyhood, who approach the most difficult part of it in the time before the serious business of housekeeping and moneymaking, and then drop it; yes, and these are your perfect philosophers! By the most difficult part I mean that which is concerned with words, dialectic. In later years, if they do consent after much persuading to listen to others engaged in this, they go as a great favour, and think they should take part in it only as a sideline. In old age, apart from a few, their light is quenched much more than the sun of Heracleitos, for their flame is never rekindled."[1]

"But how should they do?" he asked.

"Exactly the opposite. While they are boys and lads they should occupy themselves with boyish education and philosophy, and train their bodies very carefully while these are growing and coming into manhood; the lads are gaining possession of their bodies as a help to liberal education. Then as their age goes on, the time when the soul begins to be perfected, they should tune up the exercises of the soul; and when decreasing strength puts them outside politics and warfare, from then on let them pasture at will in the meadows, and practise nothing other than philosophy except as a bye-end; those, I mean, who intend to live happily, and when they come to their latter end to crown the life they have led with a fitting portion in the next world."

"In very truth, Socrates," he said, "I think you are much in earnest; however, I believe most of your hearers are even more eager to resist and will not be persuaded at all, beginning with Thrasymachos."

"Oh, don't say that," I answered, "don't make me and Thrasymachos quarrel so soon after we have made friends! But really we were not foes before. I tell you I will never give up trying until I persuade him and all the rest, or at least until we achieve something useful towards that life when they shall be born again and there meet with discussions like this."

---

[1] Heracleitos said, "A new sun every day," meaning it literally; *Fragment 32*, p. 480 of Hippocrates, vol. iv, Loeb edition.

"That will be quite soon, of course, from your words!" he said.

"A mere nothing," said I, "compared with all time. It is no wonder that the multitude do not believe what we are saying. For they have never seen in existence the project now being discussed; instead they have heard a lot of phrases (such as these),[1] arranged in an artificial assonance, not falling together into their natural pattern like ours do; and a man, balanced and equated with virtue as nearly as possible to perfection in word and deed, and, moreover, holding sovereignty in a city perfectly equated with him, this they have never seen; they have seen neither one man, nor more men than one. Don't you agree?"

"I do; they never have."

"And, on the other hand, they have never cared to listen, bless you, with sufficient attention, to words beautiful and generous, words able to seek out the truth attentively by every means for the sake of knowing, which keep a respectful distance from the clever sophistries that lead nowhere except to opinion and strife both in courts of law and in private discussions."

"They listen to nothing of that sort," he said.

"This I foresaw, let me tell you, and this is the reason why I was afraid that time; nevertheless I spoke, because truth constrained me; and I dared to say that no city or constitution, or likewise man either, will ever become perfect until the philosophers take charge of the state, those few now dubbed 'not bad but useless'[2]—if some necessity of fortune throws it upon them, whether they wish or not, and compels the city to listen to them, or if true love for true philosophy comes over the sons of those who now are potentates and kings or the men themselves, by some divine inspiration. It is not impossible that one or both of these things might happen; there is no reason in saying that they cannot, or we should fairly be laughed at as pious dreamers. Don't you agree?"

"I do."

"If, then, it has ever happened in the extreme past times, or if it now is so in some barbaric place somewhere far out of our ken, or if it ever shall be, that some necessity brings the highest philosophic natures to take charge of a city, then we are ready to maintain to the end our contention that the described constitution has been and is, yes and shall be, realised, whenever this Muse gains power over a city. For the thing is not impossible, and we are not speaking of impossibili-

---

[1] Socrates here imitates the artificial style of Gorgias. See *Banquet*, p. 93, n. 5.
[2] On page 288.

ties; difficulties there are indeed—even *we* admit that."

"I think so too," said he.

"But the multitude," said I, "do not think it possible—is that what you will say?"

"Perhaps," he said.

"Bless you," said I, "don't be so hard on the multitude. They will surely change their opinion if you soothe them without controversy; if you undo this prejudice against the love of learning by showing what you mean by philosophers, and if you define their nature and their practice as we have lately done and convince the multitude that you do not mean those whom they now regard as philosophers. As soon as they see this, surely you will admit they will get a different opinion and answer in a different way. Who will quarrel with the unquarrelsome, who will grudge the ungrudging, if he is himself ungrudging and gentle? I take the words out of your own lips, and say that I believe a nature so quarrelsome and unkind exists only in a few, not in the many."

"So I believe also," he said; "be sure of that."

"Then you surely believe also that the many are now unkind to philosophy only because of that gang of outsiders who have come rioting in where they have no business, abusing each other, behaving like lovers of wrangling, and always indulging in personalities, which is the thing least like philosophy?"

"Very true," he said.

"For the truth is, my dear Adeimantos, one who really keeps his mind on the things which are has no leisure to look below upon the transactions of mankind, and, battling with them, to be infected by jealousy and ill will; but by seeing and contemplating things which are well ordered and ever unchangeable,[1] each thing neither wronged nor wronging another, but all things in concord and regulated by reason, we surely imitate these things and make ourselves most like to them; or is it possible in any way, do you think, *not* to imitate what one converses with and admires?"

"Impossible," he said.

"Then conversing with the divine and orderly,[2] the philosopher becomes orderly and divine so far as a man can; but there is much unbalance[3] in all men."

"Indeed there is."

"Then," said I, "if he feels any constraint not only to mould himself, but to practise bringing into human customs both

---

[1] and [2] Like the order of the stars and the cosmos (universe).
[3] διαβολή, root meaning "throw-over"; probably contrasted here with "cosmos" or "order" mentioned three times in this passage; possibly suggesting a shooting star, and here a tendency to evil. Usual meaning, "calumny."

publicly and privately what he sees there, do you believe he will be a bad craftsman for the people, of temperance and justice and all civic virtue?"

"By no means," he said.

"But if the multitude really perceive that we speak the truth about him, will they indeed be angry with philosophers, and disbelieve us when we say that a city could never be happy and fortunate unless it could be painted by these artists using the divine model?"

"Oh no," he said, "they will not be angry if they really perceive the truth. But tell me, please, how the painting will be done."

"They would take a city of men and manners, as it were, already sketched on a panel," I said, "and they would begin by wiping the panel clean, which is not at all easy; but then be sure that here they would at once differ from others—they will not want to put a finger to city or man, or inscribe a law, until they make the panel clean themselves or get a clean one."

"And quite right, too," said he.

"The next thing would be to make a sketch of the constitution; don't you think so?"

"Why, what else!"

"After that, I should say, they would work out the picture. They must cast a glance constantly this way and that; they must look now upon what is just in its real nature, or good or temperate, and so forth, and now again upon what they are implanting in mankind, mixing and mingling from various practices the man's tint for the man's image, judging from that which Homer called, when it appeared in human beings, the likeness divine and tint divine."[1]

"Well said," he replied.

"Here they will erase, no doubt, and here they will insert, until as far as possible they will make human manners as like as men can be to those that God loves."

"A beautiful painting, at least, that would be," he said.

"Well now," said I, "are we beginning to convince that army which you said was eagerly marching to attack us, that such an artist of constitutions is the very man whom we were praising to them, and about whom they were so angry because we were proposing to put the cities into his hand? Are they growing any gentler at all for listening to our talk?"

"Much gentler," said he, "if they have any sound sense."

"Why, how indeed will they find any objection to make?

---

[1] In *Iliad* i. 131, Achilles is the "image of God," and such epithets are common. See also *Odyssey* iii. 416.

Will they say the philosophers are not enamoured of truth, and that which really is?"

"Absurd, that would be," he said.

"That their nature, as we described it, is not akin to the best?"

"No, they could not say that."

"Well, can they deny that such a nature, if it be given the practices which suit it, will be perfectly good and philosophic if any can be? Or will they declare that those whom we excluded are better?"

"I don't think that likely."

"Then will they still be wild if we say that until the philosophic character is master of a city there will be no rest from misery for either city or citizens, and the constitution which we describe in words in our fable will never be accomplished in fact?"

"Not so wild, perhaps."

"Not so wild!" said I. "Please don't let us say that; let us say they have become wholly gentle and convinced, so that they agree for very shame if not for any other reason."

"By all means," he said.

"Very well, then," said I, "let us take it they are convinced of this. Next, will anyone deny that kings or potentates might possibly have sons philosophic in nature?"

"No one could deny that," he said.

"If such were born, can anyone say it is absolutely necessary that they must be corrupted? It is difficult that they should be preserved, we admit that ourselves; but will anyone maintain that in all time, out of them all, not even one would be preserved?"

"How could that be said?"

"Well then," I said, "one is enough, if he has an obedient city, to make real all that now seems incredible."

"One is enough," said he.

"For no doubt," said I, "if a ruler laid down the laws and practices which we described, I don't suppose it is impossible that the citizens would be willing to obey."

"Not at all."

"Then is it impossible, or even surprising, that others should think as we think?"

"I don't believe it is," said he.

"And further, we have sufficiently shown already, as I believe, that it is best, if it really is possible."

"Quite sufficiently."

"Very well: now to sum up, it follows that what we said of

lawgiving is best if it could be done, and to do it is difficult but not impossible."

"Yes, that follows," he said.

"Now that we have finished with this after all our difficulties, we still have some more things left to discuss: what method, what learnings, and what doings, will produce these, our saviours of the constitution, and keep them among us—and the age when each group shall take up each?"

"We have," said he.

"My little trick," said I, "came to nothing, when I left out some time ago that troublesome business about possessing women and getting children and the appointment of rulers, because I knew that the wholly true way was difficult and offensive. You see it has come—I am obliged to discuss it now all the same. The women and children have been disposed of, but the rulers must be considered almost from the beginning. We said, if you remember, that they must be proved patriotic while tested in pleasures and pains; they must prove that they did not throw away that faith in hardship or in fear or in any other vicissitude, and he that did not endure was to be dismissed; but he that came out everywhere pure, like gold tested in the fire, was to be established ruler—honours were to be given him both in life and after death, and prizes too; something like that was said as our tale crept by with veiled head, fearing to stir up what is now before us."

"Very true," he said. "I remember."

"I shrank, my friend," said I, "from saying what I have now had the audacity to say: now let us dare to say that we must establish philosophers as the most perfect guardians, the rulers."

"Let that be understood," he said.

"Observe then, that you will naturally find only a few. For they must have the nature we described, and its parts will not be born all together very often, but generally it is born in pieces."

"What do you mean?" he asked.

"Those who love knowledge, and have good memory, the quick-witted and sharp, and all else that goes with these qualities, and stirring men magnificent in mind, these you know are not usually born also willing to live modestly in quietude and steadiness; such men are carried anywhere and everywhere by their quickness, and all steadiness is gone from them."

"True," he said.

"On the other hand, that steady character not easily swayed, which one would choose to use as trustworthy, which in war also is not easily moved to fear, behaves in the same way towards learning; it is hard to move and hard to teach, as if benumbed, and it is full of sleep and yawns whenever it must do work of that kind."

"That is true," he said.

"But we say that a man must have a good, handsome share of both kinds, or we must not give him part in the most complete education or honour or rule."

"Rightly too," he said.

"Then don't you think it will be a rare thing?"

"Of course I do."

"He must be tested then, you see, in both kinds; in the labours and fears and pleasures, which we described before, and besides, as you see now, in what we omitted then; we must practise their nature in learning many different things, and watch if it is able to endure the hardest studies, or whether it will flinch as men flinch in games and sports."[1]

"We ought certainly to watch them so," he said; "but what do you mean by the hardest studies?"

"You remember, I suppose," said I, "that when we distinguished three parts in the soul, we deduced definitions of justice, temperance, courage and wisdom."

"If I did not remember," said he, "I should have no right to hear the rest."

"Do you remember what went before that?"

"What, pray?"

"We said, I fancy, that to gain the best possible view, another and a longer roundabout way was necessary which would show all clearly, if we took it, but that it was possible to proceed by tacking onto our argument proofs which followed from what we said before. You all said that would do, and consequently we went on; what we said lacked exactness, as it appeared to me, but if you were satisfied you might say so."

"It satisfied me in a measure," he said, "and the others thought the same."

"But, my friend," said I, "short measure is no measure; in such matters you cannot be satisfied in a measure less than the reality, because an imperfect measure measures nothing, although some people think that it is well enough and there is no need to seek further."

"Yes indeed," he said, "a good few feel in that way because of laziness of mind."

"That feeling," I said, "is the last thing in the world we ought to find in a guardian of city and laws."

---

[1] Accepting Orelli's conjecture ἄθλοις. The mss. have ἄλλοις, "in matters other than intellectual."

"That is fair enough," he said.

"Well then, my comrade," said I, "such a one must go round the longer way, and he must labour as hard over learning as he does in bodily exercise; or else, as we said just now, he will never come to the end of that greatest task which is proper to him."

"What!" said he, "are not these the greatest tasks? Is there another still greater than justice and the other things we have described?"

"Not only so," said I, "but of these very things we need to do more than examine our present sketch; we must not omit the most complete working out. Surely it is ridiculous not to exact the greatest accuracy in the greatest things, when for others of small value we strain every nerve to make them as exact and clear as they can be!"

"Certainly," he said; "but do you believe anyone can let you get off without asking what this greatest task is, and what it is all about?"

"Oh dear, no," said I, "just ask me. Certainly you have heard it often enough, but now either you don't understand it, or else you want to make difficulties for me by interrupting! That's what I rather think; for you have often heard that the greatest task is to learn the perfect model of the good,[1] the use of which makes all just things and other such become useful and helpful. And now you know pretty well that I am about to speak of this, and to say, besides, that we do not know the model sufficiently; but if we do not know it, you know it will not be of any advantage to us to understand all the rest perfectly without this model,[2] just as it is no advantage to possess anything without the good. Do you suppose there is any gain in possessing everything in the world without possessing the good? Or to understand everything in the world except the good?—to understand nothing of the beautiful and the good?"

"No indeed, by heaven," said he.

"Further, you know that the many think pleasure to be the good, and the smarter sort say understanding."[3]

"Certainly."

"You know also, my friend, that those who say 'understanding' cannot tell us what understanding, but they are compelled at last to say the understanding of the good."

"Silly fools!" he said.

"Yes," I said, "silly indeed, if they first blame us for not

---

[1] ἡ τοῦ ἀγαθοῦ ἰδέα, the "idea," or perfect ideal of goodness.
[2] Cf. St. Paul: "though I bestow all my possessions to feed the poor . . . and have not love, it profits me nothing." I Cor. xiii:3.
[3] φρόνησις, practical wisdom.

knowing the good, and then talk to us as if we do know it. For they call this an understanding of good—our knowing what they mean whenever they utter the word 'good.'"

"Very true," he said.

"Well then, are those who define pleasure as a good any less infected by error than the others? Are they not equally compelled to admit that there are evil pleasures?"

"Undoubtedly."

"It follows then that they admit the same things to be both good and evil; isn't that true?"

"Of course."

"It is plain, then, that there are many great controversies about it."

"Yes, indeed."

"And again: Is it not plain also about things just and beautiful that many would choose what seem so even if they are not—would still prefer such things to do and to possess and to seem; but about good things none are content to possess what seems good, but they seek what really is good, and here at last everyone despises the seeming?"

"Assuredly," he said.

"Then what of a thing which every soul pursues, and will do anything and everything to get, divining that it really is something but being puzzled because he cannot understand what it is, and cannot find any sufficiently lasting confidence about that as he does about other things; and through this he loses all the advantage which may be in the other things? Are we to say that such a thing, so great a thing, should be kept in the dark, even from those best men of all in whose hands we are to place everything?"

"No indeed," said he.

"I believe, at least," said I, "that if it is unknown in what way just things and beautiful things are good,[1] these things will not have gained a guardian of themselves worth much, in one who does not know this himself; and I prophesy that no one will understand them satisfactorily before he does."

"You are a true prophet," he said.

"Then will not our constitution be perfectly arranged only if such a one is guardian in charge, one who does know these things?"

"That must be so," he said. "But what do you say yourself, Socrates? Is knowledge the good, or pleasure, or something else?"

"A nice fellow this!" I said. "I saw through you long ago!

[1] Such as laws and customs.

I knew you would never be satisfied with what other people think about it."

"Well, Socrates," he said, "it does not appear to me fair, to be able to give other people's opinions, but not your own, when you have been busy so long about the matter."

"What's that?" I said. "Is it fair for a man to speak about what he doesn't know as if he does?"

"No, no," he said, "not as if he does, but he ought fairly to be willing to speak these things which he believes, as believing them."

"Very well," I said. "You have noticed that opinions without knowledge are all ugly. The best of them are blind. Don't you think that those who, without intelligence, have a true opinion are like blind men going along on the right road?"

"Just like them," he said.

"Then do you choose to contemplate ugly things, blind and crooked things, when you could hear brilliant and beautiful things from others?"

"In God's name, Socrates," said Glaucon, "don't back out as if you had come to the end. We shall be satisfied if you will explain the good as well as you explained justice and temperance and the rest."

"So shall I be, my good man," said I, "and very well satisfied. But I am afraid I shall not be able and my clumsy eagerness will only make a fool of me. But bless you, my friends, let us pass by the question what the good is, just for the present; I fear my present impulse is not strong enough to carry me as far as what I think on that subject now. But there is an interesting offspring of the good, as it seems to me, and very like it; I am willing to speak of that, if you care, or not if you don't care."

"Do go on," he said, "you can pay up your account of the father another time."

"I only wish," I said, "that I could pay it up and you two could pocket the whole, and not merely the offspringing interest as now.[1] Anyway, put in your pockets this interest and offspring of the good itself; only be careful that I may not cheat you and myself by paying spurious coin in the account."

"Oh, we'll be careful," said he, "as far as we can; only go on."

"So I will," said I, "as soon as we have come to an agreement. May I remind you of something already said in our talk and often on other occasions?"

"What?" he asked.

[1] The same Greek word means "offspring" and "interest on money."

"We speak of there being many beautiful things and many good things and so on; that is how we describe it."

"Yes indeed."

"And we speak of beauty by itself and good by itself—and so on for each of all those things which we have just put as many; again, moreover, we say that these[1] are related to one single perfect ideal for each, and we put each as a portion of a single essence, and each is really what we name."[2]

"That is true."

"Further, we say that those 'many' things are seen[3] but not thought, and the ideals appeal to the mind, though not seen."

"Most assuredly."

"Now by what part of ourselves do we see things seen?"

"Sight."

"And so," I said, "we hear things by hearing, and perceive all other things perceived by the other senses of perception?"

"Of course."

"Now, have you noticed," said I, "with what great extravagance the creator has created this power of seeing and being seen?"

"Not particularly," he said.

"Look here, then. Do hearing and sound need anything else besides to hear and be heard, so that if this third be absent, hearing will not hear and sound will not be heard?"

"Nothing," he answered.

"And I believe," said I, "that most, if not all, the other powers need nothing more. Can you tell me of one?"

"No, I cannot," he said.

"But don't you notice that the power of sight and the visible do need something else?"

"How so?"

"If sight is in the eyes, and the possessor tries to use it, and if colour is in the things, you know, I suppose, that it will see nothing and the colours will be unseen unless a third thing is there specially created for this very purpose."

"What is that?" he asked.

"Of course," I said, "that which you call light."

"True," said he.

"Then how great is the conception[4] through which the sense of sight and the power of being seen have been united by a

[1] "Beauty by itself" and "good by itself" and so on.
[2] For example—there are many beautiful things, beautiful to the eye; each of these has intrinsic beauty appealing to the mind only; this "beauty by itself" is related to the perfect ideal of beauty, and is a portion of the universal essence of beauty, and is really what we name "beauty." Cf. *Phaedo*, p. 506.
[3] This means apprehended by one or other of the senses.
[4] Literally, "With no slight 'idea' have the sense of sight . . . been united."

more precious bond than the other pairs!—unless light is quite without worth."

"Oh no," said he, "far from that."

"Then which of the gods in heaven can you put down as cause and master of this, whose light makes our sight see so beautifully and the things to be seen?"

"The same as you do," said he, "and everyone else; it is plain that you mean the sun!"

"Shall I suggest how sight is related to this divinity?"

"Well, how?"

"Sight itself is not the sun, nor is that in which it is, which we call eye."

"It is not."

"But sight is the most sunlike, I think, of the organs of sense."

"Much the most."

"Moreover, the power which it has is always being dispensed by the sun like an inundation, and sight possesses it?"

"Certainly."

"Then again the sun is not sight, but the cause of sight, and is seen by sight itself."

"That is quite correct," he said.

"Surely, now," I said, "my meaning must appear to be that this, the offspring of the good which the good begat, is in relation to the good itself an analogy, and what the good effects, by its influence, in the region of the mind, towards mind and things thought, this the sun effects, in the region of seeing, towards sight and things seen."

"How?" he asked, "please explain further."

"When a man turns his eyes," I said, "no longer to those things whose colours are pervaded by the light of day, but on those pervaded by the luminaries of night, the eyes grow dim and appear to be nearly blind, as if pure sight were not in them."

"Yes, they do," he said.

"But whenever he turns them to what the sunlight illumines, they see clearly, and sight appears to be in these same eyes."

"Certainly."

"Understand then, that it is the same with the soul, thus: when it settles itself firmly in that region in which truth and real being brightly shine, it understands and knows it and appears to have reason; but when it has nothing to rest on but that which is mingled with darkness—that which becomes and perishes, it opines, it grows dim-sighted, changing opinions up and down, and is like something without reason."

"So it is."

"Then that which provides their truth to the things known, and gives the power of knowing to the knower, you must say is the idea or principle of the good, and you must conceive it as being the cause of understanding and of truth in so far as known; and thus while knowledge and truth as we know them are both beautiful, you will be right in thinking that it is something different, something still more beautiful than these. As for knowledge and truth, just as we said before that it was right to consider light and sight to be sunlike, but wrong to think them to be sun; so here, it is right to consider both these to be goodlike, but wrong to think either of them to be the good—the eternal nature[1] of the good must be allowed a yet higher value."

"What infinite beauty you speak of!" he said, "if it provides knowledge and truth, and is above them itself in beauty! You surely don't mean that it is pleasure!"

"Hush!" I said. "But here is something more to consider about its likeness."

"What?"

"The sun provides not only the power of being seen for things seen, but, as I think you will agree, also their generation and growth and nurture, although it is not itself generation."

"Of course not."

"Similarly with things known, you will agree that the good is not only the cause of their becoming known, but the cause that knowledge exists and of the state of knowledge,[2] although the good is not itself a state of knowledge but something transcending far beyond it in dignity and power."[3]

Glaucon said very comically, "O Lord, what a devil of a hyperbole!"

"All your fault," said I, "for compelling me to say what I think about it."

"Oh, please don't stop!" he said. "At least do finish the comparison with the sun, if you are leaving anything out."

"Oh yes," I said, "I am leaving a lot out."

"Not one little bit, please!" he said.

"I'm afraid I must leave out a good deal," said I; "but I won't willingly leave out anything now if I can help it."

"Please do not," he said.

"Conceive then," I said, "that there are these two, as we say; and one reigns over the region and things[4] of the mind, the

---

[1] ἕξις, a permanent condition or state.
[2] Literally, "but the cause that they are, the cause of their state of being, although the good is not itself a state of being. . . ."
[3] "The ideas are only specific determinations of the good: the first principle of all existence must itself be underived." J. Adam; see p. 344, n. 2.
[4] γένους. Literally, "the region and class of things of the mind."

other over those of the eye—not to say the sky, or you will think I am playing on the word![1] Now then, you have these two ideas distinct—'seen' and 'thought.'"

"I have."

"Suppose you take a line [AE],[2] cut into two unequal parts [at C] to represent in proportion[3] the worlds of things seen and things thought, and then cut each part in the same proportion[4] [at B and D]. Your two parts [AB and BC] in the world of things seen will differ in degree of clearness and dimness,[5] and one part [AB] will contain images; by images I mean first of

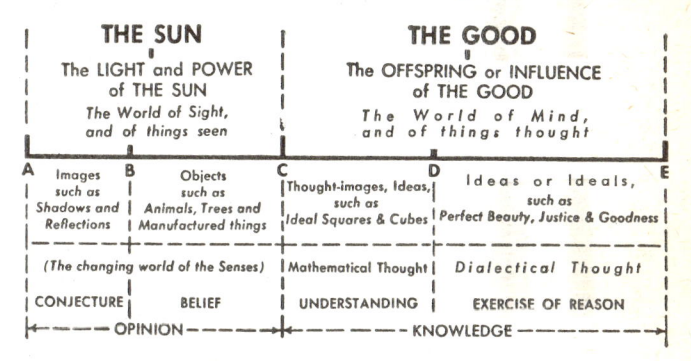

	THE SUN		THE GOOD	
	The LIGHT and POWER of THE SUN		The OFFSPRING or INFLUENCE of THE GOOD	
	The World of Sight, and of things seen		The World of Mind, and of things thought	
A	B	C	D	E
Images such as Shadows and Reflections	Objects such as Animals, Trees and Manufactured things	Thought-images, Ideas, such as Ideal Squares & Cubes	Ideas or Ideals, such as Perfect Beauty, Justice & Goodness	
(The changing world of the Senses)		Mathematical Thought	Dialectical Thought	
CONJECTURE	BELIEF	UNDERSTANDING	EXERCISE OF REASON	
←————— OPINION —————→		←——————— KNOWLEDGE ———————→		

LENGTH REPRESENTS DEGREE OF CLEARNESS, NOT SIZE OF CLASS.

Note:—since $\frac{CE}{AC} = \frac{DE}{CD} = \frac{BC}{AB}$, it follows that $BC = CD$.

THE DIVIDED LINE

---

all shadows, then reflections in water and in surfaces which are of close texture, smooth and shiny, and everything of that kind, if you understand."

"Yes, I understand."

"Take the second part of this [BC] for the things which the images resemble, the animals about us and all trees and plants and all kinds of manufactured articles."

"Very good," said he.

[1] Plato puns on the words ὁρατός, visible, and οὐρανός, the heavens or sky; some authorities did derive one of these words from the other.

[2] See diagram; the diagram (and lettering) is of course not in the Greek text. For a discussion of the Divided Line and its connection with the allegory of the Cave which follows in Book VII, readers may consult the article by J. E. Raven, in the *Classical Quarterly*, Jan.-Apr. 1953, pp. 22-32.

[3] and [4] A numerical value for this proportion can only be assumed. Socrates refers again to this proportion on p. 333, and there proposes to Glaucon to "leave aside" the value of the proportion, as involving too much discussion.

[5] See p. 310, n. 1.

"Would you be willing to admit," said I, "that in respect of truth and untruth there is the same distinction between the opinable and the knowable as there is between the image and its model?" [1]

"Oh yes, certainly," he answered.

"Now then, consider how the section for 'things thought' should be divided."

"How?"

"This way. In the first part [CD] the soul in its search is compelled to use as images the things imitated [2]—the realities of the former part [BC]—and from things taken for granted [3] passes not to a new beginning, a first principle, but to an end, a conclusion; in the second part [DE] it passes from an assumption to a first principle free from assumption, without the help of images which the other part [CD] uses, and makes its path of enquiry amongst ideals themselves by means of them alone."

He answered, "I don't quite understand that."

"Let us try again," I said; "you will understand easier when I have said some more first. I suppose you know that students of geometry and arithmetic and so forth begin by taking for granted odd and even, and the usual figures, and the three kinds of angles, and things akin to these, in every branch of study; they take them as granted and make them assumptions [4] or postulates, and they think it unnecessary to give any further account of them to themselves or to others, as being clear to everybody. Then, starting from these, they go on through the rest by logical steps until they end at the object which they set out to consider."

"Certainly I know that," he said.

"Then you know also that they use the visible figures and give lectures about them, while they are not thinking of these they can see but the ideas which these are like; a square *in itself* is what they speak of, and a diameter [5] *in itself*, not the one they are drawing. It is always so; the very things which they model or draw, which have shadows of their own and images in water, they use now as images; but what they seek is to see those ideals which can be seen only by the mind."

"True," he said.

"This ideal, then, that I have been describing belongs to the first part [CD] of things thought, but the soul, as I said, is compelled to use assumptions in its search for this; it does not

---

[1] These two statements are referred to later, p. 311, n. 1.
[2] Reading μιμηθεῖσιν.
[3] ἐξ ὑποθέσεων, from or out of hypotheses, from assumptions.
[4] ὑποθέσεις.
[5] The Greeks spoke of a diameter of a square; we say "diagonal."

THE REPUBLIC Book VI (510B–511E)

pass to a first principle because of being unable to get out clear above the assumptions, but uses as images the very things [in *BC*] which are represented by those below [in *AB*] and were esteemed and honoured as bright compared with those."[1]

"I understand," he said, "that you speak of what belongs to geometry and its kindred arts."

"Now, then, understand," I said, "that by the other part [*DE*] of things thought I mean what the arguing process itself grasps by power of dialectic, treating assumptions not as beginnings, but as literally hypotheses,[2] that is to say steps and springboards for assault, from which it may push its way up to the region free of assumptions and reach the beginning of all,[3] and grasp it, clinging again and again to whatever clings to this; and so may come down to a conclusion without using the help of anything at all that belongs to the senses, but only ideals themselves, and, passing through ideals, it may end in ideals."

"I understand," said he, "though not sufficiently, for you seem to me to describe a heavy task; but I see that you wish to lay down that a clearer perception of real being and the world of mind is given by knowledge of dialectic, than by the so-called 'arts' which start from pure assumptions. It is true that those who view them through these are compelled to view them with the understanding and not the senses, but because they do not go back to the beginning in their study, but start from assumptions, they do not seem to you to apply a reasoning mind about these matters, although with a first principle added they belong to the world of mind. The mental state of geometricians and suchlike you seem to call understanding, not reason, taking understanding as something between opinion and reason."

"You have taken my meaning quite sufficiently," I said. "Now then, accept these four affections of the soul[4] for my four divisions of the line: Exercise of Reason for the highest, Understanding for the second; put Belief for the third and Conjecture for the last. Then arrange the divisions in proportion, believing they partake of clearness just as the affections which they represent partake of truth."

"I understand," said he, "and I agree, and I arrange them as you tell me."

---

[1] I.e., compared with the images in *AB;* cf. page 310, n. 1.

[2] ὑποθέσεις; root meaning is "a placing-under." The words which follow seem to suggest an assault on a fortress wall, using steps and clinging to ropes or the backs of other men, reaching the top, and dropping down on the other side to finish the fight.

[3] ἐπὶ τὴν τοῦ παντὸς ἀρχήν.

[4] On p. 333, Socrates mentions again these four "affections of the soul."

BOOK VII

"Next, then," I said, "take the following parable of education and ignorance as a picture of the condition of our nature. Imagine mankind as dwelling in an underground cave with a long entrance open to the light across the whole width of the cave; in this they have been from childhood, with necks and legs fettered, so they have to stay where they are. They cannot move their heads round because of the fetters, and they can only look forward, but light comes to them from fire burning behind them higher up at a distance. Between the fire and the prisoners is a road above their level, and along it imagine a low wall has been built, as puppet showmen have screens in front of their people over which they work their puppets."

"I see," he said.

"See, then, bearers carrying along this wall all sorts of articles which they hold projecting above the wall, statues of men and other living things,[1] made of stone or wood and all kinds of stuff, some of the bearers speaking and some silent, as you might expect."

"What a remarkable image," he said, "and what remarkable prisoners!"

"Just like ourselves," I said. "For, first of all, tell me this: What do you think such people would have seen of themselves and each other except their shadows, which the fire cast on the opposite wall of the cave?"

"I don't see how they could see anything else," said he, "if they were compelled to keep their heads unmoving all their lives!"

"Very well, what of the things being carried along? Would not this be the same?"

"Of course it would."

"Suppose the prisoners were able to talk together, don't you think that when they named the shadows which they saw passing they would believe they were naming things?"[2]

"Necessarily."

"Then if their prison had an echo from the opposite wall, whenever one of the passing bearers uttered a sound, would they not suppose that the passing shadow must be making the sound? Don't you think so?"

"Indeed I do," he said.

"If so," said I, "such persons would certainly believe that

[1] Including models of trees, etc.
[2] Which they had never seen. They would say "tree" when it was only a shadow of the model of a tree.

there were no realities except those shadows of handmade things."[1]

"So it must be," said he.

"Now consider," said I, "what their release would be like, and their cure from these fetters and their folly; let us imagine whether it might naturally be something like this. One might be released, and compelled suddenly to stand up and turn his neck round, and to walk and look towards the firelight; all this would hurt him, and he would be too much dazzled to see distinctly those things whose shadows he had seen before. What do you think he would say, if someone told him that what he saw before was foolery, but now he saw more rightly, being a bit nearer reality and turned towards what was a little more real? What if he were shown each of the passing things, and compelled by questions to answer what each one was? Don't you think he would be puzzled, and believe what he saw before was more true than what was shown to him now?"

"Far more," he said.

"Then suppose he were compelled to look towards the real light, it would hurt his eyes, and he would escape by turning them away to the things which he was able to look at, and these he would believe to be clearer than what was being shown to him."

"Just so," said he.

"Suppose, now," said I, "that someone should drag him thence by force, up the rough ascent, the steep way up, and never stop until he could drag him out into the light of the sun, would he not be distressed and furious at being dragged; and when he came into the light, the brilliance would fill his eyes and he would not be able to see even one of the things now called real?"[2]

"That he would not," said he, "all of a sudden."

"He would have to get used to it, surely, I think, if he is to see the things above. First he would most easily look at shadows, after that images of mankind and the rest in water, lastly the things themselves. After this he would find it easier to survey by night the heavens themselves and all that is in them, gazing at the light of the stars and moon, rather than by day the sun and the sun's light."

"Of course."

"Last of all, I suppose, the sun; he could look on the sun itself by itself in its own place, and see what it is like, not reflections of it in water or as it appears in some alien setting."

"Necessarily," said he.

---

[1] Shadows of artificial things, not even the shadow of a growing tree: another stage from reality.
[2] To the next stage of knowledge: the real thing, not the artificial puppet.

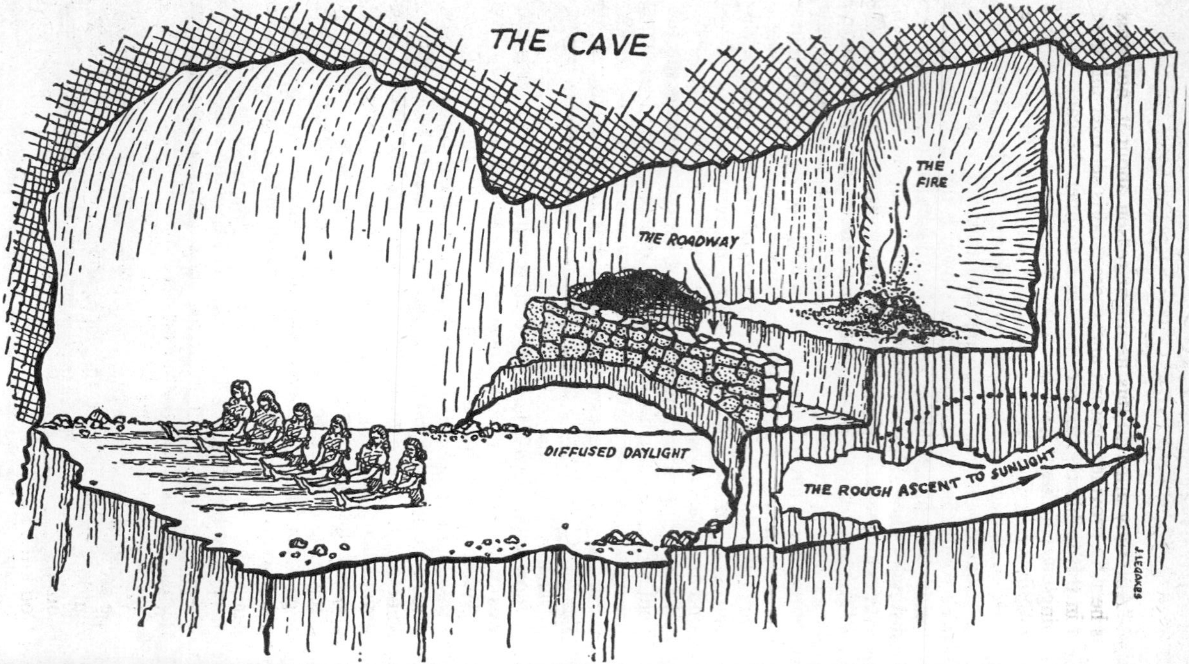
THE CAVE
THE FIRE
THE ROADWAY
DIFFUSED DAYLIGHT
THE ROUGH ASCENT TO SUNLIGHT
J. LEGAKES

"And only after all this he might reason about it, how this is he who provides seasons and years, and is set over all there is in the visible region, and he is in a manner the cause of all things which they saw."

"Yes, it is clear," said he, "that after all that, he would come to this last."

"Very good. Let him be reminded of his first habitation, and what was wisdom in that place, and of his fellow-prisoners there; don't you think he would bless himself for the change, and pity them?"

"Yes, indeed."

"And if there were honours and praises among them and prizes for the one who saw the passing things most sharply and remembered best which of them used to come before and which after and which together, and from these was best able to prophesy accordingly what was going to come—do you believe he would set his desire on that, and envy those who were honoured men or potentates among them? Would he not feel as Homer says,[1] and heartily desire rather to be serf of some landless man on earth and to endure anything in the world, rather than to opine as they did and to live in that way?"

"Yes indeed," said he, "he would rather accept anything than live like that."

"Then again," I said, "just consider; if such a one should go down again and sit on his old seat, would he not get his eyes full of darkness coming in suddenly out of the sun?"

"Very much so," said he.

"And if he should have to compete with those who had been always prisoners, by laying down the law about those shadows while he was blinking before his eyes were settled down—and it would take a good long time to get used to things—wouldn't they all laugh at him and say he had spoiled his eyesight by going up there, and it was not worth-while so much as to try to go up? And would they not kill anyone who tried to release them and take them up, if they could somehow lay hands on him and kill him?"[2]

"That they would!" said he.

"Then we must apply this image, my dear Glaucon," said I, "to all we have been saying. The world of our sight is like the habitation in prison, the firelight there to the sunlight here, the ascent and the view of the upper world is the rising of the soul into the world of mind; put it so and you will not be far from my own surmise, since that is what you want to hear; but God knows if it is really true. At least, what appears to me is,

[1] *Odyssey* xi. 489.
[2] Plato probably alludes to the death of Socrates. See *Apology*, p. 444.

that in the world of the known, last of all,[1] is the idea of the good, and with what toil to be seen! And seen, this must be inferred to be the cause of all right and beautiful things for all, which gives birth to light and the king of light in the world of sight, and, in the world of mind, herself the queen produces truth and reason; and she must be seen by one who is to act with reason publicly or privately."

"I believe as you do," he said, "in so far as I am able."

"Then believe also, as I do," said I, "and do not be surprised, that those who come thither are not willing to have part in the affairs of men, but their souls ever strive to remain above; for that surely may be expected if our parable fits the case."

"Quite so," he said.

"Well then," said I, "do you think it surprising if one leaving divine contemplations and passing to the evils of men is awkward and appears to be a great fool, while he is still blinking—not yet accustomed to the darkness around him, but compelled to struggle in law courts or elsewhere about shadows of justice, or the images which make the shadows, and to quarrel about notions of justice in those who have never seen justice itself?"

"Not surprising at all," said he.

"But any man of sense," I said, "would remember that the eyes are doubly confused from two different causes, both in passing from light to darkness and from darkness to light; and believing that the same things happen with regard to the soul also, whenever he sees a soul confused and unable to discern anything he would not just laugh carelessly; he would examine whether it had come out of a more brilliant life, and if it were darkened by the strangeness; or whether it had come out of greater ignorance into a more brilliant light, and if it were dazzled with the brighter illumination. Then only would he congratulate the one soul upon its happy experience and way of life, and pity the other; but if he must laugh, his laugh would be a less downright laugh than his laughter at the soul which came out of the light above."

"That is fairly put," said he.

"Then if this is true," I said, "our belief about these matters must be this, that the nature of education is not really such as some of its professors say it is; as you know, they say that there is not understanding in the soul, but they put it in, as if they were putting sight into blind eyes."

"They do say so," said he.

[1] The end of our search.

"But our reasoning indicates," I said, "that this power is already in the soul of each, and is the instrument by which each learns; thus if the eye could not see without being turned with the whole body from the dark towards the light, so this instrument must be turned round with the whole soul away from the world of becoming until it is able to endure the sight of being and the most brilliant light of being: and this we say is the good, don't we?"

"Yes."

"Then this instrument," said I, "must have its own art, for the circumturning or conversion, to show how the turn can be most easily and successfully made; not an art of putting sight into an eye, which we say has it already, but since the instrument has not been turned aright and does not look where it ought to look—that's what must be managed."

"So it seems," he said.

"Now most of the virtues which are said to belong to the soul are really something near to those of the body; for in fact they are not already there, but they are put later into it by habits and practices; but the virtue of understanding everything really belongs to something certainly more divine, as it seems, for it never loses its power, but becomes useful and helpful or, again, useless and harmful, by the direction in which it is turned. Have you not noticed men who are called worthless but clever, and how keen and sharp is the sight of their petty soul, and how it sees through the things towards which it is turned? Its sight is clear enough, but it is compelled to be the servant of vice, so that the clearer it sees the more evil it does."

"Certainly," said he.

"Yet if this part of such a nature," said I, "had been hammered at from childhood, and all those leaden weights of the world of becoming knocked off—the weights, I mean, which grow into the soul from gorging and gluttony and such pleasures, and twist the soul's eye downwards—if, I say, it had shaken these off and been turned round towards what is real and true, that same instrument of those same men would have seen those higher things most clearly, just as now it sees those towards which it is turned."

"Quite likely," said he.

"Very well," said I, "isn't it equally likely, indeed, necessary, after what has been said, that men uneducated and without experience of truth could never properly supervise a city, nor can those who are allowed to spend all their lives in education right to the end? The first have no single object in life, which they must always aim at in doing everything they do, public or private; the second will never do anything if they can help it, believing they have already found mansions abroad in the Islands of the Blest."[1]

"True," said he.

"Then it is the task of us founders," I said, "to compel the best natures to attain that learning which we said was the greatest, both to see the good, and to ascend that ascent; and when they have ascended and properly seen, we must never allow them what is allowed now."

"What is that, pray?" he asked.

"To stay there," I said, "and not be willing to descend again to those prisoners, and to share their troubles and their honours, whether they are worth having or not."

"What!" said he, "are we to wrong them and make them live badly, when they might live better?"

"You have forgotten again, my friend," said I, "that the law is not concerned how any one class in a city is to prosper above the rest; it tries to contrive prosperity in the city as a whole, fitting the citizens into a pattern by persuasion and compulsion, making them give of their help to one another wherever each class is able to help the community. The law itself creates men like this in the city, not in order to allow each one to turn by any way he likes, but in order to use them itself to the full for binding the city together."

"True," said he, "I did forget."

"Notice then, Glaucon," I said, "we shall not wrong the philosophers who grow up among us, but we shall treat them fairly when we compel them to add to their duties the care and guardianship of the other people. We shall tell them that those who grow up philosophers in other cities have reason in taking no part in public labours there; for they grow up there of themselves, though none of the city governments wants them; a wild growth has its rights, it owes nurture to no one, and need not trouble to pay anyone for its food. But you we have engendered, like king bees[2] in hives, as leaders and kings over yourselves and the rest of the city; you have been better and more perfectly educated than the others, and are better able to share in both ways of life. Down you must go then, in turn, to the habitation of the others, and accustom yourselves to their darkness; for when you have grown accustomed you will see a thousand times better than those who live there, and you will know what the images are and what they are images of, because you have seen the realities behind

[1] Cf. *Banquet*, p. 77, n. 3.
[2] Both the Greeks and Romans spoke always of "king," not "queen," of a hive.

just and beautiful and good things. And so our city will be managed wide awake for us and for you, not in a dream, as most are now, by people fighting together for shadows, and quarrelling to be rulers, as if that were a great good. But the truth is more or less that the city where those who are to rule are least anxious to be rulers is of necessity best managed and has least faction in it; while the city which gets rulers who want it most is worst managed."

"Certainly," said he.

"Then will our fosterlings disobey us when they hear this? Will they refuse to help, each group in its turn, in the labours of the city, and want to spend most of their time dwelling in the pure air?"

"Impossible," said he, "for we shall only be laying just commands on just men. No, but undoubtedly each man of them will go to the ruler's place as to a grim necessity, exactly the opposite of those who now rule in cities."

"For the truth is, my friend," I said, "that only if you can find for your future rulers a way of life better than ruling, is it possible for you to have a well-managed city; since in that city alone those will rule who are truly rich, not rich in gold, but in that which is necessary for a happy man, the riches of a good and wise life: but if beggared and hungry, for want of goods of their own, they hasten to public affairs, thinking that they must snatch goods for themselves from there, it is not possible. Then rule becomes a thing to be fought for; and a war of such a kind, being between citizens and within them, destroys both them and the rest of the city also."

"Most true," said he.

"Well, then," said I, "have you any other life despising political office except the life of true philosophy?"

"No, by heaven," said he.

"But again," said I, "they must not go awooing office like so many lovers! If they do, their rival lovers will fight them."

"Of course they will!"

"Then what persons will you compel to accept guardianship of the city other than those who are wisest in the things which enable a city to be best managed, who also have honours of another kind and a life better than the political life?"

"No others," he answered.

"Would you like us, then, to consider next how such men are to be produced in a city, and how they shall be brought up into the light, as you know some are said to go up from Hades to heaven?"

"Of course I should," said he. "Remember that this, as it

seems, is no spinning of a shell,[1] it's more than a game; the turning of a soul round from a day which is like night to a true day—this is the ascent into real being, which we shall say is true philosophy."

"Undoubtedly."

"We must consider, then, which of the studies has a power like that."

"Of course."

"Then, my dear Glaucon, what study could draw the soul from the world of becoming to the world of being? But stay, I have just thought of something while speaking—surely we said that these men must of necessity be athletes of war in their youth."

"We did say so."

"Then the study we seek must have something else in addition."

"What?"

"Not to be useless for men of war."

"Oh yes, it must," he said, "if possible."

"Gymnastic and music[2] we used before to educate them."

"That is true," said he.

"Gymnastic, I take it, is devoted to what becomes and perishes, for it presides over bodily growth and decay."

"So it appears."

"Then this, I suppose, could not be the study we seek."

"No indeed."

"Is it music, then, as far as we described that?"

"But if you remember," said he, "music was the counterbalance of gymnastic. Music educated the guardians by habits, and taught them no science, but a fine concord by song and a fine rhythm by tune, and the words they used had in them qualities akin to these, whether the words were fabulous tales or true. But a study! There was nothing in it which led to any such good as you now seek."

"Thanks for reminding me," said I. "What you say is quite accurate; it had nothing of that sort in it. But, my dear man, Glaucon, what study could there be of that sort? For all the arts and crafts were vulgar, at least we thought so."

"Certainly we did, but what study is left apart from gymnastic and music and the arts and crafts?"

"Look here," I said; "if we can't find anything more outside these, let us take one that extends to them all."

"Which?" he asked.

---

[1] A game. Boys in two groups would spin a shell, black on one side and white on the other, and according as it fell, one party would run and the other chase. The one who tossed called out, "Night or Day!"
[2] In their wide meanings, of course.

THE REPUBLIC Book VII *(521C–523B)*

"This, which they have in common, which is used in addition by all arts and all sciences and ways of thinking, which is one of the first things every man must learn of necessity."

"What's that?" he asked again.

"Just this trifle," I said—"to distinguish between one and two and three: I mean, in short, number and calculation. Is it not always true that every art and science is forced to partake of these?"

"Most certainly," he said.

"Even the art of war?"

"So it must," said he.

"At least," I said, "Palamedes[1] in the plays is always making out Agamemnon to be a perfectly ridiculous general. Haven't you noticed that Palamedes claims to have invented number, and with this arranged the ranks in the encampment before Troy, and counted the ships and everything else, as if they had not been counted before and as if before this Agamemnon did not know how many feet he had, as it seems if he really could not count? Then what sort of general do you think he was?"

"Odd enough," said he, "if that was true!"

"Then shall we not put down this," I said, "as a study necessary for a soldier, to be able to calculate and count?"

"Nothing more so," said he, "if he is to understand anything at all about his own ranks, or, rather, if he is to be even anything of a man."

"I wonder," said I, "if you notice what *I* do about this study."

"And what may that be?"

"It is really one of those we are looking for, those which lead naturally to thinking; but no one uses it rightly, although it draws wholly towards real being."

"What do you mean?" he asked.

"I will try to explain," said I, "what I, at least, believe. Whatever points I distinguish in my own mind as leading in favour of or against what we are speaking of, pray look at them with me and agree or disagree; then we shall see more clearly if this study is what I divine it to be."

"Do indicate them," said he.

"That is what I am doing," I said. "If you observe, some things which the senses perceive do not invite the intelligence to examine them, because they seem to be judged satisfactorily by the sense; but some altogether urge it to examine them because the sense appears to produce no sound result."

---

[1] A chief in the Grecian army before Troy, and a proverbial master of inventions. All three tragedians brought him into their plays, and he was credited with the invention of number, among other things. Plato is bored with Palamedes.

"Obviously you mean," he said, "things seen from a distance, or in shadow drawing."[1]

"You have not quite caught my point," I said.

"Then what do you mean?" he asked.

"I mean by those which do not invite thought," I said, "all those which do not pass from one sensation to its opposite at the same time. Those that do, I put down as inviting thought, that is, when the sensation shows two opposites equally, whether its impact comes from near or from far.[2] I can explain what I mean more clearly. These are three fingers, we say, little finger and second and middle."

"Just so," said he.

"Suppose now that I speak of them as seen close by. Just ask yourself this, please—"

"What?"

"Each of them appears to be equally a finger, and in this respect there is no difference whether the one seen is in the middle or on the outside, whether it is white or black, thick or thin, and so forth. In all these things the soul of most men is not forced to call on thought and ask, 'Whatever is a finger?' for the sight does not signal to it at all that the finger is the opposite of a finger."

"No indeed," said he.

"Then it is not likely," said I, "that such a case would invite or arouse thought."

"Not at all likely."

"Very good. What of their bigness and smallness? Does the sight see these sizes adequately, and does it make no difference to it that one is in the middle or on the outside? Thickness or thinness again, and softness or hardness, does the touch feel these surely enough? So with the other senses—are they not also defective in what they show? Or rather what happens is this: In the first place, the sensation which is appointed to judge the hard must also be appointed over the soft, and as it goes on feeling, it reports to the soul that the same thing is both hard and soft."[3]

"Just so," said he.

"Then," said I, "is it not necessary that the soul is puzzled in such cases, as to what, indeed, the sensation signifies to it by 'hard' if it says the same thing is 'soft'; and so with the feeling of light and heavy, what light or heavy means, if the sensation declares the heavy light and the light heavy?"

[1] σκιαγραφία, meaning perhaps scene painting; but see p. 402, n. 1.
[2] Referring to the distant view mentioned above.
[3] When it feels that one thing is harder than a second, and softer than a third; so it is both hard and soft. So with the other qualities.

"Really," he said, "these explanations are queer for the soul, and need examination."

"It is likely, then," I said, "that it is in such cases the soul first calls in calculation and reasoning, and tries to examine whether one thing or two things are reported to it each time."

"Of course."

"If it appears to be two, then, each appears to be distinct from the other, and one?"

"Yes."

"And if each appears to be one, and both together two, it will conceive of the two as separate because they are two, or else it would have conceived of one, not two, if they were inseparable."

"Quite right."

"Sight, again, saw big and small, we say, but as something compounded, not separate; don't you agree?"

"Yes."

"But, on the other hand, to make this something clear, as in fact big and small, reason was compelled to see it not as compounded but separate, the opposite of what sight saw."

"True."

"So from some beginning like this we first think of asking the question, 'Then what, after all, is bigness and smallness?'"

"Undoubtedly."

"And that, you know, is how we came to call one thing a thing of the mind[1] and another a thing of sight."

"Quite right," said he.

"Then this is what I was trying to say just now, when I said that some things provoke thought and some do not; I distinguished as provocative of thought those which bring their opposites with them when they fall upon the senses, and, as not awaking the intelligence, all such as do not bring in their opposites."

"I understand you at last," he said, "and I think so too."

"Very good. Which class does number belong to, and the 'one'?"

"I have no notion," he said.

"Start from what has been said already, and reason it out. If the 'one' is sufficiently seen in itself and by itself, or if it is sufficiently apprehended by any other sense, it could not draw towards real being, as we described in the case of the finger; but if some opposite is always seen along with it so that it appears to be no more than the opposite, at once it would need a critic to decide; the soul would be forced to be puzzled over it and enquire by stirring thought within itself, and to ask,

---

[1] I.e., we call a thought-provoking thing a thing of the mind.

'What, after all, is the one in itself?' So the study of the 'one' would be one of the studies which lead and divert the soul towards the contemplation of real being."

"But surely," he said, "an opposite is just what the 'one' especially has when it is examined by sight; for we can at the same time see the same thing both as one and as an infinite number."[1]

"Then if that is true of one," said I, "the same happens with all number."

"Of course."

"But the science of numbers and the art of calculation are wholly concerned with numbers."

"Undoubtedly."

"Number, then, appears to lead towards the truth."

"That is abundantly clear."

"Then, as it seems, this would be one of the studies we seek; for this is necessary for the soldier to learn because of arranging his troops, and for the philosopher, because he must rise up out of the world of becoming and lay hold of real being or he will never become a reckoner."

"That is true," said he.

"Again, our guardian is really both soldier and philosopher."

"Certainly."

"Then, my dear Glaucon, it is proper to lay down that study by law, and to persuade those who are to share in the highest things in the city to go for and tackle the art of calculation, and not as amateurs; they must keep hold of it until they are led to contemplate the very nature of numbers by thought alone, practising it not for the purpose of buying and selling like merchants or hucksters, but for war, and for the soul itself, to make easier the change from the world of becoming to real being and truth."

"Excellently said," he answered.

"And besides," I said, "it comes into my mind, now the study of calculations has been mentioned, how refined that is and useful to us in many ways for what we want, if it is followed for the sake of knowledge and not for chaffering."

"How so?" he asked.

"In this way, as we said just now; how it leads the soul forcibly into some upper region and compels it to debate about numbers in themselves; it nowhere accepts any account of numbers as having tacked onto them bodies which can be seen or touched.[2] For of course you know that experts in these mat-

---

[1] Glaucon refers back to his "things seen from a distance," p. 322, n. 2; a company of one hundred men might be looked upon as one company or as one hundred men (or might appear to be two hundred at a distance).
[2] Thus one, or two, not one man, or two men.

ters laugh at anyone who tries in discussion to cut unity itself, and they do not accept this; but if you chop it into bits they multiply them,[1] taking care lest the unit should ever appear not a unit but a lot of little pieces."

"Very true," he said.

"Then suppose, Glaucon, that someone should say to them, 'Numbers indeed! You people surprise me. What are you talking about—numbers in which all your ones are equal each to each, and not a bit different, and have within them no parts?' What do you think they would answer?"

"Just this, I think, that they are speaking of what can only be conceived in the mind, which it is impossible to deal with in any other way."

"You see then, my friend," said I, "that really this seems to be the study we need, since it clearly compels the soul to use pure reason in order to find out the truth."

"So it most certainly does," he said.

"Very well. You have seen already that natural calculators are sharp, for the most part, in all studies, and the slow ones have only to be educated and practised in this to become sharper than before, every one of them, even if they get no other benefit?"

"That is true," said he.

"And besides, I don't believe you could easily find studies which give more hard work than this in learning and in practice, not many at least."

"No indeed."

"For all these reasons, then, we must not omit this study, but the best natures must be trained in it."

"I agree," he said.

"Then let us take that as point one settled," I said. "Let us see, secondly, if what comes next to this is proper for us."

"What is that?" he said. "Do you mean geometry?"

"Just that,"[2] said I.

"Clearly it is proper," said he, "as far as it is concerned with warfare. In measuring encampments and assaulting strongholds, in closing up and extending the order of troops, and all other arrangements men make in armies in actual battles or on the march, it would make a great difference whether a general was a geometrician or not."

"But for all this at least," I said, "a very little geometry and calculation would be enough. We have to consider if the greater and higher part of the study tends towards our end, to make it easier to see the idea of the good. All does tend to this,

[1] I.e., back into unity.
[2] He refers to the three divisions of mathematics, line, surface and solid. See note on Pythagoreans on p. 327.

we say, which compels the soul to turn round towards that region in which is the happiest and most fortunate part of real being, which the soul by all means must see."

"You are right," said he.

"So if it compels the soul to contemplate being, it is proper; if to contemplate becoming, it is not proper."

"So we say."

"Well then, no one who has any knowledge of geometry will deny to us that the science goes clean contrary to the way the geometricians talk."

"How?" he asked.

"They speak in a very laughable and forced style, for they speak as if they were really doing and achieving something, as if their words had some action in view, talking loudly about squaring and applying and adding and all the rest of it; but the fact is, of course, that the whole study has only knowledge in view."[1]

"No doubt of it," said he.

"But must we not agree to this further?"

"What?"

"That the knowledge they seek is not knowledge of something which comes into being for a moment and then perishes, but knowledge of what always is."

"Agreed with all my heart," said he, "for geometrical knowledge is of that which always is."

"A generous admission! Then it would attract the soul towards truth, and work out the philosopher's mind so as to direct upwards what we now improperly keep downwards."

"As certainly as can be," he said.

"Then you must ordain as certainly as can be that in your City Beautiful they shall not neglect geometry by any means, for even its bye-ends are not small."

"What bye-ends?" he asked.

"What you mentioned," I said; "all that concerns warfare; and moreover as regards the better taking in of all studies, we doubtless know that it will make all the difference in the world whether one has grasped geometry or not."

"Yes," he said, "all the difference in the world."

"So this is the second study we must lay down for our young people?"

"Yes," said he.

"Very well: Shall we put astronomy third? Or don't you think so?"

"I do," said he; "for to have a good sense of seasons, of months and years is proper not only for husbandry and navi-

[1] They use common words of action for processes of thought, and can find nothing better.

THE REPUBLIC Book VII (526E–528C)

gation, but for strategy in war no less."

"I like that!" said I. "You seem to fear that the multitude may think you to be ordaining studies which are useless. It is no petty thing in fact, but hard to believe, that in every man's soul there is an instrument which is purified by these studies and enkindled, but corrupted and blinded by the other practices; an instrument more important to preserve than countless eyes, for by this alone can truth be seen. Those then who agree with you will think this to be abundantly true; but those who have never perceived it at all[1] will naturally think you are talking nonsense, for naturally they see no practical benefit in them worth mention. Very well, make up your mind on the spot which class you are speaking to. Or perhaps to neither? Perhaps you are stating your opinions chiefly for your own sake, although you would not grudge another if he could find use in them?"

"That is what I choose," he said; "I speak, ask and answer mostly for my own sake."

"Come back a little, then," said I, "for see, we were wrong in taking the study of astronomy next after geometry."

"How were we wrong?" he asked.

"After the plane surface," I said, "we took solids already in revolution, before we examined them by themselves; but the right way is to take the third increase[2] next after the second. This study relates of course to cubic increase and to forms having depth."

"Quite so," he said; "but it seems that those problems have not yet been solved."

"For two reasons," I said. "Because no city holds them in honour, they are weakly pursued, being difficult. Again, the seekers lack a guide, without whom they could not discover; it is hard to find one in the first place, and if they could, as things now are, the seekers in these matters would be too conceited to obey him. But if any whole city should hold these things honourable and take a united lead and supervise, they would obey, and solutions sought constantly and earnestly would become clear. Indeed even now, although dishonoured by the multitude, and held back by the seekers themselves having no conception of the objects for which

[1] That is, the usefulness of the "useless," things of no use to the practical man.
[2] αὔξην, increase. We should say "dimension." "Third increase" or "cubic increase" meant to the Greeks the change of plane squares into solid cubes; "forms having depth" refers to solids other than cubes.
These are Pythagorean terms; the Pythagoreans considered the point as the symbol of the unit, the line of numbers. The point, one, multiplied by its "first increase" (say 10) became the line, ten; this by "second increase" (i.e., multiplied again by 10 and so brought to a square) became the plane square, one hundred; this by "third increase" (i.e., brought to a cube) became the solid cube, one thousand.

they are useful, these things do nevertheless force on and grow against all this by their own charm, and I should not be surprised if they should really come to light."

"Yes, indeed," he said, "the charm in them is remarkable. But tell me more clearly what you mean by what you were just saying. You put down geometry as the study of the plane surface."

"Yes," I answered.

"Next after this," he said, "at first you put astronomy, but afterwards you drew back."

"Yes," I said, "hastening to go through everything quickly —the less I speed.[1] The treatment of solids[2] does come next, but it is dealt with so ridiculously through neglect that I passed that by and put next to geometry astronomy, that is solids in motion."

"Quite right," said he.

"Very well, let us put astronomy the fourth study, assuming that solid geometry, which we leave aside now, is there for us if only the city would support it."

"That is reasonable," said he, "and now I will tell the advantages of astronomy in the way you regard it, Socrates; you blamed me for praising it in the vulgar way just now. I think it is plain to everyone that this compels the soul to look on high, and leads it away yonder from things here."[3]

"Everyone except me, perhaps," I said, "for I don't think so."

"Then what do you think?" he asked.

"As it is treated now by those who would lead us to the heights of philosophy, I think it makes the soul look down very much indeed."

"What do you mean?" said he.

"A grand conception you truly seem to have," said I, "of the study of things on high. For if anyone should throw back his head and learn something by staring at the varied patterns on a ceiling, apparently you would think that he was contemplating with his reason, when he was only staring with his eyes. Your opinion may be right, I may be only a simpleton; but on the contrary, I cannot but believe that no study makes the soul look on high except that which is concerned with real being and the unseen. Whether he gape and stare upwards, or shut his mouth and stare downwards, if it be things of the senses that he tries to learn something about, I declare he never could learn, for none of these things admit of knowledge: I say his soul is looking down, not up, even

[1] Evidently a Greek proverb resembling ours.
[2] Literally, "increase consisting of depth."
[3] He takes this in the physical sense of looking at the stars.

THE REPUBLIC Book VII (528D–530B)

if he is floating on his back on land or on sea!"[1]

"It serves me right," he said, "I deserved the reproof. But what did you mean by saying that they ought to be taught astronomy differently if their learning it is to be useful for what we want?"

"This is what I meant," said I. "Those lovely patterns in the heavens are decorations in the visible world, so they may well be thought most beautiful and perfect of visible things; but they fall far short of those which are true, far short of the movements by which a real quickness and a real slowness in true number and in all sorts of true forms move about in relation to one another and carry about what is in them. These I tell you can be apprehended by reason and by thought, but not by sight. Don't you think so?"

"I do," said he.

"Then," I said, "one must use the intricate decorations of the heavens as models to help in the study of those others, as one would do if he happened upon excellently drawn and elaborated diagrams[2] by Daidalos[3] or some other great craftsman or painter. For a man acquainted with geometry on seeing such things would think they were exquisite in workmanship, but that only a fool would study them in earnest and expect to find in them the realities of equals or doubles or of some other proportion."

"Indeed he would be a fool to expect it," he said.

"Then don't you think the true astronomer will have the same feelings when he gazes at the movements of the stars? He will believe that the great architect of the heavens has framed the heavens and all that is in them as beautiful as such works can possibly be; and when he reflects how night and day are fitted together, and these with month and month with year, and the other stars with these and one another, will he not consider it absurd to believe that these things, which both have bodies and are visible, exist as they are forever without any change, and absurd to seek with all his power to grasp reality in these?"

"I think so at least," he said, "when I hear you now."

"So then," I said, "we will pursue problems in astronomy as we do in geometry, and leave the starry heavens alone, if we mean to tackle astronomy truly and to make useful instead of useless the natural power of thinking in the soul."

"What a multiplication of work," he said, "you prescribe

---

[1] The words used imply that Plato repudiates the caricature of Socrates in the *Clouds* of Aristophanes, where Socrates is hung up in a basket contemplating the sun, and one of his students is made to relate how, when Socrates was "gaping up at the moon" at night, a house lizard spattered on him from the roof.

[2] Such as an orrery, or planetarium.

[3] For note on this mythical craftsman, see Meno, p. 64.

for astronomy, compared with present practice!"

"Yes," I said, "and I believe we shall prescribe a lot of other work also in the same way, if we are to be of any use as lawgivers."

"But what have you to suggest," I said, "in the way of proper studies?"

"I can't think of one just now," said he.

"Yet surely," I said, "movement offers not one but several. All of them, perhaps, it would need a very wise man to tell; but two are obvious to us."

"What two, please?"

"Besides astronomy," I said, "its counterpart."

"What?"

"It seems," I said, "that just as our eyes were made[1] for astronomy, so our ears were made for harmonic movements, and these two are sister sciences, as the Pythagoreans aver, and as we, Glaucon, agree, don't we?"

"We do," he said.

"Then," said I, "since the task is great, let us ask them what they have to say about it, and other things too, perhaps; but all the while we will keep our own purpose in view."

"What is that?"

"Never to let any of our pupils try to study anything not perfect, anything which does not always arrive at that end which all studies ought to reach, as we said just now about astronomy. Don't you know the Pythagoreans do the same sort of thing again about harmony? They measure up against one another the sounds and concords which are heard, the same ineffectual labour as in astronomy."

"So they do, by heaven," he said, "enough to make one laugh;[2] they give names to certain close intervals, and stick out their ears as if they were eavesdropping on a voice next door; some say they can still hear a note in between and that is the smallest interval to measure by; some will have it the notes now sound alike—both trust their ears rather than their mind!"

"Ah, but you," said I, "you mean those worthy persons who make life unpleasant for gutstrings, tormenting them and racking them round the pegs—not to mention the beatings administered with plectrum and the loud accusals, expostulations and braggings[3] of the strings—but I will stop so as

[1] τέτηγεν; fixed in.
[2] Socrates has spoken of the Measurers; Glaucon mistakes him and speaks of the Listeners, a rival school, empiricists.
[3] It is difficult to do justice to this comic scene. The poor strings are racked and beaten in court, and they and their masters abuse each other!

THE REPUBLIC Book VII (530C–532B)

not to carry the metaphor too far, and will only say that I don't mean these, I mean those whom we proposed to question about harmonics. They do just the same as people engaged in astronomy. They search for the numbers in the concords which are heard, but they do not come up as high as problems, so as to discover which numbers are concordant and which not, and why in each case."

"A devil of a job that is!" he said.

"Say rather a useful job," I answered, "if pursued in seeking for the beautiful and the good, but if pursued otherwise, useless."

"That's reasonable," said he.

"Besides," I said, "if indeed our examination of all these arts which we have been discussing brings us to consider the community and kinship between them and if it shows in what way they are related to one another, then I think the study of them does bring us a bit further on towards what we want, and our labour is not in vain, but otherwise it is."

"So I surmise also," he said; "but it is a gigantic task, Socrates."

"Do you mean the preamble," I asked, "or what? Surely we know that all these are only preambles, approach paths leading to the law itself, which we need to learn about? For I don't suppose you think that the experts in these things know anything of dialectics."

"By God they don't!" said he, "except a very few of those I have met."

"But did you ever meet any that could not give and take in argument, whom you thought likely to know anything of what we say they ought to know?"

"No, as before," said he.

"Then, my dear Glaucon," said I, "is this the law at last, which dialectic brings out to its final meaning,[1] and which being the *law* of *mind* would have a likeness in the *power*[2] of *sight* trying, as we described it,[3] to look at last upon living things themselves, and the stars themselves, and finally upon the sun itself? Just so when a man tries by discussion to get a start towards the real thing, through reason and without any help from the senses, and will not desist until he grasps by thought alone the real nature of good itself, he arrives at the very end of the world of thought, as the other before was at the end of the world of sight."

"Undoubtedly," said he.

[1] Literally, "brings out to the finish." I.e., dialectic enables the mind to grasp the unfolding to it of the guiding law of the good: p. 311.
[2] See pp. 307, 308 and 311. Light, the "power" which illumines sight, bears an analogy with the "law" of good, which influences the mind.
[3] In the story of the cave.

"Very good: Don't you give the name dialectic to this progress of thought?"

"Of course."

"Well," said I, "*there*[1] was release from chains, and turning away from the shadows to the images and the light, and an upward passage from underground to the sun; and there still no ability to look at living things and plants and sunlight, but only upon godlike reflections in water and shadows of real things, not now shadows of images cast from another light such as, compared with the sun, was as shadowy as they were. All this diligent study of the arts—those we have been discussing—has this power, a stirring up and bringing out of the best in the soul to survey the best in things which really are, just as there it brought the clearest thing in the body to survey the most brilliant things in the bodily world of vision."

"I accept that," he said; "but all the same it seems to me hard to accept, yet again in another way hard not to accept. However, don't let us hear this only now at this moment—we must return to it again often; so let us assume what has been said, and go on to the law itself, and discuss it, as we have discussed the preamble. Then pray tell us what is the character of the power of dialectic, and what are its various kinds, and lastly what are its methods. For the methods, as it seems, would be ways ready to lead us to that very place where we may rest from the road and come to our journey's end."

"You will not be able," I said, "to follow me further, my dear Glaucon, although on my part there would be no want of good will. I should be glad to show you, if I could, no longer an image of what we speak of, but the truth as it appears to me, at least—though whether really so or not, I dare not say for certain; but I must certainly say that what we should see is something like that. Don't you agree?"

"Of course."

"And we could say also that only the power of discussion could show it, and only to one with experience of the studies which we have just described, and in no other way is it possible?"

"This too," he said, "one might say for certain."

"At any rate," I said, "no one will ever contradict us when we say that it is some method of investigation different from these, which tries to ascertain step by step about everything what each really is in itself. Nearly all the other arts are concerned with the opinions and desires of men, or generation and composition, or the care of things growing

[1] In the story of the cave.

and being compounded; and the few which do take hold of truth a little, as we said, geometry and those which go with it, we see are in dreamland about real being, and to perceive with a waking vision is impossible for these arts so long as they leave untouched the hypotheses which they use and cannot give any account of them. For when a beginning is something a man does not know, and the middle and end are woven of what he does not know, how can such a mere admission ever amount to knowledge?"

"Impossible," said he.

"Then the dialectic method proceeds alone by this way, demolishing the hypotheses as it goes, back to the very beginning itself, in order to find firm ground; the soul's eye, which is really buried deep in a sort of barbaric bog,[1] it draws out quietly and leads upwards, having the arts we have described as handmaids and helpers. These we have often termed sciences from habit, but they need another name, one clearer than opinion and dimmer than science. We have defined it already somewhere as understanding; but we are not debating about names when we have before us things so great to examine."

"No, indeed," said he.[2]

"We are content, then," said I, "as before to call the first part science,[3] and the second understanding, and the third belief, and the fourth conjecture: these last two together we may call opinion, and the first two exercise of reason. Opinion is concerned with becoming, and exercise of reason with being; and what being is to becoming, that exercise of reason is to opinion, and what exercise of reason is to opinion, that science is to belief, and understanding to conjecture. But let us leave aside, Glaucon, the proportion[4] between lines which represent these, and the division of opinable and reasonable[5] each in two, or we shall have our fill of many times the number of discussions we had before."

"Oh, well, for myself," he said, "I agree with you about the other things, as far as I can follow."

---

[1] According to the Orphic myth the impious and unjust souls were buried in mud in Hades. See p. 160.
[2] A sentence of about fifteen words, for which the Greek text is unreliable, is omitted here.
[3] These four correspond with the "affections of the soul" on p. 311 except that there Socrates put Exercise of Reason (instead of science) "for the highest." See the diagram of the Divided Line, p. 309. Here Exercise of Reason takes the place occupied by Knowledge on the diagram.
[4] The proportion described can be followed in the table below; each time it is the same. Socrates "leaves aside" discussion of the numerical value of the proportion; it is $CE:AC$ of the Divided Line, see p. 309 n. 3, 4.

| Reasonable | 1st Science
2nd Understanding | Exercise of Reason, concerned with being. |
| Opinable | 3rd Belief
4th Conjecture | Opinion, concerned with becoming. |

[5] I.e., of Opinion and Knowledge.

"Then one who exacts an account of the real being of each thing, you call the man of dialectic? And one who cannot, you will say, has not understanding of this, in so far as he cannot give an account of it to himself and to another?"

"Why, how could I say he has?" was the reply.

"Exactly the same about the good. If a man cannot distinguish by reasoning, and isolate the idea of the good from all other things, you will declare that he does not know the real good at all. He must behave like a soldier in battle; through all tests he must push, determined to test things not according to opinion but according to reality, and in all these things pass through without a fall in his reasoning. If not, you will say that he does not know either the good or any good thing; if he does somehow get hold of an image[1] of it, he holds it by opinion, not by knowledge; and he lives the present life sleeping and dreaming, never awaking in this world, until he comes to the house of Hades for his long, eternal sleep."

"Yes, by God," he said, "that is just what I shall say."

"And further, if you ever in fact had sons of your own to foster and train, as you now are training children in our discourse, you would not let them remain 'as irrational as pen strokes'[2] to rule in the city and be masters of the highest things."

"That I should not," said he.

"You will lay down, then, in the law, that they must adhere chiefly to the education which makes them able to question and answer most scientifically."

"So I will," he said, "with your help."

"Then do you agree," said I, "that we place dialectic on top of our other studies like a coping-stone; that no other study could rightly be put above this, and that here our discussion of studies is ended?"

"I do," said he.

"Now then, distribution," said I. "That is what remains for us; as to who shall be given these studies, and how."

"Clearly," he said.

"Do you remember, then, the choice of rulers we made before, what sort we chose?"

"Of course," he said.

"So in general," said I, "those are the natures which ought to be our choice; we must prefer the steadiest and the bravest, and as far as possible the most handsome. But besides

---

[1] Or phantom.
[2] ὥσπερ γραμμάς. Alternatively this may refer to certain lines which geometricians called "irrational."

that we must seek not only those who are generous and beefy[1] in character, but they must have in their nature all that suits this education."

"What are you thinking of particularly now?" he asked.

"Keenness, bless you!" I said. "They must have that for their studies, and they must not find learning difficult. The soul flinches much more, let me tell you, in hard study than in athletics; the labour goes more home to the soul, its very own, not shared by the body."

"True," he said.

"And we must seek the man who has a good memory and doggedness, and is a lover of all sorts of hard labour. Else how do you think anyone would want both to work hard with his body and to complete all that study and practising as well?"

"No one would," he said, "unless of a fine all-around nature."

"At any rate, the mistake of today," said I, "and the dishonour which has fallen upon philosophy, comes from what I said before, that they cannot approach her as equals: for bastards, we said, ought not to touch her, only true-born sons."

"How so?" he asked.

"In the first place," I said, "no one should come near her lame in diligence, half of him loving hard work and half idle. This happens whenever one loves athletics and hunting and loves all hard work which involves the body, but does not love learning or listening or enquiring; in fact hates all that kind of work. He is equally lame who puts hate and love of work the opposite way."

"Very true," said he.

"So again with truth," I said, "we will set down as a soul maimed for truth one which hates only the intended lie, and will itself have nothing to do with that and is very angry with others who are false; and yet easily accepts the unintended falsehood, and is not vexed when detected in some ignorance, but rolls in the mud of ignorance like a pig."

"Most certainly," he said.

"And with regard to temperance," I said, "and courage and magnificence, and all the parts of virtue, we must be most careful to distinguish bastard and true-born. For when a city, or a person indeed, does not know how to examine things of that sort, they use unconsciously for any of their purposes cripples and bastards for rulers or friends, as the case may be."

"Certainly that is true," he said.

[1] Literally, "hairy," a vulgar term.

"But we shall have to be most cautious," I said, "in all such matters. If we bring those of sound body and sound mind to this great study and this great practice, and so educate them, we shall save both city and constitution, and justice herself will have no fault to find with us; but if we bring in aliens our lot will be altogether contrary, and we shall let loose a still greater flood of ridicule on philosophy."

"That would indeed be an ugly thing," said he.

"It certainly would," I said. "But I—here's a funny thing happening to me again!"

"What?" he asked.

"I forgot we were playing," I said, "and I spoke too strongly. As I was speaking I glanced at philosophy, and saw her unworthily trampled underfoot; I suppose it provoked me and I spoke as I did, like an angry man, too seriously against those who were to blame."

"Not too seriously for me," said he, "as a hearer."

"Ah, but for me," I said, "as a speaker. But we must not forget that in our former choice we chose old men, but in this one that will not be possible. We must not believe Solon[1] that a man can learn many things while growing old. He is less able to learn than to run; most of the labours, and all the hard ones, are for young men."

"That comes of necessity," said he.

"Then what belongs to calculations and geometries and all the education which is necessary as a prelude to dialectic must be set before them while still young, and not as a scheme of instruction which they must be compelled to learn."

"Why, pray?"

"Because," I said, "the free man must not learn anything coupled with slavery. For bodily labours under compulsion do no harm to the body, but no compulsory learning can remain in the soul."

"True," said he.

"No compulsion then, my good friend," said I, "in teaching children; train them by a kind of game, and you will be able to see more clearly the natural bent of each."

"There's reason in that," he said.

"Well," said I, "you remember we said that the children must be brought to war on horseback as spectators, and if there were a safe place they must be brought near and taste blood, like dogs?"

"I remember," said he.

"Then in all these things," I said, "in labours and learnings

[1] Solon, fragment 18, *Elegy* and *Iambic* (Loeb), p. 134.

and fears, whoever always appears most ready and active must be enrolled in a class apart."

"At what age?" he asked.

"The age," I said, "when they are released from compulsory gymnastics. For in this time, two or three years as it may be, they can do nothing else; labour and sleep are enemies to learning, and besides, how they will prove themselves in these exercises is one of our chief tests."

"Certainly," said he.

"After this time, then," said I, "those who are judged best of the twenty-year-olds will receive greater honours than the rest; and these must gather together into one connected view all the studies which they followed without order in their education in childhood, to disclose the relationship of the studies to one another and to the nature of real being."

"At any rate," he said, "only such learning as that could remain firm in those who have it."

"And it is also," I said, "the chief test of the dialectic nature and the reverse: for the 'synoptic' person is a 'dialectic' person;[1] anyone else is not."

"I agree with you," said he.

"Then these are the matters," I said, "which you must supervise, and you must see which most of all among them have these qualities, and are steadfast in their studies, steadfast in war and in their other duties. When these pass their thirty years, choose the best in this select class and give them greater honours; then test them in the power of dialectic, to discover which has the power to shake off sight and the other senses and pass onwards to real being in very truth. And now you must be especially careful, my comrade."

"Why, I wonder!" said he.

"Do you not notice," I said, "what a mighty danger there is now in the use of dialectic?"

"What danger?" he asked.

"They get filled with lawlessness," said I.

"So they do," he said.

"Well, do you think that what happens to them is at all surprising," I said; "can you find no excuse?"

"What excuse?" he asked.

"Just suppose," I said, "a changeling son brought up in great wealth in a great family and surrounded by flatterers; when he grew up to be a man, suppose he should perceive that he was no son to those who called themselves parents but he could not find out who the real ones were. Can you

[1] A "synoptic" means one who can bring all into one connected view; a "dialectic" means one fit for logical reasoning.

imagine how he would feel towards the flatterers and towards his supposed parents during the time when he did not know of his substitution, and again when he did? Perhaps you would like to hear me imagine."

"I should," said he.

"I imagine, then," I said, "that while he did not know the truth, he would be more likely to honour his father and mother and his other apparent relatives than to honour the flatterers, and less ready to leave them in want, less ready to say or do anything lawless to them, less ready to disobey them in great matters than to disobey the flatterers."

"That is likely," he said.

"But, on the other hand, when he found out the facts, I imagine that he would be remiss in the honour and care due to these and increase it towards the flatterers, he would obey the flatterers more than before and live now after their fashion, he would associate openly with them and care nothing for that old father and the adoptive relatives, unless he had a particularly generous nature."

"That is exactly what would happen," said he; "but how does that picture suit those who are tackling the study of words?"

"I will tell you how," I said. "We have, I suppose, been influenced from childhood by settled opinions about just and beautiful things, opinions amongst which we have been brought up, obeying and honouring them, as if in subjection to parents."

"We have."

"And also there are other practices contrary to these, which have pleasures in them, and these flatter our soul and draw it towards themselves; yet they do not convince those who are at all decent, who still honour the old traditions and obey them."

"That is true."

"Very good," said I.

"Suppose a question comes along to someone in that condition, asking him, 'What is the beautiful?' Suppose he answers what he used to hear from the lawgiver, but argument begins to pick holes, and tests the answer this way and that way over and over again and drives him into the opinion that the thing is no more beautiful than ugly; if the same thing happens about the just and the good and whatever he held most in honour—what do you think he will do then about honour and obedience?"

"Neither honour nor obey as before, that's a necessity."

"Very well," said I; "he no longer thinks the old opinions

honourable and of his own kith and kin, as he did once, and he cannot find the true ones. What other life do you expect him to give himself up to? Will he not probably go straight over to the life of flatterers?"

"That he will," said he.

"From law-abiding, then, it seems likely he will have become lawbreaking, I think."

"It must be so."

"So that is likely to be the experience of those who take up word study in this way, and, as I said just now, there should be much excuse for it."

"And pity too," he said.

"Therefore, so that there may be none of this pity on behalf of your thirty-year-olds, the study of words must be tackled most cautiously in every way."

"Very much so, indeed," he said.

"And one great safeguard is not to let them taste these things while they are young, isn't it? For I am sure you have not failed to notice that as soon as youngsters get a first taste of words in their mouth, they treat them as a game, and misuse them, always words against words; they copy people who refute them, and themselves refute others in the same way, as happy as a lot of puppies to worry and tear with their words those who happen to be nearest to them."

"They do love it vastly!" said he.

"So they refute many, and many refute them, and in the end they tumble headlong into a strong disbelief of all they used to believe. The result is, as you see, that they get a bad name everywhere, and the whole cause of philosophy is prejudiced."

"Most true," he said.

"But the older man," I said, "would never want to share such insanity. He will rather choose to imitate those who wish to argue and search for the truth, not those who make it a game and contradict for fun. So he will be a more moderate man, and he will make his pursuits appear more honourable, not more dishonourable."

"Quite right," said he.

"And surely what we laid down before this was also said with a view to this caution—I mean that we must choose decent and steady natures to teach the art of words, and we must not have any chance comer taking it up who may be unsuitable."

"I quite agree," he said.

"Well now, for the study of words is it enough if a man sticks to it constantly and intently, and does nothing else but exercise himself in it, just as was done in the exercises for his body, but for twice as many years as then?"

"Six years do you mean," he said, "or four?"

"Oh, well," said I, "put it down as five; for after that they must be taken down again into that cave, and compelled to rule in the affairs of war and the other offices of young men, that they may not be behind the others in experience. Even in these also they must be further tested, to see whether they will stand firm when attracted in all directions, or will in the least give way."

"How long," said he, "do you put for that?"

"Fifteen years," I said. "And when they are fifty years old, those who have come safely through and distinguished themselves everywhere in everything, both action and knowledge, must now be brought to the last task. They must be made to uplift the brilliant radiance of the soul and to fix their gaze on that which provides light for all; then, beholding the good in itself, and using that as a standard, they must adorn city and men, yes themselves also, for the rest of their lives each in turn. Most of the time must be spent in philosophy, but when their turn comes, they must labour hard yet again in politics; rulers they must each be, for the city's sake, doing it not as a beautiful thing but as a necessity. And so educating others to be like them, they must leave them as guardians of the city in their place, then depart and dwell in the Islands of the Blest; the city shall make public monuments and sacrifices in their honour, as holy spirits, if the Pythian oracle concurs, or else as men happy and divine."

"A noble row of rulers you have made, Socrates," he said, "like a sculptor making statues!"

"And don't forget the women, Glaucon," I said, "they may be rulers, too! Don't suppose that what I have said was meant only for men; women too, as many as are born among us with natures sufficiently capable."

"Quite right," he said, "if they are to share all in common with men, as we described."

"Very well," I said; "you agree that what we said of the city and its constitution was not altogether a pious prayer. Difficult it is indeed, but possible somehow, and only in the way we said, when those who are truly philosophers become potentates whether one or more in the city, men who despise what are now honours, believing them to be ignoble and worthless, but hold the right of most value and the honours which come from that; men who hold the greatest and most necessary thing to be justice, and, steadfastly serving and exalting justice, set their city into complete order."

"How?" he asked.

"All above ten years of age in the city," said I, "must be sent out into the country; and all the children among them must be taken charge of and kept outside their present surroundings and the ways of life led by their parents; and the reformers must bring them up in their own ways and customs, which are such as we have described already. Thus most easily and most quickly, don't you agree, the city and constitution we described will be established and prosper and be happy, and the nation in which it exists will receive most benefit?"

"Yes, by far," said he; "and I think, Socrates, that you have well explained how that could be done, if ever it should be done."

"Then we have said enough now," I went on, "about this city and of the man who is like it, haven't we? For it is also clear, I take it, what sort of person we shall expect him to be."

"Quite clear," said he, "and, to answer your question, I think we have come to the end."

BOOK VIII

"Very well. So far we are agreed, Glaucon. The city which is to be arranged in the best possible way must have women in common, children in common and all education in common. So also its practices must be common to all, both in war and peace; kings among them must be those who have shown themselves best both in philosophy and in warfare."

"So far we are agreed," said he.

"And further, we agreed as to what the rulers are to do when appointed. They will take the soldiers and settle them in such lodgings as we described, common to all without any thing private. Besides the lodgings, if you remember, we agreed what property they should have."

"Yes, I remember," said he; "we thought they should have no property at all such as other people now have, but, as being athletes of war and guardians, they were to receive a wage for their guarding from the others, namely the year's keep for these purposes, and their duty was to take care of the rest of the city and themselves."

"Quite correct," I said; "but now that we have finished that matter, let us recall where we turned off on the path which led us here, and go by the old road."

"That is not difficult," said he, "you were then saying very much the same as now. You assumed that the city had been fully described, and went on to say that you would call such a city good, and a man like it good, although you could describe a better city and a better man; then, further, that if this one were right all other cities were wrong. The constitutions remaining, as I remember it, you said were of four kinds; and it was worth-while to take account of these and see their faults, and to observe the men resembling them; thus by examining all these, and agreeing about the best and worst man, we might consider whether the best man was happiest and the worst most miserable, or otherwise. Then I asked what these four constitutions were. There Polemarchos and Adeimantos broke into the discussion; then you resumed, and so you have arrived at this stage."

"Quite correct," I said, "you have a good memory."

"Then give me the same hold again, like a wrestler, and when I ask the same question, try to say what you were going to say then."

"If I can!" said I.

"Well, indeed," said he, "I do desire to hear for myself what you meant by the four constitutions."

"That will not be difficult," I said, "you shall hear; these are what I mean, as far as they have names. First, your Cretan and Laconian,[1] which are generally praised. The second is called oligarchy, the rule of the few, which is praised in the second place, a constitution full of many evils. Next after this comes democracy, the rule of the people, its antagonist, which naturally follows; and last, far removed from all these, that glorious thing tyranny, fourth—the extremest pestilence which a city can have. Can you name any other kind of constitution that stands in a distinct class? There are principalities, I suppose, and purchased royalties, and constitutions of such kinds somewhere in between these—one could find more of them among barbarians than Hellenes."

"A good few indeed," he said, "and strange ones, as they are described."

"Well then," said I, "you know there must be as many kinds of men as constitutions. You don't suppose the constitutions grow out of a tree or a stone;[2] no, they grow out of men's manners in the cities, whichever manners tip the scales down, so to speak, and draw the others after them."

"True indeed," said he, "that's where they come from."

"Then if there are five kinds of constitutions, there should be five conditions of soul of private men."

"Of course."

"We have already described the man who is like aristocracy,

[1] Spartan.
[2] A proverb of the origin of mankind, e.g., *Odyssey* xix. 163.

'the rule of the best,' the one whom we properly describe as good and just, the best man."

"We have."

"Then what next—should we describe the inferior sorts? One imperious and greedy of honour, answering to the Laconian state; one again the member of a ruling class—oligarchy, and the democratic man, and the natural tyrant? What we want is to compare the most unjust to the most just, and that will end our enquiry as to how justice unmixed stands to injustice unmixed in the possessor, whether he is happy or miserable. Are we to obey Thrasymachos and pursue injustice, or to obey the argument which is now appearing, and pursue justice?"

"Yes, that is what we should do next," said he, "by all means."

"We began by examining the manners in states before taking persons, as being clearer there; shall we do the same now, and examine first the honour-loving constitution? I can't find any other word for it in our Greek language; it must be called timocracy or timarchy, the power or rule of honour. Then we will consider the man of that kind; after that oligarchy and the oligarchical man, and then again democracy and the democratical man. And fourthly we will come to the city under a tyranny and look at that, turning our eyes towards the tyrannic soul. Last of all, we will try to be competent judges of the one question which we have set before us."

"I must say at least," he answered, "that would be a reasonable way to examine and to judge."

"Come, then," said I, "let us try to say how a timocracy would grow out of an aristocracy. One thing is plain, I think; change in a constitution always begins from the governing class when there is a faction within; but so long as they are of one mind, even if they be a very small class, it is impossible to disturb them."

"That is true."

"Very well, Glaucon," I said, "how will our city be disturbed? How will the assistants and the rulers quarrel with one another and themselves? Would you like us to beseech the Muses, as Homer does, to tell us 'how first fell faction among them';[1] and should we imagine the Muses mouthing their words in the lofty tragic vein, while really they are playing up mock-heroic and teasing us as if we were children?"

"How?"

"Like this more or less. 'It is difficult indeed to disturb a city thus constituted; but destruction comes to everything existing,

[1] Cf. *Iliad* xvi. 112.

and therefore even a fabric like this will not endure for ever, but it must be dissolved. The dissolution will be thus. In plants which grow in the earth, and also in animals which live on the earth, there is bearing and barrenness both in soul and bodies when the rounding circles of each come completely round, a short course for the short-lived and a long course for the long-lived; but in your race, mankind,[1] the city leaders whom you have educated will never succeed in procuring the fine births and the barrenness, however wise they are, by reasoning combined with sensation, but these will escape them, and they will sometimes beget children when they should not. For a divine birthling the circle is comprehended by a perfect number,[2] for a human birth by the first number in which increases by root and square are given three dimensions, with four marking-points[3] of things that make like and unlike, that wax and wane, and make all commensurable together and rational, from which numbers, three and four wedded with five[4] and cubed produce two harmonies, one square, so many times a hundred, one oblong: one side being one hundred squares of the rational diameter of five[5] less one each, or of the irrational diameter less two; the other side one hundred cubes of three. This whole number, geometrical, master of gestation on earth,[6] is controller of better and worse births. And when your guardians, not knowing this, bring brides and bridegrooms together unseasonably, the children will not be of fine nature or fine fortune. The best of them will be established in office by their predecessors, it is true; but still, being unworthy, when they come in turn into their fathers' powers, they will begin to neglect us as guardians, first slighting music more than is

---

[1] The Muses are speaking.

[2] The exact meaning of this depends on an elaborate arithmetical sum, which, however, is clear. Those who wish to understand the details may find them in Adam's admirable excursus to Book VIII, to which I am much indebted. The general idea is that every birth is symbolised by a circle with a moving circumference. At the beginning is the begetting: and if the circumstances are all favourable, the birth takes place when the circumference completes the circuit; if not, all goes wrong. The numbers are the numbers of days in the seven-months birth $3^3 + 4^3 + 5^3 = 216$, and the numbers of days in a divine birth $(3 \times 4 \times 5)^4 = 3,600 \times 3,600$ (a square) $= 4,800 \times 2,700$ (an oblong) $= 12,960,000$. The perception the number is connected with Pythagorean beliefs; Cf. p. 399, n. 4. These things belong to a commentary, not to a translation; and I am content to give renderings of the mathematical terms, which no doubt delighted the Athenian audience, who loved such speculations. See J. Adam, *The Republic of Plato*, Cambridge University Press, 1902, Vol. II, pp. 264 ff. (In Appendix to Book VIII.) Also, J. Adam, *The Vitality of Platonism and Other Essays*, Cambridge University Press, 1911.

[3] The points marking the development of a certain parallelogram in the Greek method of drawing.

[4] $3 \times 4 \times 5 = 60$, $3^3 + 4^3 + 5^3 = 216$; square numbers were called like, and "oblong" numbers (for the numbers were thought of as figures) unlike. The words have also a philosophic association, the cycles of the universe. "Wedded," because the first "masculine" number, 3, and the first "feminine" number, 2, multiplied together, make 6, called "marriage" by the Pythagoreans.

[5] The diameter of a square of 5 is $\sqrt{50}$, and the nearest rational number is 7; the alternative is 50 l s

[6] It is not only geometrical, but it controls all human gestation.

THE REPUBLIC Book VIII *(546A–547D)* 345

proper, secondly gymnastic; whence your young people will care less for us Muses. And the rulers appointed from them will not behave like very good guardians in testing the breeds among you, Hesiod's golden and silvern and brazen and iron:[1] iron will be mixed with silver and brass with gold, and so unlikeness and unevenness unharmonised will come up; and if these grow up, wherever they grow up, they also bring forth war and hatred. From this generation I tell you[2] is begotten faction, whenever and wherever faction appears.'"

"'Well answered, indeed, Muses!' shall be our reply," he said.

"As you might expect," said I, "since they are Muses."

"Well, what next?" he asked, "how do the Muses go on?"

"When faction comes up," said I, "there is a tug of war between the two breeds among the guardians; iron and brazen pulling towards moneymaking and freehold property and riches of silver and gold; and on the other side, the silvern and golden, being themselves naturally rich in their souls, not poor, pull towards virtue and the ancient tradition. So, after a violent struggle together they compromise the matter; they would share land and houses among themselves in private possession, and then make slaves of those whom they had been guarding in freedom, their friends and supporters, keeping them now as yeomen[3] and servants, and themselves managing war and guardianship over them?"

"Yes," he said, "that seems how the change comes about."

"Accordingly," said I, "this would be a constitution between aristocracy and oligarchy."

"Exactly."

"Thus, then, the change will come about. But after the change, how will it go on? Obviously, it will imitate partly the old constitution, and partly oligarchy, being between them, and it will also have something of its own."

"Just so," he said.

"Then in honouring the rulers, and in keeping away from agriculture and handicrafts and moneymaking that part which fights for the city, in establishing messes and attending to gymnastic and training for war, in all such things it will imitate the old constitution?"

"Yes."

"But in many ways it will also have special customs of its own; thus, it will fear to bring the wise into places of govern-

[1] Hesiod, *Works and Days*, 109, describes the Four Ages of Man as under four metals.
[2] From *Iliad* vi. 211.
[3] *Perioikoi*, provincial yeomen, the second class in Laconia, subject to the noble Spartans, but free inhabitants of the provincial towns and farms. The lowest class were helots or serfs.

ment, because the men of that sort which it has are no longer simple and earnest but a mixture; it will incline to the high-spirited and more single-minded men, those whose nature is rather for war than for peace, and it will hold in honour warlike stratagems and contrivances and spend the whole time in war."

"Yes."

"Covetous, again, such men will be," said I, "covetous of riches as those in oligarchies are, with a fierce love in the darkness for gold and silver, now they are possessed of storehouses and private treasuries to store and hide these things in; they will build habitations about them to dwell in, nothing less than little nests for themselves, in which they can spend fortunes lavishing money on their women and any others they may wish."

"Most true," said he.

"And so they will be misers with their own money, because they value it so and have to keep it hidden, but spendthrifts with the money of others, because of their desires; they will enjoy their pleasures in secret, running away from the law like boys who run from their father, since force and not persuasion has educated them, all because they have neglected the true Muse, the comrade of reason and philosophy, and have honoured gymnastic with greater reverence than music."

"Assuredly," said he, "this constitution is a mixture of both evil and good."

"Yes, a great mixture," said I, "but most manifest in it is one thing only, because the high-spirited part is predominant, I mean the desire to be first[1] and the passion for honour."

"Decidedly," said he.

"Well, then," I said, "this is the constitution, and this is how it arises, and such would be a general sketch of it without going into details exactly; even the sketch is enough to show the most just and the most unjust man, and our task would be unmanageable to describe all constitutions and all characters without leaving out any."

"You are quite right," said he.

"What of the man corresponding to such a constitution? How does he come up, and what sort of person is he?"

"My notion is," said Adeimantos, "that he comes pretty near to our friend Glaucon in the wish to be first."

"Perhaps," I said, "as far as that goes; but there are some things where they are different."

"What are those?"

"He must be more self-willed than Glaucon," said I, "and

[1] Everyone wishes to be boss; not a general quarrelsomeness.

a little less cultured, yet a lover of music; fond of hearing speakers, yet in no way a speaker himself. Such a man would be brutal to slaves, instead of treating slaves with disdain, as a man properly educated would do; but he is gentle to the freeborn. He would be very obedient to rulers, with a passion for rule himself, and for honour; but he would claim the right to rule not because he could talk or anything of that sort, but because of his deeds of war and practice of warlike exercises, and being fond of gymnastic and hunting."

"Yes," he said, "because that is the character of this constitution."

"As to money, too," I said, "such a man would despise it in youth, but the older he grew, the more he would love it, because he has a bit of the money-loving nature within him, and is not single-minded for virtue—his best guardian has left him."

"What guardian?" asked Adeimantos.

"Reason," said I, "mingled with music; this alone when it grows within dwells throughout life in the possessor as the saviour of virtue."

"Well said!" he answered.

"There then," said I, "is the character of the timocratic youth, like to the city of the same kind."

"By all means."

"And this is how he is produced, more or less," I said. "Sometimes he is the young son of a good father, a father who lives in a city without a good constitution, who eschews honours and offices and lawsuits, and all such meddlesomeness, and is willing to be overreached so long as he can be spared trouble."

"And how does he become what he is?"

"It begins," I said, "when he hears his mother grumbling that her husband is not one of the governing class and so the other women look down upon her. Then she sees that her husband does not worry much about money, and will not fight and rail in private lawsuits and in parliament; he takes all that quietly, and she notices he is always attending to himself and doesn't pay much respect to her, though he is never rude to her. So the boy just listens, and she goes on grumbling, because of all this, that father is no man and only slack, and all the other grievances which women love to harp on."

"You're right," said Adeimantos, "no end of grievances, that's just like the women."

"Then you know too," said I, "that the servants of such people, servants who seem to be loyal, sometimes say the same sort of thing to the sons quietly; and if they see someone in their debt and the father will not prosecute, or any other wrong they may see, they exhort the boy to punish them all when he grows up, and be more of a man than father; and out of doors he hears and sees other things of the same sort—those in the city that attend quietly to their own business being called simpletons and thought little of, while those who meddle in other business are honoured and praised. Then as the young man hears and sees all this, and hears on the contrary what his father says and compares his ways with the others, he is attracted by both: his father waters[1] and fosters the reasoning part in his soul, the others the desiring and high-spirited part. So, because his nature is not evil, but is influenced by the evil natures of his companions, he is dragged into the middle by both these, and yields the governance of himself to the mean, the self-asserting and high-spirited part, and becomes an ambitious and honour-loving man."

"I think you have got it exactly," said he; "that is how such a man is produced."

"Then," said I, "there we have the second constitution and the second kind of man."

"We have," said he.

"Next, then, shall we tell of 'another man set up against another city,'[2] as Aeschylus might say—or rather take the city first, according to our system?"

"By all means," he said.

"Well, the next constitution, I think, would be oligarchy."

"But what sort of establishment," said he, "would you call oligarchy?"

"A constitution," I said, "according to property, in which the rich govern and the poor man has no share in government."

"I understand," said he.

"Then shall I explain first how timocracy changes into oligarchy?"

"Yes."

"Yet a blind man could see that," I said.

"How?"

"That storehouse full of gold," said I, "which every man has, destroys such a constitution. First they invent ways of spending for themselves, and neither they nor their wives obey the laws, but they pervert them to support this."

"That is likely," said he.

"After that," I said, "they observe each other and rival each other, and make the whole body of the people like themselves."

"Quite likely."

---

[1] Irrigates like a farmer, a favourite metaphor of Plato.
[2] Cf. Aeschylus, *Seven against Thebes*, 451 and 570.

"By and by, then," said I, "they push ahead with their moneymaking, and the more they value money the less they value virtue; in truth, we may imagine riches and virtue as always balanced in scales against each other."

"Just so," said he.

"And when riches are honoured in a city, virtue and the good people are less honoured than the rich."

"That is clear."

"Now what is honoured anywhere is practised, and what is dishonoured is neglected."

"Just so."

"Thus in the end they have become lovers of money and moneymaking and no longer aim at honour and ambition; they praise the rich man and admire him and bring him into places of government, and the poor man they dishonour."

"Certainly."

"So then they lay down a law of limitation in the constitution; they fix a sum of money, greater or less, according as the oligarchy is more or less complete, and proclaim that no one may share in the government unless his property comes up to the assessment. This they carry out by force of arms, or they have used terror before this to establish such a constitution. Don't you think so?"

"Yes, I do."

"Then that is how it is established, more or less."

"Yes," he said, "but how does the constitution work? And what are those faults which we said it had?"

"First of all," said I, "look at the character of this very limitation. Suppose pilots were chosen on board ship by their property, and no poor man could be chosen even if he were a better pilot."

"A bad voyage," said he, "is what I should prophesy for them."

"Would it not be the same with any other form of government?"

"I think so."

"Except government of a city?" said I, "or does it hold for a city too?"

"Most of all for a city," said he, "for that government is the greatest and the most difficult."

"This, then, is one great fault in an oligarchy."

"So it appears."

"Very well; there is another just as bad."

"What?"

"That a city of that sort is not one but two by necessity, a city of the rich and a city of the poor, living together and always plotting against each other."

"Indeed, that is just as bad as the first," said he.

"And there is something besides which is not good. They may be unable perhaps to wage some war, because then they are compelled either to arm the populace and to fear them more than the enemy, or not to use them, and so to see themselves literally oligarchs in the very process of battle, with precious few to rule. And remember that they are money-lovers, and so they will not be ready to pay levies."[1]

"Not at all good, that!"

"Very well, what about another thing which we have already condemned? They meddle in many businesses, the same people farmers and traders and fighters all at once under such a constitution; do you think that right?"

"By no manner of means."

"Just consider now; is not this constitution the first which admits the greatest of all these evil things?"

"What do you mean?"

"That a man may sell all his goods, and another may get hold of them, and the seller may go on living in the city when he is no part of it at all, neither trader nor craftsman, neither horse soldier nor foot soldier, but simply dubbed pauper and destitute."

"Yes, this is the first," said he; "certainly nothing is done to prevent it in oligarchic states, or else some people would not be extremely rich and others utter paupers."

"Quite right. Look here again. When such a man was rich and spent his money, was he of any more use then to the city for what we spoke of just now? He was thought then one of the governing class, but isn't it the truth that he was neither governor nor servant of the city, but only a consumer of stores?"

"Exactly," said he; "he was nothing but a consumer, whatever he was thought!"

"Then, if you please," I said, "we will call him a drone in the home, where he is produced to be a plague to the city, as a drone in the honeycomb is a plague to the hive!"

"Excellent, Socrates!" he said.

"All drones with wings, my dear Adeimantos," I said, "God has made without stings; but some of these drones with two legs have terrible stings, although some have none. Those who reach old age at last as beggars come from the stingless ones; all the people called criminal come from the stinging ones."

"Most true," he said.

"It is clear, then," said I, "that wherever you see beggars in any city, you may be sure that hidden somewhere not far

[1] E.g., for hiring mercenary troops.

off are thieves and cutpurses and sacrilegious persons, and craftsmen of all crimes of that sort."

"Yes, that is clear," said he.

"Very well, then," said I, "don't you see beggars in oligarchical cities?"

"Nearly all are beggars," he said, "except the government."

"Then are we not to believe," I said, "that there are plenty of criminals in them with stings, whom the governors take great care to hold down by force?"

"We must certainly believe that."

"Shall we say, then, that the reason why such creatures are produced there is lack of education and bad nurture and a bad constitution of the state?"

"Yes."

"Very well, then; such would be the oligarchic state, and such the evils in it, perhaps even more."

"Something like that," said he.

"So much then," said I, "for this constitution called oligarchy, which chooses its rulers according to property. Now let us examine the man who is like this city, and ask how he is produced and what his character is."

"By all means," he said.

"First, perhaps, I may suggest how our timocratic man changes into the oligarchic."

"How?"

"When a son is born to the timocratic man, he first imitates his father and follows in his footsteps. Then he sees him suddenly wrecked against the state like a ship on a sunken reef, and himself and his cargo washed overboard; he may have been at the head of an army or in some other great post and then thrown into the law court, ruined by false informers, and put to death, or banished, or outlawed and all his estate confiscated."

"That is likely enough," said he.

"And when the young man sees this, my friend, after such an experience, and being robbed of all he had, he kicks out that love of honour and that high spirit from his soul's throne head over heels; he is humbled by poverty and turns greedily to trading, and, little by little, by miserly savings and hard work he collects money. Don't you suppose such a man will then seat upon that empty throne Coveting and Greed, and will make a Great Mogul within himself, crowned with tiaras, collars about its neck and scimitars at its sides?"

"That I do!" said he.

"And beneath, I suppose, he will put, squatting on the floor like a couple of slaves, Reasoning on the right and Passion on the left; and to reasoning he allows no other task than to calculate how less money shall be made into more, and passion may admire nothing and honour nothing but riches and the rich, and be ambitious for no single thing in the world but getting money and whatever leads to that."

"Ah, yes," he said, "no change is so swift and sure as from love of honour to love of money for the young man."

"Then," said I, "is this the oligarchic man?"

"At least his change is from a man like the constitution whence the oligarchy came."

"Let us consider, then, if he would be like it himself."

"Very good," said he.

"Firstly, then, he would be like in prizing money most highly?"

"Of course."

"And further, in being parsimonious and hard-working, in fulfilling only the necessary desires of his household, and refusing all other expenditure, and enslaving his other desires as vain."

"Certainly."

"A shabby creature," said I, "and a hoarder, making profit from everything. Those are the ones the multitude praises. Would not such be the man who is like such a constitution?"

"Yes, at least I think so," he said; "at least money is chiefly honoured both by the city and by such a man."

"Oh, yes," I said, "and that, I think, is because he has not attended to education."

"So I think," he said, "or else he would not have put a 'blind-eyes'[1] to lead the dance and thus chiefly honoured him."

"Good!" said I. "But consider this. May we not suppose that dronish desires come up in him because of this lack of education, some beggarly and some criminal, which are restrained forcibly by his general carefulness?"

"Undoubtedly," said he.

"And do you know where to look in order to discover the criminal acts of those men?"

"Where?" he asked.

"Guardianships of orphans, if they ever get such a thing, because these allow ample freedom to act unjustly."

"True."

"This makes it clear then, that in his other contracts where he has won a good name for seeming honest dealing, he is using force, but this time a sort of decent force, upon himself, to restrain other evil desires which are within him; he does not persuade them that 'it is better not,' nor tame them

[1] Plutus, god of riches (Gr. *ploutos*), was depicted as blind.

THE REPUBLIC Book VIII (553D–555B)

by reasons, but does it by compulsion and terror, trembling for his other property."

"Exactly so," said he.

"And I do declare, my friend," said I, "that whenever they have to pay out the money of others, you will find in most of them desires akin to the drone."

"I agree heartily."

"Then he would not be without faction within himself; he is not one, but a kind of double creature, with desires overpowering desires, the better overpowering the worse, on the whole."

"That is true."

"This, you see, is the reason why such a man would make a better outside show than many, but true virtue would flee afar from him—that comes when the soul is in concord and one with itself."

"So I think."

"But the thrifty man would be a feeble competitor in person against his fellow-citizens, for victory in the games or any other fine ambition; he would be unwilling to spend money for a fine name and such competitions, he fears to excite the spending desires if he summons them to be allies in his desire for victory, and so he brings only a few[1] parts of himself into the war, and like an oligarch loses most of his fights and keeps his riches."

"Just so," said he.

"Then have we any doubt left," said I, "that there is a likeness and correspondence between the thrifty money-maker and the oligarchic city?"

"None at all," said he.

"Democracy,[2] then, as it seems, is the next thing to examine: how it arises, and what character it has. Then again we may observe the character of that kind of man and parade him for comparison."

"That, at least, would be our usual method of procedure," said he.

"Well then," said I, "the oligarchy changes into a democracy something in this way: through its insatiate desire for that which it sets before itself as a good and a duty—to become as rich as possible."

"How do you mean?"

"The rulers hold their position, I take it, because of their great possessions; and they will not make laws against un-

[1] *oligois*.
[2] Used in the sense of rule by a city's whole free male people, where all adult men are members of parliament, and attend it in person, and give their votes there. Modern democracy would not be democracy to a Greek of ancient times.

disciplined young men to prevent any who may turn up from running through their fortunes. They hope to lend money on the property of such men, and then buy it up, and so to become richer and more honourable than ever."

"Only too true!"

"Well, we have already clearly seen that to honour riches, and at the same time to acquire enough temperance, is a thing impossible for the citizens in a city; they must of necessity neglect one of the two."

"That is pretty clear," said he.

"So in the oligarchies by overlooking or even encouraging intemperance, they have sometimes compelled men not ignoble to become paupers."

"Very true indeed."

"And there they sit idle, I suppose, in the city, stings ready—that is, fully armed; some in debt, some disfranchised, some both, hating and plotting against those who have gotten their goods and everybody else, in love with revolution."

"That is true."

"And there are the moneymakers, stooping as they go and pretending not to see them; when any of the others submits, they wound him with a shot of money and carry off multiplicated interest, the offspring of the parent loan, and so they fill the city with drones and beggars."

"Yes indeed!" said he.

"Here is a fire of evil," said I, "blazing up, which they do not want to quench, although they could in two ways: one is what I suggested, by preventing a man from turning his property to any purpose he likes; the other is this—by doing away with such evils by a different law."

"And what is that other law?"

"The next best law, one that compels the citizens to care for virtue. For if it laid down that in most of the voluntary contracts a man must act on his own risk, people in the city would not be so shameless in their dealings, and not so many of those evils we have mentioned would come up at all."

"Far fewer," he said.

"But as things are," I said, "and for all such reasons, you see what a state the rulers have brought the ruled into; and as to themselves and their sons, are not the young people luxurious and lazy in matters concerning both body and soul? Are they not too soft to stand firm before both pleasures and pains, and idle?"

"Of course."

"And themselves—are they not careless of all else but

THE REPUBLIC Book VIII (555C–557B)

making money, and do they not care no more for virtue than the poor do?"

"No more, indeed."

"So when, thus prepared, rulers and ruled are thrown together, on the march perhaps or in some other association, whether for festival or campaign, shipmates or tentmates, or even amidst the dangers of battle, then they can observe each other, and then the poor are not despised by the rich at all! Often enough a sinewy, sun-browned poor man may be posted in battle beside a rich man fostered in shady places, encumbered with alien fat, and sees him panting and helpless. Don't you suppose he reflects that his own cowardice has allowed such men to be rich? Will not one pass the word to another, when they meet together in private, 'We've got the fellows! There's nothing in them!' "

"I'm quite sure," said he, "that's what they do!"

"You know that an unhealthy body needs only to have a small push from without to make it fall ill, and sometimes even without that the body rebels against itself: just so a city which is in the same state as that body needs only a small excuse; if one party invites outside help from some oligarchic city, or another from a democratic city, it falls ill in the same way and fights against itself, or sometimes even without those outside develops internal strife."

"Only too true."

"So democracy, I suppose, comes into being when the poor conquer, and kill some of the other party and banish others, and share out the citizenship and government equally with the rest; and the offices in it are generally settled by lot." [1]

"Yes," he said, "that is how democracy is established, whether by force of arms, or by fear, as when the other party go out and escape."

"Well, then," I said, "how do these people live? And how does this constitution also work? For it is clear that such a man will prove to be the democratic."

"That is clear," said he.

"First of all, then, they are free men; the city is full of freedom and liberty of speech, and men in it may do what they like."

"So it is said, at least," he replied.

"Where there is liberty of action, it is clear that each man would arrange his own private life in it just as it pleased him."

"Yes, that is clear."

"Consequently, I suppose, all varieties of men would be

[1] As they were in Athens.

produced under this system more than anywhere else."

"Of course."

"In fact," I said, "this is the most beautiful of constitutions. It is decked out with all sorts and conditions of manners, as a robe of many colours is embroidered with all the flowers of the field, and what could be more beautiful! Yes, perhaps," I went on, "many would judge it most beautiful, staring at it like a lot of women and children admiring a pretty frock!"

"Yes, indeed," said he.

"Yes indeed, bless you!" said I, "this is the city in which to look for a constitution."

"Why, if you please?"

"Because of this liberty! All sorts of constitutions are there; and if anyone wants to fit up a city, as we have been doing, it is only necessary for him to go to a city governed by a democracy, and choose whatever fashion of constitution pleases him, as if he had come to a bazaar of constitutions; then, having picked out his pattern, he can make his city accordingly."

"Perhaps at least," he said, "there would be plenty of patterns there."

"No necessity to be governor there," said I, "even if you are fit for it, no need to be ruled if you don't like it; you need not go to war if they fight, you need not keep the peace if the others keep it, unless you desire peace; if a law forbids you to be a magistrate or a judge, you may be magistrate and judge all the same if you take it into your head—what a lovely, heavenly life, while it lasts!"

"Yes, while it lasts," he said.

"And what a sweet temper there is in the convicts! Isn't it delightful? Haven't you seen in such a city nothing less than men condemned to death or banishment calmly remaining and mixing in society; and how a man can go about like a hero returned from the dead, nobody noticing him or seeing him?"

"I've seen that often enough," he said.

"Toleration! No worrying in democracy about a trifle! What contempt of the solemn proclamations we made in founding our city, that no one could become a good man unless he had a superlative nature—unless from a boy he should play among beautiful things and study beautiful practices! How magnificently it tramples all this underfoot, and cares nothing what he practises before entering and living political life, but gives him honour if he only says he is loyal to the people!"[1]

[1] All the Greek votes of thanks recorded in the inscriptions make particular mention of "loyalty to the people," and the orators appeal to their juries for this.

"What a noble constitution!" he exclaimed.

"These things, then," I said, "and other such like them are in democracy; a delightful constitution it would be, as it seems: no governor and plenty of colour; equality of a sort, distributed to equal and unequal alike."

"Oh yes, we know all that," said he.

"Now," said I, "look and see what kind of man corresponds in private character. Shall we begin as we did with the constitution, and ask how he is produced?"

"Yes," said he.

"Well, then, surely, in this way. The thrifty oligarchic man would have a son, I suppose, brought up under his father in his father's manners."

"Of course."

"But he, like his father, rules his own pleasures by force, those of them which are called unnecessary, those which cause spending and are not moneymaking."

"Clearly," said he.

"Now don't let us talk in the dark; suppose we first explain what we mean by desires necessary and not necessary."

"I am quite willing," said he.

"Then would it not be right to call those necessary which we cannot turn away, and those which benefit us when fulfilled? For it is plain necessity that we reach after both by our very nature. Don't you think so?"

"Certainly I do."

"Then we shall be right in giving these the title necessary."

"We shall."

"Very good. Those which a man could get rid of if he trained himself to do it from youth up, which also do no good by being in him—indeed some do harm—we should be right in saying that all these are unnecessary, shouldn't we?"

"Quite right."

"Suppose we take an example of each class to get a general notion."

"So we should."

"Then the desire of eating would be a necessary one, the desire for simple bread and meat,[1] enough for health and vigour."

"So I think."

"The desire for bread is necessary on both counts, both because bread is beneficial and because a living man cannot suppress the desire for it."

"Yes."

---

[1] The word ὄψον properly means relish, usually meat or fish, eaten with bread.

"And the desire for meat, if it provides any help towards vigour."

"By all means."

"Very well. And we might fairly name any further desire unnecessary, a desire for other viands than those we have mentioned, one that can be corrected and trained from youth and can be got rid of by most people, which does harm to the body and harm to the soul as regards wisdom and temperance."

"Most rightly, indeed."

"And may we not call these desires spending desires, and the others moneymaking because they are useful in production?"

"Certainly."

"We will say the same of love-making and so forth."

"Just so."

"Well, didn't we name that fellow a drone just now, the one laden with such pleasures and desires and ruled by the unnecessary desires, and we called the one ruled by the necessary desires thrifty and oligarchic?"

"Sure enough we did."

"Now we just go back," said I, "and explain how the democratic man is produced. Here, it seems to me, is the usual way."

"What?"

"A young man brought up as we described, in parsimony and ignorance, gets a taste of the drones' honey, and finds himself among wild beasts fiery and dangerous, who are able to provide pleasures of every variety and complexity and condition; there you must see the beginning of his inward change from the oligarchic to the democratic."

"No doubt about that," said he.

"As the city then was changed by the alliance coming from without to assist one party within, like to assist like, so the young man changes by a crowd of desires from without coming to assist one of the parts within him, a crowd akin and alike."

"Undoubtedly."

"And if another alliance comes from somewhere to assist the oligarchic part in the man—from the father, perhaps, or others of the family, who warn and reproach him—then there is faction and anti-faction and a battle ensues within him against himself."

"To be sure."

"And sometimes, I suppose, the democratic part retreats before the oligarchic, some of the desires are destroyed, and some are banished; a little shame comes up in the young man's soul, and it is brought into order again."

"That does happen sometimes," he said.

"Then again, I take it, when the desires are banished others grow up unnoticed, through the father's lack of knowledge of right upbringing, and these become many and strong."

"Yes," he said, "at least that is what generally happens."

"Then they draw him back to the same associations, and they spawn secretly and breed a multitudinous brood."

"Yes, to be sure."

"So in the end, I think, they storm the fortress of the young man's soul, and they find it empty of learning and beautiful practices and without words of truth, which are indeed the best sentinels and guardians in the minds of men whom the gods love."

"By far the best," said he.

"Now liars and impostors, I suppose, false words and opinions, charge up and occupy the place of the others in such a man."

"So they do," said he. "So then the young man comes back among these lotos-eaters[1] and makes his home there openly; if any support comes from his family for the thrifty part of his soul, those bragging words bar up the gates of the royal castle in him, and will not let in even these allies, nor even receive any embassy of words from his older friends in private life. A battle follows, and they win; Shame they dub Silliness and cast it forth, a dishonoured outlaw; Temperance they dub Cowardice, trample it under foot and banish it; they persuade the man that moderation and decent spending are clownishness and vulgarity, and drive them out beyond the border by the help of a gang of unprofitable desires."

"Indeed they do!"

"And so having purged and swept clean of such things the soul of this man, who is now in their power and being initiated into their grand Mysteries,[2] they proceed at once to bring home again Violence and Anarchy and Licentiousness and Immodesty with a long train of attendants, resplendent with garlands about their heads; and they glorify them and call them by soft names—Violence is now Good Breeding, Anarchy is Liberty, Licentiousness is Magnificence, Immodesty is Courage. There," said I, "you see more or less how the young man who was being trained among necessary desires is led into the emancipation and release of unnecessary and unprofitable pleasures."

[1] Cf. *Odyssey* ix. 83 ff; 91 ff; Tennyson's *"Lotus-Eaters."*
[2] Alluding to the Eleusinian Mysteries, where the initiates were cleansed in the sea.

"And a very clear picture it is," he said.

"And so he lives, I think, after this, spending money and pains and study upon unnecessary pleasures no less than the necessary. But if he is fortunate and not too dissolute, if as he grows older the great riot abates a bit, he receives back again parts of the exiles, and does not yield himself wholly to the intruders; he carries on his pleasures, maintaining if you please a sort of equality among them; he gives over the rule of himself to any pleasure that comes along, as if it had gained that by lot[1]—until he has had enough, then to another again, without disrespect for any, but cherishing all equally."

"Quite so."

"And not a word of truth," I said, "does he receive into the fortress of his soul, he will not even let it into the guardhouse. If anyone tells him that some pleasures belong to beautiful and good desires, others to those which are vile; some he should practise and respect, others he should chasten and enslave—at all such warnings, he nods his head up[2] and says, 'Not at all, they are all equal, and to be respected equally.'"

"Exactly," says he, "that's what he does in such a state of things."

"And so," said I, "he spends his life, every day indulging the desire that comes along; now he drinks deep and tootles on the pipes, then again he drinks water and goes in for slimming; at times it is bodily exercise, at times idleness and complete carelessness, sometimes he makes a show of studying philosophy. Often he appears in politics, and jumps up to say and do whatever comes into his head. Perhaps the fame of a military man makes him envious, and he tries that; or a lord of finance—there he is again. There is no discipline or necessity in his life; but he calls it delightful and free and full of blessings, and follows it all his days."

"Upon my word," said he, "that's a lifelike picture of the man who is all for equal laws."

"So you see," said I, "this, I think, is a variegated man, full of all sorts of conditions and manners, this is the beautiful, many-coloured man exactly like that city, one whose life many a man and many a woman would envy, having in himself patterns innumerable of constitutions and characters."

"That's the man!" said he.

"Very well. Let such a man be ranked beside our democracy as the democratic man rightly so called."

"Yes, let him be ranked there!" said he.

"And now for the most beautiful constitution," said I, "and

[1] Alluding to the election of magistrates by lot in Athens.
[2] The Greek gesture for no; p. 236, n. 1.

the most beautiful man—that's what is left for us to describe, tyranny and the tyrant."

"Exactly so," said he.

"Tell me then, my dear friend, how does tyranny come about? Of course democracy changes into this, so much is clear enough."

"Quite clear."

"Then does tyranny come out of democracy more or less in the same way as democracy comes out of oligarchy?"

"How?"

"What they set before them as their good," said I, "and through which oligarchy was established—that was riches, wasn't it?"

"Yes."

"So, then, oligarchy was destroyed by the insatiate desire of riches, and disregard of everything else for the sake of moneymaking."

"True," said he. "Then is democracy also dissolved by insatiate desire for that which it defines as good?"

"What do you say it so defines?"

"Liberty," I said. "That, I suppose, you would always hear described as most beautiful in the democratic city, and therefore this is the only city where a man of free nature thinks life worth living."

"Oh yes," he said, "that word is on every tongue."

"Is it true then, as I was going to say, that the insatiate desire for this, and disregard of everything else, transforms the constitution here also and makes it want a tyranny?"

"How?" he asked.

"When a democratic city athirst for liberty gets worthless butlers presiding over its wine, and has drunk too deep of liberty's heady draught, then, I think, if the rulers are not very obliging and won't provide plenty of liberty, it calls them blackguards and oligarchs and chastises them."

"So they do," said he.

"Yes," I went on, "and any who obey the rulers they trample in the dust as willing slaves and not worth a jot; and rulers who are like subjects, and subjects who are like rulers, come in for the votes of thanks and the honours, public and private. In such a city must not your liberty go to all lengths?"

"Of course it must."

"And it must go creeping, my friend," said I, "into private houses too, and the end is, their anarchy even gets into the animals!"

"Why, how can that be?" he exclaimed.

"This is how," said I. "The father gets into the habit of

behaving like the son and fears his own children, the son behaves like a father, and does not honour or fear his parents, 'must have liberty' he says. Settler is equal to citizen and citizen to settler, the foreigner is the same."

"Yes, that's what happens," he said.

"And there are these other trifles too," I said. "Teacher fears pupil in such a state of things, and plays the toady; pupils despise their teachers and tutors, and in general, the young imitate their elders and stand up to them in word and deed. Old men give way to the young; they are all complaisance and wriggling, and behave like young men themselves so as not to be thought disagreeable or dictatorial."

"Just so," said he.

"And behold the topmost pinnacle!" said I. "Mob liberty can go no further in such a city, when slaves bought with money, both men and women, are no less free than the buyers! Ah, I almost forgot to tell how great equality and liberty there is between women and men, between men and women!"

"Shall we say what now cometh to our lips," he rejoined, "as Aeschylus put it?"[1]

"By all means," I said, "so I will. The domestic animals—how much more free-and-easy they are in a city like this than in others, no one would believe who had not seen it. There's really nothing to choose between missus and bitch, as the proverb goes.[2] Horses and asses, if you please, adopt the habit of marching along with the greatest freedom and haughtiness, bumping into everyone they meet who will not get out of the way; and all the other animals likewise are filled full of liberty."

"Oh, that's just my own dream come true!"[3] said the other. "That often happens to me when I'm going out into the country."

"To sum up," said I, "observe what comes of all these things together: how touchy it makes the people! They fret at the least hint of servitude, and won't have it; for at last, you know, they care nothing for the laws written or unwritten, that no one may be their master in anything."

"Oh yes, I know that," said he.

"This then, my friend," said I, "is the beginning from which tyranny grows, such a beautiful, bright beginning!"

"Bright and gay indeed," he said, "but what comes after that?"

"The same as in the oligarchy," said I; "the same disease which destroyed that gets in here, stronger and more violent

[1] In one of the lost plays.
[2] Literally, "the bitches become just like their mistresses."
[3] A proverb.

from this liberty, and enslaves democracy. And in fact that is what generally happens in the world. To do anything too much tends to take you to the opposite extreme, in weather and in plants and in living bodies, and so also in constitutions most of all."

"That is likely," said he.

"For too great liberty seems to change into nothing else than too great slavery, both in man and in city."

"Yes, that is likely."

"Then it is likely," said I, "that democracy is precisely the constitution out of which tyranny comes; from extreme liberty, it seems, comes a slavery most complete and most cruel."

"Yes," he said, "there is reason in that."

"But I think that is not what you asked about," I said; "you asked what kind of disease it was which grows up the same both in oligarchy and in democracy, and enslaves democracy."

"True," said he.

"Well, then," I said, "what I meant was that class of idle and extravagant men, of which the most manly part leads and the most unmanly part follows. You remember we likened them to drones, some with stings and some without."

"And quite right, too," said he.

"These two, then," said I, "make a mess of every constitution they get into, like hot phlegm and cold gall in the body; the good physician must beware of them both in good time, and so must the good lawgiver in the city, no less than the skilful beemaster. It is best not to let them get in at all; but if they do, cut them out, honeycombs and all."

"The very thing," said he, "the whole lot of them."

"Then let us take it in this way," said I, "so that we may see what we want more clearly."

"How, pray?"

"Let us assume that a democratic city is made up of three parts, as it really is. One, a class such as we have described, grows here because of democratic licence, no less than in the oligarchic city."

"That is true."

"And indeed much fiercer here than there."

"How so?"

"There they get no training and gather no strength, because they are excluded from the government as being held in no honour; but in democracy this is the dominant class, all but a few. The fiercest part of them talk and act while the others swarm round the platform and buzz; they never tolerate anyone who speaks on the other side, so that all business of state is managed by this class, with a few exceptions."

"Exactly," he said.

"Another class, besides, is always being separated from the mass."

"What class?"

"When all are busy in making money, the most orderly by nature, I suppose, generally become richest."

"That is likely."

"From them, I think, comes the most honey for the drones, and they are most easy to squeeze."

"Of course," he said; "how could one squeeze it out of those that have little?"

" 'The rich' is the name they go by, you see, drones' fodder."

"Pretty nearly," he said.

" 'People' will be the name of the third class; all who are handiworkers and outside politics, without much property of their own. This is the largest and most sovereign class in democracy, when it combines."

"So it is," he said, "but it does not often care to combine unless it can get a bit of the honey."

"Well, it does get a bit from time to time," I said, "depending on the ability of the presidents, in taking the property away from those who have it and distributing it among the people, to keep most of it themselves."

"Yes, it gets a share to that extent," he said.

"So those whom they plunder have to defend themselves, I suppose, by speaking before the people and taking action in what way they can."

"Of course."

"And so they are accused by the other party of plotting against the people, even if they have no wish to revolt, and they are said to be reactionary oligarchs."

"To be sure."

"In the end, when they see the people, ignorant and completely deceived by the false accusers, trying recklessly to do them wrong, then at last willy-nilly they become truly oligarchic, not willingly, but this evil thing also is put in them by that drone stinging them."

"Exactly so."

"Then come impeachments and sentences and lawsuits between them."

"Yes, indeed."

"So the common people will always put up for itself some special protector,[1] whom it supports and magnifies?"

"Yes, that's its way."

[1] "Protector of the people" was a recognised title of the leading demagogue. Pericles himself had it. Cromwell assumed it.

"One thing is clear then," I said, "that when a tyrant appears, he grows simply and solely from a protectorship as the root."

"That is quite clear."

"Then what is the beginning of this change from protector to tyrant? Isn't it when the protector begins to do like the man in the fable about the temple of Lycaian Zeus in Arcadia?"

"What fable?" he asked.

"That whoever tasted the one bit of human entrails minced up with all the sacrificial meat must be changed into a wolf. Haven't you heard the story?"

"I have."

"This is just the same. When the Protector of the People finds a very obedient mob; when he will not abstain from shedding tribal blood; when he drags someone into court by the usual unjust accusations, and incurs bloodguilt by destroying the life of a man; when, with unholy mouth and tongue, he tastes a kinsman's gore; when he banishes and executes, when he hints at abolition of debts and partition of estates—surely for such a one the necessity is ordained that he must either perish at the hands of his enemies, or become a tyrant, and be a wolf instead of a man?"

"Such must be his fate of necessity," said he.

"That is the man then," said I, "who comes to lead a party against those who possess property."

"That's the man," said he.

"He may be banished then, and return in despite of his enemies a tyrant finished and complete?"

"That is clear."

"And if they are unable to banish him, or to accomplish his death by setting the mind of the city against him, they may plot violent death for him in secret?"

"At least that often happens," he said.

"And to prevent this those who get so far always hit on the tyrant's notorious plea—they beg the people to give them a bodyguard, in order that the people's champion may be kept safe for themselves."

"They do indeed," said he.

"So the people grant the bodyguard; fearing for him, I suppose, but quite easy about themselves."

"Exactly."

"And when a man sees this who has money and with his money the repute of being a people-hater, then my friend, that man thinks of the oracle given to Crœsus;[1] and

[1] Herodotus, I, 55.

> Along the pebbly Hermos
> He flees, he does not wait, he has no shame
> To be a coward."

"Not he!" said the other. "He would have no second chance to be ashamed."

"And anyone caught," I said, "would be done to death."

"Naturally."

"Meanwhile your Protector himself does not lie low, grand in his grandeur,[1] at all; no, he knocks down crowds of others and stands towering in the coach of state, Protector no longer but Tyrant finished and complete."

"That's a matter of course," he said.

"Now suppose we describe the happiness," said I, "happiness of man and city, in which such a creature would make his appearance."

"By all means," he said, "let us describe that."

"Well, then," I said, "at first, in the early days, he greets everyone he meets with a broad smile; says he is no tyrant, and promises all sorts of things in private and in public, frees them from their debts and parcels out the land to the people and to those about him, pretends to be gracious and friendly to all the world."

"He has to do it," said he.

"As to outside enemies, when he has made terms with some and destroyed others, I take it, and when all is quiet from that source, he is forever stirring up some war in order that the people may want a leader."

"That is likely."

"And, moreover, in order that they may become poor by having to pay taxes, and stick to their daily round, and be less likely to plot against him."

"That's clear."

"And if he suspects that any harbour a free spirit and will not endure his rule, he wants an excuse to destroy them by exposing them to the enemy. For all these reasons the tyrant must always be stirring up war."

"So he must."

"Then by doing this he becomes more and more detestable to the citizens."

"Of course."

"You may expect that some of those who helped to set him up, the bravest of them, being now in power themselves, will speak freely before him and among themselves, and reproach him with what is happening."

"Quite likely."

[1] *Iliad* xvi. 776 and elsewhere.

"So he must quietly get rid of all these if he is to rule, until not a single one is left, either friend or foe, who is of any use."

"That is clear."

"He must look sharp to see, then, who is brave, who is magnanimous, who is prudent, who rich; and so happy and fortunate he is that he is bound to be enemy to all these whether he likes it or not, and to scheme against them until he has purged the city."

"A fine purge that!" said he.

"Yes," I said, "the opposite of what doctors do for the body; they clear away the worst and leave the best; he does just the opposite."

"He can't help it, as it seems," said he, "if he is to remain ruler."

"And so a blessed necessity binds him," said I, "which commands him to have worthless creatures about him for the most part, and to be hated by them too, or else to live no longer."

"Blessed indeed," said he.

"Consequently, the more the citizens detest him for doing this, the more bodyguards he will need and the more trusty."

"Of course."

"Well, who are his trusty guards, and where will he find them?"

"They will come of themselves," he said, "plenty of them, on wings of the wind, if he pays their wages."

"Drones!" I said. "Drones, by the Dog! That is what you seem to mean again, mercenaries from anywhere."

"True," said he, "that's what I mean."

"What!" I asked, "no recruits from home? Won't he want—"

"Whom?"

—"the slaves; he will take them from the citizens, and set them free, and add them to the bodyguard about his person."

"Sure enough," he said, "those will be the most trusty of all."

"Oh, what a blessed thing is your tyrant!" I exclaimed.

"What friends he has, what men he trusts, now that he has destroyed that first lot!"

"Yes truly," he said, "those are the kind of men he has."

"And these comrades even admire him," I said, "and the new citizens are his companions; but the decent ones hate him and flee!"

"They are sure to do it."

"There must be good reason," I said, "why most people think that tragedy is full of wisdom and Euripides is at the head of it."

"Why so, pray?"

"Here is one of his pronouncements, typical of his profound thought,

> Tyrants are wise by company with the wise.[1]

He meant of course that those are wise whom they keep company with."

"Yes," he said, "and often Euripides lauds the tyrant as a ruler like God in heaven,[2] and many such things he said; so do the other poets."

"Therefore," said I, "the tragic poets, being wise men, will see some excuse for us, and for those who have politics rather like ours, when we refuse to receive them into the city as singing the praises of tyranny."

"I think they will," said he, "all that are agreeable men."

"And there they go, I think, all round the cities, collecting the people into crowds; they hire lovely, loud, persuasive voices and drag the cities over to tyrannies and democracies."

"Exactly so."

"And, besides, they get rewards and honour for this, chiefly from tyrants, as you might expect, secondly also from democracy; but the higher they ascend the steps of Mount Constitution, the more their honour fails, as if it could go no further for want of breath."

"Just so."

"But here we have digressed," I said. "Let us go back to the tyrant's army, so fine and large and variegated, always changing, and ask how it is to be fed."

"It is clear," he said, "that if there are any temple treasures in the city, he will spend these, and the goods of his victims as far as they will go; so the people will not have to contribute so much."

"And what when these fail?"

"It is clear," said he, "he will use his own father's property to maintain himself and his boon-companions and his boy friends and girl friends."

"I understand," said I; "you mean that the people who begat this tyrant will feed him and his companions."

"That is plain necessity," said he.

"But look here," I said. "What if the people objects, and says that 'a grownup son cannot fairly ask his father to keep him, but the opposite—the son ought to keep the father! And he didn't beget the brat and set him on his feet only to be a slave to his own slaves when the boy grew up, and have to support

---

[1] This is attributed also to Sophocles. The poet meant that tyrants learn wisdom from the wise men who frequent their courts, where literary men, at least, were often seen.
[2] Euripides, *Troades*, 1169.

the boy himself and the slaves along with a rabble of foreigners. He meant, with his son as Protector, to get free from the rich and the "gentlemen," as they are called in the city. Now he is telling him to get out of the city with his companions, like a father turning a son out of doors with a drunken company who are making themselves a nuisance.'"

"Ah, then the people will find out, by God," said he, "just what they are, and what a monster they have bred, and nursed in their bosom, and raised to greatness; and that they, the weaker, are now talking of throwing out the stronger!"

"What's that you say?" I exclaimed. "Will the tyrant dare to use violence against his father, and thrash him if he won't obey?"

"Yes," said he, "after taking away his arms."

"Patricide!" I said. "That's what you call a tyrant, and a cruel neglecter of aged parents. We have tyranny here unconcealed, the people will run from the smoke into the fire, as the proverb goes, from slavery under free men into despotism under slaves. That perfect and unseasonable liberty has been exchanged for a new dress, the most cruel and most bitter slavery under slaves."

"Yes, indeed," said he, "that is exactly what happens."

"Very well, then," I said. "Have we sufficiently explained how democracy changes into tyranny, and, when tyranny has come, what its character is? Can we say yes with confidence?"

"We can," said he; "it is quite sufficient."

BOOK IX

"What is left now to examine," said I, "is the tyrannic[1] man himself: how he arises out of the democratic, and what his character is, and how he lives, whether wretched or in bliss."

"Yes, he is still left," said the other.

"But still," I said, "there is something I miss."

"What is that?"

"The desires: what are they, and how many. I don't think we have defined them properly; our enquiry will not be clear enough if we leave that unfinished."

"Isn't this still a good opportunity?" he asked.

"Yes, by all means. See here, this is what I want to look into about them. I feel that some of the unnecessary desires and pleasures are lawless; they are born in everyone, it is true, but when they are chastened by the laws and the better desires

[1] By a tyrant the ancient Greeks meant a man who made himself absolute ruler by usurpation and used force to maintain his position.

with reason's help, some people can get rid of them wholly, or only a few remain and weak, although in others they are more and stronger."

"What are these, pray?" he asked.

"Those which are aroused in sleep," said I, "whenever the rest of the soul, all the reasonable, gentle and ruling part, is asleep, but the bestial and savage, replete with food or wine, skips about and, throwing off sleep, tries to go and fulfil its own instincts. You know there is nothing it will not dare to do, thus freed and rid of all shame and reason; it shrinks not from attempting in fancy to lie with a mother, or with any other man or god or beast, shrinks from no bloodshed, refrains from no food—in a word, leaves no folly or shamelessness untried."

"Only too true," he said.

"But I think that anyone healthy and temperate in himself, before going to sleep, should arouse his reasoning part, and feast it with beautiful sayings and meditations and search out his own inmost thoughts; he should neither starve his desiring part nor stuff it full, that it may rest, and may not with its joys or sorrows disturb the best part; whenever he does that, he allows the best part to remain pure and self-contained, to ponder and to reach after something, to perceive something which he did not know, past or present or future. In the same way he tames the passionate part, he does not fly into a rage with someone just before going to sleep, so as to have his temper stirred; but he has quieted these two parts, and stirred up the third in which reason is native. When he thus takes his rest, you know that in such a state of soul he touches truth most nearly, and the visions of his dreams are least likely to be lawless."

"I am wholly with you," said he.

"Well, we have really gone out of our way in saying these things; but what we want to notice is this, what a dreadful savage lawless brood of desires is in everyone, even in some of us who are thought decent people; and these, it appears, are shown clearly in sleep. See if you think there is anything in what I say, and if you agree."

"Oh yes, I agree."

"Recall, then, what we said was the democratic man's character. He was produced, you remember, as the son of a thrifty father, and brought up from youth by him, a father who honoured the moneymaking desires alone, and despised the unnecessary ones, which exist only for pastime and finery. Is that correct?"

"Yes."

"Then, mixing in more fashionable society with men full of

THE REPUBLIC Book IX (571C–573C)

the desires we have just described, he rushed into riot of all kinds and behaviour after their style, through hatred of his father's parsimony; but his nature was better than his corruptors', and so, swinging to and fro, he settled in the middle between these two characters. Thus he enjoyed each, in what he thought moderation, if you please, and went on living a life neither lacking in freedom nor lawless. So the oligarchic became democratic."

"Yes," he said, "that was and is our opinion."

"Suppose then again," said I, "that when such a man grew older, he had a young son in his turn brought up in his ways."

"Very good."

"Suppose again that the same happens to this boy as to his father. He is led into complete lawlessness, which those leading him call complete liberty; his father and the rest of the family support these intermediate desires, but his leaders again support the other side. When these terrible magicians and tyrant-makers see no hope of holding the young man in any other way, they contrive to implant in him some passion to be the protector of his idle and spendthrift desires, a huge, winged drone; what else is the ruling passion in such men?"

"Nothing else," he said, "just that."

"Now the other desires come buzzing around the huge drone, laden with incense and perfumes and garlands and wines, and the dissolute pleasures which are found in such companies, magnifying and nursing him to the uttermost, and they implant in him a sting of unsatisfied craving; then this protector of the soul takes madness for his bodyguard and runs wild; if he finds any opinions or desires in himself accounted honest and modest, he slays them and casts them out of himself, until he has purged himself of temperance and filled himself with foreign frenzy."[1]

"Exactly so," said he, "that is how the tyrannic man is produced."

"Is this the reason," I asked, "why Love has of old been called a tyrant?"

"No doubt," he replied.

"And also," said I, "a drunken man has a sort of tyrannical spirit, hasn't he?"

"Yes, he has."

"And one who is mad and somewhat deranged in mind fancies that he can rule not men only but gods also, and does his best in that direction?"

"Undoubtedly," said he.

"Then here's a surprise for you, my friend: a man becomes

[1] Like foreign mercenaries in a city.

tyrannical in the exact sense, when he is drunken and lustful and insane, whether by nature or habit or both."

"Just so."

"Thus is he produced then, as it seems, and such is his character; but what is his life?"

"*You* had better tell *me* that," he replied, "as they say in the game."[1]

"Here goes, then," said I. "The next thing is, I suppose, there are feastings among them and revellings, festivities and pretty girls and all the rest of it, wherever Love the tyrant makes his home within and steers the soul according to his will!"

"That must be so," he said.

"How many dire desires do sprout up beside the tyrant Love every day and every night! How many things they want!"

"Very many indeed."

"The revenues, if there are any, are soon spent, then."

"Of course."

"Then come borrowings and levyings off the estate."

"Certainly."

"And when all these fail, what must happen now! What a deafening cackle of the chicks, the desires which have made their nests in him, thick and strong! And these men, driven and goaded by the other desires, and specially by Love itself, the leader, as it were, of all the others as bodyguards, run wild, and hunt for someone to rob of something by deceit or by violence!"

"Exactly," said he.

"Then they must lift spoil from anywhere and everywhere, or else be afflicted with great travails and pains."

"They must."

"He will do as the pleasures did. The pleasures sprang up in him and got the better of the old ones and robbed them of what they had; so he too will claim the right to have the better of father and mother, although he is younger than they are, and to rob them, taking pieces of his father's estate after he has spent his own share."

"What else would you expect?" said he.

"And if they will not put up with it, won't he try first to deceive his parents and to steal?"

"By all means."

"Whenever he fails to do that, he would proceed to rob with violence?"

"So I think," said he.

"And if the old man and old woman resist and fight, my

[1] A proverbial tag, for one who does not know the answer, if the questioner does.

worthy friend, what scruples will he have? Will he spare to do anything that a tyrant would do?"

"I don't feel quite happy," he said, about the parents of such a man."

"But in God's name, my dear Adeimantos!" I said, "do you think he would strike his own mother, so long dear and necessary to him, for the sake of some new darling not necessary at all, who has become his mistress? Would he strike his own father, an old man in his latter years, necessary to him and most ancient of all dear friends, for the sake of a pretty youth but newly his dear and not necessary at all? Would he make them both slaves and subject them to these others, bringing these into the same house?"

"Yes, by God!" said he.

"A most blessed thing it seems to be," said I, "to have a tyrannical son!"

"Yes, indeed!" said he.

"Then what will happen when such a man finds the goods of his parents beginning to fail him, and there is all that swarm of pleasures collected within him? Surely he will first get in touch with some house-wall,[1] or the cloak of someone walking about late at night, and then sweep clean a temple or so! And all the while the beliefs which he had from boyhood about what is beautiful and ugly, which were held to be right and just, will be mastered by those lately emancipated from slavery, aided by the ruling passion whose bodyguard they are—those that used to be let loose in the vision of sleep, when he was under law himself and under his father, still democratic in himself. But now under the tyranny of the ruling passion, he becomes always in broad daylight such as he used to be now and then in dreams; he will abstain from no dreadful deed, no murder, no forbidden food. That passion lives in him as a tyrant, sole sovereign alone with no government or law to restrain it; and so it will lead the man, whom it occupies like a conquered city, into every audacity by which it can support both itself and the racket of desires around it, partly introduced from without from evil company, and partly let loose at liberty from within by similar habits and by the tyrant passion itself. Is not this the life of such a man?"

"It is, indeed," said he. "And if there are only a few such in the city," I said, "and the rest of the people are temperate, out they go and bodyguard some other tyrant, or serve as his mercenaries if a war is going on somewhere; but if they appear when there is peace abroad and quiet at home, they stay there in the city and do no end of evil in small things."

[1] That is, break through as a burglar, or rob on the highway.

"What things?" he asked.

"They steal, they are burglars and cutpurses, they strip travellers, they rob temples, they kidnap; sometimes they blackmail and slander, if they are able speakers, bear false witness and take bribes."

"Oh yes," he said, "those evils are small, if such men are few."

"Indeed small things," I said, "are small only as compared with great things, and all these small crimes, you know, compared with a tyrant, in respect of the wickedness and wretchedness caused in a city, 'don't come anywhere near him in scope,' as the saying is. For, you see, when such men, with their followers, become numerous in a city, and when they perceive their own numbers, then with help of the people's folly these produce the tyrant; and he is just that man among them who has the tyrant in his own soul most mighty and prevailing."

"Very likely," said he, "for he would be the most tyrannical."

"Then if the people are willing to yield, well and good; but if not, he will treat the city as the man did mother and father: he will import new comrades and chastise it if he can; he will keep and maintain his own fatherland and once dear motherland, as the Cretans call it, in slavery under these foreigners. So this would be the final consummation of such a man's desire."

"So it would," said he, "no doubt about that."

"Well then," said I, "what is the private character of such men, as they show it even before they are rulers? Whom do they mix with? Either with flatterers who are ready to do anything for them; or if they want something, they themselves grovel and condescend to any grimaces of friendship—but when they have got what they want, they don't know you!"

"Exactly."

"So all their lives they are absolutely friendless, either slavemasters or slaves of someone; the tyrannic nature has never a taste of true freedom and friendship."

"Quite so."

"Then should we not be right in calling such men faithless?"

"Of course we should."

"And as unjust as unjust can be, if we were right in our former conclusions about the nature of justice."

"We were certainly right," said he.

"Then let us sum up the most evil character," I said. "He is, I take it, the man who would be living in broad daylight such as that man was in dreams."

"By all means."

THE REPUBLIC Book IX (575B–577B) 375

"Then this is what the man becomes, who is most tyrannic naturally and gains sole power, and the longer he lives as a tyrant the more like that he becomes."

"That is certain," said Glaucon, taking up the argument.

"Is it true, then," said I, "that whoever shall be proved most wicked will also be proved most miserable? And whoever is tyrant longest and most fully will be most and longest miserable in truth? There are many different opinions about this."

"So much at least," he said, "must certainly be true."

"Then surely," I said, "the tyrannical man would be in one likeness with the city under a tyrant, and the democratical man with the city under democracy, and so with all the others."

"Why, what else!"

"Then what city is to city as to virtue and happiness, that man is to man."

"Of course."

"And what, in respect of virtue, is a city under a tyrant compared with a city under a king as we first described it?"

"Exactly the opposite," he said: "for one is best, the other worst."

"I will not ask which is which," said I, "for that is clear. But in happiness or misery—do you judge in the same way, or not? And don't let us be dismayed by keeping our eyes on that one man, the tyrant, or the few he may have about him; we must dive into every part of the city and see it as a whole, and then give our opinion."

"A fair challenge," he said; "everyone can see that no city is more miserable than under a tyrant, and none happier than under a king."

"Very good," said I; "then in comparing the two men it would be a fair challenge, in the same way, if I asked that the judge should be one who can dive deep into human nature and understand it in his mind; he must not be, like a boy, dismayed by the sight of the tyrannical façade, by the pomp which they display outside, but he must see through that and properly understand. Could I fairly think that we all must listen to him—one not only able to judge but who also has lived under one roof with the man, has been by his side and seen his doings at home, how he behaves before the members of his household one and all, those who could best see him naked of stage costume, or again has seen him in public perils? Could we fairly call on one such who had seen all this and bid him declare how the tyrant compares with others in happiness or misery?"

"Nothing could be fairer than that," he said.

"Then may we pretend," I said, "that we are of those who

would be able to judge and have already mingled with such men, in order that we may have someone to answer our questions?"

"By all means."

"Come along, then," said I, "just consider it in this way. Remember the likeness between city and man, and examine everything in turn, and tell me what happens to each of these two."

"What happens?" he asked.

"First of all," said I, "take the city: Will you call it free or enslaved under a tyrant?"

"The most slavish of slaves," he said.

"However, you do see slavemasters and free men in it."

"I do," he said, "just a small number; but in that city the whole in general is in slavery, and the most decent part of it is in dishonour and misery."

"Then if man is like city," I said, "there must be the same arrangement in him; his soul must be laden full of slavery and ungenerousness, and those parts of the soul which were most decent are enslaved, but the small part most mad and abominable is master."

"That must be so," he said.

"Well, will you say such a soul is free or slave?"

"Slave, surely, that is what I think."

"Very good. The city which is a slave under the tyrant least of all does what it wishes?"

"Decidedly."

"So also the soul under tyranny least of all will do what it wishes, to speak of the soul as a whole; but it is always that gadfly drives it violently about, and it is full of confusion and repentance."

"Of course it is."

"Rich or poor—which must the city be under a tyrant?"

"Poor."

"Then the tyrant soul must also be poverty-stricken and even unsatisfied."

"So it must," said he.

"Again then, must not such a city and such a man be laden full of fear?"

"Yes, indeed."

"Lamentations and groanings, dirges and anguish—do you think you will find more in any other city?"

"By no means!"

"And in the man—who else do you think will have such things more in him than the one maddened by desires and passions, this man of tyranny?"

"Who else indeed!"

"Then as to the city, with these considerations and others of this sort in view, you judged it most miserable of all cities."

"And rightly so, don't you agree?" said he.

"Most rightly," said I; "but the tyrannical man[1]—what say you of him, with regard to the same things?"

"Most miserable of all men by far," said he, "that is what I say."

"Ah no," said I, "you are no longer right there."

"How so?" he asked.

"You have not yet found the most miserable of all," I said.

"Why, who else could be?"

"Here is someone perhaps that you will consider more miserable still."

"Who is he?"

"The tyrannical man," said I, "who does not live a private life, but has a bad piece of luck: if some chance provides for him so that he becomes a tyrant himself."

"I infer from what has been previously said," he replied, "that you speak truth."

"Yes," I said; "but such things ought not to be a matter of opinion; we must thoroughly examine them by continuing our reasoning. For this is in truth the supreme question, the good and the evil life."

"Quite right," said he.

"Then consider," said I; "see if there is some reason in what I have to say. I think we ought to get some notion about the man from examining certain persons."

"What persons?"

"Each and any of the private citizens who are rich and possess many slaves. For these are like tyrants, in having many to rule; the difference is—a tyrant has the numbers."

"Quite so, that is the difference."

"You understand that these are in security and do not fear their household servants."

"Of course—what could they fear?"

"Nothing," I said, "but do you understand why?"

"Yes," he said, "because the whole state is ready to help each one of the private persons."

"You are quite right," I said. "Very well, then: Take one man with fifty or more slaves, and suppose a god from heaven should pick him up out of the city, wife and children and all, and set him down with his servants and all his other possessions in a desert where none of the free men could

[1] The man under the tyranny of his passions.

help him, what consternation would be his! How fearful he would be for himself and his wife and children, lest all might be destroyed by the servants!"

"I should think he would," said he, "exceedingly."

"Wouldn't he be obliged to wheedle some of the slaves themselves, and make them many promises and even undertake to set them free, when he did not wish to? Would he not stand forth as flatterer of his own servants?"

"He couldn't help it," said he, "if he wanted to remain alive."

"Next suppose," I said, "that the god planted a lot of neighbours about him, who would never allow any one man to claim to be master of another, but if they caught one trying to do that would punish him with the extreme penalty?"

"He would be altogether worse off still, I think," said the other, "with only enemies all round him on guard."

"And is not that the sort of prison where the tyrant lies in chains? His nature is what we have described, and he is filled with all manner of terrors and passions; dainty and greedy of soul, he alone of all in the city may never travel abroad or see any of the sacred festivities which other free men desire to see, but he lives for the most part entombed in his own house like a woman, and envies the other citizens if someone goes abroad and sees anything good!"

"Yes, that is his life exactly," said he.

"Is not, then, the harvest of evils much greater for that man to reap who has an evil constitution in himself, the tyrannical man whom you have just judged to be most miserable, if he does not live out his life as a private person, but if he is compelled by some chance to be tyrant himself, and tries to rule others when he cannot be master of himself? It is just as if one sickly in body, and so not master of himself, should be compelled to live his life not in private but always contending with other bodies, at war his whole life long."

"Most assuredly, Socrates," he said, "they are exactly alike, it is quite true."

"Then, my dear Glaucon," said I, "his whole condition is absolutely miserable, and the tyrant lives more wretchedly than the one whom you judged most wretched."

"There's no doubt of it," said he.

"So in very truth, whatever anyone may think, the real tyrant is a real slave to all coaxings and slaveries of the basest; he must flatter the most worthless of mankind, and never can satisfy his own desires in the least; no, he stands in direst need of most things, and turns out to be truly a pauper, if one knows how to estimate the soul as a whole;

all his life laden with fear he is full of spasms and pains, if his condition indeed is like the city he rules—and he is like it, isn't he?"

"Very much like it indeed," said he.

"And in addition we will also grant the man all that we mentioned before—namely, he must of necessity be, and become, because of his rule, more than ever envious, faithless, unjust, friendless, wicked, the universal innkeeper and fosterfather of all the vices. So for all these reasons, he must be most wretched himself, and make those about him wretched."

"No one with sense in his head will deny that," he replied.

"Here you are, then, Glaucon," said I, "like the final judge in musical contests;[1] you can give the deciding vote who is first in your opinion in happiness, and who second, and so on, among the five men—royal, timocratic, oligarchic, democratic, tyrannic."

"Oh, that decision is easy," said he: "I judge them in order as they come on the stage, like choruses, for virtue or vice, and for happiness or unhappiness."

"Let's hire a herald then," said I, "or I'll do it myself. Oyez! Mr. Bestmanson[2] has judged as Happiest: the best and justest man, and that same is the most wholly royal man, who reigns king of himself. And he has judged as Most Miserable: the most wicked and unjust man, and that same is he who, most tyrannical in himself, is most completely tyrant both over himself and over the city."

"Take that as your proclamation," said he.

"Shall I add," I said, "to my proclamation, 'This holds good whether all earth and heaven know them to be such, or whether they do not'?"

"Pray add that to the proclamation," he said.

"Very good," said I. "This would be one of our proofs;[3] now see whether there seems to be anything in our second."

"What is that?"

"Since just as the city," said I, "has been divided into three classes, and thus also the soul of each person is divided in three parts,[4] it seems to me the soul will provide a way for a second proof."

"What, if you please?"

"Listen. These three parts have three pleasures, as it appears to me, one peculiar to each, and three desires and governances likewise."

---

[1] There was an elaborate system of judging in the contests of drama and music and dance. The victor's name was solemnly proclaimed by a herald.
[2] "Son of Ariston" (best). Glaucon's father's name was Ariston. Plato puns on the name. Cf. p. 164, n. 2.
[3] Of the proposition that the just man is the happiest and most fortunate.
[4] See pp. 239-241.

"What do you mean?" he asked.

"One part, we say, was that by which a man learns, one by which he is angry and spirited; the third has many forms, and we could not give it a proper name of its own, but we named it by what was greatest and strongest in it. We have called it the desiring part because of its powerful desires for food and drink and love-making and all that attends these, yes and money-loving too, because these desires are fulfilled mostly through money."

"And quite right too," said he.

"Then if we should say that its pleasure and affection is in gain, we should very fairly bring them all under one head and have this for our argument to rest on; we should have so much clear between us when we named that part of the soul, and we should be right in calling it the money-loving and gain-loving part?"

"I think so at least," said he.

"Very well. The high-spirited part certainly aims wholly at victory and glory, isn't that what we say?"

"Exactly."

"Then if we should call it victory-loving and honour-loving, would that be unsuitable?"

"No, most suitable."

"Moreover, the part we learn with—anyone can see that it is always bent on knowing what the truth is in everything; and this cares least of them all for money and fame."

"Far the least."

"So learning-loving and wisdom-loving would be proper terms for it?"

"Certainly."

"Now," I went on, "sometimes one and sometimes another rules in the souls of men, just as it happens."

"Just so," said he.

"So that is why we say that the first great classes of men too are three, wisdom-loving, victory-loving, gain-loving?"

"Exactly so."

"And so pleasures also are of three kinds, one belonging to each of these?"

"Certainly."

"Now you know," said I. "that if you should question men of each of these classes in turn, which of these lives is most delightful, each will praise his own most; the money-maker, at any rate, will say that, compared with getting gain, the pleasure of honour or of learning is worth nothing at all, unless perhaps there is a bit of money in them."

"True," said he.

"Isn't the honour-lover the same?" said I. "Doesn't he see something vulgar in the pleasure that comes from money? And indeed the pleasure of learning too, unless learning brings honour with it, he thinks only smoke and nonsense?"

"Just so," said he.

"But the philosopher!" said I. "The lover of wisdom! What are we to suppose he thinks of the other pleasures as compared with that of knowing the truth as it is, and always being a learner in that school? Will he not think them far indeed from true pleasure, and call them strictly necessary pleasures, since he wanted none of these others unless there was necessity for them?"

"We should be sure of that," he said.

"Since there is dispute, then," I said, "about the pleasures of each class, and the life of each class, not only which leads to the more beautiful or ugly existence, or the better or worse, but which, indeed, is more pleasant and free from pain, how could we know which of them speaks most truly?"

"I really can't say," he answered.

"Well, look at it this way. What must we judge by if we are to judge properly? Surely experience and intelligence and reason! Could one find a better standard than those?"

"How could one!" said he.

"Just think now; here are three men—which is most experienced in all the pleasures we mentioned? Has the gain-lover more experience of the pleasure of knowledge by striving to learn the nature of truth, than the philosopher has of the pleasure that comes from gain?"

"There is a great difference," he said: "the philosopher must have tasted the other pleasures from boyhood up; but there is no necessity for the gain-lover to learn the real nature of things, or to taste and gain experience of that pleasure and to know how sweet it is—indeed he would not find if easy even if he tried."

"Then there is a great difference," I said; "the philosopher far surpasses the gain-lover in experience of both pleasures."

"Yes, far," said he.

"And how does he compare with the honour-lover? Which has more experience, the philosopher of the pleasure of being honoured, or the honour-lover of the pleasure of being wise?"

"The truth is," he said, "that if they each accomplish their aims, honour follows them all. For the rich man is honoured by many, and so is the brave man, and so is the wise man; thus all have experience of the pleasure which comes from honour. But how great is the pleasure of contemplating things as they are, none but the philosopher can ever taste."

"Then as far as experience goes," I said, "he is the best judge in the world."

"Far the best."

"And besides, his experience alone has intelligence with it."

"Undoubtedly."

"And further, the instrument through which judgment must be made belongs to the philosopher, not the gain-lover nor the honour-lover."

"What instrument?"

"Reasoning through words, we said, ought to be the way of judging, didn't we?"

"Yes."

"And words are chiefly the philosopher's instrument?"

"Of course."

"Well, if the things judged were best judged by riches and gain, the judgments of the gain-lover in praise or blame would necessarily be most true."

"Undoubtedly."

"And if it were by honour and victory and bravery, the honour-lover and the victory-lover would judge most truly?"

"That is clear."

"But since it is by experience and wisdom and reasoning?"

"Then necessarily," said he, "the praise of the philosopher, the lover of wisdom and words, must be most true."

"There are these three pleasures, then, and the pleasure of that part of the soul by which we learn would be most pleasurable, and the life of that man among us most pleasurable in whom this part rules?"

"How can it be otherwise," he said: "At least the intelligent man is a competent judge in praising his own life."

"And what life," said I, "and what pleasure does the judge put second?"

"The warlike and honour-loving, that is clear; for his pleasure is nearer to him than the gain-lover's pleasure."

"So the gain-lover's comes last, as it seems."

"Certainly," said he.

"There, then, are two falls in the wrestling in succession; twice the just man has beaten the unjust; now third and lastly in Olympian fashion, here's to Zeus[1] Olympian and the Saviour! Please observe that only the understanding man's pleasure is all-truthful and pure, not that of the others; theirs

[1] These two proofs are from politics and psychology; now comes the third, and greatest, from metaphysics. At feasts, the libations were poured regularly (1) to Olympian Zeus and the Olympian gods, (2) to the heroes, (3) to Zeus Saviour. Cf. Odysseus in the palace of Alcinoös: *Odyssey* vii The Olympian Games are also alluded to here. In the contest of five events, the victor had to win three; in wrestling, which is mentioned here specially, two falls out of three. Plato seems to have all these things in mind.

THE REPUBLIC Book IX *(582D–583E)*

is 'a sort of rough sketch,'[1] as I seem to have heard from one of the wise. I beg to inform you that this would be the greatest and most decisive of the falls."

"Oh yes, much the greatest; but please tell me how?"

"I shall find out how," I said, "if you help my search with your answers."

"Ask away," said he.

"Now then, tell me this," I said. "We say that pain is the opposite of pleasure, don't we?"

"Certainly."

"And there is such a thing as being neither glad nor sorry?"

"There is."

"Something in the middle between these two, a kind of quietude in the soul as regards them? Don't you agree that it is something like that?"

"I do," said he.

"I suppose you remember how sick people talk when they are ill."

"What do they say?"

"That there is no greater pleasure than to be well, but they had never noticed it was the greatest until they fell ill."

"I remember," said he.

"And don't you hear people suffering some great pain say that there is no greater pleasure than for the pain to cease?"

"Yes, I do."

"And you often see people, I think, in other conditions like that; when they are in great distress, they vow that relief from their distress is the greatest of pleasures, not joy, just quietude from the state they are in?"

"Yes," he said, "at the time perhaps this really becomes pleasurable and longed for, just quietude."

"And whenever someone ceases being joyful," I said, "the quietude from the pleasure will be painful."

"Perhaps," he said.

"So then," I went on, "what we said just now to be between the two, quietude, this will be sometimes both, pain as well as pleasure."

"So it seems."

"But can that which is neither become both?"

"I don't think so."

"Now, the pleasure arising in the soul and the pain are both a kind of emotion,[2] aren't they?"

"Yes."

---

[1] σκιαγραφία, see p. 402, n. 1.
[2] He explains this further on; pp. 384 and 385.

"But that which is neither pain nor pleasure is quietude surely, and we have just seen that it comes between these, haven't we?"

"Yes, we have."

"Then how can it be right to believe that not to be in pain is pleasurable, or not to be joyful is grievous?"

"It cannot be right."

"Then this is not really so, but only seems to be so," said I; "seems at the time to be pleasant beside the pain, and seems to be painful beside the pleasure, this quietude; and such fancies are all unsound as compared with the real truth of pleasure, they are only a sort of enchantment."

"At any rate," said he, "our reasoning signifies that."

"Now," said I, "glance at those pleasures which do not arise out of pain; for you must not suppose from the present instance that this is a law of nature, I mean that pleasure is a cessation of pain and pain a cessation of pleasure."

"What pleasures," he asked, "and where are they?"

"There are many others," I said; "notice the pleasures of smell as a good example. They appear suddenly in overwhelming strength without previous pain, and when they cease they leave no pain behind."

"Very true," said he.

"Then do not let us believe that pure pleasure is riddance of pain, or pain riddance of pleasure."

"By no means."

"But surely," I said, "the so-called pleasures that reach the soul through the body are of this kind, riddances of pain, at least nearly all and the strongest of them."

"So they are."

"And the same may be said of the anticipatory pleasures and pains of expectation which precede them?"

"Just the same."

"Do you know what sort of pleasures these are, and what they are really like?" said I.

"What?" he said.

"Do you believe," said I, "that there is in nature an up and a down and a middle?"

"I do."

"If someone is carried from below to the middle, don't you suppose he would believe he is being carried up? And while he stands in the middle looking down to the place from which he has been brought, won't he think he is up, never having seen that which really is up?"

"Upon my word," said he, "I don't imagine he could think otherwise."

"But if he were carried back," I said, "he would think he was going down, and that would be thinking the truth?"

"Naturally."

"Wouldn't he feel all this because he had no experience of what was truly up and middle and down?"

"Certainly, that is clear."

"Thus, if people without experience of the truth hold unsound opinions about many other things, would you be surprised how they feel about pleasure and pain and what lies between? When they are carried towards pain they have true opinion and they really are in pain; but when they are carried from pain towards the middle, they fully believe they are coming to fulfilment of pleasure—they compare the painless to pain, and they are deceived by their inexperience of pleasure, as if they were comparing grey with black, having no experience of white. Would that surprise you?"

"Not at all, I vow," said he. "I shall be much more surprised if it is not so."

"Look at the matter in this way," said I. "Are not hunger and thirst and so forth each a sort of emptiness in the bodily condition?"

"Quite so."

"And ignorance and unwisdom again an emptiness in the soul's condition?"

"Certainly."

"So would not the man who takes sustenance and the man who gets sense both be filled?"

"Of course."

"And which is the truer filling, to be full of that which more really *is*, or of that which less really *is*?"

"Clearly of that which more really *is*."

"Then which class of things do you think has a greater share of real being, things like food and drink and meat and nourishment in general, or things like true opinion and knowledge and reason, and, in a word, virtue of all kinds? In forming your judgment ask yourself which you think more really *is*, that which is connected with the always unchanging and immortal, with truth, being itself of the same nature and produced in something of the same nature; or that which is always changing and mortal, being itself of the same nature, and produced in something of the same nature."

"Far superior," he said, "is that connected with the unchanging."

"Then does the changeable partake any more of real being

than knowledge does?"[1]

"Not at all."

"More of truth then?"

"Nor that."

"For in fact if something has less of truth, it has also less of real being?"

"Necessarily."

"Then in general, the classes of things concerned with the care of the body have less of truth and real being than the classes of things concerned with the care of the soul?"

"Much less."

"Don't you believe the same of body itself as compared with soul?"

"I do."

"Then soul, which itself more really *is*, being filled with what more really *is*, is filled with more real fulfillment than body, which itself less really *is*, being filled with what less really *is*: don't you agree?"

"Of course I do."

"Then if to be filled with what is proper to nature is pleasant, that which is more really filled with what is more real would be made more really and truly to rejoice with true pleasure; but that which partakes of what less really *is*, would be less truly and abidingly filled, and would partake of pleasure less trusty and less true."

"That is quite inevitable," said he.

"Then those who have no experience of wisdom and virtue, who are always at their feastings and so forth, are being carried downwards, as it seems, and back again to the middle region, and there they wander about all their lives; as to passing above this limit, they have never even cast a look to the true upwards and never been there, never been filled with what really is or had a taste of pure and abiding pleasure. Like brute beasts, they look ever downwards, and feed stooping over the ground and poking their noses into their tables, cropping and coupling; and to get more and more of these things they kick and butt with iron horns and hooves and kill one another because of their insatiate desire, since they fail either to satisfy with real things the real part of themselves, or to fill up that vessel, their body."

"A perfect picture of most men's lives," Glaucon said; "you speak like an oracle, Socrates!"

"Then must not the pleasures they live with be of necessity

[1] Literally, "Does the real being of the changeable partake any more of real being than the real being of knowledge does?" Two words of the Greek text are doubtful here.

always mingled with pains, phantoms of true pleasure and rough sketches which take shade and colour from each other by contrast, so that both pleasures and pains seem intense and beget in fools frantic loves of self; phantoms to be fought for, as in Troy Stesichoros tells us the phantom of Helen was fought for[1] through ignorance of the truth."

"Something like that is quite inevitable," said he.

"Very well: Now the high-spirited part; must not the same happen, when a man acts to gratify that part, seeking his fill of honour and victory and temper without reason or sense, whether by envy through ambition, or by violence through contentiousness, or by anger through ill-temper?"

"What happens must inevitably be much the same," said he.

"Very good," said I, "may we make bold to declare that both in the gain-loving and in the victory-loving parts, those desires which follow knowledge and reason, and pursue their pleasures in company with these, and take only those that good sense prescribes, will receive the truest pleasures which they are capable of, inasmuch as they follow truth, as well as their own special pleasures, if the best for everything is also its very own."[2]

"Yes indeed," he said, "that is its very own."

"So while the whole soul follows the wisdom-loving part and there is no quarrel within, the result is not only that each part does its own business, and is just, but moreover each part enjoys its own pleasures, the best pleasures, and the truest as far as it is capable."

"Exactly so."

"But, on the other hand, whenever one of the other two parts gets control, the result is that not only it cannot find its own pleasure, but it compels the others to pursue pleasures alien and untrue."

"Just so," said he.

"Now what is farthest away from wisdom and reason would be most likely to have that effect?"

"Much the most likely," said he.

"And farthest from reason is that which is farthest from law and order?"

"So much is clear."

"But it was proved that the passionate and tyrannical desires were farthest away?"

---

[1] This follows a legend that only a phantom of Helen went to Troy, while she herself stayed in Egypt.

[2] For instance, the honour-loving soul finds its best pleasure in honour, but if it has sought honour legitimately and wisely it will receive true pleasure in honour as well as its own special pleasure, if its own is good for it.

"Much the farthest."

"And least far away were the kingly and orderly desires?"

"Yes."

"Then the tyrant will be found farthest away from true and proper pleasure, and the king least far."

"Necessarily."

"So the tyrant's life," I said, "will be the most unpleasant, and the king's the most pleasant."

"Inevitably."

"Do you know, then," I asked, "how much unpleasanter the tyrant's life is than the king's?"

"Would you please tell me?" said he.

"There are three pleasures, as it seems, one genuine, two spurious. The tyrant deserts law and reason, and crosses the line beyond the spurious ones, and there lives with a mercenary bodyguard of slavish pleasures; and how much inferior he is it is not very easy to tell, except perhaps in this way."

"How?" he asked.

"I suppose the tyrant comes third from the oligarch, for the democratic man was between them."

"Yes."

"Then the phantom of pleasure he lives with would be, as regards truth, the third from that man, if what we said is true."

"That is so."

"But the oligarchic man is again third from the kingly man, if we put aristocratic[1] and kingly into the same series."

"Yes, third."

"Three times three, then," said I, "is the arithmetical distance between the tyrant and true pleasure."

"So it seems."

"Now then," said I, "the *phantom* of tyrannical pleasure,[2] it seems, according to the number of its magnitude, would be a plane figure."

"Exactly."

"So square this and bring it to a cube,[3] and you will see what the distance becomes!"[4]

[1] Thus inserting aristocrat in the series similarly to democrat.
[2] In other words, three times three (9) is the arithmetic distance between the tyrant and the kingly man, but whereas the kingly man has true pleasure, the tyrant's is a mere phantom of pleasure and the effect of this must be taken into account.
[3] Literally, "by third increase," which to the Greeks meant changing a square into a cube. The Greeks used to think of numbers as figures, because they had no such helps to calculation as we have in Arabic numerals and algebraic formulae.
[4] We already had 9. Socrates says square this for the phantom effect ($9 \times 9 = 81$) and bring it to a cube (81×9), and we get 729.

THE REPUBLIC Book IX (587B–588C)

"I dare say," said he, "a mathematician could see it!"

"Conversely, if one wanted to say how far off the king is from the tyrant in true happiness, when he has done his multiplication sum he will find that the king lives sevenhundredandtwentyninetimes[1] more happily than the tyrant, and the tyrant justthesamenumberoftimes more wretchedly!"

"Ho!" said he, "what a tempestuous tornado of a number you have poured over our heads in your differentiation of these two gentlemen, the good man and the bad man, and their pleasures and pains!"

"My dear sir!" I said, "a true number and a proper number for men's lives, if days and nights and months and years are proper to them!"[2]

"Oh yes," he said, "they are proper enough."

"Then if in pleasure the good and just man beats the bad and unjust man as much as that, no one can measure how much more he will beat him in graciousness of life and beauty and virtue."

"Ah, no one will measure that, by God!" said he.[3]

"So much for that," I said. "Now that we have got that far in discussion, let us recall our first statement that brought us here. Someone was saying, I think, that it paid to be unjust, if one was perfectly unjust but was believed to be just. Was not that said?"

"Certainly."

"Now, then," said I, "it is time to reason with him again, since we have now agreed on the real meaning of doing justly and doing unjustly."

"How?" he asked.

"Let us draw a word picture of the soul, that the one who made that proposition may know what he was saying."

"What sort of picture?" he asked.

"Like one of those old creatures in the fables," I said, "Chimaira and Scylla and Cerberos[4] and plenty more, said to be a number of shapes grown together into one."

"Yes," he said, "we have heard of them."

"Mould me, then, the shape of a multiform, many-headed

---

[1] The long Greek number and long Greek words used were no doubt part of the jest.

[2] Philolaos reckoned the year as 364½ days; add 364½ nights and you have 729. He spoke also of a "great year" of 729 months, if that be alluded to here.

[3] It is of no use to ask why these numbers are squared and cubed and so forth. Plato loves to jest about numbers; and Socrates is jesting here all the time although he uses the correct Greek technical terms, but even good old Glaucon sees through him at the end. And Plato's raillery does produce the overwhelming effect which he wanted. It suggests that degradation increases at terrible speed.

[4] Chimaira, lion, goat and serpent; Scylla, witch with tentacles ending in dogs' heads; Cerberos, dog of Hades, usually described as having three heads, though Hesiod gives him fifty. In the allegory which follows, the many-headed monster, of course, represents the desires, the lion the temper.

monster, with heads of tame and wild animals round him in a ring, all of which he has the power to change about or make them all grow out of himself."

"That's a job for a clever modeller," he said; "however, words are easier to model in than wax; suppose the model's made."

"Now, one of a lion, if you please, and one of a man, the lion much the largest, the man second."

"Those are easier," said he; "they're done!"

"Now join the three into one, so that they grow together somehow."

"All joined!" said he.

"Now then, mould round them on the outside a single form like the man's, so that to a person unable to see the insides, but only the outside skin, it may appear one creature —a man."

"Skin moulded!" said he.

"Now let us answer the person who says that it pays this man to be unjust, and it is not profitable to him to do justice. Tell him that he is simply saying it pays to feed up his multiform monster, and by so doing make the lion and all about it strong, but to starve the man inside and make him weak so as to be dragged wherever either of the others leads him; and not make either of them friends of each other and intimates, but leave all the creatures to bite and fight and eat each other."

"Yes, not a doubt of it," he said, "that's what the man would really mean by praising injustice."

"On the contrary, one who says that justice pays would be telling us we ought to do and say what will make our inside man completely master of the whole man, and give him charge over the many-headed monster, like a farmer, cherishing and tending the cultivated plants, but preventing the weeds from growing; he must make an ally of the lion's nature, and care for all the creatures alike, making them friendly to each other and to himself, and so he will nourish the whole."

"Yes, that is exactly what the praise of justice means."

"You see the one who sings the praises of justice would speak the truth in every way, and the one who praises injustice would be a liar. And if you regard pleasure and fair fame and benefit, the advocate of justice speaks truth, and he who blames it has no health in him and does not know what he is blaming."

"So I think," said he, "not one little bit."

"Then let us persuade him gently," said I, "for he does not

willingly err. Let us ask him, 'Bless you, my friend! Should we not say that whatever rules of behaviour are accepted as beautiful and ugly are so accepted because of an arrangement such as this? The beautiful are those which make the bestial part of our nature subject to the man, or rather, perhaps, to the divine within us; the ugly are those which make the gentle part slave to the savage?' Will he agree, or what?"

"He will," said the other, "if he takes my advice."

"Then is there anyone," said I, "according to this reasoning, whom it will pay to take gold unjustly, if the consequence is that by taking the gold he enslaves at the same time the best in him to the worst? If by taking a sum of gold he were selling a son or a daughter to be a slave, and the slave of savage and wicked men, it would not pay him, not if he got a mint of money for such a thing; and if he pitilessly enslaves the divinest part of himself under the most impious and detestable part, surely he is miserable, and he accepts the golden bribe for a ruin far more terrible than Eriphyle's,[1] who took that necklace as the price of her husband's life?"

"Indeed he is much more miserable," said Glaucon, "for I will answer instead of the man."

"And don't you believe that this is why loose living has been so long in disrepute, because in it that terrible, that huge, multiform monster is let loose too much?"

"Clearly," said he.

"When men are blamed for wilfulness and ill-temper, has not the lionish and snakish in them been allowed to grow out of proportion to the rest?"

"Undoubtedly."

"And slackening and loosening of this same part, when they cause cowardice in a man, bring the blame of luxury and softness."

"What else could it be?"

"So, also, flattery and vulgarity, when a man subjects the same high-spirited part to that vulgarian monster, when for the sake of money, and to fill its insatiable maw, he accustoms that part to be treated with contumely from youth up, and turns lion into ape?"

"Quite true," said he.

"And what makes commonness, and the work of our hands, a reproach, do you think? Surely, we shall say, only when a

[1] The seven champions were about to lead an expedition against Thebes; and the great prophet Amphiaraos foretold that it would fail. Polyneices of Thebes, banished from Thebes by his brother, got up this expedition in order to recover the crown and he presented the famous necklace of Harmonia to Eriphyle, the wife of Amphiaraos, to persuade him to join the expedition. She did so, and he perished.

man has his best part naturally weak, so that it could not rule the brood within him but only coax them, and could learn nothing but the ways to flatter them?"

"So it seems," he said.

"Then such a man ought to be ruled; and that he may have a ruler like the ruler of the best man, we say he ought to be the slave of that best man, who has the divine as ruler within himself. We do not believe, as Thrasymachos did about ruling subjects, that he should be ruled for his own hurt; we think it better for everyone to be ruled by the divine and wise, if possible having this as his own within himself, if not, imposed from without, in order that we may all be equal and friendly as far as possible, all having the same guide."

"And quite rightly too," said he.

"And it is clear," I said, "that the law has the same intention, being the ally of all in the city; and so has the rule of children, too, not to leave them to be free until we have established a constitution within them, as in a city, until we have fostered the best in them by the best in us, and established a like ruler and guardian to take our place; then, and not before, we leave a child free."

"Yes, that is clear," said he.

"Then how indeed, and for what reason, Glaucon, can we say that it pays a man to be unjust or to live loosely or to do anything ugly, by which he will gain more money or some other power, and become worse himself?"

"There is none at all," said he.

"Or to be unjust without being found out and punished, how can that pay? If he is not found out, he becomes still worse; if he is found out and chastened, his bestial part is made quiet and gentle, and the gentle is let free, and the whole soul settles down into the best nature. It acquires more property, I mean temperance and justice along with wisdom; and its new condition is worth more than that of the body when it gets beauty and strength along with health, by so much as the soul is worth more than the body. Doesn't that pay?"

"By all means!" he said.

"Then a man of sense will strain every nerve to this end while he lives. In the first place he will honour the studies which will make his soul such as we have said, and he will disregard the others."

"That is clear," said he.

"Next," I said, "he will not yield his bodily habit and nurture to bestial and unreasoning pleasure, and live turned in that direction—far from it! He will not even fix his eyes on health, and think first and foremost how to be strong or healthy or handsome, unless these things will bring temperance, too; but he will ever seek harmony and proportion, and tune himself to concord in the soul—there shall be no mistake about that."

"Yes, by all means," he said, "if he is to be truly musical."

"And will he not seek," said I, "the same proportion and concord in getting money? He will not be impressed by mere bulk of quantity, just because the multitude think that bliss; he will not increase his riches to infinity, and find it infinity of evil!"

"I think not," said he.

"No," said I, "he will keep his eyes fixed upon the constitution within himself, and keep watch that he may disturb nothing there because of the magnitude or smallness of his property; thus he will guide his voyage, adding to his property and spending from it as well as he can."

"Exactly so," said he.

"And the same with honours, he will keep the same thing in view; he will partake of some and enjoy them frankly, whichever he believes will make him better; but any which will dissolve his present condition he will avoid, both public and private."

"So if he cares for that," he said, "he will keep clear of politics."

"Yes, by the Dog!" quoth I; "certainly in *his own* city—yet perhaps not in his native city, unless some divine dispensation should intervene."

"I understand you," he said, "you mean in our city, the city which we have described and founded in words, for I do not think it exists anywhere on earth."

"Well," said I, "in heaven, perhaps, a pattern of it is indeed laid up, for him that has eyes to see, and seeing to settle himself therein. It matters nothing whether it exists anywhere or shall exist; for he would practise the principles of this city only, no other."

"That seems likely," said he.

BOOK X

"Now I see," said I, "reflecting on many other aspects of our city, that we arranged it most admirably in general, but I say this especially when I think about poetry."

"What was that?" he said.

"Not to let in the imitative part of it. Since we have clearly distinguished the parts of the soul, I think it is now most abundantly clear that this must not be let in."

"How do you mean?"

"Between ourselves—for I'm sure you will not betray me to the tragic poets and the other imitators—all such things are the ruin of the hearers' minds, unless they possess the antidote, knowledge of what such things really are."

"What is your notion, exactly, in saying this?" he asked.

"Yes, I must speak out," I said, "although a certain affection and veneration for Homer, which I have had from boyhood, checks my utterance; for he seems to be the first leader and teacher in all these beauties of tragedy. However, one must not honour a man above the truth, but what I am saying must be spoken."

"By all means," he said.

"Listen then, or rather answer."

"Ask away."

"What is imitation really, could you tell me? The fact is I'm not quite certain myself what it means."

"And then you expect me to be certain!" said he.

"Nothing very odd in that," said I; "dim eyes often see things before sharp eyes do."

"That does happen," said he; "but in your presence I could have no desire to say what appears to me: look yourself!"

"Then shall we go on and begin our enquiry following our usual method? I think we have usually assumed a general form or idea, one idea, in each class of many particulars to which we give the same name. You understand, don't you?"

"I do."

"Now, take any class of many particulars you please, for instance, if you like, there are many beds and tables."[1]

"By all means."

"These have ideas, I suppose, underlying them—two in fact: one of the bed, one of the table."

"Yes,"

"Well, we usually say that the craftsman, in making either of these articles of furniture, keeps his eye upon the idea, and so makes the beds or tables which we use accordingly, and so with other things. For I suppose no craftsman makes the idea itself; how could he?"

"He could not."

"Now please consider how you define this Craftsman."

[1] Readers must consult commentators for the "idea" of artificial things. The Indians had a similar notion; "the pothood of the pot" is a commonplace of Indian philosophy.

"What one?"

"The one who makes everything that separate handicraftsmen make."[1]

"What a wonderful, clever man you speak of!"

"Wait a minute—you will say that more than ever directly. This same handicraftsman can make not only furniture, but he makes all that grows in the earth and fashions all living creatures, all these including himself, and, besides, earth and heaven and gods, and all that is in heaven above and in Hades under the earth—he fashions all!"

"There's a marvel!" said he, "a real professor of knowledge!"[2]

"Don't you believe me?" said I: "just inform me—do you deny flatly that there could be such a Craftsman? Or do you think that in one way there could be, and in another way there could not be, a maker of all these things? Don't you see that there is a way in which you could make all these things yourself?"

"And what way, if you please?" he asked.

"An easy way," I said, "craftsman-made everywhere and quickly too; most quickly, I think, if you just pick up a mirror and carry it about everywhere. You will then quickly make a sun and all there is in the heavens, quickly an earth, quickly yourself and the other animals and furniture and plants and everything else I mentioned."

"Oh yes," he said, "appearances, but not things really existing anywhere."

"Splendid!" I said. "Just what is needed to help our argument! The painter is one of these craftsmen, isn't he?"

"Why, yes."

"But you will say, I think, that there is no truth in what he makes. Yet, in a way at least, even the painter makes a bed, doesn't he?"

"Yes," he said, "and that is an appearance too."

"And what of the maker of beds?[3] Surely you said just now that he does not make the idea which we say is the bedhood of a bed, but only some particular bed?"

"Yes, I did."

"Then if he does not make the bedhood, he would not be making real being but only something resembling real being, but not itself real. But if anyone should say the cabinet-maker's work, or any other handicraftsman's work, really

---

[1] A general definition of "craftsman."
[2] *Sophistes.* Each Sophist professed to be master of some branch of knowledge.
[3] The cabinet maker.

exists in the full and perfect sense, he simply would not be telling the truth?"

"He would not be," said he, "in the opinion of those who practise reasoning such as ours."

"Then don't let us be surprised, if this also is really dim as compared with the truth."

"Not at all," said he.

"Then shall we use these very same things in enquiring about this imitator, what he is?"

"If you like," said he.

"Good. Here are three different beds: one in the nature of things, bedhood, which we would say God[1] made, as I think. Or who else?"

"Nobody."

"And one that the carpenter made."

"Yes," he said.

"And one that the painter made, eh?"

"I don't mind."

"Painter then, and maker of beds, and God, there are three superintendents of three kinds of beds."

"Yes, three."

"God, then, whether it was his will, or whether some necessity was upon him not to complete more than one in the nature of things, at any rate God made one only, that very Bed which a[2] bed really is; two or more such were not made by God and never shall be, world without end."

"How so?" he asked.

"Because," I said, "suppose he made *two* only, again one would become apparent of which both those two would have the idea; and that would be the real true Bed, not these two."

"Quite so," said he.

"God knew this then, I think, and he wished really to be maker of actual bedhood, not of a particular bed, not to be a mere bed-maker; consequently he created one bed unique in the nature of things."

"So it seems."

"What shall we call him, then? Its creator in nature, or something like that?"

"That would be right enough, I think, since he has made this and all the rest in the nature of things."

[1] To Plato, God and the Idea or nature of Good are the same. Readers must be careful not to think that the name called up the same associations for him as it has for us.
[2] That is, every.

"And what shall we call the carpenter? The craftsman who made the bed—will that do?"

"Yes."

"And the painter—is he craftsman and maker of that sort of thing?"

"Not at all."

"Then what will you say he is to the bed?"

"I think the fairest name would be imitator of the thing of which the others were craftsmen."

"Very good," I said, "you call him the imitator in the third generation from nature?"

"Exactly," he said.

"So the tragedy-maker also will be, then, if he is an imitator, third in succession from the Great King—the truth,[1] and so will be all the other imitators."

"That is the fact."

"So we are agreed about the imitator. But I have something more to ask about the painter; do you think each painter tries to imitate that very reality in the nature of things, or the particular works of the craftsmen?"

"The craftsmen's works," he said.

"As they are, or as they seem? Define this also, if you please!"

"What do you mean?" he said.

"This: A bed, when you look at it from the side, or when you look at it from the front, or however you look at it, the bed may appear to be different, but is there any difference in it, really? So also with anything else, of course."

"Just so," he said, "it appears to be different, but there is no real difference."

"Then here is the point for you to consider. With what object has the painting been made in each case; has it been made to imitate the real thing as it is, or appearance as it appears; is it imitation of appearance or of truth?"

"Appearance," he said.

"Then imitative art is a long way from truth, and, as it seems, that is why it reproduces everything, because it touches only a little part of each, and even that an image. For example, the painter, as we say, will paint us a cobbler, or a carpenter, or any other craftsman, although he understands nothing of any of these arts; but all the same if he is a good painter, he could deceive children and fools if he showed them his painting of a carpenter from a distance, and he

[1] This may be a common expression in terms of the Persian throne; for Plato, the King here is God.

could make them think it was a real carpenter."

"Of course he could."

"But we ought, I think, to remember in such cases, my friend, if anyone should announce to us that he had met with a man who knows all the arts and crafts as well as each particular man knows them, knows everything about them better than all the world—we ought to retort to such a man that he must be a simple soul, and he seems to have met a magician and an imitator who tricked him into believing he was all-wise; when the fact is he is at fault himself, because he himself cannot tell the difference between knowledge and ignorance, or see what imitation is."

"Very true," he said.

"The next thing we have to do," I said, "is to consider tragedy[1] and its leader, Homer; since we hear some say that these poets understand all arts, and all human things concerned with virtue and vice, and things divine, too; it is plain necessity, they say, that the good poet must know what he brings into his poetry, if he is to compose fine poems; or else he is not at all fitted to do so. So then we must consider whether those poets they have come across were not imitators, whether they have not been deceived, when they saw their works and did not perceive that their works were three removes away from reality, and something easy to make without knowing the truth; for the poems are appearances and not real. Or perhaps there is something in what they say, and in reality the good poets do know the things which the multitude think they speak well about?"

"By all means," he said, "we must examine that."

"Then if someone could make both, the thing he is to imitate and the image of it as well, do you think he would hasten to give himself up to the manufacture of images, as the serious business and the aim of his life and the best thing he had?"

"No, I don't."

"No, so I think; but if he really knew in truth about the things which he imitates, he would make the real things his business far more than he would the imitations; he would try to leave many beautiful real things behind him as his memorials, and rather to be the praised than the praiser."

"I think so," he said, "for both the honour and the benefit are greater."

"Very well, that is not how we must question Homer or any other poet. Don't let us call them to account, and ask if one of them was a medical man and not a mere imitator of medi-

[1] Plato often uses "tragedy" as a general expression, as we might use drama, or poetry.

cal talk; whether any of the poets, ancient or modern, is said to have cured people, as Asclepios did, or left behind him pupils in medicine, as Asclepios left his descendants; let that alone, and don't let us ask them about the other arts and crafts. We must take the greatest and finest things which Homer tries to describe, wars and campaigns and the government of cities and the education of man, and it would surely be fair to ask him a question like this: 'My dear Homer, if you are not really at a distance three removes from truth in the matter of virtue, just the manufacturer of images whom we defined as an imitator, but if you are even at the second, and were able to know what pursuits make men better or worse in public and private life, tell us this: What city was ever governed better because of you, as Lacedaimon was because of Lycurgos, and many other cities, both great and small, because of many other persons? What city gives you the credit of being a good lawgiver who has done them good? Italy and Sicily can name Charondas;[1] we can name Solon—who names *you*?' Will he be able to mention one?"

"I think not," said Glaucon; "none are spoken of—not even by Homerids[2] themselves!"

"Well, is there any war of Homer's time recorded as being successful with Homer in command or Homer in council?"

"None."

"Think again of all the ingenious devices in arts or other achievements, such as you might expect in one of practical ability; you remember Thales of Miletos and Anacharsis the Scythian?"[3]

"Homer did nothing of this kind."

"He did nothing in public matters, then; what of private life? Is Homer reported to have been himself a leader of education for any, while he lived? Did any enjoy being in his company, and did they hand down to posterity any Homeric method of life? Pythagoras, you know, was especially revered for this; his followers even now use the title Pythagorean Way of Life,[4] and they have a shining place among the rest of men."

---

[1] Of Catana in Sicily.

[2] There was a group in Chios called the Homeridai, "the clan or family of Homer," who claimed descent from him.

[3] Thales was credited with discoveries in geometry and good advice in politics; he was a very great philosopher, and one of the Seven Wise Men. See Diogenes Laertius, i. 23 ff.
Anacharsis was said to have invented the anchor and the potter's wheel. Diogenes Laertius, i, 105.

[4] A very important and interesting society. All they said and did was kept a profound secret. The members were severely tested and trained, and the popular idea of them was that they were ascetics. Those who were fit studied physics and metaphysics, music and religion; their science of numbers was remarkable, and Plato is fond of alluding to it. Cf. p. 344, n. 2.

"No," he said, "nothing of that kind, either. Perhaps, my dear Socrates, Homer's friend Creophylos would seem even more ridiculous than his own name Meatyclan,[1] as a specimen of good education, if what is said about Homer is true. You know it is said that this very man[2] showed a vast neglect of Homer while he was alive."

"Yes, that is said," I replied. "But if Homer really could educate men and make them better, if he had been able to understand and not simply to imitate, do you suppose he would not have gathered a band of disciples who would have honoured and loved him? Protagoras of Abdera we see, Prodicos of Ceos, and no end of others, are able to impress on persons of their own times, just by being with them in private life, that these persons must place them in charge of their own education, or else these will not be capable of managing their own house or city; and they are so beloved for this precious wisdom that their disciples almost carry them about on their shoulders! Then, if Homer had been able to bless men with virtue, would the men of his time have let him or Hesiod travel about reciting poetry? Would they not rather have clutched them closer than gold, and compelled them to reside with them in their homes? Or if they could not persuade them so far, they would themselves have attended them like children as they went around, until they got enough education?"

"There is no doubt about that, Socrates, it is true."

"We may take it, then, that all the poetic company from Homer onwards are imitators of images of virtue and whatever they put in their poems, but do not lay hold of truth. Indeed, as we said just now, the painter will fashion an apparent cobbler, although he knows nothing of cobbling himself, nor do his viewers, who judge from the colours and shapes."

"By all means."

"Just so, I think, we shall say that the poetic workman dabs on certain colours by using the words and phrases of the various arts, but all he knows himself is how to imitate; so that others as ignorant as himself, taking their view from words, think he is speaking magnificently when he talks in metre and rhythm and pitch about cobbling, or about strategy or anything else. So great is the natural charm in this manner of speaking. For if the sayings of the poets have their musical colours stripped off, I think you know how they look when told alone in plain words; you have noticed it, no doubt."

"Yes, I have," he said.

[1] This is a translation of the Greek name Creophylos.
[2] An ancient annotator says he was an epic poet, but we do not know what this allusion means.

"Are they not," said I, "like the faces of people in youthful prime, but not beautiful, as it is possible to see when the bloom leaves them?"

"Most certainly," he said.

"Look here, then: The maker of the image, the imitator, as we say, knows nothing of the real thing, but only the appearance. Don't you agree?"

"Yes."

"Then don't let us leave it half said; let us take a full view."

"Go on," he said.

"A painter, we say, will paint reins and bit."

"Yes."

"But the maker will be the saddler or the smith."

"Certainly."

"Then does the painter know what the reins and bit ought to be? Does even the maker know, the saddler and the smith, or only the horseman, who knows how to use them?"

"The horseman, yes, of course."

"Shall we not say the same about everything?"

"What?"

"That each of these has three arts concerned with it, one that will use, one make, one imitate."

"Yes."

"Then virtue and beauty and rightness in each article or animal or action refers only to the use, for which each is made or created?"

"Just so."

"It follows, then, of sure necessity that the user of each has most experience, and he informs the maker what good or mischief the instrument does in use. For example, the piper, of course, informs the pipe-maker about the pipes, which of them are useful in piping; the user will direct him what sort of pipes he must make, and the other will serve him."

"Of course."

"So the one who knows informs the other about good and bad pipes, and the other will believe him and make them accordingly."

"Yes."

"Then for every article the maker will have right belief about fineness and badness, by associating with the man who knows, and by being compelled to listen to the man who knows; and the user will have knowledge." [1]

"Exactly."

"But what of the imitator? Will he have knowledge, from use of what he describes, to say whether it is beautiful and

---

[1] The craftsman is on a higher stage than the imitator; belief, not opinion.

right or not? Or will he have right opinion, through being obliged to associate with the man who knows, and to take his orders as to what he must write?"

"Neither!"

"Then the imitator will neither know nor have right opinion about what he imitates, as regards fineness or badness?"

"So it seems."

"What a nice, pretty person your poetic imitator must be, with respect to true wisdom about what he makes!"

"Not nice at all!"

"But imitate he will all the same, although he does not know how his work is good or bad; but, as it seems, he will just make something which appears beautiful to the many who know nothing—there's his imitation!"

"Yes, what else would he do!"

"Very well, we are agreed so far, as it seems; the imitator knows nothing worth mentioning about what he imitates, but his imitation is a kind of play, not earnest; and those who take up tragedy in iambic or epic verse are imitators in the highest possible degree."

"By all means."

"Then, in the name of heaven, just think!" I said. "This imitation is only concerned with the third remove from truth, isn't that so?"

"Yes."

"Well, what part of man's nature is it aimed at, with all this power?"

"What part are you speaking about?"

"This will explain. The same object sighted from near and from far does not, I take it, appear to us an equal magnitude."

"No, it does not."

"And the same things appear bent or straight seen through water or in the air, and concave or convex by similar error of vision about colours, and there is clearly this sort of general confusion in our souls; indeed, in its play upon the weakness of our nature, shadow-drawing[1] is nothing short of magic, and also juggling and the many other such devices."

"True."

"Well, measuring and counting and weighing were invented very nicely to help us in such cases; thus we are not ruled by appearance, what seems to be greater or less or more or heavier, but by what has been counted and measured or even weighed."

---

[1] σκιαγραφία, painting in light and shade; here, however, it may refer to the distortions of forms cast by shadows on the ground or walls; the Greeks may have amused themselves by drawing in these shapes. For other uses of the word see p. 322 and p. 383; also *Phaedo*, p. 472.

"Certainly."

"Well, surely this would be the work of the reasoning part of the soul."

"Certainly, so it would."

"And when this has measured and signified that certain things are some greater or less than others, or equal, very often the contrary *appearances* are shown at the same time about the same things."

"Yes."

"And did we not say[1] that the same part of the soul could not possibly hold contrary opinions at the same time about the same things?"

"And we were quite right there."

"Then that in the soul which opines contrary to the measures could not be the same as that which opines according to the measures."

"Certainly not."

"But further, that which trusts measure and reasoning would be the best part of the soul."

"Of course."

"So that which goes contrary to this would be one of the inferior parts in us."

"It must be so."

"This is what I wished to have admitted, when I said that painting, and imitative art in general, works far away from truth in doing its own work, and joins hands and makes bosom friends with that part in us which is far away from wisdom, for no healthy and true end."

"I agree with you fully," he said.

"Then imitative art is an inferior uniting with an inferior and breeding inferior offspring."

"So it seems."

"Is that true of the sight only, or also of the hearing, the art which we call poetry?"

"The same with hearing also, probably."

"Now, don't let us trust only to the analogy from painting; let us in turn go straight to that very part of the mind which poetic imitation joins hands with, and see if that part is good or bad."

"So we must."

"Put it in this way, then: Men in action is what poetic imitation imitates, we say, acting freely or against their will, and believing themselves to have done well or ill from the action, and in all this feeling either grief or joy. Was there anything else besides this?"

[1] P. 235.

"Nothing."

"In all this, then, is a man of one mind with himself? Or is there rebellion within him, is he at war with himself in his doings—as, where sight was concerned, there was internal strife, and he had contrary opinions within him about the same things at the same time? Oh, I remember, now, we need not come to agreement about that again; for we have already agreed sufficiently about all this in our former discussion; that our soul is laden with thousands of such contradictions which exist all at once."

"We were right," he said.

"Yes, right enough," I said, "but I think it is necessary now to discuss something we left out then."

"What was that?" said he.

"A decent man," I said, "whose fortune it is to have lost a son or something he prized very highly, will bear it more easily than any of the others; I think we said that before."

"Certainly."

"But now further, let us consider whether he will feel no sorrow; or, that being impossible, will he be moderate in his grief?"

"That is more like the truth," he said.

"Very good, answer me this now about him: Do you think he will be more likely to fight and struggle with his grief when he is observed by his equals, or when he is in solitude by himself?"

"Much more," he said, "when he is observed."

"Ah, but left alone, I think, he will dare to say many things of which he would be ashamed if someone heard him; and he will do much that he would not like anyone to see him doing."

"That's how it is," said he.

"Now, that which exhorts him to resist is reason and law; but that which draws him towards grief is the affliction itself?"

"True."

"But when there is a contrary movement in the man, we say there must be two things in him."

"Naturally."

"And the one is ready to obey the law as the law leads him?"

"How so?"

"The law tells him, I suppose, that it is best to be calm in his misfortunes and not to resent them, since the good and the evil of such things is not clear; he would get no further at all by bearing them hardly, and nothing that happens to man matters very much; grief becomes a hindrance to that which ought in misfortunes to come to our help as soon as possible."

"And what is that?" he asked.

"Deliberation," I said. "We should think over what has happened, and when the dice fall we should arrange our business according to what turns up, in the way that reason takes for the best; we should not be like children who have tumbled down and clutch the part which is hurt and waste their time in crying, but we should always accustom the soul to set about raising up the fallen and curing the hurt, and by healing make wailing disappear."

"That's the right way, at least," he said, "to behave in face of the fortunes of life."

"Then the best part, we say, is willing to follow this reason."

"Surely that is clear."

"But that which draws you to lamentation and brooding over past troubles incessantly, we will say is unreasoning and idle and the friend of cowardice."

"Just so."

"And does not this regretful and resentful part allow of imitation in great variety? But the wise and calm character, being nearly always the same and self-composed, is not easy to imitate, and when imitated is not readily understood, especially by a festival assembly of all sorts and conditions of men gathered in a theatre; for the condition of mind imitated is, I should think, alien to them."

"Altogether alien."

"So the imitative poet is clearly not naturally suited to imitate this part of the soul, and his skill is not set upon adapting itself to it, if he is to be popular with the multitude, but rather to imitate the resentful and complex character, because that can be imitated well."

"Clearly."

"Then we can rightly catch hold of him at once, and place him beside the painter as his counterpart, for he is like the painter in making things which are inferior in point of reality; he is also like him in being intimate with an inferior part of the soul, not the best part. Thus we are justified at once in refusing to let him into a city which is to be ordered well; because he arouses and fosters and strengthens this part of the soul, and destroys the rational part, just as in a city, when by putting bad men in power one hands over the city to them and ruins the finer people. The imitative poet, we will say, does just the same with each private person; he establishes an evil constitution in his soul; he gratifies the unthinking part of it which does not know the difference between greater and less, but which believes the same things to be now great and now small, by imaging images very far away indeed from the truth."

"Undoubtedly."

"But we certainly have not come yet to the strongest accusation against imitation. For it is surely monstrous that it is able to corrupt even the decent people, with very few exceptions."

"Monstrous, indeed, if it really does that!"

"Listen and see. I suppose when the best of us hear Homer or any other of the makers of tragedy imitating one of the heroes, deep in mourning and making a long speech in his lamentations, when he shows them chanting and beating their breasts, you know we are delighted and yield ourselves; we go with him in sympathy, we take all in earnest, and praise as a really good poet one who can make us feel most like that."

"Of course, I know."

"But when we have a private affliction ourselves, you notice that we pride ourselves on just the opposite, if we can only keep calm and endure, believing that this is manly, and that what we praised before is womanly."

"Yes, I notice that," he said.

"Then is this praise right and proper," I said—"to watch such a man as one would not like to be oneself, indeed one would be ashamed, and then to rejoice and praise him instead of being disgusted?"

"No, by God," he said, "that doesn't seem reasonable."

"It's quite right," I said, "if you would think back a moment."

"How?" he asked.

"If you would bear in mind that the part which the poets feed up and delight is the very one which, as we said, is forcibly restrained in private misfortunes, and hungers to be satisfied with tears and a good hearty cry, being by nature such as to desire these things; the naturally best part of us, since it has not been properly educated by reason or habit either, relaxes the guard over this lamenting part, because it is a spectator of the sufferings of others; it feels no shame for itself in praising and pitying another man who, calling himself a good man, weeps and wails unseasonably; it considers this pleasure as pure gain and would not consent to sacrifice it by despising the whole poem. Indeed, very few, I think, are able to reflect that the enjoyment must react from others upon oneself; for when a man has fed pity, on the sufferings of others, until it has grown strong, he cannot easily restrain it in his own afflictions."

"Very true," he said.

"Does not the same reasoning hold about the ridiculous? If you would be ashamed to make certain jests yourself, but if you thoroughly enjoy listening to such things in comic representations on the stage, or even at home, instead of hating them as immoral, surely you are doing the same as in the case of pity. For again what you restrained in yourself by reason when you wished to make jests, because you feared to be thought a buffoon, then also you release; you make it vigorous there, and at home you are often carried so far as to become a comedian without noticing it."

"Yes, indeed," said he.

"And the same with love-making and anger and all the desires and griefs and pleasures in the soul which we say go along with our every action—poetical imitation produces all such things in us. For it nourishes them by watering what it ought to dry up, and makes them rulers in us, when they ought to be ruled that we may become better and happier instead of worse and more miserable."

"I cannot deny it," he said.

"Then, Glaucon," said I, "when you hear people singing the praises of Homer, and telling you that this poet has educated Hellas, that we should take him and learn him by heart for all the conduct and culture of human life, that we should regulate all our own lives by this poet, just salute them and welcome them as doing the best they can, and admit that Homer is chief of poets and first of tragedians; but remember that we must give poetry entry into our city as far only as hymns to the gods and encomiums of the good are concerned. But if you receive the honeyed Muse in lyric or epic, be sure that pleasure and pain will be kings in your city, instead of law and whatever reasoned argument the community shall approve in each case to be best."

"Very true," he said.

"So much then," said I, "for our defence, having returned to the consideration of poetry, that, being such as we have shown her to be, we were justified before in banishing her from our city. For it was reason which led us on. And lest she condemn us as rather harsh and rough, let us tell her that there is an ancient feud between philosophy and poetry.[1] There are thousands of traces of the ancient quarrel: 'That yelping

[1] The old philosophers were always railing against Homer and other poets; but scarcely anything on the other side has survived.

bitch barking at her master,' and 'mighty in the empty babble of fools,' and 'the rabble master of too-too-wise heads,' and 'the highbrows are all hungry,' and so on.[1] But let it be said plainly that if imitation and poetry made to please can give some good reason why she ought to be in a well-ordered city, we should be glad indeed to receive her back home, since we are quite conscious of her enchantment for us. Yet to betray the truth as we see it would be very wrong. Tell me, my friend, aren't you enchanted by poesy yourself, especially when you see her through Homer?"

"I should think so!"

"Then may she have the right to return from her exile, when she has defended herself in some lyric or any metre you like?"

"By all means."

"And perhaps we may allow those other champions of hers who are not poets but poet-lovers to plead for her in prose, that she is not only delightful but helpful for constitutions and human life, and we will hear them with favour. For I suppose it will be just so much gain for us if she is proved to be helpful also as well as delightful."

"That it surely will," he said.

"But if not, my dear fellow, we shall do as people who once were in love with somebody, if they believe their love to be no good to them: they don't want to give it up, but they must. And we shall do the same. We shall be glad, indeed, that she should be proved good and true in the highest degree, through the love which has been inbred in us for such poetry by the education which these grand city-constitutions of ours provide; but as long as she cannot make out her case, we will still listen to her, but while we listen we will chant over to ourselves this argument of ours, this, our reasoned incantation, careful not to fall again into that childish passion for her which the many have. We will listen, I say, knowing that we must not take such poetry seriously, as if it were a serious thing that held fast to truth, but the listener must be ever careful, must fear unceasingly for the city within himself, and he must believe what we have said about poetry."

"I agree with you completely," he said.

"Yes, my dear Glaucon," said I, "great is the struggle, great indeed, not what men think it, between good and evil, to be a good man or a bad man: no exaltation from honours or riches or power or anything soever, no, not from poetry itself, is worthy to make us careless of justice and all other virtue."

[1] These tags have not been traced.

"I agree with you," he said, "after this our discussion, and so would anyone else, I think."

"And yet," I said, "we have not yet mentioned the greatest wages and prizes offered for virtue."

"They must be prodigious, indeed, according to you," he said, "if there are others greater than those already mentioned."

"Ah, what could be great," I said, "in such a little time! For all this time from boy to old man would be little indeed compared with all time."

"Nothing, rather!" said he.

"Well then, do you believe an immortal thing ought to be serious about such a little time, and not rather about all time?"

"About all time, I think," he said; "but what is this that you mean?"

"Have you not perceived," I said, "that our soul is immortal and never dies?"

He looked me full in the face, and said, surprised, "No indeed, that I have not; have *you?* Dare *you* say that?"

"If I'm an honest man," I said; "and so can you, I believe; it's nothing difficult."

"*I* find it so," he said, "but I should like to hear this not-difficult thing from you."

"Listen then," I said.

"Only go on," said he.

"You speak of good and evil?" I said.

"I do."

"I wonder if you understand them as I do."

"Pray how is that?" he asked.

"That the evil is all that which destroys and corrupts, and the good is what preserves and benefits."

"Yes, I agree," he said.

"Very well. Do you agree that each thing has its evil and good? For instance, ophthalmia for the eye, and disease for the whole body, mildew for corn and rot for wood, rust for iron and bronze—pretty well everything, as I say, has its natural evil and disease?"

"I agree," he said.

"So whenever one of these appears in anything, it injures whatever it gets into, and in the end it dissolves and destroys it."

"Of course."

"The natural evil of each thing, then, and its own vice, destroys it, and if this does not destroy it nothing else can corrupt it. For I don't suppose the good can ever destroy anything, nor can what is neither good nor evil."

"Why, how could it?" he said.

"Then, if we find something in existence which has its own evil, but one which can only do it harm, yet cannot dissolve or destroy it, we shall know at once that there is no destruction for such a nature?"

"That is probable," he said.

"Very good," said I. "The soul has something which makes it evil, hasn't it?"

"Yes indeed," said he, "all the things we have discussed—injustice, intemperance, cowardice, ignorance."

"Now does anyone of these dissolve and destroy it? Reflect lest we should be deceived by thinking that the unjust and foolish man, when caught doing injustice, then perishes by his injustice, which is the vice of the soul. Take it like this: As disease, which is the vice of the body, wastes and dissolves the body and makes it at last to be body no longer, so all the other things we mentioned are brought to nothingness by their own proper vice, which clings to them and abides within and corrupts them—is not that so?"

"Yes."

"Come then, consider the soul in the same way. Injustice and other vice existing in it clings to it and abides within and corrupts and withers it, until it brings it to death and separates it from the body—is that true?"

"No, not at all," he said.

"Well, it is certainly unreasonable," said I, "that the vice of something else should destroy anything, when its own does not."

"Quite unreasonable."

"Just consider, my dear Glaucon," said I. "We do not suppose the badness of the foods must destroy the body, whatever may be their own particular badness, staleness or rottenness or whatever else; but if the particular badness of the foods themselves engenders in the body the body's own corruption, we shall say that it perishes by its own vice, which is disease, through the foods; but we will never admit that the body is destroyed by the badness of the foods, which are things different from the body, that is, by the alien vice of another thing, unless it engenders in it the natural vice."

"You are quite right," he said.

"According to the same reasoning then," I said, "if badness of the body does not engender vice of soul in the soul, we must never allow that the soul can be destroyed by the vice of anything else without its own badness, one thing by another's vice."

"That is reasonable," he said.

"Then we must either prove that the reasoning is wrong; or so long as that is not proved, we must never say that by fever, or any other disease, or cold steel, or even if you cut up the whole body into the smallest possible pieces, a soul would ever by reason of these things be more liable to destruction, until it is proved that the soul itself becomes more unjust and more impious through these afflictions of the body; if a foreign evil appears in something else,[1] and a thing's[2] own proper evil is not engendered, we must never allow anyone to say that a soul or anything else is being so destroyed."

"Ah, but certainly," he said, "no one will ever prove that the souls of the dying become more unjust through death."

"Ah, but suppose," I said, "that someone dares to tackle that argument, and says the dying man does become more wicked and unjust, merely to avoid having to admit that souls are immortal, what then? If the man who says this is speaking truth, we shall, of course, expect the injustice to be fatal to him that has it like a disease, and that those who catch it would die just by this, because it kills them by its own nature; those would die quicker who take it worst, those who take it lighter would die more slowly; instead of dying—as the unjust die now on account of this disease—by the hand of others inflicting punishment."

"Upon my word," he said, "then injustice will turn out to be no very great terror if it brings death to the man who has it; that would only be a release from evils. But I rather think it will prove to be exactly the opposite; that injustice goes on killing other people if it can, but makes the possessor very lively, and not only lively but unsleeping. So far away, it seems, is its tent pitched from being deadly to him!"

"Well stated!" I said. "Since its own badness and its own evil cannot kill and destroy a soul, the evil which is appointed for the destruction of another thing could hardly destroy soul or anything else except that for which it is appointed."

"Hardly," he said, "that's not probable."

"Then, since it is not destroyed by any evil at all, neither its own evil nor foreign evil, it is clear that the soul must of necessity be always in existence; and if always in existence, then immortal."

"A necessary consequence," he said.

"Then let that be taken as settled," I said, "and if so, you notice that the souls would be always the same. For they

---

[1] E.g., the body.
[2] E.g., the soul's.

could not become fewer, if none perishes, nor again more:[1] since, if any part of what is immortal should become more, you know it must come from the mortal, and all things in the end would become immortal."

"That is true."

"But we must not believe that," I said, "for reason will forbid; nor again must we believe that in its true and real nature a soul is such as to be full of ever-changing diversity and difference in itself."

"What do you mean?" he asked.

"It is not easy," I said, "for anything to be everlasting—as the soul has now been shown to us to be—which is composite of many things, unless it possesses the most beautiful composition."

"Not easy or likely."

"So then, that the soul is a thing immortal we should be compelled to believe both by the argument just concluded and by the others;[2] but as to what its nature really and truly is, we ought not to examine when it is contaminated by union with the body and other evils, as we are doing now. No, what it is in its pure state, such is what must be thoroughly and completely examined by reasoning; and then it will be found much more beautiful, and we shall distinguish much more clearly the opinions about justice and injustice and all the other matters we have discussed. But now we have told the truth about it as far as appears at this present; only we have contemplated it in a state like the sea-god Glaucos;[3] his original nature would no longer be easily discerned by those who catch glimpses of him, because some of the old parts of his body have been broken off, and some worn and crushed and altogether marred by the waves, and others have molluscs grown on and seaweeds and stones, so that he looks like any monster rather than what he naturally was. That is just what the soul looks like as we examine it, marred by a thousand evils. But we must look elsewhere, Glaucon."

"Where?" he asked.

"To its love of wisdom: we must notice what it clings to and what company it seeks; how it is akin to the divine and immortal and that which always exists, and what it would become if it followed the divine wholly, if it could be carried by this impulse out of the deep where it now is, the stones and molluscs all beaten off—all the many wild, stony, earthy

---

[1] Plato believed in reincarnation.
[2] Such as those in the dialogue *Phaedo*, and in the dialogue *Phaedrus*, which is not included in this book.
[3] A fisherman transformed into a sea-god.

things, since earth is the food it feasts on, which have grown about it from its happy entertainments, as they are called. Then we could see its true nature, is it multiple or simple, how it is and what it is. But now I believe we have described pretty well what happens to it in human life and what shapes it takes."

"We have, undoubtedly," said he.

"Very well," I said; "we have cleared ourselves of all the other things in our discussion, and we have not brought in the wages and the reputation of justice, as you said Homer and Hesiod do,[1] justice itself we have found to be best for the soul itself, and the soul must act justly whether it has the ring of Gyges or not, and the cap of Hades too."[2]

"Very true," he said.

"Very well, my dear Glaucon," said I, "now we can, in addition to our previous conclusions, without offence assign the wages to justice, and virtue in general—what wages, how rich wages, it provides for the soul from gods and men alike, both while the man lives and when he has made an end!"

"By all means," he said.

"Then will you all grant me back what you borrowed in our discussion?"

"What exactly?"

"I granted to you that the just man should be thought unjust, and the unjust just. For you considered that this ought to be granted for the sake of argument, even if it were impossible really to hide it from gods and men, in order that justice itself might be distinguished from injustice itself. Don't you remember?"

"It would be wrong of me if I did not," said he.

"Now they have been distinguished, then, I ask you in the name of justice to return me her reputation as it is held in heaven and earth; let us admit about her that she is really reputed so, that she may receive the prizes which she wins by that reputation and hands over to those who possess her, since it has been proved that she does also give them the blessings that come from really being just and does not deceive those who really win her."

"That is only fair," said he.

"Then won't you grant me back this, first of all," I said, that the gods do not fail to know each of these two men— what his real character is?"

"We will grant that back," he said.

---

[1] See p. 161.
[2] *Iliad* v. 844; it made the wearer invisible: the word Hades (Ἀΐδης) was popularly associated with the word ἀειδής, unseen; see *Phaedo* p. 483, n. 1.

"If the gods know, then one would be god-beloved and the other god-hated, as we agreed at the beginning."

"Quite so."

"One whom the gods love will have everything of the best as far as the gods can give it, if there was not some evil inevitably belonging to him from a former sin.[1] Shall we agree there?"

"By all means."

"Then this is what we must believe about the just man: If he is born in poverty, if disease be his portion, or any other evils as men regard them, all these will work together for his good in the end, while he lives or even when he is dead. For the gods of a surety never neglect one who earnestly desires to be just, and by practising virtue to become as like to God as it is possible for man to be."

"It may be expected," he said, "that such a man would not be neglected by one who is like him."

"And we should believe the opposite of this about the unjust man?"

"Most certainly."

"Such prizes, then, come from the gods for the just man."

"That is my opinion, at least," he said.

"From men, then," said I, "what does he get from *them?* Surely this is how we should see it, if we are to present the real truth: Clever and unjust men behave like racers, who make a good run of it from the start, and collapse on the way from the turn; they leap away in a spurt at first, but end up by being laughed at like a lot of fools, and run away uncrowned with their ears down on their shoulders;[2] but real racers keep on to the finish, and win the prizes and the crown. Isn't that what generally happens to the just? At the finish of every action and association, and of life itself, they are held in high esteem, and gain the prizes from mankind?"

"Very true indeed."

"Then will you allow me to say of these just ones what you said yourself of the unjust? Listen now: I shall say that the just, when they grow older, attain high office in the state, if they wish, they take a wife from such family as they wish, they give a daughter in marriage into such family as they wish, and all you said of the unjust I now say of these; on the contrary, I say of the unjust that even if they are not found out in youth, at the finish of the race most of them are caught and laughed at for fools; when they are old they are spurned in their misery by strangers and their fellow-citizens

[1] In some earlier life.
[2] Like dogs or horses tired out.

alike, and flogged, and all the other things you truly said were too coarse to mention—kindly take them as heard from me—that's what they suffer. But see if you will allow my statement?"

"Most certainly," he said, "your statement is quite fair."

"Such, then," I said, "would be the prizes and wages and gifts which come to the just man in his lifetime from gods and men alike, besides those good things that justice itself provides."

"By all means," he said, "fine things and quite certain."

"But these," I said, "are nothing in number or magnitude, compared with what awaits each after death. Those also must be announced, that each of these, the just and the unjust, may have received in full the awards which by the judgment of our argument are due to be announced." [1]

"Speak on," he said, "there are few things which I would more gladly hear."

"Indeed, I have no 'mighty long tale of Alcinoös' to tell you," [2] said I, "but the tale of a mighty man, Er, son of Armenios, a Pamphylian by nation.[3] He met his end in battle once upon a time; and when the dead were taken up after ten days, the bodies already decayed, he was found whole; taken home and about to be buried on the twelfth day, while he lay on the pyre, he came to life again, and alive again he told what he had seen in the other world. When his soul went forth, he said, it travelled with many others, until they reached a wonderful region, in which were two openings in the earth side by side, and two others in the heaven above facing them. Between these judges were seated.[4] These gave judgment, and, according to the judgment, they commanded the just men to proceed to the right and upwards through heaven, after hanging on the breasts of the judged ones tokens to show the judgment; the unjust they sent down to the left, these also having tokens hanging behind of all they had done. When he himself approached they told him he must become a messenger[5] to mankind of things there, and they commanded

---

[1] χρή...ἀκοῦσαι......ἀκοῦσαι—the proclamation of the final judgment.
[2] The proverbial title of the long story told to Alcinoös by Odysseus, *Odyssey* ix. to xii.
[3] Plato puns on the name Alcinoös by the title "mighty," *alcimos*. Even Pamphylian (a native of Pamphylia in Asia Minor) means "of every nation," so here "a native of Everyland." There were many such legends, but Plato puts his own stamp upon this. Scholars give a number of references and parallels. One of the ancestors of Joseph, the husband of Mary, was named Er; Luke iii: 28.
[4] The wonderful region was a sort of meadow, like Homer's meadow of asphodel, where the judges sat. On the right were two heavenly openings, on the left, two earthly openings. By one of each pair, souls departed, by the other of each pair, souls came back; some from earth and some from heaven for new lives, some to earth and some to heaven to serve their sentences.
[5] Ἄγγελος, the same word as "angel."

him to hear and see everything in the place. So here he watched the souls departing by two of the openings of heaven and earth when sentence had been passed on them, and, by the other two, souls returning, those coming up out of one in the earth[1] covered with dirt and dust, others coming out of the other down from heaven pure and clean. The souls which arrived from time to time appeared to have come from a long journey, and were glad to come out into the meadow; there they encamped as at a fair, and any that were acquainted greeted each other; the souls that came out of the earth asked the others news of their part, and the souls from heaven asked those what befell in their place. They recounted their histories to each other; those, weeping and lamenting when they recalled what they had suffered and seen in their sojourn underground—the sojourn, they said, lasted a thousand years; on the other hand, the souls out of heaven told of bliss and sights incredibly beautiful. It would take a long time, Glaucon, to tell the whole history, but the sum of his tale he said was this. Each had paid satisfaction to all persons that he had wronged, and for each offence in turn ten times, that is to say, once in each hundred years, taking a hundred years as the length of a human life, so as to make the payment for each wrong tenfold. For example, if any had been the cause of many deaths, or betrayed cities or armies, and cast men into slavery, or had part in some other villainy, for all these things they received pains for each, tenfold; if again any had done good deeds of benefaction, and if they had been just and religious, they received recompense in the same proportion. He spoke also of those who had died at birth or after a short life, but that is not worthy of record. For piety and impiety toward gods and parents, and personal homicide, he described still heavier retribution. Thus he was by, he said, when one asked another where was Ardiaios the Great. This Ardiaios had been tyrant of a city in Pamphylia a thousand years before that time; he had murdered his old father and his elder brother, and done many other abominable things, as was reported. Then the one who had been questioned answered, 'He has not come here, and verily he never will. Indeed, this was one of the dreadful sights which we saw, when we were near the mouth and just about to go up after all we had suffered, we suddenly saw that man and a number of others, mostly tyrants I think, but there were some other great sinners from private life. These believed they were about to go up, but the mouth would not receive them; it

[1] Not the newly dead, but those returning from discipline in the bowels of the earth.

THE REPUBLIC Book X (614D–616E) 417

bellowed aloud whenever one incurably wicked in this way, or one who had not paid in full for his wickedness, attempted to go up.' And there they could see standing by, he said, savage men and fiery all through to look at, who understood the sound, and seized some and carried them away; but Ardiaios and others they bound hand and foot and head, threw them down, and dragged them along by the wayside, flaying their skins off by carding them on thorn bushes like wool, and proclaiming to all the passers-by why this was, and how they were being taken away to be thrown into the bottomless pit. Then indeed, he said, after their many awful terrors of all kinds this last terror went beyond all, each fearing lest the bellow should sound against him as he came up, and how overjoyed each one was if it were silent and let him go up.

"Such, then, were the kinds of penalties and punishments, or, on the other hand, the corresponding blessings, which they received. Seven days each company was allowed to remain in the meadow, and on the eighth they must rise up and proceed.[1] Then on the fourth day they come to a place whence they can see stretching from above through all the earth and sky a light straight like a pillar, most resembling the rainbow but more brilliant and pure. To this light they came in a day's march; and there at the middle of the light[2] they saw the ends of its chains stretched from heaven; for this light was the bond of heaven and held together all the revolving vault like the undergirdings of ships-of-war.[3] From the ends was extended the Spindle of Necessity, through which all the orbits were turned; its shaft and hook were of adamant, the whorl of adamant with a mixture of other things. This is how he described the whorl. The shape is like ours of this earth; but to judge from what he said, it is as if there were one great whorl[4] hollow and scooped out right through, and another one smaller fitting exactly within it, and a third and a fourth and four more, fitted into each other like a nest of boxes, for there were eight whorls in all fitting each into the next, and they showed their rims from above in circles, forming together one solid whorl around the shaft; and the shaft was driven right through the eighth. The first whorl,

[1] What follows is a poetical and symbolical description, not an exact astronomy. Plato seems however to regard earth as in the centre, and sun, moon and planets revolving around it.
[2] The light passed through the earth, so this was the middle point of the earth too.
[3] In storms merchant ships were "undergirded" to strengthen them, as described by St. Paul in Acts xxvii:17. Greek triremes probably had permanent strengthening; for information about their structure see *A Dictionary of Greek and Roman Antiquities* by W. Smith and others.
[4] Almost like a sphere sliced through the middle, and showing a flat surface there.

the one on the outside, had the circle of its rim widest, the rim of the sixth was second widest, the fourth third widest, the eighth fourth widest, the seventh fifth widest, the third sixth widest, the seventh widest, the second eighth widest.[1] The rim of the widest was spangled,[2] that of the seventh most brilliant, that of the eighth took its colour from the seventh shining upon it, those of second and fifth were alike, and more yellow than these two, the third had the whitest colour, the fourth was reddish, the sixth was second in whiteness. The spindle revolved turning as a whole in the same movement, but within the whole as it revolved the seven inside circles revolved quietly in the opposite direction to the whole; of these seven, the eighth moved most quickly; second in speed and together, seventh and sixth and fifth; third in speed (as it appeared to them) revolved the fourth in the contrary direction; fourth in speed the third, and fifth the second. The spindle itself was turned on the knees of Necessity.[3]

"Perched above upon each of the circles is a Siren carried round along with it, and singing one sound, one note, so that from all the eight there was one concord.[4] Others were seated around at equal distances, three, each on her throne, daughters of Necessity, the Portioners,[5] robed in white, with ribands upon their heads, Lachesis and Clotho and Atropos,[6] singing to the concord of the Sirens, Lachesis the past, Clotho the present, Atropos what is to come. And Clotho with a touch of the right hand helped in moving the outside orbit of the spindle, stopping from time to time, and Atropos again with the left hand helped with the inner ones in like manner; Lachesis takes hold of either in turn, with one or the other hand.[7]

"When they arrived, he went on, they had to go straight before Lachesis. Then an interpreter first arranged them in order. There were lots, and little models of lives, lying upon the lap of Lachesis, and he took some of these and went up on a high platform, and spoke, saying: 'Thus saith the Virgin Lachesis, daughter of Necessity. Souls of a passing day, here beginneth another cycle of mortal life that leads to death. No

---

[1] These are the orbits or places of (1) Fixed Stars, (2) Venus, (3) Mars, (4) Moon, (5) Sun, (6) Mercury, (7) Jupiter, (8) Saturn; counted according to the width of the rims. The width of the rims means the distances of the planets from each other. The order from the outside is: (1) Fixed Stars (2) Saturn, (3) Jupiter, (4) Mars, (5) Mercury, (6) Venus, (7) Sun, (8) Moon. Plato rightly believed the moon to be lighted by the sun.

[2] The poet's regular description of the sky is "spangled with burning stars." The other rims are described as the planets generally are.

[3] Who was therefore seated in the centre of the universe.

[4] The Pythagoreans held that the seven-planets gave forth each one note of the heptachord; later the eighth of the fixed stars was added. Hence the music of the spheres.

[5] The Fates.

[6] Lotter and Spinner and Neverturnback.

[7] Each of these details has some philosophical meaning.

Destiny[1] shall cast lots for you, but you shall all choose your own Destiny; let him that draws the first lot first choose a life, and thereto he shall cleave of necessity. But Virtue knows no master: as each honours or despises her he shall have more or less of her. The blame is for the chooser; God is blameless.'

"Having spoken thus, the Interpreter threw the lots before them all, and each one picked up that which fell near him, except Er himself; they forbade him. It was clear to each one picking up what number his lot was. After this again he laid out the models of lives on the ground before them, many more in number than those present, all sorts and kinds of them; there were lives of all kinds of animals and all sorts and conditions of men. For there were tyrannies among them, some lasting to the end, others destroyed in the middle and ending in penury and banishment and beggary; and there were lives of famous men, some renowned for beauty of looks or form or else for strength and prowess of any sort, some for high birth and the virtues of ancestors, and other lives ignoble on the same accounts: so also, lives of women. There was no regulation of soul in the lives, because a soul must become different of necessity, according to what life is chosen; but all the other things were commingled together and mixed with riches and poverty, with disease and health, and some were intermediate among these.

"There indeed, my dear Glaucon, is the whole danger for man. Therefore we must take most care that each one of us shall disregard all studies, except this one study, and in this he shall be both seeker and student, to see if he shall be able to learn and discover in any place one who shall give him the ability and intelligence to know a good life from a bad, and to choose always and everywhere the best that the conditions allow; taking into account all we have spoken of, and comparing and distinguishing them for their effect towards virtue in life: one who shall teach him how thus to know what beauty mingled with poverty or riches in union with what state of soul will work evil or good; what will be the effect of high birth or low birth, private station or governing station, strength or weakness, cleverness or dullness in learning, and all such qualities of the soul natural or acquired—what effects they will have when commingled together; so that it will be possible for him, by taking account of all these things, to make his choice: keeping his gaze fixed all the while on the nature of the soul, and considering both the worse and the better life, calling it worse if it so leads the soul that it becomes more

---

[1] *Daimōn*, meaning here the "genius" or "double" of a man—a spirit supposed to attend upon each man through life.

unjust, and better if it leads the soul to become more just. All else he will leave alone; for we have seen that this is the best choice, both for living and for dying. Holding fast, then, to this faith like adamant, he must go to the house of Hades, that there also he may be unshaken by riches and such evil things; that he may not fall into tyrannies and other such activities and do many incurable evils, and suffer even greater evils himself; but that he may know how to choose always the life that lies in the mean of such things, and to flee from excess on either side, both in this life as far as possible and in all the life to come. For thus does a man become happiest and most fortunate.

"To pass on, then, the messenger from the other world declared that the interpreter then spoke and said: 'Even for the last comer there remains a life which is not evil but agreeable, if he chooses with good sense and lives with good effort. Let not the first choose heedlessly, let not the last despair.' After this proclamation, Er said the drawer of the first lot went straight up and chose the greatest tyranny, but in his folly and greed he did not in choosing examine all the details properly, so he never saw that he was fated in it to devour his own children, amongst other horrible things; when he examined it at his leisure he beat his breast and lamented the choice, ignoring the interpreter's forewarning, for he laid the blame for his ills not on himself but on luck and destiny, and anything instead of himself. And he was one of those who had come down out of heaven; he had lived his former life in a well-ordered community, with some share of virtue which came by habit without philosophy. Indeed, one might say, not less than half[1] those caught in such ways had come out of heaven, because these had no practice in bearing trouble; but most of those who came out of the earth were in no hurry to choose, because they had both felt trouble themselves and seen others in trouble. That was why most of the souls had an exchange of evil and good things, as well as because of the luck of the lot. Yet if a man, when he came back into life on earth, always studied a sound philosophy, and if his lot of choice was not among the last, he would have a good chance of being happy here, according to this report from the next world; and not only that, but his journey from this world to that and back again would not be underground and rough but smooth and through heaven. For this was a sight worth seeing, he said, how the different souls chose their lives, a pitiable sight, and ridiculous, and very strange. They mostly chose according to their experience in the former life. He said he saw the soul

[1] An understatement meaning more than half.

which had been Orpheus choosing a swan's life, through hatred of womankind, because women killed him, and therefore he would not be conceived and born of a woman. He saw the soul of Thamyras[1] choosing to be a nightingale. And he saw a swan changing to a man's life for its choice, and other musical creatures doing the same. The soul that drew the twentieth lot he said chose a lion's life; that was Aias, Telamon's son, who shrank from becoming a man because he remembered the award of the arms.[2] Next after him was the soul of Agamemnon,[3] this also hated the human race for its sufferings, and chose to be an eagle. The soul of Atalanta had one of the middle lots; she caught sight of the great honours of a man who was an athlete, and she could not pass them by, she took them. After this soul, he saw the soul of Epeios,[4] Panopeus' son, entering into the nature of a craftswoman. Far away among the last lots he saw the soul of that buffoon Thersites[5] putting on the ape. As chance had it, the soul of Odysseus had the last lot of all, and went up to make its choice; remembering his former toils and troubles,[6] it had thrown off all ambition, and went hunting around for a long time for a quiet, retired life, until it found one at last lying somewhere which no one else wanted. The soul chose it gladly, and said, 'That's my choice—I'm glad! I should have done the same if I had had the first lot.'

"So with other creatures, the beasts; some passed into men and some into one another, the unjust beasts changing into savage ones, the just into gentle ones, and there were all sorts of mixtures. When, therefore, all the souls had chosen their lives in the order of their lots, they went in turn before Lachesis and she sent with each the Destiny[7] he had chosen, to be his guardian through life and to fulfill all his choice. First this spirit led the soul to Clotho, passing under her hand and the turn of the circling spindle, thus ratifying the fate which he had chosen for his lot; then, after touching her, the spirit next brought the soul to the spinning of Atropos Neverturnback—to make the threads now spun to be never reversed,[8] and from there he went, without casting one look back, below the throne of Necessity, and passed through it.

[1] A singer, like Orpheus.
[2] The arms of Achilles were awarded to Odysseus. Aias (Ajax) thought they were due to him, and he went mad and then killed himself.
[3] His wife murdered him.
[4] He built the Wooden Horse.
[5] The ugliest man in the army before Troy, and a ranting agitator. *Iliad* ii. 212 ff.
[6] See Homer's *Odyssey*, the story of the wanderings, adventures, toils and troubles of Odysseus.
[7] *Daimon*, see p. 419, n. 1.
[8] To make the fated future irreversible.

Then after the others[1] had passed through, all travelled into the Plain of Oblivion through terrible stifling heat; for the plain is bare of trees and all that grows on the earth. There he said they camped, as evening was coming on, beside the River of Neglectfulness, whose water no vessel will hold. Everyone was compelled to drink a measure of this water; but those who were not saved by prudence drank more than the measure, and whoever drank forgot everything. When they were laid to sleep and midnight came, there was thunder and earthquake and then suddenly they were carried upward this way and that to birth, like shooting stars. Er was himself prevented from drinking the water; yet how and by what way he came again to his body, he knew not, only he suddenly opened his eyes in the morning and saw himself lying upon the pyre.

"And so, Glaucon, the story was saved and not lost; and it would save us, if we would be guided by it, and we shall safely cross the River of Oblivion, and we shall not stain the soul. But if we will follow my advice, believing the soul immortal, and able to undergo all evil things and all good things, we will hold ever to the upward road, and we will practise in every way justice along with wisdom, in order that we may be friends to the gods and to ourselves as well, both while we remain here on earth, and when we receive the rewards of virtue, like the victors in the games going round collecting their prizes; and that both here and in the thousand-year journey, which I have told you of, all may be well with us."

[1] The other spirits and their charges.

THE APOLOGY

(The Defence of Socrates)

Introductory Note

The trial of Socrates took place in 399 B.C., when he was seventy years old. Meletos, Anytos and Lycon (Anytos is one of the characters in the Meno) *accused him of impiety and of corrupting the young men.*

The court which tried Socrates was composed of 501 citizens, and was a subdivision of the larger court of six thousand citizens, chosen by lot, which dealt with such cases. There were no judge and jury in the modern sense; the decision of the court was that of the majority vote.

When the court had pronounced Socrates guilty, the law required him to propose his own penalty, as an alternative to the death penalty proposed by Meletos; no penalty was prescribed by law for his offence. The court then had to choose, by a second vote, between the proposals of the accuser and the accused.

From the mention on page 439 it appears that Plato himself was present at the trial.

How you felt, gentlemen of Athens, when you heard my accusers, I do not know; but I—well, I nearly forgot who I was, they were so persuasive. Yet as for truth—one might almost say they have spoken not one word of truth. But what most astonished me in the many lies they told was when they warned you to take good care not to be deceived by me, "because I was a terribly clever speaker." They ought to have been ashamed to say it, because I shall prove them wrong at once by facts when I begin to speak, and you will see that I am not a bit of a clever speaker. That seemed to me the most shameless thing about them, unless of course they call one who speaks the truth a clever speaker. If that is what they mean, I would agree that I am not an orator of their class. Well then, these men, as I said, have spoken hardly one word of truth; but you shall hear from me the whole truth; not eloquence, gentlemen, like their own, decked out in fine words and phrases, not covered with ornaments; not at all—you shall hear things spoken anyhow in the words that first come. For I believe justice is in what I say, and let none of you expect anything else; indeed it would not be proper, gentlemen, for an old man like me to come before you like a boy moulding his words in pretty patterns. One thing, however, gentlemen, I beg and pray you most earnestly; if you hear me using to defend myself here the same words which I speak with generally, in the market or at the banker's counter, where many of you have heard me, and elsewhere, do not be surprised and make a noise on that account. The fact is, this is the first time I ever came up before a court, although I am seventy years old; so I am simply quite strange to the style of this place. If I were really a stranger, a foreigner, I suppose you would not be hard on me if I used the language and manner which I had been brought up to; then I beg you to treat me the same way now, and, as seems fair, to let pass my manner of speaking; perhaps it might be better, and perhaps it might be worse; but please consider only one thing and attend carefully to that—whether my plea is just or not. For that is the merit of the juryman, but the merit of the orator is to speak the truth.

First, then, gentlemen, it is proper for me to answer the first false accusations made against me, and the first accusers; next, to answer the later accusations and accusers. Indeed, I have had many accusers complaining to you, and for a long time, for many years now, and with not a word of truth to say; these I fear, rather than Anytos and his friends, although they, too, are dangerous; but the others are more dangerous, gentlemen, who got hold of most of you while you were boys, and persuaded you, and accused me falsely, and said, "There is a certain Socrates, a highbrow; brainy in skylore, has investigated what is under the earth, makes the weaker argument the stronger." These, gentlemen, who have broadcast this reputation, these are my dangerous accusers; for those who hear believe that anyone who is a student of that sort of lore must be an atheist as well. Yes, these accusers are many, and they have been accusing me for a long time, still saying the same, and moreover saying it to you at an age when you would be most likely to believe, when some of you were children or at least lads, really accusing in a case which goes by default, with no one to defend. The most unreasonable thing is that it is impossible to know their names or to tell who they are—unless one of them happens to be a comic poet.[1] But those who have deluded you from envy and malice,

[1] Aristophanes was one of them. In *The Clouds* he represented Socrates as an old man hung up in a basket observing the sun, and in other comic situations.

APOLOGY (17C–19E)

or some who are convinced themselves and try to convince others, these are the hardest to deal with. For there is no possibility of having them produced here, or of cross-questioning any one of them, but having to defend oneself against them is just like being compelled to fight with shadows, and cross-question with none answering. Pray remember, then, that my accusers are of two kinds, as I say, one, those who have accused me now, and the other, the old ones I mention; and consider that I must answer the old ones first. You heard them first, you see, and much more than the new ones. Very good; I must answer them, gentlemen, and try to get rid of the prejudice which you have had so long, with only a short time to do it. I hope indeed I may remove it, if it is better so both for you and for me, and I hope my defence may have some success; but I think it is difficult, and I am quite aware what a task it is. All the same, in this let God's will be done; I must obey the law, and make my defence.

Let us go back to the beginning, and see what the accusation is, whence came the prejudice against me, which Meletos believed when he brought this indictment. Very well; what did the calumniators say who calumniated me? I will pretend to read a pretended affidavit of my accusers: "Socrates is a criminal and a busybody, prying into things under the earth and up in the heavens, and making the weaker argument the stronger, and teaching these same things to others." It is something like that; for that is what you saw in the comedy[1] of Aristophanes, a certain Socrates there being carried about, and claiming to be treading on air and talking much other nonsensical nonsense about which I don't understand one jot or tittle. Don't suppose that in saying this I mean to disparage knowledge of that kind, if anyone does know about such things: may I never be prosecuted by Meletos on serious charges such as that! But I have nothing to do with such things, gentlemen. I appeal to most of you to bear me out, and I ask you to inform and tell one another, as many as have ever heard me conversing—and those of you who have heard me are many—tell one another, then, whether any of you has ever heard me conversing about such things, either much or little. Then you will recognise from this that the other things are just the same which people say about me.

But, indeed, as none of these things is true, neither is it true, even if you have heard it from someone, that I undertake to educate people, and take fees. I must say I think it is a grand thing for anyone to be able to educate people as Gorgias of Leontini, and Prodicos of Ceos, and Hippias of

[1] *The Clouds.* See also p. 329, n. 1.

Elis do. For each of these, gentlemen, is able to go to any city, and persuade the young men, who can associate for nothing with any one they like of their fellow-citizens, to leave the society of those and to associate with themselves, and to pay for it and thank them besides. Indeed, there is in this place another man, one from Paros, an able man, who I found out was staying here in Athens; for I happened to meet a man who has paid more money to Sophists[1] than all the rest put together, Callias, Hipponicos' son, so I asked him —he has two sons of his own—"Callias," I said, "if your two sons were colts or calves, we should know how to hire and pay a manager for them, to make them well-bred in the virtue proper to those animals; he would be a horse-trainer or a farmer; but now, since they are human beings, whom have you in mind to be their manager? Who is an expert in such virtue, human or political? For I think you have looked for one because you have sons. Is there one," said I, "or not?"

"Certainly there is," said he.

"Who?" said I, "and where does he come from, and what's his fee for teaching?"

"Euenos," he said, "from Paros, my dear Socrates, five minas." [2]

And I said Euenos is a happy man, if really and truly he has this art and teaches it for such a modest fee. I, at least, should give myself fine airs and graces if I had this knowledge. But I have not, gentlemen.

Some one of you then might put in and ask perhaps, "Well, Socrates, what is your business? Where did these calumnies come from? For all this talk about you, and such a reputation, has not arisen, I presume, when you were working at nothing more unusual than others do; it must be you were doing something different from most people. Then tell us what it is, that we may not be rash and careless about you." That seems to be quite fair, if anyone says it, and I will try to show you what this is which has got me this name[3] and this prejudice. Listen, then. And perhaps some of you will think I am jesting, but be sure I will tell you the whole truth: a sort of wisdom has got me this name, gentlemen, and nothing else. Wisdom! What wisdom? Perhaps the only wisdom that man can have. For the fact is, I really am wise in this wisdom; but it may be that those I just spoke of are wise in a wisdom greater than man's, or I can't think how to describe it—for I don't understand it myself, but whoever says I do, lies, and speaks in

[1] See note on *Meno*, p. 49.
[2] About the equivalent of £60, or $180.
[3] Of Sophist.

calumny of me. And do not protest, gentlemen, even if you should think I am boastful; for what I am going to tell you is not my word, but I will refer it to a speaker of sufficient authority; I will call the god in Delphi as witness of my wisdom, whether indeed it is wisdom at all, and what it is. I suppose you know Chairephon. He has been my friend since I was young, and a friend of your people's party, and he was banished with you lately and with you was restored. And you know, doubtless, what sort of man he was, how impetuous in all he tried to do. Well, once he went to Delphi and dared to ask this question of the oracle—don't make an uproar, gentlemen, at what I say—for he asked if anyone was wiser than I was. The priestess answered, then, that no one was wiser. His brother is here, and he will bear witness to this, as Chairephon is dead. But let me tell you why I say this; I am going to show you where that calumny came from. Well, when I heard that reply I thought: "What in the world does the god mean? What in the world is his riddle? For I know in my conscience that I am not wise in anything, great or small; then what in the world does he mean when he says I am wisest? Surely he is not lying? For he must not lie." I was puzzled for a long time to understand what he meant; then I thought of a way to try to find out, something like this: I approached one of those who had the reputation of being wise, for there, I thought, if anywhere, I should test the revelation and prove that the oracle was wrong: "Here is one wiser than I, but you said I was wiser." When I examined him, then—I need not tell his name, but it was one of our statesmen whom I was examining when I had this strange experience, gentlemen—and when I conversed with him, I thought this man seemed to be wise both to many others and especially to himself, but that he was not; and then I tried to show him that he thought he was wise, but was not. Because of that he disliked me and so did many others who were there, but I went away thinking to myself that I was wiser than this man; the fact is that neither of us knows anything beautiful and good, but he thinks he does know when he doesn't, and I don't know and don't think I do: so I am wiser than he is by only this trifle, that what I do not know I don't think I do. After that I tried another, one of those reputed to be wiser than that man, and I thought just the same; then he and many others took a dislike to me.

So I went to one after another after that, and saw that I was disliked; and I sorrowed and feared; but still it seemed necessary to hold the god's business of the highest importance, so I had to go on trying to find out what the oracle meant, and approaching all those who had the reputation of knowledge. And by the Dog, gentlemen—for I must tell you the truth—this is what happened to me: Those who had the highest reputation seemed to me nearly the most wanting, when I tried to find out in the god's way, but others who were thought inferior seemed to be more capable men as to common sense. You see I must show you my wanderings, as one who had my own Labours[1] to prove that the oracle was unimpeachable. For after the statesmen, I approached the poets, the composers of tragedies and the composers of dithyrambs,[2] and all the rest as well; there I expected to find myself caught in the act as more ignorant than they were. So I took up their poems, those which I thought they had taken most pains to perfect, and questioned them as to what they meant, and I hoped to learn something from them at the same time. Well, gentlemen, I am ashamed to tell you the truth; but I must. Almost all the bystanders, with hardly an exception, one might say, had something better to say than the composers had about their own compositions. I discovered, then, very soon about the poets that no wisdom enabled them to compose as they did, but natural genius and inspiration;[3] like the diviners and those who chant oracles, who say many fine things but do not understand anything of what they say. The poets appeared to me to be in much the same case; and at the same time I perceived that because of their poetry they believed they were the wisest of mankind in other things as well, which they were not. So I left them also, believing that I had the same superiority over them as I had over the statesmen.

At last I approached the craftsmen; for here I was conscious that I knew nothing, one may say, but these I was sure to find knowing much of real value. I was not deceived in that; they knew what I did not, and here they were much wiser than I was. But, gentlemen, they seemed to make the same mistake as the poets, even good workmen; because they could manage their art well, each one claimed to be very wise in other things also, the greatest things, and this fault of theirs appeared to obscure their real wisdom. So I asked myself on behalf of the oracle, whether I should prefer to be as I am, not wise with their wisdom nor ignorant with their ignorance; or to have what they have, both. I answered myself and the oracle, that it was best for me to be as I am.

From this enquiry, gentlemen, many dislikes have arisen against me, and those very dangerous and crushing, so that

[1] Like Heracles (Hercules).
[2] See p. 192 n.
[3] See also *Ion*, p. 18, and generally.

many calumnies have come out of them, and I got the title of being wise. For the bystanders always believe that I am wise myself in the matters on which I test another; but the truth really is, gentlemen, that the god in fact is wise, and in this oracle he means that human wisdom is worth little or nothing, and it appears that he does not say this of Socrates, but simply adds my name to take me as an example, as if he were to say that this one of you human beings is wisest, who like Socrates knows that he is in truth worth nothing as regards wisdom. This is what I still, even now, go about searching and investigating in the god's way, if ever I think one of our people, or a foreigner, is wise; and whenever I don't find him so, I help the god by proving that the man is not wise. And because of this busy life, I have had no leisure either for public business worth mentioning or private, but I remain in infinite poverty through my service of the god.

Besides this, the young men, those who have most leisure, sons of the most wealthy houses, follow me of their own accord, delighted to hear people being cross-examined; and they often imitate me, they try themselves to cross-examine, and then, I think, they find plenty of people who believe they know something, when they know little or nothing. So in consequence those who are cross-examined are angry with me instead of with themselves, and say that Socrates is a blackguard and corrupts the young; and whenever someone asks them, "By doing what and teaching what?" they have nothing to say; they do not know, but, unwilling to own that they are at a loss, they repeat the stock charges against all philosophers, "underground lore and up-in-the-air lore, atheists, making the weaker argument the stronger." For they would not like, I think, to say the truth, that they are shown up as pretending to know when they know nothing. So I think, because they are ambitious, and pushing, and many in number, and they speak in battalions very plausibly about me, they have deafened you long since and now calumniate me vigorously. From among these Meletos has set upon me, and Anytos and Lycon, Meletos being angry on behalf of the poets, and Anytos for the craftsmen and statesmen, and Lycon for the orators. The result is, as I began by saying, that I should be surprised if I could erase this prejudice from you in so short a time when it has grown so great. This, gentlemen, is the truth; I have hidden nothing great or small, and dissembled nothing. And I know well enough that these same things make me disliked; which is another proof that I am speaking the truth, and that this is the prejudice against me, and these are the causes. Whether you examine this now or afterwards, you will find the same.

As regards the accusations of my first accusers, let this defence suffice for you; next I will try to answer Meletos, the good patriot, as he calls himself, and the later accusers. Once more, then, let us take their affidavit, as if they were another set of accusers. This is how it runs: It says that Socrates is a criminal, who corrupts the young and does not believe in the gods whom the state believes in, but other new spiritual things instead. Such is the accusation; let us examine each point in this accusation. It says I am a criminal who corrupts the young. But I say, gentlemen, that Meletos is a criminal who is making a jest of serious things by prosecuting people lightly, by pretending to be serious and to care for things which he has never cared about at all. That this is true, I will try to show you also.

Meletos, stand up here before me, and answer: Don't you think it very important that the younger generation should be as good as possible?

"I do."

Then tell these gentlemen, who is it makes them better? It is clear that you know, since you care about it. You have found the one who corrupts them, as you say, and you bring me before this court here and accuse me; now then, say who makes them better, inform the court who he is. You see, Meletos, you are silent, you cannot say. Yet does it not seem disgraceful to you, and a sufficient proof of what I am just saying, that you have cared nothing about it? Come, say my good man, who makes them better?

"The laws."

That's not what I ask, dear sir; what *man*, who in the first place knows this very thing, the laws?

"This jury, Socrates."

What do you mean, Meletos? The gentlemen of the jury here are able to educate the young and make them better?

"Yes indeed."

All of them, or only some?

"All."

Excellently said, by Hera, quite an abundance of benefactors. Well, what of the people here listening to us, do they make the young better, or not?

"Yes, they do too."

What about the Councillors?[1]

"The Councillors too."

Oh, indeed, Meletos, is it possible that the Commons corrupt

---

[1] The members of the upper house; see p. 438, n. 1.

the younger generation? Or do they also make them better, all of them?"

"They do."

Then the whole nation of the Athenians, it seems, makes them fine gentlemen,[1] except me, and I alone corrupt them? Is that what you say?

"Yes, that is exactly what I do say."

What bad luck for me! You charge me with my great bad luck! Answer me now: Are horses in the same case, do you think? All the men in the world are making them better, and only one corrupting them? Isn't the truth quite the opposite of this: There is one, perhaps, able to make them better, or very few—the horse-trainers, but most people, if they have to do with horses and use them, spoil and corrupt them? Isn't that the case, Meletos, both with horses and with all other animals? Most certainly, whether you and Anytos say no or whether you say yes. What a blessing it would be for young people, if only a single one corrupts them, and all the rest do them good! But really, Meletos, that is enough to show that you never were anxious about young people; you show clearly your own carelessness—you have cared nothing about the things you impeach me for.

I have another question for you; in God's name attend, Meletos. Is it better to live among good citizens or bad ones? Answer me, good sir. There's nothing difficult in my question. Don't the bad ones do some harm to those who are at any time nearest to them, and the good ones some good?

"Certainly."

Then is there anyone who wants to be damaged by his associates rather than to be helped? Answer, my good man; the law commands you to answer. Is there anyone who wants to be damaged?

"No, certainly."

Very well. You bring me here as one who corrupts the young generation and makes them worse: Do you say that I mean to do it, or not?

"You mean to do it is what I say."

Oh dear me, Meletos! I so old and you so young, and yet you are so much wiser than I am! You know that bad men always do harm to those who are nearest about them, but good men do good; yet look at me—have I indeed come to such a depth of ignorance that I do not know even this—that if I make one of my associates bad I shall risk getting some evil from him—to such a depth as to do so great an evil intentionally, as you say? I don't believe you there,

[1] Literally, "Beautiful and good."

Meletos, nor does anyone else in the world, I think; but either I do not corrupt, or if I do, I corrupt without meaning to do it. So you are speaking falsely on both counts. But if I do it without intent, there is no law to bring a man into court for accidental mistakes such as this; on the contrary, the law is that one should take him apart privately and instruct and admonish him: for it is plain that, if I learn better, I shall stop what I do without intent. But you shirked meeting me and instructing me; you would not do that, and you bring me to this court, where it is the law to summon those who need punishment, not instruction.

Well now, gentlemen, thus much is plain by this time, as I said, that Meletos has never cared for these things, not one little bit. All the same, kindly tell us, Meletos, how do you say I corrupt the young? It seems plain from the indictment which you made that it is by teaching them not to believe in the gods which the state believes in, but in other new spirits. Don't you say that it is by teaching this that I corrupt them?

"I do say so, and no mistake about it."

In the name of those gods, then, the very ones we speak of, Meletos, make it still clearer to me and these gentlemen. I can't understand whether you say I teach them to believe in some gods—in that case I do believe myself that there are gods, and I am not a complete atheist, nor am I a criminal in that sense —but that I do not believe in the same gods which the state believes in, but others, and this is what you accuse me of, that I believe in others: or, secondly, do you say that I disbelieve in gods altogether and teach this to other people?

"This is what I say, that you believe in no gods at all."

O you amazing creature, Meletos! What makes you say that? Then I don't believe even the sun and the moon are gods, like everyone else in the world?

"No, by Zeus, he does not, gentlemen of the jury, he says the sun is a stone and the moon is earth."

Is Anaxagoras before you, my dear Meletos? Do you think you are accusing him? Do you despise these gentlemen so much, do you think them so illiterate, as not to know that the books of the great Anaxagoras of Clazomenae are full of this lore? And so the young men learn this lore from me, when they might often buy a ticket for one drachma at the most in the orchestra,[1] and have a laugh at Socrates if he says this lore is his, especially when it is so odd! By Zeus, is that what you

---

[1] The "orchestra" was the space in front of the stage (corresponding roughly to the orchestra's place in a modern theatre) used by the chorus in Greek drama. The reference here is probably to the orchestra of the theatre of Dionysus, where spectators might see plays presenting doctrines of Anaxagoras. The drachma is the ancient drachma—say about 3 shillings or 50 cents now.

think of me, that I don't believe in any god?

"No, by Zeus, you don't, not one little bit."

Well, Meletos, no one can believe you, and, to my mind, in this matter you don't believe your own words. What I think, gentlemen, is that this man seems to be an impudent bully, and he has made this indictment in the reckless violence of wild youth. He is like one who has made a riddle to test me: Will Socrates the so-called Wise guess that I am jesting and contradicting myself? Or shall I deceive him and the others who hear it? For the man seems to me to be contradicting himself in the indictment, which might be put "Socrates is a criminal for not believing in gods but believing in gods." Truly this is a game he is playing.

Now come with me, gentlemen, while I examine how he seems to me to mean this. You answer us, Meletos, and you gentlemen, remember not to make an uproar, as I asked you before, if I speak in my usual manner.

Is there any man, Meletos, who believes there are human things, but does not believe in human beings?—Let him answer, gentlemen, and let him not go on interrupting again and again. Is there anyone who does not believe in horses, but does believe in horsey things? Or does not believe in pipers, but does believe in things which pipers do? No, there is not, my good friend; I will answer it for you to the court, if you won't answer yourself. But answer what comes next: Is there anyone who believes in spiritual things, but not in spirits?

"No, there is not."

Many thanks for the answer, wrung from you by the court here. Now then, you say I believe in spiritual things and teach them, whether new or old, at any rate spiritual things; I believe in them according to your words, indeed you even swore to it in the indictment. But if I believe in spiritual things, surely it is absolutely necessary that I believe in spirits. Is not that right? It is then, for I put you down as agreeing since you do not answer. And spirits, do we not believe them to be either gods or the sons of gods? Yes or no?

"Certainly."

I believe in spirits then, as you say; then if spirits are a kind of gods, this would be your riddle or jest which I spoke of, that you said I do not believe in gods and yet again I do, because I believe in spirits; if, again, spirits are sons of gods, a sort of bastards from nymphs or whatnot, as they are said to be, who in the world would believe in sons of gods if they did not believe in gods? It would be just as odd as believing in sons of horses or asses, but not in horses or asses! Well, Meletos, there's no question about it—you were just pulling our legs in making this indictment; perhaps you did not know a true crime to put in; but for you to persuade any man with even a grain of sense that the same man can believe in divine things and in spiritual things, and yet not in gods and spirits and heroes, that is absolutely impossible.

Well, gentlemen, I am no criminal according to Meletos's indictment; that needs no long defence from me to prove, but this is enough. However, when I said some time ago that I was heartily disliked by many, you may be sure that it is quite true. And this is what will convict me, if anything does, not Meletos or Anytos but the prejudice and dislike of so many people. The same thing has convicted many other good men, and I think will do so again; there is no fear it will stop with me. But perhaps someone may say: Are you not ashamed then, Socrates, at having followed such a practice that you now run a risk of a sentence of death? I would answer such a one fairly: You are wrong, my friend, if you think a man with a spark of decency in him ought to calculate life or death; the only thing he ought to consider, if he does anything, is whether he does right or wrong, whether it is what a good man does or a bad man. For according to your argument, in the Trojan War those of the demigods who died would have been poor creatures, particularly Thetis' son, Achilles; he so despised danger in comparison with undergoing disgrace that when he wished to kill Hector, and his mother (a goddess herself) said thus to him, if I remember, "My son, if you avenge the slaughter of your friend Patroclos and kill Hector, you will be killed yourself, for 'right after Hector death is ready for you,"[1]—when he heard this, he belittled danger and death, and much rather feared to live as a coward who would not avenge his friends, and replied, "Right after this let me die, when I have punished the offender; I don't want to stay here a laughingstock beside the ships, a burden to the earth."[2] You cannot think he cared about danger and death? And this is true, gentlemen, wherever a man places himself, believing it to be the best place, or wherever he has been placed by his captain, there he must stay, as I think, and run any risk there is, calculating neither death nor anything, before disgrace.

Then, gentlemen, I should have been acting strangely, if at Poteidaia and Amphipolis and Delion[3] I stayed where I was posted by the captains whom you had chosen to command me, like anyone else, and risked death; but where God posted me, as I thought and believed, with the duty to be a

[1] *Iliad* xviii. 96.
[2] *Iliad* xviii. 98, 104.
[3] In the years 432-429, 424, 422 B.C. These places were scenes of battles in the great war between Athens and Sparta.

philosopher[1] and to test myself and others, there I should fear either death or anything else, and desert my post. Strange indeed it would be, and then truly anyone might have brought me to court justly and affirmed that I did not believe in God, because I disbelieved the oracle, and feared death, and thought I was wise when I was not. For to fear death, gentlemen, is only to think you are wise when you are not; for it is to think you know what you don't know. No one knows whether death is really the greatest blessing a man can have, but they fear it is the greatest curse, as if they knew well. Surely this is the objectionable kind of ignorance, to think one knows what one does not know? But in this, gentlemen, here also perhaps I am different from the general run of mankind, and if I should claim to be wiser than someone in something it would be in this, that as I do not know well enough about what happens in the house of Hades, so I do not think I know; but to do wrong, and to disobey those who are better than myself, whether god or man, that I know to be bad and disgraceful. Therefore, in comparison with bad things which I know to be bad, rather will I never fear or flee from what may be blessings for all I know. So even if you let me go now and refuse to listen to Anytos—you remember what he said; he said that either I ought not to have been brought into court at all, or if I was, that death was the only possible penalty; and why? He told you that if I escaped, your sons "would at once practise what Socrates teaches, and they would all be utterly corrupted." Then if you were to say to me in answer to this: "We will not this time listen to Anytos, my dear Socrates; we let you go free, but on this condition, that you will no longer spend your time in this search or in philosophy, and if you are caught doing this again, you shall die"—if should let me go free on these terms which I have mentioned, I should answer you, "Many thanks indeed for your kindness, gentlemen, but I will obey the god rather than you,[2] and as long as I have breath in me, and remain able to do it, I will never cease being a philosopher, and exhorting you, and showing what is in me to any one of you I may meet, by speaking to him in my usual way: My excellent friend, you are an Athenian, a citizen of this great city, so famous for wisdom and strength, and you take every care to be as well off as possible in money, reputation and place—then are you not ashamed not to take every care and thought for understanding, for truth, and for the soul, so that it may be perfect? And if

[1] Lover of wisdom.
[2] As the apostles said, Acts v: 29, "We must obey God rather than men."

any of you argues the point and says he does take every care, I will not at once let him go and depart myself; but I will question and cross-examine and test him, and if I think he does not possess virtue but only says so, I will show that he sets very little value on things most precious, and sets more value on meaner things, and I will put him to shame. This I will do for everyone I meet, young or old, native or foreigner, but more for my fellow-citizens as you are nearer to me in race. For this is what God commands me, make no mistake, and I think there is no greater good for you in the city in any way than my service to God. All I do is to go about and try to persuade you, both young and old, not to care for your bodies or your monies first, and to care more exceedingly for the soul, to make it as good as possible; and I tell you that virtue comes not from money, but from virtue comes both money and all other good things for mankind, both in private and in public. If, then, by saying these things I corrupt the young, these things must be mischievous; but if anyone says I say anything else than these, he talks nonsense. In view of all this, I would say, gentlemen, either obey Anytos or do not obey him, either let me go free or do not let me go free; but I will never do anything else, even if I am to die many deaths.

Don't make an uproar, gentlemen, remain quiet as I begged you, hear me without uproar at what I have to say; for I think it will be to your benefit to hear me. I have something more to say, which perhaps will make you shout, but I pray you, don't do so. Be sure of this, that if you put me to death, being such as I am, you will not hurt me so much as yourselves. I should not be hurt either by Meletos or by Anytos, he could not do it; for I think the eternal law forbids a better man to be hurt by a worse. However, he might put me to death, or banish me, or make me outcast; perhaps he thinks, perhaps others think, these are great evils, but I do not; I think, rather, that what he is now doing is evil, when he tries unjustly to put a man to death. Now therefore, gentlemen, so far from pleading for my own sake, as one might expect, I plead for your sakes, that you may not offend about God's gift by condemning me. For if you put me to death, you will not easily find such another, really like something stuck on the state by the god, though it is rather laughable to say so; for the state is like a big thoroughbred horse, so big that he is a bit slow and heavy, and wants a gadfly to wake him up. I think the god put me on the state something like that, to wake you up and persuade you and reproach you every one, as I keep settling on you everywhere all day long. Such another will not easily be found by you, gentlemen, and if you will be persuaded, you will spare me. You will be vexed, perhaps, like sleepers being awaked, and if you listen to Anytos and give me a tap, you can easily kill me; then you can go on sleeping for the rest of your lives, unless God sends you such another in his care for you. That I am really one given to you by God you can easily see from this; for it does not seem human that I have neglected all my own interests, that I have been content with the neglect of my domestic affairs, all these years; while always I was attending to your interests, approaching each of you privately like a father or elder brother and persuading you to care for virtue. And indeed, if I had gained any advantage from this, and taken fees for my advice, there would have been some reason in it; but as it is, you see yourselves that my accusers, although accusing me so shamelessly of everything else, had not the effrontery or ability to produce a single witness to testify that I ever exacted or asked for a fee; and I produce, I think, the sufficient witness that I speak the truth, my poverty.

Perhaps it may seem odd that although I go about and give all this advice privately, quite a busybody, yet I dare not appear before your public assembly and advise the state. The reason for this is one which you have often heard me giving in many places, that something divine and spiritual comes to me, which Meletos put into the indictment in caricature. This has been about me since my boyhood, a voice, which when it comes always turns me away from doing something I am intending to do, but never urges me on.[1] This is what opposes my taking up public business. And quite right too, I think; for you may be sure, gentlemen, that if I had meddled with public business in the past, I should have perished long ago and done no good either to you or to myself. Do not be annoyed at my telling the truth; the fact is that no man in the world will come off safe who honestly opposes either you or any other multitude, and tries to hinder the many unjust and illegal doings in a state. It is necessary that one who really and truly fights for the right, if he is to survive even for a short time, shall act as a private man, not as a public man.

I will bring you strong proof of this, not words but facts, which you respect. Just listen to what has happened to me, and you will learn that I would never give way to anyone contrary to right, for fear of death, but rather than give way I would be ready to perish at once. I will tell you a story

[1] See also pp. 444-445.

from the law courts, tiresome perhaps, but true. I have never, gentlemen, held any office in the state but one; I was then a Councillor.[1] It happened that the tribe which was presiding was mine, the Antiochis, when you wished—illegally, as you all agreed afterwards—to try all the ten generals together for not gathering up the bodies of the dead after the sea fight.[2] Then I alone of the presidents opposed you, and voted against you that nothing should be done contrary to law; and when the orators were ready to denounce me and arrest me on the spot, and you shouted out telling them to do so, I thought it my duty to risk the danger with law and justice on my side, rather than to be on your side for fear of prison and death.[3] This happened while the government was still democratic; and when the oligarchy came in, the Thirty again summoned me and four others to the Dome,[4] and ordered us to bring Leon of Salamis from Salamis, whom they meant to put to death. Such things those people used often to do to others, wishing to make as many as possible share their guilt. Then, however, I showed again by acts, not by words, that as for death, if it is not too vulgar to use the expression, I cared not one jot, but all my anxiety was to do nothing unjust or wrong. That government did not terrify me, strong as it was, into doing injustice; but when we came out of the Dome, the other four went to Salamis and brought Leon, but I went away home. And perhaps I should have been put to death for that, if the government had not been overthrown soon. You will find many witnesses of this.

Then do you think I should have survived all these years, if I had engaged in public business, and if then I had acted as a good man should, and defended the just, and made that, as is one's duty, my chief concern? Far from it, gentlemen, nor would anyone else in the world. But through all my life I shall prove to have been just the same, both in public life, if I have done anything there, and in private life; I have never given way to anyone in anything contrary to right, including those whom my slanderers call my pupils. Yet I never was teacher to anyone; but if anyone desires to hear me speaking and doing my business, whether he be young or old, I have never grudged it to any; I do not converse for a fee and refuse without, but I offer myself both

---

[1] There were ten φυλαί, "tribes," who each elected fifty deputies to the βουλή Council or upper house of five hundred. Each tribe "presided" in turn for thirty-five or thirty-six days, and its committee of fifty selected its managing "Presidency" of ten "presidents."

[2] The battle of Arginusai, 406 B.C. The generals ought to have been tried separately.

[3] He refused to put the motion, according to Xenophon, *Memorabilia*, iv. 4.2.

[4] The round chamber where the tribal committee of fifty always met, and where the so-called Thirty Tyrants met in 404 B.C. when they were in power.

to rich and poor for questioning, and if a man likes he may hear what I say, and answer. And whether anyone becomes good after this or not, I could not fairly be called the cause of it, when I never promised any learning to anyone and never taught any; and if anyone says he ever learnt or heard anything from me privately which all the others did not, I assure you he does not tell the truth.

But why ever do some people enjoy spending a great deal of time with me? You have heard why, gentlemen; I have told you the whole truth, they enjoy hearing men cross-examined who think they are wise, and are not; indeed that is not unpleasant. And I maintain that I have been commanded by the god to do this, through oracles and dreams and in every way in which some divine influence or other has ever commanded a man to do anything. This, gentlemen, is both true and easy to test. For if I really do corrupt any of the young, or if I ever have, then either some of them as they grew older must have understood that I had once given them bad advice in their youth, so that they ought to have appeared now in this court and testified and had their revenge; or, if they did not wish to do it themselves, some of their relatives ought to have come instead—fathers and brothers and others of the family, if their own kinsmen had suffered any wrong from me—and they ought to tell it all now and have their revenge. At all events there are many of them whom I see here, first Criton yonder, my age-mate and fellow-parishioner, father of Critobulos here; then there is Lysanias the Sphettian,[1] father of Aischines here; also Antiphon the Cephisian yonder, father of Epigenes; then others yonder whose brothers have amused themselves in this way, Nicostratos, Theozotides' son and brother of Theodotos—Theodotos himself is dead, so Nicostratos could not beg him to come—and Paralos here, Demodocos' son, whose brother was Theages; here is Adeimantos, Ariston's son, whose brother Plato[2] is there, and Aiantodoros, whose brother is Apollodoros here present. Many others I can mention to you, some of whom Meletos ought certainly to have called as witnesses in his speech, and if he forgot them, let him call them up now; I give place to him; so let him speak if he has any such evidence. But you will find exactly the opposite of this, gentlemen, all of them ready to support me, the corrupter, the injurer of their relatives, as Meletos and Anytos call me. The corrupted might have some reason for supporting me; but the uncorrupted, already—elderly men, their

[1] That is, of the "deme" or parish of Sphettos in Attica.
[2] The author.

kinsmen—what other reason have they for supporting me but the right and just reason, that they know I am telling the truth and Meletos is lying?

Very well, gentlemen; the defence I could offer is this, and more perhaps of the same sort. But perhaps some one among you might be vexed when he remembers what he has done himself; he may have been in a case less important than this, and he may have entreated and prayed the jury with floods of tears, and paraded his children, to get all the pity he could, with many relatives and friends besides, but I, as it seems, will not do anything of the sort, and that too although I am probably at the last extremity of danger. Observing this perhaps someone might harden his heart against me because of it, and, being angry, might vote against me in anger. Then if any of you feels like that—I do not in the least expect it, but if he does—I may fairly say to him, My good sir, I too have relatives of my own somewhere, for to quote Homer,[1] no stick or stone is the origin of me, but humanity; so I have relatives and sons too, gentlemen—three of them, one a young man already, two still children—yet I shall parade none of them here and so entreat you to vote for my acquittal. Then why will I do none of these things? Not from obstinacy, gentlemen, not slighting you; whether I can face death confidently or not is another matter; but thinking of reputation, as regards me and you and the whole state, it does not seem to me to be decent that I should do any such thing, at my age and with my fame, whether true or false. At least it is common opinion that Socrates is in some way superior to most people. If, then, those of you who are considered superior, in wisdom or in courage or in any other virtue, are going to behave like these people, it would be a disgrace. I have often seen men of some reputation, when condemned, behaving in the strangest way, as if they thought it would be a cruel fate for them to die, as if indeed they would be immortal if *you* did not put them to death! But these seem to me to be fastening a shame about the city, so that a foreigner would naturally conceive that those of our Athenian nation who are distinguished for virtue, whom the people choose rather than themselves to place in government and office, are no better than so many women. Things of this kind, gentlemen, we who have any reputation at all should not do, and you should not allow us to do them if we tried; but you ought to show you would prefer to condemn a man who brings these pitiable exhibitions into court, and makes the city ridiculous, rather than one who behaves quietly.

[1] *Odyssey* xix. 163.

APOLOGY (34B–36B)

Apart from reputation, gentlemen, it does not seem to me right to entreat the judge,[1] or to be acquitted by entreating; one should instruct and persuade him. For why does the judge sit? Not to make a gracious gift of justice by favour, but to decide what is just; and he has sworn not to show favour as may please him, but to judge according to law. Then we must not get you into the habit of breaking that oath, nor must you let yourselves fall into that habit; one is as bad as the other in the sight of heaven. Then do not demand, gentlemen, that I should do before you such things as I hold neither honourable nor just nor permissible, most especially, by Zeus, for one who is prosecuted for impiety by Meletos here. For clearly if I should persuade you and compel you by entreaties when you are on oath, I should be teaching you not to believe in gods, and in my own defence I should actually accuse myself of not believing in gods. But I am far from that, gentlemen; I do believe, in a sense in which none of my accusers does; and I trust you, and God himself, to decide about me in the way that shall be best both for me and for you.

(The Court votes and finds him guilty, the voting being 281 for guilty, and 220 for innocent. Socrates then addresses them as to the penalty.)

You have voted for my condemnation, gentlemen of Athens; and if I am not resentful at this which has been done, many things contribute to that, and particularly that I expected this to be done which has been done. Indeed, I am much rather surprised at the actual number of votes on either side. I did not expect the voting to be so close, I thought there would be a large majority; but now, as it seems, if only thirty votes had been changed, I should have been acquitted. Even now to my mind I have been acquitted of Meletos,[2] and not only have I been acquitted, but this indeed is clear to everyone, that if Anytos and Lycon had not joined in accusing me, he would have been liable for the fine of a thousand drachmas as he did not get the fifth part of the votes.

Well, the man asks for the penalty of death. Good; and what penalty shall I propose against this, gentlemen? The proper penalty, it is clear surely? But what is that? What is proper for me to suffer or to pay, for not having the sense to be idle in my life, and for neglecting what most people care about, moneymaking and housekeeping and military appointments

---
[1] On p. 444 and elsewhere he addresses the members of the court as his judges.
[2] Socrates seems to imply that each of the three accusers should be credited with one-third of the 281 votes. One-third is less than one hundred, that is, less than one-fifth of the whole 501 votes.

and oratory, and besides, all the posts and plots and parties which arise in this city—for believing myself to be really too honest to go after these things and survive? I did not go where I thought I should be of no use either to you or to myself, but I went where I hoped I might benefit each man separately with the greatest possible benefit, as I declare; I tried to persuade each one of you to take care for himself first, and how he could become most good and most wise, before he took care for any of his interests, and to take care for the state herself first before he took care of any of her interests: that in other things also, this was the proper order of his care. Then what do I deserve, since I am such as that? Something good, gentlemen, if I am to make the estimate what it ought to be in truth; and further, something good which would be suitable for me. Then what is suitable for a poor benefactor, who craves to have leisure for your encouragement? Nothing, gentlemen, is so suitable, as that such a man should be boarded free in the town hall, which he deserves much more than any one of you who has gained the prize at Olympia with a pair of horses or a four-in-hand: for this one makes you seem to be happy, but I make you be happy, and he is not in want for food, but I am. Then if I must estimate the just penalty according to my deserts, this is my estimate: free board in the town hall.

Perhaps you think that in saying this, very much as I spoke of appeals for pity, I am just showing off; no such thing, gentlemen; I will tell you what I mean. I am convinced that I never willingly wronged anyone, but I cannot convince you, for we have conversed together only a short time. If we had a law, as other people have, that a trial for life or death is to be spread over many days and not confined to one, I think you would have been convinced; but as it is I cannot disperse great prejudices in a moment. But being convinced that I have wronged no man, I certainly will not wrong myself; I will not give sentence against myself, and say that I am worthy of something bad, I will not estimate anything bad for myself. Why should I? For fear of suffering what Meletos demands as penalty, when I say I do not know whether it is good or bad? Instead of that shall I choose one of the things which I know are bad, and propose that as penalty? Shall it be prison? And why must I live in prison, a slave to those appointed at any time as the officials of the place—the Eleven? Shall it be a fine, and prison until I pay? But that is the same to me, as I told you, for I have no money to pay. Then shall the penalty be banishment? Perhaps you might accept that penalty for me. Indeed, I should be very fond of life to choose that. Could I be so unreasonable! You, my own fellow-countrymen, could not endure my doings and my talkings, they were too burdensome and too detestable for you, so you are now trying to get rid of them; others will easily put up with them, it seems. What a notion! No, Athenians—far from it. A fine life it would be for me if I migrated, at my age, moving from city to city and living on the run. For I am quite sure that wherever I go young men will listen to my talk as they do here; and if I drive these away, they will drive me out themselves, persuading the older men to let them, but if I don't drive them away, their fathers and families will do it for their sakes.

Perhaps someone might say, Can't you go away from us, Socrates, and keep silent and lead a quiet life? Now here is the most difficult thing of all to make some of you believe. For if I say that this is to disobey the god, and therefore I cannot keep quiet, you will not believe me but think I am a humbug. If again I say it is the greatest good for a man every day to discuss virtue and the other things, about which you hear me talking and examining myself and everybody else, and that life without enquiry is not worth living for a man, you will believe me still less if I say that. And yet all this is true, gentlemen, as I tell you, but to convince you is not easy. And at the same time I have never been accustomed to think I deserve anything bad. If I had money, I would have proposed to pay all I was bound to pay, as a fine, for I should have had no harm by that; but, as it is, I have none, unless, indeed, you are willing to put it at just as much as I am able to pay. Perhaps I could pay you a mina of silver:[1] then I propose that as penalty—Plato here, gentlemen, and Criton and Critobulos and Apollodoros tell me to fix it at thirty minas, and they will be sureties: then I propose so much and these men will be sureties for the money —ample sureties in your view.

(The Court then votes again, and condemns him to death.)

You would not have had long to wait, gentlemen, but that short time will have given you the name and the blame of killing Socrates, a wise man: so those will say who wish to speak evil of our city, for they will certainly call me wise, even if I am not, when they wish to taunt you. If you had only waited a short time, this would have come to you of itself; look at my age, which is well advanced, and near death already. This I say not to you all, but to those who voted for my death; and I have something else to say to those same men. Perhaps you think, gentlemen, it was lack of words which defeated me, such words as might have persuaded you, if I had thought it right to do and say anything and everything so as to be ac-

[1] About £12 or $35.

quitted. Far from it. But it was a lack which defeated me, although not of words; it was lack of effrontery and shamelessness, and of a willingness to make you the sort of addresses you would have liked best to hear—to hear me wailing and weeping and saying and doing many things, unworthy of me, as I declare—such indeed as you are accustomed to hear from others. But then I did not think I ought to do anything servile because of my danger; and now I do not regret that such was the manner of my defence; I much prefer to die after such a defence than to live by the other sort. Neither in court nor in war ought I or anyone else to do anything and everything to contrive an escape from death. In battle it is often clear that a man might escape by throwing away his arms and by begging mercy from his pursuers; and there are many other means in every danger, for escaping death, if a man can bring himself to do and say anything and everything. No, gentlemen, the difficult thing is not to escape death, I think, but to escape wickedness—that is much more difficult, for that runs faster than death. And now I, being slow and old, have been caught by the slower one; but my accusers, being clever and quick, have been caught by the swifter, badness. And now I and they depart, I, condemned by you to death, but these, condemned by truth to depravity and injustice. I abide by my penalty, they by theirs. Perhaps this was to be so, and I think it is fair enough.

But as to the future I wish to chant this prophecy to you whose votes have condemned me; for I am now in the place where men chiefly prophesy, in sight of coming death. I foretell, gentlemen, my slayers, that a punishment will come upon you straight after my death, much harder, I declare, than execution at your hands is to me; for now you have done this, thinking to shake yourselves free from giving account of your life, but it will turn out for you something very different, as I foretell. More than one shall be those who demand from you that account, those whom I have restrained now although you did not perceive it; and they will be harder upon you inasmuch as they are younger, and you will resent it more. For if you believe that by putting men to death you will stop everyone from reproaching you because your life is wrong,[1] you make a great mistake; for this riddance is neither possible nor honourable; but another is most honourable and most easy, not to cut off lives, but to offer yourselves readily to be made as good as you can be. There is my prophecy for those who condemned me, and there I make an end.

But with those who voted to acquit me I would gladly converse about this event which has taken place here, while the

[1] See *Republic*, p. 315, n. 2.

magistrates are busy and I go not yet to the place where I must die. Pray gentlemen, be patient with me so long; for nothing hinders from storytelling a bit together while we may. To you as my friends I wish to show what is the real meaning of what has happened to me. What has happened to me, gentlemen of the jury, my judges, for you I could rightly call judges—is a wonderful thing. My familiar prophetic voice of the spirit in all time past has always come to me frequently, opposing me even in very small things, if I was about to do something not right;[1] but now there has happened to me what you see yourselves, what one might think and what is commonly held to be the extremest of evils, yet for me, as I left home this morning, there was no opposition from the signal of God, nor when I entered this place of the court, nor anywhere in my speech when I was about to say anything; although in other speeches of mine it has often checked me while I was still speaking, yet now in this action it has not opposed me anywhere, either in deed or in word. Then what am I to conceive to be the cause? I will tell you; really this that has happened to me is good, and it is impossible that any of us conceives it aright who thinks it is an evil thing to die. A strong proof of this has been given to me; for my usual signal would certainly have opposed me, unless I was about to do something good.

Let us consider in another way, how great is the hope that it is good. Death is one of two things; either the dead man is nothing, and has no consciousness of anything at all, or it is, as people say, a change and a migration for the soul from this place here to another place. If there is no consciousness and it is like a sleep, when one sleeping sees nothing, not even in dreams, death would be a wonderful blessing. For I think that if a man should select that night in which he slumbered so deep that he saw not even a dream, and should put beside that night all other nights and days of his life, and were to say, after considering, how many sweeter days and nights than that night he had spent in his whole life, I think that anyone, not only some ordinary man but the Great King of Persia himself, would find few such indeed to compare with it in the other days and nights. If, then, death is like that, I call it a blessing; for so eternity seems no more than one night. But if, again, death is a migration from this world into another place, and if what they say is true, that there all the dead are, what greater good could there be than this, judges of the court? For if one comes to the house of Hades, rid of those who dub themselves judges, and finds those who truly are judges, the same who are said to sit in

[1] See also p. 437.

judgment there, Minos and Rhadamanthys and Aiacos and Triptolemos, and the other demigods who were just in their life, would that migration be a poor thing? On the contrary, to be in company with Orpheus and Musaios and Hesiod and Homer, how much would one of you give for that? For myself, I am willing to die many times, if this is true; since I myself should find staying there a wonderful thing; then I could meet Palamedes, and Aias, Telamon's son, and any other of the ancients who died by an unjust judgment, and to compare my experience with theirs, I think, would be quite agreeable. And best of all, to go on cross-examining the people there, as I did those here, and investigating, which of them is wise, and which thinks he is, but is not! How much would one give, judges of the court, to cross-examine him who led the great invasion against Troy, or Odysseus or Sisyphos, or thousands of other men and women? To converse with them there, and to be with them, and cross-examine them would be an infinity of happiness! There, at all events, I don't suppose they put anyone to death for *that;* for in that world they are happier than we are here, particularly because already for the rest of time they are immortal, if what people say is true.

But you also, judges of the court, must have good hopes towards death, and this one thing you must take as true—no evil can happen to a good man either living or dead, and his business is not neglected by the gods; nor has my business now come about of itself, but it is plain to me that to die now and to be free from trouble was better for me. That is why my signal did not warn me off, and why I am not at all angry with those who condemned me, or with my accusers. Yet this was not their notion when they condemned and accused me; they thought they were hurting me, and that deserves blame in them. However, one thing I ask them: Punish my sons, gentlemen, when they grow up; give them this same pain I gave you, if you think they care for money or anything else before virtue; and if they have the reputation of being something when they are nothing, reproach them, as I reproach you, that they do not take care for what they should, and think they are something when they are worth nothing. And if you do this, we shall have been justly dealt with by you, both I and my sons.

And now it is time to go, I to die, and you to live; but which of us goes to a better thing is unknown to all but God.

CRITO (Criton)

Socrates, in prison; Criton, his lifelong friend.

SOCRATES: Why have you come at this time of day, Criton? Isn't it still early?

CRITON: Very early.

SOCRATES: About what time?

CRITON: Just before dawn.

SOCRATES: I wonder how the prison porter was willing to answer the door for you.

CRITON: He is used to me now, Socrates; I often come here, and I have done a little something for him.

SOCRATES: Have you just come? Been here long?

CRITON: A fairly long time.

SOCRATES: Then why didn't you wake me up, instead of sitting by me silent?

CRITON: Oh, goodness, I couldn't do that, Socrates; I wish I were not so sleepless and sad myself. But I have been wondering at you, ever so long, to see how sweetly you sleep. I took care not to wake you, that you might be as comfortable as possible. I have often thought hitherto what a happy disposition you have had all your life, but most of all in this present trouble. How easily and gently you bear it!

SOCRATES: Indeed, Criton, it would be quite out of tune to be vexed at my age if I must soon end.

CRITON: Many other people, Socrates, as old as you, are caught in troubles like this, but their age does not keep them from being vexed at their fortune.

SOCRATES: Yes, that's true. But tell me, why have you come so early?

CRITON: With news, my dear Socrates, painful news—not for you, as it appears, but for me and all your friends painful and burdensome, and I think I shall find it heavier than anyone else.

SOCRATES: What's the news? That the ship has come from Delos,[1] which means I must die?

CRITON: She has not come in yet, but I think she will today; that's what we heard from some men who had come from Sunion and left her there. Clearly then, to judge from this, she will come in today; then tomorrow it will be necessary, my dear Socrates, for you to end your life.

SOCRATES: Well, my dear Criton, good luck come with her; if that is God's will, so be it. However, I don't think she will come in today.

CRITON: What makes you think that?

SOCRATES: I'll tell you. I suppose I am to die the day after that ship comes in.

CRITON: That is what the authorities in these matters say.

SOCRATES: Thus I don't think she'll come on this day now beginning, but tomorrow. I infer this from a dream I had this very night just past, a little while ago. Really, it was most timely that you did not wake me!

CRITON: What was the dream, then?

SOCRATES: I thought a woman came to me, handsome and well grown, and dressed in white; she called to me and said, "Socrates,

"On the third day you'll reach fertile Phthia."[2]

CRITON: A strange dream, Socrates!

SOCRATES: Not at all, quite clear, Criton, as I think, anyhow.

CRITON: Too clear, it seems. But O you perverse man! Do let me persuade you, Socrates, even now, and save your life! For me it will be two troubles, not one; I shall lose such a friend as I never shall find again, and besides that, many people who do not know us well will think that I might have saved your life by spending money, and didn't care. But what can be a worse reputation than to be thought to care more for money than friends? Most people will never believe that you yourself wouldn't leave the place though we did our best!

SOCRATES: Bless you, my dear Criton, what matters it to us what the many think? All the most decent people, who are more worth consideration, will think things were done as they were done.

---

[1] Nobody could be put to death at Athens during the absence of the sacred ship, which was sent yearly to Delos. See *Phaedo*, p. 460, n. 2.
[2] *Iliad* ix. 363.

CRITON: But I suppose you see, Socrates, that we are bound also to care what the many think; even as what is happening now shows clearly that the many can work mischief—not trifles, but almost the greatest mischief possible, if one gets a bad name among them.

SOCRATES: My dear Criton, I only wish the many could do the greatest mischief, so that they could also do the greatest good! That would be well indeed. As it is, they can do neither; for they cannot make a man either wise or foolish; they do things quite at random.

CRITON: Then let that pass—be it so; but just tell me, Socrates, are you anxious about me and your other friends? Do you think that if you leave this place, the informers will give us trouble and say we stole you away, and we may be forced to lose great sums, perhaps all our property, or something worse may happen to us? If you are afraid of that, don't worry; it is right for us to risk that danger and even worse than that if need be, so long as we save you. Let me persuade you, please do!

SOCRATES: Yes, I am anxious about that, and many other things too.

CRITON: Then don't be afraid about that. After all, it is no great sum they want in order to save your life and get you out of this. Those informers again—can't you see how cheap they are? There's no need of much money for them. And all my money is yours, quite enough as I think; next, if you are troubled about me a bit, and don't think I ought to spend mine, there are these foreigners ready to help you. One has actually brought enough for the very purpose—Simmias the Theban; Cebes is ready, and plenty more. So don't be afraid about that, I tell you, don't give up trying to save yourself, and don't worry about what to do with yourself when you get free, as you said in court. They will be glad of you in many other places, wherever you go. If you like to go to Thessaly, I have friends there who will make much of you and keep you safe, so that no one in Thessaly shall hurt you.

Then again, Socrates, I do not think you are undertaking a right thing by throwing yourself away when you can be free. What's the good of taking pains to do for yourself exactly what your enemies would like to do, and what those who tried to destroy you want? Besides, I think you are betraying your own sons also; it is in your power to bring them up and educate them, and now you will go off and leave them, and so far as you are concerned, they must take their life as they find it:

they will probably get only what orphans do get in their orphan state. Either one ought not to have sons, or one ought to share their hardships in training and educating them, and you seem to me to choose the easiest way. But you ought to choose what a good and brave man would choose, especially when you are forever telling us that you cared for virtue all your life. I am ashamed myself, for my own sake and our friends; I am afraid the whole business about you may be thought to have been done because we were cowards, that the case was brought into court when it need not have been, and the whole course of the case and this end of it will be like a piece of mockery, that we lost our chance by some baseness and cowardice in ourselves—because we did not save you and you did not save yourself, when it was possible and easy if there had been the least good in us. Then think, Socrates, whether this is not bad and disgraceful too, for both you and us. Consider then what to do—or rather, there is no time now to consider, the considering ought to have been done—and there is only one plan; for in this coming night this whole thing must be finished with, and if we delay, it is impossible and we can't do it any longer. Do listen to me, Socrates, I beg and pray you—do not refuse!

SOCRATES: My dearest Crito, your anxiety would be precious if there were any right in it; otherwise, the greater it is, so much the harder to bear. Then we must examine whether we ought to do it or not; for my way is and always has been to obey no one and nothing, except the reasoning which seems to me best when I draw my conclusions. Well, what I have said in the past I must not throw overboard now because this fortune has come to me; it seems quite as reasonable to me now, I put the same things first and respect them as I did then. And if we do not find something better to say now, be sure I will not give way to you, not even if the power of the enemy plays the bugbear to us more than ever, as if we were so many children, sending us prisons and deaths and confiscations of goods. Then how could we most decently consider the matter? Let us first take up what you said about opinions, and ask whether it was always right or not—that we must attend to some opinions, but not to all? Or was it right before I was condemned to death, but now it becomes clear that we talked for the sake of talking, and it was really a game of nonsense? What I desire is, Crito, to examine along with you whether it will prove to be different now that I am in this case, or the same; and then we will say good-bye to it, or else obey it. This is very much what used to be said, I think, by those who believed they had something serious to say, and the same as I said just now: that of the opinions which people hold, we ought to value some highly, but not all. In heaven's name, Criton, don't you think that was right? For you, in all human probability, are outside; you are not going to die tomorrow; and you could not be led astray by the present circumstances. Think then: Don't you believe it was right enough to say that we must not respect all the opinions of men, but only some? And not the opinions of all men, but only of some? What do you say? Was not this rightly said?

CRITON: Quite rightly.

SOCRATES: To respect the good opinions, and not the bad?

CRITON: Yes.

SOCRATES: The good ones are those of the wise, the bad ones those of the foolish?

CRITON: Of course.

SOCRATES: Very well, how did it go on? A man practising athletics, and making that his business—ought he to pay attention to everyone's praise and blame and opinion, or only those of one, who happens to be a physician or a trainer?

CRITON: Only one.

SOCRATES: Then he ought to fear the blame and welcome the praise of that one, and not of the others.

CRITON: That is plain, surely.

SOCRATES: Then he must act and exercise and eat and drink following the opinion of that one, the overseer and expert, rather than all the others put together.

CRITON: That is true.

SOCRATES: Very well. But if he disobeys the one, and disregards his opinion and his praises, but regards those of the many who are not experts, will he not suffer harm?

CRITON: Surely he will.

SOCRATES: What is that harm, and where does it lead, and on what part of the disobedient man does it act?

CRITON: Clearly on the body, for that is what it ruins.

SOCRATES: True. Then in everything else, Criton—but we must not go into every detail—and in particular, the just and the unjust, the ugly and the beautiful, the good and the bad, which is what we now have in mind, are we to follow the opinion of the many, and to fear that, or the opinion of the one, if there is an expert whom we ought to respect and fear rather than all the others together? And if we do not follow him, we shall maltreat and destroy that which became better by justice and was ruined by injustice? Or is all this nothing?

CRITON: I think it true, Socrates.

SOCRATES: Now then, if we ruin that which is made better by health and is destroyed by disease, by obeying the opinion which is not the expert's, is life worth living when that has been destroyed? And that is the body, I suppose, isn't it?

CRITON: Yes.

SOCRATES: Then is life worth living for us with a body miserable and destroyed?

CRITON: Not at all.

SOCRATES: But is life worth living for us, with that destroyed which injustice maltreats and justice benefits? Or do we think the body more important than that?—whatever part of us it is, which is concerned with justice and injustice?

CRITON: Not at all.

SOCRATES: But this part is more precious?

CRITON: Very much more.

SOCRATES: Then, my good friend, we must not consider at all what the many will say of us, but only the expert in justice and injustice, and what he will say, the one, and truth herself. So first of all you were wrong at the beginning, when you began by saying that we must consider the opinion of the many on the just and the beautiful and the good and their opposites. "But look here," someone might say, "the many are able to put us to death."

CRITON: That also is surely clear; he might say so, Socrates. Quite true.

SOCRATES: You surprise me, my friend! This argument we have just run through seems to be still much the same as before! Here is another. I want you to see whether this one still holds for us or not; that we must value most not living, but living well.

CRITON: Yes, that holds.

SOCRATES: Well and beautifully and justly are the same? Does that hold or not?

CRITO (47D–49B)

CRITON: It holds.

SOCRATES: Then after our admissions we must examine whether it is just that I try to get out of this, or not just; and if it seems just, let us try—if not, leave it alone. But the considerations which you speak of, about spending money and public opinion and bringing up children, perhaps these may really be, Criton, speculations of people—I mean the many—who lightly put to death and would as lightly bring to life again if they were able, all with no good reason. But for us, since the argument gives us no choice, it may be that we have nothing to examine except only what we said just now: shall we be doing right in paying money to any who will get me out of this, and in thanking them too, and in getting out or being got out ourselves, or in truth shall we be doing wrong in all this; and if it proves that we shall be acting wrongly, it may be that we ought not to consider whether we ought to stay here quietly and die or suffer anything and everything else—but only the question of doing wrong.

CRITON: I think you argue well, Socrates; what are we to do, then?

SOCRATES: Let us consider together, my good friend, and if you can contradict me when I speak, do, and I will obey; if not, then cease, bless you! Don't go on singing the same old song, that I must get out of this against the will of the Athenians! I would give a great deal to act with your approval, and not against you. Look at the beginning of the investigation; see if you think it is good enough, and try to answer the question as you may think best.

CRITON: I will try.

SOCRATES: Do we say that no one should willingly do wrong in any way, or may he do wrong in some way but not in every way? That it is neither good nor beautiful to do wrong at all, as it was often admitted by us in time past? Or are all those past admissions of ours thrown away in these few days, and all this while, Criton, we old men conversing earnestly together were no better than children and never saw it? Is it not most assuredly exactly as we said then: Whether the many say so or not, and whether we may have to suffer things even harder than these or gentler than these, to do wrong is really both evil and ugly for the doer in every way—do we say this or not?

CRITON: We do.

SOCRATES: Then we must not do wrong at all.

CRITON: We must not.

SOCRATES: Not even, when wronged, wrong in return, as the many think, since we must do no wrong at all.

CRITON: It seems so.

SOCRATES: Very well. Must we injure, Criton, or not?

CRITON: We should not, I suppose, Socrates.

SOCRATES: Very well. To injure in turn when ill-treated—is that right, as the many say, or wrong?

CRITON: Certainly not right.

SOCRATES: For I suppose to do evil to people is the same as doing wrong.

CRITON: Truly said.

SOCRATES: Then we must not do wrong in return, or do evil to anyone in the world, however we may be treated by them. Take care, my dear Criton, when you agree to this, that you don't agree against your real opinion; for I know that only a few do believe it, or ever will. Then those who believe it and those who do not have no common principle, but necessarily they must despise each other when they see their different principles. Consider them carefully yourself, whether you agree with mine and believe the same, and let us begin our deliberation from that: I mean, we start from this rule—it is never right to do any injustice, or to do injustice in return, or, when one is evilly treated, to defend oneself by doing evil in return; or do you back out and deny my principle? I have always believed it, and so I do now; but if you think something else, speak up and tell me. If you abide by what we used to think, hear what follows.

CRITON: I do abide by that, I do think the same: please go on.

SOCRATES: Then I say again, the next thing—or rather I ask —Should a man do what he has agreed with someone to be right, or may he break his agreement?

CRITON: He should do it.

SOCRATES: That granted, then, look here: If we clear out from here without first getting the city's consent, are *we* doing evil, or not, to some people, and that, too, to people we least ought to harm?

CRITO (49B–51A)

CRITON: I cannot answer your question, Socrates; I don't understand it.

SOCRATES: Well, look at it like this. Suppose, just as I was about to run away from here (or whatever it should be called), the Laws and the Commonweal of the state were to appear and ask: "Tell me, Socrates, what have you in mind to do? In trying to do this, can't you see that you are trying to destroy us, the Laws, and the whole state, as far as you can do it? Or do you think it possible that a city can exist and not be overturned, where sentence given has no force but is made null by private persons and destroyed?" What shall I say, Criton, to this and other such things? For one could say much, especially an orator, in pleading about the destruction of the law which lays down that sentences given must be carried out. Or shall I answer the Laws, "The reason is that the state wronged me, and did not judge the case right"? Shall we say this, or what?

CRITON: This, of course, Socrates.

SOCRATES: What then, suppose the Laws reply, "Was that the agreement between us, Socrates? Or was it to abide by whatever judgments the state may make?" If I should be surprised at their saying this, perhaps they might say: "Socrates, do not be surprised at what we say, but answer, since you are accustomed to the use of questions and answers. If you please, what do you complain of in us and the state that you try to destroy us? First of all, did we not bring you into life, and through us your father took your mother, and begat you? Tell us then, are the marriage laws those of us you find fault with? Do you think there is something wrong with them?" "I have no fault to find," I should say. "Well, the laws about feeding the child and the education in which you were brought up. Did not those which had that duty do well in directing your father to educate you in mind and body?" "Yes," I should say. "Very well. When you had been born and brought up and educated, could you say in the first place that you were not our offspring and our slave, you and your ancestors also? And if this is so, do you think you have equal rights with us, and whatever we try to do to you, do you think you also have a right to do to us? Why, against your father you had no equal rights, or against a master, if you had one, so that you might do back whatever was done to you; if you were scolded you could not scold back, if beaten you could not beat back, and there were many other such things: but against your country, it seems, and the Laws, you shall be allowed to do it! So that, if we try to destroy you because we think it right, then you shall try to destroy us the Laws and your country, as far as you can, and you will say you do right in this, you whose care is set upon virtue in very truth? Are you so wise that you failed to see that something else is more precious than father and mother and all your ancestors besides—your country, something more reverend, more holy, of greater value, as the gods judge, and any men that have sense? You must honour and obey and conciliate your country when angry, more than a father; you must either persuade her, or do whatever she commands; you must bear in quiet anything she bids you bear, be it stripes or prison; or if she leads you to war, to be wounded or to die, this you must do, and it is right; you must not give way or retreat or leave your post, but in war and in court and everywhere you must do whatever city and country commands, or else convince her where the right lies. Violence is not allowed against mother or father, much less against your country." What shall we answer to this, Criton? Shall we say the Laws are speaking the truth, or not?

CRITON: I think they are.

SOCRATES: The Laws might say, perhaps, "See then, Socrates, whether we are speaking the truth when we say that you do wrong to us now in this attempt. We who brought you into being, who brought you up, educated you, gave you and all the other citizens a share of all the beautiful things we could, yet we proclaim, by granting permission to any of the Athenians who wishes that when he has passed the muster[1] and sees the public business and us the Laws, anyone who does not like us has leave to take what is his and go where he will. None of us Laws will stand in the way or dissuade him; if one of you does not like us and the city and wishes to go to a colony, or if he prefers to emigrate somewhere else, he may go wherever he wishes and take whatever is his. But if any one of you remains, when he sees in what manner we decide lawsuits and manage other public business, we say that he has now agreed in fact to do whatever we command; and we say that the disobedient man does wrong in three ways when he disobeys us: firstly, because we are his parents, secondly because we are his nurturers, and thirdly, because he agreed to obey us and neither obeys us nor convinces us if we do anything not right; although we give him his chance, and we do not savagely command him to do what we bid, but we leave him a choice, either to do it or to convince us—and he does neither. These charges will lie upon you also, Socrates, if you do what

[1] This was the civil scrutiny which Athenians had to undergo before they could enter upon any magistracy, to make sure that they were legitimately born and fulfilled the requirements of full citizenship.

you design; and on you more than anyone else in the whole country." Suppose I say then, "Why so, pray?"—perhaps they might retort that I have made this agreement with them more completely than anyone else in the city. "Socrates," they would say, "we have great proofs that you are pleased with us and the city. You would never have been so remarkably more constant in living here than the other Athenians, if you had not been remarkably more pleased with us. You never went out of the city to a holy festival, or anywhere else at all, except sometimes on campaign; you never made any other journey abroad like other people; you had no desire to see other cities or to know other laws, but we and our city were enough for you: so completely you chose us and agreed to live as a citizen under us, and indeed got your family in the city, which obviously pleased you. Further, in the court itself, it was open to you to propose the penalty of banishment, if you wished, and to do with the consent of the city what you now attempt to do without it. Then you gave yourself airs, and pretended that you did not object to die, but you chose death before banishment, as you said; and now are you not ashamed of that talk, when you do not respect us Laws, trying as you are to destroy us, but you do what the commonest slave would do, you try to take to your heels, contrary to the agreements and contracts by which you consented to live as a citizen with us. First then, answer us even this, whether we tell the truth when we say you agreed to live in conformity with us, in fact although not in word, or whether that is not true." What are we to say to this, Criton? Must we not agree?

CRITON: We must indeed, Socrates.

SOCRATES: They would say then: "And so you are breaking your bargains and agreements with us, which you made under no compulsion, and not deceived; you were not compelled to decide in a short time, but you had seventy years in which you could have gone away, if you did not like us, or if the agreements did not seem to you just. But you did not prefer Lacedaimon[1] or Crete, which you always declare to be under good laws, nor any other city, Hellenic or barbarian; but you were less out of town than the lame or the blind or the others who are maimed: so much more remarkably than the other Athenians you liked the city and us, the Laws, that is clear—for what city could please without laws? And now then, will you not abide by your agreements? Yes, if you obey us, Socrates, and do not make yourself ridiculous by leaving the city.

"For consider again: Suppose you do thus break and violate

[1] Sparta.

any bit of them, what good will you do to yourself or your friends? It is plain enough that your friends themselves also will risk being banished and deprived of their citizen's rights, or losing all their property. And you yourself, if you go to one of the cities nearest, Thebes or Megara—for both are under good laws—you will come as an enemy, Socrates, to their constitution, and whoever have care for their own cities will think you a destroyer of laws, and look askance at you, and you will confirm the judges in their opinion, so that they will believe they decided aright in their judgment; for whoever is a destroyer of laws would surely be thought to be a corrupter of young men and foolish people. Then will you avoid well-governed cities and the most decent men? If you do, will your life be worth living? Or will you approach these, and will you be shameless enough to talk—how, Socrates? The same sort of talk as here, how virtue and justice is most precious for mankind, and law and order? Don't you think that the whole business of Socrates will be a notorious, nasty story? You must think so. And suppose you decamp from these places, and go to the friends of Criton in Thessaly. The greatest disorder and laxity is found there, and perhaps they would like to hear from you how comically you played truant from that prison with some disguise on, how you changed your looks with a rough cloak or such things as runaways wrap round them. Won't someone say, 'You, an old man, with probably only a short time left for life; did you dare to break the greatest laws and do you still shamefully desire to live?' Perhaps no one will, if you do not make yourself disagreeable to anyone; if you do, Socrates, you will hear plenty of ugly names to your disgrace. So you will live, at every creature's beck and every creature's slave; and what will be your business?—eating and drinking in Thessaly, as if you had travelled abroad to dine in Thessaly! Where will your talks be, our talks about justice and all the other virtues? Suppose you want to live for the children's sake, to bring them up and educate them. Will you take them to Thessaly, and bring them up and educate them there, and make them foreigners, that they may enjoy that too? Perhaps not, but if they are brought up here while you live, will they be better brought up and educated better while you are separated from them? Yes, for your friends will care for them. Will they care for them then if you migrate to Thessaly, but not if you migrate to Hades? Oh yes, we must believe that they will, if there is any good in those who say they are your friends.

"Then listen to us, Socrates, who reared you; do not value children or life or anything else above the right, so that when you come to the world below you may have all these things to plead before the magistrates there. For if you do what you intend, things clearly do not seem any better for you in this world, and you will find no more justice and piety here, nor will any of your people; and when you come to the next world it will be no better. As things are, if you depart, you will depart wronged not by us, the Laws, but by human beings; but if you escape in this ugly way, after requiting wrong with wrong and damage with damage, and after breaking your own bargains and agreements with us, and doing evil to those you least ought to wrong, yourself and your friends and your country and us, then we shall be angry with you living, and in the next world our brothers the Laws in the house of Hades will not receive you as a friend, for they will know that you tried to destroy us as far as you could. But do not let Criton persuade you to do what he said; let *us* rather persuade you."

This, I assure you, my dear comrade Criton, is what I seem to hear, as the mystic revellers think they hear the pipes; so in my ears the sound of these words keeps humming and makes me deaf to other things. As far as I can see, you may be sure that whatever you say contrary to this, you will say in vain. However, if you think you can do any good, speak.

CRITON: But, my dear Socrates, I have nothing to say.

SOCRATES: Then let it be, Criton, and let us do in this way, since in this way God is leading us.

PHAEDO (Phaidon)

The Death of Socrates, 399 B.C.

Echecrates, Phaidon.

Apollodoros, Socrates, Cebes, Simmias, Criton.

ECHECRATES: Were you there yourself, Phaidon, with Socrates, on the day when he took the poison in prison, or did you hear about it from someone?

PHAIDON: I was there myself, Echecrates.

ECHECRATES: Then what was it our friend said before his death? And how did he end? I should be glad to hear. You see no one at all from our part of the world[1] goes now to visit in Athens, and no visitor has come to us from there this long time who might be able to tell us properly what happened; all they could say was, he took the poison and died; no one could tell us anything about the other details.

PHAIDON: Then you never heard how things went at the trial?

ECHECRATES: Yes, somebody did bring news of that, and we were surprised how long it seemed between the sentence and his death. Why was that, Phaidon?

PHAIDON: It was just a piece of luck, Echecrates; for the day before the trial it so happened that the wreath was put on the poop of the ship which the Athenians send to Delos.

ECHECRATES: What ship is that?

PHAIDON: That is the ship, as the Athenians say, in which Theseus once went off to Crete with those "twice seven," you know, and saved them and saved himself.[2] The Athenians vowed to Apollo then, so it is said, that if the lives of these were saved, they would send a sacred mission every year to Delos; and they do send it still, every year ever since that, to honour the god. As soon as the mission has begun, then, it is

[1] Phlius, a small town in the Peloponnesus (Morea) about sixty miles from Athens.
[2] In Athenian legend, Athens because of a past misdeed had to send seven youths and seven maidens every ninth year to King Minos in Crete to be devoured by the Minotaur. Theseus of Athens went to Crete and killed the monster.

PHAEDO (57A–59A)

their law to keep the city pure during that time, and to put no one to death before the ship arrives at Delos and comes back again here; this often takes some time, when the winds happen to delay them. The beginning of the mission is when the priest of Apollo lays a wreath on the poop of the ship, and this happened, as I say, the day before the trial. Accordingly Socrates had a long time in prison between the trial and his death.

ECHECRATES: Then what about the death itself, Phaidon? What was said or done, and which of his friends were with him? Or did the magistrates forbid their presence, and did he die alone with no friends there?

PHAIDON: Oh no, friends were with him, quite a number of them.

ECHECRATES: That's just what I want to know; please be so kind as to tell me all about it as clearly as possible, unless you happen to be busy.

PHAIDON: Oh, I have plenty of time, and I will try to tell you the whole story; indeed, to remember Socrates, and what he said himself, and what was said to him is always the most precious thing in the world to me.

ECHECRATES: Well, Phaidon, those who are going to hear you will feel the same; pray try to tell the whole story as exactly as you can.

PHAIDON: I must say I had the strangest feeling being there. I felt no pity, as one might, being present at the death of a dear friend; for the man seemed happy to me, Echecrates, in bearing and in speech. How fearlessly and nobly he met his end! I could not help thinking that divine providence was with that man as he passed from this world to the next, and on coming there also it would be well with him, if ever with anyone that ever was. For this reason I felt no pity at all, as one might at a scene of mourning; and yet not the pleasure we used to have in our philosophic discussions. The conversation was certainly of that sort, but I really had an extraordinary feeling, a strange mixture of pleasure and pain at once, when I remembered that then and there that man was to make his end. And all of us who were present were very much in the same state, sometimes laughing, sometimes shedding tears, and one of us particularly, Apollodoros[1]—no doubt you know the man and his ways.

ECHECRATES: Oh yes, of course.

[1] See *Symposium*, introductory note.

PHAIDON: Well, he behaved quite as usual, and I was broken down myself, and so were others.

ECHECRATES: But who were they, Phaidon?

PHAIDON: Of our countrymen[1] there was this Apollodoros I have mentioned, and Critobulos and his father, and, besides, Hermogenes and Epigenes and Aischines and Antisthenes; there was also Ctesippos the Paianian and Menexenos, and others of our countrymen; but Plato was ill, I think.

ECHECRATES: Were any foreigners present?

PHAIDON: Yes, Simmias the Theban and Cebes and Phaidondes; and from Megara, Eucleides and Terpsion.

ECHECRATES: Oh, were not Aristippos and Cleombrotos present?

PHAIDON: No, they were said to be in Aegina.

ECHECRATES: Was anyone else there?

PHAIDON: I think these are about all who were present.

ECHECRATES: Very well; tell me, what did you talk about?

PHAIDON: I will try to tell you the whole story from the beginning. You see we had been accustomed during all the former days to visit Socrates, myself and the rest. We used to gather early at the court where the trial had been, for that was near the prison. We always waited until the prison was opened, passing the time together, for it was not opened early; and when it was opened we went in to Socrates and generally spent the day with him. That day, however, we gathered earlier than usual; for the day before, after we left the prison in the evening, we learnt that the ship had come in from Delos; so we warned one another to come as early as possible to the usual place. We came early, then, and the porter who used to answer the door came out to us, and told us to wait and not to go in till he gave the word; for, he said, "The Eleven[2] are knocking off his fetters and informing him that he must die today."

After a short while he came back and told us to go in. So we went in, and found Socrates just released, and Xanthippe,[3] you know her, with his little boy, sitting beside him. Then when Xanthippe saw us, she cried out in lamentation and said as women do, "O Socrates! Here is the last time your friends will speak to you and you to them!"

[1] Athenians.
[2] In charge of the prison and of executions.
[3] Socrates' wife.

Socrates glanced at Criton and said quietly, "Please let someone take her home, Criton."

Then some of Criton's people led her away crying and beating her breast. Socrates sat up on his bed, and bent back his leg and rubbed it with his hand, and said while he rubbed it, "How strange a thing it seems, my friends, that which people call pleasure! And how wonderful is its relation to pain, which they suppose to be its opposite; both together they will not come to a man, yet if he pursues one of the pair, and catches it, he is almost compelled to catch the other, too; so they seem to be both hung together from one head. I think that Aesop would have made a fable, if he had noticed this; he would have said they were at war, and God wanted to make peace between them and could not, and accordingly hung them together by their heads to the same thing, and therefore whenever you get one, the other follows after. That's just what it seems like to me; first came the pain in my leg from the irons, and here seems to come following after it, pleasure."

Cebes took up here, and said, "Upon my word, Socrates, I am much obliged to you for reminding me. About your poems, I mean, when you put into verse Aesop's fables, and the prelude for Apollo; many people have asked me, for example Euenos, the other day, what on earth put it in your mind to make those poems after you came into prison, although you never made any before. Then if you care that I should be able to answer Euenos, next time he asks me, and I'm sure he will, tell me what to say."

"Tell him then, Cebes," he said, "just the truth: that I did not want to rival him or his creations when I did it, for I knew it would not be easy; but I was trying to find out the meaning of certain dreams, and getting it off my conscience, in case they meant to command me to attempt that sort of composition. The dreams went like this: In my past life, the same dream often used to come to me, in different shapes at different times, but saying the same thing, 'Socrates, get to work and compose music!'[1] Formerly I took this to mean what I was already doing; I thought the dream was urging and encouraging me, as people do in cheering on their own men when they are running a race, to compose—which, taking philosophy to be the highest form of composition, I was doing already; but now after the trial, while the festival was putting off my execution, I thought that, if the dream should really command me to work at this common kind of composition, I ought not to disobey the dream but to do so. For it seemed safer not to go away before getting it off my conscience by composing poetry,

[1] "Music" included poetry. See *Republic*, p. 174, n. 1.

and so obeying the dream. So first of all I composed in honour of the god[1] whose festival this was; after the god, I considered that a poet must compose fiction if he was to be a poet, not true tales, and I was no fiction-monger, and therefore I took the fictions that I found to my hand and knew, namely Aesop's, and composed the first that came. Then tell Euenos that, Cebes, and bid him farewell, and tell him to follow me as soon as he can, if he is sensible. I am going away, as it seems, today; for so the Athenians command."

"What advice, Socrates," he said, "to give to Euenos! I have often met the man; from what I have seen of him so far he will be the last man to obey!"

"Why," said he, "is not Euenos a philosopher?"

"I think so," said Simmias.

"Then Euenos will be willing enough, and so will everyone who goes properly into the subject. But perhaps he will not do violence to himself; for they say that is not lawful."

As he spoke, he let down his legs on to the ground, and sat thus during the rest of the talk. Then Cebes asked him, "What do you mean, Socrates, by saying, that it is not lawful for a man to do violence to himself, but that the philosopher would be willing to follow the dying?"

"Why, Cebes," he said, "have not you and Simmias heard all about such things from Philolaos, when you were his pupils?"

"Nothing clear, Socrates."

"Well truly, all I say myself is only from hearsay; however, what I happen to have heard I don't mind telling you. Indeed, it is perhaps most proper that one who is going to depart and take up his abode in that world should think about the life over there and say what sort of life we imagine it to be: for what else could one do with the time till sunset?"

"Well then, why pray do they say it is not lawful for a man to take his own life, my dear Socrates? I have already heard Philolaos myself, as you asked me just now, when he was staying in our parts, and I have heard others too, and they all said we must not do that; but I never heard anything clear about it."

"Well, go on trying," said Socrates, "and perhaps you may hear something. It might perhaps seem surprising to you if in this one thing, of all that happens to a human being, there is never any exception—if it never chances to a man amongst the other chances of his life that sometimes for some people it is better to die than to live; but it does probably seem surprising to you if those people for whom it *is* better to die may not

[1] Apollo.

PHAEDO (61B–63A)

rightly do this good to themselves, but must wait for some other benefactor."

And Cebes answered, with a light laugh. "True for ye, by Zeus!" using his native Doric.

"Indeed, put like this," said Socrates, "it would seem unreasonable; but possibly there is a grain of reason in it. At least, the tale whispered in secret about these things is that we men are in a sort of custody, and a man must not release himself or run away, which appears a great mystery to me and not easy to see through. But I do think, Cebes, it is right to say the gods are those who take care of us, and that we men are one of the gods' possessions—don't you think so?"

"Yes, I do," said Cebes.

"Then," said he, "if one of your own possessions, your slave, should kill himself, without your indicating to him that you wanted him to die, you would be angry with him, and punish him if there were any punishment?"

"Certainly," said he.

"Possibly, then, it is not unreasonable in that sense, that a man must not kill himself before God sends on him some necessity, like that which is present here now."

"Yes indeed, that seems likely," said Cebes. "But you said just now, Socrates, that philosophers ought cheerfully to be willing to die; that does seem unreasonable, at least if there is reason in what we have just said, that God is he who cares for us and we are his possessions. That the wisest men should not object to depart out of this service in which we are overseen by the best overseers there are, gods, there is no reason in that. For I don't suppose a wise man thinks he will care better for himself when he is free. But a foolish man might well believe that he should run away from an owner; and he would not remember that from a good one he ought not to run away but to stay as long as he could, and so he would thoughtlessly run away, while the man of sense would desire always to be with one better than himself. Indeed, in this case, Socrates, the opposite of what was said would be likely: It is proper that wise men should object to die, and foolish men should be glad."

Socrates, hearing this, was pleased, I thought, at the way Cebes dealt with the matter; and, glancing away at us, he said, "Cebes is always on the hunt for arguments, and won't believe straight off whatever one says."

And Simmias added, "But I tell you, Socrates, I think I now see something in what Cebes says, myself; for what could men want, if they are truly wise, in running away from owners better than themselves, and lightly shaking them off? And I really think Cebes is aiming his argument at you, because you take it so easily to leave both us and good masters, as you admit yourself, gods!"

"Quite right," said he. "I think I must answer this before you just as if you were a court!"

"Exactly," said Simmias.

"Very well," said he, "I will try to convince you better than I did my judges. I believe, my dear Simmias and Cebes, that I shall pass over first of all to other gods, both wise and good, secondly to dead men better than those in this world; and if I did not think so, I should do wrong in not objecting to death; but, believing this, be assured that I hope I shall find myself in the company of good men, although I would not maintain it for certain; but that I shall pass over to gods who are very good masters, be assured that if I would maintain for certain anything else of the kind, I would with certainty maintain this. Then for these reasons, so far from objecting, I have good hopes that something remains for the dead, as has been the belief from time immemorial, and something much better for the good than for the bad."

"Then," said Simmias, "do you mean to keep this idea to yourself and go away with it, or will you give us a share? This good find seems to be a case of findings is sharings[1] between us, and don't forget you are on your defence, to see if you can convince us."

"Well, I'll try," he said.

"But first I see Criton here has been wanting to say something ever so long; let's ask what it is."

"Only this," Criton said, "the man who is to give you the poison keeps telling me to advise you not to talk too much. He says people get hotter by talking, and nothing like that ought to accompany the poison; otherwise people who do that often have to take two or three potions."

And Socrates said, "Oh, let him be; he must just be ready to give me two, or three if necessary."

"I guessed as much," said Criton, "but he keeps bothering me."

"Oh, let him be," said he. "Now then, I want to give the proof at once, to you as my judges, why I think it likely that one who has spent his life in philosophy should be confident when he is going to die, and have good hopes that he will win the greatest blessings in the next world when he has ended: so Simmias and Cebes my judges, I will try to show how this could be true.

"The fact is, those who tackle philosophy aright are simply and solely practising dying, practising death, all the time, but

[1] A proverb.

nobody sees it. If this is true, then it would surely be unreasonable that they should earnestly do this and nothing else all their lives, yet when death comes they should object to what they had been so long earnestly practising."

Simmias laughed at this, and said, "I don't feel like laughing just now, Socrates, but you have made me laugh. I think the many if they heard that would say, 'That's a good one for the philosophers!' And other people in my city would heartily agree that philosophers are really suffering from a wish to die, and now they have found them out, that they richly deserve it!"

"That would be true, Simmias," said Socrates, "except the words 'found out.' For they have not found out in what sense the real philosophers wish to die and deserve to die, and what kind of death it is. Let us say good-bye to them," he went on, "and ask ourselves: Do we think there is such a thing as death?"

"Certainly," Simmias put in.

"Is it anything more than the separation of the soul from the body?" said Socrates. "Death is, that the body separates from the soul, and remains by itself apart from the soul, and the soul, separated from the body, exists by itself apart from the body. Is death anything but that?"

"No," he said, "that is what death is."

"Then consider, my good friend, if you agree with me here, for I think this is the best way to understand the question we are examining. Do you think it the part of a philosopher to be earnestly concerned with what are called pleasures, such as these—eating and drinking, for example?"

"Not at all," said Simmias.

"The pleasures of love, then?"

"Oh no."

"Well, do you suppose a man like that regards the other bodily indulgences as precious? Getting fine clothes and shoes and other bodily adornments—ought he to price them high or low, beyond whatever share of them it is absolutely necessary to have?"

"Low, I think," he said, "if he is a true philosopher."

"Then in general," he said, "do you think that such a man's concern is not for the body, but as far as he can he stands aloof from that and turns towards the soul?"

"I do."

"Then firstly, is it not clear that in such things the philosopher as much as possible sets free the soul from communion with the body, more than other men?"

"So it appears."

"And I suppose, Simmias, it must seem to most men that he who has no pleasure in such things and takes no share in them does not deserve to live, but he is getting pretty close to death if he does not care about pleasures which he has by means of the body."

"Quite true, indeed."

"Well then, what about the actual getting of wisdom? Is the body in the way or not, if a man takes it with him as companion in the search? I mean, for example, is there any truth for men in their sight and hearing? Or as poets are forever dinning into our ears, do we hear nothing and see nothing exactly? Yet if these of our bodily senses are not exact and clear, the others will hardly be, for they are all inferior to these, don't you think so?"

"Certainly," he said.

"Then," said he, "when does the soul get hold of the truth? For whenever the soul tries to examine anything in company with the body, it is plain that it is deceived by it."

"Quite true."

"Then is it not clear that in reasoning, if anywhere, something of the realities becomes visible to it?"

"Yes."

"And I suppose it reasons best when none of these senses disturbs it, hearing or sight, or pain, or pleasure indeed, but when it is completely by itself and says good-bye to the body, and so far as possible has no dealings with it, when it reaches out and grasps that which really is."

"That is true."

"And is it not then that the philosopher's soul chiefly holds the body cheap and escapes from it, while it seeks to be by itself?"

"So it seems."

"Let us pass on, Simmias. Do we say there is such a thing as justice by itself, or not?"

"We do say so, certainly!"

"Such a thing as the good and beautiful?"

"Of course!"

"And did you ever see one of them with your eyes?"

"Never," said he.

"By any other sense of those the body has did you ever grasp them? I mean all such things, greatness, health, strength, in short everything that really is the nature of things whatever they are: Is it through the body that the real truth is perceived? Or is this better—whoever of us prepares himself most completely and most exactly to comprehend each thing which he examines would come nearest to knowing each one?"

PHAEDO (65A–67A)

"Certainly."

"And would he do that most purely who should approach each with his intelligence alone, not adding sight to intelligence, or dragging in any other sense along with reasoning, but using the intelligence uncontaminated alone by itself, while he tries to hunt out each essence uncontaminated, keeping clear of eyes and ears and, one might say, of the whole body, because he thinks the body disturbs him and hinders the soul from getting possession of truth and wisdom when body and soul are companions—is not this the man, Simmias, if anyone, who will hit reality?"

"Nothing could be more true, Socrates," said Simmias.

"Then from all this," said Socrates, "genuine philosophers must come to some such opinion as follows, so as to make to one another statements such as these: 'A sort of direct path, so to speak, seems to take us to the conclusion that so long as we have the body with us in our enquiry, and our soul is mixed up with so great an evil, we shall never attain sufficiently what we desire, and that, we say, is the truth. For the body provides thousands of busy distractions because of its necessary food; besides, if diseases fall upon us, they hinder us from the pursuit of the real. With loves and desires and fears and all kinds of fancies and much rubbish, it infects us, and really and truly makes us, as they say, unable to think one little bit about anything at any time. Indeed, wars and factions and battles all come from the body and its desires, and from nothing else. For the desire of getting wealth causes all wars, and we are compelled to desire wealth by the body, being slaves to its culture; therefore we have no leisure for philosophy, from all these reasons. Chief of all is that if we do have some leisure, and turn away from the body to speculate on something, in our searches it is everywhere interfering, it causes confusion and disturbance, and dazzles us so that it will not let us see the truth; so in fact we see that if we are ever to know anything purely we must get rid of it, and examine the real things by the soul alone; and then, it seems, after we are dead, as the reasoning shows, not while we live, we shall possess that which we desire, lovers of which we say we are, namely wisdom. For if it is impossible in company with the body to know anything purely, one thing of two follows: either knowledge is possible nowhere, or only after death; for then alone the soul will be quite by itself apart from the body, but not before. And while we are alive, we shall be nearest to knowing, as it seems, if as far as possible we have no commerce or communion with the body which is not absolutely necessary, and if we are not infected with its nature, but keep ourselves pure from it, until God himself shall set us free. And so, pure and rid of the body's foolishness, we shall probably be in the company of those like ourselves, and shall know through our own selves complete incontamination, and that is perhaps the truth. But for the impure to grasp the pure is not, it seems, allowed.' So we must think, Simmias, and so we must say to one another, all who are rightly lovers of learning; don't you agree?"

"Assuredly, Socrates."

"Then," said Socrates, "if this is true, my comrade, there is great hope that when I arrive where I am travelling, there if anywhere I shall sufficiently possess that for which all our study has been pursued in this past life. So the journey which has been commanded for me is made with good hope, and the same for any other man who believes he has got his mind purified, as I may call it."

"Certainly," replied Simmias.

"And is not purification really that which has been mentioned so often in our discussion, to separate as far as possible the soul from the body, and to accustom it to collect itself together out of the body in every part, and to dwell alone by itself as far as it can, both at this present and in the future, being freed from the body as if from a prison?"

"By all means," said he.

"Then is not this called death—a freeing and separation of soul from body?"

"Not a doubt of that," said he.

"But to set it free, as we say, is the chief endeavour of those who rightly love wisdom, nay of those alone, and the very care and practice of the philosophers is nothing but the freeing and separation of soul from body, don't you think so?"

"It appears to be so."

"Then, as I said at first, it would be absurd for a man preparing himself in his life to be as near as possible to death, so to live, and then when death came, to object?"

"Of course."

"Then in fact, Simmias," he said, "those who rightly love wisdom are practising dying, and death to them is the least terrible thing in the world. Look at it in this way: If they are everywhere at enmity with the body, and desire the soul to be alone by itself, and if, when this very thing happens, they shall fear and object—would not that be wholly unreasonable? Should they not willingly go to a place where there is good hope of finding what they were in love with all through life (and they loved wisdom), and of ridding themselves of the companion which they hated? When human favourites and wives and sons have died, many have been willing to go down to the grave, drawn by the hope of seeing there those they used to desire, and of being with them; but one who is really in love with wisdom and holds firm to this same hope, that he will find it in the grave, and nowhere else worth speaking of —will he then fret at dying and not go thither rejoicing? We must surely think, my comrade, that he will go rejoicing, if he is really a philosopher; he will surely believe that he will find wisdom in its purity there and there alone. If this is true, would it not be most unreasonable, as I said just now, if such a one feared death?"

"Unreasonable, I do declare," said he.

"Then this is proof enough," he said, "that if you see a man fretting because he is to die, he was not really a philosopher, but a philosōma—not a wisdom-lover but a body-lover. And no doubt the same man is money-lover and honours-lover, one or both."

"It certainly is so, as you say," he replied.

"Then, Simmias," he said, "does not what is called courage belong specially to persons so disposed as philosophers are?"

"I have no doubt of it," said he.

"And the same with temperance, what the many call temperance, not to be agitated about desires but to hold them lightly and decently; does not this belong to those alone who hold the body lightly and live in philosophy?"

"That must be so," he said.

"You see," said he, "if you will consider the courage and temperance of others, you will think it strange."

"How so, Socrates?"

"You know," said he, "that everyone else thinks death one of the greatest evils?"

"Indeed I do," he said.

"Then is it not fear of greater evils which makes the brave endure death, when they do?"

"That is true."

"Then fear, and fearing, makes all men brave, except philosophers. Yet it is unreasonable to become brave by fear and cowardice!"

"Certainly."

"And what of the decent men? Are they not in the same case? A sort of intemperance makes them temperate! Although we say such a thing is impossible, nevertheless with that self-complacent temperance they are in a similar case; because they fear to be deprived of other pleasures, and because they desire them, they abstain from some because they are mastered by others. They say, of course, intemperance is 'to be ruled by pleasures'; yet what happens to them is, to master some pleasures and to be mastered by others, and this is much the same as what was said just now, that in a way intemperance has made them temperate."

"So it seems."

"Bless you, Simmias! This is hardly an honest deal in virtue—to trade pleasure for pleasure, and pain for pain, and fear for fear, and even greater for less, as if they were current coin; no, the only honest currency, for which all these must be traded, is wisdom, and all things are in truth to be bought with this and sold for this.[1] And courage and temperance and justice and, in short, true virtue, depend on wisdom, whether pleasure and fear and all other such things are added or taken away. But when they are deprived of wisdom and exchanged one for another, virtue of that kind is no more than a make-believe,[2] a thing in reality slavish and having no health or truth in it; and truth is in reality a cleansing from all such things, and temperance and justice and courage, and wisdom itself, are a means of purification. Indeed, it seems those who established our mystic rites were no fools; they in truth spoke with a hidden meaning long ago when they said that whoever is uninitiated and unconsecrated when he comes to the house of Hades will lie in mud, but the purified and consecrated when he goes there will dwell with gods. Indeed, as they say in the rites, 'Many are called but few are chosen',[3] and these few are in my opinion no others than those who have loved wisdom in the right way. One of these I have tried to be by every effort in all my life, and I have left nothing undone according to my ability; if I have endeavoured in the right way, if we have succeeded at all, we shall know clearly when we get there; very soon, if God will, as I think. There is my defence before you gentlemen on the bench, Simmias and Cebes, showing that in leaving you and my masters here, I am reasonable in not fretting or being upset, because I believe that I shall find there good masters and good comrades. So if I am more convincing to you in my defence than I was to the Athenian judges, I should be satisfied."

When Socrates had thus finished, Cebes took up the word: "Socrates," he said, "on the whole I think you speak well; but that about the soul is a thing which people find very hard to believe. They fear that when it parts from the body it is nowhere any more; but on the day when a man dies, as it parts from the body, and goes out like a breath or a whiff of smoke, it is dispersed and flies away and is gone and is nowhere any

---

[1] Plato's text is doubtful here, and in the next two sentences.
[2] σκιαγραφαί, literally, a shadow-drawing.
[3] The Greek means "Wand-bearers are many, inspired mystics are few."

more. If it existed anywhere, gathered together by itself, and rid of these evils which you have just described, there would be great and good hope, Socrates, that what you say is true; but this very thing needs no small reassurance and faith, that the soul exists when the man dies, and that it has some power and sense."

"Quite true," said Socrates, "quite true, Cebes; well, what are we to do? Shall we discuss this very question, whether such a thing is likely or not?"

"For my part," said Cebes, "I should very much like to know what your opinion is about it."

Then Socrates answered, "I think no one who heard us now could say, not even a composer of comedies,[1] that I am babbling nonsense and talking about things I have nothing to do with! So if you like, we must make a full enquiry.

"Let us enquire whether the souls of dead men really exist in the house of Hades or not. Well, there is the very ancient legend which we remember, that they are continually arriving there from this world, and further that they come back here and are born again from the dead. If that is true, and the living are born again from the dead, must not our souls exist there? For they could not be born again if they did not exist; and this would be sufficient proof that it is true, if it should be really shown that the living are born from the dead and from nowhere else. But if this be not true, we must take some other line."

"Certainly," said Cebes.

"Then don't consider it as regards men only," he said; "if you wish to understand more easily, think of all animals and vegetables, and, in a word, everything that was birth, let us see if everything comes into being like that, always opposite from opposite and from nowhere else; whenever there happens to be a pair of opposites, such as beautiful and ugly, just and unjust, and thousands of others like these. So let us enquire whether everything that has an opposite must come from its opposite and from nowhere else. For example, when anything becomes bigger, it must, I suppose, become bigger from being smaller before."

"Yes."

"And if it becomes smaller, it was bigger before and became smaller after that?"

"True," he said.

"And again, weaker from stronger, and slower from quicker?"

"Certainly."

[1] As Aristophanes had done in his play *The Clouds*.

"Very well, if a thing becomes worse, is it from being better, and more just from more unjust?"

"Of course."

"Have we established that sufficiently, then, that everything comes into being in this way, opposite from opposite?"

"Certainly."

"Again, is there not the same sort of thing in them all, between the two opposites two becomings, from the first to the second, and back from the second to the first; between greater and lesser increase and diminution, and we call one increasing and the other diminishing?"

"Yes," he said.

"And being separated and being mingled, growing cold and growing hot, and so with all; even if we have sometimes no names for them, yet in fact at least it must be the same everywhere, that they come into being from each other, and that there is a becoming from one to the other?"

"Certainly," said he.

"Well then," he said, "is there something opposite to being alive, as sleeping is opposite to being awake?"

"There is," he said.

"What?"

"Being dead," he said.

"Well, all these things come into being from each other, if they are opposites, and there are two becomings between each two?"

"Of course."

"Then," said Socrates, "I will speak of one of the two pairs that I mentioned just now, and its becomings; you tell me about the other. My pair is sleeping and being awake, and I say that being awake comes into being from sleeping and sleeping from being awake, and that their becomings are falling asleep and waking up. Is that satisfactory?"

"Quite so."

"Then you tell me in the same way about life and death. Do you not say that to be alive is the opposite of to be dead?"

"I do."

"And that they come into being from each other?"

"Yes."

"From the living, then, what comes into being?"

"The dead," he said.

"And what from the dead?"

"The living, I must admit."

"Then from the dead, Cebes, come living things and living men?"

"So it appears," he said.

"Then," said he, "our souls exist in the house of Hades."

"It seems so."

"Well, of the two becomings between them, one is quite clear. For dying is clear, I suppose, don't you think so?"

"Oh yes," said he.

"Then what shall we do?" he said. "Shall we refuse to grant in return the opposite becoming; and shall nature be lame in this point? Is it not a necessity to grant some becoming opposite to dying?"

"Surely it is," he said.

"What is that?"

"Coming to life again."

"Then," said he, "if there is coming to life again, this coming to life would be a being born from the dead into the living."

"Certainly."

"It is agreed between us, then, in this way also that the living are born from the dead, no less than the dead from the living: and since this is true, there would seem to be sufficient proof that the souls of the dead must of necessity exist somewhere, whence we assume they are born again."

"It seems to me, Socrates," he answered, "from our admissions that must of necessity be true."

"Another way of looking at this, Cebes," he said, "shows, as I think, that we were right to make those admissions. If opposites did not return back continually to replace opposites, coming into being just as if going round in a circle, but if birth were something going direct from the opposite once only into the exact opposite and never bent back and returned back again to its original, be sure that in the end all things would get the same form and go through the same process, and becomings would cease."

"How do you mean?" he asked.

"What I mean is nothing difficult to understand," said he. "For example, if there were falling asleep, but waking up did not return back in its place, coming into being from the sleeping, be sure that in the end Endymion[1] would be nowhere and this would show his story to be nonsense, because everything else would be in the same state as he, fast asleep. And if everything were combined and nothing split up, the result would be the Chaos of Anaxagoras, 'all things together.' In the same way, my dear Cebes, if everything died that had any life, and when it died, the dead things remained in that state and never came to life again, is it not absolutely necessary that in

---

[1] The Moon fell in love with Endymion, most beautiful of men, and kept him in a perpetual sleep on Mt. Latmos, so that she could embrace him nightly.

the end all things would be dead and nothing alive? For if the living things came into being from things other than the dead, and the living died, all things must be swallowed up in death, and what device could possibly prevent it?"

"Nothing could possibly prevent it, Socrates, and what you say I think perfectly true."

"Yes, Cebes," he said, "I think this is all perfectly true, and we are not deceived in admitting what we did; but in fact coming to life again is really true, and living persons are born from the dead, and the souls of the dead exist."[1]

"Another thing," said Cebes, putting in, "you know that favourite argument of yours, Socrates, which we so often heard from you, that our learning is simply recollection: that also makes it necessary, I suppose, if it is true, that we learnt at some former time what we now remember; but this is impossible unless our soul existed somewhere before it was born in this human shape. In this way also the soul seems to be something immortal."

Then Simmias put in, "But, Cebes, what are the proofs of this? Remind me, for I don't quite remember now."

"There is one very beautiful proof," said Cebes, "that people, when asked questions, if they are properly asked, say of themselves everything correctly; yet if there were not knowledge in them, and right reason, they would not be able to do this. You see, if you show someone a diagram[2] or anything like that, he proves most clearly that this is true."

Socrates said, "If you don't believe this, Simmias, look at it in another way and see whether you agree. You disbelieve, I take it, how what is called learning can be recollection?"

"Disbelieve you," said Simmias, "not I! I just want to have an experience of what we are now discussing—recollection. I almost remember and believe already from what Cebes tried to say; yet none the less I should like to hear how *you* were going to put it."

"This is how," he answered. "We agree, I suppose, that if anyone remembers something he must have known it before at some time."

"Certainly," he said.

"Then do we agree on this also, that when knowledge comes to him in such a way, it is recollection? What I mean is something like this: If a man has seen or heard something or perceived it by some other sense, and he not only knows that, but thinks of something else of which the knowledge is not the

[1] Socrates' theory of a conservation of life is somewhat like our familiar theory of the conservation of energy.
[2] Compare *Meno*, p. 43 ff.

PHAEDO (72D–74A)

same but different, is it not right for us to say he remembered that which he thought of?"

"How do you mean?"

"Here is an example: Knowledge of a man and knowledge of a lyre are different."

"Of course."

"Well, you know about lovers, that when they see a lyre or a dress or anything else which their beloved uses, this is what happens to them: they know the lyre, and they conceive in the mind the figure of the boy whose lyre it is? Now this is recollection; just as when one sees Simmias, one often remembers Cebes, and there would be thousands of things like that."

"Thousands, indeed!" said Simmias.

"Then is that sort of thing," said he, "a kind of recollection? Especially when one feels this about things which one had forgotten because of time and neglect?"

"Certainly," he said.

"Very well then," said Socrates. "When you see a horse in a picture, or a lyre in a picture, is it possible to remember a man? And when you see Simmias in a picture, to remember Cebes?"

"Yes indeed."

"Or when you see Simmias in a picture, to remember Simmias himself?"

"Oh yes," said he.

["These being either like or unlike?"

"Yes."

"It makes no difference," he said. "Whenever, seeing one thing, from sight of this you think of another thing whether like or unlike, it is necessary," he said, "that that was recollection."

"Certainly."][1]

"Does it not follow from all this that recollection is both from like and from unlike things?"

"It does."

"But when a man remembers something from like things, must this not necessarily occur to him also—to reflect whether anything is lacking or not from the likeness of what he remembers?"

"He must."

"Consider then," he said, "if this is true. We say, I suppose, there is such a thing as the equal, not a stick equal to a stick, or a stone to a stone, or anything like that, but something independent which is alongside all of them, the equal itself, equality; yes or no?"

---
[1] The bracketed passage has been transposed from 74 C-D of the Greek text, p. 478, where it would appear to be meaningless.

"Yes indeed," said Simmias, "upon my word, no doubt about it."

"And do we understand what that is?"

"Certainly," he said. "Where did we get the knowledge of it? Was it not from such examples as we gave just now, by seeing equal sticks or stones and so forth, from these we conceived that, which was something distinct from them? Don't you think it is distinct? Look at it this way also: Do not the same stones or sticks appear equal to one person and unequal to another?"

"Certainly."

"Well, did the really-equals ever seem unequal to you, I mean did equality ever seem to be inequality?"

"Never, Socrates."

"Then those equal things," said he, "are not the same as the equal itself."

"Not at all, I think, Socrates."

"Yet from these equals," he said, "being distinct from that equal, you nevertheless conceived and received knowledge of that equal?"

"Very true," he said.[1]

"Well," said he, "how do we feel about the sticks as compared with the real equals we spoke of just now; do the equal sticks seem to us to be as equal as equality itself, or do they fall somewhat short of the essential nature of equality; or nothing short?"

"They fall short," he said, "a great deal."

"Then we agree on this: When one sees a thing, and thinks, 'This which I now see wants to be like something else—like one of the things that are, but falls short and is unable to be such as that is, it is inferior,' it is necessary, I suppose, that he who thinks thus has previous knowledge of that which he thinks it resembles but falls short of?"

"That is necessary."

"Very well, do we feel like that or not about equal things and the equal?"

"Assuredly we do."

"It is necessary then that we knew the equal before that time when, first seeing the equal things, we thought that all these aim at being such as the equal, but fall short."

"That is true."

"Well, we go on to agree here also: we did not and we could not get a notion of the equal by any other means than by seeing or grasping, or perceiving by some other sense. I say the same of equal and all the rest."

[1] See p. 477, n.

"And they are the same, Socrates, for what the argument wants to prove."

"Look here, then; it is from the senses we must get the notion that all these things of sense aim at that which is the equal, and fall short of it; or how do we say?"

"Yes."

"Then before we began to see and hear and use our other senses, we must have got somewhere knowledge of what the equal is, if we were going to compare with it the things judged equal by the senses and see that all things are eager to be such as that equal is, but are inferior to it."

"This is necessary from what we agreed, Socrates."

"Well, as soon as we were born we saw and heard and had our other senses?"

"Certainly."

"Then, we say, we must have got knowledge of the equal before that?"

"Yes."

"Before we were born, then, it is necessary that we must have got it."

"So it seems."

"Then if we got it before we were born and we were born having it, we knew before we were born and as soon as we were born, not only the equal and the greater and the less but all the rest of such things? For our argument now is no more about the equal than about the beautiful itself, and the good itself, and the just and the pious, and I mean everything which we seal with the name of 'that which is,' the essence, when we ask our questions and respond with our answers in discussion. So we must have got the proper knowledge of each of these before we were born."

"That is true."

"And if having got the knowledge, in each case, we have not forgotten, we must continue knowing this and know it through life; for to know is, having got knowledge of something, to keep it and not to lose it; dropping knowledge, Simmias, is what we call forgetfulness, isn't it?"

"Just so, Socrates," he said.

"But, I think, if we got it before birth, and lost it at birth, and if afterwards, using our senses about these things, we recover the knowledge which once before we had, would not what we call learning be to recover our own knowledge? And this we should rightly call recollection?"

"Certainly."

"For, you see, it has been shown to be possible that a man perceiving something, by sight or hearing or some other sense, thinks, from this perception, of some other thing which he has forgotten, to which he compares this as being like or unlike. So as I say, there is choice of two things: either we were all born knowing them and we all know them throughout life; or afterwards those who we say learn just remember, and nothing more, and learning would be recollection."

"That is certainly true, Socrates."

"Which do you choose then, Simmias? Were we born knowing, or do we remember afterwards what we had got knowledge of before?"

"I can't choose all at once, Socrates."

"Another question, then; you can choose, and have some opinion about this. When a man knows anything, could he give an account of what he knows or not?"

"He must be able to do that, Socrates."

"Do you think that all could give account of the matters we have been discussing?"

"I would that they could," said Simmias, "but so far from that, I fear that tomorrow at this time there may be no one left in the world able to do that properly."

"Then, Simmias, you don't think that all know them?"

"Oh, no!"

"Then are they trying to remember what they once learnt?"

"It must be so."

"When did our souls get the knowledge of these things? For surely it is not since we became human beings."

"Certainly not."

"Then before."

"Yes."

"So, Simmias, our souls existed long ago, before they were in human shape, apart from bodies, and then had wisdom."

"Unless, indeed, we get all these knowledges at birth, Socrates; for this time is still left."

"Very well, my comrade; at what other time do we lose them? For we are not born having them, as we admitted just now. Do we lose them at the very same time as we get them? Can you suggest any other time?"

"Oh no, Socrates, I did not see I was talking nonsense."

"Is this the case then, Simmias?" he asked. "If all these exist which we are always harping on, the beautiful and the good and every such essence; and if we refer to these essences all the things which our senses perceive, finding out that the essences existed before and are ours now, and compare our sensations with them, it necessarily follows that, just as these exist, so our soul must have existed before our birth; but if they do not exist, this argument will be worthless. Is this true, and is there equal necessity that these things exist and our souls did before our birth, or if they do not exist, neither did our souls?"

"I am quite convinced, Socrates," said Simmias, "that there is the same necessity; our argument has found an excellent refuge when it maintains equally that our soul exists before we are born, and the essences likewise which you speak of. Nothing is clearer to me than this, that all such things exist most assuredly, beauty and good and the others which you named; and I think it has been sufficiently proved."

"And what thinks Cebes?" said Socrates. "We must convince Cebes too."

"It is good enough for him," said Simmias, "as I believe; but he is the most obstinate man in the world at disbelieving what is said; however, I believe he really is convinced that our soul existed before our birth.

"Yet will it exist after death too?" he went on. "I don't think myself that has been proved yet, Socrates. We are confronted still with what Cebes said just now: Can it be that when the man dies his soul is scattered abroad and that is the end of it, as so many say? For supposing it is composed from somewhere or other, and comes into existence before it even enters a human body; what hinders it, when it has entered and finally got rid of that body, from ending at that moment also, and being itself destroyed?"

"Well said, Simmias," said Cebes. "It does seem that half of what ought to be proved has been proved, that our soul exists before our birth; it must also be proved that when we die it will exist no less than before our birth, if the proof is to be completed."

"It has been proved already, my dear Simmias and Cebes," said Socrates, "if you choose to combine this argument with what we agreed to before it, that all the living comes from the dead. For if the soul exists before, and if it is necessary that when coming into life and being born it comes from death and from nothing else at all, it must certainly be necessary that it exists even when one dies, since it must be born again. Well then, what you said has in fact been proved already. Still, I think you and Cebes would be glad to investigate this argument yet further, and you seem to me to have the fear which children have—that really, when it leaves the body, the wind blows it away and scatters it, especially if anyone dies not in calm weather but in a great tempest."

Cebes laughed, and said. "Then think we are afraid of that, Socrates," he said, "and try to convince us against it; or better, don't think *we* are afraid, but imagine there is a kind of child in us which has such fears; then let us try to persuade this child not to fear death as if it were a bogey."

"No," said Socrates, "you must sing incantations over it every day, until you charm it out."

"My dear Socrates," he said, "where shall we get a good charmer of such things, since you are leaving us?"

"Hellas is a big place, my dear Cebes," he replied, "and there are many good men in it, and there are many barbarian nations too; and you must search through them all looking for such a charmer; you must spare neither money nor pains, since you could not spend money on anything more important. And you must not forget to search among yourselves; for perhaps you could not easily find any better able than yourselves to do that."

"Oh, that shall be done, of course," said Cebes; "but let us go back to where we left off—if you would like to."

"But certainly I should like to," he said; "of course I should!"

"That's well said," said Cebes.

"Very well then," said Socrates, "we must ask ourselves what sorts of things properly undergo this; I mean, what sorts of things are dissolved and scattered, for what sorts we must fear such an end, and for what not; next we must consider which sort the soul belongs to. We shall know then whether to be confident or fearful for our own soul."

"True," he said.

"Isn't it to the composite, which is by nature compounded, that dissolution is proper—I mean it is dissolved just as it was composed? And, on the other hand, an uncompounded thing, if indeed such exists, is least of all things naturally liable to dissolution?"

"That seems to me correct," said Cebes.

"Then what is always the same and in the same state is likely to be the uncompounded, but what is always changing and never keeps in the same state is likely to be the compounded?"

"I think so."

"Let us turn to what we have discussed already," he said. "This essence which we describe in all our questions and answers as existing—is it always in the same state or does it change? I mean the equal itself, the beautiful itself, everything which exists by itself, that which is—does it admit of any changes whatever? Or is it true that each thing that so exists, being of one form and itself alone, is always in the same state, and never admits of any change whatever in any way or at any time or in any place?"

"It must necessarily be always in the same state," said Cebes.

"And what of the many particulars, men or horses or dresses or what you will, things equal or beautiful and so forth, all that have the same name as those essences? Are they always in the same state; or, quite opposite to the essences, are they not constantly changing in themselves and in relation to each other, and, one might say, never keep in the same state?"

"That again is right," said Cebes, "they never keep in the same state."

"These, then, you could touch or see or perceive by the other senses, but those which continue in the same state cannot be grasped by anything except intellectual reasoning, and such things are unseen[1] and not visible?"

"Certainly that is true," he said.

"Shall we lay down, then, that there are two kinds of existing things, one visible, one unseen?"

"Yes," he said.

"And the unseen is always in the same state, but the visible constantly changing?"

"Yes to that also," he said.

"Now come," said he, "in ourselves one part is body and one part soul?"

"Just so," he said.

"Then which kind do we say the body would be more like and akin to?"

"The visible," he said, "that is clear to anyone."

"And the soul—is it visible, or unseen?"

"Not visible to mankind at least, Socrates," he said.

"But when we say visible and not visible, we mean to human senses, don't we?"

"Yes, we do."

"Then what of the soul—do we say that is visible or invisible?"

"Not visible."

"Unseen, then?"

"Yes."

"Then soul is more like to the unseen, and body to the visible."

"It surely must be."

"Now you remember that we were saying some time ago that the soul, when it has the body to help in examining

---

[1] The word used is ἀειδής, unseen or without form. Plato introduces it here because it sounds significantly like the word Ἀιδης, Hades, suggesting that the unchanging essences are immaterial and belong to the other world. The association between the two Greek words is also brought out on pp. 485 and 486.

things, either through sight or hearing or any other sense—for to examine something through the body means through the senses—then it is dragged by the body towards what is always changing, and the soul goes astray and is confused and staggers about like one drunken because she is taking hold of such things."

"Certainly."

"But when she examines by herself, she goes away yonder to the pure and everlasting and immortal and unchanging; and being akin to that, she abides ever with it, whenever it becomes possible for her to abide by herself. And there she rests from her wanderings, and while she is amongst those things she is herself unchanging because what she takes hold of is unchanging: and this state of the soul has the name of wisdom?"

"Most excellent and true, Socrates."

"Then which of the two kinds is she more like and more akin to, judging from what we said before and what we are saying now?"

"Everyone, even the most ignorant, would admit, I think, Socrates," he said, "from that way of reasoning, that soul is wholly and altogether more like the unchanging than the changing."

"And the body?"

"More like the changing."

"Look at it in this way also: When soul and body are together, our nature assigns the body to be slave and to be ruled, and the soul to be ruler and master; now, then, further, which of the two seems to be like the divine, and which like the mortal? Don't you think the divine is naturally such as to rule and to guide, and the mortal such as to be ruled and to be a slave?"

"I do."

"Then which is the soul like?"

"It is clear, Socrates, that the soul is like the divine, and the body like the mortal."

"Consider now, Cebes, whether it follows from all that we have said, that the soul is most like the divine and immortal and intellectual and simple and indissoluble and self-unchangeable, but on the contrary, the body is most like the human and mortal and manifold and unintellectual and dissoluble and ever-changing. Can we say anything to contradict that, my dear Cebes, or is that correct?"

"We cannot contradict it."

"Very well. This being so, is it not proper to the body to be quickly dissolved, but on the contrary to the soul to be wholly indissoluble or very nearly so?"

"Of course."

"You understand, then," he said, "that when the man dies, the visible part of him, the body—that which lies in the visible world, and which we call the corpse, for which it is proper to dissolve and disappear—does not suffer any of this at once but instead remains a good long time, and if a man dies with his body in a nice condition and age, a very long time. For if the body is shrivelled up and mummified like the mummies in Egypt it lasts almost whole, for an incredibly long time. And some portions of the body, even when it decays, bones and sinews and so forth, may almost be called immortal."

"Yes."

"But the soul, the 'unseen' part of us, which goes to another place noble and pure and unseen like itself, a true unseen Hades, to the presence of the good and wise God, where, if God will, my own soul must go very soon—shall our soul, then, being such and of such nature, when released from the body be straightway scattered by the winds and perish, as most men say? Far from it, my dear Simmias! This is much more likely: If it is pure when it gets free, and drags nothing of the body with it, since it has no communion with the body in life if it can help it, but avoids the body and gathers itself into itself, since it is always practising this—here we have nothing else but a soul loving wisdom rightly, and in reality practising death—don't you think this would be a practice of death?"

"By all means."

"Then, being thus, it goes away into the unseen, which is like itself, the divine and immortal and wise, where on arrival it has the opportunity to be happy, freed from wandering and folly and fears and wild loves and all other human evils, and, as they say of the initiated, really and truly passing the rest of time with the gods. Is that what we are to say, Cebes?"

"Yes indeed," said Cebes.

"But if contrariwise, I think, if it leaves the body polluted and unpurified, as having been always with it and attending it and in love with it and bewitched by it through desires and pleasures, so that it thinks nothing to be true but the bodily —what one could touch and see and drink and eat and use for carnal passion; if what is darksome to the eyes and 'unseen' but intellectual and to be caught by philosophy, if this, I say, it is accustomed to hate and fear and flee; do you think a soul in that state will get away pure and incorrupt in itself?"

"By no possible means whatever," he said.

"No, I think it is interpenetrated by the bodily, which the association and union with it of the body has by constant practice made ingrained."

"Exactly."

"A heavy load, my friend, we must believe that to be, heavy and earthy and visible; and such a soul with this on board is weighed down and dragged back into the visible world, by fear of the unseen,[1] Hades so-called, and cruises[2] about restless among tombs and graves, where you know shadowy apparitions of souls have often been seen, phantoms such as are produced by souls like this, which have not been released purely, but keep something of the visible, and so they are seen."

"That is likely, Socrates."

"Indeed it is likely; and likely that these are not the souls of the good, but souls of the mean, which are compelled to wander about such places as a penalty for their former way of life, which was evil; and wander they must until by desire for the bodily which is always in their company they are imprisoned once more in a body. And they are imprisoned, as is likely, into the same habits which they had practised in life before."

"What sort of habits do you mean, Socrates?"

"It is likely, for example, that those who have practised gluttony and violence and drunkenness and have not taken heed to their ways enter the bodies of asses and suchlike beasts, don't you think so?"

"Very likely indeed."

"Those, again, who have preferred injustice and tyrannies and robberies, into the bodies of wolves and hawks and kites; or where else do we say they would go?"

"No doubt," said Cebes, "they pass into creatures like these."

"Then it is clear," said he, "that the rest go wherever they do go, to suit their own likenesses and habits?"

"Quite clear, of course," he said.

"Then of these the happiest people," he said, "and those who go to the best place, are those who have practised the public and political virtues which they call temperance and justice, got from habit and custom without philosophy and reason?"

"How are these happiest, pray?"

"Why, isn't it likely that they pass into another similar

[1] See p. 483, n. 1.
[2] Literally "rolls about" (like a ship at sea).

PHAEDO (81C–83B)

political and gentle race, perhaps bees or wasps or ants; or even into the same human race again, and that there are born from them decent men?"

"Yes, that is likely."

"But into the family of gods, unless one is a philosopher and departs wholly pure, it is not permitted for any to enter, except the lover of learning. Indeed, it is for the sake of this purity, Simmias and Cebes, my two good comrades, that those who truly seek wisdom steadfastly abstain from all bodily desires and refuse to give themselves over to them, not from having any fear of ruin of their home or of poverty, as the money-loving multitude has; and again, not from being afraid of dishonour, or a bad reputation for wickedness, as the honour-lovers and power-lovers are; that is why these abstain from them."

"No, Socrates," said Cebes, "that would not be proper."

"Not at all, by heaven," said he. "Therefore those who care at all for their own soul and do not live just serving[1] the body say good-bye to everyone of that kind and walk not after guides who know not where they are going; for they themselves believe they must not act contrary to philosophy, and its deliverance and purification, and so they turn to philosophy and follow by the way she leads them."

"How, Socrates?"

"I will tell you," he said.

"The lovers of learning understand," said he, "that philosophy found their soul simply imprisoned in the body and welded to it, and compelled to survey through this as if through prison bars the things that are, not by itself through itself, but wallowing in all ignorance; and she saw that the danger of this prison came through desire, so that the prisoner himself would be chief helper in his own imprisonment. As I say then, lovers of learning understand that philosophy, taking possession of their soul in this state, gently encourages it and tries to free it, by showing that surveying through the eyes is full of deceit, and so is perception through the ears and the other senses; she persuades the soul to withdraw from these, except so far as there is necessity to use them, and exhorts it to collect itself together and gather itself into itself, and to trust nothing at all but itself, and only whatever of the realities each in itself the soul itself by itself can understand; but that whatever of what varies with its environs the soul examines through other means, it must consider this to be no part of truth; such a thing, philosophy tells it, is a thing of the senses and of the visible, but what it sees itself is a

[1] This word is doubtful in the Greek text.

thing of the intellect and of the 'unseen.' So the soul of the true philosopher believes that it must not oppose this deliverance, and therefore abstains from pleasures and desires and griefs and fears as much as possible, counting that when a man feels great pleasure or fear or pain or desire, he suffers not only the evil that one might think (for example, being ill or squandering money through his desires), but the greatest and worst of all evils, which he suffers and never counts."

"What is that, Socrates?" asked Cebes.

"That the soul of every man suffers this double compulsion: At the same time as it is compelled to feel great pleasure or pain about anything, it is compelled also to believe that the thing for which it specially feels this is most clearly real and true, when it is not. These are generally the visible things, aren't they?"

"Certainly."

"Then in this state especially the soul is imprisoned by the body?"

"Pray how?"

"Because each pleasure and pain seems to have a nail, and nails the soul to the body and pins it on and makes it bodily, and so it thinks the same things are true which the body says are true. For by having the same opinion as the body, and liking the same things, it is compelled, I believe, to adopt the same ways and the same nourishment, and to become such as never could come pure to the house of Hades, but would always go forth infected by the body; so it would fall again quickly into another body and there be sown and grown, and therefore would have neither part nor lot in communion with the divine and pure and simple."

"Most true, indeed," said Cebes.

"So then it is for these reasons, Cebes, that those who rightly love learning are decent and brave, not for the reasons which the many give; what do you think?"

"Certainly not."

"No indeed. Such would be the reasoning of the philosopher. His soul would not think it right that philosophy should set her free, and that while being set free she herself should surrender herself back again in bondage to pleasures and pains, and so perform the endless task of a Penelope unweaving the work of her loom.[1] No, she thinks she must calm these passions; and, following reason and keeping always in it, beholding the true and the divine and the certain, and nourishing herself on this, his soul believes that she

[1] Penelope prolonged her task for three years by unweaving at night what she wove by day. *Odyssey* xix. Bodily indulgence is unweaving and the soul would have to weave it up again.

ought to live thus, as long as she does live, and when she dies she will join what is akin and like herself, and be rid of human evils. After nurture of this kind there is nothing to fear, my dear Simmias and Cebes, and she need not expect in parting from the body to be scattered about and blown away by the winds, and to be gone like a bird and be nowhere any more."

There was a long silence after Socrates had ended; Socrates himself was deep in these thoughts, or appeared to be, and so were most of us. But Cebes and Simmias whispered together a bit, and when Socrates noticed them he said, "What's the matter? Surely you don't think our argument has missed anything? Indeed, there are a good many suspicions and objections, if one is to go through it thoroughly. If, then, you are considering something else, I say nothing; but if you are at all puzzled about what we have been saying, don't hesitate to speak yourselves. Go through it, and see if you think it might have been improved; and take me with you through it again if you think I can help you any more at all in your difficulties."

Simmias answered, "Well then, Socrates, I will tell you the truth. We have been puzzled for a long time, both of us, and each pushes on the other and bids him ask; because we wish to hear and don't want to be a nuisance, in case you are feeling unhappy about the present misfortune!"

Socrates laughed gently as he heard this, and said. "Bless me, my dear Simmias! Surely I could hardly persuade others that I don't think the present fortune a misfortune, when I can't persuade even you, but you fear I am more fretful now than I have been in my past life. Apparently it seems to you that I'm a worse prophet than the swans. When they perceive that they must die, you know, they sing more and better than they ever did before, glad to be going away into the presence of that god whose servants they are. But men tell lies against them because they fear death themselves, and they say that the swans are mourning their death and singing a dirge for sorrow; men don't take into account that no bird ever sings when it is hungry or cold or feels any other pain, not the swallow or the hoopoe or even the nightingale, which they say all sing a dirge for sorrow. But I don't believe those birds do sing in sorrow, nor do the swans, but these, I think, because they belong to Apollo, are prophets and know beforehand the good things in the other world, and sing and rejoice on that day far more than ever before. Indeed I think myself that I am the swans' fellow-slave, and sacred to the same god, and I think I have prophecy from my master no less than they have, and I depart from life no more dispirited than they do. No, as far as that matters, you should speak and ask what you will, so long as we have leave of the Athenian Board of Eleven."

"Good," said Simmias, "then I will speak out, and tell you my difficulty, and Cebes too, where he does not accept all you have said. For I think, as perhaps you do, Socrates, that to know the plain truth about such matters in this present life is impossible, or at least very difficult; but only a very soft man would refuse to test in every possible way what is said about them, and would give up before examining them all over till he was tired out. I think a man's duty is one of two things: either to be taught or to find out where the truth is, or if he cannot, at least to take the best possible human doctrine and the hardest to disprove, and to ride on this like a raft over the waters of life and take the risk; unless he could have a more seaworthy vessel to carry him more safely and with less danger, some divine doctrine to bring him through. So now I will not be ashamed to ask, since you tell me yourself to do it; and I shall not blame myself afterwards because I did not now say what I think. Well, my opinion is, Socrates, when I consider what has been said in my own mind and with Cebes here, that it is not quite satisfactory."

Socrates said, "Perhaps, my comrade, your opinion is true. But say where it is not satisfactory."

"Here," said he: "That one could say the same about harmony[1] and a harp with strings; that the harmony is invisible and bodiless and all-beautiful and divine on the tuned harp; but the harp itself and the strings are bodies and bodily and composite and earthy and akin to the mortal. So when someone breaks the harp, or cuts and bursts the strings, suppose he should maintain by the same argument as yours that it is necessary the harmony should still exist and not perish; for it would be just as impossible that the harp should still exist when the strings are broken, and the strings should still exist which are of mortal kind, as that the harmony should perish —harmony, which is of the same kith and kin as the divine and immortal, perishing before the mortal; no, he would say, the harmony must necessarily exist somewhere, and wood and strings must rot away first, before anything could happen to the harmony! Well, Socrates, I think you yourself must have noticed that we conceive the soul to be something like this—that our body being tuned and held together by hot and cold and dry and wet and suchlike, our soul is a kind of mixture and harmony of these very things, when they are

[1] Or tune.

well and harmoniously mixed together. If, then, our soul is a kind of harmony, it is plain that when the body is slackened inharmoniously or too highly strung, by diseases and other evils, the soul must necessarily perish, although it is most divine, just as the other harmonies do, those in sounds and those in all the works of craftsmen, but the relics of each body will remain until it rots or is burnt. Then consider what we must answer to this argument, if anyone claims that the soul is a mixture of the things in the body, and at what is called death, it is the first to perish."

Socrates gazed at us with his eyes wide open, as he usually did, and said, smiling, "What Simmias says is quite fair. Then if any of you is readier than I am, why didn't he reply? I think he tackles the question neatly. But before the answer comes, I think we ought to hear Cebes first, what fault he, too, has to find with our argument. Then there will be a little time and we can consider what to say; afterwards, when we have heard them, we ought to agree with them if they seem to be in tune with us, or if not, we should continue as before to defend our doctrine. Come along, Cebes," he said, "speak! What worried you?"

"I'll tell you," said Cebes. "I think the argument is where it was, and has the same objection which I made before. That our soul existed before it came into this form, I do not retract; it was a nice, neat proof, and quite satisfactory, if I may say so without offence; but that when we are dead the soul will still exist somewhere, I can't say the same of that. However, I do not agree with the objection of Simmias, that the soul is not stronger and much longer-lasting than the body; for I think it is very far superior in all those respects. 'Well,' the argument might say to me, 'why do you still disbelieve? You can see when the man is dead the weaker part still existing, and don't you think the longer-lasting must necessarily survive during this time?' Well, see if you think anything of this answer of mine; really, it seems that I also want a simile, like Simmias. I think all this is very much the same as saying as follows of a weaver who died old: The man is not dead but exists somewhere safe and sound, and here is a proof one might offer—here is the cloak which he wove himself, and used to wear, safe and sound, and it has not perished. If someone disbelieved, one might ask him, 'Which kind of thing is longer-lasting, a man, or a cloak in use and wear?' If the answer was, 'A man lasts longer than a cloak,' one might imagine that this proved that the man was certainly safe and sound, since the shorter-lasting thing had not perished. But I don't think that is right, Simmias; just consider what I have to say now. Everyone would understand that such an argument is silly; for this weaver had woven and worn out many such cloaks and died later than all except the last, when he died before it, yet for all that a man is neither inferior to a cloak nor weaker. Soul and body might admit of the same simile, and one might fairly say the same about them, I think, that the soul is long-lasting, the body weaker and shorter-lasting; but one might say more, that each of the souls wears out many bodies, especially if it lives many years. For if the body wastes and perishes while the man still lives, but the soul always weaves anew what is worn away, it would, however, be necessary that when the soul perished it would happen to be wearing the last body and it would perish before this last only, and when the soul perished, the body would show at once the nature of its weakness and would quickly rot and vanish in decay. This argument, then, is not yet enough to give confidence that when we die our soul exists somewhere. For if one should grant your supporter even more than what you say, and admitted to him not only that our souls existed in the time before our birth, but that nothing hindered the souls of some of us from still existing when we die, and continuing to exist, and from being born and dying again and again, for so strong is its nature that the soul endures being born many times: one might admit that, and yet never admit that it does not suffer in these many births, and at last in one of its deaths does not perish outright. But one might say that no one knows which death and dissolution of the body brings death of the soul; for it is impossible for any one of us to distinguish it beforehand. Now if this is correct, it follows that anyone who is confident about death is foolish in his confidence, unless he can show that the soul is wholly immortal and imperishable; for if he cannot show this, it is necessary that he who is about to die must always fear for his soul lest at the present separation from the body it may utterly perish."

When we had heard these two we were very unhappy, as we told one another afterwards. We had been firmly convinced by the earlier arguments, and now we seemed to be thrown back by the speakers into confusion and disbelief; we distrusted not only the earlier arguments but those which were coming, and we thought that either we were worthless judges, or else there could be nothing to trust in the whole thing.

ECHECRATES: By heaven, Phaidon, I feel with you. As I heard you tell such a story, I felt like asking myself, "Then what argument can we trust any longer?" That one seemed quite convincing when Socrates spoke, but now it has fallen into distrust. This notion has a wonderful hold of me and always did, that our soul is a kind of harmony, and when you spoke of it I was, one might say, reminded that I had once thought so too. Now again we must start from the beginning, for I very much want another argument to persuade me that the soul of the dead does not die with him. Tell me this in heaven's name, how did Socrates follow up the discussion? Was he also put out like the rest of you? Did he show it or not? If not, did he quietly defend the reasoning? And did he defend it enough, or too little? Tell us the whole story as exactly as you can.

PHAIDON: Well, I must say, Echecrates, I always wondered at Socrates, but I never wondered at him more than when I was with him then. To have something to say was perhaps no novelty in that man; but what most surprised me was, how pleasant and friendly and respectful he was in welcoming the speculations of the young men, and then how sharply he saw how we were affected by what was said, and then how well he treated us, and rallied us like a lot of beaten runaways, and headed us back to follow the argument and examine it along with him.

ECHECRATES: Well, how?

PHAIDON: I will tell you. I happened to be sitting on his right hand, on a low stool beside his bed, and his seat was much higher than mine. Then he stroked my head and pinched together the hair on my neck—he used occasionally to play with my hair—and said, "Tomorrow perhaps, Phaidon, you'll cut off this pretty hair."[1]

"It seems like it, Socrates," I said.

"Well, you won't, if you will listen to me."

"But why?" said I.

"Today," he said, "you shall cut off this, and I mine, at least if our argument comes to its latter end and we can't bring it to life again. In fact if I were you, and if the argument escaped me, I would swear an oath like the Argives,[2] never to let my hair grow long again till I renew the fight with Simmias and Cebes and beat their argument."

"But Socrates," I said, "two to one! Not even Heracles could be a match for two, as they say!"[3]

"Then," he said, "call me in as your Ioleos, while there is daylight still."

---

[1] In mourning for Socrates.
[2] Herodotos, I. 82. They swore not to let their hair grow till they reconquered Thyreai.
[3] A proverb. Heracles was fighting the hydra, and saw a crab coming up to help the hydra. He then called in Ioleos.

"I call you to help, then," said I, "not as Heracles did to Ioleos; but like an Ioleos to Heracles."

"That will be the same thing," he said. "But first let us be careful against a danger."

"What is the danger?" said I.

"Don't let us be 'misologues,' hating argument as misanthropes hate men; the worst disease one can have is to hate arguments. Misology and misanthropy come in the same way. Misanthropy is put on from believing someone too completely without discrimination, and thinking the man to be speaking the truth wholly and wholesomely, and then finding out soon afterwards that he is bad and untrustworthy and quite different; when this happens often to a man, especially from those he thought to be his closest and truest friends, at last, after so many knocks, he hates everybody, and believes there is no soundness in anyone at all. Haven't you noticed that happening?"

"Oh yes," I said.

"Then that is an ugly thing," he said, "and it is clear such a man tries to deal with men when he has no skill in human affairs. For if he had that technical skill when he dealt with them, he would take them as they are, and believe that the very good and very bad are few, but most are betwixt and between."

"What do you mean?" I asked.

"As with very big and very small men. Don't you think the rarest thing is to find a very big or a very small man, or dog, or anything else? So with quick and slow, ugly and handsome, white and black? Don't you see that in all these the extremes are few and rare, but the betweens plenty and many?"

"Oh, yes, indeed," I said.

"Then," said he, "if there were a competition in wickedness, there, too, the prize-winners would be few?"

"Quite likely," I said.

"Yes, quite likely," said he, "but in that respect arguments are not like men. I have been following your lead so far, but I think the likeness lies in this: when a person without technical skill in words believes an argument to be true, and soon afterwards thinks it false, sometimes when it is and sometimes when it is not, and so again one person after another—and especially those who spend their time arguing against each other—you know that in the end they think they are the wisest men in the world, and that they alone understand how there is nothing sound and wholesome either in practical affairs or in arguments, but all real things are just like a Euripos,[1] a tide moving up and down and never remaining the same."

[1] The strait between Euboia and the mainland, where there are several "tides" or currents of water every day.

PHAEDO (89C–91D)

"That is truly stated indeed," I said.

"Then, Phaidon," he said, "it would be a pitiable disease, when there *is* an argument true and sound and such as can be understood, if through the pain of meeting so many which seem sometimes to be true and sometimes not, instead of blaming himself and his own clumsiness a man should in the end gladly throw the blame from himself upon the arguments, and for the rest of his life should continually hate and abuse them, and deprive himself of the truth and the knowledge of what is real."

"Yes, I do declare," said I, "it would be pitiable."

"First, then, let us be careful," he said, "and let us not admit into our souls the belief that there really is no health or soundness in arguments. Much rather let us think that we are not sound ourselves, let us be men and take pains to become sound: you and the others to prepare you for all your coming life, I to prepare myself for death. For in fact as regards this very matter I am just now no philosopher, I am a philovictor— I want to win, as much as the most uneducated men do. Such men, you know, when there is difference of opinion, care nothing how the truth stands in a question, but do their very best to make their audience believe whatever they have laid down. Just now I am the same as they are, with only one difference: I shall do my very best to convince of the truth—not my audience, except by the way, but to convince myself that what seems true to me is perfectly true. For, my dear comrade, see how selfishly I reckon it up! If what I say is really true, then it is well to be convinced; but if for the dead nothing remains, then at least for just this time before death, I shall not be disagreeable to you here by lamentations. And this ignorance[1] of mine will not last, which would be an evil thing, but very soon it will perish. Thus prepared, then," he said, "my dear Simmias and Cebes, I proceed to the question; but you, if you please, do not be anxious about Socrates, not a bit, but be very anxious about truth; if you think I say anything true, agree with me, and if not, oppose me with all your might, that my eagerness may not deceive both myself and you—I don't want to be like a bee and leave my sting in you when I go.

"Forward, now," he went on. "First remind me what you said, if I don't seem to remember. Simmias, as I think, disbelieves, and fears that the soul, although something more divine and beautiful than the body, may perish before the body like a sort of harmony. Cebes I thought admitted with me that soul was at least longer-lasting than body, but everyone must doubt whether the soul has already worn out many bodies, and now,

[1] Another reading is "folly."

leaving the last body, it may perish itself; and death may be just this, the destruction of soul, since body is perishing continually and never stops. Are not these the matters which we must consider, Simmias and Cebes?" Both agreed to this. "Well, do you reject all the earlier arguments, or only some?"

"Some only," they replied.

"And what of that one," said he, "when we said learning was recollection, and that therefore our soul must exist somewhere before being imprisoned in the body?"

"That one," said Cebes, "seemed to me wonderfully convincing, and I abide by it now as by no other argument."

"Yes, and so do I, too," said Simmias, "and I should be surprised if I could ever think otherwise about that."

Socrates answered, "Well, my good friend from Thebes," he said, "you must think otherwise, if the notion holds that harmony is a thing composite, and soul is a harmony arising from all the elements strung and tuned in the body. For you will not allow yourself to say that a composite harmony existed before the elements from which it had to be composed—eh, Simmias?"

"Oh dear me no, Socrates!"

"You perceive, then," said he, "that this is what you really affirm, when you say that the soul existed before it came into human shape and body, and that it existed composed of things which did not exist. But see, harmony is not such a thing as you likened it to; no, first the harp and the strings and their tones not yet harmonised come into being, and last of all the harmony is composed, and it is first to perish. Then how will your argument be in tune[1] with that?"

"It will not," said Simmias.

"And yet," said he, "it ought to be in tune with the argument about harmony, if with any at all."

"So it ought," said Simmias.

"Then your argument," he said, "is not in tune. But look here: Which of the two do you choose—is learning recollection, or is the soul a harmony?"

"I much rather choose the first," said he. "Perhaps the other came without proof from a likely comparison that looked good, which makes most people pleased with it; but I am conscious that arguments proved from likelihood are humbugs, and if we are not careful they deceive us, in geometry and everything else. But the argument about recollection and learning has been shown to stand on a good foundation. What was said, I think, was that our soul existed before coming into the body just as that essence exists which has the name of 'real

[1] Literally, "sing together," i.e., accord.

PHAEDO (91D–93D)

being.' This I have accepted, I am convinced, with right and sufficient reason. I must therefore refuse now, as it seems, to accept for myself or anyone else that account of the soul which calls it a harmony."

"Very well, Simmias," said he. "What do you think of this: Is it proper for a harmony, or any other composite thing, to exist in any other state than the state of its component parts?"

"No," he said.

"Again, it cannot do, or be done to, anything else than they do or are done to?" He said no. "Then it is proper that a harmony does not lead the things which compose it, but follows?" He agreed. "Then a harmony cannot be moved and cannot sound or do anything else in opposition to its own parts?"

"Impossible," he said.

"Well, is not each harmony naturally so much a harmony according as it is harmonised?"

"I don't understand," he said.

"Listen," said he, "if it is more harmonised and more intensely, supposing that to be possible, would it be more a harmony and more intense, and if less harmonised and less intensely, would it be less a harmony and less intense?"

"Certainly."

"Is this true, then, of soul—that even in the smallest degree one soul can be more intensely and more completely, or less intensely and less completely, that very thing, a soul, than another is?"

"Not in the least," he said.

"Very well, then," he said, "in God's name: Is it said that one soul has sense and virtue and is good, but another has folly and wickedness and is bad, and is this true?"

"Quite true," he said.

"Then what will they say, those who lay down that soul is harmony, what will they say these things are which are in the souls, virtue and vice? Will they say these are yet another harmony, and a discord? And say that one soul is harmonised, the good one, and, being itself harmony, has in it another harmony, but the other is discordant itself and has in it no other harmony?"

"I can't say," said Simmias, "but it is clear that one who laid that down would say something of that kind."

"But we agreed before," said Socrates, "that one soul is not more or less soul than other; that means it is agreed that one is not more or less harmony than another, nor to a greater or less degree that another. Is that so?"

"Certainly."

"But that which is neither more nor less harmony has been

neither more nor less harmonised. Is that true?"

"That is true."

"When it is neither more nor less harmonised, can it partake of harmony to a greater or less degree, or only the same?"

"The same."

"Then soul, since one is no more than another what we actually mean by soul, consequently is neither more nor less harmonised?"

"Just so."

"In this condition, it would have no greater share of discord or harmony?"

"No, indeed."

"Then in this condition one would not partake of vice or virtue more than another, if vice is discord and virtue harmony?"

"No more."

"Rather I think, Simmias, according to right reasoning, no soul will partake of vice, if it is really harmony; for harmony which is wholly this very thing harmony could never partake of discord."

"Never, surely."

"Nor could soul partake of vice, if it is wholly soul."

"How could it, after what we admitted?"

"By this our reasoning then, all souls of all living creatures will be equally good, if they are equally and actually souls."

"I think so, Socrates," he said.

"Do you think that is correct," said he, "and do you think our argument would have come to this state, if the foundation were right, that is, that soul is harmony?"

"Not in the least," he said.

"Well now," said Socrates, "of all that there is in man, would you say anything rules but soul, especially a wise one?"

"No, not I."

"A soul which gives way to the feelings of the body, or one that even opposes them? I mean something like this—suppose fever be in the body and thirst, would you say soul drags it in the opposite way, so as not to drink, and if hunger be in it, not to eat? And we see the soul opposing the body in thousands of other things, don't we?"

"We do."

"Well then; did we not moreover agree earlier, that if it be indeed a harmony it would never sound a tune opposing the elements from which it arises, according as they are strung tight or loose, and twangled, and however else they are treated? It must follow these, it could never lead them?"

"Yes," he said, "we did agree. Of course."

"Very well: Don't we see it now doing the very opposite, leading all the things from which it is said to be composed, and opposing almost always all through life, a tyrant in every way, punishing them sometimes harshly and with bodily pain, that is, through gymnastic and physic, sometimes gently, giving now threats and now advice, talking to desires and angers and fears just as if it was different from them and they from it? Remember, too, Homer's lines in the Odyssey, where he says somewhere of Odysseus[1]

> Striking his chest, he thus reproached his heart,
> My heart, bear up! You have borne worse than this!

Do you think when he composed this he regarded the soul as a kind of harmony, something to be led by the body's feelings? —surely not, but as something able to lead these and play the tyrant, something much more divine than a harmony!"

"Yes indeed, Socrates, I agree," he said.

"Then, my good sir," he said, "it is quite wrong altogether to say that the soul is a harmony; for it appears we should contradict Homer, the divine poet, and ourselves too."

"Just so," he said.

"So much for that, then," said Socrates. "Our Theban Harmonia[2] has been appeased, it seems, pretty well; but what of Cadmos? My dear Cebes," he said, "how shall we appease Cadmos? What argument will do?"

"You'll find one, I think," said Cebes; "this one at least, against the harmony, was amazingly unexpected. When Simmias was telling what he was puzzled about, I wondered very much if anyone could deal with his argument at all, and to my surprise it couldn't stand your argument's first attack. I shouldn't wonder if the same happened to the argument of Cadmos."

"My good man," said Socrates, "don't tempt Providence, or some evil eye may overturn the argument which is coming. But God will care for that; let us charge into the fray like Homeric heroes, and try if there's anything in your contention. This is the sum of what you seek: You demand that it be proved that our soul is imperishable and immortal, if a student of philosophy, being about to die, and being confident, and believing that after death he will be better off in that world than if he had lived to the end a different life, is not to be found foolish and senseless in this confidence. But to show that the soul is something strong and godlike and existed before we were born men, all this you say may be no more than to indi-

[1] *Odyssey* xx. 17.
[2] Wife of Theban Cadmos in Greek story.

cate, not immortality, but that the soul is something long-lasting, and that it existed somewhere before for an immeasurable time, and knew and did many things; but it is not really any more immortal, but in fact its entry into the body of a man was the beginning of destruction for it, like a disease; it lives this life in distress, and last of all, at what is called death, it perishes. So there is no difference at all, you say, whether it comes once into the body or often, at least as regards our feeling of fear; for fear is proper, if one is not senseless, for him that knows not and cannot prove that the soul is immortal. That is very much what you say, Cebes; and I repeat it often on purpose that nothing may escape us; pray add or subtract if you wish."

And Cebes replied, "No, there is nothing I wish to add or subtract now; that is what I do say."

Socrates was silent for some time, thinking to himself; then he said, "That is no trifle you seek, Cebes; we are bound to discuss generally the cause of generation and destruction. If you allow me, I will run through my own experience in these matters. Then if anything of what I shall say seems useful, you shall use it to prove whatever you may say."

"By all means," Cebes said.

"Then listen, and I will tell you. When I was a young man, Cebes, I was most amazingly interested in the lore which they call natural philosophy. For I thought it magnificent to know the causes of everything, why it comes into being and why it is destroyed and why it exists; I kept turning myself upside down to consider things like the following: Is it when hot and cold get some fermentation in them, as some said,[1] that living things are bred? Is it the blood by which we think,[2] or air[3] or fire;[4] or whether it is none of these, but the brain is what provides the senses of hearing and sight and smell, and from these arise memory and opinion, and from memory and opinion in tranquillity comes knowledge; again I considered the destructions of these things, and what happens about heaven and earth. At last I believed myself as unfitted for this study as anything could be. I will tell you a sufficient proof: I found myself then so completely blinded by this study that I unlearned even what I used to think that I knew—what I understood clearly before, as I thought and others thought—about many other things and particularly as to the reason why man grows. I used to think that this was clear to all—by eating and drinking; for when from his foods flesh was added to flesh, and

[1] Anaximandros, Anaxagoras and others.
[2] Empedocles.
[3] Anaximenes.
[4] Heracleitos.

bones to bones, and in the same way the other parts each had added to them what was their own, then what was the little mass before became great later, and so the small man became big. That is what I believed then; isn't it a natural opinion?"

"I think so," said Cebes.

"Look next at this, then. I believed that when a big man stood by a small man, it was correct enough to suppose that he was bigger by the head, and so horse and horse; more clearly still, I thought ten was greater than eight because two was added to it, and the two-cubit bigger than the one-cubit because it overreached it by half."

"But now," said Cebes, "what do you think about them?"

"I'm very far, I swear, from thinking I know the cause of any of these things, for I can't agree with myself, even when one is added to one, either that the one to which it was added has become two, or the one which was added has become two, or that the one added and the one it was added to become two, by the adding of the one to the other; for I am surprised that when they were apart from each other each was one and they were not then two, but when they approached each other this was the cause of their becoming two, the meeting, their being near together. Or again, if a one is cut in half I cannot be convinced any longer that this, the cutting, was the cause of its becoming two; then it was because they were brought close together and one was added to the other, now because one is taken away and separated from the other. Nor can I even convince myself any longer that I know how the one is generated, or in a word how anything else is generated or perishes or exists; I can't do it by this kind of method, but I am muddling along with another of my own[1] and I don't allow this one at all.

"Well, I heard someone reading once out of a book, by Anaxagoras he said, how mind is really the arranger and cause of all things; I was delighted with this cause, and it seemed to me in a certain way to be correct that mind is the cause of all, and I thought that if this is true, mind arranging all things places everything as it is best. If, therefore, one wishes to find out the cause of anything, how it is generated or perishes or exists, what one ought to find out is how it is best for it to exist or to do or feel everything; from this reasoning, then, all that is proper for man to seek about this and everything is only the perfect and the best; but the same man necessarily knows the worse, too, for the same knowledge includes both. Reasoning thus, then, I was glad to think I had found a teacher of the cause of things after my own mind in Anaxag-

[1] The logical method.

oras: I thought he would show me first whether the earth is flat or round, and when he had shown this, he would proceed to explain the cause and the necessity, by showing that it was better that it should be such; and if he said it was in the middle of the universe, he would proceed to explain how it was better for it to be in the middle; and if he would explain all these things to me, I was prepared not to want any other kind of cause. And about the sun too I was equally prepared to learn in the same way, and the moon and stars besides, their speed as compared with one another, their turnings, and whatever else happens to them, how these things are better in each case for them to do or to be done to. For I did not believe that, when he said all this was ordered by mind, he would bring in any other cause for them than that it was best they should be as they are. So I thought that, when he had given the cause for each and for all together, that which is best for each, he would proceed to explain the common good of all; and I would not have sold my hopes for anything, but I got his books eagerly as quick as I could, and read them, that I might learn as soon as possible the best and the worse.

"Oh, what a wonderful hope! How high I soared, how low I fell! When as I went on reading I saw the man using mind not at all; and stating no valid causes of the arrangement of all things, but giving airs and ethers[1] and waters as causes, and many other strange things. I felt very much as I should feel if someone said, 'Socrates does by mind all he does'; and then, trying to tell the causes of each thing I do, if he should say first that the reason why I sit here now is, that my body consists of bones and sinews, and the bones are hard and have joints between them, and the sinews can be tightened and slackened, surrounding the bones along with flesh and the skin which holds them together; so when the bones are uplifted in their sockets, the sinews slackening and tightening make me able to bend my limbs now, and for this cause I have bent together and sit here; and if next he should give you other such causes of my conversing with you, alleging as causes voices and airs and hearings and a thousand others like that, and neglecting to give the real causes. These are that since the Athenians thought it was better to condemn me, for this very reason I have thought it better to sit here, and more just to remain and submit to any sentence they may give. For, by the Dog! these bones and sinews, I think, would have been somewhere near Megara or Boeotia long ago, carried there by an opinion of what is best, if I had not believed it better and more just to submit to any sentence which my city gives than to take

---

[1] Air is the lower air about the earth, ether the upper air of heaven.

to my heels and run. But to call such things causes is strange indeed. If one should say that unless I had such things, bones and sinews and all the rest I have, I should not have been able to do what I thought best, that would be true; but to say that these, and not my choice of the best, are the causes of my doing what I do (and when I act by mind, too!), would be a very far-fetched and slovenly way of speaking. For it shows inability to distinguish that the real cause is one thing, and that without which the cause could not be a cause is another thing. This is what most people seem to me to be fumbling after in the dark, when they use a borrowed name for it and call it cause! And so one man makes the earth remain under the sky, if you please, by putting a rotation about the earth; another thinks it is like the bottom of a flat kneading-trough and puts the air underneath to support it; but they never look for the power which has placed things so that they are in the best possible state, nor do they think it has a divine strength, but they believe they will some time find an Atlas[1] more mighty and more immortal and more able than ours to hold all together, and really they think nothing of the good which must necessarily bind and hold all things together. How glad I should be to be anyone's pupil in learning what such a cause really is! But since I have missed this, since I could not find it myself or learn it from another, would you like me to show you, Cebes," he said, "how I managed my second voyage in search for the cause?"

"Would I not!" said he: "more than anything else in the world!"

"Well then," he said, "it occurred to me after all this—and it was then I gave up contemplating the realities—that I must be careful not to be affected like people who observe and watch an eclipse of the sun. What happens to them is that some lose their sight, unless they look at his reflection in water or something of that sort. This passed through my mind, and I feared that I might wholly blind my soul by gazing at practical things[2] with my eyes and trying to grasp them by each of the senses. So I thought I must take refuge in reasoning, to examine the truth of the realities. There is, however, something not like in my image; for I do not admit at all that one who examines the realities by reasoning makes use of images, more than one who examines them in deeds and facts. Well anyway, this is how I set out; and laying down in each case the reasoning which I think best fortified, I consider as true whatever seems to harmonise with that, both about causes and about every-

[1] The Titan who upheld the heavens.
[2] Natural phenomena, etc.; see p. 500.

thing else, and as untrue whatever does not. But I wish to make it clearer, for I think you do not understand yet."

"Indeed I do not," said Cebes, "not well."

"Well, this is what I mean," he said, "nothing new, but the same as I have been saying all this time in our conversation, and on other occasions. I am going to try to show you the nature of the cause, which I have been working out. I shall go back to the old song and begin from there, supposing that there exists a beautiful something all by itself, and a good something and great and all the rest of it; and if you grant this and admit it, I hope from these to discover and show you the cause, that the soul is something immortal."

"I grant it to you," said Cebes; "pray be quick and go on to the end."

"Then consider," he said, "what follows, and see if you agree with me. What appears to me is, that if anything else is beautiful besides beauty itself, what makes it beautiful is simply that it partakes of that beauty; and so I say with everything. Do you agree with such a cause?"

"I agree," said he.

"Very well," he said, "I can no longer recognise or understand all those clever causes we heard of; and if any one tells me that anything is beautiful because it has a fine flowery colour or shape or anything like that, I thank him and let all that go; for I get confused in all those, but this one thing I hold to myself simply and completely, and foolishly perhaps, that what makes it beautiful is only that beauty, whether its presence or a share in it or however it may be with the thing, for I am not positive about the manner, but only that beautiful things are beautiful by that beauty. For this I think to be the safest answer to give to myself or anyone else, and clinging to this I think I shall never fall, but it is a safe answer for me and everyone else, that by that beauty all beautiful things are beautiful. Don't you think so?"

"I do."

"And by greatness the great things are great, and the greater greater, and by smallness small things are small?"

"Yes."

"So you would not accept it if you were told that one person was greater than another by a head, or less by the same, but you would protest that you say every greater is greater than another because of greatness alone, and the smaller is smaller by reason of smallness alone; you would fear, I think, that a contradictory reasoning might meet you if you said someone is greater or less by a head, first that the same thing is making the greater greater and the lesser lesser, and next that a small

PHAEDO (100B–102A)

thing like a head is making the greater greater, which is a monstrosity—that a small thing should make anyone great. Would you not fear that?"

And Cebes said, with a laugh, "I should!"

"So," said he, "you would not dare to say that ten is more than eight by two, but you would say it is more by number and because of number?—and the two-cubit measure greater than the cubit not by half, but by length? For you would fear the same each time."

"Certainly," he said.

"Well, if one has been added, you would be careful not to say the addition caused the two, or if one is divided, the division caused the two. And you would shout that you do not know how each thing comes to be, except by partaking of its own proper essence, whatever each partakes of; in these examples, you see for instance no other cause for becoming two but partaking of twohood, and whatever is to be two must partake of this, and of onehood whatever is to be one, while these splittings and addings and such niceties you would just bow to and let them go, leaving cleverer men than you to answer. For you would be frightened of your own shadow, as people say, your inexperience, and you would cling to that safe supposition,[1] and so you would answer. If anyone should attack the supposition itself, you would let him be and would not answer, until you examined the consequences to see if they were in agreement or discord together; and when you must give account of that supposition itself, you would do it in the same way by supposing another supposition, whichever seemed best of the higher suppositions, until you came to something satisfactory; at the same time you would not make a muddle like the dialecticians, by confusing arguments about the beginning with arguments about the consequences of the beginning, if you wished to find out something of reality. For those people, perhaps, think and care nothing at all about this; they are clever enough to make a mess of the whole business and yet to be pleased with themselves; but if you are a true philosopher, I believe you would do as I say."

"Very true," said Simmias and Cebes together.

ECHECRATES: Reasonable too, I do declare, Phaidon. Amazingly clear he makes it, as anyone with a grain of sense can see.

PHAIDON: Yes indeed, Echecrates, and all of them thought so who were present.

[1] I.e., the "safe answer"; p. 504.

ECHECRATES: So do we who were not present, but are hearing of it now. But what was said after that?

PHAIDON: As I think, when this was granted, and all agreed that each of these ideal qualities has a kind of existence, and the particular things that partake of them get their name from them,[1] next he asked: "Well then," said he, "if that is what you agree, when you say Simmias is bigger than Socrates, and smaller than Phaidon, you say that both are in Simmias, both bigness and smallness?"

"I do."

"But all the same you agree that for Simmias to overtop Socrates is not true as the words describe it. For Simmias, I suppose, does not naturally overtop Socrates by being Simmias, but by the bigness which he happens to have; nor does he overtop Socrates because Socrates is Socrates, but because Socrates has smallness as against the other's bigness."

"True."

"Nor again is he overtopped by Phaidon because Phaidon is Phaidon, but because Phaidon has bigness as against the smallness of Simmias?"

"That is right."

"Thus, then, Simmias has the title of being both small and great, being between both, in the first case submitting his smallness for the other's bigness to surpass, in the second offering his bigness which surpasses the other's smallness. At the same time," he said, smiling, "I seem to speak like a lawyer's deed, but that is very much how things are." He said yes. "I say this," he added, "because I want you to agree with me. For it appears to me that bigness itself never consents to be big and small at the same time, and not only that, even the bigness in us never accepts smallness and will not be surpassed; but one of two things, it must either depart and retreat whenever its opposite, smallness, comes near, or else must perish at its approach; it does not consent to submit and receive the smallness, and so to become other than what it was. Just so I, receiving and submitting to smallness, am still the man I am, I'm still this same small person; but the bigness in me, being big, has not dared to become small! In the same way, the smallness in us does not want to become or be big, nor does any other of the opposites, being still what it was, want to become and be the opposite; but either it goes away or it is destroyed in this change."

"Certainly," said Cebes, "that is what I think."

One of those present, hearing this, said—I do not clearly remember who it was— "Good heavens, didn't we admit in

[1] Cf. *Republic*, p. 306, n. 2.

our former discussion the very opposite of what we are saying now—that the greater came from the less and the less from the greater, and in fact this is how opposites are generated, from opposites? Now it seems to be said that this could never be."

Socrates bent down his head to listen, and said, "Spoken like a man! I thank you for reminding me, but you don't understand the difference between what we are saying now and what we said then. For then[1] we said that the practical opposite thing is generated from its practical opposite, but now we are saying that the opposite quality itself could never become the quality opposite to itself, either in us or in nature. Then, my friend, we were speaking of things which have opposites, these being named by the name of their (opposite) qualities, but now we are speaking of the opposite qualities themselves, from which being in the things, the things are named: those qualities themselves, we say, could never accept generation from each other." Then, with a glance at Cebes, he added, "Is it possible that you too, Cebes, were disturbed by what our friend spoke of?"

"No, not by this," replied Cebes, "but I don't deny that I get disturbed a good deal."

"Well, then, are we agreed," said Socrates, "simply on this, that nothing will ever be opposite to itself?"

"Quite agreed," he said.

"Here is something else," he said, "see if you will agree to this. You speak of hot and cold?"

"Yes."

"Is it the same as fire and snow?"

"Not at all."

"But the hot is something other than fire, and the cold other than snow?"

"Yes."

"Well, I suppose you agree that snow receiving fire (to use our former way of putting it) will never be what it was, snow, and also be hot, but when the hot approaches it will either retreat from it or be destroyed."

"Certainly."

"Fire, also, when the cold approaches, will either go away from it or be destroyed, but it will never endure to receive the coldness and still be what it was, fire, and cold too."

"True," said he.

"Then it is possible," he said, "with some such things, that not only the essence is thought worthy of the same name forever, but something else also is worthy, which is not that

[1] See p. 473.

essence but which, when it exists, always has the form of that essence. Perhaps it will be a little clearer as follows. Odd numbers must always be called odd, I suppose, mustn't they?"

"Yes."

"Of all things do we use this name only for oddness, for that is what I ask, or is there something else, not oddness, but what must be called always by that name because its nature is never to be deserted by oddness? For example, triplet and so forth. Now consider the triplet: Don't you think it should be called always both by its own name and also by the name of odd, although oddness is not the same as triplet? Still it is the nature of triplet and quintet and half of all the numbers, that each of them is odd although it is not the same thing as oddness; so also two and four and all the other row of numbers are each of them always even, although none is the same thing as evenness; do you agree?"

"Of course," he said.

"Now attend, this is what I want to make clear. It seems that not only those real opposites do not receive each other, but also things which not being opposites of each other yet always have those real opposites in them, these also do not look like things which receive that reality which is opposite to the reality in them, but when it approaches they either are destroyed or retire. We shall say, for example, that a triplet will be destroyed before any such thing happens to it, before it remains and becomes even, while it is still three?"

"Certainly," said Cebes.

"Nor, again," he said, "is twin the opposite of triplet."

"Not at all."

"Then not only the opposite essences do not remain at the approach of each other, but some other things do not await the approach of the opposites."

"Very true," he said.

"Then shall we distinguish what sorts of things these are," he said, "if we can?"

"Certainly."

"Then, Cebes, would they be those which compel whatever they occupy not only to get their own essence but also the essence of some opposite?"

"How so?"

"As we said just now. You know, I suppose, that whatever the essence of three occupies must necessarily be not only three but odd."

"Certainly."

"And the essense opposite to that which does this we say could never come near such a thing."

"It could not."
"And what has done this? Was not it oddness?"
"Yes."
"And opposite to this is the essence of even?"
"Yes."
"Then the essence of even will never approach three."
"No."
"So three has no part in the even."
"None."
"Then the triplet is uneven."
"Yes."

"Now for my distinction. What things, not being opposite to something, yet do not receive the opposite itself which is in that something? For instance now, the triplet is not the opposite to the even, yet still does not receive it because it always brings the opposite against it; and a pair brings the opposite against the odd, and fire against cold, and so with very many others. Just look then, if you distinguish thus, not only the opposite does not receive the opposite, but that also which brings anything opposite to whatever it approaches never receives the opposite to that which it brings. Recollect once more; there's no harm to hear the same thing often. Five will not receive the essence of even, or its double ten the essence of odd; yet this same double will not receive the essence of odd, although it is not opposite to anything. Again, one and a half and other such things with a half in them will not receive the essence of whole, nor will one-third and all such fractions, if you follow and agree with me in this."

"I do agree certainly, and I follow."

"Once more, then," he said, "go back to the beginning. And don't answer the questions I ask, till I show you how. I want something more than the first answer I mentioned, the safe one; I see a new safety from what we have been saying now. If you ask me what must be in any body if that body is to be hot, I will not give you that safe answer, the stupid answer, 'Heat,' but a more subtle answer from our present reasoning, 'Fire'; or if you ask what must be in a body if it is to be diseased, I will not answer 'Disease,' but 'Fever'; or if you ask what must be in a number if it is to be odd, I will not say 'Oddness,' but 'Onehood,' and so forth. Now then, do you know clearly enough what I want?"

"Oh yes," he said.

"Answer then," said he, "what must be in a body if it is to be living?"

"Soul," said he.

"Is this always true?"

"Of course," he said.

"Well now, whatever the soul occupies, she always comes to it bringing life?"

"She does, indeed," he said.

"Is there an opposite to life, or not?"

"There is."

"What?"

"Death."

"Then soul will never receive the opposite to that which she brings, as we have agreed already."

"Most assuredly," said Cebes.

"Well, what name did we give just now to that which did not receive the essence of the even?"

"Uneven," he said.

"And what name to that which does not receive what is just, or to that which does not receive music?"

"Unmusical," he said, "and unjust the other."

"Very well. What do we call that which does not receive death?"

"Immortal," he said.

"And the soul does not receive death?"

"No."

"Then the soul is a thing immortal?"

"It is," he said.

"Very well," said he. "Shall we say this has been proved? Or what do you think?"

"Proved, and amply proved, Socrates."

"Now then, Cebes," he said, "if the uneven were necessarily imperishable, would not three be imperishable?"

"Of course."

"And if the not-hot were necessarily imperishable, when someone brought a hot thing to snow, the snow would retire safe and unmelted? For it would not be destroyed, nor would it remain and receive the heat."

"Quite true," he said.

"So also if the not-cold were imperishable, when something cold was brought to fire, the fire would not be quenched or destroyed, but it would go away safe."

"That is necessary," he said.

"And is it equally necessary to say that of the immortal? If the immortal is also imperishable, it is impossible for the soul to be destroyed when death comes to it; for death it will never receive, by our argument, and it will never be dead, just as we showed that the three would never be even, nor the odd be even, nor indeed would fire, or the heat in the fire, ever be cold. But someone might say, 'The odd will not become even, when the even comes near, as we have agreed, but what is to hinder its being destroyed and an even being made instead?' In answer to the man who said that, we could not maintain that it is not destroyed; for the uneven is not imperishable; since if that had been granted us we could easily maintain that when the even approached, the odd, and the three, go clean off; and we could do the same about fire and heat and all the rest, couldn't we?"

"Certainly.

"So about the immortal, if we agree that this is imperishable, the soul would be imperishable as well as immortal; but if we do not, we need a new argument."

"There's no need of that in this case," said he, "nothing could escape destruction if the immortal, which is everlasting, could be destroyed."

"God himself, I think," said Socrates, "and the very essence of life, and whatever else is immortal, would be admitted by all never to suffer destruction."

"Yes, admitted by all indeed," he said, "by men of course and still more, I think, by the gods."

"Then, since the immortal is also imperishable, the soul if it is immortal would be imperishable too?"

"That must certainly be."

"So when death approaches a man, the mortal in him dies, as it seems, but the immortal part goes away undestroyed, giving place to death."

"So it seems."

"Then beyond all doubt, Cebes," he said, "soul is immortal and imperishable, and in fact our souls will exist in the house of Hades."

"I have nothing else to say to the contrary, Socrates," he answered, "and I cannot disbelieve you in any way."

"But now if Simmias has something to say, or anyone else, it is well not to be silent. I don't know what better opportunity we could have; we can't put it off now; there is only this chance if anyone wishes to say or hear more about such matters as this."

"No, indeed," said Simmias, "I can't find anything myself to disbelieve after what has been said. But in the momentous matter which we are discussing, I do distrust human weakness, and I am compelled to have a little incredulity in my mind about what we say."

"Not only that, Simmias," said Socrates; "you are quite right, and you ought still to scrutinise our first suppositions and see if you can trust them; and if you test them sufficiently, you will follow our reasoning, I think, as well as it is possible for man to follow it; and if only this be made clear, you will seek nothing further."

"True," he said.

"Well, here is something more, gentlemen," said Socrates, "that we ought to understand. If the soul is immortal, she needs care, not only for the time which we call life, but for all time, and the danger indeed would seem to be terrible if one is ready to neglect her. For if death were release from everything, a great blessing it would be for evil men to be rid of the body and their own wickedness along with the soul. But since, as things are, she appears to be immortal, there could be no escape from evil for her and no salvation, except that she should become as good and wise as possible. For when the soul comes to Hades she brings with her nothing but her education and training; and this is said to do the greatest help or hurt to the dead man at the very beginning of his course thither. What men say is this. At death the guardian spirit of each, to whom each was allotted for life, undertakes to lead each to a certain place; there those gathered must stand their trial, and then pass on to the house of Hades with the guide whose duty it is to conduct them hence to that place. When they have met there what they must meet with, and remained such time as they should, another guide again brings them back after many long periods of time. The journey is not as Telephos describes in Aeschylus, for he says that a simple way leads to Hades, but this appears to me neither simple nor single. If so, there would be no need of guides, for no one could miss one way to anywhere. But really, it seems to have many breaks and branches; I judge by the pious offerings made to the dead among us.[1] The wise and decent soul follows and understands the circumstances; but the soul which has desire for the body, as I said once before, flutters about it for a long time and about the visible world, resisting much and suffering much, and the appointed spirit drags her away by force not easily. When she comes where the others are, the unpurified soul, which has done deeds like herself, which has touched unjust murders, or done other such deeds which are akin to these and are the acts of kindred souls, is avoided by all; each one turns from her and will neither be fellow-traveller nor guide, but she wanders by herself in complete helplessness, until certain times come: when they come she is carried by necessity to her proper dwelling place. But the soul which has passed through life purely and decently finds gods for fellow-travellers and

[1] Food and the like were laid on shrines where roads joined; he therefore assumes that the roads below were like that.

PHAEDO (107B–109C)

leaders, and each soul dwells in her own proper dwelling place. There are many wonderful regions in the earth, and the earth itself is not of such a quality or such a size as it is thought to be by those who are accustomed to describe the earth, so a certain man has convinced me."

Then Simmias asked, "What is this you say, Socrates? I have heard much about the earth myself, but not this story that convinced you. So I should be very glad to hear it."

He answered, "Why indeed, Simmias, I am afraid I lack a Glaucos' handbook[1] to tell you all that! But truly I think it is too hard for Glaucos' book, and besides my not perhaps being equal to it, at the same time even if I understood it, my life, Simmias, seems to me insufficient for such a long story. But what I believe to be the shape of the earth and its regions, I can tell you, there's nothing to hinder that."

"Well," said Simmias, "that will do."

"I believe, then," said he, "that first, if it is round and in the middle of the heavens, it needs nothing to keep it from falling, neither air nor any other such necessity, but the uniformity of the heavens,[2] themselves alike all through, is enough to keep it there, and the equilibrium of earth itself; for a thing in equilibrium and placed in the middle of something which is everywhere alike will not incline in any direction, but will remain steady and in like condition. First I believe that," he said.

"Quite right too," said Simmias.

"Next, I believe it is very large indeed, and we live in a little bit of it between the Pillars of Heracles[3] and the river Phasis,[4] like ants or frogs in a marsh, lodging round the sea, and that many other people live in many other such regions. For there are everywhere about the earth many hollows of all sorts in shape and size, into which have collected water and mist and air; but the earth itself is pure and lies in the pure heavens where the stars are, which is called ether by most of those who are accustomed to explain such things; of which all this is a sediment, which is always collecting into the hollows of the earth. We then, who lodge in its hollows, know nothing about it, and think we are living upon the earth; as if one living deep on the bottom of the sea should think he was at the top, and, seeing through the water sun and stars, should think the sea was heaven, but from sluggishness and weakness should never come to the surface and

---

[1] A proverb: probably some discoverer or inventor.
[2] The universe is homogeneous and of one density, so there is no reason why the earth should move this way or that.
[3] Mts. Calpe and Abyla, on the straits of Gibraltar; Calpe is the modern Rock of Gibraltar.
[4] The river Rion which flows into the eastern part of the Black Sea.

never get out and peep up out of the sea into this place, or observe how much more pure and beautiful it is than his own place, and should never have heard from anyone who saw it. This very thing has happened to us; for we live in a hollow of the earth and think we live on the surface, and call the air heaven, thinking that the stars move through that and that is heaven; but the fact is the same, from weakness and sluggishness we cannot get through to the surface of the air, since if a man could come to the top of it, and get wings and fly up, he could peep over and look, just as fishes here peep up out of the sea and look round at what is here, so he could look at what is there, and if his nature allowed him to endure the sight, he could learn and know that that is the true heaven and the true light and the true earth. For this earth and the stones and all the place here are corrupted and corroded, as things in the sea are by the brine so that nothing worth mention grows in the sea, and there is nothing perfect there, one might say, but caves and sand and infinite mud and slime wherever there is any earth, things worth nothing at all as compared with the beauties we have; but again those above as compared with ours would seem to be much superior. But if I must tell you a story, Simmias, it is worth hearing what things really are like on the earth under the heavens."

"Indeed, Socrates," said Simmias, "we should be glad to hear this story."

"It is said then, my comrade," he went on, "that first of all the earth itself looks from above, if you could see it, like those twelve-patch leathern balls,[1] variegated, with strips of colour of which the colours here, such as are used by painters, are a sort of specimens; but there the whole earth is made of such as these, and much brighter and purer than these; one is sea purple wonderfully beautiful, one is like gold, the white is whiter than chalk or snow, and the earth is made of these and other colours, more in number and more beautiful than any we have seen. For indeed the very hollows full of water and mist present a colour of their own as they shine in the variety of other colours, so that the one whole looks like a continuous coloured pattern. Such is the earth, and all that grows in it is in accord, trees and flowers and fruits; and again mountains and rocks in like manner have their smoothness and transparency and colours more beautiful, and the precious stones which are so much valued here are just chips of those, sard and jaspers and emerald and so forth, but there every single one is

[1] Leathern balls with coloured patches. He is thinking also of the twelve Signs of the Zodiac, hence twelve.

such and they are still more beautiful. The cause of that is that those stones are pure and not corroded or corrupted as ours are by the rot and brine of stuff which has gathered here, which bring ugliness and disease on stones and earth and everything else, living creatures and plants. But the real earth is adorned with all these and with gold and silver and all such things as these. For there they are clearly to be seen, being many in number and large and all over the earth, so that to see it is a sight for happy spectators. Animals there are on it many and various, and men too, some living inland, some round the air as we do round the sea, some in islands surrounded by the flowing air near the mainland; in a word, what water and sea are to us for our use, the air is to them, and what the air is to us, ether is to them. The seasons have such temperature that the people there are free from disease and live a much longer time than we do, and in sight and hearing and intelligence and so forth they are as different from us as air is different from water and ether from air in purity. Groves of the gods also they have and sanctuaries, and the gods really dwell in them, and there are between them and the gods voices and prophecies and perceptions and other such communions; sun and moon and stars are seen by them as they are, and their happiness in all other respects is according.

"This, then, is the nature of the whole earth and all that is about it; but there are many regions in it and hollows of it all round, some deeper and spreading wider than the one we live in, some deeper but having their gap smaller than ours, some again shallower in depth than ours and wider; but these are all connected together by tunnels in many places narrower or wider, and they have many passages where floods of water run through from one to another as into a mixing-bowl, and huge rivers ever flowing underground both of hot waters and cold, where also are masses of fire and great rivers of fire, and many rivers of liquid mud, some clearer, some muddier, like the rivers of mud which run in Sicily before the lava,[1] and the lava itself. And each of these regions is filled with this, according as the overflow comes in each case. All these things are moved up and down by a sort of seesaw which there is in the earth, and the nature of this seesaw movement is this. One of the chasms in the earth is largest of all, and, besides, it has a tunnel which goes right through the earth, the same which Homer speaks of when he says,

> Far, far away, where is the lowest pit
> Beneath the earth,[2]

[1] From Mount Etna in eruption.
[2] *Iliad* viii. 14.

and which elsewhere he and many other poets have called Tartaros. For into this chasm all the rivers flow together, and from this again they flow out, and they are each like the earth through which they flow. The cause which makes all the streams run out from there and run in is that this fluid has no bottom or foundation to rest on. So it seesaws and swells up and down, and the air and wind about it do the same; for they follow with it, both when the rivers move towards that side of the earth, and when they move towards this side, and just as the breath always goes in and out when men breathe, so there, too, the wind is lifted up and down with the liquid and makes terrible tempests both coming in and going out. Therefore whenever the water goes back into the place which is called 'down,' it rushes in along those rivers and fills them up like water pumped in; but when, again, it leaves that part and moves this way, it fills up our region once more, and when the rivers are filled they flow through the channels and through the earth, and, coming each to those places where their several paths lead, they make seas and lakes and rivers and fountains. After that they sink into the earth again, some passing round larger regions and more numerous, some round fewer and smaller, and plunge again into Tartaros, some far below their source, some but little, but all below the place where they came out. Some flow in opposite where they tumbled out, some in the same place; and there are others which go right round the earth in a circle, curling about it like serpents once or many times, and then fall and discharge as low down as possible. It is possible from each side to go down as far as the centre, but no farther, for beyond that the opposite part is uphill from both sides.

"All these rivers are large, and they are of many kinds; but among these many are four in especial. The greatest of these, and the outermost, running right round, is that called Ocean; opposite this and flowing in the contrary direction is Acheron, the River of Pain, which flows through a number of desert places, and also flowing under the earth comes to the Acherusian Lake, to which come the souls of most of the dead, and when they have remained there certain ordained times, some longer and some shorter, they are sent out again to birth in living creatures. The third of these rivers issues forth in the middle, and near its issue it falls into a large region blazing with much fire, and makes a lake larger than our[1] sea, boiling with water and mud; from there it moves round turbid and muddy, and rolls winding about the earth as far as another place at the extreme end of the Acherusian Lake, without

[1] The Mediterranean.

mingling with the water; when it has rolled many times round it falls into a lower depth than Tartaros. This is what they call Pyriphlegethon, the River of Burning Fire, and its lava streams blow up bits of it wherever they are found on the earth. Opposite this again the fourth river discharges at first into a region terrible and wild, it is said, all having the colour of dark blue; this they call the Stygian, the River of Hate, and the lake which the river makes they call Styx. But the river, falling into this and receiving terrible powers in the water, plunges beneath the earth and, rolling round, moves contrary to Pyriphlegethon and meets it in the Acherusian Lake on the opposite side. The water of this, too, mixes with none, but this also goes round and falls into Tartaros opposite to Pyriphlegethon. The name of this, as the poets say, is Cocytos, the River of Wailing.

"Such is the nature of the world. So when the dead come to the place whither the spirit conveys each, first the judges divide them into those who have lived well and piously, and those who have not. And those who are thought to have been between the two travel to the Acheron, then embark in the vessels which are said to be there for them, and in these come to the lake, and there they dwell, being purified from their wrongdoings; and after punishment for any wrong they have done they are released, and receive rewards for their good deeds each according to his merit. But those who are thought to be incurable because of the greatness of their sins, those who have done many great acts of sacrilege or many unrighteous and lawless murders or other such crimes, these the proper fate throws into Tartaros whence they never come out. Those who are thought to have committed crimes curable although great, if they have done some violence to father or mother, say, from anger, and have lived the rest of their lives in repentance, or if they have become manslaughterers in some other such way, these must of necessity be cast into Tartaros; but when they have been cast in and been there a year the wave throws them out, the manslaughterers by way of Cocytos, the patricides and matricides by way of Pyriphlegethon; and when they have been carried down to the Acherusian Lake, there they shriek and call to those whom they slew or treated violently, and, calling on them, they beg and beseech them to accept them and let them go out into the lake; if they win consent, they come out and cease from their sufferings; if not, they are carried back into Tartaros and from there into the rivers again, and they never cease from this treatment until they win the consent of those whom they wronged: for this was the sentence passed on them by the judges. But those who are thought to have lived in especial holiness, they are those who are set free and released from these places here in the earth as from a prison house, and come up into the pure dwelling place and are settled upon earth. Of these same, again, those who have purified themselves enough by philosophy live without bodies altogether forever after, and come into dwellings even more beautiful than the others, which it is not easy to describe nor is there time enough at this present. But for the reasons which we have given, Simmias, we must do everything so as to have our share of wisdom and virtue in life; for the prize is noble and the hope great.

"No sensible man would think it proper to rely on things of this kind being just as I have described; but that, since the soul is clearly immortal, this or something like this at any rate is what happens in regard to our souls and their habitations—that this is so seems to me proper and worthy of the risk of believing; for the risk is noble. Such things he must sing like a healing charm to himself, and that is why I have lingered so long over the story. But these are the reasons for a man to be confident about his own soul, when in his life he has bidden farewell to all other pleasures, the pleasures and adornments of the body, thinking them alien and such as do more harm than good, and has been earnest only for the pleasure of learning; and having adorned the soul with no alien ornaments, but with her own—with temperance and justice and courage and freedom and truth, thus he awaits the journey to the house of Hades, ready to travel when the doom ordained shall call. You indeed," he said, "Simmias and Cebes and all, hereafter at some certain time shall each travel on that journey: but me—'Fate calls me now,' as a man might say in a tragedy, and it is almost time for me to travel towards the bath; for I am sure you think it better to have a bath before drinking the potion, and to save the women the trouble of washing a corpse."

When he had spoken, Criton said, "Ah well, Socrates, what injunctions have you for these friends or for me, about your children or anything else? What could we do for you to gratify you most?"

"What I always say, Criton," he said, "nothing very new: Take good care of yourselves, and you will gratify me and mine and yourselves whatever you do, even if you promise nothing now. But if you neglect yourselves, and won't take care to live your lives following the footsteps, so to speak, of both this last conversation and those we have had in former times, you will do no good even if you promise ever so much at present and ever so faithfully."

"Then we will do our best about that," he said; "but how are we to bury you?"

"How you like," said he, "if you catch me and I don't escape you." At the same time, laughing gently and looking towards us, he said, "Criton doesn't believe me, my friends, that this is I, Socrates now talking with you and laying down each of my injunctions, but he thinks me to be what he will see shortly, a corpse, and asks, if you please, how to bury me! I have been saying all this long time, that when I have drunk the potion, I shall not be here then with you; I shall have gone clear away to some bliss of the blest, as they call it. But he thinks I am talking nonsense, just to console myself, yes and you too. Then go bail for me to Criton," he said, "the opposite of the bail he gave to those judges. He gave bail that I would remain; you please, give bail that I will not remain after I die, but I shall get off clear and clean, that Criton may take it more easily, and may not be vexed by seeing my body either being burnt or buried; don't let him worry for me and think I'm in a dreadful state, or say at the funeral that he is laying out or carrying out or digging in Socrates. Be sure, Criton, best of friends," he said, "to use ugly words not only is out of tune with the event, but it even infects the soul with something evil. Now, be confident and say you are burying my body, and then bury it as you please and as you think would be most according to custom."

With these words, he got up and retired into another room for the bath, and Criton went after him, telling us to wait. So we waited discussing and talking together about what had been said, or sometimes speaking of the great misfortune which had befallen us, for we felt really as if we had lost a father and had to spend the rest of our lives as orphans. When he had bathed, and his children had been brought to see him—for he had two little sons, and one big—and when the women of his family had come, he talked to them before Criton and gave what instructions he wished. Then he asked the women and children to go, and came back to us. It was now near sunset, for he had spent a long time within. He came and sat down after his bath, and he had not talked long after this when the servant of the Eleven came in, and standing by him said, "O Socrates! I have not to complain of you as I do of others, that they are angry with me, and curse me, because I bring them word to drink their potion, which my officers make me do! But I have always found you in this time most generous and gentle, and the best man who ever came here. And now too, I know well you are not angry with me, for you know who are responsible, and you keep it for them. Now you know what I came to tell you, so farewell, and try to bear as well as you can what can't be helped."

Then he turned and was going out, with tears running down his cheeks. And Socrates looked up at him and said, "Farewell to you also, I will do so." Then, at the same time turning to us, "What a nice fellow!" he said. "All the time he has been coming and talking to me, a real good sort, and now how generously he sheds tears for me! Come along, Criton, let's obey him. Someone bring the potion, if the stuff has been ground; if not, let the fellow grind it."

Then Criton said, "But, Socrates, I think the sun is still over the hills, it has not set yet. Yes, and I know of others who, having been told to drink the poison, have done it very late; they had dinner first and a good one, and some enjoyed the company of any they wanted. Please don't be in a hurry, there is time to spare."

But Socrates said, "Those you speak of have very good reason for doing that, for they think they will gain by doing it; and I have good reasons why I won't do it. For I think I shall gain nothing by drinking a little later, only that I shall think myself a fool for clinging to life and sparing when the cask's empty.[1] Come along," he said, "do what I tell you, if you please."

And Criton, hearing this, nodded to the boy who stood near. The boy went out, and after spending a long time, came in with the man who was to give the poison[2] carrying it ground ready in a cup. Socrates caught sight of the man and said, "Here, my good man, you know about these things; what must I do?"

"Just drink it," he said, "and walk about till your legs get heavy, then lie down. In that way the drug will act of itself."

At the same time, he held out the cup to Socrates, and he took it quite cheerfully, Echecrates, not a tremble, not a change in colour or looks; but looking full at the man under his brows, as he used to do, he asked him. "What do you say about this drink? What of a libation to someone?[3] Is that allowed, or not?"

He said, "We only grind so much as we think enough for a moderate potion."

"I understand," he said, "but at least, I suppose, it is allowed to offer a prayer to the gods and that must be done, for

---
[1] There's a proverb:

    Cask full or failing, drink; but in between
    Spare if you like; sparing at bottom's mean.

Hesiod, *Works and Days*, 368.

[2] The poison was hemlock.

[3] The custom was for the butler to spill a drop into the cup which the drinker then spilt on the ground as a libation with a prayer; then the butler filled and the man drank.

good luck in the migration from here to there. Then that is my prayer, and so may it be!"

With these words he put the cup to his lips and, quite easy and contented, drank it up. So far most of us had been able to hold back our tears pretty well; but when we saw him begin drinking and end drinking, we could no longer. I burst into a flood of tears for all I could do, so I wrapped up my face and cried myself out; not for him indeed, but for my own misfortune in losing such a man and such a comrade. Criton had got up and gone out even before I did, for he could not hold the tears in. Apollodoros had never ceased weeping all this time, and now he burst out into loud sobs, and by his weeping and lamentations completely broke down every man there except Socrates himself. He only said, "What a scene! You amaze me. That's just why I sent the women away, to keep them from making a scene like this. I've heard that one ought to make an end in decent silence. Quiet yourselves and endure."

When we heard him we felt ashamed and restrained our tears. He walked about, and when he said that his legs were feeling heavy, he lay down on his back, as the man told him to do; at the same time the one who gave him the potion felt him, and after a while examined his feet and legs; then pinching a foot hard, he asked if he felt anything; he said no. After this, again, he pressed the shins; and, moving up like this, he showed us that he was growing cold and stiff. Again he felt him, and told us that when it came to his heart, he would be gone. Already the cold had come nearly as far as the abdomen, when Socrates threw off the covering from his face—for he had covered it over—and said, the last words he uttered, "Criton," he said, "we owe a cock to Asclepios;[1] pay it without fail."

"That indeed shall be done," said Criton. "Have you anything more to say?"

When Criton had asked this, Socrates gave no further answer, but after a little time, he stirred, and the man uncovered him, and his eyes were still. Criton, seeing this, closed the mouth and eyelids.

This was the end of our comrade, Echecrates, a man, as we would say, of all then living we had ever met, the noblest and the wisest and most just.

---

[1] A thank-offering to the god of healing. The cock is the poor man's offering. The touching beauty and restraint of this account is heightened still more, if Plato, who was ill and unable to be present at the death of his dearest friend, took this last request to have been made for his sake.

The Greek Alphabet and Its Pronunciation

Alpha	A	α	ă (as in German *hat*), ā (as *ah*)
bēta	B	β	b
gamma	Γ	γ	g (as in *good*)
delta	Δ	δ	d
epsīlon	E	ε	e (as in *wet*)
zēta	Z	ζ	dz
ēta	H	η	ē (as in French *fée*)
thēta	Θ	θ	th (as in *think*)
iota	I	ι	i (as in French *lie*, *lit*)
kappa	K	κ	k
lambda	Λ	λ	l
mū	M	μ	m
nū	N	ν	n
xī	Ξ	ξ	x
omīcron	O	ο	o (as in *pot*)
pī	Π	π	p
rhō	P	ρ	r or rh'
sīgma (san)	Σ	σ, ς final	} s (as in *sing*, *ass*)
tau	T	τ	t
upsīlon	Υ	υ	u (as French u, or as oo in *foot*)
phī	Φ	φ	ph, f
chī	X	χ	ch (as in Scotch *loch*)
psī	Ψ	ψ	ps
Ōmega	Ω	ω	ō (as *awe*)

Notes

The names epsīlon (ε), omīcron (ο), upsīlon (υ), and ōmega (ω) are of later date, and were not used by the Greeks of the classical age.

γ before γ, κ, ξ, χ is sounded *ng*.

αι should be pronounced as in *aisle*, ει as two short sounds together, ἔῠ, οι as in *foil*, υι as French *oui;* αυ as *ow* in *cow*, ευ as two short sounds together *ĕŭ*, ου as *oo* in *fool;* ᾳ, ῃ, ῳ, ("with iota subscript") simply as ā, η, ω.

A vowel or diphthong marked ‛ at the beginning of a word is pronounced as aspirated with h, but if marked ’ is not aspirated. Thus ὑπό is pronounced "hupo," but ἄλφα is pronounced "alpha."

Every Greek word, except a few such as εἰς, "into," was written with an accent; this marked a raising of the tone of voice on that syllable, not stress as in English. ⁀ denoted a raising followed by lowering on that vowel, as we do in "No!", the English expression of surprise.

The Greek question mark was ; like our semicolon. Their colon or semicolon was · like a period at the top of the line.

Pronouncing Index

This index shows the correct quantities of the vowels in the names, and an accent ′ is placed to suggest how the reader may pronounce them as if English names (vowels are short if not marked long):

> c always sounded as k.
> ch always sounded as kh.
> g always sounded hard (as in *good*).
> th always sounded as in *think*.

a, e, i, o, u as in Italian properly, but for convenience they may be sounded as in English, the final syllable of names such as Odysseus, Orpheus, Atreus being pronounced as we pronounce the first syllable of the name Eustace.

Vowels marked ā, ē, etc. are of double length.
˚ mark on ê means that it is not mute, but forms a syllable.

Ab–dĕr′–a
A–chil′–lēs
A–dei–man′–tos
Ad–mē′–tos
A–dras–tei′–a
Ae–gī′–na
Aes′chylus
A–ga–mem′–nōn
A′–gath–ōn
A–gla–i′–ōn
Ag–la′–o–phōn
Ai′–a–cos
Ai–an–to–do′–ros
Ai′–ās
Ais′–chin–ēs
Al–ci–bī′–a–dēs
Al–cin′–o–ös
A–lex–i–dēm′os
Am–phi–ar′–ā–os
Am–phi′–polis
An–ach–ar′–sis
An–ax–ag′–or–ās
An–dro′–ma–chē
An–tē′–nōr
An–the′–mi–ōn
An–ti′–lo–chos
An–ti′–o–chis

An′–ti–phōn
An–ti′–sthen–ēs
A′–ny–tos
A–phro–dī′–tē
A–pol′–lō
A–pol–lo–dō′ros
Ar–chi′–lo–chos
Ar′–gos
Arist–eid′–ēs
Arist–ip′–os
Aristo–dēm′–os
Arist′–on
Aristo′–phan–ēs
Aristō′–ny–mos
Ar–men′–ios
As–clē′–pi–os
Ā′–tē
Athē′na
A′–treus
A′–tro–pos
Au–to′–ly–cos

Bacch–yl′id–es
Bī′–ās

Cal–li′–ās
Cat–an′–a

Ceb'-ēs
Ce'-os
Ceph'-al-os
Cēph-is'-ian
Chai'-reph-ōn
Chal-cē'-dōn
Chal'-cis
Char-ōnd'-ās
Char-man'-tid-ēs
Chi-mai'-ra
Chi'-os
Chrȳ'-sēs
Claz-om'-enai
Clei'-to-phōn
Cle-om'-brot-os
Cle-oph'-ant-os
Clō'-thō
Cō-cȳ'-tos
Cre-ō'-phil-os
Crit'-o-būl'-os
Cri'tōn (Anglicised Crī'tō)

Dai'-da-los
Dē'-li-on (Dēlium)
Dē'-los
Del'-phī
Dē-mo'-do-cos
Di-o'-gen-ēs (g soft in English)
Di'-o-mēde (pron. *meed* in English)
Di-o-ny'-sia
Di-o-nȳ'-sos
Dō'ri-an

Ech-ecr'-at-ēs
E'-leu-sis
Ē'-lis
Em-ped'-o-clēs
Em'-pū-sa
E-pei'-os
Ephē-s'ian, Eph'e-sus
Epi-dau'-rians
Epi'-gen-ēs (g soft in English)
Er
Eri-phȳ'-lē
E-ryx-im'-ach-os
Eu-clīd'-ēs
Eu-dō'-ros
Eu'-ē-nos
Eur-i'pid-ēs
Eu-rīp'-os

Eu-ry'-py-los
Eu-thy-dē'-mos

Glau'-cōn
Gor'-gi-ās
Gȳ'-gēs

Ha'des
Har-mon'-ia
He-ca-mē'-dē
He'-cu-ba
He'llas (Greece)
He'llen-es (Greeks)
Hē-phais'-tos
Hē'-ra
Hē-ra'-clē-a
Hē-ra-cleid'-ēs
Hē-ra-cleit'-os
Hē'-ra-clēs (Herculēs)
Her-mo'-gen-ēs (g soft in English)
Hē-rod'-ic-os
Hē'-si-od
Hipp-i'-ās
Hip-po'-crat-ēs
Hip-po'-lyt-ē
Hippo'-nīc-os
Hom-ēr'-id-ai
Hom-ēr'-ids

I'-nach-os
I'-ōn
I-ōn'-i-an
I'-tha-ca
Is-mēn'-i-ās

La-ce-dai'-mōn
Lach'-ēs
Lach'-es-is
La-cōn'-i-an
La-ert'-i-os
La'-mi-a
La-ri'-ssa (town, pron. Larē-ssa)
Le'-on
Le-on-tī'-ni
Ly'-cōn
Lyd'-i-a, Lyd'-i-an
Lȳ-sān'i-ās
Ly-sim'-ach-os

524

Ma–chā′–ōn
Me′–ga–ra
Mel′–ĕt–os
Me–ne–lā′–os
Men–ex′–en–os
Me–noi′–ti–os
Men′–ōn (Anglicised Mē′no)
Mĕt′–i–ōn
Met–rod–ōr′–os
Mī–lēt′–os
Mī–nos
Mō′–mos
Mū–sai′–os

Nem–e′–an
Nem′–es–is
Nīc–ēr′–atos
Nī′–ci–ās
Nīc–os′–trat–os
Ni′–ob–ē

O–dys′–seus
Omph′–al–os
Orph′–eus

Pai–ān′–ian
Pal–a–mēd′–ēs
Pa′–no–peus
Par′–al–os
Par–men′–id–ēs
Pa′–tro–clos
Pau–sā′ni–ās
Pē′–leus
Pēn–el′–op–ē
Per–dic′–cās
Pe–ri–and′–ros
Per′–ic–lēs
Per–seph′–on–ē
Phai′–dōn (Anglicised Phae′do)
Phai′–dros
Phal–ēr′–on
Phan–o′sthen–ēs
Phĕ′–mi–os
Phil–o–lā′–os
phil–o′–soph–os
Pho–cyl′–id–ēs
Phoi′–bos
Phthī′–ā
Pit′–tac–os
Pol–em–arch′–os
Pol–y′–crat–ēs

Pol–y–gnōt′–os
Pot–eid–ai′–a
Pri′–am
Pro′–dic–os
Prō–ta′goras
Prō′–teus
Pu–ly′–dam–ās
Pȳ–ri–phle′–ge–thōn
Pȳth–ag′–or–ās
Pȳth–ag–or–e′ans

Rha–da–man′–thys

Scyth′–i–an (pron. Ssith–i–an in English)
Ser–ī′–phi–an
Si–mōn′–id–ēs
Sī′–sy–phos
Sō′–crat–ēs
Sol′–ōn
Soph′–ist
So′phoc–lēs
Stē–sim′–brot–os
Styx, Sty′–gi–an

Tei–rē′–si–ās
Te′–la–mōn
Thal′–ēs
Tha–myr′–ās
Thas′–i–an
The–ag′–ēs
Thē′–ban
The′–mis
Them–is′–to–clēs
Theo–dōr′–os
Theo′–dot–os
Theo–zō′–tid–ēs
Ther–sī–tēs
The′–tis
Thra–sy′–mach–os
Thū–cy′di–dēs (c soft in English)
tīm–o–crat′–ic
Trip–tol′–em–os
Trō′–ad–es
Tyn–nich–os

Xan′–thi–ās
Xan–thip′–pē
Xan–thip′–pos
Xe′nophōn

Other MENTOR Books on Philosophy

SCIENCE AND THE MORAL LIFE *by Max C. Otto, introduction by E. C. Lindeman.* (#MD139—50¢)
A noted American philosopher sounds a positive approach to morals in a scientific age.

PHILOSOPHY IN A NEW KEY *by Susanne K. Langer.* (#MD475—60¢)
A study of the symbolism of reason, rite, and art, presented in a clear, readable style.

ADVENTURES OF IDEAS *by Alfred North Whitehead.* (#MP419—60¢)
A history of mankind's greatest thoughts, tracing the development of crucial ideas from ancient times to the present.

SCIENCE AND THE MODERN WORLD *by Alfred North Whitehead.* (#MD162—50¢)
A penetrating study of the influence of three centuries of scientific thought on world civilization.

THE NEXT DEVELOPMENT IN MAN *(revised) by Lancelot Law Whyte.* (#MP399—60¢)
Art, politics, economics and science are integrated into a "unitary" way of thinking in this stimulating book.

ON THE NATURE OF MAN *by John Langdon-Davis.* (#MD334—50¢)
An analysis of man's nature, both physical and psychological, and his relation to the world around him.

MAN IN THE MODERN WORLD *by Julian Huxley.* (#MD148—50¢)
A collection of stimulating essays on all phases of our natural science involvement, and their relation to our contemporary situation.

CHINESE THOUGHT *by H. G. Creel.* (#MD269—50¢)
Tracing Chinese philosophy from Confucius to Mao Tse-Tung, Professor Creel shows how traditional attitudes shape the policies of China today.

The Mentor Philosophers

The entire range of Western speculative thinking from the Middle Ages to modern times is presented in this series of six volumes. Each book contains the basic writings of the leading philosophers of each age, with introductions and commentary by noted authorities.

"A very important and interesting series."
—*Gilbert Highet*

THE AGE OF BELIEF: The Medieval Philosophers
edited by Anne Fremantle. (#MT463—75¢)
"Highly commendable . . . provides an excellent beginning volume."   —*The Classical Bulletin*

THE AGE OF ADVENTURE: The Renaissance Philosophers
edited by Giorgio de Santillana. (#MT437—75¢)
"The most exciting and varied in the series."
—*New York Times*

THE AGE OF REASON: The 17th Century Philosophers
edited by Stuart Hampshire. (#MT367—75¢)
"His (Hampshire's) book is a most satisfactory addition to an excellent series."   —*Saturday Review*

THE AGE OF ENLIGHTENMENT: The 18th Century Philosophers *edited by Sir Isaiah Berlin.* (#MT473—75¢)
"(Sir Isaiah) has one of the liveliest and most stimulating minds among contemporary philosophers."
—*N. Y. Herald Tribune*

THE AGE OF IDEOLOGY: The 19th Century Philosophers
edited by Henry D. Aiken. (#MT421—75¢)
". . . perhaps the most distinct intellectual contribution made in the series."   —*New York Times*

THE AGE OF ANALYSIS: 20th Century Philosophers
edited by Morton White. (#MT353—75¢)
"No other book remotely rivals this as the best available introduction to 20th century philosophy."
—*N. Y. Herald Tribune*

TO OUR READERS: If your dealer does not have the SIGNET and MENTOR books you want, you may order them by mail, enclosing the list price plus 5¢ a copy to cover mailing. If you would like our free catalog, please request it by postcard. The New American Library of World Literature, Inc., P. O. Box 2310, Grand Central Station, New York 17, N. Y.

THE BEST READING AT REASONABLE PRICES

mentor ▶MENTOR▶ paperbacks

MENTOR BOOKS *The earliest of "quality paperbacks," this distinguished publishing program presents sound, scholarly works in history, international affairs, the arts, archaeology, anthropology, psychology, philosophy, science, religion, and many other fields. Among the authors are Margaret Mead, Rachel Carson, Charles Darwin, Whitehead, Jung, Veblen, William James, and many other authorities of the past and present.*

MENTOR CLASSICS *The timeless works of Homer, Aeschylus, Plato, Vergil, Dante, Goethe, and other great writers, in superb English translations by eminent scholars, poets, and writers.*

MENTOR-OMEGA BOOKS *A new series presenting major works of Catholic scholarship, religious classics in translation as well as contemporary Catholic books of lasting value. Among the authors are Jacques Maritain, Christopher Dawson, Karl Adam, Etienne Gilson.*

Long-Range Publishing Programs

Unique, long-range editorial programs include *The Mentor Religious Classics*, presenting basic scriptures of Christianity, Judaism, Mohammedanism, Buddhism, and other world religions; *The Mentor Philosophers*, consisting of six volumes from the Middle Ages to the 20th Century; *Mentor: Ancient Civilizations*, offering archaeological discoveries of past centuries in six or more volumes; *The Mentor History of Scientific Thought*, a projected five-volume series tracing the unfolding of the scientific mind from the 5th Century B.C. to Einstein; and many other multi-volume series published in conjunction with UNESCO (including the new *Mentor-Unesco Art* books), university presses, and outstanding hardcover publishers.